Principles and Practice of Social Marketing

This fully updated edition combines the latest research with real life examples of social marketing campaigns the world over to help you learn how to apply the principles and methods of marketing to a broad range of social issues. The international case studies and applications show how social marketing campaigns are being used across the world to influence changes in behaviour, and reveal how those campaigns may differ according to their cultural context and subject matter. Every chapter is fully illustrated with real life examples, including campaigns that deal with racism, the environment and mental health. The book also shows how social marketing influences governments, corporations and NGOs, as well as individual behaviour. The author team combine research and teaching knowledge with hands-on experience of developing and implementing public health, social welfare and injury prevention campaigns to give you the theory and practice of social marketing.

ROB DONOVAN is Professor of Behavioural Research at the Centre for Behavioural Research in Cancer Control in the Faculty of Health Sciences, Adjunct Professor of Social Marketing and co-director of the Social Marketing Research Unit at Curtin Business School, Curtin University, Western Australia.

NADINE HENLEY is Professor of Social Marketing, director of the Centre for Applied Social Marketing Research and Associate Dean of Research and Higher Degrees for the Faculty of Business and Law at Edith Cowan University, Western Australia.

Principles and Practice of Social Marketing

An International Perspective

Rob Donovan and Nadine Henley

CAMBRIDGE
UNIVERSITY PRESS

CAMBRIDGE UNIVERSITY PRESS
Cambridge, New York, Melbourne, Madrid, Cape Town, Singapore,
São Paulo, Delhi, Dubai, Tokyo, Mexico City

Cambridge University Press
The Edinburgh Building, Cambridge CB2 8RU, UK

Published in the United States of America by Cambridge University Press, New York

www.cambridge.org
Information on this title: www.cambridge.org/9780521167376

First published 2010

Printed in the United Kingdom at the University Press, Cambridge

A catalogue record for this publication is available from the British Library

ISBN 978-0-521-19450-1 Hardback
ISBN 978-0-521-16737-6 Paperback

CONTENTS

TABLES

FIGURES

PREFACE

In the first edition of this book, we adopted the original definition of social marketing as the application of marketing principles and tools to the achievement of socially desirable ends. In our view, while there are clear differences between commercial marketing and social marketing (as there are between marketing fast moving consumer goods to domestic consumers and marketing industrial products to manufacturers), social marketing is simply an area of application of marketing techniques. Hence, this edition remains firmly based on the basic principles of marketing. This grounding reminds public health and other social change agents who have enthusiastically adopted commercial marketing techniques, that marketing – when applied correctly – is more than just a bag of advertising and promotional tools; it is both a philosophy and a set of principles about how to achieve mutually satisfying exchanges between marketers and consumers. Marketing, and therefore social marketing, relies on a comprehensive and fully integrated approach to achieving a campaign or programme's objectives.

At the same time, the first edition broadened the definition and domain of social marketing by addressing two issues: first, to pre-empt debate about 'who decides what is socially desirable', the first edition proposed the UN Charter on Human Rights as the authoritative source for defining what constitutes a *socially desirable* goal; second, and following the UN Charter, the *social* in our social marketing emphasises the social determinants of individual and population health and wellbeing. Social marketing not only targets individual behaviour change, but also attempts to 'go upstream' and target individuals and groups in legislative bodies, government departments, corporations and non-profit organisations, who have the power to make policy, regulatory and legislative changes that protect and enhance people's health, wellbeing and quality of life. From this perspective, social marketing attempts to bring about changes in *products* to reduce harm and enhance wellbeing; changes in *places* to facilitate adoption of desirable behaviours and inhibit undesirable behaviours; and changes in the *political* allocation of resources to bring about changes in the social and structural factors that impinge on an individual's opportunities, capacities and the right to have a healthy and fulfilling life.

The 2003 edition illustrated the principles of social marketing with numerous examples of practical application from the field. In this edition we do likewise. However, while the first edition emphasised much of our own work and Australian-based examples, this international edition contains not only updated material, but also provides numerous examples from around the globe. In particular, we have added a chapter on advocacy with a special emphasis on environmental issues; the marketing mix chapter is expanded to include reference also to policy and partnerships; the two previous case chapters have been replaced by a case on promoting positive mental health and well-being (a major emerging area in public health). What remains the same is the book's use of examples from a broad range of topics, not just the usual lifestyle risk behaviours, and the synthesis of both previously published and unpublished on-going research projects and interventions.

The book is a blend of the authors' practical commercial marketing know-how, hands-on experience in developing and implementing social marketing campaigns and extensive involvement in formative and evaluative research across a broad variety of health and social policy areas. This book is intended to be useful for anyone involved in social marketing or health promotion, public health interventions, injury prevention or public welfare in general, whether as teachers, students, practitioners or researchers.

Students in particular will benefit from the book's sequencing of earlier chapters dealing with overall principles and the later chapters dealing with specific components of the marketing plan. They will also benefit from the book's evidence-based approach; the continual referral to concrete examples to illustrate concepts, principles and approaches; the use of boxes to elaborate issues or provide succinct examples that might be a little out of the ordinary; the questions and recommended readings at the end of each chapter; and the companion website.

ACKNOWLEDGEMENTS

Geoffrey Jalleh, Associate Director of the Centre for Behavioural Research at Curtin University, contributed significantly to Chapters 7 (Research) and 13 (Sponsorship), as well as assisting considerably in other ways for which we are very grateful. Chapter 13 draws on the work of Professor Billie Giles-Corti and other colleagues at the University of Western Australia, and Chapter 15 draws on the work of colleagues at Mentally Healthy WA, particularly Ray James. We would like to thank the anonymous reviewers of the proposal and completed text for their insightful comments. We also acknowledge the support of the Cancer Council Western Australia and Healthway, the Western Australian Health Promotion Foundation. We are grateful to Dr Anne Aly at Edith Cowan University for developing the website materials, Lynda Fielder who assisted with referencing and numerous other administrative details, research assistants Lynn Smith and Jeremy D'Gama, Sandra Voesenek for assistance in seeking permissions, Paul Watson for proofing the initial drafts, and Judy McDonald for her meticulous indexing. We also thank our colleagues who contributed to the first edition, and the ongoing contributions of Ross Spark and Garry Egger.

Finally, a personal thank you to Cobie and Peter for all their patience and support, and to our publisher, Paula Parish, for her faith in the book and her gentle nudging from the early concept to the finished product.

The authors would also like to thank the following institutions and individuals for permission to reproduce copyright material:

Chapter 4:

Sage Publications and Mr Trevor Shilton (Figure 4.1); Greenpeace (Figure 4.2); Professor Edward Maibach, Dr Connie Roser-Renouf and Dr Anthony Leiserowitz (Figure 4.3); WE ACT (Figure 4.4); Sage Publications (Box 'Shilton's ten-point plan for physical-activity advocacy').

Chapter 5:

Professor John R. Rossiter and Dr Larry Percy (Figure 5.2); Cancer Council (Figure 5.4); Rape, Abuse & Incest National Network (Figure 5.5); Australian Government Department of Health and Ageing, Canberra and Department of Pathology, the University of New South Wales, Sydney (Box on health warnings on cigarette packs: 'Smoking causes blindness', Smoking causes lung cancer', 'Smoking doubles your risk of a stroke', and 'Smoking causes mouth and throat cancer').

Chapter 6:

Professor Paschal Sheeran, Dr Paul Norman, Professor Marc Connor, Professor Charles Abraham and Open University Press (Figure 6.1); University of Chicago Press (Figure 6.4); Professor John R. Rossiter and Dr Larry Percy (Figure 6.6, Tables 6.1, and 6.2); Road Safety Operations Branch (No Seatbelt No Excuse logo).

Chapter 7:

Elsevier (Figure 7.1); Taylor & Francis (Figure 7.2.); Professor Ross Spark (Figures 7.4(a), and 7.4(b)); Heartline Bali 92.2 FM (Figure 7.5.); Australian Market and Social Research Society (Tables 7.1(a), and 7.1(b)).

Chapter 8:

American Marketing Association (AMA's Statement of Ethics); United Nations Office of the High Commissioner for Human Rights (excerpts from UN Universal Declaration of Human Rights in Box, 'Who determines what is the social good?').

Chapter 9:

Unilever Australasia (Figure 9.1); Fonterra (Figure 9.3); Adbusters (Figure 9.4); Campaign for a Commercial-Free Childhood (Figure 9.5); The National Heart Foundation of Australia (Box on Heart Foundation's Tick Programme).

Chapter 10:

Professor Edward Maibach, Dr Connie Roser-Renouf and Dr Anthony Leiserowitz (Figures 10.1, 10.2 and 10.3); American Marketing Association (Table 10.2); Taylor & Francis (Figure 10.4); Sage Publications (Figure 10.5); Professor Rod K. Dishman (Table 10.5); Oxford University Press (Box 'Targeting opinion leaders'); Texas Department of Transportation (Box 'Targeting heavy litterers'); Wiley-Blackwell (Box 'Targeting by risk factor profile', 'Skin cancer – have you been checked?').

Chapter 11:

Queensland Health (Figures 11.2, 11.3 and 11.4); Professor Anne Peterson (Box 'Cookin' chitlins for littluns – putting it all together'); Proteines – EPODE International Coordination Unit (Images Box 'EPODE Campaign: Product', Box 'EPODE Campaign: Place' and Box 'EPODE intermediaries and partners').

Chapter 12:

Australian Government Department of Health and Ageing, Canberra (Figure 12.1); McGraw-Hill Australia (Table 12.1); Soul City (Figure 12.6); Oxford University Press (Figure 12.7); Commonwealth of Australia (Figure 12.8); Kevin Casey (Figure 12.9); Asia Injury Prevention Foundation, Ogilvy & Mather (Vietnam) and Mr Dusit Pongkrapan (Figure 12.10).

Chapter 13:

Australian Associated Press (Figure 13.2); Taylor & Francis (Figure 13.3); Healthway (Figures 13.4, 13.5, 13.6 and 13.9); Taylor & Francis (Figure 13.7).

Chapter 14:

Annual Reviews (Figure 14.1); Academy for Educational Development (Figure 14.2); McGraw-Hill Companies (Figure 14.3); BioMed Central Ltd (Figure 14.4.); Figure 14.5 with permission of John Wood (http://www.costaricabybus.com/); McGraw-Hill Australia (Table 14.1).

Chapter 15:

Mentally Healthy WA (Figures 15.1, 15.2, 15.3, 15.4 and 15.5); Department of Sport and Recreation (Figure 15.6); Centre for Well-being/New Economics Foundation (Figure 15.7); Public Health Institute of Iceland (Box '10 commandments of mental health').

1 Social marketing and social change

Social marketing is just one 'branch' of marketing, where the branches reflect the area of application: for example, sports marketing; business to business or industrial marketing; not-for-profit marketing; religious marketing; political marketing and so on. However, social marketing is more than just the application of marketing to social *issues*: the key point of difference to all other branches of marketing, is that the social marketer's goals relate to the wellbeing of the *community*, whereas for all others, the marketer's goals relate to the wellbeing of the marketer (sales and profits, members and donations, political representation, etc.). If the wellbeing of the community is not the goal, then it isn't social marketing.

Social marketing is concerned with helping to achieve and maintain desirable social change. Sometimes social change occurs unplanned, and with generally benign or even positive effects, such as in the introduction of the printing press, the telephone, or the worldwide web. In other cases, change can be violent as in the French and Russian revolutions of the eighteenth and twentieth centuries, respectively, or have devastating health effects as in the industrial revolution's underground mining and unsafe factories. More recently, social and economic changes in countries previously constituting the Soviet Union have led to a marked increase in heart disease in these countries, especially among the unemployed and underemployed, with alcohol abuse being the major proximal contributor to deaths (Zaridze *et al.* 2009a, 2009b). Hence, social marketers and other social change practitioners are called on to use their skills not only to achieve socially *desirable* change, but also to *counter undesirable* social change.

Social marketing is best viewed within a broad context of social change

We would argue that the value of social marketing is that it is the one discipline to embody, within the one framework, most of the principles, concepts and tools necessary for the development and implementation of effective social change campaigns.

While ideological and religious causes are still catalysts for social change in many parts of the globe, most social change is occurring as a result of changes in technology – with implications not only for the developed countries where these changes originated, but also for developing countries where they are often applied.

Changes in communication technology lead to cultural intrusions, usually US-based, and to names like McDonald's, Paris Hilton and Nike being known in even the most remote parts of the globe, and particularly among the young. Changes in industrial technology lead to unemployment or redeployment, with subsequent social upheaval.

Technological changes have consequences for health, such as the marked decline in physical activity as a result of labour-saving devices in the home and workplace, and the advent of computer-driven home entertainment systems. As our colleague Garry Egger has said, 'It's not just Ronald McDonald who's causing the current obesity epidemic in developed countries, it's also Bill Gates!'

Social change practitioners are involved in a wide variety of areas, from changing practices and cultures within corporations, government bureaucracies and institutions, to achieving change within local communities and broader state and national groupings. For example, environmentalists such as Greenpeace are seeking to change the way people treat the environment; public health professionals are attempting to change the way politicians view preventive health versus medical 'cures'; progressive educationists are attempting to change the way teachers view learning and conduct their classes; and organisational psychologists are attempting to change the way workers react to changing technology and work practices. In this book we will argue that social marketing has much to contribute to all these areas, and that social change practitioners in these areas can assist social marketers in developing comprehensive social marketing campaigns.

According to Ross and Mico (1980), social change can be brought about through any or all of several different methods. These vary from passive to active acceptance by the community, for example:

- the diffusion of ideas, products and services throughout society, often led by opinion leaders and mass media;
- consensus organising by interested parties;
- planned or political action – such as lobbying, legislation and election campaigns;
- confrontational methods via threats of reactive action if agreement is not reached;
- non-violent disruptive protests (e.g., boycotts, strikes); and
- violent disruption through riots and revolution.

Social marketing has a major contribution in understanding and facilitating social change in all the non-confrontational methods noted above, but particularly in facilitating diffusion and adoption.

Marketing and business

Just as business in general relies on marketing tools to attract (and satisfy) customers, so too does the business of social change. While no business relies solely on marketing (i.e., finance, production, transport and warehousing, etc., are essential), without marketing of some sort the company could not survive. No matter how good a product is, if consumers are not made aware of how it could meet their needs, and if it is not readily available and affordable, the company will fail. In short, marketing is a necessary, but not sufficient, factor for success.

All other things being equal (e.g., costs of production and distribution, etc.), the most successful businesses are those with the best marketing. By 'best marketing', we don't just mean the best ads or high incentive promotions, but the best use of techniques to: identify consumer needs; develop products and services tailored to deliver benefits that satisfy the needs of different market segments; reach and attract the attention of the target audience and make access to the products and services easy, at prices that customers consider equitable.

Like any other business, the business of social change relies on the use of marketing tools to achieve its goals of attracting and satisfying its target groups. No matter how intrinsically good is our product, say energy conservation, we still need to do the following effectively to get people to 'buy' and act on our message:

• inform people as to *why* energy conservation is necessary;
• show them *how* they can buy products or adopt behaviours that conserve energy *without* undue cost or effort;
• *demonstrate* how energy conserving behaviours meet individual and community *needs*; and
• in a way that *attracts* and holds their *interest*.

Similarly, we need to do the same for legislators and corporations if we want to achieve regulatory, policy and product changes that provide support for individual behaviour change.

What is marketing?

Marketing has been variously defined. The American Marketing Association's (AMA) current definition (October 2007) is very broad: 'Marketing is the activity, set of institutions, and processes for creating, communicating, delivering, and exchanging offerings that have value for customers, clients, partners, and society at large.' The AMA's previous definition is more concrete: 'Marketing is the process of planning and executing the conception, pricing, promotion, and distribution of ideas, goods, and services to create exchanges that satisfy individual and organisational goals.' It is noteworthy that 'ideas' was included in 1985.

For many people, 'marketing' is simply the tactics used by companies to sell their products and services; that is, the first half of the AMA's previous definition – 'the process of planning and executing the conception, pricing, promotion, and distribution of ideas, goods and services'. However, the second half of this definition – 'to create exchanges that satisfy individual and organisational goals' – is the essence of marketing and the basis for what has been called the 'marketing concept' or 'marketing philosophy' approach to doing business. The key words here refer to 'satisfying exchanges' – for both the buyer (the benefits derived from the product or service meet the customer's needs) and the seller (at a price that meets costs and returns a profit).

The marketing concept proposes that company profits are gained via the identification and satisfaction of consumer needs. This emphasis, known as a 'consumer orientation', is on maximising consumer satisfaction, with resultant repeat purchasing and favourable word-of-mouth contributing to the company's ongoing success. The orientation is long term and aims to establish an ongoing relationship with the customer. In this sense, marketing is distinguished from the 'selling orientation', where the emphasis is on the short-term goal of making the sale, regardless of whether the item is best suited to meet the customer's needs. The quote attributed to Henry Ford is often cited as demonstrating the selling orientation ('They can have any colour they want so long as it's black'), as are the tactics of time-share and door-to-door encyclopaedia salespeople. Other orientations contrasted with marketing's customer orientation are the 'product' and 'production' orientations. The former focuses on developing the best possible product – with little attention paid to whether customers want or can afford such a product; the latter focuses on obtaining the most cost-efficient production, packaging and distribution processes – with scant regard for how this might affect the consumer. Obviously, excluding monopoly or cartel situations, commercial organisations that do not place sufficient emphasis on a consumer orientation will fail in the long run. We will have more to say on a consumer orientation in Chapter 2.

Defining social marketing

Social marketing was originally named – as were other sub-branches of marketing such as business-to-business or industrial marketing – to refer to a specific sub-area of marketing. In practice, what occurred was that modern marketing techniques developed for consumer products began to be applied by other areas of business as they saw the apparent success of these techniques. These sub-disciplines were demarcated because, although the principles and tools of marketing could be applied in the different areas, the 'marketplaces' were very different for each. Marketers in these areas required an understanding of these marketplaces in addition to their understanding of marketing *per se*. Hence, we now have texts and courses entitled industrial or business-to-business marketing, services marketing, financial services marketing, government or public sector marketing, events marketing, sports marketing, and even religious marketing. Social marketing came about as marketers and social change practitioners began to apply marketing techniques to achieve socially desirable goals.

Religious marketing?

While there may be some argument as to whether the Church of Scientology (COS) constitutes a genuine religion, the Church recently commenced a television advertising campaign promoting Scientology as the answer to those seeking the 'truth'. Interestingly, given the Church's strident opposition to medication, the execution of the ad has been described as very similar to a much prescribed anti-depressant drug (with the implication that it offers the same benefits) (Edwards 2009a).

Free beer at church?

Taking a different approach, concerns over the lack of men attending services year-round has led Church of England clergy in the UK to offer a range of incentives for fathers attending church on Father's Day, including free beer, bacon rolls and chocolate bars. Men at St Stephen's church in Barbourne, Worcester, for example, will be handed bottles of beer by children during the service – although we are reassured that a prayer will be said for the fathers before the beer is distributed. (No doubt the singing will benefit.)

Not unexpectedly, the plan to distribute beer has upset groups working against alcohol abuse, but the Bishop of Worcester said that it could help churches to attract more men, arguing that the free beer was intended to be symbolic of "the generosity of God" (Wynne-Jones 2009).

What distinguished early social marketing efforts from other areas, was that they were not for commercial profit, nor were they promoting a particular organisation (the domain of not-for-profit marketing). Rather, social marketing campaigns appeared to be conducted for the common good.

Incidentally, just as many original applications of consumer goods marketing to other business areas failed (see Baker 1996), so too have many attempts to apply marketing to social causes. However, this is not because the principles and tools of marketing are inappropriate in these areas, but because marketing concepts and techniques have been misinterpreted or poorly applied. Too many early (and recent) social marketing campaigns were conducted by health and social policy professionals who lacked marketing expertise, or were led by marketing or advertising professionals who lacked an understanding of the health or social policy area in question. Given that the most visible aspect of consumer goods marketing was advertising, many 'uses' of marketing simply involved the addition of advertising to the organisation's promotional strategy. A classic example was that of the early adoption of 'marketing' by universities to compete for students. This generally involved the appointment of a 'marketing manager', the creation of a slogan and the advertising of their various courses – with too little regard for factors such as teacher quality, timetabling, job opportunities, relevance of course content, etc.

Social marketing was first defined by Kotler and Zaltman (1971) as 'the design, implementation and control of programmes calculated to influence the acceptability of social ideas and involving considerations of product planning, pricing, communications and market research'. They referred to social marketing as simply the application of the principles and tools of marketing to achieve *socially* desirable goals, that is, benefits for society as a whole, rather than for profit or other organisational goals

An often cited definition in the past decade has been Andreasen's (1995): 'Social marketing is the application of commercial marketing technologies to the analysis, planning, execution, and evaluation of programmes designed to influence the voluntary behaviour of target audiences in order to improve their personal welfare and that of their society.' We have previously preferred Kotler and Zaltman's definition because of its simplicity and wide generalisability. For example, in this view, a health promoter's use of sponsorship (a marketing tool) to ensure that entertainment venues are smoke free or that healthy food choices are available, is an example of 'social marketing'. Kotler and Zaltman's definition also avoids unnecessary and generally unhelpful definitional debates.

We consider Andreasen's definition unduly constrictive in its apparent emphasis on *voluntary* behaviour change of individuals in the general population and their own welfare. For example, a social marketing campaign with an end goal of individuals consuming less saturated fat, might also target biscuit manufacturers to persuade them to replace saturated fats in their products with polyunsaturated fats. While this requires a voluntary behaviour change among the food company executives, the end consumers' change in saturated fats intake is involuntary. Furthermore, from our point of view, if the social marketers lobbied legislators to enforce such substitutions (i.e., individual voluntary behaviour by legislators, involuntary by food manufacturers and their consumers), this would still be social marketing.

Defining social marketing

The social marketing listserv has a burst of activity every so often with respect to 'defining social marketing'. Much of this is semantic, with various contributors taking perhaps perverse intellectual delight in trying to think of exceptions to whatever definition is proposed by someone else. We think that the vast majority of social marketing practitioners have been doing quite well without a precise definition of each and every word, and pedantic posturing serves little useful purpose.

This 'voluntary' restriction is somewhat inconsistent with the practice of marketing anyway. For example, commercial sponsors of events often negotiate exclusive merchandising arrangements, such that the customer has little or no choice but to consume the sponsor's product at the sponsored event. For example, commercial sponsors in US schools have exclusive merchandising contracts, and for the 2000 Olympics, the only credit card accepted by the ticketing agency was Visa (an

Olympic sponsor). Similarly, health promoters use sponsorship agreements to ensure that healthy food choices are available in entertainment venues, that the venues are smoke free and that access is available to people with disabilities (see Chapter 13). That is, individuals who are in a position to make policy or regulatory decisions are important target audiences, in addition to individuals changing their own risky behaviours.

Hence, we would modify Andreasen's definition by adding 'involuntary' and expanding it to include those who make decisions that affect the welfare of others, thus de-emphasising the targeting of individuals to change their personal risk behaviours in keeping with Andreasen's (2006) emphasis: 'Social marketing is the application of commercial marketing technologies to the analysis, planning, execution, and evaluation of programmes designed to influence the voluntary or involuntary behaviour of target audiences in order to improve the welfare of individuals and society.'

We further extend this definition to accommodate two key points underlying this book's approach to social marketing, especially as we wish the field to develop:

• First, much of the debate about defining social marketing and the common good centres on how to establish this so-called 'common good' in pluralistic societies (i.e., 'who decides what is "good"?'). While we believe that this is rarely an issue in practice, we propose the UN Universal Declaration of Human Rights (www.unhchr.ch) as our baseline with respect to the common good.

• Second, most social marketing to date, particularly in the public health and injury prevention areas, has focused on achieving individual behaviour change, largely independent of the individual's social and economic circumstances. There is now overwhelming evidence that various social determinants influence health over and above individual behavioural risk factors and physical environment risk factors (Wilkinson and Marmot 1998). These social determinants result from the social structure of society in (interrelated) areas such as the workplace, education, literacy and community cohesion. Hence, we see a primary future goal of social marketing as achieving changes in these social determinants of health and wellbeing (Donovan 2000b; Mechanic 1999).

That is, our view is that the domain of social marketing is not just the targeting of individual voluntary behaviour change and changes to the environment that facilitate such changes, but the targeting of changes in social structures that will facilitate individuals reaching their potential. This means ensuring individuals' access to health services, housing, education, transport and other basic human rights that clearly impact on health status (Gruskin, Plafker and Smith-Estelle 2001). This will require the targeting of individuals in communities who have the power to make institutional policy and legislative change (Andreasen 2006; Hastings, MacFadyen and Anderson 2000).

Social marketing's beginnings

Social marketing has its roots in public education campaigns aimed at social change. Kotler and Roberto (1989) report campaigns in ancient Greece and Rome to free the slaves, and history records many attempts by governments in particular to mobilise public opinion or educate the public with respect to health or edicts of the government of the day. These efforts perhaps reached a peak of sinister sophistication with the expertise of Goebbels in Nazi Germany in the 1930s, and similar attempts by the Allies to rally their own populations to the war efforts in the 1940s (see Chapter 12). The propaganda expertise developed in the 1940s was then applied, initially mainly in the United States, to a series of topic areas such as forest fire safety, crime prevention, cardiovascular disease, and so on; and is perhaps most evident in the anti-smoking and HIV/AIDS campaigns of the 1990s that continue today.

Although some would argue that many of these early public education campaigns were primarily media campaigns rather than comprehensive 'social marketing' campaigns (Fox and Kotler 1980), they appeared to promote socially desirable products (e.g., war bonds) and attitudes (e.g., towards women working) in ways indistinguishable from commercial marketing. In any case, social marketing was being applied far more comprehensively in developing countries than in developed countries in the 1970s (Manoff 1985), in areas such as family planning, rat control and other hygiene/sanitation areas, agriculture and attitudes towards women (Rice and Atkin 1989).

The 1980s saw rapid growth, especially in Canada and Australia, in the application of marketing concepts to public education campaigns across a broad range of activities, including injury prevention, drink-driving, seat belt usage, illicit drugs, smoking, exercise, immunisation, nutrition and heart disease prevention (Egger, Donovan and Spark 1993; Fine 1990; Kotler and Roberto 1989; Manoff 1985; Walsh *et al.* 1993).

Egger and colleagues (1993) point to a number of factors influencing this:

- the realisation by behavioural scientists and health professionals that, while they were expert in assessing what people *should* do, they were not necessarily expert in *communicating* these messages, nor in *motivating* or *facilitating* behavioural change;
- the observed apparent success of marketing techniques in the commercial area, and the observation that the discipline of marketing provided a systematic, research-based approach for the planning and implementation of mass intervention programmes;
- epidemiological research findings about the relationships between habitual behaviours and long-term health outcomes led public health experts to implement campaigns aimed at preventing behaviours that resulted in the so-called 'lifestyle' diseases such as heart disease and cancer; and
- a focus on lifestyle diseases initially led to an emphasis on individual responsibility and individual behaviour change (Egger and colleagues imply that this was an undue emphasis), a view consistent with the capitalist philosophy of individualism and rational free choice, which many saw as synonymous with commercial marketing.

Some critics of social marketing (and health promotion) campaigns have claimed that this individual focus philosophy largely ignores the social, economic and environmental factors that influence individual health behaviours. While some social marketing campaigns deserve this criticism, this is not an inherent characteristic of marketing. One of the fundamental aspects of marketing – and, hence, *social* marketing – is an awareness of the total environment in which the organisation operates, and how this environment influences, or can itself be influenced, to enhance the marketing activities of the company or health agency (see Andreasen 2006; Buchanan, Reddy and Hossain 1994; Hastings and Haywood 1994). Our definition of social marketing explicitly acknowledges the influence of the social and physical environments on individual behaviour.

Social marketing: what it is – and what it is not

Although some argue about what is and is not *social* marketing, we take an eclectic, pragmatic and parsimonious view that what distinguishes social marketing from other areas of marketing is the primary end goal of the campaigners. If the Hungarian National Heart Foundation (HNHF), as part of the European Heart Health Charter were to undertake a campaign to reduce cardiovascular disease in the population by reducing the amount of trans-fats in people's diets, using advertising and promotions aimed at increasing fruit and vegetable consumption, and via lobbying manufacturers and fast-food outlets to reduce their use of saturated fats, this would be *social* marketing. The intended goal is increased health and wellbeing in the population at large. If the HNHF formed a partnership with various fruit and vegetable marketers in the above campaign, these commercial partners would not be engaging in social marketing. While the impact of increased fruit and vegetable consumption would have a desirable population health outcome, this is not the commercial partners' goal: their goal is increased profit via the partnership.

Not-for-profit marketing: This refers to not-for-profit organisations using marketing to achieve organisational goals. If Cancer UK were to undertake a fundraising and volunteer recruiting drive using direct mail and mass media advertising, this is not-for-profit marketing. While Cancer UK's overall aims are for the common good, raising funds in competition with other charitable organisations is an organisational goal rather than a 'common good' aim. Similarly, if a library used marketing techniques to build its customer base and attract funds to achieve its goals of growth and its positioning of having an up-to-date library of music videos and DVDs, this would be not-for-profit marketing. However, if the library undertook to increase the literacy of people in the community it served, and this was the primary aim of the programme, it would be engaging in social marketing. Such a programme might, of course, result in increased use of the library, but this would be a means to the primary goal.

Cause-related marketing: This refers to a commercial entity forming a partnership with a pro-social organisation or cause, such that sales of the commercial organisation's products benefit the pro-social cause (Webb and Mohr 1998). In some ways this is similar to sponsorship (or pro-social marketing; see below), where the pro-social organisation allows the commercial entity to promote its association with the pro-social organisation in order to improve people's attitudes towards the company and its products. The difference is that in cause-related marketing, the return to the pro-social organisation is directly related to product sales. Again this is not social marketing as the commercial organisation's main aim is to achieve increased sales or some other marketing objective; it is simply using the social goal as a means to this end.

Cause-related marketing has become relatively popular in the United States ever since 1983 when American Express offered to donate one US cent to the restoration of the Statue of Liberty for every use of its card, and US$1 for every new card. The company gave US$1.7 million to the restoration as consumer card usage increased by 27 per cent and new applications by 45 per cent. Recent examples are Dove's successful and much-lauded 'real women, real beauty' campaign that funds a self-esteem foundation for women, and P&G's 'One Pack = One Vaccine' campaign – where Pampers makes a donation to UNICEF equivalent to the cost of one tetanus vaccine for each pack of specially marked Pampers sold (Cone 2008). That initiative began in 2006 in the United Kingdom, and has since expanded to other countries in Western Europe, North America and Japan.

The 2008 Pampers campaign in North America, which featured actress and new mother Salma Hayek as spokesperson, reportedly generated funding for over 45 million vaccines. The initiative has expanded across Europe, Africa, the Middle East, Asia and North America, with approximately 100 countries participating in the 2008–9 campaign (www.unicefusa.org/hidden/pampers-usfund.html; accessed 16 June 2009).

Pink cans double soup sales

While projects like the Pampers UNICEF campaign have obvious benefits to the recipients of the vaccination, these campaigns can be very profitable to the marketers. Campbell's soup sales to the Kroger supermarket chain doubled during the pink labelled Breast Cancer Awareness Month in 2006. After deducting 3.5 cents per can, this presumably leaves Campbell with a hefty profit from the promotion (Thompson 2006).

Pro-social marketing: This refers to a commercial organisation promoting a pro-social cause related in some way to its target audience. For example, Kellogg in Australia featured messages on its cereal products about bullying, targeting young children, and a message about folate from the Northcott Society for Crippled Children on its Guardian pack. It is also a major sponsor of the Surf Life Saving Association (Kellogg's 'Surf Safe Summer'). Pro-social marketing is similar to sponsorship in that the commercial organisation hopes to achieve an increase in positive attitudes to itself and its products through an association with the pro-social organisation or issue.

In many cases, an apparent concern for a social issue is directly related to the commercial organisation's interests: for example, a condom manufacturer providing information on HIV transmission; insurance companies promoting screening; and cereal manufacturers providing information on fibre and colorectal cancer. A variation on this is where the commercial organisation joins with its critics to minimise the harm done by its products: for example, alcohol marketers mounting or supporting responsible drinking campaigns; packaging companies supporting and promoting recycling and 'clean up' campaigns; and Phillip Morris funding domestic violence shelters and related projects. For example, Philip Morris International (PMI) supports the 'Violence: que faire' website run by the Swiss organisation, Vivre sans Violence, claimed by PMI to be the first website to offer information and advice for victims of domestic violence in French-speaking Switzerland. In many cases, we suspect the primary motive is to avert criticism or regulation rather than achieving a socially desirable goal (www.philipmorrisinternational.com/PMINTL/pages/eng/stories/f012_CHViolence.asp; accessed 16 June 2009).

Societal marketing: This is sometimes confused with social marketing. Kotler *et al.* (1998) use this term to refer to companies that act in socially responsible ways in the achievement of their profit goals (e.g., companies that voluntarily use biodegradable products in production processes, recyclable packaging, etc.). This was considered an extension of the original marketing concept from profit through identification and satisfaction of consumer needs, to profit through identification and satisfaction of consumer needs 'in a way that preserves or improves the consumer's and the society's wellbeing' (Kotler *et al.* 1998).

Today there is much talk of corporate social responsibility (CSR), originally associated with companies such as the Body Shop and Ben & Jerry's, but now claimed by companies such as Nike and McDonald's (Doane 2005). In some cases this seems like corporate philanthropy, such as GlaxoSmithKline's donation of anti-retroviral medications to Africa and Hewlett-Packard's corporate volunteering programmes. Others seem to be based on values, such as Starbucks' purchases of fair-trade coffee. Doane (2005) seems rather sceptical of CSR motives – and we would agree.

Corporate philanthropy: Corporate philanthropy, such as Body Shop's secondment of staff to Romanian orphanages and McDonald's Ronald McDonald houses, is viewed as altruistic, with no direct link to increased sales or other commercial goals. However, corporate philanthropy has direct and indirect benefits to the company's profitability via positive effects on employees, external stakeholders and the community (Collins 1993), and, along with social responsibility and an interest in social causes, appears to be on the increase (Drumwright 1996; Osterhus 1997). Qantas raised almost AUD$5 million from 1991 to 2000 for UNICEF; its staff are raising money for aid projects in Zimbabwe and Thailand, and it raised AUD$410,000 for the Starlight Children's Foundation in 1998 through sales of a Christmas carols CD (McCoy 2000).

Social marketing and social change tools

Social marketing as proposed by many social marketers (mainly by academics, less so by practitioners), has been restricted to the classical marketing techniques and originally excluded areas such as lobbying, legislative and policy action and structural change. However, marketers use a number of tools to achieve sales and profit goals. Business lobbies government for policies and legislation that facilitate business operations, such as restricting competition – especially from imports, tax breaks for research and development of new products, plant and retail location incentives, fuel subsidies and so on, all of which have a bearing on the company's marketing efforts. For example, Australian margarine manufacturers lobbied long and hard for legislation to allow margarine to be coloured like butter to increase its acceptance by consumers – a move vigorously opposed by the dairy industry. Similarly, anti-tobacco campaigners have lobbied government to ban tobacco advertising, to increase tax on tobacco and to restrict smoking in public places. Is lobbying for the social good 'social marketing'? From our point of view, if the lobbyist considers the interaction an exchange and is concerned with the needs of the lobbied (i.e., the politician or legislator), then it is social *marketing*. Hopefully Andreasen's (2006) book on influencing policymakers and legislators will increase the acceptance of these areas as within a marketing approach.

Such lobbying is, of course, consistent with commercial marketing anyway – as noted above – since actions like lobbying are included in the promotion 'P' of the marketing mix in terms of influencing the environment in which exchanges take place (Kotler *et al.* 1998). Furthermore, if the key core concept of marketing is the *exchange process*, whereby one party exchanges something of value with another party to the perceived benefit of each, then much of human activity – not just that of commercial organisations – could be termed 'marketing'. In this sense we agree with Piercy (2008) and Baker (1996) that virtually all organisations engage in some form of marketing (i.e., attempting to achieve satisfying exchanges with stakeholders), although many would not label it as such, and some would make more efforts with some stakeholders than others. For example, many government department CEOs expend far more effort in keeping their minister happy than they do in keeping their clients satisfied.

Education, motivation and regulation

There are three major campaign strategies to facilitate desired behaviour changes:

- to educate (information and skills);
- to motivate (persuasion); and
- to advocate (socio-political action).

Education and persuasion are aimed at individual behaviour change, while advocacy is aimed at achieving structural change – at the social, physical and legislative environmental levels. We distinguish education/information and motivation/persuasion in much the same way that health education is distinguished from health promotion. Health education involves the provision of information in a more or less dispassionate, objective scientific manner, where the target audience is left to make an 'informed choice'. Education can be effective in achieving behaviour change when ignorance is the major barrier.

However, information *per se* is often insufficient to bring about behaviour change. Persuasion involves the provision of information, products and services so as to directly influence the target audience to adopt the source's recommendations. In health education we would dispassionately inform the target audience of the constituents of inhaled tobacco smoke, how the lung cells metabolise this smoke and how tobacco is related to a number of illnesses. In health promotion, we would dramatise the ill-health effects and attempt to increase the target audience's perception of the severity of the illness and the likelihood of personally being afflicted, stress that quitting smoking would vastly reduce if not eliminate the possibility of suffering a smoking-related illness and offer nicotine replacement therapy products. We could also lobby to restrict tobacco advertising and institute non-smoking areas in public places. That is, health promotion is also concerned with the influence of social and physical environment factors.

Rothschild (1999) proposed three overall methods for achieving desirable social change: education, motivation and legislation. Rothschild's framework appears similar to ours, although he views 'motivation' as the domain of social marketing and differentiates it from education and legislation. He sees all three as complementary, and, where relevant, co-operating means of achieving desirable social change. However, in our view, education/information is part of marketing, as are attempts to achieve a legislative context that facilitates the marketing effort. Hence, while different professionals might be necessary to help implement these three methods, they are all part of what we would call a comprehensive social marketing campaign. In the case of tobacco noted above, legal restrictions on advertising and promotion, mandatory packaging requirements and no-smoking areas would constitute the legislative component of a comprehensive approach.

This more comprehensive view of social marketing reflects our background in the public health area, where advocacy for legislative and policy change has played a major role in areas such as tobacco and gun control and environmental protection. Furthermore, the law has long been used to assist in public health areas, from mandatory notification of various infectious diseases and indicators of child abuse, to restrictions on the sexual behaviour of HIV positive persons, requirements for food handling and food processing, mandatory seat belt use and so on. Similarly, racial vilification and anti-discriminatory laws are used to influence social norms in tolerance campaigns. Although some social commentators question the use of so-called 'educative laws' to achieve changes in cultural mores or morality, in our opinion, such laws can be a positive force for change, especially if accompanied by education as to why the laws are there.

Social marketing campaigns in many areas exploit existing laws or can be used to create or simply result in favourable public opinion supporting further enforcement strategies (e.g., road safety, illicit drug use, underage alcohol and cigarette purchases, etc.). This is particularly so in road safety campaigns in the United Kingdom, Northern Ireland, Australia and New Zealand, where shockingly graphic advertising and accompanying publicity have been used to create public support – or at least neutralise opposition – to regulatory measures such as increased fines, hidden cameras and compulsory random breath testing.

Today, social marketing techniques are being used to achieve policy and legislative change at local, state, national and international levels of government. In 2000, the European Union Parliament adopted policies on tobacco packaging to apply to all member countries (Smith 2000). Furthermore, public health lobbyists are attempting to achieve international agreements on a broad range of issues that impact social welfare and public health, from tobacco to human trafficking.

Social marketing and health promotion

As noted above, attempts to achieve social change have been around for a long time. While these may not have been called 'social marketing', they share many of the same techniques and principles. Consider the case of 'health promotion'. Health promotion has been defined as a more proactive stance than 'health education', in that whereas health education attempted to inform people – and then left them to make a so-called 'informed choice' – health promotion attempts not only to inform, but also to persuade people to cease unhealthy behaviours and to adopt healthy behaviours. Health education focused on biomedical information, risk factors and diseases in a fairly dispassionate format. Health promotion, on the other hand, uses highly graphic, emotion arousing appeals to dissuade people from unhealthy habits such as smoking. It also uses positive appeals to wellness, self-esteem and mental alertness to persuade people to adopt healthy behaviours.

Health promotion also places considerable emphasis on environments in which health promotion takes place (e.g., health promoting schools, health promoting workplaces, health promoting cities, etc.). The Ottawa Charter (see below) explicitly states that health promotion should not only target individual undesirable behaviours, but also act to create social, political, health service and legislative environments that support communities and individuals to make desirable changes.

Health promotion: The Ottawa Charter

• Build Healthy Public Policy
• Create Supportive Environments
• Strengthen Community Actions
• Develop Personal Skills
• Re-orient Health Services

Adopted at an international conference on health promotion, 17–21 November 1986, Ottawa, Canada.

A perusal of health promotion campaigns and health promotion texts might give a marketing savvy reader the sense that 'only the name has been changed'. Interestingly, some of these texts include a section or chapter on 'social marketing' as just one way of approaching a health promotion campaign (including ones co-authored by the first author of this book: see Egger, Donovan and Spark 1993; Egger, Spark and Donovan 2005).

Social marketing, the public health approach and social medicine

A common call today by health and social policy professionals is for 'a public health approach' to almost every health and social ill, from the obesity problem, violence, adolescent substance use and increasing physical activity to reducing medical malpractice errors (just Google Scholar 'public health approach' and you will see what we mean). Much of this has arisen from the success of the public health approach in controlling infectious diseases (and environmental hazards) and applying the same principles and methods to the lifestyle behaviour of tobacco use.

Public health is concerned with preserving, promoting and improving health, with an emphasis on prevention: primary prevention refers to preventing problems occurring in the first place (universal interventions); secondary prevention refers to interventions targeting at-risk groups before the problem is established (selective interventions); and tertiary prevention refers to interventions that attempt to prevent the problem re-occurring (indicated interventions). Hence, relationship programmes for young males about respecting women are an example of primary prevention; interventions aimed at young males whose father or male carer was abusive represent secondary prevention; behaviour change programmes for men who have physically abused their partner represent tertiary intervention (Donovan and Vlais 2006).

The steps in a public health approach can be described as follows:

(1) Determine what is the problem via systematic data collection ('surveillance') (e.g., extent and nature of violence against women, prevalence of substance use among

'tweens and teens). This is particularly important for setting relevant goals, including behavioural objectives.

(2) Identify risk and protective factors via epidemiological analyses and attempt to identify causes (by experimental and other methods) and the health and other effects in various groups. Such analyses are particularly important for target audience identification.

(3) Develop and implement interventions to see what works, why and for which groups.

(4) Apply the efficacious interventions population wide, assess their impact and their cost-effectiveness.

(5) Continue surveillance, data analyses and modification of interventions.

A public health approach incorporates an acknowledgement of all environmental influences on health and welfare, and, from its beginnings as 'social medicine' in Europe, social inequalities in particular. This is epitomised in Virchow's famous statement that social conditions influence health, and hence political action is necessary to restructure society and remove these social conditions (see Chapter 3). Virchow stated 160 years ago that 'medicine is a social science, and politics nothing more than medicine on a grand scale'. He meant that a society's health is very much dependent on the way that society structures itself. Factors affecting the health of populations may be different to those affecting the health of individuals. While the health care system deals with the proximate 'causes' of illness, broader social change is necessary to deal with population cause (Mackenbach 2009).

Social medicine is most associated in the twentieth century with South America, and with names like Salvador Allende (the military–CIA deposed Chilean leader) and Ernesto 'Che' Guevara (Waitzkin *et al.* 2001) (see the movie 'Motorcycle Diaries' for Guevara's 'discovery' of the relationship between poverty and ill-health).

Social marketing and social mobilisation

Based on social change programmes in developing countries, McKee (1992) defines social mobilisation as 'the process of bringing together all feasible and practical intersectoral social allies to raise people's awareness of and demand for a particular development programme, to assist in the delivery of resources and services and to strengthen community participation for sustainability and self-reliance'. He lists legislators, community leaders (religious, social and political), corporations and the target audience themselves (the 'beneficiaries') as targets via lobbying, mass media, training, participation in planning, sponsorship, study tours and so on, to bring about the 'mobilisation' of all these groups to ensure a programme's success. In this sense, McKee sees social mobilisation as incorporating and supporting a social marketing campaign with specific objectives. In our view, we see the terms as synonymous, with his list of mobilisation targets simply being the list of necessary stakeholders to engage for maximal impact.

McKee's framework is particularly relevant in developing countries where inter-sectoral alliances and government support for programmes are relatively weak, or where there may even be hostility towards the programme. In developed countries, government departments, NGOs, corporations and community organisations are more likely to be positive towards the programme – although moving these positive attitudes into co-operative action still requires considerable effort.

Major target groups for social marketing/social mobilisation	
National, and state policy makers, legislators:	Political mobilisation
Service providers, funders:	Government mobilisation
Opinion leaders, NGOs, local government, unions:	Community mobilisation
Businesses, business organisations:	Corporate mobilisation
Individuals and groups that will benefit from the programme:	Beneficiary mobilisation

McKee's framework is useful because it highlights all the target groups for any campaign, although their relevance will vary by issue, resources and campaign objectives. For example, a bullying campaign implemented in a Western Australian town was initiated by the then member of the state Legislative Assembly; it had a board consisting of representatives of several state government departments and the Commonwealth Government (e.g., education, family and children's services), and community organisations; major companies in the area were approached for financial support; schools were incorporated in the programme; and individual parents, children and members of the community were consulted and participated in the campaign.

Another example of a social marketing approach which embodies the principles of social mobilisation is the US Centers for Disease Control and Prevention's (CDC's) (1996) Prevention Marketing Initiative. This HIV prevention programme targeting adolescents in five locations used media, skills workshops, contests, condom distribution, promotional merchandise, public events and influential opinion leaders to reach its goals.

Mindful of all of the above we propose an additional '4Ps' that represent the goals of social marketing [see Cohen, Scribner and Farley (2000 and Maibach, Abroms and Marosits (2007) for similar frameworks]. These goals are:

- changes in **population** prevalence of individuals' undesirable behaviours;
- changes in **products** people use or consume that impact on health and wellbeing;
- changes in **places** where people live, work and play so as to reduce harm and enhance wellbeing; and
- changes in the **political** structure that ensures equality of access and opportunity in society.

Hence:

to achieve **population prevalence** changes,

- social marketing targets individuals to encourage them to change their risky, unhealthy and undesirable beliefs, attitudes and behaviours to achieve changes in the prevalence of behaviours in the general population, and, where relevant, specific sub-populations (e.g., encouraging smokers to quit, violent men to seek help, householders to reduce electricity use, changing racist or gender or mental illness stereotypes, etc.);

to achieve desirable changes in **products and services**,

- social marketing targets individuals with the power to influence the manufacture and marketing of consumer and industrial products and their regulation so as to eliminate, modify or restrict access to unhealthy and undesirable products and promote the development and marketing of healthy alternatives (e.g., regulation of 'sin' products, including guns, making motor vehicles safer in collisions, safer toys, stricter building regulations, low alcohol/fat/sugar/salt alternatives, mandatory additives in some products, carbon emission reduction technology, slower operating poker machines, etc.);

Baby product makers asked to not use bisphenol A (BPA)

BPA is used in the manufacture of lightweight plastic containers, including baby bottles and baby formula containers. Although scientists disagree on the harmful effects of BPA, it is a toxic chemical and some studies suggest that BPA can attach to food in heated containers. Hence, attorneys general in several US states are asking companies that make baby products to voluntarily not use BPA. Some manufactures have already ceased using the chemical and are promoting their BPA-free baby bottles (*Wall Street Journal* 2008).

to achieve desirable changes in **places**,

- social marketing targets individuals with the power to make changes to and regulate activities in places where people congregate (e.g., work sites, schools, recreational areas, institutions/hospitals, etc.) to facilitate healthy, positive behaviours and reduce risky behaviours (e.g., safe exercise areas, safe serving practices in bars, shade sails over swimming pools, reduction of lead emissions, safe rail crossings, canteens with healthy foods, no-smoking areas, urban design to reduce crime);

to achieve **political** changes in the allocation of resources,

- social marketing targets individuals who have political power to determine the allocation of a society's financial and other resources and to change public institutions, such as the media and the law, and government bureaucracies, such as education and health services, to ensure equality of access and opportunity as per the Universal Declaration of Human Rights.

Taking road safety, for example, our additional 4Ps would involve a multifaceted approach to reducing road crashes and subsequent harm, including:

- mass media advertising and publicity to encourage individuals to adopt safe driving practices, increased driver education before and after obtaining a licence, enhanced driving skills for dangerous situations;
- encouraging (or mandating) motor vehicle modifications such as shock absorbing panels, air bags front and back, enhanced stabilisers and braking systems, immobilisers under conditions such as driver seat belt not engaged, breath alcohol measured, etc.;
- road modifications to enhance road holding and visibility, separation of traffic, normative campaigns against speeding, drink driving and non-use of restraints, bars to promote skipper or designated driver strategies (where one member of a group abstains to drive the others home), promotion of public transport acceptability and accessibility, etc.;
- legislation to enforce motor vehicle and road standards, allocation of resources to driver education and public transport, etc.

Product safety concerns in China

Since the 2008 scandal over baby milk formula, product safety has been a growing concern among Chinese consumers. And with good reason. A recent government survey in April and June 2009 in Guangdong Province of 202 items found that 51 per cent were substandard or dangerous to consumers' health. The government came under heavy criticism because they did not release details of which products were OK and which were not (New Tang Dynasty Television 2009).

In June 2009 a thirteen-storey block of flats in Shanghai collapsed, prompting questions about shoddy building practices and corruption in the construction industry (Foster 2009). Such collapses are not uncommon in inland areas of China.

Concluding comments

In short, there are a number of principles, concepts and tools that are, or should be, used to develop and implement effective social change campaigns. These are drawn from disciplines such as psychology, sociology, social research and communication. We would argue that the value of social marketing is that it is the one discipline to embody most of these principles, concepts and tools within the one framework.

Social marketing can be viewed as a bag of tools or technologies adapted mainly from commercial marketing and applied to issues for the social good. In our view, a key point of the marketing concept or 'philosophy' is that it emphasises the perspective of the target audience as the basis for achieving mutually satisfying exchanges. From a broader viewpoint, the end goal of any social marketing campaign should also be to contribute to achieving health and wellbeing via a socially just society. That is, this book retains the definition of social marketing as derived from the key concepts of commercial marketing, but broadens the *domain* of social marketing from the application of commercial marketing techniques to the achievement of socially desirable goals to the application of the marketing concept, commercial marketing techniques and other social change techniques to achieving individual behaviour changes and societal structural changes that are consistent with the UN Universal Declaration of Human Rights.

Social marketing seeks to *inform* and *persuade*, and, where deemed necessary, *legislate* to achieve its goals. The relative emphasis on each of these will depend on formative research, resources, the nature of the issue and the prevailing socio-cultural norms and values. For example, mandatory seat belt usage was met with considerable resistance in the United States because this was viewed as an infringement of citizens' rights. In some cases therefore, social marketing campaigns are undertaken to bring about positive community attitudes to facilitate legislative change. For example, road safety advertising and publicity campaigns serve to convince the public that increased fines and surveillance and detection methods are necessary.

The broader approach we advocate is consistent with the articles of the Ottawa Charter, the public health paradigm and the US National Academy of Sciences' Institute of Medicine 2000 report into social and behavioural intervention strategies for health. The Academy's report acknowledges that health and wellbeing is a function of the interaction between **biology** (genetics), **behaviour** (lifestyle, risk factors) and the **environment** (physical, social), and where the context is shaped by factors such as age and gender, race and ethnicity, and socio-economic status. They conclude that interventions need to:

- 'Focus on generic social and behavioural determinants of disease, injury and disability' (i.e., societal level phenomena);
- 'Use multiple approaches (e.g., education, social support, laws, incentives, behavior change programmes) and address multiple levels of influence simultaneously' (i.e., individuals, families, communities, nations);
- Involve sectors 'that have not traditionally been associated with public health promotion efforts, including law, business, education, social services, and the media.'

The report concluded that although environment-based strategies have greatest population effect, far more progress had been made in developing individual-oriented interventions than environmental-oriented interventions (Orleans *et al.* 1999). We feel there is a clear need for social marketing to help redress this situation; and other social marketers have also pointed this out (Goldberg 1995; Hastings, MacFadyen and Anderson 2000). To achieve this turnaround, we see future applications of social marketing working alongside practitioners in, and incorporating lessons and principles from, areas such as social activism, social entrepreneurship, social medicine and liberation theology.

Hence, *social* marketing extends marketing's borrowings from psychology (e.g., mental health and happiness), sociology (e.g., war and conflict, social movements) and economics (e.g., globalisation effects), and further draws on disciplines and concepts that are related to community wellbeing, such as public health and health promotion, criminology, social policy and social welfare and environmental sustainability. However, regardless of these elaborations, and regardless of whether we are targeting individual consumers or those in power to make regulatory changes, the primary paradigm is that of marketing.

Just like any marketing campaign, a social marketing campaign works when it is based on good research, good planning, relevant attitudinal and behavioural models of change, when all elements of the marketing mix are integrated, and when the socio-cultural, legislative and structural environments facilitate (or at least don't inhibit) target audience members from responding to the campaign. A well-planned social marketing campaign stimulates people's motivations to respond, removes barriers to responding, provides them with the opportunity to respond, and, where relevant, the skills and means to respond.

QUESTIONS

● What are the major differences between commercial marketing and social marketing?

● How does social marketing differ from cause marketing?

FURTHER READING

Andreasen, A. R. 2006. *Social Marketing in the 21st Century*. Newbury Park, CA: Sage.

Doane, D. 2005. The Myth of CSR: The Problem with Assuming that Companies can do Well While Also Doing Good is that Markets don't Really Work that Way, *Stanford Social Innovation Review*, Stanford Graduate School of Business, Stanford University.

Maibach, E. W., Abroms, L. C. and Marosits, M. 2007. Communication and Marketing as Tools to Cultivate the Public's Health: A Proposed 'People and Places'

Framework, *BMC Public Health* 7:88, available from: www.biomedcentral.com/1471–2458/7/88.

Waitzkin, H., Iriart, C., Estrada, A. and Lamadrad, S. 2001. Social Medicine Then and Now: Lessons from Latin America, *American Journal of Public Health* 91:10, 1592–601.

2 Principles of marketing

As defined in Chapter 1, social marketing is the application of the concepts and tools of commercial marketing to the achievement of socially desirable goals. Marketing is characterised by things like a consumer orientation, segmentation and targeting, advertising and sales promotions, and much research with customers and potential customers to ensure that things like packaging and pricing are appropriate for the product, and that the advertising is believable, relevant and motivating. Research and negotiations are also undertaken with intermediaries such as retailers, and with stakeholders such as unions and government, to ensure that making the product attractive, available and affordable will be facilitated by distributors and not hampered by structural and regulatory restrictions. In all these areas, the notion of an exchange process between the 'buyer' (target) and the 'seller' (marketer) forms a platform of operation.

Chapter 1 emphasised the 'social' in social marketing. This chapter emphasises the 'marketing' in social marketing by briefly reviewing the major principles of marketing. It is these principles that form the core of a social *marketing* approach. Unfortunately, many campaigns that have been labelled 'social marketing' have not been based on an adequate understanding of these principles, leading to unjustified criticisms of social marketing and unjustified claims of ineffectiveness.

For many health and social change professionals, social marketing is seen as synonymous with the use of media advertising and publicity to promote socially desirable causes. Given that the basic 'product' or primary resource of many social marketing campaigns is information (Young 1989), this view is not unexpected. However, the use of media is only one component of a total marketing process: the product or service must be designed to meet the customer's needs; it must be packaged and priced appropriately; it must be easily accessible; it should be 'trial-able' (if a large commitment is required); intermediaries such as wholesalers and retailers must be established; and, where relevant, sales staff must be informed and trained.

In the same way, a campaign that aims to promote improved parenting behaviour must be based on more than just advertising that perhaps models positive practices as a replacement for coercive practices. Programmes and strategies are required at community level; parenting courses must be developed and offered; self-instruction materials made available; the activities promoted must be 'do-able' (that is, within the target group's capacities) or 'learn-able' (that is, skills must be defined and training must be available for specific activities); and the courses and materials must be easily accessible and affordable. In fact, many marketers use very little mass media advertising, particularly marketers of illicit drugs. While it may be considered unusual to think of a criminal behaviour involving marketing, as we see in the example below, the same principles apply in terms of attracting and satisfying customers. In fact, it could be argued that the notion of establishing a good relationship with buyers is even more important for marketing of illegal products and services.

Allen Long and cannabis marketing

In the 1970s, before cocaine and the Columbian cartels introduced extreme violence into the illicit drug business, cannabis marketing was often overseen by hippie-type business school dropouts or graduates with an intuitive or learned marketing approach. Allen Long was such an individual. He established direct links with his Columbian growers (which increased his margin) and built good relationships, because he not only exchanged dollars for the crops but also 'gifts' not easily obtained in rural and remote areas in South America, such as Sony Trinitron TV sets, Adidas running shoes, Heineken, Marlboros and Swiss Army knives (Sabbag 2003). This understanding of his suppliers meant that Long could be assured of a steady supply in times of poor harvest.

Long also introduced product quality and branding. The crop yield was sorted into high quality (Columbian Gold) and lesser quality (Columbian Red) and priced accordingly. The customer was assured of consistent quality according to the branding, thus increasing customer loyalty. Long also ensured that the product's packaging could withstand immersion in the ocean (an oft-used tactic to avoid detection) yet arrive without deterioration. Furthermore, Long appreciated the need to keep all his intermediaries happy, so the packaging was also designed to make it easy for the loaders to handle these bulky packages.

Successful drug dealers must also establish loyalty in their customers – not just to ensure that they can sell their products, but also to avoid being reported to the police. This is done by appreciating that customers – many with severe addictions – may require 24-hour access, deliveries while in prison and credit terms when times are tough. That is, pricing and distribution issues are also important. The other point to note is that illicit drug marketing does not rely on any paid media advertising or publicity – it's all word-of-mouth.

Marketing is all about satisfying one's customers. Marketing therefore permeates (or should) all areas of an organisation:

- it affects the finance department with regard to prices customers are prepared to pay, how they would like to pay (online, cheque, credit card or cash), and what sort of credit terms are desired;
- it affects the production department in terms of desired product varieties and packaging;

- it affects transport and distribution in terms of where customers prefer to buy the product, and the attitudes of retailers to stocking arrangements and in-store promotions;
- it affects staff training in terms of what factors enhance or detract from customer satisfaction – for example, how the receptionist treats a customer, how staff are dressed and how clean are the premises – can have as much to do with customer satisfaction as the actual service the organisation provides. And it is customer satisfaction that will ensure the success and profitability or otherwise of an organisation.

Given that marketing is often defined in terms of delivering products and services that meet customers' needs, and that profitability results from customer satisfaction, British author Nigel Piercy (2008) considers that any organisation with customers (or clients) relies on a marketing process, whether they call it that or not.

Marketing basics

There is much jargon and perhaps some mystique attached to the term 'marketing'. Some social change practitioners are cynical about its philosophical appropriateness and its potential effectiveness, while others have a blind, optimistic faith in its ability to achieve all sorts of objectives. Each of these views stems from an objectification of marketing as either an individual-based, capitalistic approach or a bag of highly successful manipulative techniques, or both.

Piercy (2008) takes a very pragmatic view on what marketing really is in that as every organisation has customers, at the end of the day the only thing that really matters is the long-term satisfaction of customers. Hence, every organisation relies on a marketing process. We discuss each of these premises in turn.

Every organisation has customers even though it may sometimes be difficult to decide just who they are. For a public housing department, identifying its customers (or 'clients') appears relatively easy: all existing and potential tenants and purchasers who qualify for public housing assistance. However, taxpayers and society in general are also interested in the type and location of public housing. Many public housing projects of the 1960s and 1970s, especially high-rise blocks, ended up as 'ghettos' of crime and social disorder, that pleased neither the primary customers, nor their neighbours, nor the taxpayer who paid not only for the bricks and mortar, but also for the social ills exacerbated by these developments.

The police service also has quite diverse customers: criminals in their care; the general public; shop and property owners, and so on. The Department of (Road) Transport has a broad variety of customers: road users – cyclists, motorcyclists, car, truck and bus users; road transport firms; organisations and communities that rely on road transport; pedestrians, and so on. All these different groups have needs – some of which are conflicting – and, hence, demand different products and services to meet these needs.

Determining priorities of needs is one of the major issues facing government departments, and one of the major ethical problems for social marketers.

For all organisations, at the end of the day, the only thing that really matters is the long-term satisfaction of customers. This is the only reason for the existence of an organisation, whether commercial, non-profit or government, and the only way it can survive. Take customers away and organisations cease to exist. Customers' long-term satisfaction is often more difficult to define and achieve in the public and NGO sectors than the private sector. Nevertheless, the point is that if public sector and non-profit organisations really wish to achieve their vision and mission statements, they must first identify, and then satisfy, their customers' needs.

In past experience with the public sector, it was evident that many such organisations put organisational goals ahead of client satisfaction goals. For example, public housing was designed, located and built primarily to achieve financial and productivity indicators, not the long-term satisfaction of users (and often with disastrous effects as noted above). Similarly, road transport departments would focus on miles of road built and maintained rather than on measures such as road safety indicators, traffic noise and road users' satisfaction with traffic flow and convenience. Fortunately, with the rise of 'Customer Charters', many government organisations around the globe are at least aware of customer needs, even if they only pay lip service to satisfying these needs.

Therefore, every organisation relies on a marketing process – but the most important marketing tasks are not necessarily carried out by a specialist marketing department or person, but by front-counter staff, telephone answering staff or delivery staff.

A customer's impression of an organisation is based on their experiences with the people who represent that organisation, whether they are an accounts person responding to a customer querying their account, or the person who delivers the product to their home or factory, or the person answering the phone. Good marketing means that each of these organisation staff recognises the need to treat the customer with dignity and respect. Too many organisations fail to appreciate that all their staff influence customer satisfaction. Public sector organisations, in particular, need to implement a marketing orientation within their organisations before they can properly adopt social marketing to meet their campaign objectives. That is, a Family and Children's Services Department dealing with troubled or neglected children should first understand the need to treat its captive clients as customers before it can maximise the effectiveness of adopting a social marketing approach to, say, attracting parents to enrol in parenting courses.

Piercy further states that marketing is very simple in concept (i.e., common sense), but very difficult to implement in practice. Even for those with a will it's not that easy. A survey of marketers at the American Marketing Association's Customer Satisfaction Congress in 1994 found that only 16 per cent said their company had a very successful customer satisfaction strategy (Services Marketing Today July/August 1994).

We couldn't find a recent survey, but suspect that things would not have changed much. Similarly, although many public sector (and commercial) organisations now have Customer Charters, many have failed to fully – or even partly – implement these charters. Piercy claims – and we agree – that the reason is a lack of real commitment by senior management. How many public sector heads actually spend time at the front counter? How many take the time to attend community meetings? How many read whatever customer research their department does undertake? In the authors' experience, very few.

Principles and practices of marketing

A number of aspects of product and service marketing such as market segmentation, market research, competitive assessment, the use of product, price, promotion and distribution tactics, pre-testing and on-going evaluation of campaign strategies, and models of consumer behaviour adapted from the psychological and communications literature, have been discussed in the context of social marketing (e.g., Andreasen 1995; Hastings 2007; Kotler, Roberto and Lee, 2008; Lefebvre and Flora 1988; Manoff 1985).

Those we consider most relevant are shown in Figure 2.1 and outlined below (see also Donovan and Owen 1994).

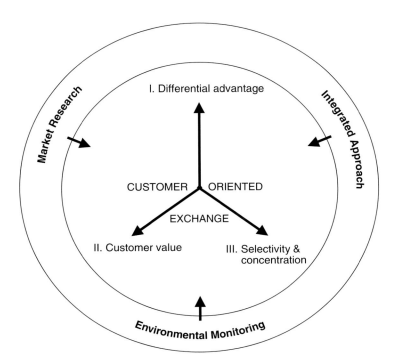

Figure 2.1 Basic principles of marketing

Marketing can be considered to incorporate two fundamental concepts, three principles that guide the planning and implementation of marketing in practice, and three defining features that inform and integrate the fundamental concepts and implementation principles:

• Two fundamental concepts:	Consumer orientation
	Exchange
• Three implementation principles:	Customer value
	Selectivity and concentration
	Differential advantage
• Three defining features:	Use of market research
	Integrated approach to implementation
	Monitoring and influencing environmental forces

We will present and illustrate each of these in turn.

A consumer orientation (the 'marketing concept')

Piercy's major point is that marketing is about focusing an organisation on identifying its customers and its customers' needs, and then directing resources to meeting those needs. It is this 'customer orientation' view of marketing that we most endorse and that permeates all of the other principles and concepts dealt with below. Beverley Schwartz of Ashoka in Washington DC expresses the consumer orientation in social marketing in her statement that 'the problem is not what to *tell* people, but what to *offer* them to make them want to change'.

This 'customer orientation' is also known as 'the marketing concept'. Organisations with a consumer orientation are contrasted with organisations that have production, product or sales orientations. These orientations focus on the needs of the seller rather than the buyer (Kotler 1988). In contrast, a customer focus seeks profits through the identification of customer needs, the development of products and services to meet these needs, and the pricing, packaging, promotion and distribution of these products in accordance with consumer habits, aspirations and expectations.

The first author (RJD) was once employed by the Swan Brewery which, at that time (the 1970s), enjoyed a near-monopoly in Western Australia. In 1971 the Swan Brewery employed its first marketing manager, and in 1972, RJD was employed as the company's first market research officer (MRO). However, while the company had employed a marketing manager, they had not yet embraced the marketing concept. They saw the marketing function as just a more sophisticated sales department that would design more stylish can and bottle labels, develop professional-looking (and expensive) television ads, and sell more beer in overseas markets by lavishly entertaining import agents in various countries. The company was still largely in the hands of the brewers, the finance people and the production/packaging managers. The brewers' dominance meant that the consumer got what the brewers considered beer should look and taste like – regardless of consumer research indicating different preferences; the dominance of the production/packaging manager meant that packaging was dictated by what was easiest and least costly rather than what consumers preferred (e.g., an initial reluctance to introduce six-packs); and the dominance of the finance people meant that credit terms were inflexible to hoteliers and liquor store owners, and that all areas of the brewery first considered cost implications rather than customer satisfaction implications. For example, the MRO's research revealed that retailers and customers were complaining about cartons coming apart. Nevertheless, it took considerable effort to persuade the production people to apply two applications of glue rather than one, because of the increased cost.

Even the marketing manager had not fully adopted a consumer orientation. While he was concerned about customer satisfaction in some areas, he was dominated more by a desire to reach quarterly and annual sales goals (against which his performance was assessed) rather than by achieving long-term customer satisfaction. When customer research revealed that many (older) beer drinkers wanted only one or two glasses of a 750-ml bottle per night, and hence looked for all sorts of ways to stop the remainder going flat, the MRO suggested a screw top for 750-ml bottles. The marketing manager dismissed this outright and delivered his mantra: 'Mr Heinz made his fortune not from the mustard people ate, but from the mustard they left on their plate.'

Can social marketing really be based on customers' needs?: A basic distinction between social and commercial marketing is that social marketing campaigns are often *not* based on needs experienced by consumers, but on needs identified by experts. This is true. Communities might prefer their resources to be spent on hospitals rather than on disease prevention, and on tougher prisons rather than rehabilitation. Similarly, although epidemiological evidence indicates that smoking and physical inactivity are greater causes of morbidity and mortality, a government might allocate far more resources to anti-drug campaigns, because a majority of voters considers drug taking a more important issue. That is, government resource allocation is informed not only by experts, but also by party philosophy, lobbying from various specific interest groups and voter opinion polling.

At the same time, there is at least the appearance of increasing community consultation on priorities for health and social policies. 'Citizen Juries' are sometimes used in a number of countries to obtain community input to decisions about health care resource allocation or to simply listen to community concerns. Citizen Juries apparently originated with the Jefferson Center (2009), whose website reports that a similar method called the 'Planungszelle' was developed by a Peter Dienel, working out of the Research Institute for Citizens Participation and Planning Methods at the University of Wuppertal in Germany. These juries consist of small convenience samples of citizens who are presented with information by experts, then asked to consider the information and make recommendations on priorities for policy-making or resource allocation. For example, after listening to Citizen Juries in Bristol in 2007, the Prime Minister of the UK claimed that his Government had 'changed their mind' on casinos and cannabis as a result (BBC News, 6 September 2007).

The Center for Advances in Public Engagement (Public Agenda 2008) in the United States has a professional and sophisticated approach to involving the public in decision-making and creating greater capacity in communities to solve problems and engage with public officials. Their public-engagement primer (available at www.publicagenda.org/public-engagement-materials/public-engagement-primer-public-agenda) demonstrates a good understanding of a consumer orientation: the first of its ten core principles of public engagement is: begin by listening

Organ donation and a consumer orientation

Although a person might agree that his or her organs should be donated on their death, in reality, many relatives refuse consent. Follow-up research shows that many of these people later regret that decision, suggesting that it is situational, temporary factors that drive refusal. Good research that looks at the situation from the grieving relatives' view can provide clues as to how to minimise refusals when a donor dies. Factors found to be important in a UK review are: the timing of the request – specifically separating the request from notification of the death; making the request in a very private setting; information about the concept of brain stem death; not rushing the decision; and a joint approach by a trained professional from an organ procurement organisation and a member of the hospital staff (Simpkin *et al.* 2009).

Regardless of who decides the priorities, a marketing approach emphasises that the development, delivery and promotion of the message and products or services must be carried out in accordance with consumer needs. For example, messages about immunisation must be in a language consumers understand, the promised benefits must be relevant and the messages must be placed in media that consumers attend to. A number of studies have shown that although things are improving, much health education and other literature emanating from government departments is written at a readability level far higher than the average reader level, and contain jargon understandable only to other professionals in the area (Rudd, Moeykens and Colton 1999). It appears that many of the authors of such material are attempting to meet their peers' approval rather than attempting to make the literature easily comprehensible to end consumers. In a later publication, Rudd and his colleagues provide a case study of how they rewrote a state water resource authority report to make it readable by laypersons. We recommend that study for practical tips for improving the readability of public documents (Rudd *et al.* 2004).

In the 1970s, the first author's research company was commissioned by the then West Australian State Housing Commission (SHC) to assist them in implementing an urban renewal programme in public housing areas (Donovan *et al.* 1979). We suggested the then radical step of having the Commission's architects actually meet with the people for whom they were designing homes and units, and recommended that the Commission should open 'information centres' in areas to be renewed. We also suggested that the CEO and other senior executives appear at an open meeting in the renewal area to answer residents' questions. To ensure that the SHC executives could answer these questions, we recommended a small survey of residents to determine what questions residents would be likely to ask. Hence, the SHC could prepare appropriate answers. The SHC accepted all these suggestions, but initially as a means of mollifying the residents rather than out of a genuine concern for the residents' needs.

However, as a result of participating in these activities and seeing the benefits first-hand (e.g., reduced resident anger and complaints, feelings of goodwill arising from listening and co-operating, etc.), a profound cultural shift occurred among the Commission staff involved. The renewal programme then proceeded with a distinct and genuine consumer orientation, to the extent that Commission staff took over the social marketing role that the research company had previously performed.

Perhaps the most important outcome of this project was that it at least temporarily removed the confrontational 'them versus us' attitude that still pervades in many public sector organisations, where staff view the customer or client as the 'enemy'. Perhaps the reason why universities are still struggling with their marketing programmes is that many staff still believe their job would be so much better if it weren't for the students.

Good service people make their customers feel important

From a social marketing view, a consumer orientation means viewing individuals, regardless of their position or circumstances, as equal human beings, with a right to dignity and respect. This requires an empathy with their needs and a caring, compassionate approach to their immediate situational as well as long-term needs. This is particularly important when dealing with disadvantaged people.

The concept of exchange

The concept of exchange has long been described as the core concept of marketing: 'Marketing is the exchange which takes place between consuming groups and supplying groups' (Alderson 1957). An essential factor differentiating exchanges from other forms of need satisfaction is that each party to the exchange both gains and receives value, and, at the same time, each party perceives the offerings to involve costs. Hence, it is the ratio of the perceived benefits to the costs that determines choice between alternatives (Kotler and Andreasen 1987).

> **Save the crabs, then eat 'em**
>
> Funded by the Chesapeake Bay Program, the Academy for Educational Development
> implemented a campaign to reduce nutrient pollution flowing into Chesapeake Bay from
> the greater Washington DC area. The primary campaign goal was to convince area residents
> not to fertilise their lawns in the spring, when fertiliser run-off is most damaging to the Bay,
> but to do so in the fall, if at all. The campaign message was not framed as an environmental
> appeal; rather, the campaign offered a continued supply of Chesapeake Bay seafood (crabs
> in particular) in exchange for residents changing their lawn fertilising practices (Landers
> *et al.* 2006).

Kotler (1988) lists the following as necessary conditions for *potential* exchange:

- there are at least two parties;
- each party offers something that might be of value to the other party;
- each party is capable of communication and delivery;
- each party is free to accept or reject the offer; and
- each party believes it is appropriate or desirable to deal with the other party.

There is some debate as to whether the exchange concept is truly present in many social marketing areas and, if not, 'is it really social *marketing*?' Elliott (1995) takes the view that a voluntary exchange as it occurs in commercial marketing differs from the exchange that takes place in social marketing, and that it is an 'intellectual contortion' to consider that 'exchange' means the same as when a consumer exchanges dollars for a refrigerator and when a smoker gives up smoking for a longer, healthier life (Elliott 1995).

Elliott has a point. In the commercial world, the exchange is generally between two parties; in social marketing, depending on the issue, the 'exchange' of something of value may appear to take place within rather than between the parties. For behaviours such as immunisation, time and effort on the part of the consumer is exchanged for a healthy life through prevention of diseases; for the health organisation, resources are exchanged for lower morbidity and premature mortality, and lower health costs. Consistent with Maibach (1993), we take the view that some sort of exchange is usually always present, even if primarily intra-individual, somewhat complex or ill-defined. Nevertheless, neither our definition in Chapter 1, nor those of Andreasen (1995) and Kotler and Zaltman (1971) relies on the inclusion of an explicit exchange in the definition of social marketing.

More pragmatically, the lessons for social marketers from the exchange concept are that we must:

- offer something perceived to be of value to our target audiences;
- recognise that consumers must outlay resources such as time, money, physical comfort, lifestyle change or psychological effort in exchange for the promised benefits;

- acknowledge that all intermediaries enlisted to support a campaign also require something of value in return for their efforts (De Musis and Miaoulis 1988).

In short, 'the social marketer's task is to maximise the perceived benefits and minimise the perceived costs associated with the advocated change' (Goldberg 1995).

In Piercy's terms, the customers (or target audiences) for a physical activity campaign are not only inactive individuals, but include GPs, commercial health club operators, local government recreational officers, community health instructors, health promotion and fitness professionals' associations, volunteer workers, sponsors, and so on. For example, health promoters have too often assumed that the medical and para-medical professions' shared common goal of public health enhancement would be sufficient to ensure their support. But each intermediary should be considered a distinct target market with their own needs and values that must be included in an exchange process. Hence, promotions to GPs asking them to recommend exercise to their patients must be designed with the GPs' needs in mind; that is, materials distributed to GPs should be easy to use, easy to distribute and should improve patients' understanding of the relationship between physical activity and physical and mental health.

Customer value: the concept of the marketing mix

The principle of customer value emphasises that products and services are purchased not so much for themselves, but for the benefits they provide to the buyer (Lancaster 1966). This point was reportedly well made by Revlon's Charles Revson in his statement that '... in the factory we make cosmetics; in the store we sell hope'. Levitt's more mundane example was that although people may buy a ¼-inch drill what they want is a ¼-inch hole (Kotler 1988).

Customer value is provided not just by the tangible product or the service *per se*, but by all the so-called '4Ps' that constitute what is known as the marketing mix. The 4Ps are:

- **p**roduct (brand name and reputation, packaging, product range, etc.);
- **p**rice (monetary cost, credit terms, payment methods, etc.);
- **p**romotion (advertising, sales promotion, publicity and public relations, personal selling, product placement, etc.); and
- **p**lace or distribution (number and type of outlets, opening hours, atmosphere in outlets, accessibility by car, availability of public transport, availability and ease of parking, etc.).

The marketing manager's task is to blend these 4Ps to provide maximal value to selected market segments. For example, customer value can be increased by: reducing time and effort costs in obtaining the product (e.g., wide distribution, vending machines in appropriate locations, Internet ordering); rapid replacement of stocks before depletion; easy handling and storing packaging; making the product trial-able before commitment (for example, sample packs, in-office/in-home demonstrations, *'seven days free trial'*); easy to pay for (e.g., credit-card acceptance, lay-by, hire purchase, online payment); and easy to use (e.g., user-friendly packaging, instructions on use, free training courses). The total value of a particular perfume is determined not only by its fragrance, but – and arguably more so – by its packaging, brand name, brand positioning (i.e., brand image), price and outlet reputation.

A fifth P – **p**eople – is often added for services marketing (Baker 1996), given the frequent inseparability of the service provider and the actual service. In social market-ing, for example, of counselling services, people aspects are crucial. The lesson from commercial services marketing is that staff training, especially in interpersonal skills, is essential for successful completion of the exchange transaction. For example, unless domestic violence counsellors have empathy with their clients and have the ability to maintain rapport, perpetrators will discontinue counselling.

A concept that ties the two aspects of customer benefits and the 4Ps together is Kotler's concept of the *core* product, the *augmented* product and the *tangible* product. For example, the *tangible* product might be a computer. The *augmented* product involves after-sales service, training, warranties, associated software, a widespread consumer user network and so on. The *core* product is better management decision-making. In fact, many companies compete more on augmented product features than on tangible product features.

In the promotion of physical activity, the core product might be a longer, healthier life through cardiovascular disease risk reduction; the actual product might be an aer-obics class; and the augmented product might include a crèche, off-peak discount rates, clean hygienic change rooms and a complimentary towel.

The notion of augmented product emanates directly from a consumer orienta-tion: an approach that continually seeks to identify customers' needs and attempts to meet them. Many public sector welfare organisations often have large numbers of clients waiting, many of whom are women with young children who have probably arrived somewhat tired and frazzled – especially in the summer – after some time on public transport. A social marketing consumer orientation would result in these organisations' waiting areas having an area for children to play, the provision of toys and games, refrigerated water fountains, adequate and comfortable seating, and easily accessible toilets and washrooms.

Freedom from Fear campaign products

The Freedom from Fear campaign encouraged men who used violence against their female partner to seek help to end their violence.

The core product – the end benefit being offered to violent men in relationships – was the opportunity to keep their relationship (family) intact by ending the violence towards their partner (and its impact on their children).

Actual products consisted of the Men's Domestic Violence Helpline and Counselling Programmes. The Helpline was staffed by trained counsellors who offered counselling over the phone and encouraged men to enter a counselling programme. The counselling programmes were delivered by private service providers, subsidised by the Government. Prior to this campaign there was no Helpline specifically for perpetrators who voluntarily sought help, nor were counselling programmes promoted. Self-help booklets provided tips on how to control violence and how to contact service providers. These self-help booklets were also provided on audio-cassettes for men with literacy difficulties (Donovan, Paterson and Francas 1999).

Market (or customer) segmentation: the principle of selectivity and concentration

Market segmentation is probably the most important and most established concept in marketing. At a fundamental level it is obvious that the young differ from the old in product requirements and tastes, as do the sexes. But there are far more and sometimes better ways than demographics to segment markets to maximise campaign resources. For example, some people rarely read newspapers, others are avid TV watchers, and different people respond to different types of appeals. Some respond only to self-interest appeals, others to civic duty appeals, some to fear, others to guilt; some are already positive towards the use of water conservation devices, others see them as too costly and ineffectual, and so on.

Market segmentation involves dividing the total market into groups of individuals that are more like each other than they are like individuals in other groups. The fundamental issue is to identify groups that will respond to different products or marketing strategies, and, for commercial organisations, to select and concentrate on those segments where the organisation can be most competitive.

The segmentation process involves three phases:

(1) dividing the total market into segments and developing profiles of these segments;
(2) evaluating each segment and selecting one or more segments as target markets;
(3) developing a detailed marketing mix (that is, the 4Ps) for each of the selected segments.

The concept of market segmentation derives directly from a consumer orientation. To segment adequately clearly requires a comprehensive understanding of customers and is therefore heavily dependent on appropriate market research. Segmentation is fundamental to developing social marketing campaigns and is dealt with in Chapter 10.

Competition and the principle of differential advantage

In marketing, this refers to an analysis of the marketer's resources versus those of the competition with the aim of determining where the company enjoys a differential advantage over the competition. Companies are most likely to be successful in areas where they enjoy a differential advantage. Commercial organisations regularly carry out SWOT analyses on themselves and their competitors – audits of the organisation's strengths and weaknesses, and identification of current and future opportunities and threats in the environment. Social marketers should do likewise, remembering that strengths and weaknesses cover financial, human and technological resources. Many social marketing campaigns directed at youth fail simply because the people involved have little understanding of youth culture.

This principle is useful at even the most basic stage of identifying just who or what is the 'competition' in a particular instance. Interestingly, and particularly with (global) moves towards privatisation and outsourcing, many public sector organisations are now realising that competitors are being forced upon them, or they face growing competition from the private sector expanding into traditionally public areas. For example, while private detective agencies have been around for many years, recent years have seen a dramatic increase in private security organisations, such that police services are expressing concern about 'protecting their turf' (Harvey 2001). Furthermore, in what some might consider a bizarre anomaly, private contractors appear to have had more responsibility for security such as protecting diplomats and even senior military officers in Iraq than the US military (see Congress of the United States 2008).

What is the competition to increasing physical activity? The answer is any other leisure time activity, such as watching TV, movies, hobbies, Internet time and electronic games. The strategy of attempting to increase physical activity levels via day-to-day activities recognises that allocating a set period of time for 'exercise' faces far more formal competition than does an attempt to increase incidental physical activity.

In a wider sense, the principle of differential advantage relates to monitoring and understanding competitive activity, sometimes to emulate or follow such activity, or, in other cases to pre-empt or counter competitors' activities. A study of alcohol advertising and promotion, for example, can assist in understanding appeals to young people. Similarly, advocacy groups need to monitor industries such as the tobacco industry and attempt to pre-empt expected industry moves.

Monitoring the competition: messages in alcohol advertising

Jones and Donovan (2001) analysed the messages young people perceived in ads for UDL's vodka-based drink. They showed that these ads promoted the drink as a facilitator of social relationships by removing inhibitions, especially those with the opposite sex, and that the drink had direct mood effects such as inducing relaxation, removing worries and making the drinker 'feel good'. These messages are consistent with the reasons for young people's consumption of alcohol in general. Jones and Donovan point out that these messages are, in fact, against the alcohol industry's self-regulatory code, and that public health professionals need to be vigilant with regard to the alcohol industry's activities.

The use of market research

It should be apparent that effective marketing is a research-based process with ongoing research in various areas: testing new products; surveys to identify consumer dissatisfaction with current offerings and opportunities for improvement; pre-testing advertising and promotions; surveys of attitudes to competitors' offerings; pricing and packaging research; feedback from distributors and intermediaries, and so on.

The major use of research in social marketing campaigns to date has been in understanding target audiences' beliefs, attitudes and behaviours, the development and pre-testing of communication materials (advertising, posters, brochures, PSAs), measures of exposure to campaign materials, and pre-post surveys or periodic surveys to assess changes in attitudes, beliefs and behaviour over the duration of campaigns.

Examples of some basic research questions we have looked at to inform various social marketing campaigns include the following:

- what are food vendors' attitudes to including healthy food alternatives on their menus?
- what healthy lifestyle issues (e.g., exercise, dietary fat reduction, smoking cessation, etc.) do the community perceive as priorities for action?
- what *tangible* products can be developed to facilitate the adoption of health promoting behaviours or to reduce risk (e.g., no-tar cigarettes, low-fat foods, quit smoking kits, exercise videos, etc.)?
- what factors influence GPs' use of health promoting brief interventions?
- what would increase residents' participation in urban renewal decisions?
- what would increase residents' involvement in a recycling programme?
- what do people understand by the term 'bullying'?
- what would influence mental health professionals to support a positive mental health promotion campaign?
- what do people believe are factors influencing good and poor mental health?
- what would motivate domestic violence perpetrators to seek help?
- what social and structural facilitators and inhibitors need to be taken into account when promoting increased physical activity?
- what would influence legislators' attitudes to tobacco control measures?
- who are the relevant influencers of youth fashion and music preferences?
- what motivates young people's alcohol, tobacco and illicit drug use?
- how do men in different ethnic populations view campaigns about violence against women?
- what messages about Indigenous people are most likely to neutralise negative stereotypes?
- what socio-cultural factors influence eating behaviours in different ethnic populations?

Our framework for campaign evaluation is based on that of Coyle, Boruch and Turner (1989), who delineated four types of evaluation designed to answer four questions:

- Formative research: What message strategies and materials would work best?
- Efficacy research: Could the campaign actually make a difference if implemented under ideal conditions?
- Process evaluation: Was the campaign implemented as planned?
- Outcome evaluation: What impact, if any, did the campaign have?

Research in social marketing not only requires an understanding of consumer research methods, but, increasingly, an understanding of epidemiological research methods, as many campaigns are based on such data. Also, given the greater complexity of social marketing areas, research designs can often be more complex, or require more in-depth analysis and a broader variety of approaches than research into commercial products. Furthermore, we believe that the researchers themselves should have some background in the social sciences, not just marketing or economics. Research and evaluation are covered in Chapter 7.

An integrated process

The marketing process is an *integrated* process, such that elements of the marketing mix, the organisation's resources, the use of market research and the selection and concentration on specific market segments, are all combined to maximise the value of the organisation's offerings to the consumer and profit to the company.

In simple terms, a perfume's packaging must be consistent with its price, its brand image and its retail distribution. An expensive perfume clearly must be accompanied by expensive looking packaging, and an elegant stylish image rather than, say, an outdoors or disco fun image, and be available only in upmarket outlets (such as Harrods in London). Market research is needed to ensure a viable target segment exists for the perfume; outlets and shelf space must be negotiated for distribution of the product; and advertising and publicity timed to take advantage of gift buying seasons – and certainly not until distribution has been completed. Such a simple adage of 'not advertising until the product is on the shelf', is often forgotten by commercial and social marketers. Many campaigns in the social welfare area (for example, domestic violence, child abuse) often lead to services being overloaded, because demand was underestimated, was not adequately planned for, or because there was insufficient time to put them in place because the minister or CEO wanted to do something quickly simply to be seen to be doing something.

An integrated approach implies the need for a systematic strategic planning process: the setting of clearly defined overall goals; the setting of measurable objectives to meet the overall goals; the delineation of strategies and tactics to achieve these objectives; and management and feedback systems to ensure that the plan is implemented as desired, and to avert or deal with problems as they arise. Egger, Spark and Donovan (2005) have presented what they called the SOPIE approach to campaign planning: **s**ituational analysis; **o**bjective setting; **p**lanning; **i**mplementation; and **e**valuation. This will be covered, along with other planning methods, in Chapter 14.

The environment

Commercial marketers are keenly aware that the marketing process takes place in a changing environment, and that this environment must be monitored continually to identify potential opportunities and to avoid potential and actual threats to the company and its products or services. Aspects of the environment that influence commercial and social marketing include:

- **political–legal** (e.g., exhaust emission requirements, anti-monopoly laws, food labelling regulations and rulings on the use of words like 'natural', 'fresh', etc.);
- **economic** (e.g., the introduction of low priced alternatives during recession periods, changes in spending patterns such as reduced petrol consumption – and, hence, reduction in distance driven and number of accidents);
- **technological** (e.g., changes in packaging and production methods, whole product categories such as typewriters becoming obsolete);
- **social and cultural** (e.g., the demand for environmentally friendly packaging and products, the consumer movement, 'yearnings' for traditional values); and
- **demographic trends** (e.g., increase in single person and single parent households, changes in ethnic composition due to different birth rates, ageing of the population).

However, social marketing takes a broader view in that it recognises that the environment plays a role in bringing about or exacerbating poor health and anti-social behaviours, and that individual behaviour change is often limited, if not impossible to achieve or sustain without concurrent or preceding environmental change. For example, people's levels of physical activity are related to opportunities in their immediate physical environment. This is not just in terms of access to facilities such as squash and tennis courts, swimming pools and commercial health centres (i.e., 'gyms'), but also in terms of whether attractive parks are nearby, whether the neighbourhood is safe to go walking, jogging or cycling (in terms of traffic and likelihood of assault/harassment), whether the footpaths are maintained and so on (Corti 1998; Sallis *et al.* 1990; Stokols 1992).

Similarly, a community's or individual's response to a delinquency programme or a positive parenting practices programme will be dependent on factors such as the level of unemployment in the community, the level of income and home ownership, educational opportunities (Hawkins *et al.* 1992) and other measures commonly known as 'social capital' (Putnam 2000). An ecological perspective considers the role the environment can play regardless of individual risky behaviours. We will cover wider environmental implications in Chapter 3. One of the major events near the end of the last century was the death of Princess Diana and the rather extraordinary reaction among people around the globe. Various health and road safety spokespersons attempted to exploit the situation by highlighting the individual's behaviours. However, there was another – environmental – issue.

Who killed Princess Diana?

Would Princess Diana be alive today ...
... if her driver hadn't been affected by alcohol?
... if the vehicle hadn't been speeding?
... if she'd been wearing her seat belt?

An individual, voluntary behaviour focus would emphasise the above questions.

An environmental perspective would add ...
... if French authorities had followed standard practice and installed guard rails between the concrete pillars in the tunnel?

Differences between commercial and social marketing

Many years ago, Wiebe (1952) questioned whether marketing principles and practices could be applied to non-commercial areas: 'Can we sell brotherhood like we sell soap?'. Clearly the answer has been 'yes', although there are perhaps obvious differences between 'selling' soap and 'selling', say, alcohol moderation, just as there are obvious differences between selling high involvement products such as fashion clothing, life insurance and earth-moving equipment, and low involvement products such as laundry detergent, insecticides and ice cream. Consumers' buying decisions, sources of influence, amount of effort involved and so on are clearly quite different across these product categories, and hence so too are the marketing approaches. Nevertheless, while specific tools and tactics may differ, the overall principles of commercial marketing are applicable to all areas, including selling socially desirable products.

The major differences between social and commercial marketing, as noted by various social marketers and commentators (Bloom and Novelli 1981; McKee 1992; Rangan, Karim and Sandberg 1996; Rothschild 1979) and from our own experiences, can be summarised as follows:

- Defining and communicating the 'product' is far more difficult in social marketing, especially when different experts may have different views on the subject. *Developing the National Physical Activity Guidelines for Australians* went through ten drafts following development by two key stakeholder workshops and then being mailed three times to a large sample of health and physical fitness professionals, as well as undergoing scrutiny by a twelve-member scientific advisory committee (Egger *et al.* 2001).

- The 'product' in social marketing is often information designed to bring about attitudinal and behavioural change; less frequently do social marketers have tangible products to sell, and even where they do, the primary task is to sell the 'idea' (or core product). For example, people must first be convinced that water conservation (the 'idea') is desirable (and that their contribution would be meaningful) before they can be persuaded to purchase water limiting attachments to their plumbing.
- Commercial products tend to offer instant gratification, whereas the promised benefits of many social marketing campaigns are often delayed. This especially applies to many health behaviours. Furthermore, some social marketing campaigns (such as de-stigmatisation and anti-racism campaigns) appear to offer little, if anything, in return.
- The exchange process is far easier to define in commercial marketing than in social marketing.
- Social marketing attempts to replace undesirable behaviours with behaviours that are often more costly in time or effort, and, at least in the short term, less pleasurable or even unpleasant. Changes in parenting practices require considerable patience and persistence; withdrawal from addictive substances can be physiologically very traumatic; breaking long-established social and sub-cultural influences can be difficult.
- Behaviours targeted in social marketing campaigns are often very complex, both at a personal and social level, and far more so than are the behaviours involved in purchasing most commercial products. Racist beliefs, attitudes and behaviours are far more complex than any purchasing behaviour.
- Many targeted behaviours, especially health behaviours, are inconsistent with social pressures. Consuming alcohol is a normative behaviour in most Western countries, with excess consumption not only condoned but encouraged among young males in some population segments. Social marketing aims to shift some behaviours such as recycling and condom use from unusual to normative behaviours, maintain others such as children's immunisation as normative behaviours, and shift some normative behaviours in some groups (say, doping in cycling) to being seen as aberrant behaviours.
- Social marketing often asks the target group to accept a reduction in personal benefits or increase in personal costs to achieve a societal benefit from which they may or may not directly benefit. This applies particularly to corporations in areas such as packaging, land clearing and toxic waste disposal.
- Commercial marketing mostly aims at groups already positive towards the product category and its benefits, whereas social marketing is often directed towards hard-to-reach, at-risk groups or to entrenched bureaucrats and others with vested interests who are antagonistic to change.
- Intermediaries and stakeholders in commercial marketing are far fewer in type and generally far easier to deal with (although perhaps more costly) than in social

marketing. Anti-drug campaigns targeting youth involve a broad variety of inter-mediaries: health department staff, youth drug workers, drug clinics, school author-ities, local government authorities, the police, sport coaches and youth entertainment operators. Commercial retailers can be influenced by monetary and promotional incentives in a straightforward negotiating process. Influencing medical practition-ers to co-operate in a health promotion campaign is far more complex and gaining co-operation from different government departments or NGOs requires substantial skills.

- Political considerations are far more frequent in social marketing. This applies not only to more obviously sensitive areas such as HIV/AIDS and illicit drugs, but also to all areas that are vulnerable to political party philosophy and governments desiring to stay in power. Large corporations and industry bodies clearly influence govern-ment policy in a variety of areas affecting health and wellbeing, and particularly in areas such as environmental degradation, alcohol marketing, pharmaceuticals, gambling, gun ownership, health insurance and processed foods.

- Commercial marketing mainly operates within social systems that are conducive to the marketers' goals and that facilitate the marketing and purchasing processes. Commercialisation, privatisation, sponsorship and the dominance of brand names in sport and entertainment all support a consuming culture. On the other hand, social marketing is operating in many areas where social systems not only inhibit success, but actually exacerbate the targeted problem, and possibly contributed to the prob-lem in the first place. Hence, social marketing is often – and should be *more* often – directed not just towards changes in individual behaviour, but towards changes in systems and social structures that operate to the detriment of the wellbeing of popu-lations. For example, is there any point in running anti-smoking campaigns or posi-tive parenting campaigns in communities with high unemployment, extensive drug use, high rates of domestic and street violence and poor and overcrowded housing? (On the other hand, is it ethical *not* to run anti-smoking campaigns in these areas if other communities are getting the campaign?)

- Ethical questions and issues of equity are far more complex and important in social marketing (for example, victim blaming). Commercial marketing practices would suggest that non-smokers should be offered a discount on their life insurance pol-icies. Given that a high proportion of smokers are lower income people likely to suf-fer from greater morbidity than upper income people anyway, is it ethical for health professionals to encourage private health insurers to offer this incentive?

- Social marketing programmes are often limited in comprehensiveness, duration and evaluation by available funds.

- Successful commercial marketers have a genuine concern for their customers' needs – not just their money. Social marketers share this concern, but at a deeper level. Social marketers' transactions with their clients have the underlying goals of enhanced self-esteem, empowerment and enhanced wellbeing.

Concluding comments

Although the techniques and principles of marketing are applicable to any consumer decision, their effective application to health and social policy areas requires an understanding of marketing and the content areas in which it is to be applied. In practical terms this requires close co-operation between marketing experts and staff within the content areas, as well as behavioural scientists with expertise in programme design and implementation, research and evaluation, communication theory, and attitude and behaviour change.

With regard to the above principles of marketing, in our opinion, it is the consumer orientation that most defines a marketing approach. It is a consumer orientation that forms the basis for many of the other marketing concepts and that distinguishes social marketing from other frameworks for achieving social change. What the discipline and philosophy of marketing also provides is a comprehensive planning framework for the development, implementation and evaluation of campaigns. It brings together concepts that are not necessarily new to those working for social change, but demands that they be considered.

QUESTIONS

● Which of the characteristics of a marketing approach do you think is most important? Why?

● Choose a cereal manufacturer. Match the range of products they make to the market segments they are targeting.

● If you were going to develop a programme targeting young people to moderate their alcohol consumption, what would be among the first things you would do?

FURTHER READING

Donovan, R. J., Paterson, D. and Francas, M. 1999. Targeting Male Perpetrators of Intimate Partner Violence: Western Australia's 'Freedom from Fear' Campaign, *Social Marketing Quarterly* 5(3): 127–43.

Public Agenda. 2008. Public Engagement: A Primer from Public Agenda, Essentials, No. 01/2008, Center for Advances in Public Engagement, available at: www.publicagenda.org/public-engagement-materials/public-engagement-primer-public-agenda.

Rudd, R. E., Kaphingst, K., Colton, T., Gregoire, J. and Hyde, J. 2004. Rewriting Public Health Information in Plain Language, *Journal of Health Communication* 9(3):195–206.

Sabbag, R. 2003. *Smokescreen*. Edinburgh: Canongate.

3 Social marketing and the environment

As noted in Chapter 2, commercial marketing has always been mindful of environmental factors that impinge on the consumer and on business in general. However, the regulatory and structural environment for commercial marketers is generally facilitative as governments tend to encourage commerce to maintain economic growth. However, that is not necessarily the case for social marketers who often have to lobby hard and long for regulatory and structural changes that enhance health and wellbeing.

In this chapter we look at aspects of the environment that are relevant to social marketers. First, we briefly discuss the legal, technological, political and socio-cultural aspects of the environment within which social marketers operate. Then we look in more depth at the ways in which the environment impacts on people's health, that is, the environmental determinants of health.

Reflecting the prevailing values of many social marketers to date, there has been a strong focus in social marketing on the individual's responsibility for adopting healthy lifestyle behaviours. This view is particularly popular with politicians, who abdicate responsibility for making structural changes by blaming the 'victims' rather than the conditions in which they live (Hastings, MacFadyen and Anderson 2000). This individual focus is called a 'downstream' approach, whereas a focus on environmental factors is called an 'upstream' approach. While some social marketers have been calling for more emphasis on upstream factors for some years, there has been little response in practice. However, current social marketing texts now acknowledge upstream factors more; Alan Andreasen has a text solely devoted to upstream social marketing (Andreasen 2006), and Kotler and Lee (2009) have a book devoted solely to poverty reduction.

In this chapter, we outline the evidence that social, economic and built environment factors beyond the individual's control have a powerful effect on overall health. For example, disadvantageous social factors outside the individual's control can foster unhealthy behaviours such as substance abuse and addictions. In short, the individual should not be left with the whole responsibility of their behaviour (Wilkinson and Marmot 1998).

The upstream/downstream metaphor comes from a frequently cited fable in public health involving people and a river. Clinical medicine is seen as rescuing people who have fallen into the river and been swept downstream. Preventive medicine is seen as going upstream to erect fences on the edge of the river so that people won't fall in. A variation on this fable is the 'ambulance in the valley' as in the box 'A Fence or an Ambulance', below – which also shows that an awareness of the benefits of prevention is hardly new, nor is the difficulty in getting politicians and others to accept the benefits of prevention. As Chapman and Lupton (1994) explain, the downstream approach involves heroic rescues, racing ambulances, new technologies, grateful patients and many opportunities for dramatic news stories and political capital. Upstream prevention approaches have much less news value because, as they point out, successful prevention strategies result in *nothing happening*.

The downstream approach addresses the individual person with recommended behaviours that will help them negotiate the river safely, that is, skills to stay afloat or swim; hence, a focus on educational approaches to eating right, exercising, refusing illicit drug offers, etc. The upstream approach addresses preventive measures that can be put in place by agencies and organisations that will bring about desired individual behaviours, sometimes without the individual's conscious volition; for example, a reduction in smoking can be achieved by banning cigarette advertising and taxing cigarettes. Hollingworth *et al.* (2006) calculate that in the United States, a tax-based 17 per cent increase in the price of alcohol could reduce deaths from harmful drinking by 1,490, and that a complete ban on alcohol advertising would reduce deaths by 7,609.

Upstream approaches targeting legislators can be much more cost-effective than downstream approaches targeting individuals. For example, in South Africa, the decision was taken in 1995 to legislate that all salt should be iodised in order to ensure universal access to iodised salt (Marks 1997). At the time, only 30 per cent of households used iodised salt, which was slightly more expensive than ordinary salt. Rural and low income people were less likely to have access to the iodised version or to purchase it. The alternative 'downstream' approach of a lifestyle modification programme to educate the whole population to choose iodised salt would have been much more costly and inevitably fallen short of the 100 per cent compliance obtained by the upstream approach.

Social marketers can increase the effectiveness of their campaign strategies by being aware of these determinants and adopting upstream approaches that create changes in the environment as well as downstream approaches targeting individuals' undesirable behaviours. In fact, Smith (1998) argued that social marketers should consider environmental change *first*. Only when all possible structural changes have been adopted to make it easier for people to change should we resort to trying to persuade individuals to change their behaviour.

Going upstream: restricting pack sizes of over-the-counter drugs to reduce self-poisoning in the United Kingdom

Paralleling increases in sales, misuse of paracetamol has been a major cause of liver poisoning in the United Kingdom and has led to a number of deaths. In September 1998, legislation was introduced that limited pack sizes of paracetamol, salicylates and their compounds in pharmacies to thirty-two tablets (previously no limit) and elsewhere to sixteen (previously twenty-four). Specific warnings were added to the packs and to a leaflet inside the pack. The rationale for this legislation was that analgesic self-poisoning is often impulsive, associated with low suicidal intent and little knowledge of the possible severe consequences. Hence, limiting availability was expected to lead to less misuse.

In the year following introduction of the legislation, deaths from paracetamol and salicylates poisoning decreased by 21 per cent and 48 per cent, respectively; liver transplant rates after paracetamol poisoning declined by 66 per cent. Furthermore, the number of tablets taken in overdoses decreased by 7 per cent and the proportion involving thirty-two or more tablets decreased by 17 per cent and 34 per cent for paracetamol and salicylates, respectively (Hawton *et al.* 2001). These results persisted with large overdoses reduced by 20 per cent and 39 per cent for paracetamol and salicylates in the second and third years after legislation was introduced (Hawton *et al.* 2004).

Stokols (1996) has argued that there will inevitably be 'blind spots' in focusing on either the individual or the environment. He advocates *social ecological analyses* that complement current approaches in health promotion by focusing on the interplay between the environment and the individual. His approach will be discussed later in the chapter.

Environmental monitoring

As with marketing in general, the success of a social marketing campaign depends in part on the marketer's accurate analysis of the complex environment in which the campaign appears. The purpose of the environmental analysis is to understand and monitor the environmental factors, predict the impact of these factors on the organisation's performance and make strategic decisions that will enhance competitiveness. Environmental factors include: political–legal; demographic–economic; social–cultural; and technological–physical environment factors (Kotler 2001). These factors are described separately, but must be analysed in terms of their interactions. For example, a demographic change such as population growth will have impacts on the physical environment by depleting resources and increasing pollution. All these factors are subject to change and, in our contemporary world, are changing at an ever-increasing rate. Environmental analysis takes account of the current environment, but also tries to anticipate future trends and developments (Kotler 2001).

Like any other marketers, social marketers must continually monitor the environment so as to be aware of competitive activities, opportunities for exploitation, factors requiring pre-emption and changes in attitudes, values and practices. Similarly, but more importantly than for commercial marketers, social marketers must focus on ways of changing the environment, because these physical, social, legal, technological and political environments may passively or actively inhibit desirable social change.

Political–legal

Monitoring the political–legal environment means being alert to possible changes in legislation, government priorities and the influence of numerous pressure groups that lobby government (Kotler 2001). An upstream approach open to social marketers is to increase the level of political will to make policy changes by changing social norms and increasing salience and concern over social issues in the general population (Henry 2001).

Changes in government may have an effect on social marketing priorities. This was seen in the Bush administration in the United States, where there were changes in policy relating to the physical environment (greenhouse gas emissions) and abortion, as well as a change in the inclusion and exclusion of organisations in the process of making health policy decisions (DeYoung 2001). Conversely, the election of Obama is expected to see greater government intervention in climate issues and health care.

Social marketing is often used to complement changes in legislation as well as to reinforce existing legislation. For example, domestic violence campaigns around the globe are commonly associated with changes in legislation (Donovan and Vlais 2005); the introduction of compulsory random breath testing (RBT) laws in Australia was supplemented with campaigns to inform people about the new law; and a campaign in Vietnam advocating the benefits of wearing a bicycle helmet preceded and facilitated the introduction of a law making it compulsory (Clegg 2009).

Demographic–economic

The demographic environment is analysed by noting trends in population growth, distribution (e.g., urban–rural) and movement, as well as demographics of age, gender, education, household characteristics and ethnicity. Marketers need to understand the characteristics of the ageing baby boomers (born between 1941 and 1960) as well as Generation X (born about 1961–81), Generation Y (born about 1982–2002), and (the future) Generation Z (born from 2003–23). These generations differ on many dimensions, such as their preference for green products and packaging, interest in recycling, music and entertainment tastes, and their attitudes towards convenience foods.

Economic trends associated with demographics include income, disposable income and patterns in savings, debt and credit (Kotler 2001). As unemployment goes up, the economy slows down and companies may respond by abandoning the development of luxury products in favour of low cost, generic alternatives. If the price of petrol goes up, people may drive less. A reduction in road fatalities might have more to do with the price of petrol than with a road safety campaign. Hence, a failure to analyse the environment might lead to an inflated assessment of the value of a campaign. Conversely, in the current global economic crisis with most developed countries showing negative growth, there is considerable stress on the already poor and the capacity of charities to meet the needs of the newly poor. Hence, campaigns trying to persuade people affected by the current economic climate to buy healthier foods at higher prices than less healthy foods face an uphill battle.

Social–cultural

The social–cultural environment includes the broad beliefs, values and social norms that people hold, how persistent the core values are over time, how norms shift over time and the existence of sub-cultures (Kotler 2001). Core values are reinforced by the family and all the major social institutions, including schools and churches. It is unlikely that social marketers would be able to change core values in campaigns of limited duration and scope. It reportedly took 250 years of campaigning to abolish slavery and 150 years to achieve the vote for women. Attempts in the United States to ban the sale of alcohol in the Prohibition era were unsuccessful, indicating that a core value was being targeted. On the other hand, social norms, or secondary values, may be more accessible to change, such as changing perceptions about drink-driving. People have been amenable to accepting a new social norm in most Western developed countries that drink-driving is not acceptable.

An example of a social marketing campaign sensitive to socio-cultural factors is a US campaign to prevent illness in young children associated with the preparation of a holiday dish, chitterlings (Peterson and Koehler 1997). It is safer to cook chitterlings by pre-boiling them for five minutes and this simple change in cooking method is effective in preventing a severe form of diarrhoea that was killing African-American children. However, it was recognised that this method of cooking chitterlings would be non-traditional for many families. The problem was overcome by enlisting the support of African-American grandmothers, who were able to recommend the new method as being safer for children with no difference in taste (confirmed in a taste test by the researchers). It also made cleaning up afterwards easier. The success of this campaign was measured in the fewer deaths of young children and the number admitted to hospital after the bacterium incubation period following Thanksgiving and Christmas holiday festivities. (This campaign is noted again in Chapter 11.)

Technological–physical

Technological trends also need to be considered, including the rate of change, the budgets available for technological innovations and the commercial opportunities for new technologies (Kotler 2001). From the social marketer's viewpoint, campaign effectiveness can be enhanced with appropriate technology (e.g., to iodise salt, manufacture safe helmets, measure consumption of alcohol in a breath test, etc.). Recent techno-logical advancements mean that we now have fast-response ambulances equipped with life saving machines resulting in a decline in deaths from cardiovascular disease and road accidents. On the other hand, high production-value advertisements for fast cars equipped with safety items such as air bags evoke a sense of thrill and invulnerability that has to be counteracted with effective road safety messages, often at a fraction of the car manufacturer's advertising budget.

The physical environment is affected by technological change, usually in a negative way. Raw materials are being used up, particularly finite, non-renewable resources such as oil. Finite renewable resources such as forests may be depleted and even resources that are seen as infinite, such as air and water, appear at risk in the long-term from pol-lution (Kotler 2001). The physical environment includes the climate, which can have a major effect on people's behaviour and, hence, their risk factors. For example, people might feel less like being physically active in the winter and might eat foods higher in fat. People in tropical climates need to be protected against malaria, while people in northern Canada would need to know how to protect against frostbite.

The physical environment exerts a powerful influence on what people do. Making a simple change to the environment is sometimes more effective than running an expensive campaign. For example, if pedestrian injuries at a junction can be traced to inebriated people stumbling out of a tavern on the corner, it will be more efficient to put up a barrier than to run a campaign to moderate their drinking or their behaviour as pedestrians.

Food for thought: a monitoring example

The influence of each of these aspects of the environment and the interaction between them can be illustrated by looking briefly at some of the many issues relating to food in contemporary times: 'fast' or 'convenience' food, 'green' or 'clean' food, 'GM (gen-etically modified) foods', and 'functional' food. We have chosen to illustrate the influ-ence of the environment using food as a case study because individual choices around food are powerfully affected by the environment in which they are made and have an equally powerful effect on the health of the individual who makes them. Healthy food choices will be made only in an environment where healthy food is accessible and affordable (Story *et al.* 2008).

Fast or convenience food includes takeaways, drive-throughs, casual dining, delis and pre-prepared supermarket meals (Hollingsworth 2001). Green or clean foods are organic, preservative free, all-natural and free of genetic modification (GM). GM foods, also emotively called 'Frankenstein foods' (Johnson *et al.* 2007), are foods where some alteration has been made to the plant or animal DNA. The term functional food is used where there is some beneficial effect beyond normal nutrition, particularly if it can help to reduce or prevent disease (Roberfroid 2002). It could be a naturally occurring food (e.g., high in dietary fibre), or one modified by adding something (e.g., a vitamin), or taking away something (e.g., unhealthy fats), or by making the nutrients more available to the body (Roberfroid 2002).

The term 'functional food' dates from the 1980s to refer to a fibre drink marketed in Japan, but the practice goes back much further – adding iodine to salt to prevent thyroid disease, adding thiamine to rice or bread for iron and adding fluoride to water for dental health (Dixon, Hinde and Banwell 2006). Claims for functionality relate to heart health (particularly in the United States and Europe), intestinal health (particularly in Japan and Europe), enhancing the body's defences and improving energy levels (Weststrate, van Poppel and Verschuren 2002), and preventing cancer, osteoporosis, and perhaps obesity (St-Onge 2005).

The *political–legal* environment around food has included major issues in Europe relating to 'mad-cow disease' and foot-and-mouth disease, and subsequent European import restrictions, with considerable impact on the economic environment. The European Union has passed the EU Food Law (2002), placing the responsibility for food safety with the European Commission and setting up the European Food Safety Authority (Todt *et al.* 2009). Other food scares include hormones in milk, e-coli in meat, fruit and vegetables (Finch 2006), and melamine in baby formula, milk and pet food coming from China (ABC News 2008).

Genetic modification has been a major issue, with regulations imposed on GM crops and moves in many countries to clearly label whether products contain any GM ingredients. Consumers have not readily accepted GM foods, especially in countries where labelling is required, perceiving the technologies to be risky and expressing moral concerns that it is wrong to interfere with nature (Frewer, Scholderer and Lambert 2003). Consumers may be worse off if the cost of separating out GM seeds from other crops has to be passed on, and producers may lose if consumer aversion to GM foods is not satisfactorily addressed (Fulton and Giannakas 2004).

Safety concerns are another issue, with calls for some products such as caffeine drinks to be restricted, especially for children and young people. There are serious health concerns as many of the ingredients, for example, of functional beverages, have not been tested, and may have adverse effects. For example, kava is suspected of causing liver toxicity and has been banned in Switzerland; St John's wort can reduce the effectiveness of prescribed drugs; and gingko biloba can interact with anticoagulants, including aspirin (Morales 2002).

There are legal issues about what health claims can be made for functional foods on the nutrition labels (Sloan 2000a), and whether such products should come under the definition of food or drugs as regulations relating to drugs are much more stringent. The lobbying power of the food industry has consistently blocked public health attempts to address dietary issues. For example, in 2000, the US Department of Agriculture attempted to include in official dietary guidelines a recommendation to limit consumption of sugar. The sugar industry lobbied on the basis that it would hurt their business and there was no proof of a link between sugar and obesity. The word 'limit' was not included in the guidelines (Brownlee 2001).

One opportunity for upstream social marketing is to encourage governments to use its influence in the lives of children – by providing healthy school lunches to children, sponsoring programmes and curricula on nutrition and requiring the provision of healthy food choices at school recreational events (Chou, Rashad and Grossman 2005). In Italy the provision of school meals is recognised as a way of educating children about food, as well as a way of supporting nutrition and health (Morgan and Sonnino 2007). Italy's Law 281, passed in 1998, sets high standards for the quality and safety of food given to children, as well as stressing the importance of educating children about food as part of their cultural heritage (Morgan and Sonnino 2007).

In the United Kingdom, partly in response to celebrity chef Jamie Oliver's television programme *School Dinners*, the accompanying publicity and a 300,000-signature petition, the Labour Government committed £280 million in additional funding (Jamie's School Dinners 2009) and introduced compulsory nutritional standards for school lunches (Morgan and Sonnino 2007).

In the *demographic–economic* environment, organic foods are perceived as being expensive and purchased by a young, affluent, well-educated and health-conscious demographic (Finch 2006), while functional foods appeal to baby boomers as they move into their fifties and sixties and become concerned with ageing and lifestyle disease risks (Frost and Sullivan 2008). Value is now being added to ordinary grocery foods by cutting the planning and preparation time of cooking, as seen in the variety of prepared salads and vegetables in the supermarket today.

It would seem that consumers generally prefer 'clean foods', foods that do not contain preservatives or GM modifications (Sloan 2001). With so much research and development into GM, it will be necessary to consider the public concerns and whether they can be overcome if a market is to be successfully constructed for the product (Frewer, Scholderer and Lambert 2003; Fulton and Giannakas 2004). At present, consumers are afraid of the risks involved in GM foods and sceptical about regulations which they perceive to have been influenced by industry (Todt *et al.* 2009). Consumers are concerned that non-GM crops may be contaminated by GM seeds (Fulton and Giannakas 2004), reducing public confidence in basic food products.

In the *social–cultural environment* there are trends to fast foods, convenience foods, vegetarianism, organic and clean foods. In the West, we now have a generation of adults who grew up entirely in the fast-food era. Fast food, with its high fat content, is frequently blamed for the epidemic of obesity in developing countries. The CARDIA study, a fifteen-year study of young adults in the United States, from both black and white ethnic types, investigated the consumption of fast food and found that it did correlate positively with gaining weight and becoming more resistant to insulin (a precursor to diabetes) (Pereira *et al.* 2005). Yet fast-food franchises have moved into some US hospitals (as well as many US schools), so that it is now possible to enjoy a Big Mac and fries before checking out after a triple by-pass operation (Brownlee 2001). Some have argued that children in hospital will recover faster being able to eat familiar food that 'brings back fun memories', but some hospitals have declared their intention not to renew contracts with fast-food franchises (Santora 2004). In the People's Republic of China, there is an increasing demand for Western-style convenience foods as incomes increase and the availability of foods and refrigeration has improved; additionally, as Western culture is fashionable, convenience food is seen as Western and therefore fashionable (Curtis, McCluskey and Wahl 2007).

There has also been an increase in the consumption of pre-prepared foods. The main reason given for serving pre-prepared foods at home is lack of time, with only 25 per cent of people planning meals before 9 am, and 50 per cent waiting until after 4 pm (Sloan 2000b). This is in keeping with the change in work patterns and household characteristics, with more women in the workforce and smaller family units. However, the home environment is a key aspect in children's food choices; there is evidence that children's consumption of healthy foods, such as fruits and vegetables, is strongly related to parental modelling of the behaviour, an authoritative parenting style that encourages healthy feeding but in a nurturing way, as well as parents making healthy foods available in the home (Story *et al.* 2008).

In the *technological–physical environment* there have been major developments in food science. Phytochemicals in common foods such as garlic, liquorice, cruciferous vegetables (e.g., broccoli and cauliflower) and soybeans have been found to inhibit the growth of cancer tumours (Caragay 1992). Soy phytoestrogens such as genistein have been shown to be particularly effective in suppressing mutant breast cancer cells (Privat *et al.* 2008).

The advances in genetic modification of foods, such as built-in pesticides may please farmers and produce healthy yields, but generally have not been readily accepted by consumers (Frewer, Scholderer and Lambert 2003; Lehrman 1999). There may be no discernible difference in taste, but consumers object on a cognitive level. However, if there is a difference in price, there is evidence from France to suggest that consumers are prepared to buy GM products provided they are inexpensive (Noussair, Robin and Ruffieux 2004).

Environmental determinants of health and wellbeing

We now address the influence of environmental determinants on health and wellbeing. It has long been known that the poor and disadvantaged have poorer health than their richer counterparts. The differences have largely been attributed to:

- *differences in risk behaviours*, such as poor diet, smoking, alcohol and drug abuse and poor personal hygiene, or
- *differences in the physical environment*, such as poor sanitation, overcrowded housing, lack of adequate heating, exposure to pollution, or
- *both* individual and environmental factors.

Other factors that affect health include lower rates of literacy and reduced access to medical services, both linked to lower socio-economic status (Wilkinson and Marmot 1998).

Obesogenic environments

Swinburn, Egger and Raza (1999) have proposed a framework to identify obesogenic environments: environments that promote or facilitate obesity in the population. The basic framework analyses physical factors (what foods and physical opportunities are available), economic factors (what are the costs), political factors (what are the 'rules') and socio-cultural factors (what are the attitudes and beliefs).

However, differences in lifestyle, deprivation and the physical environment only partly account for differences in health status. Poverty clearly contributes to poor health at the bottom of the scale, but in developed countries most people have access to adequate food, clothing, shelter and medical care. Comparisons between countries suggest that it is not the average level of income that determines health status, but *the size of the gap* between rich and poor within a country (Donovan 2000b; Wilkinson and Marmot 1998).

Physical and built environment determinants

The connections between land use and people's health have long been established in developed countries (Purdue, Gostin and Stone 2003), with perhaps the most obvious being between poor sanitation and diseases such as yellow fever in times past. Current connections between the built environment and health include designing for injury prevention (e.g., road design, building design and safety codes), exposure to toxins (e.g., lead in paint and petrol, pesticide and fertiliser run-off, incinerator emissions), violence and crime reduction and exercise and recreation (Peek-Asa and Zwerling 2003; Purdue, Gostin and Stone 2003). Given the interdependence of factors, there are also strong relationships between the built environment and mental wellbeing, with psychological distress, including depression, associated with traffic stress (Song *et al.* 2006) and crime (Curry, Latkin and Davey-Rothwell 2008). Obesity has also been associated with stress resulting from neighbourhood disorder (Burdette and Hill 2008).

Improved housing reduced illness in children in Malawi

The importance of housing standards for health is well accepted, but few studies have provided rigorous data on this effect. A well-designed study of a Habitat for Humanity Housing project in Malawi showed that improvements in housing were accompanied by a significant reduction in respiratory, gastrointestinal or malarial illnesses among children under five years compared to children in traditional homes (Wolff, Schroeder and Young 2001).

Many physical environment factors that cause ill-health are associated with socio-economic status. Poverty is associated with poor and overcrowded housing, inadequate sanitation and rubbish removal, lack of plumbing and clean water supplies, insufficient protection against temperature extremes and exposure to toxic fumes (Marmot 2000).

On a broader scale, certain geographical regions are more prone to various diseases than others, so that mosquito control is far more important in tropical regions than in temperate zones. Similarly, vaccination with HIB to protect against meningococcal meningitis is far more important in some parts of Africa than in Australia. Given the poor physical conditions in which many Indigenous people live in remote communities, environmental health workers (EHWs) play a crucial and different role in these communities than do EHWs in the suburbs.

Given the current focus on the so-called 'obesity epidemic', physical activity is receiving increasing attention from an ecological perspective. It is now widely accepted that participation in physical activity is likely to be influenced by the quality and design of the physical environment (Committee on Environmental Health 2009; Doyle *et al.* 2006; Humpel, Owen and Leslie 2002; Owen *et al.* 2004). Stairwells have been a popular setting in which to show the impact on use by drawing people's attention to stair use (point-of-decision prompts) and improving the ambience in the stairwell (Boutelle *et al.* 2001; Kerr *et al.* 2004).

Improving stairwell ambience increases use

Kerr and colleagues (2004) assessed the impact on stair use of four sequential environmental interventions: installing new carpet and painting the walls; adding framed artwork on stair landings; displaying motivational signs throughout the building; and adding a stereo system and playing various types of music in the stairwell. Appropriately enough, the setting was the main stairwell in the Centers for Disease Control and Prevention's (CDC) Rhodes Building in Atlanta, Georgia. Proximity sensors monitored traffic in the stairwell. Motivational signs and music both significantly increased stair use by 8.9 per cent over baseline. The increase in sign use occurred in the first three months of the intervention, whereas the increase in music occurred after the first three months.

The physical environment affects participation in two ways: *incidental* physical activity is encouraged or discouraged through energy-inducing or energy-reducing design of the urban environment, buildings and household appliances; and *planned* physical activity is encouraged (or discouraged) by providing (or not providing) accessible, convenient, safe, affordable and appealing recreational opportunities (Hahn and Craythorn 1994; King *et al.* 1995; Sallis *et al.* 1990). Automatic opening gates, escalators and elevators, push-button appliance controls (including windows in cars), the expansion of electronic entertainment devices and the provision of parking close to worksites and entertainment venues, all serve to decrease incidental physical activity. Attractive parks and walkways, safe cycleways separated from vehicular traffic and beach access serve to increase planned physical activity. All these examples suggest that if we want to increase physical activity and lessen obesity, we need the active involvement of disciplines and sectors outside health, including local government, urban planning, architectural design, transport and property developers.

Safety is of particular importance. For example, the Marin County, California 'Safe Routes to School Program' identifies safe routes to schools and invites community involvement. By its second year the programme served over 4,500 students in fifteen schools. Schools reported a 64 per cent increase in walking to school, a 114 per cent increase in biking and a 91 per cent increase in car-pooling. There was a 39 per cent reported decrease in private vehicle trips carrying only one student (Staunton, Hubsmith and Kallins 2003).

Crime prevention is one area that has received considerable environmental design input for many years – and with some success (Mair and Mair 2003). More than forty years ago, Jeffery (1971) introduced the concept of 'crime prevention through environmental design' (CPTED). This concept remains intact today, although updated and extended by Crowe (2000). Jeffery's recommendations were largely related to reducing the opportunity for, or increasing the difficulty of crime, particularly robbery of retail and transportation outlets. Factors such as lighting, cleanliness, escape routes, cash register location, employee training, alarms, cameras, grilles and bullet-resistant barriers have been found to markedly reduce crime (Casteel and Peek-Asa 2000).

Crime prevention through environmental design

A team of city planners, police officers and architects analysed land-use data and crime statistics in an area of Sarasota, Florida. Following consultation with local businesses, residents and community leaders, area redevelopment was encouraged using 'crime prevention through environmental design' (CPTED) principles along with increased police patrols to reduce prostitution. Compared with the rest of Sarasota, this area experienced reduced calls for police assistance, fewer crimes against persons and property and less prostitution (Carter, Carter and Dannenberg 2003).

Social determinants

Wilkinson and Marmot's (1998) landmark documentation of the social determinants of health (*The Solid Facts*, 2nd edition, 2003) listed ten areas that contributed significantly to people's health:

(1) the social gradient
(2) stress
(3) early life
(4) social exclusion
(5) work
(6) unemployment
(7) social support
(8) addiction
(9) food
(10) transport

Wilkinson and Marmot's publication attracted worldwide attention, and, given time, hopefully may lead to increased government attention to these determinants instead of the still current emphasis on individual risk behaviours. Health indicators that have been found to correlate with social class include mortality rates, birth weights, incidence of obesity, heart disease, lung disease, asthma, cancer, diabetes, lower back pain, sick days, smoking, alcoholism, teeth brushing, seat belt use, physical activity, television watching, diet, accident rates, suicide, depression and mental health (Henry 2001; Marmot and Wilkinson 1999, 2006; Wilkinson and Marmot 1998, 2003; Yen and Syme 1999).

Despite the popular notion that chief executives suffer more stress and are more likely to die of a heart attack, evidence clearly indicates that people in higher positions are *less* likely to suffer from disease. People on the lower rungs of the social ladder have generally twice the risk of serious illness and premature death than those near the top (Wilkinson and Marmot 2003). Interestingly, a continuous gradient has been found between each level, so that health declines progressively the further down the ladder you go (Henry 2001; Wilkinson and Marmot 2003).

Social determinants of health

The Whitehall studies (Marmot *et al.* 1978, 1991) followed 10,000 British civil servants with a twenty-five-year mortality follow-up. These showed a social gradient related to all-causes morbidity and mortality: there was a fourfold difference in mortality between men in the bottom grade of the civil service compared with men in the top grade; and each higher level in the employment hierarchy was associated with less morbidity and mortality even when holding all other factors constant. A large number of European and US studies show relationships between a number of social factors and health. For example, in one study, the best predictors of coronary heart disease were social isolation, depression, anxiety and low control at work; others have shown HDL cholesterol levels to be related to employment grade – independently of other risk factors.

Link and Phelan (1995, 1996) in the United States suggest that the differences are due to differences in resources such as knowledge, money and social connections that allow people to avoid risks and minimise disease consequences. However, this explains only the lower risk factor rates among higher social classes. Other researchers (e.g., McEwen in the United States; Marmot in the United Kingdom) have begun to look at the body's physiological response to stress (i.e., immune and hormonal responses) in terms of the relationship between these responses and causes of morbidity and mortality.

People with low control of their work, those living in poverty, those experiencing racism and those with little social support generally experience far greater sustained or chronic stress than those higher up the social scale. Marmot and others postulate that it is the additional and sustained stress experienced by those lower down the social scale that not only increases an individual's vulnerability to lifestyle risk factors, but also, through effects on the hormonal and immune system, independently contributes to morbidity and mortality. A number of studies – both with humans and animals – support the notion that higher status individuals not only experience less stress (in terms of physiological responses), but also recover more quickly than do those of lower status (Wilkinson and Marmot 1998).

Whatever the 'cause' might be, it is clear that some fundamental factors are operating to sustain the social gradient of disease.

Data from the British civil service in the 1960s showed that there were significant differences in health across the five classes of public servants, all of which were relatively affluent (Marmot *et al.* 1978). In a follow-up study in the 1980s, Marmot and colleagues found the same differences in morbidity still existed twenty years later among the classes of British civil servants (Marmot 2000; Marmot *et al.* 1991).

The work environment can have a major impact on health (Wilkinson and Marmot 2003). Health improves as people have greater control over their work environment, more opportunity to use their skills and greater rewards (including money, status and self-esteem). The negative effects of a poor work environment can be mitigated somewhat in a workplace where there is strong social support. Interestingly, studies of primates and humans show greater risk of cardiovascular disease in those in subordinate positions (Henry 2001; Wilkinson and Marmot 1998).

Healthy food availability may depend on where you live

Using a healthy food availability index (HFAI), researchers assessed the availability of healthy foods in 226 neighbourhood stores in 159 neighbourhoods in Baltimore. They found that 43 per cent of predominantly black neighbourhoods and 46 per cent of lower-income neighbourhoods were in the lowest tertile of healthy food availability versus 4 per cent and 13 per cent in predominantly white and higher-income neighbourhoods, respectively. The authors conclude that these differences may contribute to racial and economic health disparities (Franco *et al.* 2008).

Social class and self-efficacy

Self-efficacy is the individual's sense that they can exert control over their environment and the sense that they are able to perform deliberate and conscious behaviours, such as quitting smoking, if this is what they want to do. The concept of self-efficacy has received much attention in the threat appeals literature, where it is theorised to be a critical factor in determining whether a threat appeal will motivate the recipient to take appropriate action (when self-efficacy is high) or to adopt a maladaptive response (when self-efficacy is low) (Snipes, LaTour and Bliss 1999; Witte 1998; Witte and Allen 2000).

Perhaps not unexpectedly, given less access to power and resources, self-efficacy has been found to be associated with social class. Lower-class respondents have been found to have a limited sense of mastery, a greater sense of perceived constraints and a more fatalistic attitude towards their health. This fatalistic, pessimistic view of the future leads to limited planning for the long term and less persistence of long-term healthy behavioural patterns (Henry 2001).

Economic determinants

It is tempting to think that all that is needed to reduce the effect of social determinants is a more equal distribution of wealth. Mayer (1997) studied the effect of income on children whose basic material needs were already being met through income support programmes. She concluded that doubling the income of low income families would improve some outcomes (such as raising children's test scores by a couple of points and the years of education by a couple of months), but it would not have a significant effect on health outcomes unless accompanied by changes in the non-economic domain, such as the years of parents' education, the age of young mothers, the experience of racism and single parenthood (Mayer 1997). That is, income support programmes must be accompanied by educational programmes for long-term success, such as in conditional cash transfer (CCT) programmes.

Families enrolled in CCT programmes receive cash for complying with conditions, such as attending nutrition education courses, regular school attendance and regular community clinic checks on the children. The aim is to ensure better health and educational outcomes for the children in particular and, hence, prevent health and social problems later on. CCT programmes in areas of extreme poverty appear to be successful in increasing the health of children in these programmes, which aim to not only alleviate poverty in the short term, but also, by increasing the children's health, break intergenerational poverty and increase human capital.

There are several CCT programmes in place in Latin America, including *Oportunidades* in Mexico, *Bolsa Alimentação* in Brazil, *Red de Protección Social* in Nicaragua, *Programa de Asignación Familial* in Honduras, *Familias en Acción* in Colombia and *Subsidio Unico Familiar* in Chile (Fernald, Gertler and Neufeld 2008). A CCT programme is reportedly planned for New York City (Cardwell 2007). In general, these programmes have been associated with significant health improvements in the short term for the children involved.

Fernald, Gertler and Neufeld (2008) demonstrated that the cash component significantly contributes to these positive health outcomes. Perhaps more importantly given our next section, Fernald and Gunnar (2009) showed that involvement in *Oportunidades* was associated with favourable changes in salivary cortisol levels – which are related to activity of the stress-sensitive hypothalamic–pituitary–adrenocortical (HPA) system. They state that this is strong evidence that a family's economic circumstances can affect a child's developing stress system and, hence, the child's life-course risk for physical and mental health disorders.

At a broader level, micro-financing represents a means for low income groups to access finance to begin small enterprises. This has been very successful since its inception in Bangladesh in 1976 in the form of Muhammad Yunus' Grameen Bank Project (Yunus and Jolis 1999).

Muhammad Yunus and Grameen Bank

Following a field trip to a poor village, Professor Muhammad Yunus saw at first-hand how the poor could make little headway by borrowing at the rates they were charged. However, using his own money, he found it was possible with very small amounts that people could not only survive, but could create the spark of personal initiative and enterprise necessary to pull themselves out of poverty. In 1983 he formally formed the Grameen Bank, meaning 'village bank' founded on principles of trust and solidarity. The Grameen website in April 2009 reported that Grameen has 1,084 branches in Bangladesh, with 12,500 staff serving 2.1 million borrowers in 37,000 villages. Of the borrowers, 94 per cent are women and more than 98 per cent of the loans are paid back, a recovery rate higher than any other banking system. Grameen methods are applied in projects in fifty-eight countries, including the United States, Canada, France, the Netherlands and Norway (www.grameen-info.org).

Other groups attempt to help low income groups with savings plans, budgeting, keeping track of their finances and so on. These are not targeted at just low income groups. For example the UK Financial Services Authority's 'Moneymadeclear' provides a number of resources for people wishing to improve their financial capabilities in plain, jargon-free language (www.moneymadeclear.fsa.gov.uk). The Australian 'Foodcents' programme is a way of addressing nutrition issues in low income groups. The Foodcents programme shows low income groups how to eat healthily and save money. It incorporates lessons on budgeting, cooking and shopping (www.foodcentsprogram.com.au).

Importance of early childhood

In the past three decades there has been a substantial amount of research in the neurobiological, behavioural and social sciences about the importance of early childhood – including pre-natal conditions – in predicting health and other outcomes in later life (Shonkoff and Phillips 2000). This has led to increasing attention around the globe to the need to ensure that children's neurological and socio-emotional development proceed optimally. For example, the UK Childcare Act of 2006 committed to a national network of children's centres, based on results of the Sure Start programme. The centres are also expected to link parents to training and education opportunities, and with health services such as ante-natal and post-natal support, smoking cessation support, and speech and language therapy. By 2009, some 3,000 Sure Start Children's Centres, providing services for 2.3 million children were in operation (Halfon *et al.* 2009).

However, some countries are more likely than others to actually implement policies and programmes to enhance early childhood. For example, in the 1990s, almost 100 per cent of French and Belgian children were enrolled in an educational pre-school programme by age three, compared with 28 per cent of Spanish and Portuguese children and less than 6 per cent of Swiss children of that age (Boocock 1995). UNICEF publishes 'a league table of early childhood education and care in economically advanced countries', based on ten criteria such as extent of parental leave, the existence of a national plan with priority for disadvantaged children, training of child-care staff, amount of GDP spent on early childhood services and so on. The results are presented as a Report Card (see box; UNICEF 2008) and reflect a country's understanding of neurological–environmental interactions and a willingness for governments to do something about a country's investment in its human capital.

UNICEF Report Card			
Top six countries (8+)		Bottom seven countries (3−)	
Sweden	10	Mexico	3
Iceland	9	Spain	3
Denmark	8	Switzerland	3
Finland	8	United States	3
France	8	Australia	2
Norway	8	Canada	1
		Ireland	1

Taking an economic view of human capital, Heckman (2006) lists four evidence-based core concepts that underpin the importance of good early childhood policy:

(1) the architecture of the brain and the process of skill formation are influenced by an interaction between genetics and individual experience;
(2) the mastery of skills essential for economic success and their underlying neuro pathways follow a hierarchical process such that later developments are based on foundations laid earlier;
(3) cognitive, linguistic, social and emotional competencies necessary for success in life are interdependent and heavily influenced by childhood experiences;
(4) the development of human abilities follows a predictable sequence of sensitive periods in which the neural circuits and associated behaviour are most subject to environmental influences.

Hence, some countries have introduced policies and programmes purporting to acknowledge such facts, most noticeably articulated in programmes targeting pre- and early school children in disadvantaged areas, for example, Head Start (US), Healthy Start (Hawaii), Sure Start (UK) and Building Blocks (Australia).

Hawkins, Catalano and colleagues in the United States have demonstrated the importance of protecting children in early childhood from risk factors that could lead to crime, violence, teenage pregnancy and substance abuse. They have developed a prevention planning system, Communities That Care (Harachi *et al.* 1996; Hawkins, Catalano and Miller 1992), to promote the positive development of children, based on community involvement. In 2002 they claimed that more than 400 communities have used their system over the previous thirteen years with positive results. The programme is offered by the Channing Bete Company (www.channing-bete.com). The aim of this prevention strategy is to mobilise and train communities to reduce risk factors and increase protective factors that reduce the incidence of uptake of substances such as tobacco, alcohol and illicit drugs. The programme has three phases:

- the recruitment and training of key community leaders to drive the process, act to recruit other community members and to oversee the operation of the other phases, such as data collection, analysis and intervention planning and implementation;
- a risk-and-resources assessment in order to complete an inventory of the community's health. This phase allows communities to determine which risk and protective factors are important to target for intervention;
- planning and implementation of intervention strategies that meet the needs of the community, and that have been shown to impact upon the significant risk and protective factors that are relevant to the community.

Process and formative evaluations indicate that this approach is effective in bringing communities together to assess risk and protective factors for substance abuse and then implement evidenced-based strategies to reduce such problems. For example, Manger *et al.* (1992) describe a state-wide implementation of this approach in twenty-eight communities in Washington State resulting in reductions in adolescent drug abuse. Harachi *et al.* (1996) describe a replication of this process in 31 communities in Oregon.

Social determinants: the gangs of New York

The gangster whose reign ended with the murder of Kid Dropper was primarily a product of his environment: poverty and disorganisation of home and community brought him into being, and political corruption and all its attendant evils fostered his growth. He generally began as a member of a juvenile gang, and lack of proper direction and supervision naturally graduated him into the ranks of the older gangsters …

Moreover, his only escape from the misery of his surroundings lay in excitement, and he could imagine no outlets for his turbulent spirit save sex and fighting.

And many a boy became a gangster solely because of an overwhelming desire to emulate the exploits of some spectacular figure of the underworld, or because of a yearning for fame and glory which he was unable to satisfy except by acquiring a reputation as a tough guy and a hard mug. Of course, there were exceptions … but in the main the gangster was a stupid roughneck born in filth and squalor and reared amid vice and corruption. He fulfilled his natural destiny. Herbert Asbury, 5 January 1928 (in Asbury 2002).

Factors that protect children from risk are: a strong bonding to school, family and friends; healthy beliefs and expectations of success; clear standards against criminal behaviour and early sexual activity; as well as individual characteristics, such as resilience, intelligence (though intelligence does not protect against substance abuse) and a sociable disposition (Lehman *et al.* 1994). It is estimated that children develop some of these individual characteristics in early childhood, sometimes as early as two years of age. Children's 'habitual ways of responding', such as with persistence and enthusiasm have been developed by age two. This is also the critical period for learning emotional control, while social competence with peers begins around age three and continues to six or seven years (Williams, Zubrick and Silburn 2001).

Figure 3.1 suggests that disturbed attachments in early childhood are likely to lead to adult ill-health via substance abuse and other risky behaviours, and/or through experiencing greater stress in life. Even if a child achieves adequate attachments in early childhood, the loss of the ability to maintain social supports can result in adult ill-health. Hence, it is crucial to act early, especially in low socio-economic circumstances. Such programmes are available if there is the political will to implement them. For example, a low cost home visiting programme in South Africa had significant impact on mother–infant bonding and the child's emotional development (Cooper *et al.* 2009).

The influence of two protective environmental factors, social bonding to family and to school, was investigated in a non-randomised, controlled study conducted in a high crime area in Seattle (Hawkins *et al.* 1999). It provided a multi-component intervention for children in grades 1–6, with a follow-up six years later. The intervention consisted of in-service training for teachers, parenting classes offered to parents and developmentally appropriate social competence training for children. The aim was to

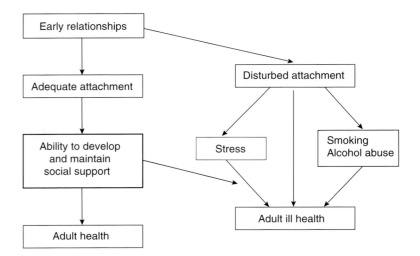

Figure 3.1 Importance of early life experiences and social support on adult health

increase the children's sense of bonding with family and school. There was no attempt to develop competencies relating to health risk behaviours, such as 'how to say no to drugs'. The children were not informed at the time that they were part of a study, and at the follow-up six years later they would not have known whether they were in the intervention or control group, minimising possible 'halo' effects.

For a cost per child of US$2,991, there were significant positive effects relating to school achievement and behaviour. Positive effects had endured at the follow-up at 18 years: significantly fewer in the intervention group had committed violent delinquent acts by age 18, used alcohol heavily and had had multiple sex partners (Hawkins *et al.* 1999). These positive outcomes were generally maintained at 21 years (Lonczak *et al.* 2002).

The Triple-P Positive Parenting Programme, developed by Sanders and colleagues in Queensland, is a behavioural family intervention that has been shown to be an effective clinical intervention suitable for adaptation as a population-based strategy. The programme aims to reduce or prevent emotional and behavioural problems in children by targeting their parents with a multi-level parenting programme. The programme develops knowledge, skills, confidence and teamwork in parents (Sanders 2001). A randomised controlled trial was conducted with parents of three-year-olds at high risk for developing behaviour problems, with a follow-up one year later. Parents who received training in parenting strategies observed a significant decrease in disruptive behaviour in their children, compared with the control group (Sanders *et al.* 2000; Sanders, Markie-Dadds and Tully 2001). It has been estimated that if such behavioural family interventions were to be adopted as a universal strategy to reach all eligible families, it would reduce the number of children with behaviour problems by 37 per cent in two years (Zubrick *et al.* 2005). The Triple-P has been successfully tested with Japanese parents (Matsumoto, Sofronoff and Sanders 2007) and in Germany and Switzerland (Cina *et al.* 2006).

The World Health Organisation (WHO) suggested six policies that would significantly improve the health of future adults:

(1) reduce parents' smoking;

(2) increase parents' knowledge of health and understanding of children's emotional needs;

(3) introduce pre-school programmes not only to improve reading and stimulate cognitive development, but also to reduce behaviour problems in childhood and promote educational attainment, occupational chances and healthy behaviour in adulthood;

(4) involve parents in pre-school programmes to reinforce their educational effects and reduce child abuse;

(5) ensure that mothers have adequate social and economic resources; and

(6) increase opportunities for educational attainment at all ages, since education is associated with raised health awareness and improved self-care. Wilkinson and Marmot (1998).

Social capital

It has been suggested that the effect of relative deprivation and income inequality may be a reflection of low social capital, and that it is the effect of low social capital that causes negative health effects (Kawachi *et al.* 1997). This idea is receiving growing attention among social marketers (Donovan 2000b; Hastings, MacFayden and Anderson 2000), and is discussed more fully below.

Social capital was defined by Robert Putnam as 'features of social organisation such as networks, norms and trust, that facilitate co-ordination and co-operation for mutual benefit' (1995b). It refers to the degree of interaction between people, both formal and informal, and the levels of civic engagement, trust, mutual obligation and caring in the community. Some people now believe social capital to be the most important determinant of health (Lomas 1998).

Greater health is associated with a sense of belonging and being valued (Wilkinson and Marmot 1998). Indicators of social capital, such as trust, reciprocity and participation in voluntary organisations have been associated with reduced mortality rates. Kawachi *et al.* (1997) attempted to quantify the effect of social capital. They estimated that an increase in overall trust by 10 per cent in the population would lead to a reduction in the age-adjusted mortality rate of about 67 per 100,000 people per year. Improvements in health can be achieved with increases in community involvement and supportive networks that reduce isolation and foster cohesion. Perhaps social capital improves health by increasing people's sense of self-worth (Berkman 1995, cited in Henry 2001). Wilkinson and Marmot (1998, p. 21) concluded that 'in all areas of personal and institutional life, practices should be avoided that cast others as socially inferior or less valuable'.

Social capital protects against binge drinking

Weitzman and Kawachi (2000) found a 26 per cent lower risk for binge drinking (three or more drinks at a time) for individuals on campuses with higher than average levels of social capital, where social capital was measured by the average time committed to volunteering aggregated to the whole campus. That is, on campuses where there was generally more volunteering, the incidence of individual binge drinking was lower. Interestingly, as might be expected, the incidence of social drinking (one or two drinks at a time) was higher on campuses with higher social capital.

Although this association is correlational, not causal, a college administration concerned about the level of students' binge drinking may wish to consider implementing initiatives that are intended to increase the level of volunteerism on campus. This strategy may be at least as effective as, and may be more effective than, trying to change individual behaviour.

Social cohesion is in part the product of the physical structure, such as the design of housing estates, and social structure, including community centres and opportunities for meeting and interaction (Lomas 1998). Small changes at a local level could make a substantial difference to social capital, for example, by increasing the number and size of public spaces or encouraging architects to design homes with verandas on the *front* of houses rather than the back, or by subsidising local clubs (Lomas 1998).

Bearing in mind the current thinking about social capital, social marketers can build in to their communication strategies messages that *reinforce* social bonds. For example, the director of a drink-driving rehabilitation centre in Queensland reported that high-risk offenders reacted with hostility to the drink-driving campaign slogan 'If you drink and drive, you're a bloody idiot', feeling personally insulted. However, they seemed to respond more favourably to messages such as 'Mates don't let their mates drink and drive'. She said: 'Offenders ask to be shown gory videos, thinking that will help, but most of them have been in multiple crashes already, may even have been responsible for fatalities; they've lived through worse than we could ever show them and that hasn't worked. What works is being drawn into the community, being included' (Donovan *et al.* 1995).

Racism and ill-health

Discrimination and stigmatisation of any sort causes considerable psychological distress, which can then influence mental and physical wellbeing. Race and self-reported racism is clearly associated with mental and physical illness (Karlsen and Nazroo 2002; Paradies 2006), yet is largely ignored as an upstream intervention.

Social ecology

The theory of social ecology in health promotion is another example of the shift from the downstream, individual-focused, lifestyle-modification approach to a broader understanding of health protective factors. Stokols (1996) advocated the theory of social ecology as one of three complementary perspectives on health promotion:

- targeting the individual with behaviour-change recommendations relating to lifestyle issues such as smoking, substance use, diet, exercise and safety;
- changing the environment to maximise health protective factors by creating a safe place, free from contagious disease and unhealthy levels of stress (caused by environmental factors such as pollution, racism or violence), in which healthy behaviours are actively facilitated and where people have access to health care; and
- social ecological analyses that attempt to understand the interplay between the environment and the individual, emphasising the interdependence of multiple environments and the contributions of many, diverse disciplines.

Thus, while the individual behaviour-change approach may be concerned with persuasion theories and health communication, and the environmental-change approach may consider urban planning and injury control, the social-ecological approach focuses on aspects such as cultural-change models of health, medical sociology, community health and public policy (Stokols 1996). The major contribution of the social-ecological approach is that it provides a systems framework within which behavioural and environmental factors can be integrated, thereby eliminating the 'blind spots' inherent in focusing on either the individual or the environmental approach (Stokols 1996). A typical ecological health evaluation involves different levels of analysis and multiple methodologies, from individual medical examinations to environmental assessments to epidemiological analyses (Stokols 1996).

Cohen, Schribner and Farley (2000) provide a useful framework based on ecological theory. They postulate four categories of structural factors that influence individuals' behaviours: the availability of protective or harmful consumer products (e.g., tobacco, alcohol, guns, fatty foods, condoms, fruit and vegetables, etc.); physical structures and physical characteristics of products (e.g., buildings, neighbourhood design, lighting, seat belts, childproof medicine containers, etc.); social structures and policies (e.g., strict versus lax enforcement of laws and policies, unsupervised youth, social norms, etc.); and media and cultural messages (e.g., advertising messages re materialism, depictions of violence, racism, etc.). Hence, with regard to firearms in the United States, there is relatively easy availability; fear and perceived likelihood of crime facilitate purchasing; safety locks can make guns safer – other modifications make them more lethal; and television shows and movies suggest that guns are a good – and normative – way to resolve conflicts.

Concluding comments

There is now a growing movement in public health and injury prevention to address environmental determinants of health in the areas of education, employment and income by influencing government policy on a broad scale. Social marketing practitioners need to recognise this fundamental shift in public health strategy, and to become part of it. Just as public health professionals have needed to familiarise themselves with fundamental marketing principles, so social marketers now need to better understand the fundamental principles and philosophies of public health if we are to play a role in changing the social determinants of health. As Donovan and Hastings have pointed out both separately and jointly (Hastings and Donovan 2002) the emphasis of social marketing should shift from marketing voluntary healthy behaviours to individuals in the general population to targeting community leaders, who have the power and influence to make major institutional policy and legislative changes.

If we are to have an impact on social determinants, social marketers will need to think in terms of group and system effects rather than just individual effects. This may require a cultural shift from thinking of health as the individual's responsibility to seeing it as a collective social responsibility. Thus, the slogan of a major US initiative targeting children and educators 'Healthy children make healthy communities' would be reversed: we need to build healthy communities if we are to have healthy children. Or, as the allegedly African saying goes: 'It takes a village to raise a child'.

To influence policymakers and legislators to address upstream strategies will require a supportive public. However, to date there have been few systematic attempts to increase the public's awareness of the importance of social determinants of health. One exception is the Peterborough County–City Health Unit in Ontario, Canada. The unit ran a poverty and health campaign in 2007–8 featuring three television ads that dealt with the relationship between income and health, housing and health and access to nutritious food and health. The website offers extensive relevant information on the social determinants of health and tips on how to take action (www.pcchu.ca/PH/PH-SDH.html).

A Fence or an Ambulance?

'Twas a dangerous cliff, as they freely confessed,
Though to walk near its crest was so pleasant;
But over its terrible edge there had slipped
A duke and full many a peasant.
So the people said something would have to be done,
But their projects did not at all tally;
Some said, 'Put a fence round the edge of the cliff,'
Some, 'An ambulance down in the valley.'

'For the cliff is all right, if you're careful,' they said,
'And, if folks even slip and are dropping,
It isn't the slipping that hurts them so much
As the shock down below when they're stopping.'
So day after day, as these mishaps occurred,
Quick forth would those rescuers sally
To pick up the victims who fell off the cliff,
With their ambulance down in the valley.

Then an old sage remarked: 'It's a marvel to me
That people give far more attention
To repairing results than to stopping the cause,
When they'd much better aim at prevention.
Let us stop at its source all this mischief,' cried he,
'Come, neighbours and friends, let us rally;
If the cliff we will fence, we might almost dispense
With the ambulance down in the valley.'

'Oh he's a fanatic,' the others rejoined,
'Dispense with the ambulance? Never!
He'd dispense with all charities, too, if he could;
No! No! We'll support them forever.
Aren't we picking up folks just as fast as they fall?
And shall this man dictate to us? Shall he?
Why should people of sense stop to put up a fence,
While the ambulance works in the valley?'

But the sensible few, who are practical too,
Will not bear with such nonsense much longer;
They believe that prevention is better than cure,
And their party will soon be the stronger.
Encourage them then, with your purse, voice, and pen,
And while other philanthropists dally,
They will scorn all pretence, and put up a stout fence
On the cliff that hangs over the valley.

Joseph Malins (1895)

QUESTIONS

● What are the major technological trends at the moment? How will they influence how we communicate with different target audiences?

● What are the major economic trends at the moment? How will they influence the social determinants of health?

● What are the major social and physical environmental factors that inhibit people being more physically active? How might we reduce those barriers?

FURTHER READING

Cohen, D. A., Scribner, R. A. and Farley, T. A. 2000. A Structural Model of Health Behaviour: A Pragmatic Approach to Explain and Influence Health Behaviours at the Population Level, *Preventive Medicine* 30: 146–54.

Donovan, R. J. and Vlais, R. 2005. Review of Communication Components of Social Marketing/Public Education Campaigns Focusing on Violence Against Women, Report to VicHealth, Melbourne, Australia.

2006. A Review of Communication Components of Anti-racism and Pro Diversity Social Marketing/Public Education Campaigns, Report to VicHealth, Melbourne, Australia.

Fernald, L. C. H., Gertler, P. J. and Neufeld, L. M. 2008. Role of Cash in Conditional Cash Transfer Programmes for Child Health, Growth, and Development: An Analysis of Mexico's Oportunidades, *Lancet* 371: 828–37

Humpel, N., Owen, N. and Leslie, E. 2002. Environmental Factors Associated with Adults' Participation in Physical Activity, *American Journal of Preventive Medicine* 22(3): 188–99.

Yunus, M. and Jolis, A. 1999. *Banker to the Poor: the Autobiography of Muhammad Yunus, Founder of the Grameen Bank.* London: Aurim Press.

Wilkinson, R. G. and Marmot, M. 2003. *The Solid Facts*, 2nd edn, available at: www.euro. who.int/DOCUMENT/E81384.PDF.

4 Advocacy and environmental change

Following on from our discussion in the previous chapter about the need to address social determinants with upstream strategies, in this chapter we look more closely at how social marketers can use advocacy to achieve change, and, specifically, how advocacy can be and is being used to address the world's challenges relating to environmental change. As Margaret Mead is reported to have said: '*Never doubt that a small group of thoughtful, committed citizens can change the world; indeed, it is the only thing that ever has.*' However, Hubert (2000) pragmatically reminds us that most successes by NGOs result from strategic alliances with positive governments or politicians.

Advocacy is about actively supporting a person or cause. In the legal context, an advocate is a lawyer who defends someone who is accused of a crime. In the context of public health, the World Health Organization has defined advocacy as 'a combination of individual and social actions designed to gain political commitment, policy support, social acceptance and systems support for a particular health goal or programme' (WHO 1995). Another definition of advocacy from the public health literature is 'action taken on behalf of individuals and/or communities to overcome structural barriers to health' (Nutbeam 1998).

Advocacy 'uses the media to strategically apply pressure for policy change. It provides a framework for moving the public health discussion from a primary focus on the health behavior of individuals to the behavior of the policymakers whose decisions structure the environment in which people act' (Wallack and Dorfman 1996). These definitions from the public health literature could be made to apply more generally in terms of overcoming barriers to other issues, for example, social inclusion, environmental sustainability and so on.

Despite numerous calls for advocacy to be used more fully in social marketing, it is still a neglected area. Chapman (2004) points out that there are few postgraduate courses teaching the principles of advocacy and no journals dedicated to disseminating academic findings about what works and what doesn't. There is some literature that discusses what has worked in the past, for example, Chapman's (2007) book, *Public Health Advocacy and Tobacco Control: Making Smoking History*, and Susan Braun's (2003) article, 'The History of Breast Cancer Advocacy'.

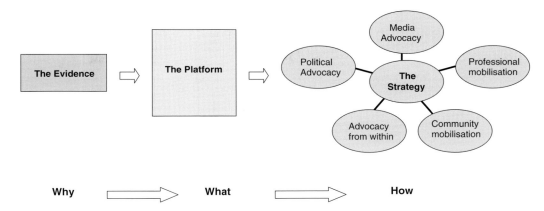

Figure 4.1 A three-step – why, what and how – model of advocacy
Shilton (2006).

One of the problems with advocacy is that it is often very difficult to evaluate the specific effects of particular advocacy strategies as they are usually accompanied by other approaches, take place over time, use a diverse range of actions, are directed at different targets and often with delayed effects (Fawcett *et al.* 1997). Some measurements can be made of media advocacy efforts – how many media stories on a topic, whether the coverage is positive or negative, whether is it is prominent (e.g., large item on page one of a major newspaper or beginning of a news broadcast) or not, and so on – but this does not measure whether it has been heard, understood or had any effect on the audience (Stead, Hastings and Eadie 2002). A comprehensive framework for evaluating media advocacy outcomes can be found in Stead, Hastings and Eadie (2002). Shilton's (2006) model (see Figure 4.1 above) is a useful starting point for planning advocacy strategy, depicting the why, what and how of advocacy.

The 'why' relates to the evidence on which we choose to advocate – in public health terms this could be epidemiological evidence, such as the effect of sedentariness on the health of a population. It might also include evidence that more people walking to work or taking public transport helps the environment, which might be more persuasive than the evidence around health benefits, either with the public or with politicians who want to remain popular with the media and the electorate.

The 'what' platform is the determination about what will be advocated – in social marketing terms, this could be seen as getting the right message. It can include a prioritised list of actions – a ten-point plan to achieve the desired outcome. In the context of physical activity, for example, this could involve obtaining high-level government endorsement for national guidelines about the recommended levels of activity for children, adults and seniors.

Then there is the 'how' – the advocacy strategy itself – and that has several components – what strategy will be used in a political sense, with the media to mobilise the professionals or experts, to mobilise the community or public, and how to advocate from within. These five components are incorporated in Shilton's ten-point plan for physical activity advocacy (see box below) and will each be discussed below in the context of advocating for physical activity.

Shilton's (2006) ten-point plan for physical activity advocacy

(1) Establish a task force or government body of some sort that will have high level support in government and that includes the whole of the community.
(2) Design and implement a comprehensive strategy for physical activity.
(3) Ensure the strategy is fully resourced.
(4) Provide support for regular monitoring of population level data on physical activity levels in different target markets, e.g., children, adults and seniors.
(5) Resource mass media campaigns to promote physical activity.
(6) Resource proven programmes that will include participation on a large scale, tailored to different target audiences.
(7) Resource transport programmes to encourage walking and cycling for transport.
(8) Liaise with the planners whose decisions about new developments will make a difference to the activity levels of the people who live and work in them.
(9) Look at the needs of different segments and the life stages they are in, and plan to intervene at key points, e.g., with children, with young women, with seniors.
(10) Make physical activity in schools mandatory and resource teacher training to ensure high-quality programmes.

Political advocacy: This should be the central driving element, which is why the ten-point plan begins with forming a high-level political board or task force, supported by, if possible, the head of government or head of state, and including senior government ministers with responsibilities for health, the environment, planning and infrastructure, sport, tourism and recreation. This is a first step, and a necessary platform for further engaging opportunities for policy decisions that can increase physical activity in the community, such as policies relating to public transport and town planning.

Professional or workplace mobilisation: Professionals or experts in the discipline are all potential allies. In the context of physical activity, professionals could be mobilised from health, education, sport and recreation, planning, transport and the environment.

Community mobilisation: Depending on the context, the community may be more or less inclined to support the issue. In the context of physical activity, the community as a whole is generally in agreement with promoting physical activity messages and can be mobilised through sporting clubs, parents' organisations, community centres and so on.

Advocacy from within: People can be encouraged to advocate outwards to the media, to their council and MPs, but also encouraged to recognise more immediate opportunities to advocate within their own organisation. An advocate who lobbies colleagues and key decisionmakers within their organisation, for example, can improve physical activity opportunities by asking for showers to be installed at the workplace, and for the provision of a secure bicycle parking area.

Media advocacy: The media has a major influence on public opinion and can be mobilised to present positive news stories about the benefits of physical activity. Well-researched mass media campaigns, based on sound theoretical principles can be effective in persuading people to be more active. As media advocacy is the most easily available to social marketers, we discuss this element in more depth below.

CASE STUDY

The landmine ban: a study in humanitarian advocacy

Don Hubert's (2000) case study is a must read for anyone interested in advocacy at a global level. The widespread and indiscriminate use of landmines in late Cold War conflicts (e.g., Afghanistan, Angola and Cambodia) and other conflict zones throughout the world, particularly in Africa, produced an inevitable number of civilian fatalities and amputees during conflicts, but particularly *after* conflicts, had ended or moved elsewhere. Much arable land also is affected.

Many states and belligerents viewed the weapon as an essential component of their military strategy and tactics and, hence, considerable opposition to any landmine control was anticipated by those seeking such actions. Nevertheless, by the 1990s, the mines issue had become a leading component of the global humanitarian agenda, greatly facilitated by relentless ongoing publicity in major media showing amputee victims and the development of a broadly-based transnational NGO coalition, the International Campaign to Ban Landmines (ICBL). This group advocated a comprehensive ban on the production, export and use of these weapons. The campaign's efforts, combined with those of the International Committee of the Red Cross (ICRC) and interested United Nations agencies, such as the UN Department of Humanitarian Affairs (UNDHA) and the UN Children's Fund (UNICEF), and joined eventually by a growing coalition of sympathetic states, produced the landmines treaty in 1997. The treaty was a striking achievement, not least because, as Hubert documents, much of it was resisted by the most powerful state in the international system – the United States. Hubert identifies the following as key attributes of this successful advocacy. We can also map these into Shilton's frameworks above:

Credibility. Advocacy rooted in practical experience in the field is more credible and stands a greater chance of success. The campaign was led by a group of organisations that had considerable expertise in working with mines issues in the field, including surgeons, de-miners and specialists in prosthetics. A number of prominent military officers who supported the ban lent further credibility to the campaign. In Shilton's terms, this is establishing the credibility of the evidence (the why) and 'professional mobilisation'.

Co-ordination. Unity of action if not of perspective was essential. Although comprising a very diverse set of organisations, the various members subordinated their differences to the pursuit of the central objective. Hence, all communications were focused on the primary messages without contradictions or confusions. In Chapter 11 under partnerships, we define this as the highest level of partnering.

Pressure and persuasion. Advocacy generally involves efforts to alter politicians' views of cost and benefit and their understandings of issues. Hubert states that this partly involved simply providing better and more comprehensive information and increasing their perception of the seriousness of the problem. However, the major task was to reframe landmines from a military and arms control issue to a humanitarian issue. Once this reframing was achieved, states found it difficult to resist acting. Hubert reports that innovative use of visual media was significant in reinforcing this reframing, along with print media. In Shilton's framework, this is the 'what' along with political and media advocacy.

The division of labour. To be successful, the campaign had to be truly global in scope. This required recognising and exploiting the various strengths and weaknesses of the various organisations involved in different parts of the globe. NGO-based advocacy networks worked well in developed countries, but campaign partners such as the ICRC and the UN agencies took the lead in areas such as East Asia, the Middle East and parts of Africa. This is part of Shilton's professional mobilisation.

Building from below. Consistent with the ubiquitous (but true) 'think global, act local', considerable effort was made to disaggregate the process through regional meetings to build support in smaller groups. This is part of Shilton's community mobilisation.

The state as partner. At the same time as building from below, this advocacy also required seeking partners at the state level, because solving the landmines problem required the consent of states that held, sold and deployed them. Moreover, it was realised that states are themselves formidable advocates and may well be taken more seriously than non-state actors by other states. In this case, a number of states were sympathetic to the cause and assumed an active partner role. The involvement of states such as Canada and Norway in prominent advocacy roles resulted in a situation where other states were being lobbied both from below by civil society organisations and by significant international peers. This is Shilton's political mobilisation, but at a national rather than individual politician level.

Overall, the success of this advocacy demonstrates that professional, well-organised and sustained advocacy can be successful in achieving change for a specific well-defined issue. However, as Hubert notes, it is never guaranteed even with these characteristics, and particularly where the issues are broader.

Media advocacy: targeting socio-political change

The ultimate goal of media advocacy is to create changes in policies that improve the health and wellbeing of communities (Wallack 1994). It seeks to do this by developing and shaping ('framing') news stories in ways that build support for public policies, and ultimately influence those who have the power to change or preserve laws, enact policies and fund interventions that can influence whole populations (Chapman 2004). It can also be described as the use of media, usually via unpaid publicity, to place a particular point of view before the public with regard to some controversial issue, with the aim of involving the public in the resolution of that issue. That is, a major aim of media advocacy is to empower the public to take part in policy-making (see Rogers *et al.* 1995).

The media can discover and publicise the existence of a social problem; raise the issue on the public agenda; outline choices and help choose possible courses of action; promote solutions; and help monitor the impact of interventions (Andreasen 2006).

Those most associated with media advocacy to date – the quit smoking lobby – have used the media to redefine smoking as a public health issue of concern to all, and to attack the morals and motives of tobacco companies' marketing techniques (Chapman and Lupton 1994; Wallack *et al.* 1993).

Specific advocacy-related communication objectives for the media are as follows:

- increasing community awareness of the issue and placing the issue on the community's agenda ('agenda setting');
- creating or increasing community awareness of a particular point of view with regard to the issue ('framing' the community agenda);
- creating or maintaining a favourable attitude towards this particular view;
- creating a view that the issue is a significantly serious one for community concern ('legitimising' the issue);
- generating a positive community mood within which regulatory and other policies can be introduced with minimal opposition and/or maximal support.

Soundbites for the media

In this age of brief news reporting on television, a useful media strategy is to formulate 'soundbites': 'pithy, memorable, and repeatable summations that can come to epitomise a debate'.

- 'the [tobacco] industry is to lung cancer what mosquitoes are to malaria'
- 'a non-smoking section of a restaurant is like a non-urinating section of a swimming pool' (Chapman 2004).

Some writers view media advocacy as an alternative to, and hence separate from, social marketing (Wallack 1990). However, we and others (Slater, Kelly and Edwards 2000), view media advocacy as part of a comprehensive social marketing approach. Furthermore, advocacy *per se* involves far more than just media components, and is a major tool for achieving change at the 'upstream', broader societal level.

Individual and structural change objectives should be part of any comprehensive social change campaign. In some cases it is likely that individually targeted campaigns must have some impact first, not only on individual beliefs and attitudes towards the issue *per se*, but also on social norms towards the recommended behaviour, before advocacy objectives can be achieved. For example, it is unlikely that efforts to frame smoking as a public health issue would have been as successful without prior 'Quit' campaigns that emphasised the ill-health effects of smoking and encouraged individual smokers to cease smoking. Similarly, graphic road safety ads targeting individual drivers' behaviours served to create a positive social context within which harsher penalties and surveillance methods, such as speed cameras and random breath testing, could be introduced with minimal public opposition.

Advocacy – a global phenomenon?

Advocacy organisations have proliferated on a global scale via the Internet. For example, Avaaz.org – The World in Action (www.avaaz.org) – describes itself as 'a community of global citizens who take action on the major issues facing the world today. The aim of Avaaz.org is to ensure that the views and values of the world's people shape global decisions. Avaaz.org members act for a more just and peaceful world and a globalisation with a human face.'

At the time of writing, the Avaaz homepage calls for action against the government crackdown in Iran, action to protect Indigenous rights in the Amazon, action to support Obama's call to 'stop the settlements' in the Middle East, and action to free Aung San Suu Kyi in Myanmar. Action can be in the form of signing petitions, donating money or simply telling your friends about the website. For example, alongside amateur mobile phone photos of what is happening in Iran, there is a call:

> Sign the petition below, and forward this email to friends and family – **let's build a massive global outcry of 1 million voices** against the crackdown …

And the petition reads:

> **To the Organization of Islamic Conference, the Non-Aligned Movement, and all UN member states**: As citizens of Iran and countries around the world united in common appeal, we call on you to condemn the violent crackdown on peaceful Iranian protesters, and withhold recognition of any new government until the Iranian people's rights to peaceful protest, justice and democratic process are protected.

However, we question the efficacy of websites or advocacy groups that exist primarily in cyberspace. Simply generating chatter on Facebook, tweeting on Twitter, or blogging all over may increase awareness of, or discussion of, an issue (usually from people on both sides who have already made up their minds), but perhaps little else. In our view, advocacy happens on the ground: in communities, in corridors, in meetings, in town halls, in forests, in the streets and in court rooms – as recognised by global advocacy groups such as the United Nations' campaign to reach the eight Millennium Development Goals, the Gaia Foundation (which has been working for over twenty years to protect and enhance biological and cultural diversity www.gaiafoundation. org), and the Friends of the Earth, who have been campaigning even longer on environmental issues, and celebrated their fortieth year in 2009.

We are the first generation that can end poverty (but will we?)

In 2000, the United Nations identified eight Millennium Development Goals to be reached by 2015:

- Eradicate extreme poverty and hunger.
- Ensure all boys and girls complete primary school.
- Promote gender equality and empower women.
- Reduce by two-thirds child mortality of under 5s.
- Reduce by three-quarters the ratio of women dying in childbirth.
- Halt and reverse the spread of HIV/AIDS, malaria and other major diseases.
- Ensure environmental sustainability.
- Create a global partnership for development, ensuring developed countries play their part to help developing countries end poverty (www.endpoverty2015.org/goals).

Advocacy for environmental change

In *Sustainability Marketing: A Global Perspective* (2009), Beltz and Peattie identify these major challenges for our century: population growth; poverty; health; urbanisation; peak oil; ecosystem damage; food; water; and climate change. Sustainability means using the earth's resources at a pace that allows them to be renewed or, if not renewable, at a pace that allows adequate substitutes to be invented; and creating waste products at a pace that the earth can absorb without being damaged.

Figure 4.2 Greenpeace energy evolution

The United Nations is committed to ensuring environmental sustainability as one of the Millennium Development Goals, but there is no comprehensive, systematic, co-ordinated global campaign to change people's behaviour. However, there are numerous examples of community-based environmental activities, and these are ongoing around the globe in communities everywhere, from the rainforests in South America to the 200-year-old forests in the Ukraine. Social marketers to date have not been involved in many of these campaigns, but we expect that they will be in the future as advocacy becomes more embedded in social marketing, and the principles of marketing become more appreciated by activists. Having a global presence as social marketers will also probably help (see Box below for an advocacy effort by a group of social marketers to achieve just that).

An e-petition to further the cause of a global social marketing organisation

See http://fusomar.epetitions.net for the e-petition to support the creation of a global social marketing organisation. The site was created by Craig Lefebvre, in conjunction with other social marketing academics and practitioners. The first signature was Professor Phil Kotler's.

- 'The Future of Social Marketing: A Call for Collective Engagement for the Creation of a Global Organization: We, the undersigned, agree that the moment has arrived for the development of a social marketing organization. We will support, in words and actions, the creation of a global social marketing organization by July 2010. To work towards this end, we share the following core principles.
- Social marketing starts from the personal perspectives of the people with whom we work.
- Social marketing is a well-established professional discipline with a strong academic and practical foundation.
- Social marketing is a systematic approach to large-scale behavior and social change.
- Social marketing is a "community of practice" that is open to all disciplines and types of practitioners and can be applied to a range of environmental, public health and social issues.
- The development of a professional social marketing organization should be a widely participatory and transparent process.
- A social marketing organization should represent the views of practitioners, organizations, academics, researchers, donors, policymakers and others who advocate for, practice, and support the use of social marketing applications to address social problems ...' http://socialmarketing.blogs.com/r_craiig_lefebvres_social/2009/04/the-future-of-social-marketing-a-call-for-collective-engagement-for-the-creation-of-a-global-organiz.html.

Researching environmental campaigns

Research is essential for ensuring an effective environmental campaign. The Yale Project on Climate Change and the George Mason University Center for Climate Change Communication have published a major report on Americans' beliefs about

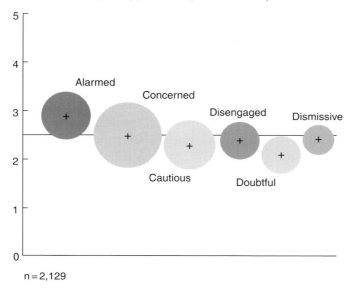

Number of actions that respondent does 'always' or 'often' from the following list of five: turning off unneeded lights; raising the thermostat to 76 or higher or using less air conditioning is summer; lowering the thermostat to 68 or cooler in winter; walking or biking instead of driving; using public transportation or car pools

n = 2,129

Figure 4.3 Environmental behaviours by attitude segmentation

Maibach, Roser-Renouf and Leiserowitz (2009)

and attitudes towards various climate change issues: *Global Warming's Six Americas 2009: An Audience Segmentation Analysis* (Maibach, Roser-Renouf and Leiserowitz 2009). The fundamental premise of the study is that effective communication has to begin with understanding the different target audiences – in this case, 'the different psychological, cultural, and political reasons for acting – or not acting – to reduce greenhouse gas emissions'.

The six distinct target groups identified were given these names: the Alarmed; the Concerned; the Cautious; the Disengaged; the Doubtful; and the Dismissive. The segmentation is discussed more fully in Chapter 10, but here we focus on what this segmentation means in terms of people's behaviour around environmentally favourable behaviours such as turning off lights, adjusting the thermostat to use less energy and finding ways to avoid driving. According to the report (see Figure 4.3 above), there isn't much difference in the behaviours of the different segments: the Alarmed are not engaged in much more desirable activity than the Concerned, and people who are Dismissive appear to engage in more environmentally favourable activities than the Doubtfuls. It may well be that given their lower income status, they are more frugal and are turning lights/heat etc. off to save money rather than for environmental reasons.

These data are consistent with studies in the United States (Kollmuss and Ageyman 2002) and the United Kingdom (Barr and Gilg 2006) showing a significant gap between people's expressed attitudes towards environmental issues and how they actually behave. It seems that the threats and negative consequences of failing to act are yet to be experienced or are seen to be too far in the future to motivate action.

Retallack (2006) points to the need to frame climate change issues in such a way that people will translate their concerns into action. He claims, for example, that framing global warming in a weather change context leads to inaction because people see the weather as out of their control. Similarly, claiming large-scale effects of global warming and then encouraging small actions like changing a light bulb as the solution is seen to undermine the credibility of the claim. We clearly need considerable research to develop appropriate framings for action.

There are a number of social marketing campaigns such as the 'Reduce, Reuse, Recycle' campaign that have attempted to change people's behaviour. In a qualitative study of people who 'reduce, reuse and recycle' waste and people who don't, Bonniface and Henley (2008) found that all the participants expressed pessimistic views about the abilities of others to perform pro-environmental behaviours. However, the people who did perform the behaviours were quite positive that a collective effort would be effective (*many drops will fill up the bucket*), while people who didn't perform the behaviours felt strongly that the problem would still exist even if everyone performed waste minimising behaviours (*it's just a drop in the bucket*). Behaviour change interventions might be more effective if they focus on convincing people that a concerted, collective effort *will* be effective in solving environmental problems such as waste management.

In his testimony before the US House Science and Technology sub-committee on research and science education, psychologist Robert Cialdini (whom we'll meet again in Chapter 5), stated that one of the most effective messages to motivate environmental action is that others are taking such action. For example, guests in an upscale hotel were asked to re-use their towels via four messages: 'help save the environment'; 'help save resources for the future'; 'partner with us to save the environment'; and 'join your fellow citizens in helping to save the environment; the majority of hotel guest do re-use their towels'. Compared with the first three messages, the social norm message increased towel re-usage by 34 per cent (APA Public Affairs Office 2007).

All the above examples refer to research with members of the general public. We also need research on decisionmakers so we can better present issues to them that will result in desired policy changes. This is where learning from case studies is helpful.

CASE STUDY

Reducing diesel bus emissions in Harlem

This campaign was led by the West Harlem Environmental ACTion group (WE ACT; www.weact.org), supported by the Columbia University's Center for Children's Environmental Health. WE ACT serves Northern Manhattan, where about 600,000 mostly low to mid-income African-Americans and Hispanics live. The area has high rates of disability and premature death, with mortality rates from asthma being among the highest in the United States. Much of the poor air quality that contributes to respiratory diseases and asthma was due to the levels of diesel exhaust in the area, which in turn was because six of the eight Manhattan diesel bus depots were located in this area.

Beginning in the mid-1990s, the two partners began their campaign to get the transit authority to convert the bus fleet to gas, with the university providing the expert information on concentrations of elemental carbon from diesel exhaust particles in various locations throughout the area, and the medical scientific links of such to diseases in the area.

Some characteristics of this case study with regard to formulating the desired policy to advocate for were as follows:

Clear problem identification and definition: Air pollution and its link to respiratory health was the clearly defined problem, with a credible link to fine particulate matter and elemental carbon exposure provided by the researchers.

Setting an agenda and creating awareness: WE ACT mounted a substantial campaign to make the community and policymakers aware of, and arouse their interest in, this environmental issue. A strong visual image was used in bus shelter ads, buttons, posters and brochures; this showed two children in gas masks on a busy

Father Robert Castle (formerly of St Mary's Episcopal Church in Harlem) speaks at a press conference announcing the launch of WE ACT's MTA Campaign; page 16 of 'WE ACT for Environmental Justice - 17th Anniversary Report' (summarises WE ACT's activities from 1988 to 2005)

Figure 4.4 'If you live uptown, breathe at your own risk' poster

corner with the slogan: 'If you live uptown, breathe at your own risk' (see Figure 4.4)

Constructing policy alternatives and identifying relevant policymakers to target: Following a thorough analysis of policy alternatives, the group identified three government entities with the power to make relevant policy changes: the Metropolitan Transit Authority (MTA); the governor; and a state legislative oversight committee. They then developed various policy scenarios for each of these.

Deciding on the policy to pursue: Following the guidelines for a policy goal that is specific, achievable and easy to articulate, WE ACT identified its primary policy goals as 300 new compressed natural gas buses in 2000–4 and having all new MTA depots converted to compressed natural gas.

Policy advocacy: On-the-ground activities included getting 10,000 postcards signed by residents and sent to the governor and the chair of the MTA after the MTA refused to meet with WE ACT. WE ACT also joined a legal action charging the MTA with racial discrimination by disproportionately locating bus depots in these neighbourhoods.

While WE ACT is yet to achieve conversion of buses to compressed natural gas, the MTA is converting its entire fleet to 'clean' ultra-low sulphur diesel and the government is undertaking regular air monitoring in previously unmonitored areas of Northern Manhattan.

Source: adapted from Vasquez, Minkler and Shepard (2006)

The principles above fit closely with a community-based social marketing approach such as that espoused by Doug McKenzie-Mohr and William Smith (1999). Their approach involves 'identifying barriers to a sustainable behavior, designing a strategy that utilizes behavior change tools, piloting the strategy with a small segment of a community, and finally, evaluating the impact of the program once it has been implemented across a community'.

Environmental cases from Central and Eastern Europe

Although the emphasis in the following cases was on mediation as a tool for public participation and conflict resolution, they introduce the important role that legal advocates can play in advocacy.

CASE STUDY

Ukraine: returning protected status to forest areas in the Lviv region

In December 1999 the Lviv Regional Council decided to remove the status of several protected forest areas, thus opening to door to commercial exploitation by timber cutting. One area in particular, the Kornalovychy reserve, was established in the 1970s to protect an unique oak forest that was now about 200–210 years old. This decision was made following a proposal from the state forest management association, Lvivlis, and was supported by the Lviv Regional Department of Environment and Natural Resources. Under law, such a decision needs to be supported by scientific evidence. In this case, it was claimed that the forest was losing its economic value and tree felling was needed to maintain its healthy condition.

However, several environmental NGOs and scientists protested the decision, which they considered illegal without a valid scientific basis. The first protests and actions started in 2000, immediately after the decision was passed, organised mainly by NGOs in the form of media campaigns. They were joined by scientists and others when Lvivlis started cutting old oak trees in the former Kornalovychy reserve. This was particularly important in order to initiate legal proceedings, NGOs needed the support of scientists.

The public interest environmental law organisation Ecopravo-Lviv (EPL) spent about two years collecting documents and evidence that showed that the decision was illegal, violated procedures and lacked proper scientific grounds. These analyses were then presented to the relevant authorities.

In 2002 the Lviv Regional Department of Environment and Natural Resources announced that they would consider returning the protected status to the Kornalovychy reserve, but took no action.

In June 2005 the journalism NGO, WETI, organised a press tour of the former Kornalovychy reserve for about forty journalists, scientists, governmental officials, environmental prosecutors, NGOs and foresters. There they were able to see first-hand huge, recently cut, old oak trees. WETI also distributed the legal analysis of the December 1999 decision, which showed the various deficiencies in that process. The main aim of the tour was to raise public awareness of the issue and to place pressure on the local government to reverse the 1999 decision and return protected status to the valuable natural territories. It was also important to show the damage that had already been caused to arouse emotions and interest.

There was wide representation from different national and local media (TV, newspapers and radio) and the story received wide national and local distribution. The day after the press tour, the environmental prosecutor began inspecting recently visited areas.

As a result of this pressure, a roundtable was organised where the various pro and con groups presented their positions. During the roundtable a consensus was reached that the former Kornalovychy reserve should be protected. A commission of different stakeholders was created with fifteen members (eight scientists, two NGOs, one journalist, one legal expert, two representatives from Lvivlis and one representative from the Lviv Regional Department of Environment and Natural Resources). In August 2005, the commission visited Kornalovychy and agreed to prepare a scientific document in favour of returning protected status to the forest territories that had not been cut yet. They also proposed that a new protected area be created in the Kornlovychy forest.

The advocates reflected that it was largely the media attention that led to the authorities being prepared to reconsider the original decision – although they always denied that there was anything improper or illegal about the decision. It was felt that without the media spotlight, the authorities would have continued to refuse any reconsideration of the original decision. Hence, while a strong legal case and strong scientific support were necessary conditions for success, they were not sufficient. It was the media advocacy that resulted in these strengths being able to have an impact.

Source: A report for the Regional Centre for Central and Eastern Europe and the Austrian society for the Environment and Technology (OGUT: Osterreichische Gesellschaft fur Umwelt und Technik) (Handler *et al.* 2005).

CASE STUDY

Czech Republic: persuading car manufacturers to adhere to corporate social responsibility (CSR) practices

The Toyota Motor Company and PSA Peugeot Citroen joint venture plant in Kolin is reportedly the biggest direct foreign investment in the Czech Republic. One can understand why local and national government authorities might be reluctant to upset them. It was claimed by local groups that a willingness to accommodate the corporates resulted in an inadequate environmental impact assessment, leading to negative effects such as noise, wells drying up, air pollution and traffic congestion for residents. Furthermore, road works were planned that would impact on a nature reserve, as well as on local residents.

The cause was taken up by the Environmental Law Service (ELS) of the Global Alliance for Responsibility Democracy and Equity (GARDE), along with thirty local NGOs and numerous local people. The main weapons available to the advocates were negative publicity for the car makers and the threat of legal action.

While GARDE–ELS and the residents did achieve some important concessions and promises of consultation in future developments, the general conclusion was that corporate social responsibility is actioned only when it is in the interests of the corporation – not civic society. In the words of the case authors: 'their CSR practices are nothing more than greenwash'.

The major features of this case were comprehensive legal analyses, co-ordinated action by a number of NGOs with a strong lead agency, and use of the media to draw (negative) attention to the opposition.

Source: Handler *et al.* (2005).

CASE STUDY

Estonia: stopping pollution of the Baltic Sea by a pulp factory

In December 2001, the company AS Estonian Cell decided to build a pulp plant in Kunda, with effluent running into the Baltic Sea. To do this the company required an integrated environmental permit (IPPC permit), which controlled such effluent and its impact on marine life. However, it was alleged by those opposing the building of the plant that the IPPC was based on incorrect data, that the application included false information and that the emissions of chemical oxygen that had been permitted exceeded emissions levels in the regulations.

The opposition was led by the Estonian Fund for Nature (ELF), which disputed the IPPC in court, with scientific support from the Marine Systems Institute with regard to the impact on marine flora and fauna. In this case, the company opened negotiations directly with ELF – probably because it was

seeking funds from the European Bank for Reconstruction and Development and involvement in protracted court action could have jeopardised that funding. The company agreed to change the IPPC permit in accordance with most – but not all – of ELF's recommendations.

This case demonstrates, once again, that corporations will tend to act out of self-interest. Advocates would do well to consider what low-cost actions or fortuitous events can be used to influence companies to negotiate and compromise, rather than to resist and reject advocacy efforts. The case took place in the absence of publicity (a trade-off with the company), but again shows a strong reliance on credible scientific support.

Source: Handler *et al.* (2005).

Planning for advocacy

Social marketers can make a significant contribution to the global effort to address the major challenges of the twenty-first century, both by advocating for policy and regulatory change, and by persuading individuals to adopt environmentally favourable behaviours. Some argue that it is governments that are the primary target:

> It doesn't matter if we save energy because we care about the earth or our money or our neighbors; we just need to save energy. The government just needs to provide the right rules, incentives and nudges to help us make the right choices. It would be nice if Obama could change our social norms so that green living and healthy eating and financial responsibility would be new ways of keeping up with the Joneses. But it would be enough if he changed Washington's social norms. We need better policies, not better attitudes. (Grunwald 2009)

Based on survey research with politicians, the UK non-profit group, nfpSynergy, provides a number of tips for lobbying individual MPs (nfpSynergy 2005).

Ten campaigning tips for lobbying MPs

(1) Be specific about what you want from your campaign.
(2) Timing, timing, timing.
(3) Constituency focus should be more readily exploited.
(4) Encourage and empower your supporters to lobby.
(5) Keep up the pressure – create a memorable and powerful campaign brand and continually refresh it.
(6) Direct personal contact with MPs is essential.
(7) Send MPs targeted, concise letters and regular, punchy news.
(8) Ensure both long-term and short-term commitment from MPs.
(9) Use the media and public area more widely – think of the bigger picture.
(10) Join forces where necessary.

nfpSynergy (Flatt 2005)

On the other hand, politicians and governments will often act only if they see that their constituents are interested in the issue and that the desired action will help them retain their seat in Parliament or their ruling party in government. Media advocacy emerges as a primary factor supporting advocacy efforts. The noted opinion pollster Daniel Yankelovich (1992) reminds us of the various stages that the public goes through before being actively engaged in an issue. This is a useful framework for planning strategies to move through these stages – which we will meet again in Chapter 10. As Maibach and others have shown, with regard to environmental issues, most people have moved past stage 1, but there are still substantial numbers at each of the other stages.

Yankelovich's seven stages of public opinion

(1) **Dawning awareness**: people begin to become aware of an issue, usually through television and newspaper reports.

(2) **A sense of urgency**: people advance from simply being aware of an issue to developing a sense of urgency about it.

(3) **Discovering the choices**: people start to explore choices for dealing with the issue, although the depth of their understanding varies.

(4) **Resistance**: wishful thinking and incomplete knowledge often lead citizens to reach for easy answers and resist facing costs and trade-offs.

(5) **Weighing the choices**: in this stage, people can more rationally and realistically weigh the pros and cons of alternatives.

(6) **Taking a stand intellectually**: at this stage, many people endorse an option in theory but do not make good on it in their personal lives.

(7) **Making a responsible judgement morally and emotionally**: at this final stage, citizens are willing to endorse a course of action, accept its costs and tradeoffs, and live with the consequences of their beliefs (Yankelovich 1992)

Concluding comments

The major lessons to be learned for a successful advocacy initiative are as follows:

- Define a specific, concrete problem that can be clearly articulated to both people in general and to decisionmakers.
- Ensure credible scientific support and expertise to justify the urgency and severity of the problem – and the proposed policy solutions.
- Policy solutions must be concrete, supported by the evidence, have the support of the community and must be within the capacity of those asked to implement them.
- Media support is usually essential, particularly where opponents will suffer from negative publicity.
- In keeping with 'one picture is worth a thousand words', graphic visual images can mobilise and motivate all target groups.
- Use legal advocates where there are legal issues involved, and particularly to expose procedural irregularities where they may exist.
- Be persistent and operate at several levels with as many co-operating partners as relevant.
- Remember that the opposition will be acting in their best interests – attempt to find and use how the opposition can actually benefit from, or avoid negative consequences by, adopting the recommended policy.

QUESTIONS

● A company plans to build a chemical processing plant in a run-down area of a major city. The residents ask you to help them block the plan. What would you recommend they do?

● What do you think are the major reasons why many people express concern about environmental issues, but don't personally do much to conserve energy or water?

FURTHER READING

Belz, F-M. and Peattie, K. 2009. *Sustainability Marketing: A Global Perspective.* Chichester: Wiley.

Chapman, S. 2007. *Public Health Advocacy and Tobacco Control: Making Smoking History.* Oxford: Blackwell.

Hubert, D. 2000. The Landmine Ban: A Case Study in Humanitarian Advocacy, Occasional Paper No. 42, The Thomas J. Watson Jr. Institute for International Studies, Brown University, Providence, RI.

Maibach, E., Roser-Conouf, C. and Leiserowitz, A. 2009. Global Warming's 'Six Americas': An Audience Segmentation, available at: www.climatechangecommunication.org.

McKenzie-Mohr, D. and Smith, W. 1999. *Fostering Sustainable Behavior: An Introduction to Community-Based Social Marketing*, available online at McKenzie-Mohr's website (www.cbsm.com/public/world.lasso). This website contains resources (articles, cases, strategies and forums) for five main environmental areas: agriculture and conservation; energy efficiency; transportation; waste reduction and pollution; and water efficiency.

Shilton, T. 2006. Advocacy for Physical Activity – From Evidence to Influence, *Promotion and Education* 8(2): 118–26.

Vasquez, V. B., Minkler, M. and Shepard, P. 2006. Promoting Environmental Health Policy through Community-based Participatory Research: A Case Study from Harlem, New York, *Journal of Urban Health: Bulletin of the New York Academy of Medicine* 83(1): 101–10.

5 Principles of communication and persuasion

Social marketing is fundamentally concerned with bringing about behaviour change. However, in most cases this first requires bringing about changes in beliefs, attitudes and intentions. Furthermore, some components of an overall comprehensive campaign may have limited objectives, such as an increase in knowledge, or an increased belief that individuals' conservation behaviours can make a real difference, or to create a positive predisposition to act in a certain way when a relevant situation arises. The desired behaviour may then occur some time later when an appropriate situation arises. For example, a campaign to change discriminatory racist behaviours may have a component that first increases people's knowledge about a particular ethnic group, removes misperceptions about that group and creates a more positive predisposition towards that group. That might then be expressed in various ways, for example, in more friendly behaviours towards members of that group in social situations, or more positive word-of-mouth about that group in conversations with friends, or supporting anti-discriminatory legislation in a public opinion poll. That is, changes in beliefs and attitudes are usually a necessary precursor to these desired behaviours.

In this chapter we first present an overall model of the communication process, followed by a discussion of factors relevant to the first two steps of the communication process: exposure and attention. This includes aspects of how to present messages in order to have the most persuasive impact. We then present one of the most commonly used persuasion models, Petty and Cacioppo's elaboration likelihood model (the ELM). Cialdini's six 'weapons' of persuasion are then described. These 'weapons', based on the psychological literature and techniques that professional persuaders use to sell their products, can be used in interpersonal interactions as well as in the media. Finally, given that they are probably the most commonly used appeal in social marketing – particularly in health, crime, environmental degradation and road safety – we present an analysis of threat appeals (and their converse, incentive appeals). We begin with an overall summary of what factors appear to characterise successful communication campaigns.

Communication principles for successful campaigns

A number of overall principles are relevant to conducting successful communication campaigns; that is, campaigns that meet their communication and behavioural objectives (Egger *et al.* 1993; ONDCP 1997):

1. **The receiver is an active processor of incoming information:**

Paraphrasing President Kennedy's famous phrase, one ad man is alleged to have said, 'Ask not what your ad does to the consumer, but what the consumer does to your ad.' Similarly, Australian social commentator Hugh Mackay says, 'The receiver acts more on the message, than the message does on the receiver.' That is, the impact of a media message is not determined by its content alone; members of the audience are active participants in the communication process, and pre-existing beliefs, attitudes, experiences and knowledge affect attending to, interpretation of and acceptance of messages. This is particularly important in sensitive, controversial or core values areas, where existing attitudes often screen out incoming messages that contradict the individual's existing beliefs and attitudes. Hence, particular care is needed when constructing messages aimed at those antagonistic or sceptical towards the proposed idea or behaviour.

2. **Different target audiences may respond to different messages:**

Target audiences must be segmented by beliefs and attitudes before the development of targeted messages. This is dealt with in Chapter 10.

3. **Formative research, including message pre-testing is essential:**

Given the importance of existing beliefs and attitudes affecting message processing, formative research is essential to understand each target audience's beliefs and attitudes about the issue to be addressed. Also, following from the above, it is crucial that messages be pre-tested against target audiences to ensure correct message understanding and that minimal counter-argument occurs. Pre-testing is also necessary to ensure that messages aimed at primary target audiences do not have unintended negative effects on secondary audiences. Pre-testing is covered in Chapter 7.

4. **Comprehensive, co-ordinated interventions are most successful:**

Communication campaigns must be co-ordinated with other environmental and on-the-ground strategies to ensure attitudinal and behavioural success (see Figure 5.1 for the relative impact of communication campaigns versus environmental factors at various stages in the hierarchy of effects).

Effects hierarchy	Communication campaigns	Environmental factors
Awareness	Very high	Low
Attitude	High	Moderate
Intention	Moderate	High
Behaviour	Low	Very high

Figure 5.1 Relative impact of communication versus environmental factors at various stages in the hierarchy of effects

5. Use multiple delivery channels and multiple sources:

Communication campaigns involving a number of delivery channels and more than one source appear to be more successful than those that do not (Lefebvre, Olander and Levine 1999).

6. Stimulate interpersonal communications:

Mass media-led communication campaigns that stimulate interpersonal communications appear to be more successful than those that do not.

7. Campaigns must be sustained:

Communication campaigns must be sustained to achieve and maintain success.

8. Use a theoretical framework:

Campaigns that have been guided by theoretical frameworks are more successful than those that have not.

The communication process: Rossiter's and Percy's six-step model

The Rossiter–Percy model (Rossiter and Percy 1997), based on McGuire (1985), provides a conceptual framework for planning a communication strategy. This model is a simplified hierarchical six-step model relating advertising exposure to company objectives and profits (see Figure 5.2). While developed for advertising in a commercial marketing context, the model is applicable to all forms of communication.

Step 1: The hierarchy of effects commences with *exposure* of the target audience to the message. Messages may be delivered in a variety of ways (e.g., advertising, publicity, edutainment, factual information), and in a variety of media and media vehicles (e.g., websites, DVDs, newspaper articles, TV ads, billboards, radio talk back, posters, blogs, magazine articles, soap operas, hit songs, videos, or face-to-face counselling).

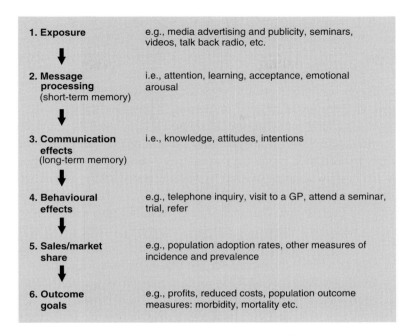

Figure 5.2 The Rossiter–Percy six-step communication process

Step 2: Attention to the message, in whatever form it appears, leads to *processing* of the message in short-term memory. This involves attention to the message content, emotional arousal, comprehension and learning, and acceptance or rejection of the message. Message execution (i.e., the use of colour and graphics), source factors (i.e., who delivers the message) and message content, all influence processing.

Step 3: Processing of the message (and subsequent related messages) results in long-term memory effects called *communication effects*. These are beliefs about, attitudes towards, and intentions with regard to the brand, message topic or promoted behaviour. The content of the message, the audience's initial attitudes and beliefs, the nature of the message exposure and the degree of repetition of the message, all affect whether, how much, and what components of the message are stored in long-term memory, and how easily these can be recalled during decision-making. (Issues with regard to attitude formation, intentions and behaviours are dealt with in Chapter 6.)

Step 4: The desired communication effects when recalled during decision-making, facilitate *behavioural effects* such as purchase of the product or trial of the recommended behaviour, or intermediate behavioural effects such as seeking further information from a website or telephone helpline. Environmental opportunities, barriers and cues to action all influence whether a behavioural response will occur.

Steps 5 and 6: These behavioural effects take place among pre-defined *target audiences* that were subject to the exposure schedule and message strategy. The accumulation of these behavioural effects among the target audiences leads to the achievement of *objectives*

and goals – which in commercial terms are usually sales and market-share objectives that contribute to profit goals. In the social and health areas, 'sales' or 'market-share' objectives may be stated in terms of participation rates or disease prevalence rates, while overall goals relate to things like risk reductions, health cost reductions or more positive life experiences for the general population (Donovan and Owen 1994).

Taking an example from commercial marketing, a teenager (*target audience*) watches a TV ad (*exposure*) for a new confectionery bar. The TV ad is aired during a show known to be popular with teens. The ad attracts and maintains our teen's *attention* because it is fast-moving, backed by a rap song and features exciting, colourful graphics. The confectionery bar is shown being shared by several cool-looking teens, who exclaim in unison that it 'tastes great'. A voiceover lists creamy caramel, milk chocolate and crunchy nuts as the ingredients. Our teen viewer is drawn into the ad, *likes* the music and talent, and *accepts* that the candy bar would probably taste good and might be worth trying (*message processing*). The ad appears twice more during the show (*repetition*). Our teen now *knows* the confectionery bar's brand name, what the wrapper looks like, what its major ingredients are and has formed a tentative positive *attitude* towards trying the confectionery bar (*communication effects*).

A few days later at the local deli, our teen sees a display of the confectionery bars on the counter and *recognises* the wrapping and the brand seen on TV. Our teen experiences a *positive feeling* towards the confectionery bar and *recalls* the promise of 'great taste' (*communication effects*). The price is slightly lower than other popular brands, and our teen has sufficient cash, so the decision is made to *buy* and *try* the confectionery bar (behavioural effects) – thus, along with thousands of others – contributing to the company's sales and profits.

Another scenario. Our high school athlete has been chosen to try out for the state basketball team (*target audience*). As part of the induction process, she attends an orientation evening (*exposure*). One part of the programme consists of an International Federation (IF) spokesperson outlining the IF's policy on performance-enhancing drugs (PEDs). A sports doctor then outlines the potential ill-health side effects of drug taking, followed by an inspiring address by a well-known athlete about 'winning without cheating' (*the messages*). A World Anti-Doping Agency (WADA) representative presents the ethical and moral basis for banning PEDs, the likelihood of being tested in and out of competition, and the sanctions for testing positive (*more messages*). Our athlete listens intently (*processing*) and goes away with a manual containing the list of banned substances, test procedures and a statement on the ethics of doping. She is somewhat confused as to what is banned and why, but feels inspired by the well-known athlete's address, and forms an implicit intention not to use PEDs (*communication effects*). The whole evening has left our high school athlete with a greater determination than ever to make the state team.

Our athlete hears little of drugs in sport from official sources over the next few months, but reads the occasional report of positive tests among cyclists and others overseas. Then, several months later, our athlete appears to have reached a plateau in performance and is competing to make the final team squad with two others who are performing slightly better. By now she has become aware that some elite athletes, not just in basketball, are using performance-enhancing drugs obtained via the health club black market. An assistant coach who has befriended our athlete and knows her situation, suggests that he may be able to get some drugs for her and supervise their use (*competing messages*). Our athlete recalls the inspiring induction address and the WADA slogan, and feels that to accept the assistant coach's offer would be wrong and inconsistent with her moral and sporting values (*communication effects recalled during decision-making*). Our athlete recalls the induction programme's tips on how to reject a drug offer and tactfully declines the offer (*communication and behavioural effect*).

This example is a reminder that our messages compete with other messages, and that a variety of influences can operate at various points in the exposure – behaviour chain that either facilitate or mitigate against our desired outcome.

Planning a communication strategy

In using the Rossiter–Percy model to plan a communication strategy, the chain is in the opposite direction to the exposure process (Figure 5.3). That is, the campaign planner asks – and then sets out to answer – the following series of questions:

Step 1:   What is the overall goal that the campaign must help achieve?

Step 2:   What specific objectives do we want this communication campaign to achieve?

Step 3:   Who do we need to impact to achieve our goal and
            What do we want them to do?

Step 4:   What beliefs and attitudes do we need to create, change or reinforce to have them behave this way?

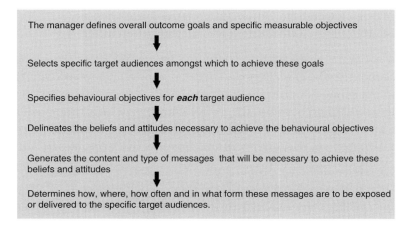

Figure 5.3 Campaign planning sequence

Step 5:   What sorts of messages do we need to create to have them adopt these beliefs and attitudes?

Step 6:   Where, how often and in what form do we need to expose these messages to reach these people?

It should be noted that this planning process is an iterative, recursive process, in that previous levels in the hierarchy may be modified as a consequence of planning considerations lower down, resulting in even further modifications and so on.

Principles of exposure and attention

People are faced with hundreds of ads per day through a proliferation of channels: milk cartons, toilet doors, blimps, bus stops, rented videos, cash-register receipts, event entry tickets, school tuck shops, projections on buildings, in the turf of football pitches, players' outfits, yacht sails, web banners and pop-ups and so on. Advertising is ubiquitous, leading agencies to urge their clients to spend more to be heard amid the din. But it's not just media weight that is needed to attract attention.

Breaking through the clutter

Australian advertising creative John Bevins uses the following to illustrate the problem of gaining attention in a modern society where individuals are continually bombarded with 'messages' or 'information' through a variety of channels (i.e., 'clutter'):

clutterclutterclutterclutterclutterclutterclutterclutterclutterclutter
clutterclutterclutterclutterclutterclutterclutterclutterclutterclutter
clutterclutterclutterclutterclutterclutterclutterclutterclutterclutter
clutterclutterclutterclutterclutterclutterclutterclutterclutterclutter
clutterclutterclamourclutterclutterclutterclutterclutterclutterclutt
clutterclutterclutterclutterclutterclutterclutterclutterclutterclutter
clutterclutterclutterclutterclutterclutterclutterclutterclutterclutter

Messages that social marketers wish to communicate are hidden in this clutter (like the single word 'clamour' in the lower left-hand side of the above). The objective is to make our message stand out more, not only through 'mechanical' or stylistic execution processes (e.g., 'clamour' would stand out from the clutter if it was in a larger and bolder typeface), but also via a knowledge of psychological factors in human information processing. The most striking such factor is selective attention. This selectivity operates in three ways:

(1) *selective exposure (or attention)*: people expose themselves or pay attention to media and messages that have a personal relevance to them, or with which they already agree;

(2) *selective perception*: when exposed to information that is not in agreement with their attitudes, individuals tend to reinterpret this information to be in accord with their existing attitudes and beliefs;

(3) *selective retention*: when information not in agreement with their attitudes is committed to memory, it is often recalled in a way more favourable towards pre-existing attitudes and beliefs.

Selective exposure and attention

Selective exposure applies at two levels: the medium or channel and the message. Some people are avid TV watchers but rarely read a newspaper; others may read only broadsheet or only tabloid newspapers; some have distinct preferences for radio stations or specific announcers; others will deliberately avoid documentary, fact-based television programmes (which is why social marketers have incorporated messages in entertainment vehicles; see Chapter 11); and many specialty magazines are read only by small, well-defined audiences. Thus, to even have a chance of reaching some target groups, we need to know their media and leisure and entertainment habits.

At the message level, people pay attention to topics in which they are interested, ignoring topics of little interest or of an opposite view. For example, voters are more likely to expose themselves to messages of the political parties to which they are already committed (Klapper 1961), and smokers who find it difficult to quit or who want to keep on smoking, tend to avoid anti-smoking messages, but pay attention to news reports that question or contradict the relationship between smoking and ill-health.

Personalising the message

According to Bevins (1988), much of the fault with public health communication is that its central orientation is:

WE

Health professionals often wrongly start from the assumption that WE know what YOU want to hear. In Bevin's terms, health authorities too often 'go around "weeing" in public' when they should be personalising the message, that is, focusing on the mirror inversion of WE or

ME

According to Bevins: 'Message begins with "me". Me singular. Indeed, there is no such thing really as mass communication. It's a contradiction in terms. Communication is an intensely personal, one-to-one process, whether you're doing it over the telephone or over the television network. Uni, Uno, One – is the very heart of communication.' In short, we must recognise that people interpret messages from the perspective of 'what's in it for me'.

Selective perception and interpretation

Even if individuals do expose themselves to a message, they may not accept that message because of the way they interpret the information. For example, the show *All in the Family* (a US version of the British show *'Til Death Us Do Part*), which featured a right-wing 'conservative' older generation couple generally in conflict with a younger generation 'liberal left-wing' couple, attracted far higher ratings than the producers expected. Subsequent surveys found that the show appealed to left-wing *and* right-wing viewers. Although the show was meant to be satirical of right-wing prejudices, right-wingers saw it as *endorsing* their views, while left-wingers saw it as endorsing *their* views (Vidmar and Rokeach 1974). Similar effects occur when supporters of opposing football teams view exactly the same incident, but disagree vehemently about which way the penalty should have been awarded. More worrying is that scientists are equally likely to selectively interpret research evidence (Kaptchuk 2003).

Inconclusive data are particularly vulnerable to selective interpretation or what is called 'biased assimilation'. Lord, Ross and Lepper (1979) found that when pro- and anti- advocates of capital punishment were presented with studies showing mixed results on the deterrent effects of capital punishment, each group interpreted the results as supportive of their own position. Similar effects are found in racism studies, where the same data are used by opposing sides to support their positions. Again this reinforces the need for pre-testing of messages – among both primary and other target groups to ensure that the desired interpretation is taking place.

Selective retention

There is evidence that 'memory' is sometimes 'reconstructed' in line with attitudes and expectations rather than being the retrieval of accurately stored information. In a classic US study, Allport and Postman (cited in Klapper 1961) showed subjects a picture of a confrontation in a subway train between a black man and a white man holding a razor. Subjects were later asked to describe the picture. As the delay from exposure to recall increased, the razor shifted from the white man to the black man's hand, illustrating the influence of prejudice on retention.

The Healthy Blokes project

Given men's general reluctance to visit their doctor 'unless it's really serious', and, hence, often too late for early intervention, one of the main aims of the Healthy Blokes project was to stimulate blue collar men over 40 to have a regular health check. The project also aimed to increase awareness for the main risk factors for heart disease, cancer and diabetes: poor diet and physical inactivity.

Qualitative research indicated that men would respond to health messages directed specifically to them; that a car maintenance analogy would be well accepted; and that health assessment 'scores' were likely to trigger action (Donovan and Egger 2000).

As part of the project, the ad in Figure 5.4 below was placed in the sporting news section of the daily newspaper, used a half-page size and a 'male interest' headline to attract attention, and included a self-assessment questionnaire to engage interaction with the message of the ad, and, hopefully, trigger some action if the 'score' indicated action was required. A telephone number was included to provide further information to those who needed it.

Is your body due for a check up and service?

TAKE FIVE MINUTES TO GIVE YOUR BODY A ROAD TEST.

Circle the number that answers each question best for you. Then add up your score at the end of each column.

NUTRITION

How many days a week do you eat at least 2 pieces of fruit?

Seven	4	One to two	1
Five to six	3	None	0
Three to four	2		

How many days a week do you eat a meal which includes vegetables?

Seven	4	One to two	1
Five to six	3	None	0
Three to four	2		

How do you spread butter or margarine on your bread?

Don't have	2	Thickly	0
Thinly	1		

How often do you eat fatty foods eg pies, pasties, sausage rolls ?

Seldom or never	3
Once or twice a week	2
Three or four times a week	1
Daily or almost daily	0

11-13: You are doing well keep up the healthy diet.
5-10: Umm... you could probably eat a bit better.
0-4: You need help. Definitely call for information.

PHYSICAL ACTIVITY

How many days a week do you participate in physical activity that makes you puff?

Seven	4	One to two	1
Five to six	3	None	0
Three to four	2		

How long do you do physical activity each time?

Thirty minutes or more	3
Fifteen up to thirty minutes	2
Up to fifteen minutes	1
I do not exercise at all	0

How many hours do you sit each day (include home and work)?

Zero to eight hours	2
Eight to twelve hours	1
Twelve or more hours	0

How often do you drive the car when you could walk?

Daily or almost daily	0
Three or four times a week	1
Once or twice a week	2
Seldom or never	3

How often do you walk the dog or the family?

Daily or almost daily	3
Three or four times a week	2
Once or twice a week	1
Seldom or never	0

11-15: Well done – you must be a fit guy.
5-10: There is always room for improvement.
0-4: Leave the remote and go for a walk – NOW!

THE CHECK UP

When was the last time you had a check up with your doctor?

Within the last year	4
One or two years ago	3
Three or four years ago	2
More than four years ago	1
Never	0

Do you know the result of your last cholesterol check?

Yes	1
No/Haven't had one done	0

Do you know the result of your last blood pressure check?

Yes	1
No/Haven't had one done	0

Do you know the result of your last blood glucose check?

Yes	1
No/Haven't had one done	0

Do you know if you are in the healthy weight range?

Yes	1
No	0

7-8: You are the full bottle about you – excellent!
3-6: A check up in the near future is a good idea.
0-2: Definitely make an appointment to see your Doctor.

Disclaimer: The purpose of this quiz is to raise awareness only of your risk factors for cardiovascular disease and type 2 diabetes and certain types of cancer. Evidence proves that early intervention can make a difference.

CANCER FOUNDATION   Healthway   Heart Foundation   HEALTHY BLOKES

Your body is like a car, and the older it gets, the more important it is to get it serviced regularly. Start by using this quiz to see if you're in need of an overhaul. If your score is low, see your doctor for some practical advice or call 13 11 20.

*Cancer Council of Western Australia

Figure 5.4 Is your body due for a check up and service?

Factors influencing the selectivity process

Three major sets of factors influence whether or not messages are attended to and how they are processed:

1. Mechanical execution factors: These factors refer to physical or sensory attributes of the message vehicle, such as colour, use of movement, size and contrast, that attract attention more or less reflexively. Mechanical factors are particularly important when messages must compete for attention against a large number of other messages or against a strong background. For example:

- eye-catching pictures greatly increase readership of print articles;
- colour stands out in largely black-and-white productions;
- larger ads attract more attention than smaller ads;

- movement gains reflexive attention (e.g., flashing lights, moving arrows, etc.); and
- isolated stimuli (as in lots of white space around a brief message in a newspaper ad) attract greater attention, as do objects placed in the centre, rather than the periphery, of the visual field.

Using mechanical execution characteristics to break through the clutter

clutterclutterclutterclutterclutterclutterclutterclutterclutterclutter
clutterclutterclutterclutterclutterclutterclutterclutterclutterclutter
clutterclutterclutterclutterclutterclutterclutterclutterclutterclutter
clutterclutterclutterclutterclutterclutterclutterclutterclutterclutter
clutterclutterCLAMOURclutterclutterclutterclutterclutterclutter
clutterclutterclutterclutterclutterclutterclutterclutterclutterclutter
clutterclutterclutterclutterclutterclutterclutterclutterclutterclutter

Novelty is included as a mechanical factor, suggesting that message executions should be continually revised and revived to prevent wear-out. For example, the pool of cigarette pack warnings that show graphic, sometimes gruesome, photos of the ill-health effects of smoking would need to be continually refreshed to prevent habituation to these warnings (Donovan 2001).

Health warning on cigarette packs

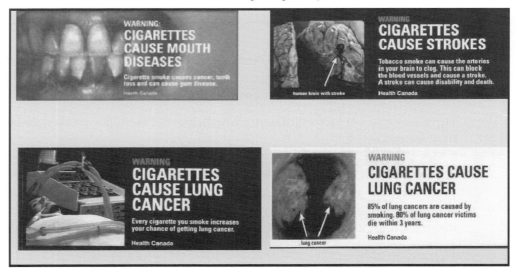

Reprinted with permission from Health Canada, British Columbia Ministry of Management Services, and Australian Commonwealth Department of Health and Aged Care.

Some factors that appear to attract attention reflexively also have some psychological aspects. For example, sensational headlines (the *New York Post*'s celebrated 'Headless body in topless bar'), sex (scantily clad women in pictures), and rare occurrences ('Man bites dog') appear to attract attention and are commonly used by sub-editors to attract readership and viewers. These appear to be socially conditioned types of response, although there does appear to be a biological basis for a novelty effect (Ornstein 1986).

2. Psychological factors: These refer primarily to factors such as personal interest, prior experiences, current attitudes and beliefs, and ability to attend to and process information. People are more willing to respond to messages relating to topics of personal interest or messages that offer a personal benefit ('Good news for frustrated golfers'), and, for 'high involvement' issues, messages that are consistent with what they already believe ('Global warming man-made, says scientist').

Expectations markedly affect interpretation in that people interpret information to be consistent with what they expect. This even affects sensory perception: people rated more expensively labelled wines much better than when the same wine is presented at a lower cost (Lehrer 2008). Expectations may also partly explain the placebo effect.

A *belief* can be defined as a perception that a certain state of affairs exists or is true. An *attitude* can be defined as the extent to which positive or negative feelings are held towards a state of affairs. A 'state of affairs' can include objects, persons, behaviours or ideas. The *salience* of a belief refers to the readiness with which that belief 'comes to mind' when the person's attention is drawn to the issue.

Most attitudes are based on a set of beliefs and an evaluation of these beliefs (see Chapter 6). Some beliefs may be negative, while others are positive. It is important to recognise that many members of a target audience may be ambivalent about an issue. For example, a woman may believe that condoms are a reliable, inexpensive, easy-to-use method for avoiding contracting a sexually transmitted disease. At the same time, she also may believe that condoms reduce pleasurable feelings for her partner, are embarrassing to purchase and present, and are difficult to dispose of afterwards.

For issues where people hold a mix of negative and positive beliefs (as for many health behaviours and in social areas such as attitudes towards ethnic groups), research suggests that the overall attitude held at a particular point in time depends on the relative salience of the various positive and negative beliefs. Hence, situations that stimulate consciousness of positive beliefs about an issue will increase the likelihood of an individual expressing a positive attitude towards that issue at that time. And vice versa. If the aim is to achieve a change in attitude towards a particular issue, the message strategy should first stimulate recall of beliefs favourable to the issue prior to the persuasive component of the message being presented. For example, a target audience may believe that exercise is beneficial to overall health, tones the body and increases energy, but may also believe that it's time consuming and hard work. The audience should be reminded of their positive beliefs before – or at the same time as – presenting 'new' reasons why they should increase their physical activity.

3. Message structure tactics (which may involve mechanical and psychological factors): The structure of more complex messages is also important. Message execution tactics, including the language, tone and style of a message, are important influences on the impact of a communication. Tactics that increase message acceptance in high involvement controversial areas include the following:

- link the desired belief to an already accepted belief (e.g., most smokers accept that tobacco smoke constituents 'can't be doing you any good'; violent men may not accept that their violence harms their partner, but they will accept that the violence affects their children);
- stay within the target audience's 'latitude of acceptance', that is, the claimed threat and/or promised benefit must be credible (Sherif, Sherif and Nebergall 1965);

Latitude of acceptance

A cartoon shows a fisherman using the distance between his hands to show his friends the size of the 'one that got away'. The fisherman's grandchild notices that the size of the fish varies according to who is being told the story. On querying this, the fisherman says: 'That's right son. I never tell a person more than I think they'll believe.'

- use two-sided messages rather than one-sided messages (i.e., accept that smoking can be enjoyable, help cope with stress and act as a social facilitator; accept that some patrons will be upset by smoking bans). This pre-empts potential counter-arguments that might otherwise distract from the message and/or lead to denigration of source credibility and hence rejection of the message;
- leave the audience to draw their own conclusions rather than 'telling' them to adopt the promoted stance (i.e., 'cool' rather than 'hot' messages) (e.g., more successful Quit smoking advertisements are those that are seen by smokers – and youth in particular – not to be 'preaching' or 'dictating' to them).

Implications for initiating the communication process

When implementing a communication campaign to create awareness of, and positive attitudes towards, a concept the first step of the campaign should focus on issues where there is most agreement between the target audience's attitudes and beliefs and those of the campaign source. In many cases, these areas of agreement may have low salience (i.e., are rarely thought about), or are weakly held. Exposure increases the salience of these attitudes and beliefs, and, depending on the persuasive power of the message, can also increase the strength of the attitudes and beliefs.

Approaching the communication process from a point of common agreement also builds source credibility and trust, and hence some form of commitment to the source and the message. This approach provides a favourable context within which to neutralise negative attitudes and beliefs, and to create positive attitudes and beliefs from a neutral position. Once this platform of credibility is established, strategies such as attaching a negative belief to a positive belief to increase the likelihood of acceptance of the negative belief can be implemented.

Targeting racist stereotype beliefs

Donovan and Leivers (1993) reported a study carried out to determine the feasibility of using paid advertising to modify beliefs underlying employment discrimination against Aborigines in a small country town in Australia.

Qualitative research with opinion leaders, employers, townspeople and local Indigenous people informed the development of the advertising. The research and the content and execution of the print and television advertising were guided by models of attitude change (Chapter 6) and various communication principles – primarily the concept of 'latitude of acceptance'.

The research showed that negative attitudes to employing Indigenous people were based on beliefs that:

- very few Aborigines had a job;
- very few Aborigines with jobs hold them for a long time; and
- very few Aborigines have skilled jobs.

These 'objective' beliefs were identified as the basis for subjective stereotypical beliefs that Indigenous people 'are lazy', 'don't want to work' and 'can't handle responsibility'.

In fact 60 per cent of local Indigenous people were employed and many had held their jobs for a considerable time. However, given the beliefs of the non-Indigenous population, promoting a 60 per cent employment rate would have met considerable scepticism from a large percentage of the non-Indigenous population. To accommodate people's different 'starting points', the advertising communication objective was defined as increasing people's beliefs about

- the percentage of Indigenous people employed,
- the percentage who remain in employment for long periods, and
- the percentage who are in skilled jobs

regardless of what percentage they currently thought fell into these categories.

Mindful of 'not telling people more than they would believe', the advertising avoided any statistical information and made no specific claims about Indigenous employment. Instead, a series of ads – television and press – simply presented the occupational details of twelve locally employed Indigenous people. The television ads, for example, pictured four people, one at a time, in their workplace. As each was pictured, their name, occupation, place of work and length of time employed appeared in print on the screen. Length of employment varied from two years to twelve years. In short, this was a 'cool' message that left the audience to draw their own conclusions from the information given.

The research had also indicated that any campaign sourced to a government organisation that simply asked people to employ Indigenous people, or extolled their virtues, and did not indicate that Indigenous people themselves were involved, would be greeted with scepticism. That is, the campaign *per se* also had to be acceptable. To provide a rationale for the campaign to the non-Indigenous population, the ad promoted an 'Aboriginal employment week', was sourced to a local Indigenous group and ended with the slogan, valued in Australian culture, and hence that no one could really argue against: 'All anyone wants is a fair go'. A post-campaign survey showed that of those aware of the campaign, 68 per cent supported it, 28 per cent had no feelings either way and only 4 per cent opposed it. The effectiveness of the campaign is reported in Chapter 12.

Cognitive processing models for persuasion: elaboration-likelihood model

Cognitive processing models attempt to describe how cognitive processing of messages explains persuasion. The two main models from a psychological perspective are the elaboration-likelihood model (ELM; Petty and Cacioppo 1983, 1986) and Chaiken's (1987) heuristic model of persuasion. Two main models from a consumer behaviour/advertising perspective are the Rossiter–Percy model (1997) and the FCB (Foote, Cone and Belding) planning model (Vaughn 1980,1986). The ELM model is briefly described here and the Rossiter–Percy model, because it emphasises motivations, in Chapter 6.

Petty and Cacioppo (1986) state that there are two routes to persuasion: the **central** route, which involves extensive consideration (or 'elaboration') of the issue-relevant arguments in the message; and the **peripheral** route, where the individual does not engage in such elaboration, but is rather persuaded by some factor(s) peripheral to the arguments such as a liking (or disliking) for the source or the music accompanying the message, or some other such cue. Peripheral processing includes the use of decision heuristics such as accepting 'seals of approval' or following 'expert advice', or such rules as 'if they advertise a lot on TV they must be a safe company'. Cialdini's principles of liking, authority and social proof can all act as heuristics for peripheral route persuasion (O'Keefe 1990).

Petty and Cacioppo claim that central route processing will occur when the individual is motivated and has the capacity to pay close attention to the message content.

This is most likely to occur when the issue has high personal relevance and high potential impact on their lives; that is, when an individual is highly involved in the issue. People generally pay far more attention to messages about issues that will affect them directly, than to messages about issues of little direct personal relevance. For example, a camera buff will pay far more attention to the technical information in camera ads, seek experts' opinions on the camera and spend considerable time and effort gathering relevant information before choosing a new camera. An amateur photographer might be more persuaded by the celebrity endorsing the product, or by the camera's styling. People who are employed directly in the timber industry, or whose employment depends on logging, will process anti-logging arguments very differently from those less impacted. The former would require two-sided messages, highly credible 'statistics', etc., whereas the latter might be persuaded simply by the sincerity of the speaker or the sheer amount of statistics – not what the statistics mean.

Using celebrities can have drawbacks

Social and commercial marketers love to use celebrities to promote their messages. Sporting heroes are particularly attractive for issues and products pertaining to youth. Unfortunately, the past is littered with such spokespersons falling out of favour because of some event or revelation of their behaviour being inconsistent with the message or just plain offensive.

Author RJD was part of an Olympic Aid (now Right to Play) GAVI (Global Alliance for Vaccination and Immunisation) vaccination promotion event in Ghana in December 2001. African-American Olympic star Marion Jones was the lead sporting celebrity to attract attention to and participation in the vaccination programme. In 2008 Jones was sentenced to six months in a US federal prison for lying to investigators about using performance-enhancing drugs and her role in a cheque fraud scam. The latest example is Kellogg spokesperson, Olympic swimmer Michael Phelps. Following a widely publicised photograph of Phelps apparently smoking marijuana through a bong, he was dumped by Kellogg and suspended from competition for three months by USA Swimming.

Similarly, people with little education in a particular area, and hence little capacity to analyse relevant information, may be persuaded by people in authority in that area or people that they trust. For example, Indigenous people with little knowledge of Western concepts of disease prevention by vaccination are more likely to be persuaded to vaccinate by the peripheral route than by scientific arguments. Similarly, most people lack the technical background to follow many political and social debates. They tend to be persuaded by source characteristics, such as the advocate's physical appearance, *apparent* sincerity and *apparent* knowledge ('she sounds as if she knows what she's talking about' … 'his deep, cultured voice sounds authoritative' … 'she's a medical doctor – she should know'). Hence, much advertising for products such as analgesics, cold remedies and toothpaste rely heavily on peripheral cues such as actors in white coats, graphs, microscopes and other apparently medico-scientific cues to support their product claims.

The ELM and other cognitive processing models remind us that messages must take into account not just the target audience's initial attitude, but their involvement or level of interest in the issue, and their motivation to process information. Questions in headlines and self-assessment tools (as in the Healthy Blokes ad above) are one way of increasing motivation to attend to a message. Where the level of involvement is high and the target attitude is currently negative, close attention must be paid to the actual message content. In fact, attitude change under these circumstances is very difficult. On the other hand, where the attitude is currently negative, but involvement in the issue is low, peripheral cues such as positive imagery can – and should – be used to achieve attitude change. Hence, a dual strategy is often required, perhaps particularly for teenagers for issues such as binge drinking, sun protection, tobacco and drug use. Many teens view these behaviours as relatively benign in the sense that the ill-health effects are distant, or because they intend to modify their behaviour before any 'permanent' damage occurs. Or the behaviours are simply of far less relevance in their lives compared with school work, boy–girl relationships, sport, computer and video games, music, fashion, physical changes in their bodies, parent conflict and so on. For example, many young Australian teens, as distinct from their Florida counterparts, and regardless of whether or not they smoke, simply do not see smoking as a 'big issue' – and certainly not one that non-smokers consider it is worth being activist about (NFO Donovan Research 2000). In this case, it is likely that peripheral cues may be more effective in inducing some teen smokers to quit.

The elaboration likelihood model of persuasion suggests that measures of personal relevance, interest in the issue and knowledge of the area are key measures for use in pre-testing messages. The model also supports the use of cognitive response measures in assessing a message's potential effectiveness (see Chapter 7).

US-funded media lack credibility in the Middle East

Alhurra (or al-Hurra; meaning 'Freedom') is a United States-based satellite TV channel. It began broadcasting on 14 February 2004 in twenty-two countries across the Middle East. Radio Sawa, a 24-hour, seven-day-a-week Arabic-language news network, began broadcasting on 23 March 2002. It originates its broadcasts from studios in the Washington, DC area and Dubai, United Arab Emirates, as well as news bureaus throughout the Middle East. Both are sponsored by the US Government. Unsurprisingly, therefore, these very costly enterprises lack credibility and influence in the populations they were supposed to win over. As Amr and Singer (2008) point out, the problem is their obvious links to the US Government which 'de-legitimises' them in the minds of most Arabs. Amr and Singer suggest that the United States should privatise the stations in order to build a bigger and more receptive audience in the area.

Cialdini's six principles of persuasion

After reviewing psychological studies of persuasion and spending some time working as a salesperson in a variety of areas, psychologist Robert Cialdini (1984, 2001) identified six principles (or sales techniques) related to the psychology of persuasion. All six principles are a result of our social conditioning and, hence, tend to operate reflexively or unconsciously. In the main, these principles are adaptive, but as Cialdini so entertainingly shows, they can be exploited by unscrupulous salespeople.

Reciprocity: 'One should be more willing to comply with a request from someone who has previously provided a favour or concession.'

The principle of reciprocity states that we should try to repay, in kind, what another person has provided. We are obligated to the future repayment of favours, gifts, invitations and so on. This is apparently a universal characteristic of human societies, exemplified in the phrase 'you scratch my back; I'll scratch yours'. Similarly, when people say 'much obliged' in response to an act of kindness, they in fact are! This principle is illustrated in the commercial area by the use of 'free gifts', 'product samples' and so on, and is clearly evident in political parties in the allocation of the spoils of government.

Given the universal functional utility of this principle, it is not surprising that it is very powerful. Politicians often find themselves in compromising situations when they have accepted gifts from certain parties who later on seek political favours. The description of the corruptor of police, politicians and others in Frank Hardy's ([1950] 1972) *Power Without Glory* puts it this way: 'Once he'd done a man a favour, he knew he was his.' The principle of reciprocity is a major reason why direct donations to political figures are (or should be) banned, and the identities of donors not revealed to legislators. The invoking of a reflexive obligation to repay is so strong that sometimes people go out of their way to avoid its triggering or feel trapped when it occurs. For example, Cialdini observes that people will cross the street to avoid someone giving out 'free' flowers and then asking for a donation, because they feel unable to accept the flower without making a donation. This illustrates another aspect of this principle: that of an obligation to accept gifts and favours when they are offered. Without this, the principle simply could not apply.

It is particularly useful to remember this principle in lobbying politicians and forming collaborative networks: provide a useful service to potential partners, funders and collaborators *before* (or at least at the same time as) asking for the favour being sought.

Reciprocal concessions: Perhaps the most powerful aspect of the reciprocity principle is this one: *an obligation to make a concession to someone who has made a concession to us.* This is particularly important in negotiating agreements where granting a concession triggers an automatic obligation for the other side to reciprocate by also making a concession: 'Would you like to buy a $50 raffle ticket? ... No? ... Well, how about a $1 donation?

Commitment and consistency: 'After committing oneself to a position, one should be more willing to comply with requests for behaviours that are consistent with that position.'

This principle states that making a commitment, particularly a *public* commitment, to a particular stance leads to greater consistency between beliefs, attitudes and behaviour. As Cialdini puts it, 'once a stand is taken, there is an almost compulsive desire to behave in ways consistent with that stand'. Hence, signing a 'pledge' to lose weight increases the likelihood of successful weight control; signing a pledge to quit smoking and displaying this on the worksite notice board leads to a greater likelihood of attempting to quit.

Marketers use this principle in many ways, including competitions where people are asked to 'write in six reasons why brand x is the most wonderful thing in their lives'. Social marketers can use this principle in a similar way by having people in workshops write out and then publicly state the reasons for adopting the recommended behaviour under discussion, regardless of their initial attitudes. Similarly, the distribution of T-shirts, car stickers and fridge magnets with energy conservation tips should lead people who accept and display these things to be consistent with their publicly apparent commitment. Whatcom County in the US state of Washington asks businesses to 'pledge' to take action to prevent pollution of watersheds. Pledgers receive an attractive pledge plaque to display their commitment to their staff and customers (www.watershedpledge.org).

This principle can be applied to extend people's commitment to a particular stance [the 'foot-in-the-door' technique; Freedman and Fraser (1966)]. For example, Healthway (the Western Australian Health Promotion Foundation) took a 'small wins' approach in its sponsorship negotiations to getting venues to go smoke-free. Healthway first asked only for areas where food is served to go smoke-free. Adjacent and other enclosed spaces were then negotiated. Finally, Healthway asked for outdoors areas also to be smoke-free. Given the organisations' earlier commitments to smoke-free areas for health reasons, the pressure to be consistent with these earlier behaviours was strong when later and greater demands were made.

Promises increase medication compliance

Half of a sample of parents of children with inner ear infection was asked to promise to administer all the prescribed medication. The other half was simply given the medication and asked to administer all of it (standard procedure). Those asked to promise were more likely to administer all the medication and their children had better recovery than those who made no promise (Kulik and Carlino 1987).

Fund raising organisations appear to make considerable use of this principle. Potential donors are first asked how good a job they think the specified charitable organisation is doing, whether they support their work, and whether they feel the organisation is an important one in the community. As a variation they might be asked to sign a 'petition' urging politicians to support the organisation. After responding favourably, the target is then asked whether they would like to make a donation. How could they refuse?

Social proof: 'One should be more willing to comply with a request for behaviour if it is consistent with what similar others are thinking or doing.'

'More doctors smoke Camel than any other cigarette' read the ad headline in a 1940s ad; 'Join the club, join the club, join the Escort Club' went a television jingle in the 1960s. Cigarette marketers were at the forefront of advertising claims that 'most' people – or those who mattered – were users of their brands.

The principle of social proof states that people look to the behaviour of others as a guide to what is appropriate or normative behaviour. This applies especially in ambiguous situations and where the others are viewed as similar to themselves. It explains the use of canned laughter in comedy shows and, more seriously, the phenomena of 'copycat' suicides and violence. For example, following a television movie about a single, isolated mother apparently about to smother her child, two women in similar circumstances made similar attempts on their children's lives, with one child dying as a result (Wharton and Mandell 1985).

This principle is the basis of current 'social norms' approaches aimed at young people. For example, campaigns attempt to inform young people that the vast majority of young people do *not* binge drink, do *not* drink and drive, do *not* do hard drugs and so on. These sort of campaigns are important as many pre-university students believe that excessive drinking is the norm on university campuses. Hence, they are more likely to feel greater pressure to binge drink when they arrive at university than if they believed the norm was moderate or light drinking (Task Force 2002).

Suicides increase following death of Princess Diana

The University of Oxford Centre for Suicide Research found that the rate of suicide among women in general rose 34 per cent, and in women aged 25–44 (Diana was 37) rose 45 per cent, in the month after her funeral. The researchers suggested that women of her age who experienced the same sort of relationship and psychological problems as she did, became more pessimistic and despondent about their capacity to solve these problems (Persaud 2000).

Similarly, campaigns attempting to prevent or reduce violence against women inform young men that the vast majority of men listen when their partner says 'no', do not believe it is ok to get a woman drunk to have sex with her, and do not believe it's ok to put women down (see also Figure 5.5).

The sale and wearing of various coloured ribbons is an example of combining the principles of commitment and consistency and social proof. Wearing a white ribbon to publicly demonstrate one's opposition to violence against women personally reinforces

Figure 5.5 Rape, Abuse and Incest National Network (RAINN): social norms poster campaign

Donovan and Vlais (2005). Posters downloadable from www.rainn.org/gcpost.html.

that opposition, and men seeing a large number of other men wearing a white ribbon reinforces their perception that many men are opposed to such violence.

Overall, the social proof principle reminds us that it is important to feed back to people the results of successful social marketing campaigns, for example, by highlighting the number of people participating in physical activity events, the number of quitters after a Quit campaign, the number of people complying with water restrictions, the number of lives saved on the roads or at worksites and so on.

Liking: 'One should be more willing to comply with the requests of friends or other liked individuals'.

The principle of liking refers to the fact that people tend to comply with the requests of those they know and like. Furthermore, liking is based on perceived and actual *similarity*: we tend to like people who have similar attitudes, beliefs and backgrounds to our own. We also tend to like people who are physically attractive with warm, friendly, outgoing personalities. Such models dominate commercial advertising. Selecting role models who have similarities with, and empathy for, the target audience is crucial in communication campaigns.

Entertainment and sporting celebrities are commonly used in commercial marketing and in social marketing campaigns to attract attention to the message and increase awareness of the issue far more rapidly that would otherwise occur. However, unless these sources are also likeable (and credible), message acceptance does not necessarily follow.

The concept of liking is related to the concept of empathy, in that we are more likely to like and to comply with requests from people whom we feel understand our situation or point of view. For example, far more women visiting a medical centre volunteered they had been sexually or physically abused when their consulting doctor wore a badge reading 'Violence against women is wrong' than when the doctor was not wearing the badge (Murphy 1994).

Authority: 'One should be more willing to follow the suggestions of someone who is a legitimate authority.'

In our society, and many others, many people have a deep-seated sense of duty and obedience to those in respected positions. This is no doubt based on the fact, learned early in life, that people in authority have superior access to information and power. This principle is exemplified in many ways, including 'automatically' following the instructions of someone in uniform or with a title like 'doctor' (as on the button '*Trust me. I'm a doctor*'). Much advertising contains testimonials from various authoritative sources, and is perhaps one of health and social marketing's greatest exploitable assets. That is, 'The Surgeon General's Report on ...' has great influence, along with the voices of 'university experts' on various matters.

Authority via experience: Boris Becker promotes condom use in Germany

In what postmodernists might call a subversion of this principle, Wimbledon tennis champion Boris Becker was recruited to front a safe sex campaign in Germany in 2006. In 2000 Becker was caught having (unprotected) sex with a Russian model in a cupboard at a London restaurant. The campaign slogan is, 'Protection is important – I should know' (Leidig 2006).

Unfortunately, health, environmental, social and other scientists do not always agree on many issues, potentially leading to people being somewhat sceptical or cynical about various 'warnings' and threats issued by 'government' organisations. However, many non-profit organisations and individuals do have high credibility. For example, a recent survey (Jalleh and Donovan 2001) showed that 66 per cent of Western Australians rated the Cancer Council of Western Australia as 'very credible', and a further 25 per cent rated it as 'somewhat credible'. Only 3per cent rated the Council as 'a little/not at all credible'. A survey of 1,000 UK respondents in 2008 showed that 65 per cent indicated they had 'quite a lot' or 'a great deal' of trust in charities, slightly higher than the police (62 per cent) and just less than the National Health Service (70 per cent) (Baker 2008).

Scarcity: 'One should try to secure those opportunities that are scarce or dwindling.'

This principle states that things in scarce supply are valued more than if they are plentiful. This principle is exemplified by the 'Only 3 left!' and 'Last chance' sales tactics, and in the country-and-western song 'The girls all get prettier at closing time'. The principle of scarcity is exacerbated when there is competition for scarce resources, accounting for the often inflated prices obtained at auctions.

This principle is related to psychological reactance: the tendency to see things as more desirable when they are restricted. Many argue that bans on various behaviours only serve to increase young people's desires for behaviours and substances to which they may not otherwise be attracted. On the other hand, loss of privileges – such as loss of a driving licence – may lead to an increased value placed on the licence and increased compliance in the future.

Tupperware parties illustrate a number of the above principles: 'free gifts' are distributed to people when they arrive; members of the audience are asked to stand and say why they have previously bought Tupperware or why they think the products are good; once one person buys, the social proof principle is activated; and people are buying from someone they know and like.

Big Pharma also uses several of these principles to great effect, such that many are worried that decisions about treatment and the costs of health care are influenced more by pharmaceutical companies than by the medical profession's concern for patient welfare (Grant and Iserson 2005; Warzana 2000). The use of gifts, hospitality, payments for advisory board membership, research grants, consultancies and conference trips are clear examples of reciprocity (Katz *et al.* 2003); the use of key opinion leaders (KOLs: specialists in various areas) to promote a drug and make known that they prescribe a drug are examples of authority and social proof; and ensuring that sales reps are trained to understand physician's career goals (via sophisticated segmentation research) and, hence, show empathy for their situations is an example of liking.

Fear arousal and threat appeals

A commonly used tactic in health promotion and social marketing campaigns is the 'fear appeal'. Fear (or threat) appeals are based on behavioural learning theory: the threatening message arouses fear (or some other unpleasant emotional state), which is then reduced by the decision to adopt the behaviour that will avert the threat (the 'fear-drive model'). Adoption of the recommended behaviour leads to fear reduction which reinforces repetition of the behaviour.

Fear appeals are common in a number of health areas (particularly anti-smoking, illicit drugs, sun protection and road safety), and in areas as diverse as energy conservation, recycling, fire control and crime control (Rice and Atkin 1989; Salmon 1989). They are also not uncommon in commercial advertising (LaTour, Snipes and Bliss 1996), particularly for insurance.

However, given conflicting findings in the literature, there is some disagreement on their efficacy (Backer, Rogers and Sopory 1992; Donovan *et al*. 1995; Hastings, Stead and Webb 2004). Nevertheless, a number of reviews of the literature have concluded that fear appeals can be effective, and that more fear is more effective than less fear – except perhaps for low esteem targets – and provided the recommended behaviour is efficacious and under volitional control (Boster and Mongeau 1984; Job 1988; Sutton 1982, 1992; Witte and Allen 2000). For us, the question is no longer *whether* fear appeals can be effective, but *when* and *for whom* fear appeals are effective.

Fear

Fear is a complex emotion that can be both attracting and repelling. People have been flocking for years to scary rollercoaster rides, sideshow 'tunnels of fear' and horror movies for the experience of fear – albeit safe in the knowledge that the experience, in movies anyway, is only vicarious (Daniels 1977). At the same time, fear can lead to panic when a threat becomes real – as when a fire breaks out (*or is thought to*) in the same cinema showing the horror movie, or when thousands of radio listeners assumed Orson Welles' production of H. G. Wells' *War of the Worlds* was an actual, not a fictional, broadcast (see Chapter 12) (Lowery and DeFleur 1995).

Two types of fear arousal: Some forty years ago, Leventhal and Trembly (1968) distinguished between two types of fear, which they labelled 'anticipatory' and 'inhibitory' fear. This distinction was highlighted by Higbee (1969) in his seminal review of the literature, but has received little attention since. Inhibitory fear, evoking feelings of nausea and horror, results from exposure to graphic, gruesome descriptions and pictures of events, such as decapitations in car crashes, bloodied and bruised bodies and removal of organs in bloody operations. The focus here is on the stimuli evoking automatic or reflexive conditioned responses of fear. Anticipatory fear results from the recipient's cognitive appraisal that the threatened consequences are likely to occur if they ignore the recommended course of action. Similar distinctions can be noted in movies. While movies such as *Chainsaw Massacre* and *Evil Dead* rely mainly on gruesome scenes of carnage to frighten (or horrify) viewers (i.e., reflexive responses), others rely more on arousing the viewers' anticipation of horrific outcomes depending on what actions the actors take (e.g., the killer is in the cellar … the lights go off … she grabs a torch and heads down the stairs to the fuse box in the cellar) (anticipatory fear).

While Higbee (1969) drew no conclusions as to the relative appropriateness of these two types of fear, Donovan (1991) has argued that it is anticipatory rather than inhibitory fear that health communicators must arouse, since it is the link between the threat and the person's continuing unhealthy behaviour that must be established. Results from the Australian national tobacco campaign relating to ads depicting the graphic squeezing of fatty deposits from an artery and the cutting in half of a brain, suggest that inhibitory fear can enhance anticipatory fear where the threatened consequence is clearly seen to result from the unhealthy behaviour (Hassard 1999).

Observation of a large number of campaigns shows that many health communicators in designing their 'scare' messages have failed to note the distinction between these two types of fear, with many simply using graphic gruesome scenes without regard to the necessary cognitive link. That is, gruesome and graphic stimuli may have aroused inhibitory fear, but failed to arouse anticipatory fear leading to a cognitive 'this could happen to me' response to the threat appeal.

'Fear appeal' or 'threat appeal'?

The terms 'fear appeal', 'fear arousal', 'threat appeal' and 'threat' are used rather loosely and interchangeably in the persuasion literature (Donovan and Henley 1997; Henley 1999). We would argue that the term 'threat appeal' is more appropriate than 'fear appeal', primarily because fear is an emotional *response* and, hence, the term fear 'appeal' confounds stimulus (i.e., message content) and response (i.e., audience reaction) variables (O'Keefe 1990; Strong, Anderson and Dubas 1993).

Focusing on the fear response also tends to distract attention from cognitive responses to threatening messages. The recipient's unprompted cognitive responses during exposure to the message (especially the degree of counter-arguing), are a major predictor of overall message effectiveness, as are prompted cognitive measures of threat appraisal such as personal relevance, credibility and 'likelihood of happening to me' (Donovan, Jalleh and Henley 1999; Rossiter and Percy 1997).

Furthermore, fear is only one of a variety of emotions that might be aroused by threat appeals and mediate audience response to the message (Bagozzi and Moore 1994; Dillard *et al.* 1996; Donovan *et al.* 1995; Stout 1989). For example, shame, guilt, sadness and remorse are emotions widely used in social areas (Bennett 1998), with many road safety ads demonstrating the effective use of guilt and remorse in the area of road safety (Donovan, Egger and Francas 1999). Although Witte (1993) defines fear appeals and threat appeals as two distinct categories, our framework defines fear appeals as a subset of threat appeals, where the targeted emotional arousal is fear rather than some other emotion.

The term 'threat appeal' is preferred to 'fear appeal' because:

(1) it encourages a broader study of potentially important mediating emotions and cognitive responses;

(2) it demands a greater focus on stimulus factors (i.e., message content and how this is communicated); and

(3) it simultaneously demands a separate and sharper focus on response factors (i.e., audience emotional and cognitive reactions to the message).

Use of the term 'threat appeal' rather than 'fear appeal' demands a more precise focus on the content of threat appeals (i.e., stimulus factors – negative outcomes, contingent behaviours) and on response factors (i.e., cognitive responses and the generation and role of emotions other than fear).

Defining threat appeals: negative outcomes, threats and threat appeals

We define a threat appeal as a communication including three major components:

(1) a negative outcome;
(2) a contingent behaviour; and
(3) a source (Donovan and Henley 1997).

The communication might be delivered in any medium and in either advertising or editorial format (i.e., a television commercial, radio or press ad, press release, news announcement), by a brochure or video, or in an interpersonal face-to-face encounter.

A threat appeal consists of a **source** stating that some negative outcome will result – or increase in likelihood – as a consequence of non-compliance with the source's recommendation. Source characteristics (likeability, credibility, relevant expertise, impartiality) are always important, but particularly for new issues where the link must be established between the threat and the behaviour in question, and for specific target audiences who might be distrusting of establishment sources (Donovan and Henley 1997; Perman and Henley 2001).

A **negative outcome** is some event that is perceived by the target audience to be harmful or undesirable (*'something bad'*), and which under normal circumstances would be avoided where possible. The loss of a loved one, blindness, a gaol sentence, loss of a limb, lung cancer, polluted waterways are negative outcomes.

A **threat** is where some harmful event is perceived by the target audience to be likely to occur to them (*'something bad could happen to you'*). Being informed of the lifetime likelihood of blindness for an individual from 'all causes' constitutes a threat; being informed of decreased future rainfall and increased land salination due to global warming constitutes a threat.

A threat becomes a **threat appeal** when a source states that the negative outcome is contingent on the recipient's behaviour and seeks to alter that contingent behaviour (*'X says that something bad could or will happen to you if you do/don't do …'*).

The difference between a threat and a threat appeal may be illustrated as follows: an ophthalmologist stating the likelihood of blindness occurring because of an existing condition constitutes a threat. Stating the likelihood of blindness occurring if an individual views an eclipse without an appropriate device constitutes a threat appeal. The weather bureau announcing a high likelihood of a cyclone occurring in the Gulf of New Orleans constitutes a threat. The local state emergency service recommending that people evacuate the area to avoid injury or loss of life constitutes a threat appeal.

Overall then, threat appeals promise the target audience that if they do not adopt the recommended behaviour or cease the undesired behaviour, then the likelihood of the negative consequences of non-compliance will be increased markedly. They work when the recommended behaviour is 'doable' by the target audience, seen to be effective and the negative consequences are seen to be severe (i.e., capable of arousing considerable emotional distress if it occurs).

De Man Met De Dwergtestikels: 'The man with the dwarf testicles'
De Man Met Vrouwen Borsten: 'The man with woman's breasts'

Dutch athletes were confronted with these graphic images on posters in their gyms illustrating the potential negative consequences of performance-enhancing drugs. The posters, part of the Eigen Kracht (true or own strength) anti-doping campaign, were in the form of old-style promotions for circus freaks. One featured a clearly 'wired' woman titled: Hyperwoman: The Woman Who Never Sleeps (www.eigenkracht.nl/lsm/ eigenkrachtcampagne/campagnemateriaals, accessed 4 July 2009).

Attributes of negative outcomes

Negative outcomes vary widely and along a number of dimensions. All these need to be considered when developing a threat appeal in a particular area. What might be an effective negative outcome in some areas for some audiences, might not be appropriate in other areas and for other audiences.

Typology of negative outcomes: There are at least four dimensions: physical (e.g., disease, disfigurement); social (e.g., ostracism, embarrassment); psychological (e.g., sense of failure, loss of self-esteem); and financial (e.g., property loss or damage, loss of job or income source). It is likely that the relative impact of these will vary by target audience.

Many negative outcomes involve several of these dimensions. For example, a car crash could cause physical injuries that result in job loss and subsequent depression. Heavy drinking, blue collar, young males who rely on their own motor vehicle for accessing employment sites are concerned about random breath testing because losing their driving licence could mean losing their job (Donovan 1995).

Degree of perceived control: Natural disasters such as earthquakes, typhoons and floods occur regardless of the individual's actions. In these cases, threat appeals focus on taking action to minimise the consequences of these events. Other negative outcomes, such as the so-called 'lifestyle diseases' and injuries, are at least partly under the individual's control. In these cases, threat appeals focus on prevention or minimising their likelihood of occurrence.

Origins: single or multiple causes: Some negative outcomes have a single cause or a set of clearly related causes (e.g., sexually transmitted diseases (STDs)). Others have multiple causes or risk factors (e.g., coronary heart disease, diabetes type 2). Messages are easier to generate and comprehend for negative outcomes with clearly defined single causes or few related causes.

Severity: Some negative outcomes have major lifestyle implications (e.g., emphysema), whereas others would have little impact on day-to-day functioning (e.g., mild hangover). Different target audiences could have vastly different views with regard to the severity of specific negative outcomes.

CABWISE – using fear to prevent rape

The use of unlicensed minicabs was a major contributor to rapes and sexual assaults of women in London. Transport authorities, the police and the City joined to increase the safety of travel at night in the city. CABWISE warns of the dangers of taking an illegal cab, and urges young women in particular to text the CABWISE number, which replies with legitimate local numbers to call. The introductory television ads showed young women in vulnerable situations and explicitly referred to and dramatised sexual assaults by unlicensed minicab drivers. The initial three-month campaign in 2006 reduced sexual assaults by unlicensed minicab drivers from an average of fourteen during the corresponding period of the previous three years to four during September–December 2006 (Okin *et al.* 2009). In the first year of the campaign, there were eighty-five fewer reported sexual assaults and twelve fewer reported rapes by illegal minicab drivers (Hoad 2008).

Reversibility: Negative outcomes can be described in terms of their permanence or 'reversibility' (Henley 1995). Amputations are non-reversible (although prostheses are available), whereas most STDs are reversible. Given awareness of coronary bypass and organ transplant successes, even some major diseases such as heart disease might be considered reversible by some people. Ease of reversibility might serve to reduce the perceived severity of a negative event (France *et al.* 1991). On the other hand, it is desirable that in some cases, such as smoking, the target audience can be assured that any damage they have suffered can be reversed (to ensure response efficacy).

Salience or familiarity: Different diseases and risk factors differ in terms of the ease with which they come to people's minds, which, in turn, is a function of media publicity,

previous educational efforts and individual circumstances. For example, there is generally continuing media publicity about road deaths, cancer and heart disease, whereas,
at least until recently, there has been far less media attention on diabetes.

Lifetime likelihood and imminence: Negative outcomes differ in their estimated lifetime likelihood independently of any contingent behaviour, and in their (perceived)
imminence (Chu 1966). In general, the more imminent the outcome, the greater the
impact on behaviour change. For example, with regard to smoking, many young people
are less deterred by death outcomes in middle age than they are by immediate effects
on their fitness or by negative cosmetic effects.

Death versus non-death: Death has been used widely as the negative outcome in
health campaigns (e.g., 'speed kills', 'smoking kills'). However, as death *per se* is inevitable, the threat appeal should focus on either *premature death* or various undesirable
attributes of death (e.g., slow, painful, etc.). Furthermore, people generally claim to be
less affected by threats of their own death and more likely to be affected by the death
of loved ones, the effect of their death on loved ones, or causing death (Henley and
Donovan 2003).

Overall then, negative outcomes being considered for inclusion in threat appeals
should first be assessed on the above attributes independently of any threat context.

'It's 30 for a reason' ('40 can kill') campaign

Research showed that many people felt that speeding is exceeding the speed limit by a
dramatic amount, whereas doing 40 mph in a 30 mph zone was of little consequence.
This UK Department of Transport campaign incorporated an ad showing a child being hit
by a car and killed and then coming to life again as the voice over states: 'If you hit me at
40 mph there is around an 80% chance I'll die. Hit me at 30 and there is around an 80%
chance that I'll live' (Lannon 2008).

Contingent behaviour complexities

In a threat appeal, adopting a recommended course of action is claimed to protect the
audience from the negative outcome. However, the choice of what behaviour to recommend needs careful consideration as there are a number of complexities to consider in
constructing the message.

Degree of protection: The recommended behaviour may prevent the negative outcome completely (e.g., abstinence from sex and STDs), or, more commonly, the recommended behaviour can only reduce the likelihood of the negative outcome occurring
(e.g., speed limit compliance and accident likelihood).

Asymmetry of effects: The contingent behaviour alternatives are often asymmetrical (e.g., while abstinence reduces the risk of an STD to zero, engaging in sexual behaviour, even unprotected, does not necessarily result in an STD).

Limits on the effectiveness of the contingent behaviour: For many negative outcomes, there is some existing base level of likelihood unrelated to the contingent behaviour, and for which there are wide individual differences (e.g., all individuals have some base level of risk for cardiovascular disease, regardless of their smoking behaviour).

Quantifying individual risk: Related to the above, the overall probability of the negative outcome (base level plus increase due to engaging in the contingent behaviour) for any particular threat appeal is generally unquantifiable for any single individual.

Behaviour target – an increase or decrease?: A major consideration is whether the focus should be on increasing a desired behaviour (e.g., eat more fruit and vegetables, increase physical activities, drive more often at the speed limit, etc.) or on decreasing an undesired behaviour (e.g., eat less fat, decrease time inactive, stop speeding, etc.). Learning theory suggests that the choice of whether to increase or decrease a behaviour has implications for the framing of the threat message (see Chapter 6).

These contingent behaviour complexities in general lead to major challenges in executing threat appeals. Together they suggest that a major aim of a threat appeal is to increase the target's perceived likelihood of some negative outcome occurring to be significantly above the perceived base level. They also highlight the strategy of focusing on a related contingent behaviour, where the main contingent behaviour may not be seen to be particularly efficacious in averting the threat. For example, rather than stressing the likelihood of a collision, in a variation of the above UK Department of Transport message, the Western Australian Office of Road Safety's 'Lady and Pram' ad emphasised the increased likelihood of being unable to stop in time, for someone stepping in front of the car, for every increase in 10 kph of speed. The ad is filmed from the position of the driver and is in three segments. In the first segment, the lady and pram step in front and the vehicle easily stops in time. In the second segment, the car is travelling a little faster, but manages to stop just short of contact. In the third segment, the car is travelling even faster and this time hits the lady and pram, with the woman's body hitting the windscreen.

This is a more concrete way of demonstrating the effect of speed than a general 'speed kills' approach, which tends to lack credibility with young male drivers. Furthermore, this approach avoids the common counter-argument of this, and other, target groups that speed *per se* does not cause accidents, although they accept that unexpected events can cause crashes. The 'lady and pram' ad was very effective: the percentage of young drivers who believed that driving 10 kph slower would reduce their risk of a crash increased from 76 per cent before the campaign to 87 per cent during the campaign.

Incentive appeals

Incentive appeals can be characterised in the same way as threat appeals: something good will happen to you if you perform the recommended behaviour. That is, incentive appeals promise the target audience that if they adopt the recommended behaviour (or cease an undesired behaviour), then the likelihood of positive consequences of compliance will be increased. They work when the recommended behaviour is doable by the target audience, is seen to deliver the benefits and the positive consequences are seen to be substantial (i.e., capable of arousing considerable positive emotions if they occur). Naturally enough, incentive (or positive) appeals dominate commercial marketing.

Perform well on test – watch teacher eat worms!

In probably the most bizarre attention grabbing incentive since that of car dealers literally throwing a radio through the window of a car as they announced 'I'll even throw in a radio', US teachers are promising all sorts of incentives if students' scores meet test standards.
In El Paso, Texas, on 21 May 2004, a school principal and assistant principal delivered on their promise that if the students met their book reading goal, they would eat worms. The children apparently 'squealed' (and probably the worms did too). The after-effects on the principals are unknown (Herrick 2004).

There are few systematic studies comparing the relative effectiveness of threat appeals versus incentive appeals for the same behaviour for the same target audience (Donovan *et al.* 1995). However, we would argue that threat appeals are far more effective than incentive appeals where the undesirable behaviour has significant negative health or other outcomes, and incentive appeals are effective where the recommended behaviour has clear positive outcomes and the undesired behaviour has only moderate or low negative outcomes.

It is likely that different individuals will respond differently not only to the two types of overall appeal, but also to different threats and to different incentives. Formative research with the target audience is necessary to identify what will motivate adoption of the desired behaviour among what proportion of the total population of interest. Gintner *et al.* (1987) found that people with a higher risk of hypertension (i.e., had a parent with hypertension), were more likely to attend a blood-pressure screening following a message that emphasised maintaining vigour and wellbeing versus a message that emphasised the severity of the illness. A study by the authors suggested that for increasing physical activity and fruit and veg consumption, threat appeals (i.e., stating the negative consequences of non-compliance such as heart disease, etc.) may be slightly more effective than incentive appeals (i.e., stating the positive consequences of compliance such as increased energy, alertness, etc.).

As we will see later, the Act–Belong–Commit campaign that promotes positive mental health and wellbeing, promises positive social, emotional and physical benefits rather than stating negative consequences of not doing things that are good for one's mental health. Threat versus incentive appeals are also covered in the next chapter in the Rossiter–Percy motivational model.

Framing effects

Consideration of positive versus negative appeals raises the issue of framing in decision-making. As used in studies of decision-making, framing generally refers to presenting one of two equivalent value outcomes to different groups of decision-makers, where one outcome is presented in positive or gain terms, and the other in negative or loss terms (Salovey and Williams-Piehota 2004). For example, a positively framed message might emphasise the benefits to be gained by adopting a promoted course of action (e.g., taking a cholesterol test allows assessment of one's risk of heart disease), while the negative frame emphasises the loss of these *same* benefits if the course of action is not adopted (e.g., not taking a cholesterol test does not allow the assessment of one's risk of heart disease) (Maheswaran and Meyers-Levy 1990). Alternatively, a probabilistic outcome might be described in terms of the positive outcome (e.g., this medical procedure has a 50 per cent chance of survival) or the negative outcome (e.g., this medical procedure has a 50 per cent chance of dying) (Wilson *et al.* 1987).

The concept of 'framing' is also used in a more general sense in terms of the context in which issues are placed. For example, the issue of HIV/AIDS was 'reframed' from a 'gay disease' to a public health infectious disease issue; hate groups attempt to frame racist comments as expressions of 'free speech'; and violence against women is now being framed as a global public health issue, not 'just a domestic' issue between intimate partners.

The results of framing studies have been mixed. For behaviours such as breast self-examination (BSE) (Meyerowitz and Chaiken 1987), mammography screening (Banks *et al.* 1995), exercise (Robberson and Rogers 1988), skin cancer detection (Rothman *et al.* 1993) and smoking (Wilson *et al.* 1987), negative framings have tended to result in greater message compliance, at least relative to controls, but not always significantly greater than positive framings.

On the other hand, a positive frame was more effective for promoting exercise as a means of enhancing self-esteem (Robberson and Rogers 1988), parents' use of children's car seat restraints and for a skin cancer prevention behaviour (Rothman *et al.* 1993). For surgical procedures, positively framed outcomes (probability of success or survival) induced greater compliance than negatively framed outcomes (probability of failure or death) (Moxey *et al.* 2003; Wilson *et al.* 1987). When the side-effects (the common 'flu) were framed positively (90 per cent chance of no side-effects) or negatively (10 per cent chance of side-effects) for a hypothetical 'new' immunisation that protected infants against respiratory complaints such as bronchitis and pneumonia, Donovan and Jalleh (2000) found the positive framing to be superior for low involved respondents (no infant and not intending to get pregnant), but there was no framing effect for high involved respondents (had an infant or intended to get pregnant in the immediate future). Other studies also suggest individual differences may interact with how people respond to different framings (Sherman, Mann and Updegraff 2005).

Rothman and Salovey (1997), referring to Kahneman and Tversky's (1979, 1982) conclusions with regard to risk aversiveness under positive framing and risk seeking under negative framing, suggest that gain frames would be more effective for disease prevention behaviours (e.g., use of sunscreen for skin cancer prevention), whereas loss frames would be more effective for disease detection behaviours (e.g., skin examination to detect early cancers). Later studies appear to support the general position that gain frames are better for disease prevention, whereas loss frames are better for disease detection (Rothman *et al.* 2006). However, our experience over a number of published (e.g., Donovan and Jalleh 2000) and unpublished framing studies, is that those based purely on variations such as 'taking a cholesterol test allows assessment of one's risk of heart disease' versus 'not taking a cholesterol test does not allow the assessment of one's risk of heart disease' are of little importance.

How Merck framed a 'bad news' clinical trial outcome as 'good news'

Message framing is ubiquitous, including in the best of journals. In Merck's report of its VIGOR trial comparing their new non-steroidal anti-inflammatory (NSAID) drug rofecoxib (Vioxx) against an existing NSAID (naproxen), the primary end points related to serious adverse gastric side-effects – a major reason for many people not being able to tolerate the older NSAIDs. Adverse cardiovascular events such as myocardial infarctions (MIs – heart attacks) were also recorded. The results were clear: Vioxx performed significantly better than naproxen on adverse gastric side-effects outcomes (the 'good news'), but significantly worse on MIs (the 'bad news'). However, that was not the way it was reported in the *New England Journal of Medicine* by Bombardier *et al.* (2000).

> We found significantly lower rates of clinically important and complicated upper gastrointestinal events in those taking rofecoxib than in those taking naproxen …

> We also found significantly lower incidence of upper gastrointestinal bleeding and bleeding beyond the duodenum in those taking rofecoxib than in those taking naproxen.

In these statements, naproxen is the benchmark comparator. Having less of something bad relative to the benchmark is 'good news' for Vioxx.

However, when reporting the MI rates, the comparator is reversed:

The rate of myocardial infarction was significantly lower in the naproxen group than in the rofecoxib group.

The result is then interpreted as a cardio-protective effect for naproxen – not 'bad news' for rofecoxib.

If the comparator had been kept constant, the MI statement would have (and arguably should have) read:

The rate of myocardial infarction was significantly higher in the rofecoxib group than in the naproxen group.

Of course, having more of something bad relative to the benchmark would have been 'bad news' for Vioxx.

Nevertheless, the good folks at the prestigious *New England Journal of Medicine* swallowed this sugar-coated pill without a murmur.

This constant comparator MI statement may also have attracted far more attention to the cardiovascular risks of Vioxx that were clearly evident in a later trial that resulted in Merck withdrawing Vioxx from the market in 2004.

However, framings of product constituents might be significant. People have more favourable purchase intentions for meat products when they are labelled with the per cent fat-free than when labelled with the per cent fat (Donovan and Jalleh 1999; Levin and Gaeth 1988). The upper graph in Figure 5.6 shows that this bias exists for 75 per cent fat-free versus 25 per cent fat; 85 per cent fat-free versus 15 per cent fat and 90 per cent fat-free versus 10 per cent fat. The lower graph in Figure 5.6 shows that the fat-free framings are all rated more lean than their percentage fat counterparts – suggesting that the framing does affect people's perception of the amount of fat in the product and hence purchase intention.

90 per cent fat-free: how much fat is that?

Jalleh and Donovan (2001) suggest that consumers need to be aware of the influence of percentage content labelling on their attitudes and purchase intention. Products with a 'fat-free' label, especially those whose fat content is less than 90 per cent, might increase their favourable perceptions and purchase intentions relative to their equivalent fat labels. Hence, when consumers are considering buying a product with a positively framed label, it is suggested that they take into account the flip side of the label. For example, in assessing mince with a 75 per cent fat-free label, consumers need to re-label the product in their mind and ask themselves how they would feel about this product if it were labelled 25 per cent fat before making a purchasing decision.

Overall, developing successful communication strategies involves two phases (Egger, Donovan and Spark 1993).

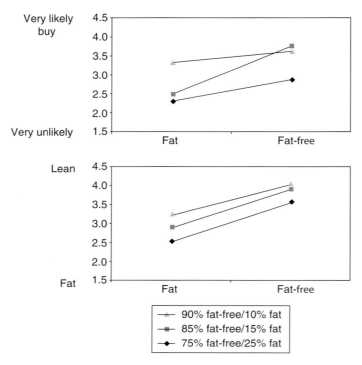

Figure 5.6 Purchase intention and fat/lean ratings by fat/fat-free framing
Jalleh and Donovan (2001)

Getting the right message and getting the message right

Getting the right message involves identifying what message will motivate the target audience to adopt the recommended action (what advertising agency people call 'the hot buttons to push'). It entails ensuring that the message content takes into account the target audience's initial knowledge, beliefs and attitudes, and has the capacity to shift beliefs, attitudes and behaviour in the desired direction. Formative research with violent men for the Freedom from Fear campaign revealed that showing the impact of their violence on their or their partner's children was the *right message* to motivate such men to seek help; showing the minister that there was overwhelming public approval for a domestic violence campaign targeting violent men to voluntarily enter counselling was the *right message* to gain government approval for the campaign; showing feminist stakeholders that the messages did not adversely affect victims was the *right message* to ensure sector support for the campaign (Donovan *et al.* 2000).

Getting the message right entails ensuring that how the message is presented attracts attention, is believable, relevant, understandable, arouses appropriate emotions and does not lead to counter-argument. The effects of domestic violence on children can be depicted in a variety of scenarios. However, such executions needed to avoid being seen by men to be judging or criticising their behaviour, a perception that would lead them to reject the ad's request for them to seek help. Pre-testing the ad was essential to ensure message understanding and credibility, as well as ensuring that the perceived tone of the ad did not antagonise men (Donovan *et al.* 2000).

Guidelines for developing communication campaigns

- Establish source credibility by seeking a common point of agreement from which to commence the communication process.
- Increase the salience and intensity of already held positive beliefs and other beliefs that provide a positive context within which to change negative beliefs.
- Link messages to which people have potentially negative responses to already held positive beliefs.
- Avoid broaching issues that generate negative responses until prior positive beliefs are firmly established.
- Attempt changes in negative beliefs slowly and in small steps, i.e., stay within the target audience's 'latitude of acceptance' – do not make extreme claims.
- Enhance source credibility by presenting apparently even-handed or two-sided approaches that pre-empt counter-arguments that would otherwise distract from the message or lead to rejection of the message.
- Draw explicit conclusions for unmotivated, naive audiences; let motivated, knowledgeable audiences draw their own conclusions.

Concluding comments

Communication strategies must not only focus on message content, but on message execution. Breaking through the clutter is essential. Like the better mousetrap, if nobody knows about it, it can hardly elicit behaviour change. To then hold attention, message construction must be based on the receiver's initial attitudes, their motivation to process the message and their ability to do so.

Communication can occur through a variety of media. The good thing about Cialdini's principles of persuasion is that they apply to interpersonal as well as media channels. And they work.

Threat appeals – and their converse, incentive appeals – constitute the major type of message in most communication strategies aimed at individual behaviour change, whether as consumers, policymakers, legislators or corporation executives. However, such appeals must be accompanied by the opportunity to adopt the behaviour, preferably in a supportive physical, social and regulatory environment.

This chapter has dealt with a number of aspects relevant to getting the right message and getting the message right, but with the emphasis on getting the message right. Chapter 6 provides further frameworks, with an emphasis on getting the right message.

QUESTIONS

● How could you use Cialdini's principles to (a) increase smokers' likelihood of success-fully quitting; (b) increase use of sunscreen at the beach; (c) increase hand washing by children?

● Look through your local newspaper at both the ads and the news. How many examples can you find of how (a) product attributes are framed in a way favourable to the prod-uct; (b) issues are framed in a particular way?

● How is the gun control debate 'framed' in your country?

FURTHER READING

Cialdini, R. B. 2001. *Influence: Science and Practice*. Needham Heights, MA: Allyn & Bacon.

Donovan, R. J. and Leivers, S. 1993. Using Paid Advertising to Modify Racial Stereotype Beliefs, *Public Opinion Quarterly* 57: 205–18.

Katz, D., Mansfield, P., Goodman, R., Tiefer, L. and Merz, J. 2003. Psychological Aspects of Gifts From Drug Companies, *Journal of the American Medical Association* 290(18): 2404–5.

6 Models of attitude and behaviour change

This chapter presents a number of models useful for developing campaign strategies. These models are generally known as 'knowledge–attitude–behaviour' change (KAB) models or 'social cognition' models (Connor and Norman 2005; Godin 1994). While each can be classified as either 'motivational', 'behavioural', 'cognitive' or 'affective' in emphasis, they all deal with conceptualising the influences on behaviour, and hence provide a framework for formative research, strategy development and campaign evaluation. In general, changes in the major components in these models, such as attitudes, norms and efficacy, have been found to be good predictors of changes in behaviours and intentions (Webb and Sheeran 2006). There are a number of such models [Darnton (2008) lists and describes over thirty]. We will briefly describe each of the models most frequently mentioned in the health promotion and social marketing literature, before presenting a synthesis of the major variables across all models. We include brief discussions on two concepts generally ignored by the KAB models: morality and legitimacy (Amonini 2001). A notable omission from this chapter is Prochaska and DiClemente's 'Stages of Change' model, which will be discussed in Chapter 10.

Most of these models are based on the assumption that an individual's beliefs about some person, group, issue, object or behaviour will determine the individual's attitude and intentions with respect to that person, group, issue, object or behaviour. These intentions, in turn, subject to environmental facilitators and inhibitors, social norms and self-efficacy, will predict how the individual actually acts with regard to that person, group, issue, object or behaviour. An understanding of KAB models provides us with directions for setting communication objectives and for generating message strategies to achieve these objectives. These processes depend on a thorough understanding of the sorts of beliefs that influence attitudes towards the recommended behaviour, how these beliefs and other facilitators and inhibitors influence intentions to behave, and when and how intentions are fulfilled or not fulfilled.

We also present Rogers' broader diffusion model as the major model for understanding how ideas and behaviours diffuse throughout a community. Rogers' model is increasingly being applied in social marketing. Behaviour modification (or applied behaviour analysis) principles are also included to further emphasise that we must translate people's beliefs, attitudes and intentions into action, and that to do this, we must be aware of the necessary environmental factors and skills that will facilitate this translation.

The health belief model

The health belief model (HBM) was perhaps the first behavioural model in health education. It was developed in the 1950s by US Public Health Service workers in an attempt to explain participation and non-participation in screening programmes for tuberculosis (Becker 1974; Maiman and Becker 1974; Rosenstock 1974). It is still widely used today. For example, Bowman, Heilman and Seetharaman (2004) developed and tested a model of general product use compliance based on the HBM. Patient compliance with instructions for prescription medicines is particularly important for health outcomes, and mental health outcomes in particular.

The model lists the following factors that are presumed to influence behaviour change in response to a potential health threat (Figure 6.1):

- the individual's perceived susceptibility to the threat;
- the individual's perceived severity of the threat;

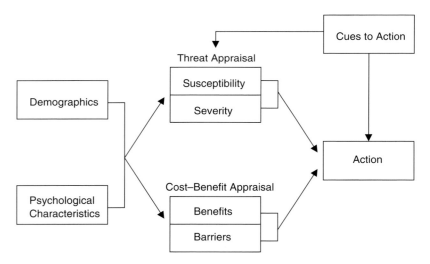

Figure 6.1 The health belief model

Adapted from Abraham and Sheeran (2005). (Note: 'health motivation' removed in this adaptation.)

- the individual's perceptions that the recommended behaviour will avert the threat (and any other additional benefits);
- the individual's perceptions of the costs of, and perceived barriers to, adopting the recommended behaviour; and
- the presence of cues to action (internal such as symptoms; external such as mass media advertising or interpersonal communications) that prompt the individual to act.

It is also assumed that demographic and psychosocial variables will moderate the above variables.

Hence, an individual is more likely to take up exercise if they consider that they are at high risk for diabetes, if they perceive diabetes as a serious disease, if they believe that increased exercise is effective in reducing the risk of diabetes, if they perceive no major barriers or costs (financial, social or physical) to increasing their level of exercise, and if a friend draws their attention to a physical activity programme commencing at a nearby community recreation centre.

As the oldest model, the HBM has been used in planning programmes in a wide variety of health areas (see Abraham and Sheeran 2005) and has been reviewed extensively (Janz and Becker 1984; Rosenstock, Strecher and Becker 1988). While Janz and Becker reported that the HBM significantly predicted health behaviours, Harrison, Mullen and Green's (1992) meta-analysis of more strictly selected studies, revealed a far weaker effect size. We would suggest this is because, while the model provides a useful framework for both research and message strategy planning, it is (like many other models) incomplete. Also, different variables may be more or less useful in different areas, and all model testing assumes that the right threats are measured. For example, seat belt use is not only motivated by a desire to avoid serious injury in a crash, but also by the perceived likelihood of being ticketed (see the US 'Click it or Ticket' campaign; Chaudhary, Soloman and Cosgrove 2004).

Explaining performance enhancing drug use

The HBM states that the recommended behaviour will occur if individuals see themselves as susceptible to a particular health problem, see this problem as a serious one, consider that the benefits of treatment are effective and not unduly costly and some event occurs to prompt action. These concepts can be applied in reverse where the behaviour under question is not a threat but a 'promise'. For example, performance enhancing drug usage will occur if athletes see themselves as unable to achieve at their desired level, if achieving at the desired level has considerable rewards, if they consider that drug use will effectively deliver the required performance without undue side effects or expense, the drugs are easily available and perhaps they learn that a rival is using performance enhancing drugs. The HBM's explicit inclusion of a cost–benefit analysis (only implied in other models) increases its potential applicability to the sport drug area (Donovan *et al.* 2002).

Protection motivation theory

Rogers' (1975) protection motivation theory (PMT) was developed originally as a model of fear arousal to explain the motivational effect resulting from 'threat' communications. The theory assumes that people are motivated to protect themselves not only from physical threats, but also from social and psychological threats (Rogers 1983). PMT also incorporates the concept of self-efficacy from Bandura's (1986) social learning theory.

PMT postulates that individuals undertake two major appraisals when confronted with a threat: a threat appraisal and a coping appraisal (Figure 6.2). As in the HBM, a threat is appraised on two major factors:

- the perceived severity of the threatened harmful event if it occurs; and
- the perceived likelihood of the threatened outcome occurring if the recommended behaviour is not adopted.

These two factors determine the individual's perceived *vulnerability*.

The coping appraisal consists of an appraisal of the recommended behaviour on the following two dimensions:

- the perceived effectiveness of the promoted behaviour to avoid or reduce the likelihood of occurrence of the threat (i.e., response efficacy); and
- the individual's self-assessed ability to perform the recommended behaviour (i.e., self-efficacy).

If an individual (a corporate executive in this case) determines that they are vulnerable to a threat (e.g., a boycott of the company's products), that the recommended behaviour (e.g., adopting recyclable packaging) would be effective in removing the threat and that they are able to carry out the recommended behaviour (i.e., the recyclable packaging and technology are available and affordable), then the recommended behaviour is likely to occur. If the threat appraisal is low, either because it is extremely unlikely to occur or not severe enough to worry about, or if the threat is seen to be significant but the recommended behaviour is not seen to be effective or within the individual's capabilities (e.g., a hostile board of directors), the recommended behaviour will not occur.

Rogers (1983) later added two further factors: *response costs* that act to inhibit adoption of the desired behaviour; and *rewards* gained from the undesirable behaviour that facilitate its continuation.

The PMT emphasises the appraisal of threatening or supposedly fear arousing communications, whereas some behaviours might be more effectively motivated, at least for some target groups, by the positive effects or benefits of adopting the recommended behaviour (as noted in Chapter 5). For example, many individuals take up

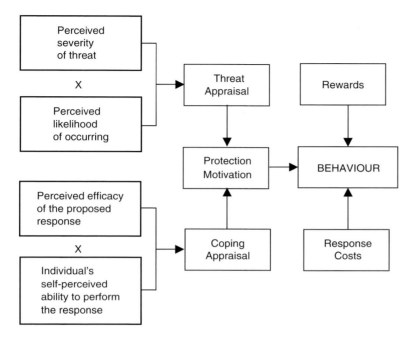

Figure 6.2 Rogers' protection motivation theory

and maintain exercise for both the positive benefits of exercising (e.g., enjoyment, social interactions, feelings of mastery, alertness, etc.), and to avoid threatened outcomes of inadequate exercise (e.g., avoidance of heart disease, diabetes risk, lose or control weight, etc.) (Donovan and Francas 1990). Hence, a more complete model would include an *incentive* appraisal: that is, the perceived attractiveness of the positive benefits to be gained by adopting the recommended behaviour. The coping appraisal in this case would be the same as for the threat: whether the recommended behaviour can deliver the promised benefits and whether the individual can perform the desired behaviour.

The PMT has been applied in a number of health areas (see Boer and Seydel 1996), including exercise, alcohol consumption, smoking, breast cancer screening and sexually transmitted diseases (e.g., Prentice-Dunn and Rogers 1986; Rippetoe and Rogers 1987; Tanner, Day and Crask 1989; Wurtele and Maddux 1987), and in predicting intentions to engage in anti-nuclear war behaviours (Wolf, Gregory and Stephan 1986), earthquake preparedness (Mulilis and Lippa 1990) and burglary prevention (Wiegman *et al.* 1992). In general, the concepts of vulnerability and coping appraisal – particularly self-efficacy – have been found to be significant predictors of intention (Boer and Seydel 1996).

Thinking positively: the importance of self-efficacy

A University of Utrecht study in the Netherlands found that in their sample of obese subjects in a weight loss programme, those who at the start perceived themselves better able to control their weight and eating behaviour lost significantly more weight than the others. Strong self-efficacy was, in fact, the best predictor of weight loss success (Squires 2005). Hence, interventions must include ways of building people's perceived (and actual) self-efficacy.

Social learning theory

At a basic level, learning occurs via a process of reinforcement: behaviours that are rewarded tend to be repeated, while behaviours that are punished tend not to be repeated. Social learning theorists believe that many learned behaviours depend on social reinforcement (e.g., peer pressure influencing taking up smoking, social norms about recycling), and that new behaviours can be learned not only by actually experiencing reinforcements, but also by *observing* reinforcements delivered to others (Bandura 1977). This is the basis of 'modelling': adopting behaviours through imitating the behaviours of others. That is, Bandura draws our attention not only to the behaviour *per se*, but also to the environment in which it takes place.

The power of a model to induce attitude and behaviour change depends on such things as the model's credibility, attractiveness, power, expertise and empathy with the audience (Rossiter and Percy 1997). It also depends on how clearly and credibly the model's behaviour is seen to be rewarded. Social learning theory is the primary rationale for testimonial communications, and for the modelling of desirable health behaviours in television advertising and entertainment vehicles such as soap operas (see Chapter 12).

Bandura (1986) has expanded his social learning theory to a comprehensive 'social cognitive' model. Many of the constructs in this model are similar to those of the HBM, with the addition of the concept of self-efficacy with regard to performing a particular behaviour. Perceived self-efficacy reflects the individual's ability and self-confidence in performing the recommended behaviour. The concept of self-efficacy is perhaps Bandura's major contribution to social cognition models (considered separately as 'self-efficacy theory' by some writers, e.g., Godin 1994). Self-efficacy has been found to be a major predictor of outcomes in a large number of studies, across a broad range of behaviours and models (as noted above), as well as independently of any particular model (e.g., Hofstetter, Hovell and Sallis 1990; McAuley and Jacobson 1991; Schwarzer and Fuchs 1996). It is particularly relevant when considering the use of threat appeals, where it is argued that if an individual experiences high anxiety as a result of the threat, but considers themselves helpless to avoid the threat, then the maladaptive behaviour (e.g., smoking, drug taking, violence) might in fact increase. The

CABWISE campaign mentioned elsewhere ensured that people had a simple way to get the phone numbers of local licensed cabs and, hence, avoid a possible sexual assault. Posters of the number to text for these local numbers were placed in strategic travel locations around the city of London – and particularly in nightlife areas, including the venues (Okin *et al.* 2009).

The theory of reasoned action

The theory of reasoned action (TRA) is perhaps the most developed of this type of model and is widely used in social psychology and consumer decision-making. It has more recently been applied to a number of health and environmental behaviours (see Conner and Sparks 1995).

Fishbein and Ajzen (1975) proposed that volitional behaviour is predicted by one's *intention* to perform the behaviour, which, in turn, is a function of *attitude* towards that behaviour and *subjective norms* with regard to that behaviour (see Figure 6.3). Attitude is a function of *beliefs* about the consequences of the behaviour weighted by an evaluation of each outcome. Subjective norms are a function of how significant others view the behaviour, weighted by the motivation to conform with each. Hence, an individual might have a positive attitude toward binge drinking, but not engage in that behaviour because their football team mates are opposed to it as it affects their chances of winning. Similarly, an individual might have a negative or neutral attitude towards separating glass, paper and metal in their rubbish, but do so because their children encourage it and all the neighbours are seen to be doing it.

Formative research is necessary to identify all of the relevant beliefs with regard to the consequences of adopting or not adopting the recommended behaviour, and

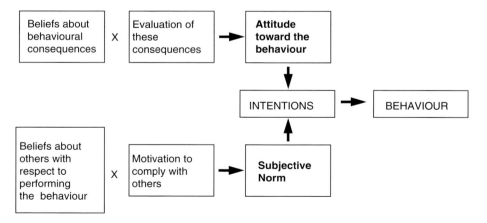

Figure 6.3 Fishbein's and Ajzen's theory of reasoned action

whether these consequences are viewed negatively, positively or neutrally. To accurately predict intentions, it is necessary to ensure that *all* relevant beliefs are uncovered. For example, it might be found that attitudes towards recycling are favourable because only beliefs that were evaluated positively were included, while many beliefs that would be evaluated negatively were unintentionally omitted. Similarly, research is needed to identify all the relevant others, how these others are perceived to feel about the recommended behaviour, and the extent to which the individual feels motivated to comply with these others. Leventhal and Cameron (1994) remind us that many beliefs might be 'common sense' or intuitive rather than objective beliefs. Commonsense beliefs are based on their own experiences and what people see, hear and feel as they go about their lives. For example, if a smoker feels fit and well, they are far less likely to be influenced by anti-smoking messages; if people live in areas where certain ethnic groups are associated with crime, they are less likely to respond to anti-stereotype tolerance campaigns.

Fishbein's model introduced two important features. First, the model requires the user to make a clear distinction between attitudes towards objects, issues or events *per se*, and attitudes towards *behaving* in a certain way towards these objects, issues, events, etc. For example, an individual may have a favourable attitude towards Porsche cars, but a negative attitude towards actually buying one because this would involve borrowing a substantial amount of money at a high interest rate (not to mention, if male, being the butt of some well-known comments about his anatomy). Similarly, an individual may have a favourable attitude towards condoms *per se*, but a negative attitude towards actually buying or carrying condoms. Hence, when exploring beliefs and attitudes to predict intentions and behaviour, it is necessary to be precise in terms of whether one is measuring attitudes towards an issue *per se* (e.g., exercise), or attitudes towards engaging in a behaviour (e.g., exercising). This aspect of the TRA forces interventionists to more precisely determine what specific behaviour they wish to change, in what context and in what timeframe (called the principle of compatibility; Ajzen 1988).

'1% or less' milk campaign in Wheeling, West Virginia

If the lead character in Neil Sedaka's 1970 hit song 'Wheeling West Virginia' returned recently he might have been surprised to see low fat milk being promoted in his old town – milk of any sort not being the usual beverage of choice of country & western devotees. The '1% or less' campaign was based on the TRA (and the compatibility principle). It resulted in a significant increase in low-fat milk share (29 per cent to 46 per cent) with 34 per cent of a Wheeling sample reporting switching versus 4 per cent of a comparison community. Analysis of the data showed that the intervention increased intention and attitude (but not subjective norm), and there were significant increases in beliefs about the healthiness, taste and cost of low-fat milk (Booth-Butterfield and Reger 2004).

Second, the TRA distinguishes between the individual's beliefs related to the object or issues *per se*, and the individual's beliefs about what other people think about the issue, and how others think they should behave towards the issue (i.e., normative beliefs). Hence, the Fishbein model incorporates social *norms* as an influence on attitudes and behaviour.

Overall then, an individual's intention towards switching from, say, regular strength beer to a reduced alcohol beer will be a function of their overall attitude to that behaviour and their subjective norm about that behaviour as follows:

Attitude: This is measured by first identifying the individual's *beliefs* about the likely consequences of drinking reduced alcohol beer, which might be: less intoxicating; fewer hangovers; increased alertness; less risk of exceeding 0.05 per cent if random breath tested; less enjoyment of full-bodied taste; less variety of beer type; less brand imagery; and so on. In research terms, individuals are asked to state *how likely* is it that each of these consequences would occur if they switched to reduced alcohol beer. This is followed by an *evaluation* of the beliefs (how positively or negatively the consequences such as fewer hangovers, increased alertness, less taste, etc.) are viewed. Attitude is then the sum of the likelihood multiplied by evaluation scores for each belief.

Social norms: This is measured by first identifying all relevant others (i.e., friends, workmates, family, sporting club mates, etc.), and then establishing how likely it is that each of these would endorse the individual switching to reduced alcohol beer (normative *beliefs*). These scores are then weighted by how likely it is that the individual would comply with each relevant other (e.g., workmates' opinions might be far more important than a spouse's opinion – or vice versa). This last point shows that the behaviour to be predicted should also be defined with regard to situation, particularly in terms of the social environment. An individual might behave quite differently depending on who else is present. Young males often moderate their drinking behaviour in the presence of young women (and perhaps stern parents), and brand choices are far more important in some bars and among some groups than others.

Predicting binge drinking

Using the theory of planned behaviour as a theoretical framework, a UK study attempted to explore the motivational and attitudinal factors underlying binge drinking, and to determine the key predictors of frequency of binge drinking. The TPB variables explained nearly 40 per cent of the variance in frequency of binge drinking, with perceived behavioural control one of the major predictors: more frequent binge drinkers were less likely to believe that their decision to binge drink was under their control (Norman, Bennett and Lewis 1998).

Fishbein and Ajzen's model has spawned a number of extensions, most notably the theory of planned behaviour (TPB; Ajzen 1988) and the theory of trying (TT; Bagozzi and Warshaw 1990). The TPB extended the TRA by adding perceived behavioural control – the extent to which the individual perceived the recommended behaviour to be easy or difficult to do (similar to self-efficacy in other models).

Both the TRA and TPB have been used quite extensively across a number of consumer purchasing, lifestyle and health behaviours (particularly smoking, exercise and STD prevention), with generally good results for all the major variables in the models in terms of predicting intentions or behaviours (Blue 1995; Conner and Sparks 1996; Godin and Kok 1996; Sheppard, Hartwick and Warshaw 1988). More recent research has provided preliminary support for the usefulness of the TPB in predicting adolescent athletes' intentions to use doping substances (Lucidi *et al.* 2004; 2008).

The theory of trying

The theory of trying (TT) has two major elements of interest. First, the focus is on goals rather than on reasoned behaviour choices in specific situations. Hence, the TT is directly applicable to most issues in health promotion and social marketing. Second, the theory focuses on *trying* to achieve these goals (i.e., attempting to quit) rather than *actual attainment* of the goals (i.e., successfully quitting). This is a far more realistic focus. For example, rather than attempting to determine the predictors of (successful) quitting, we should first determine the predictors of *trying* to quit. Many studies have failed to show a relationship between attitudes or intentions and behaviours, because the behaviours have been defined as successful outcomes (e.g., loss of weight, adoption of regular exercise, introduction of policy changes), rather than *trying* to achieve these goals. Separating trying from achieving also forces the campaign planner to consider separately what leads to trying and what factors then come into play to facilitate or inhibit a successful outcome.

The theory of trying is presented in Figure 6.4. The key points in TT are discussed below (Bagozzi and Warshaw 1990): An individual's overall *attitude towards trying* some behaviour (e.g., to lose weight) is a function of three factors:

- attitude towards succeeding and the perceived likelihood (i.e., expectation) of success;
- attitude towards failing and the perceived likelihood (i.e., expectation) of failing; and
- attitude towards the actual process of trying to lose weight.

Each of the above attitudes is measured by assessing the likelihood of various consequences occurring as a result of succeeding, failing and engaging in the process, weighted by the evaluation of these consequences. For example, the consequences of successfully losing weight might be feeling healthier, looking better, reduced risk of diabetes, and so on. The consequences of not losing weight might be feeling unhappy,

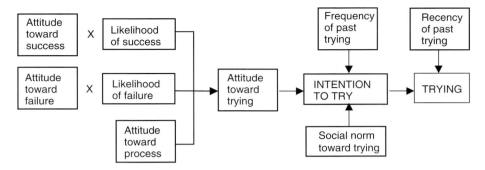

Figure 6.4 Theory of trying

Adapted from Bagozzi and Warshaw (1990)

feeling uncomfortable in one's clothes, increased risk of diabetes and heart disease, and so on. Beliefs about the consequences of the process of losing weight might include often feeling hungry, having to go without the foods one really likes, having to avoid restaurants and takeaway food, more time in preparation of food, less choice of foods, and so on. Each of these beliefs is weighted by an evaluation of these consequences and summed to provide an overall attitude.

An individual's *intention to try* to lose weight will be determined by:

- their overall attitude towards trying to lose weight as assessed above;
- social norms about trying to lose weight (i.e., beliefs about important others' attitudes towards the individual losing weight); and
- the number of times the individual has previously tried to lose weight.

Actually *trying* to lose weight will be determined by:

- the individual's intention to try to lose weight;
- the number of times the individual has previously tried to lose weight; and
- time since the last try.

Bagozzi and Warshaw (1990) showed that their model significantly and substantially predicted trying to lose weight (and was a better predictor than the TPB), although frequency of past trying was not a significant predictor of trying. On the other hand, some quitting studies have shown that frequency of past trying is a significant predictor of attempts to quit and successful quitting.

Cognitive dissonance

Cognitive dissonance is said to occur when the individual holds beliefs that are inconsistent, or when the individual's actions and beliefs are inconsistent (Festinger 1957).

For example, a politician would experience dissonance if they believed that mandatory sentencing unfairly discriminated against lower socio-economic groups or a particular ethnic group, but their party was introducing such legislation; a smoker would experience dissonance if they believed that smoking affected their pet's health.

Quit for your pet's sake

A survey of Michigan pet owners revealed that 28 per cent of smoking pet owners would try to quit when told about the effects of passive smoking on their cats or dogs. Educational campaigns informing pet owners of the risks of second-hand smoke exposure for pets could motivate these owners and non-smoking owners who cohabit with smokers to make their homes smoke-free (Milberger, Davis and Holm 2009).

Dissonance is considered to be psychologically uncomfortable and anxiety arousing. The degree of dissonance and, hence, the degree of discomfort is a function of how strongly held are the various beliefs. Individuals experiencing dissonance are assumed to take steps to reduce this dissonance. This is done by changing beliefs or actions so as to be consistent (e.g., the smoker quits), or by changing one set of beliefs (e.g., discounting the evidence that smoking causes cancer), or by generating a set of beliefs that overpower the dissonant belief (e.g., the smoker thinks of a large number of positives about smoking) (O'Keefe 1990).

Many campaigns are aimed at generating a state of dissonance in the individual, with the recommended behaviour as the means of eliminating this uncomfortable state. Such tactics are particularly appropriate for interpersonal interactions, such as workshops and lobbying. Similarly, forced behaviour adoption can result in attitude changes to be consistent with the behaviour. With regard to compulsory seat belts, this has been a desirable outcome. On the other hand, in the politician's situation above, if a conscience vote is disallowed, voting for the legislation may lead to a change in beliefs in favour of the legislation.

There has been little published on the use of this model in health and social marketing. However, it is often implied in the strategy of many campaigns and is useful to complement the more comprehensive attitude–behaviour change models.

Theory of interpersonal behaviour

Triandis' (1977) theory of interpersonal behaviour (TIB) (Figure 6.5) is similar in many respects to the theory of reasoned action, but has not received much attention outside psychology, and, hence, little systematic use in health and social marketing (Godin 1994).

The TIB includes two concepts of particular interest not included (or given little weight) in other models: the influence of habit and personal normative beliefs. The inclusion of habit demands that the social marketing practitioner distinguish between

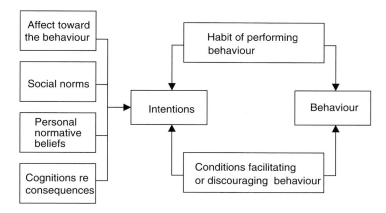

Figure 6.5 Theory of interpersonal behaviour

'new' behaviours versus established behaviours. The concept of personal normative beliefs recognises that individuals' morals and internalised values are important predictors in addition to social norms.

Triandis (1977) states that the likelihood of an individual performing a given behaviour is a function of:

• the degree to which the behaviour is already habitual;
• intentions to perform the behaviour; and
• conditions facilitating or inhibiting carrying out the behaviour.

Intentions in turn are influenced by four elements:

• the individual's anticipated emotional response to performing the behaviour (i.e., pleasure/disliking, boring/interesting, etc.);
• a cognitive summing up of the positive and negative consequences of performing the behaviour;
• perceived social norms and whether that behaviour is appropriate to the individual's social role(s); and
• felt obligation to perform the behaviour according to the individual's internalised values.

Hence, hospital doctors and nurses could be persuaded to increase their hand washing with antiseptic activity if they had positive expectations – or memories – about the proposed activity; if they considered the benefits outweighed the costs; if social norms reinforced the activity and it was considered appropriate for their age, gender and social status; and if they considered it the right thing to do (Nicol *et al*. 2009). The inclusion of role beliefs (or self-identity) is a valuable, yet little explored concept. However, the concept may be particularly relevant for stimulating community action on environmental and planning issues. It is likely that many people do not take part in advocacy activities because they see these roles as inappropriate for them.

Hohoro Wonsa – Truly Clean Hands: making hand washing a habit in Ghana

Diarrhoeal diseases result in the death of about two million children each year. It has been estimated that hand washing with soap would prevent half these deaths (Curtis 2003). However, while Ghanaians washed their hands with soap when they felt they were dirty, for example after cooking with grease, they rarely washed their hands with soap after using the toilet. In fact, toilets were a symbol of cleanliness in some places because they replaced pit latrines. Observation studies showed that only 3 per cent of mothers practised hand washing with soap after defecation, only 2 per cent after wiping their baby's bottom and less than 1 per cent before feeding them. The 'truly clean' hand washing campaign in Ghana attempted to increase hand washing with soap before eating and after toilet use. The campaign used a mix of media and interpersonal communication channels. 'Disgust' via a fear of contamination drove other hygiene behaviours, so the television ad attempted to associate disgust with unclean hands after toilet use, showing that water alone was not sufficient. The campaign significantly increased self-reported hand washing with soap, with the greatest impact on those exposed via community events and at least one mass media channel (Scott *et al.* 2008).

The Rossiter–Percy motivational model

The Rossiter–Percy model offers specific practical guidelines for developing and executing social marketing messages because of its emphasis on identifying the appropriate motivations for the target groups as the basis for attitude – and subsequent behaviour – change (Donovan *et al.* 1995; Donovan and Francas 1990; Henley and Donovan 2002).

Rossiter and Percy (1997) classify consumer decision-making in terms of two dimensions: the level of involvement associated with the decision (high or low); and the nature of the primary motivations driving the decision (positive or negative). Their framework is shown in Figure 6.6.

Involvement is defined as the degree of perceived risk – financial, functional or social – in making the wrong decision and is dichotomised as high or low. Whether a decision is high or low involvement for an individual is determined primarily through qualitative research. High involvement decision-making is inferred by a consumer's extensive pre-purchase information gathering efforts so as to reduce the risk of making a wrong decision, and the need to be convinced beforehand that they are making the 'right' decision. On the other hand, for low involvement decisions, consumers can, and generally do, adopt a 'try it and see' attitude before purchase, as the consequences of making the wrong choice are insignificant, or are perceived as such. These are similar to Petty and Cacioppo's central and peripheral routes, respectively (Chapter 5).

Type of decision	Type of Motivation	
	Positive	Negative
Low involvement		
High involvement		

Figure 6.6 Rossiter's and Percy's message strategy model

In the Rossiter–Percy model, the level of *involvement* largely determines a number of *execution* rather than message strategy elements. The main implication for communication materials is that executions must be credible for high involvement decisions, but need only arouse 'curious disbelief' (i.e., 'it might be true') for low involvement decisions.

The nature of the *motivation* largely determines the *message strategy*. Following Fennell's (1978) analysis of motivations operating in various consumption (or 'product use') situations, and imposing an overall drive induction/drive reduction framework from psychological learning theory, Rossiter and Percy (1987) proposed that motivations for behaviour can be classified as either *positive* (i.e., the goal is drive induction or increase), or *negative* (i.e., the goal is drive reduction). For positive motivations, the goal is to (temporarily) achieve a positive experience (i.e., above 'normal'), whereas for negative motivations, the goal is to remove or avoid a negative experience and return to 'normal'.

Rossiter and Percy's motivations and their goal directions are shown in Table 6.1. Two positive motives have been added by Donovan *et al.* (1995): self-approval (note Triandis' personal normative beliefs); and social conformity (note Cialdini's social proof). There is considerable evidence that social conformity in particular predicts pro-environmental behaviours. Cialdini has consistently found that messages about 'everybody's doing it' work better than messages related to saving money, being socially responsible or a concern for the earth's resources (APA 2007). The original eight motivations are described more fully in Rossiter and Percy (1997) and Rossiter, Percy and Donovan (1991).

Negative motivations relate to actions taken to solve current problems or to avoid future problems. In social marketing, the focus is usually on *problem avoidance* or *problem solution* by adopting the recommended behaviour (e.g., erecting shade cloth over swimming pools, avoiding saturated fats and heart disease, texting for a licensed cab to avoid sexual assault, recycling to reduce the energy use problem, reduction of speed to reduce severity of injuries, wearing a helmet to avoid a head injury). Mixed *approach–avoidance* motives also operate in many areas: reduced alcohol beers for those wanting to drink alcohol, but not wanting to exceed the legal blood-alcohol concentration; low fat ice-cream for those wanting the taste but not the calories, and so on. *Incomplete satisfaction* is also relevant in some areas: air bags for those seeking a safer vehicle;

Table 6.1 Rossiter's and Percy's positive and negative motivations

Energising mechanism	Goal direction
Negative or aversive origin	
(1) Current problem	Solve problem (removal or escape)
(2) Anticipated problem	Prevent problem (avoidance)
(3) Incomplete satisfaction	Continue search
(4) Mixed approach – avoidance	Reduce conflict
Mildly negative origin	
(5) Normal depletion	Maintain stable state
Positive or appetitive origin	
(6) Sensory gratification	Enjoy
(7) Intellectual needs	Explore, master
(8) Social approval	Achieve personal recognition, status
(9*) Personal values	Act consistent with personal values
Mildly positive origin	
(10*) Social conformity	Affiliate

Adapted from Rossiter and Percy (1997), with the ninth and tenth motives added by Donovan *et al.* (1995).

failing to lose weight in one programme leading to seeking a more effective weight-loss programme by some other means.

Positive motivations refer to actions taken to achieve an enhanced positive emotional state – usually temporarily because such positive states soon become overbearing, lead to 'satiation' and a return to the normal level. Much unsafe road behaviour is risk taking or sensation seeking behaviour sought for its own sake or to satisfy self-image or social approval needs. In a similar way, individuals seek risky thrills on carnival rides or in hobbies like hang-gliding (Craig-Lees, Joy and Browne 1995). While some individuals initiate drug behaviour to cope with anxieties or other personal problems, many people initiate drug taking for the expected enhanced feelings of pleasure or excitement. Of course, if the drug becomes addictive, continued use of the drug becomes necessary to solve or avoid problems associated with withdrawal and for the individual just to be able to function 'normally'.

Positive motivations are infrequently targeted in public health messages, primarily because most health behaviour adoption, for most people, is motivated by negative motivations. At the same time, the 'If you drink and drive, you're a bloody idiot' campaign approaches a 'Smart people don't drink and drive' intellectual appeal. Adoption of exercise is one health behaviour that many people adopt for positive motivations (e.g., to look better, feel more alert, increase social opportunities, compete better, or get stronger) (Donovan and Francas 1990).

We should also distinguish between motives for *adoption* of a behaviour and motives for *continuation* of the behaviour. For example, not drinking and driving or not exceeding the speed limit might be adopted initially to avoid detection and punishment, but if this compliant behaviour leads to greater feelings of relaxation and enjoyment of driving, then the compliant behaviour might be maintained for these 'approach' rewards rather than the 'avoidance' rewards. Similarly, exercise may be adopted for weight control and avoidance of heart disease, but after some time the physical activity *per se* or the accompanying social interactions may become rewarding in themselves.

It should be noted that positive motivations do not equate to positive benefits. The same positive benefit can result from quite different motives. For example, two drinking drivers might receive positive social reinforcement by their decision to take a taxi rather than drive while exceeding the legal blood-alcohol level. However, one individual might have been motivated by the need to *avoid* social *disapproval*, whereas the other might have been motivated by a desire *for* approval. Similarly, two individuals might get the same *benefit* of weight control from exercise, but for one the primary motive was to look better, while for the other, the primary motive was to reduce the risk of heart disease.

Another distinction between negative and positive motivations is that, for negative motivations consumption of the chosen product or performance of the adopted behaviour is largely a means to an end, whereas for positively motivated activities the activity is an end in itself. Speeding is often done for the thrill of the actual behaviour whereas *not* speeding is done to avoid a penalty; an analgesic is taken not because the analgesic tastes good, but because the analgesic will remove a headache; an ice-cream is (usually) not eaten to allay hunger pangs, but because the act of consumption *per se* is enjoyable. As noted above though, it is possible that negatively motivated products or behaviours initially chosen as a means to an end may generate benefits such that they become enjoyable in their own right.

The role of emotions in the Rossiter–Percy model

The Rossiter–Percy model explicitly delineates the role of emotions in message strategy. Motivation is considered to be *goal directed* (i.e., a cognitive component), with emotions being the *energising* component. Both cognitions and emotions are required for achieving the desired behavioural result. As we know, knowledge is insufficient to achieve behavioural change among many people, because this knowledge is unrelated to the underlying motivator for these people. There are two key aspects of the role of emotions in the Rossiter–Percy model:

(1) each motivation has its own relevant emotion(s), and it is crucial that communications portray the correct emotion(s); and
(2) it is the sequence of emotions that is important (for negative motives in particular), not just the arousal of single emotions.

Table 6.2 Rossiter's and Percy's hypothesised relationships linking emotions to motivations: some examples

	Negative motives	Emotional sequence
1.	Problem removal	Annoyed → relieved
2.	Problem avoidance	Fearful → relaxed
3.	Incomplete satisfaction	Disappointed → optimistic
4.	Mixed approach-avoidance	Conflicted → reassured
5.	Normal depletion	Mildly annoyed → content
	Positive motives	**Emotional sequence**
6.	Sensory gratification	Dull (or neutral) → joyful
7.	Intellectual stimulation/mastery	Bored (or neutral) → excited
		Naive (or neutral) → competent
8.	Social approval	Apprehensive (or neutral) → flattered
*9.	Social conformity	Indecisive (or neutral) → belonging
*10.	Self-approval	Conflict (or neutral) → serene, confident

Adapted from Rossiter and Percy (1997), with the ninth and tenth motives added by Donovan *et al.* (1995).

Examples of appropriate emotions (and emotion sequences) are shown in Table 6.2. Other emotions of relevance that were mentioned in Chapter 5 include disgust, shame, embarrassment and remorse.

Morality and legitimacy

Morality refers to the individual's beliefs about whether certain actions are 'right or wrong', or whether they 'should or should not' take that action. Legitimacy refers to individuals' beliefs about whether laws are justified, whether these laws are applied equally and whether punishments for transgression are fair (Tyler 1990). The concept of legitimacy applies not just to legislation, but to rules, regulations and policies. In general, people are more likely to obey rules that they believe are justified and are enforced in a fair and unbiased manner. With some reflection, and given the use of 'laws' to regulate and influence behaviour, both concepts clearly have considerable relevance in some areas of social marketing. However, they have been largely neglected in social-change models, and particularly in public health research and intervention strategies.

This neglect is surprising given the historical links between health and (religious) morality (Thomas 1997), and the fact that Fishbein's theory of reasoned action originally included the concept of moral or personal norms (Fishbein 1967; Fishbein and Ajzen 1975). Triandis (1977) included personal normative beliefs, but as noted above, his model has attracted little attention in health and social interventions. Furthermore, legislation is widely used to regulate a broad range of activities such as driving behaviours, underage alcohol and tobacco consumption, drug use, land degradation and toxic waste disposal, lighting fires in forests, littering behaviour, physical abuse, child abuse and neglect, and so on. Hence, it is important to assess people's perceived legitimacy of the laws and the authorities behind the laws in these areas. As noted in Chapter 3, crime prevention is one area where public health and anti-violence professionals are beginning to come together (WHO 2002) and some social marketers are also taking an interest (e.g., Hastings, Stead and MacFadyen 2002). Criminologists have been developing conceptual frameworks in these areas, with striking similarities to concepts in cognitive decision models as described in this chapter (e.g., Vila 1994).

Emotional appeals

Whereas the emphasis in health and injury prevention campaigns has often been on fear arousal, recent research suggests that a number of emotions other than fear are relevant in social marketing campaign messages (Bagozzi and Moore 1994; Stout and Sego 1994). For example, road safety campaigns in Britain, Northern Ireland, New Zealand and Australia often focus on the guilt and remorse experienced by drivers who injure or kill others by their speeding or drink driving.

Appropriate emotions for road safety advertising include the following (Donovan *et al.* 1995):

- sadness – at the loss or serious injury of a loved one, the impact on others of the loss or serious injury of a loved one, etc.;
- guilt or remorse – at having unintentionally caused the loss or serious injury of a loved one, for not having heeded advice that could have avoided the negative consequence, etc.;
- surprise – at information such as the 'dose'–response relationship between speed and injury, the relationship between speed and distance travelled in a 'moment's' distraction;
- anger – at the irresponsible behaviours/attitudes of speeding or drinking drivers, etc.;
- fear, anxiety – about the possibility of detection, of the loss or serious injury of a loved one, of personal injury, of loss of licence, etc.;
- shame, embarrassment – being caught for any offence, but particularly for a socially despised offence, etc.;
- acceptance, warmth, love – for complying with another's request to drive safely, protection of the vehicle's occupants (especially children), etc.;
- peace of mind, relief – at removal of anxiety and tension by compliance.

Norman and Connor (1996) found only a few studies that incorporated measures of moral norms within the public health domain. Such studies include explaining altruism and helping behaviour such as donating blood (Pomazal and Jaccard 1976; Zuckerman and Reis 1978) and intentions to donate organs (Schwartz and Tessler 1972). Other studies have found measures of moral norms to be predictive of recycling behaviour (Allen, Fuller and Glaser 1994; Vining and Ebreo 1992), eating genetically produced food (Sparks, Shepherd and Frewer 1995), buying milk (Raats 1992), using condoms (Godin and Kok 1996) and committing driving violations (Parker, Manstead and Stradling 1995).

Few public health and public policy campaigns have considered the use of moral or legitimacy appeals. In Australia, moral norms have been considered in the context of road safety behaviours (Donovan and Batini 1997; Homel, Carseldine and Kearns 1988) and in the use of performance enhancing drugs in sport (Donovan and Egger 1997; Mugford, Mugford and Donnelly 1999). Donovan (1997) included an individual's personal morality in his model of factors that influence underage drinking, but carried out no empirical studies. However, to our knowledge, no Australian (or overseas) school, community or mass media campaigns targeting substance use have been explicitly based on morality concepts or have included components on legitimacy.

On the other hand, morality and legitimacy concepts have been used in road safety campaigns for some time, beginning with campaigns to make drinking and driving dangerous to others and, hence, morally unacceptable.

No seatbelt – no excuse

This Northern Ireland (and Great Britain) campaign targeted young rear seat passengers who were least inclined to belt up. The aim was to demonstrate (in very graphic television ads) that not wearing a seat belt in a collision had serious implications for the other occupants (i.e., the unbelted individual in the back seat becomes a human missile, striking other occupants). The aim was to 'reframe the (not) wearing of seat belts from one of personal freedom to one of moral irresponsibility' (Storey 2008). The campaign had significant long-term results: back seat passenger seat belt use went from around 50 per cent in the mid-1990s to 65 per cent in 2000 and 81 per cent in 2005 (Northern Ireland Seat Belt Survey, 2005).

Legitimacy has also been part of road safety campaigns. For example, 'Buckle Up. It's the Law' in the United States appeals directly to compliance because it is a legal requirement, while the United Kingdom's 'It's 30 for a reason' can be seen as an attempt to increase people's perceived justification (legitimacy) for that speed limit in built-up areas.

In the context of performance enhancing drugs, Donovan (2009) has suggested that moral (and ethical) reasoning can be learned and, hence, could be incorporated into schools' curricula (as in the United Kingdom at West Islington school; Farrer 2000) and sporting groups' training.

An interesting report in the light of 'situational prompts' noted elsewhere in this chapter is that of Shu, Gino and Bazerman (2009). In their studies of choices in ethical dilemma scenarios, where subjects had the opportunity to carry out an unethical behaviour undetected, they found that many people almost unthinkingly chose the unethical behaviour. On the other hand, they found that increasing moral salience by simply having people read or sign an honour code significantly reduced or eliminated unethical behaviour. These findings are somewhat similar to Cialdini, Reno and Kallgren's (1990) studies, where people were found to be more likely to litter when they saw somebody else do so or where there was already considerable litter. All these types of studies continually reinforce the importance of the situational environment and perceived normative behaviours.

Given the strong body of research supporting the empirical relation of moral reasoning development to criminal behaviours (see Tyler 1990, 1997), and behaviours such as delinquency, honesty, altruism and conformity (Blasi 1980), Amonini (2001; Amonini and Donovan 2006) looked at 14–17-year-olds' use of tobacco, alcohol and marijuana, their perceptions of the morality of such use and the perceived legitimacy of the laws governing the use of these substances. Overall, while only 17 per cent of her sample of n = 611 youths considered alcohol use 'wrong under any circumstances', more than half considered tobacco (53 per cent) and marijuana (57 per cent) were wrong under any circumstances. There were strong relationships between alcohol, tobacco and marijuana use and youths' perceptions of morality and legitimacy. The bivariate correlation coefficients were all significant and substantial ($p < 0.01$): $r = 0.71$ for alcohol; $r = 0.77$ for tobacco; and $r = 0.77$ for marijuana (Amonini and Donovan 2006).

These findings are encouraging in that young people's moral perceptions are learned (Kohlberg, 1976), and therefore can be influenced (Stoll and Beller 1998). It may well be that perceptions of the morality of alcohol, tobacco and marijuana use serve as a protective factor mitigating uptake. At the very least, the data support the proposition that substance use programmes aimed at school children and adolescents should not just emphasise health effects, but also include components related to the morality of substance use and the legitimacy of the laws restricting such use among young people. Reinforcing and strengthening morality and legitimacy perceptions could significantly prevent or delay substance uptake. The challenge would be to develop appropriate interventions and at an appropriate age.

Amonini and Donovan suggest that morality and legitimacy components of substance curricula should be part of primary school interventions, and at an early age. They note that work in moral and values education suggests that such education programmes should involve substantial interactive processes and active involvement in the analysis of ethical dilemmas (Binder, 1996; Nussbaum, 1986). Regardless of specific learning strategies, there is substantial evidence that moral education interventions can be successful in advancing moral growth and teaching values (Gibbons *et al.* 1997; Gibbons, Ebbeck and Weiss 1995; Stoll and Beller, 1998). We can therefore be optimistic that appropriate interventions could yield positive results for substance use. Given that alcohol, tobacco and illicit drug use are prevalent throughout the world (2 billion adults – 48 per cent of the adult population; 1.1 billion adults – 29 per cent of the population; and 185 million adults – 4.5 per cent of the population, respectively), and that the socio-economically disadvantaged are at greater risk of harmful use, and that use is on the increase in low income countries (Anderson 2006), there is a pressing need to develop new strategies to reduce consumption of alcohol, tobacco and illicit drugs.

The Qur'an and pro-environmental behaviours in Egypt

Rice (2006) points out that the Qur'an contains a number of statements reflecting an Islamic environmental ethic, from broad statements such as 'And we have given you [humans] mastery over the earth and appointed for you therein a livelihood' (7:10), to very specific ones such as '... and do not waste in excess, for God loves those not those who waste' (6:141). The extent of environmental concerns among the public is (not unexpectedly) less in poorer countries than developed countries, even though there is a pressing need in many such countries' cities that suffer from severe air pollution, water pollution and waste disposal problems. Rice's survey of Cairo residents showed that religiosity was a significant predictor of pro-environmental behaviours, particularly public expressions of pro-environmental attitudes and actually taking some actions (such as contacting officials re environmental problems, attending meetings of local citizen environmental groups). Rice suggests that environmental movements in Islamic countries would benefit from appeals to personal ethics and the Shari'a (Islamic Law) with regard to environmental ethics.

Diffusion theory

Everett Rogers first published his book *Diffusion of Innovations* in 1962. The concept has been readily adopted in commercial marketing (to predict new product adoption), and widely used in developing countries (e.g., adoption of agricultural methods and public health measures). However, it is only in the past fifteen years or so that it has attracted much attention in the public health area in developed countries. The general concept no doubt also received an impetus from Gladwell's (2000) book *The Tipping Point*. Although the model is more of a 'process' or 'stage' model, it is included here for its concepts related to the characteristics of 'innovations' that facilitate and inhibit adoption.

Rogers (1995) defines 'diffusion' as 'the process by which an innovation is communicated through certain channels over time among the members of a social system'. Diffusion theory applies to both planned and unplanned diffusions, and to both desirable and undesirable innovations (e.g., the rapid adoption of the cocaine variant 'crack' in the United States).

Figure 6.7 shows the rate of diffusion of three innovations. From the social change practitioner's point of view, one of the major issues is how the rate of adoption of the new idea, product or behaviour can be accelerated. Figure 6.7 indicates that many

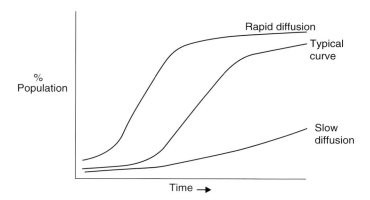

Figure 6.7 Diffusion of innovations

innovations 'take off' at about the 20 per cent adoption mark, when, according to Rogers (1995), 'interpersonal networks become activated so that a critical mass of adopters begins using an innovation'.

Each of the four main elements in diffusion, that is, the innovation, communication channels, time and the social system, will be discussed in turn.

The innovation

An innovation is an idea, product or practice that is perceived as new by the adopting population: that is, it need not be objectively 'new'. The main area of study here is on the attributes of the innovation that influence its rate of adoption. These are:

- *Relative advantage*: If the new object or practice is clearly seen to be 'better' than the old, then it will be adopted more readily. Relative advantage can be assessed in a variety of ways, including convenience, economy, prestige and time. Email is much faster than postal mail; automated rubbish trucks are perceived to be more economical than manned trucks.
- *Compatibility*: The more the new object or practice is consistent with current values and past experiences, the more readily it will be adopted. Family planning and STD prevention practices face this attribute in countries where cultural and religious values are opposed to these practices. Automated teller machines are incompatible with many people's desire for interpersonal interactions.
- *Complexity*: New practices and ideas that are easy to understand are more readily adopted than those difficult to understand or that require special skills and training. User friendly software was a major factor in the rates of adoption of office and home computers, and the new social media.
- *Trialability*: Being able to trial a new product or practice reduces the risk of the new product not delivering the promised benefits, and allows the adopter to learn about

the innovation before adoption. New grains can be trialled in limited agricultural plots. Copy machines were initially placed in offices and the owners were charged on a per copy basis. The more a product or practice can be trialled before 'purchase', the greater the rate of adoption.

- *Observability*: The more the innovation – and its results – are visible, then the greater the rate of adoption. Observability provides greater exposure as well as stimulating social discussion. Mobile phone adoption was clearly helped by visibility of use – and clear demonstration of effectiveness in communication.

Interpersonal influences: California 'Stop AIDS' project

The California 'Stop AIDS' project began with a series of group discussions to inform the development of messages for a media campaign. However, on following up group participants on another matter, the researchers noted that participants volunteered that their beliefs and attitudes about negotiating safe sex, and their safe sex practices had changed dramatically as a result of participation in the group discussions. Hence, the planned media intervention was dropped, and the funds spent on recruiting gay men to run more and more focus groups, Men in the early groups were asked if they would like to lead a similar group. Those interested were given a brief training in group moderation and further information about HIV/AIDS, and so on. This led to the SafetyNet© programme: in-home parties modelled on the Tupperware party, to educate gay men about safe sex (AIDS Action Committee 1989). (Not to be confused with the more media-based Swiss STOP AIDS programme: www.social-marketing.org/success/cs-stopaids.html.) In 2009 the California 'Stop AIDS' project is still very much a community-based project (www.stopaids.org).

Communication channels

Mass media channels are the most effective way of creating awareness for a new idea, product or practice, whereas interpersonal channels are the most effective way of getting the target audience to accept and adopt the new idea (Rogers 1995). This applies particularly to where the change agent and the target group have the same background, social status, or similar values (Cialdini 1984). Rogers states that a major impediment to most *planned* social diffusions is that the change agent and the target are quite dissimilar ('heterophilus'). Tupperware's use of party hosts to sell products to their friends is a very good example of acknowledging that persuasion occurs best between people of similar interests. Similarly, Indigenous youth prefer Indigenous people to deliver alcohol warnings and other health messages (Donovan *et al.* 1997b).

The importance of interpersonal networks in the diffusion process is one of the most important concepts of the diffusion process, and hence for community development interventions.

> **'Pass it on': Jamie's Ministry of Food**
>
> In the United Kingdom, celebrity chef Jamie Oliver featured in the 'Pass it on' campaign. This campaign appeals directly to interpersonal diffusion of healthy recipes by asking people to learn a few healthy recipes and then pass them on to family and friends. The 'Ministry of Food' website contains tips on how to 'pass it on in your community' including recipes to begin with. The campaign was helped tremendously by featuring on a TV series (www.jamiesministryoffood.com/content/c4/home.html)

Time

Time can be noted on an individual basis in the sense of the time taken to move from awareness, through persuasion, to decision and adoption. Some decision processes are relatively brief, while others may take several months.

Time also can be considered in the sense of some people adopting the innovation soon after its introduction (early adopters), while others adopt only after the vast majority have adopted ('laggards'). In general, five groups are noted: innovators (the first 2–3 per cent); early adopters (the next 10–15 per cent); the early majority (the next 30–33 per cent); the late majority (the next 30–33 per cent); and the laggards (the final 17–20 per cent). Effort expended on identifying the innovators and early adopters can result in a more efficiently planned diffusion.

Finally, as shown in Figure 6.7, the rate of adoption can vary from very rapid to quite slow.

The social system

The social structure also influences the rate of adoption. Variables here include: the extent to which communication channels exist; the presence or absence of strong opinion leaders; the prevailing social norms and their variation between parts of the system; whether the adoption decision is an individual one or must involve collective decision-making, or a single authority's decision; and whether adoption of the innovation has desirable and undesirable consequences, not just for the individual but for the social system as a whole. Rudd (2003) analyses how health policies diffuse through to general practice, given the nature of general practice and the attitudes and beliefs of general practitioners about their role in the health system. Berwick (2003) notes that innovations in health care often disseminate too slowly, probably because of managerial and organisational factors impeding the rate of adoption. Social system factors appear particularly important in developing countries (McKee 1992), and, for example, in Indigenous communities in Australia.

Table 6.3 Behaviour modification strategies		
Procedure following behaviour:		
	Deliver	**Remove**
Consequence type	**Consequence**	**Consequence**
Good/pleasant	Positive reinforcement (increases response)	Negative punishment (decreases response)
Bad/unpleasant	Positive punishment (decreases response)	Negative reinforcement (increases response)

Behaviour modification and applied behavioural analysis

Many social marketing campaigns, particularly in road safety and public health are aimed at *decreasing undesired* behaviours: don't drink and drive; don't exceed 0.05 if driving; reduce speed; eat less fat; quit smoking; reduce alcohol consumption, and so on.

At the same time, other campaigns are aimed at *increasing desired* behaviours: switch to light beer if drinking and driving; stop, revive, survive; eat more fruit and veg; be smoke-free; walk to the bus stop/up the stairs/to the shop and so on. The question in many situations, therefore, is whether the emphasis should be on increasing the desired behaviour or on decreasing the undesired behaviour. For example, for targeting obesity in children, should we focus on reducing the time spent watching TV and playing video games (i.e., reduce inactivity) or focus on increasing the children's level of physical activity? Regardless of the answer, the lesson from behaviour modification/applied behavioural analysis, is that different strategies are appropriate for increasing behaviours versus for decreasing behaviours. This is particularly important for message strategies in communication materials and for direct behavioural interventions.

The terms 'behaviour modification' and 'applied behaviour analysis' are generally interchangeable. We will primarily use the term 'behaviour modification', which is defined as 'the systematic application of principles derived from learning theory to altering environment–behaviour relationships in order to strengthen adaptive and weaken maladaptive behaviours' (Elder *et al.* 1994). Behaviour modification is based on the assumption that behaviour is determined by environmental antecedents and consequences. Hence, interventions are designed on the 'ABC' model: **a**ntecedents; **b**ehaviour; **c**onsequences (Elder *et al.* 1994; Geller 1989).

Beginning with the goal of increasing a behaviour or decreasing a behaviour, Table 6.3 delineates two methods for *increasing* a behaviour (reinforcement strategies) and two ways of *decreasing* a behaviour (punishment strategies). Each depends on whether the consequence is delivered (positive) or removed (negative) as a result of the behaviour occurring.

Reinforcement – increasing a behaviour

There are two ways of *increasing* a response:

- positive reinforcement: the behaviour is followed by a pleasant consequence (e.g., group socialising after exercise); and
- negative reinforcement: the behaviour is followed by removal of an unpleasant situation (e.g., headache and tension gone after meditation).

Punishment – decreasing a behaviour

There are two ways of *decreasing* a response:

- positive punishment: the behaviour is followed by an unpleasant consequence (e.g., speeding is followed by a fine); and
- negative punishment (or response cost): the behaviour is followed by removal of a pleasant situation (e.g., drink driving is followed by a loss of licence and, hence, limitations on mobility and socialising).

Two other processes are also relevant:

- Extinction: a behaviour will decrease if previously applied positive consequences are discontinued or barriers prevent their being obtained. For example, walking may decrease if aesthetic features of the environment are removed or friends are no longer available to walk with; blood donating behaviour will decline if donors have to visit a central location rather than donating at the worksite.
- Response facilitation: a behaviour will strengthen or re-emerge if a punishment or response cost is discontinued. For example, an athlete may revert to using performance enhancing drugs when the level of random testing is reduced; speeding behaviour returns after speed camera use declines.

In designing interventions, formative research is necessary to determine what are the appropriate reinforcers and punishments for the intervention targets. For example, Egger's GutBusters® programme for men (Egger *et al.* 1996) emphasised the 'looking good' benefit of weight loss and increased physical activity, rather than health benefits. Rossiter and Percy's motives provide a framework here; some people may be motivated primarily by social recognition rewards, others by financial incentives and others by gifts. Young males fear the loss of their driving licence more than the threat of physical harm to themselves.

Feedback on positive results, such as number of accident-free days in a workplace, is an important reinforcer. As noted in Chapter 4, advocates should remember that as well as writing to politicians and policymakers they wish to persuade, they should also write to those already on-side, with reinforcing messages thanking them for their support.

Another lesson from behaviour modification is to identify the reinforcers of the behaviours we wish to reduce or eliminate. Such an understanding is liable to lead to more sustained change if attempts are then made to either substitute benign reinforcers or take away the need for the reinforcers in the first place. For example, much alcohol and drug abuse is related to escaping from reality. Hence, interventions making reality more tolerable, or indeed enjoyable, are required.

Financial incentives can work – for some behaviours

As noted in Chapter 3, conditional cash incentives to the poor have positive health outcomes – especially for children. Kane *et al.* (2004) analysed forty-seven trials of cash incentives for preventive health behaviours such as immunisation, cancer screening, condom purchase, education session attendance, prenatal care, weight loss and tuberculosis screening. They found that these incentives were generally successful – they worked for around 73 per cent of the cases studied. In a workplace trial, around 15 per cent of workers offered $750 (over three phases) to give up smoking were smoke-free after a year compared with 5 per cent who weren't paid to quit (Gordon 2009). However, there are some ethical and sustainability issues around offering financial incentives, and there are clearly problems in determining how much the incentive should be and for how long it should be paid. Outright cash incentives appear to be more suited to one-off behaviours (such as a vaccination) rather than ongoing behaviours such as weight loss, drug use and, notwithstanding the above example, quitting smoking (Marteau, Ashcroft and Oliver 2009).

While rewards and response costs can be instituted in practice (i.e., lower insurance premiums for non-smokers, loss of driver's licence for unsafe drivers), punishments are more difficult to introduce in non-legal situations. However, all of the above strategies can be depicted and modelled in communication materials. As noted earlier, threat appeals (positive punishment and response costs) are widespread in social marketing.

Most of the above deals with the behaviour–consequence link. Interventions can also facilitate the desired behavioural response by looking at the antecedent–behaviour link (Elder *et al.* 1994; Geller 1989):

- Environments should be designed to make the behaviour change easy, such as work-site exercise rooms and showers, smaller plates in restaurants to limit food portions.
- Reminder signs can be very effective. A 'take the stairs' sign placed near a lift increased use of the stairs dramatically; 'belt up' signs at car park exits increase seat belt use; nutrition information on menus increases healthy food selections.

Point of decision prompts

Point of decision prompts are often used as visual cues to guide individuals in adopting healthy behaviours. Point of decision prompts for increasing physical activity include signs or banners posted near elevators, escalators, or moving walkways with the intention of encouraging individuals to use stairs or climb/walk rather than standing still. Such prompts have been evaluated in worksites and community settings, such as malls, airports and office buildings. (UNC Center for Health Promotion and Disease Prevention, page 2, Center of Excellence for Training and Research Translation, posted November 2007

www.center-trt.org/Downloads/Obesity_Prevention/Strategies/Physical_Activity/Point-of-decision_Prompts_for_Stairwell_Use.pdf)

- Opinion leaders, experts and celebrities can be used to demonstrate the behaviour or wear clothing promoting the behaviour.
- Target individuals can be encouraged to make public commitments to adopt the desired behaviour.
- Educational materials with behavioural tips are also useful; quitting smokers are encouraged to identify environmental cues that trigger smoking and to remove them.
- Education sessions should include interactive demonstrations rather than just passive lecturing (*Tell them and they'll forget – Demonstrate and they'll remember – Involve them and they'll understand*).

Choice architecture

The term 'choice architecture' was introduced in the book *Nudge* – which received a lot of publicity when it appeared on the shelves in 2008. The book was written by a behavioural economist and a law professor who apparently 'discovered' that people are in fact 'human', and, well, sometimes make seemingly 'bad' decisions ('mistakes'). The premise of the book is that the environment can be designed to reduce opportunities for 'bad' choices and 'nudge' people into desirable choices while retaining the US holy grail of 'freedom of choice'. Well, at least supermarket layout people, airport planners, urban designers, merchandisers, etc. now have a name for what they've been doing for years. On the positive side, the book reminds us that we can extend these ideas into better decision-making in neglected economic areas such as savings plans, insurance and retirement planning decisions (see Chapter 3; Thaler and Sunstein 2008).

While some planning models include a number of the above concepts (e.g., Green and Kreuter's (2005) PRECEDE–PROCEED model; see Chapter 14), there has been limited systematic integration of behaviour modification concepts into social marketing programmes. Geller (1989) provides an integrative example for environmental issues, while Elder *et al*. (1994) provide a number of examples of the concepts in practice.

Synthesising the models

It is clear that many of these models have similar concepts, but that no one model includes all relevant concepts. We advocate a pragmatic, eclectic approach, selecting concepts from each of the models depending on which are more or less applicable to the behaviour in question.

Assume an adult 'at risk' for diabetes type 2. The above models suggest the following questions need answering to develop appropriate interventions:

(1) What is the individual's perceived likelihood of contracting diabetes, given no change in their current behaviour?
What beliefs or perceptions underlie this perceived likelihood?
If the perceived likelihood is unrealistically low, what sort of information, presented in what way and by whom might increase this likelihood?
What is their knowledge of the causes of diabetes?

(2) What is the individual's perceived severity of contracting diabetes?
Is this realistic? If not, what sort of information, presented in what way and by whom might change this perception?

(3) What is the individual's attitude towards adopting the recommended alternative behaviours such as a change in diet or adoption of exercise?
Are some behaviours more acceptable than others? Why?
What are the perceived benefits of continuing the risk behaviours?
What are the perceived benefits and the disbenefits of the alternative behaviours?
What social and physical environment barriers inhibit adoption of the recommended dietary and exercise behaviours? What facilitators exist?

(4) What is the individual's perceived likelihood of averting the threat if the recommended behaviours are adopted?
If this is low, on what beliefs is this perception based? What information might change this perception?

(5) What are the individual's beliefs about their ability to adopt the recommended behaviours?
On what beliefs are these efficacy perceptions based?
Is skills training required?
What intermediate goals can be set to induce trial?

(6) What appear to be the major motivations that would induce trial of the recommended behaviours?
Are positive benefits (e.g., feelings of wellness, increased capacity for physical activity) more motivating than negative benefits (e.g., avoidance of disease) for some individuals or groups, and vice versa for others?

(7) What are the individual's main sources of information and advice for health?
Who are their major influencers?
Who might be additional credible sources of information and influence?

High five: the words of the experts

In a rather remarkable 'summit meeting', the US National Institutes of Mental Health managed to bring together Albert Bandura (social-cognitive learning theory), Marshall

Becker (health belief model), Martin Fishbein (theory of reasoned action), Harry Triandis (theory of subjective culture and interpersonal behaviour) and Frederick Kanfer (theory of self-regulation and self-control), in Washington DC in October 1991. The objective was to distil from all these individuals' models, implications for developing AIDS interventions (Fishbein *et al.* 1991).

The five theorists decided on a set of eight variables that predict and explain behaviour: intention; environmental constraints; ability; anticipated outcomes (or attitude); norms; self-standards; emotion; and self-efficacy (see text).

(8) How do the individual's social interactions, including their extended family, club memberships, employment and home-care role influence their health beliefs and behaviours?

(9) Does the individual exhibit any personality characteristics that might inhibit or facilitate the adoption of healthy behaviours?

(10) What are the individual's perceptions of social norms with regard to the recommended behaviours?

Who are their relevant reference groups and their relative influence?

Does the individual see the recommended behaviours as compatible with their social roles and self-image?

(11) What are the individual's perceptions of the morality of non-compliance with the recommended behaviour and consistency with internalised values?

On a broader scale:

(12) What are GPs' knowledge of diabetes risk factors and their willingness to undertake preventative measures with patients exhibiting these risk factors?

(13) What factors exist in the individual's social, economic, work and physical environment that facilitate and inhibit attendance at diabetes screening?

(14) What factors exist in the individual's social, economic, work and physical environment that facilitate and inhibit healthy eating and exercise habits?

(15) What are health bureaucrats' knowledge of diabetes and their attitudes towards allocating funds to prevention?

Behavioural scientists have now generally come to the following set of principles that guide the framework for interventions (Elder *et al.* 1994; Fishbein *et al.* 1991).

For an individual to perform a recommended behaviour:

• They must have formed an intention to perform the behaviour or made a (public) commitment to do so.
• There are no physical or structural environmental constraints that prevent the behaviour being performed.
• The individual has the skills and equipment necessary to perform the behaviour.
• The individual perceives themselves to be capable of performing the behaviour.

- The individual considers that the benefits/rewards of performing the behaviour outweigh the costs/disbenefits associated with performing the behaviour, including the rewards associated with *not* performing the behaviour (i.e., a positive attitude towards performing the behaviour).
- Social normative pressure to perform the behaviour is perceived to be greater than social normative pressure not to perform the behaviour.
- The individual perceives the behaviour to be consistent with their self-image and internalised behaviours (i.e., morally acceptable).
- The individual perceives the behaviour to be consistent with their social roles.
- The individual's emotional reaction (or expectation) to performing the behaviour is more positive than negative.

In general, Fishbein *et al.* (1991) consider that the first three are necessary and sufficient for behaviour to occur. Hence, if a violent man has formed a strong intention to call a helpline about his violence, if a telephone is easily accessible and if the call can be made in private and with assured confidentiality, it is likely that the behaviour will occur. The remainder of the above variables primarily influence intention or facilitate/inhibit translating the intention into action.

Concluding comments

The models described in this chapter apply equally to beliefs and attitudes about individuals' risky or unhealthy behaviours as well as the beliefs and attitudes about the social and political issues related to those behaviours. Hence, these models are useful not only for developing campaigns to promote healthy behaviours, but also for developing advocacy campaigns targeting policymakers and legislators. Hence, if a legislator is shown survey evidence that her constituents are overwhelmingly in favour of reduced liquor outlet hours, if there is considerable media publicity supporting such a move, if she is experienced at tabling motions at party and committee meetings and if she is personally aware of the effects of excess alcohol consumption due to extended trading hours, then it is likely that she will comply with an advocacy group's request to have the issue of liquor outlet trading hours included on the agenda of the party's next meeting.

QUESTIONS

- How would you use the health belief model to develop a programme targeting adolescent smokers to quit?
- How would you use the protection motivation model to develop a programme to increase immunisation rates in developing countries?
- How might a campaign to decrease physical inactivity differ from one to increase physical activity?

FURTHER READING

Donovan, R. J. 2009. Towards an Understanding of Factors Influencing Athletes' Attitudes towards Performance-enhancing Technologies: Implications for Ethics Education, in T. Murray, A. Wasunna, E. Parens and K. Maschke (eds.), *Enhancing Technologies in Sport: Ethical, Conceptual and Scientific Issues*. Baltimore, MD: The Johns Hopkins University Press.

Gladwell, M. 2000. *The Tipping Point*. London: Little Brown.

Pisek, P. 2000. *Spreading Good Ideas for Health Care: A Practical Toolkit*. VHA Research Series, vol. 2.

Rice, G. 2006. Pro-environmental Behaviour in Egypt: Is there a Role for Islamic Environmental Ethics?, *Journal of Business Ethics* 65: 373–90.

World Health Organisation 2002. World Report on Violence and Health: Summary. Geneva: WHO.

7 Research and evaluation

Research and evaluation require specialist technical expertise. Therefore, the aim of this chapter is to provide an overview of relevant research methods and to facilitate interaction with such experts rather than impart research skills.

We first distinguish between qualitative and quantitative research and present some of the major qualitative research methods. Qualitative research is particularly important because this is where strategy development comes from and where there is perhaps least understanding. We then describe the research framework of the US National Academy of Sciences as an overarching framework for research and evaluation.

Given that much of the application of social marketing is in public health, we then define the public health research concepts of prevalence and incidence, describe 'epidemiological' studies and note how to interpret logistic regression odds ratios – one of the major tools in public health research. Given that much formative and experimental research measures behavioural *intentions* as the dependent variable, we also comment on the relationship between intentions and behaviour, concluding with a brief discussion on research in Indigenous communities and rural communities in developing countries.

Qualitative versus quantitative research

The most common distinctions made between quantitative and qualitative research are as follows:

- Qualitative research is designed to identify, describe and explain people's points of view, whereas quantitative research is designed to measure how many people hold each of these points of view.
- Qualitative research methods consist of semi-structured, open-ended questioning techniques, where the responses are subject to varying degrees of interpretation, whereas quantitative research methods consist mostly of structured, closed-ended questioning techniques, where there is little variation in degrees of interpretation.

Qualitative research attempts to *identify* the different attitudes people hold and to *explore* how these attitudes were formed. It *probes* the influence of factors such as people's values, past experiences, sources of information, peers, family, the media and socio-cultural institutions on the development of these attitudes and their expression in behaviours. It generates 'grounded theories' or *hypotheses* about the relationships between these variables and behaviours. These theories or hypotheses can be tested in further qualitative research, but more likely, via quantitative research methods. The nature of such relationships is based on the interpretation of the researcher. Such an understanding provides 'clues' as to what type of interventions would be most effect-ive (i.e., whether 'persuasion' could be effective, whether legislation would be accepted, whether education alone would be sufficient, etc.).

The major qualitative techniques are focus groups, paired interviews (especially for children and adolescents), individual depth interviews (IDIs) and ethnographic methods such as participant and non-participant observation. Other methods include: point of use, point of purchase interviews; projective techniques (associative, TAT, pic-ture sorts, 'shopping lists'); laddering or benefit chaining; imagery generation; and cognitive response measures (including emotion measures).

The validity of qualitative interview findings is largely determined by the skill of the interviewer. Hence, it is essential that properly trained in-depth interviewers and focus group moderators should be used to gain benefit from the research and to avoid incor-rect strategies based on misinterpretation of qualitative data.

Much qualitative research questioning is open-ended, and where the interviewer asks neutral questions, avoids leading questions and is completely non-judgmental. This is very important in areas such as health and social policy, where people might give socially desirable answers (e.g., probing for racist beliefs, parenting techniques), or the areas are personally sensitive (e.g., sexual behaviours, use of violence).

Qualitative versus quantitative research methods		
	Qualitative	Quantitative
Questions:	Semi-structured	Structured
Answers:	Open-ended, para-verbal, non-verbal, non-response	Closed-ended (answer categories, rating scales, etc.)
Interviewer:	Interactive	Passive
Interviewee:	Participant	Respondent
Analysis:	Descriptive (basic), inferential (advanced)	Statistical, descriptive with some inference
Sample size:	Small (can replicate to increase reliability)	Usually large
Data sampling unit	Points of view	People, households, buying units

Quantitative research attempts to determine what proportions of the population hold the various beliefs and attitudes and behave in certain ways. Using statistical methods, it attempts to identify and quantify the extent of relationships between the identified points of view and the sort of factors listed above. Quantitative research is associated primarily with survey methods and experimental research, including randomised control trials. Quantitative analytic methods, such as regression, factor analysis and structural equation modelling, also allow the exploration of the (mathematical or statistical) relationship between variables.

Example of open-ended questioning:
Q: What is it you like about attending a festival movie?
A: *Well, it's very different from going to an ordinary movie*
Q: In what way is it different?
A: *It's more of a special event … You look forward to it more, and there's more excitement in the crowd.*
Q: How do you mean?
A: *I think there's a greater sense of expectation in the atmosphere … that the movie is going to be different from the ordinary run-of-the-mill Hollywood types.*
Q: How do you mean 'different'?
A: *I'm a bit of a movie fan, so I'm interested in different directors, how screenplays appear and things like the camera work. Some of the festival movies are interesting because they include a lot of techniques you wouldn't see otherwise.*
Q: You also mentioned a different atmosphere at festival movies. What did you mean?
A: *There's an extra buzz 'cos you feel part of the festival … like being a member of a special group – and you know the movie possibly wouldn't get here ordinarily, so you feel that you feel that you're seeing something that a lot of other people won't get to see.*
Q: Tell me a little more about 'feeling part of the festival'?
A: *Well, I suppose I don't go to many what you might call highbrow things like the theatre and ballet, but many of my friends and other people I know do. Going to a festival movie makes me feel like I am getting a bit of culture and gives me something in common with these other people – I can join in their conversations about what's going on during the festival.*

Note that as the above questions are open-ended, different interviewers might have followed up different aspects of the first response – and hence got different data. In addition, people can interpret the above statements differently. Two different researchers' conclusions appear in the next box.

Qualitative data: same data, possibly different interpretations

Researcher A
'This person primarily attends festival movies because they are seen to be far more enjoyable than mainstream movies, and because the festival offers them a chance to be among the first – or only – local people to see the particular movies. It is this opportunity of a more interesting, somewhat "exclusive", experience that is the primary motivation.'

> **Researcher B**
> 'This person primarily attends festival movies because their desired self-image, and the image they want to project to others, includes being seen to be interested in "cultural" events. However, they have little interest in, and rarely attend, any live performance event, but they do like going to movies. Hence, the festival – because of its "cultural" image and the person's perceptions of the sorts of people who attend festival events, provides an opportunity to bolster their desired self-image in a way that fits with what they already enjoy doing.'
>
> Close and Donovan (1998)

Qualitative research

Qualitative research is useful when little is known about the area and there is a need to:

- understand how attitudes are formed;
- identify motivations;
- understand how motivations are relevant;
- learn the language of the target audience.

Qualitative research is also useful for:

- exploring reactions to communication materials, merchandise or interventions;
- observing interaction among peoples;
- piloting questionnaires;
- generating new ideas;

but not pre-testing ads for go–no go decisions.

Qualitative research methods

Qualitative research methods originated from psychology, and are most associated with probing people's psyches for hidden motivations and underlying psychodynamics. Much of the early qualitative research emphasised the uncovering of such motivations – as popularised in Vance Packard's *The Hidden Persuaders* (1967) and, in research circles, by Ernest Dichter's (1964) *Handbook of Consumer Motivations*. These days, the emphasis has shifted to more of a phenomenological observation approach: that is, using qualitative research to learn how people talk about, think about and feel about various products, services and issues, rather than delving into deep Freudian or Jungian (or whoever's) interpretations of what people say.

Individual depth interviews

Individual depth interviews (IDIs) are one-on-one, usually face-to-face interviews, lasting anywhere from 45 minutes to several hours. This sort of minimum time is required to allow the interviewer to establish trust and rapport with the respondent so that the respondent feels comfortable in revealing the information sought – some of which might be very personal.

The interviewer has a list of topics to cover, but there is no requirement to stick to the order. In fact, good interviewers use the respondent's answers to follow up and explore issues, rather than sticking to a rigid sequence. Part of an IDI topic/question outline for a survey attempting to explore what motivates people to attend (or not attend) community issues meetings is shown in the box below.

IDI topic outline

- What issues in your neighbourhood and suburb concern you most? List and for each one, probe why.
- Which of these issues, if any, would you attend a community meeting on if there were going to be any local council policy changes? Probe and explore why for each one mentioned.
- How useful do you think these sorts of community meetings are? Do you think that local government takes notice of what people say? Does the state government? Who do you think they listen most to?
- Are you aware of any instances, in your suburb or anywhere else, where the ordinary people got organised and overturned a government decision? What was it? Why were they successful?
- Last community event attended – if any? Probe all details: who went with, expectations and whether or not fulfilled.

Laddering or benefit chaining questioning

One questioning procedure that is very useful, even in brief interviews, is called laddering or 'benefit chaining'. Benefit chaining attempts to go beyond first responses to identify end benefits, and beyond the physical or tangible attributes to determine what benefits these attributes give. For example, low fat is a physical attribute of an ice cream, but the end benefit sought by the consumer might be weight loss, or weight control, or less likelihood of heart disease, or being able to eat an extra piece of cake. That is, benefit chaining is useful to identify the different benefits sought by different types of consumers. In fact, benefit segmentation is a major way of segmenting some markets.

Here are two examples of a laddering question interchange, where the physical attribute 'strong' is benefit chained to establish psychological end benefits:

Q: What brand of coffee do you drink?
A: *Maxwell House.*
Q: Why do you drink Maxwell House?

A: Because it's strong coffee.

Q: What's good about strong coffee?

A: It keeps me awake.

Q: And why is that important/what's good about that?

A: I get more work done.

Q: And why is that important/what's good about that?

A: My productivity rating looks good to my manager.

Q: And why is that important/what's good about that?

A: I get praised, and it improves my promotion prospects.

Q: And why is that important/what's good about that?

A: I feel good about myself. I feel like I'm achieving my goals.

One can imagine the sort of television commercial that might result from this interview: a busy office, ambitious yuppie working into the night, a jar of Maxwell House prominently displayed on the work desk, an approving boss smiling in appreciation as the boss leaves the office while the yuppie works on, yuppie looking pleased as Punch.

On the other hand, the interview might go like this for someone else:

Q: What brand of coffee do you drink?

A: Maxwell House.

Q: Why do you drink Maxwell house?

A: Because it's strong coffee.

Q: What's good about strong coffee?

A: I just love the taste and smell of coffee. So the stronger, the better.

Again, one can imagine the sort of television commercial that might be developed to reach this segment type: terrific visuals of rich brown coffee beans pouring into a giant Maxwell House coffee jar, cut to steaming mug of rich brown coffee being held in someone's hand, pull back to show person enjoying the (presumably) rich aroma, then sipping the coffee, followed by a satisfied 'mmm …'

If the question were about physical activity, and the person said they like going for a run, the line of questioning would attempt to elicit what was liked – and why:

Q: What sorts of things do you like about going for a run?

A: I love the feeling of freedom and being alone …

Q: What's good to you about being alone?

A: I can concentrate on my breathing and get really relaxed once I hit my rhythm.

Q: And what's good about that … what do you get from that?

A: For that period of time I'm somewhere else … I'm totally oblivious to all my day-to-day problems … It's a complete escape.

Q: And what's good about that?

A: Afterwards I feel renewed … energetic, and enthused. It's a great feeling.

Research fads: 'Smile! You're on candid camera'

An increasingly common technique today is for commercial market researchers to photograph the target group as they go about their daily lives, where they 'hang out', where they work, their entertainment venues, etc. In some cases, members of the target group are given the cameras and asked to take the photographs themselves, delivering them later to the researchers. As is often the case, this new technique is being used increasingly without real consideration of what is being measured. Nevertheless, it can provide valuable additional data about the language and lifestyles of target groups for those clients who never make the time or effort to observe their target groups.

The use of photographs probably stems from Zaltman's metaphor analysis technique [ZMET: Zaltman's Meta Elicitation Technique, Zaltman and Coulter (1995)], whereby respondents are asked to select pictures from magazines and newspapers that illustrate their metaphors for the product being studied in advertising research, and bring these pictures along to a group discussion or IDI.

Photovoice

More than a fad, 'Photovoice' activities or competitions appear to be popular with health promoters for involving young people in particular. Health workers also use the technique as 'participatory research'. The data can provide an additional dimension or simply serve to stimulate discussion in groups, such as in Baker and Wang's (2006) study with chronic pain sufferers. The term was first employed by Caroline Wang, a University of Michigan professor of public health. Photovoice has also been used in advocacy efforts in places as diverse as China and Guatemala (Ying 2009).

Using projective techniques to measure attitudes

Projective techniques are a useful research tool and can be applied in qualitative and quantitative research. Projective techniques involve presenting ambiguous stimulus material (thought bubbles, pictures, ink blots, etc.) to people and asking them to interpret the situation. It is assumed that they project their own thoughts and feelings in their response. Projective techniques are useful when respondents are unable or unwilling to respond to direct questioning, or where direct questioning may yield socially desirable responses or be subject to demand characteristics.

One of the major challenges in tobacco control is that younger children appear to be opposed to smoking (sometimes vehemently so), but, at around the age of 12 to 14 years, many appear to abandon these beliefs and take up smoking. Why is this so? One reason may be that children aren't as negative as we think and might simply be giving 'socially desirable' responses to questions about smoking, especially when the questioners are adults. To assess whether this was the case, we adapted a classic projective technique used in marketing [the shopping list; Haire (1950)]. After an introduction and sample exercise about how people form impressions of other people, 8–10-year-old schoolchildren were given either one or the other of the two lists

Table 7.1(a) Using projective techniques to measure attitudes	
Pocket money expenditure lists	
List 1	List 2
Movies	Movies
Ice creams and lollies	Cigarettes
Saving for a record or cassette	Ice creams and lollies
Comic	Saving for a record or cassette
Batteries	Comic
Video games	Batteries
Hamburger	Video games
	Hamburger

Table 7.1(b) Using projective techniques to measure attitudes		
Perceptions of smokers and non-smokers		
	No cigarettes on list (%) (n = 382)	Cigarettes on list (%) (n = 240)
Someone I would (not) like	45.0	26.5*
Attractive (unattractive)	46.6	35.0*
Unpopular (popular)	26.7	36.8*
Troublemaker (well behaved)	59.4	87.4*
Smart (foolish)	33.8	13.5*
Outgoing (shy)	83.3	89.7
Grown up (childish)	30.6	29.1

* Significant at 0.05 level.
  Donovan and Holden (1985).

shown in Table 7.1(a) of what a hypothetical boy or girl their age spent their pocket money on. The only difference was that one list contained 'cigarettes'. The children were asked to write a description of 'this boy/girl' and then rate them on the bi-polar scales in Table 7.1(b). No attention was drawn to any of the items on the lists. The results show that the child spending pocket money on cigarettes was viewed far more negatively than the other child. The projective technique allowed us to rule out the possibility that negative attitudes to smoking were due to demand characteristics.

We also used a projective technique to assess people's reactions to the statements 'I have cancer' versus 'I have *a* cancer' (emphasis added here) by asking them to fill a thought bubble of a person being told this information by someone. As expected, the 'I have cancer' statement overwhelmingly elicited negative connotations of death and anxious emotional arousal. On the other hand, 'I have *a* cancer' served to distract attention from 'death' connotations to queries about the type of cancer and, hence, elicited far less anxiety in respondents (Donovan, Jalleh and Jones 2003). This is useful for doctors to know how to reduce anxiety in the patient – which facilitates the patient's processing of further information; and for cancer patients to tell their friends to facilitate rather than inhibit further conversation.

Focus group discussions

Focus groups generally work like this:

- six to nine individuals (i.e., a manageable number so everyone can join in);
- selected because of their relevance to the research objectives;
- sit around and talk about the topic of interest, under the 'control' of a group moderator;
- the moderator generally works from a topic outline in the same way as for IDIs; and
- the questioning should be flexible rather than rigidly following a set sequence of specific questions.

With the permission of the group members (usually a requirement of most market and social research profession codes) the groups are usually audio- and/or video-taped for later analysis. They may also be video-taped for the client to watch, or, at some research companies' premises, may be viewed directly via a one-way mirror. Participants are served refreshments and paid for attending. Professional or executive groups might be held over a dinner or breakfast so as not to intrude on work time.

Focus groups (or just 'group discussions') are the most used (and, some would argue – misused) technique in qualitative research. They were originally called *focus* groups, because the usual procedure was to discuss broad issues and then 'focus' in on the particular area of interest. This probably stemmed from the psychological approach, where the clinician, quite appropriately, attempted to place a person's problem in the total context of their lives, rather than treat the problem as an isolated issue.

This broad-to-specific approach is appropriate for much of what qualitative research is used for now. For example, to more fully understand a person's physical activity or eating habits, it is useful – some would say essential – to first get an overview of people's leisure and work activities in general, which would also include understanding their family and other institutional commitments.

Similarly, if we want to understand mothers' food choices for their children, we need to understand what it's like bringing up children in general. Concerns about nutrition often take second place to convenience and what the child will readily accept. When mum is busy getting the family dinner, a chocolate bar or a packet of crisps in front of the TV at least promise some peace, however temporary. This broader approach allows a better understanding of wider socio-cultural influences on motivations and behaviour.

On the other hand, group discussions are often used to get reactions to specific things such as brochures, advertisements, packaging, new products, piloting questionnaires, etc. In these cases, the group usually focuses on the specific task from the beginning.

Where do these group participants come from? – group and IDI recruiting

Most research companies either keep databases (or panels) of people who have previously expressed their willingness to take part in consumer research groups (perhaps when they have taken part in a street or home interview), or recruit via random cold calling from telephone directories, or sometimes place ads on the radio or in community newspapers.

Sometimes researchers will approach organisations (e.g., sporting or social clubs) and offer the organisation an incentive if the organisation can supply a number of people who fit the desired demographic or other characteristics. Such groups are called 'affinity' groups, and there is some disagreement among researchers as to their value. While they do have their uses, in general we recommend against using affinity groups – unless the research objective is to understand the role of that particular organisation in its members' lives and in the issue at hand.

In health and social policy areas, most of the time we are dealing with general population groups. However, we also frequently deal with professionals, such as service providers, policymakers, funders, carer support groups, physicians, nurses, pharmacists, youth workers, etc. These can be recruited from staff lists, often with the assistance of the client, or they are identifiable in the area under study. Organisations also provide access to their clients for research purposes (with the permission of the client) (e.g., people receiving income support, men in mandated counselling programmes).

Ensuring the appropriateness of the people selected to participate in the groups or IDIs is the single most important aspect of qualitative research. Hence, a screening questionnaire is administered to potential participants to ensure they fit the required characteristics.

The research objectives determine the overall characteristics of people required. Market researchers often interview people who have recently bought or used a brand for the first time (to see what motivated switching to that brand), and people who have ceased buying or using a particular brand (to probe reasons for dissatisfaction). The data provide insights into how others might be motivated to purchase a new brand and what might be done to prevent dissatisfaction with continued purchase. Hence, if the aim is to determine what differentiates full strength beer drinkers from mid strength beer drinkers, and what promotional or other incentives (if any) might be used to get full strength drinkers to switch to mid strength, groups should be chosen on the basis of current consumption – perhaps two groups of mid strength drinkers (to find out why they switched) and then two groups of full strength drinkers to assess reaction to the motives/benefits identified in the mid strength groups. Similarly, to study people's motivations to change and the decision processes they went through during these changes, we recruited two groups of people who had made a deliberate decision in the past six months to do more exercise (and had done so), and two groups with people who had made and carried out a deliberate decision to eat more healthily (Henley and Donovan 2002). Research with people who have made desirable changes provides clues to what might work on others yet to change.

A number of other aspects are important for group recruiting in particular. One of the most important relates to the homogeneity of the group. Group studies show that the more homogeneous the group (i.e., the more the group members have in common), then the better the group interaction and individual member participation. Hence, as far as possible – and depending on the research objectives, groups should be homogeneous with regard to age categories, gender and, especially where costs of activities are important such as in discussing leisure and recreation pursuits, income or socio-economic status (SES).

Existing attitudes should be a major criterion for recruiting, whether the topic is about brand choice or health and policy issues. However, given the importance of homogeneity for eliciting open discussion, homogeneity is crucial for sensitive areas and where social desirability might inhibit the expression of personal beliefs. For example, in recruiting individuals from the dominant ethnic population to talk about racial issues with regard to minority ethnic groups, it would be advisable to use a set of questions to identify those who are negative and those who are positive towards these minority groups and thus ensure like-minded individuals are in the same focus group. Screening this way allows far more negative attitudes and beliefs to be expressed by participants in the discussion as they realise they are among like-minded people. This allows the opportunity for deeper probing of the bases for these negative beliefs and how they might be countered.

Screening criteria can be dynamic

For a series of group discussions on parenting and the place of children in society, a first series of groups might be screened on basic dimensions such as children or no children, children's age, SES, single- versus two-parent household and step-parent household. If the early groups revealed that the way many parents dealt with their children was related to their own childhood, later groups might then recruited on this basis via a question like: 'Would you describe your childhood as happy, unhappy, or mixed?'

Exclusions from groups

Nothing stops a free discussion more than someone in the group declaring themselves, or being seen by the other group members to be, an 'expert' in the area. It is common practice in commercial research to exclude from groups people working in the advertising, public relations, marketing and market research industries, because they may have knowledge about the issue which consumers in general would not have, and because they may be more interested in the research process than in participating as a consumer. Other exclusions are based on the topic; for example, dentists and their families would be excluded from groups on toothpaste and oral hygiene. In the health and social policy areas, care must be taken to exclude those working in the areas under study when recruiting 'general population' groups. For example, teachers should be excluded from groups on parenting (do a group of teachers together); nurses, doctors, etc. from general population groups on health; psychologists, counsellors, etc. from groups on mental health; bureaucrats working in that particular area and so on. This requires remembering in the recruiting questionnaire to ask not just for current occupation, but for people's *previous* occupations.

When to use focus groups versus IDIs

For most issues and most occasions, focus groups are preferred to IDIs. Focus groups have a clear time – and therefore cost – advantage (it's quicker to interview eight people at a time than conduct eight separate interviews). The data also benefit from the group dynamics. IDIs are useful when sensitive issues are involved that people may not want to discuss in front of others (e.g., sexual or personal hygiene issues), when the type of person is difficult to get to come to a group (e.g., busy executives, shift workers), or when the issues are unique to individuals and require time to elicit (e.g., 'personal history' probing).

In our experience, if the groups are carefully recruited with regard to homogeneity issues, with a skilled moderator, and a careful step-by-step introduction to the specifics of the issue, then even very sensitive issues are quite readily discussed in groups.

Although focus groups are still the major qualitative technique in both commercial and social marketing, other methods are proving useful, particularly in providing convergent validity. Discreet observer and participant–observer techniques are increasingly being borrowed from anthropology and sociology as techniques to increase our understanding of behaviour and its influencers. These kind of techniques range from rubbish analysis, to hidden cameras observing TV audience behaviour, to street gang participation. In many cases though, it simply means objectively observing the behaviour under study, attempting to construct behaviour patterns and making inferences about the relationships between beliefs, attitudes, motives and behaviour. Observational methods are particularly useful for studying the influence of social factors on behaviour.

From our point of view, qualitative research is essential in determining overall strategies, with a mix of qualitative and quantitative methods useful for determining the viability of identified strategies, and quantitative indicators best for revealing outcome effects.

Research and evaluation framework

We consider the US National Academy of Sciences' research framework to be helpful in conceptualising research questions. Although the framework was developed for the development and evaluation of media campaigns, the principles apply to any type of intervention. Coyle, Boruch and Turner (1989) delineate four types of evaluation designed to answer four questions:

(1) **Formative research**: what type of intervention would work best? What mix of components would be necessary or optimal?
(2) **Efficacy trials**: could the intervention actually make a difference if implemented under ideal conditions?
(3) **Process evaluation**: was the intervention implemented as planned?
(4) **Outcome evaluation**: what impact, if any, did the intervention have? Did it make a difference? If not, why not? What worked best?

Process and outcome evaluation in this framework are often described as 'programme evaluation' when applied to ongoing comprehensive interventions such as several of those described in Hornik (2002).

Formative research: 'what is likely to work best?'

Formative research informs the development of interventions, products and communication materials. It answers questions such as:

- What strategies could be used to motivate violent men to voluntarily seek help to stop their violence?
- Can media advertising be used to change racist stereotype beliefs?
- What could motivate villagers in Ghana to use soap to wash their hands, rather than just rinsing in water?
- What approach would be most effective in stimulating concern about heart disease in rural Indigenous communities?
- What information, presented in what way, might influence a corporation to reduce the salt in their food products?
- What sort of lobbying methods have most impact on politicians?
- Are Christian and Islamic religious values congruent or incongruent with pro-environmental values?

Formative research needs to identify and explore reaction to the various means of achieving the stated objectives (e.g., getting violent men to enter counselling programmes, changing people's stereotyped beliefs about the mentally ill, increasing people's knowledge of cardiovascular (CVD) risk factors and uptake of preventive actions). It should explore not just the targeted individuals' attitudes, beliefs and behaviours, but also the social context, structural facilitators and inhibitors, and the roles and views of all relevant stakeholders with regard to potential alternative interventions.

Formative research methods can include quantitative research, such as surveys, literature reviews and epidemiological analyses, to provide background data and to generate ideas and hypotheses. However, the most valuable formative research uses face-to-face qualitative methods with all relevant stakeholders, where the reactions to potential interventions and their components can be gauged directly and indirectly. Focus groups and IDIs allow the exploration of reactions, in particular, possible ways of overcoming negative reactions. For example, qualitative research with country residents suggested that a media campaign could be successful in influencing people's attitudes towards Aborigines and employment, but would not be successful if it was simply seen as 'the government' showing positive images of Aboriginal people without some rationale. Hence, the campaign was sourced to the local Aboriginal corporation and was focused on an 'Aboriginal Employment Week' (see box below; Donovan and Leivers 1993).

Using paid advertising to counter racist stereotype beliefs: formative research

In an attempt to adopt prevention strategies, Western Australia's Equal Opportunity Commission wanted to assess the potential for a mass media-based campaign to change discriminatory practices against Aboriginal people in three areas: access to employment; access to rental housing; and entry to entertainment venues. A regional city was selected for the feasibility study.

Formative research consisted of focus group discussions with non-Aboriginal residents and small business operators, IDIs with key informants (e.g., local government councillors, police, headmasters, etc.) and individual and group interviews with key members of the Aboriginal community. The qualitative research indicated that campaigns targeting housing rental discrimination and access to entertainment venues would not be successful (few would rent a home to an Aboriginal family, there was no social support for neighbours who would and public housing was seen to be readily available anyway; and no one considered there was any discrimination with regard to access to hotels and nightclubs). On the other hand, seeking employment was admired, as were employers willing to give Aborigines a job opportunity. Furthermore, discriminatory attitudes were found to be based largely on underestimates of the numbers of Aborigines in paid employment and the length of time Aborigines stayed in a job. Hence, a media campaign was considered feasible to address these misperceptions.

Similarly, focus groups or small-scale surveys could be used to assess attitudes towards and potential purchase of water flow controlling products, and what message strategy would be appropriate to reinforce, create or alter attitudes and behaviours with regard to such devices. Matters of price, aesthetic design and impact on water flow would all need to be considered, including attitudes of manufacturers and retailers. Similarly, survey or desk research might reveal that many members of a target audience have limited literacy. Hence, if self-help materials were to be produced, they would need to be supplied on CD, DVD or audio-cassette in addition to any printed materials.

Coyle, Boruch and Turner (1989) recommend four processes in the formative stage of a communication campaign: idea generation; concept testing; setting communication objectives; and copy testing. These are discussed and elaborated on below to encompass interventions in general, although the emphasis will be on the communication elements of interventions.

Idea generation

This relates to identifying potential ways of addressing the identified problem given available resources. It explores what overall strategy or type of intervention could be effective, what sort of products might be necessary and what message strategy would motivate the desired attitude and behaviour changes. For example:

- to generate political support for tobacco control measures, the British Medical Association came up with the idea of publishing a document showing how many people died from smoking-related diseases in each MP's constituency (Lewis, Morkel and Hubbard 1993), a tactic successfully copied by anti-smoking advocates in other countries;
- the Stop it Now! campaign to prevent child sexual abuse in Vermont (and now in Minnesota; www.stopitnow.com/mn) wondered whether abusers and potential abusers would call an anonymous helpline for counselling if they knew one existed (Tabachnick 2003);
- the Road Crew team in Wisconsin wanted 21–30-year-old drinkers in rural bars to take a ride home rather than drive their own cars;
- health workers in Ghana thought basing a campaign on the emotion of disgust would be a far more effective motivator of hand washing with soap than knowledge of disease prevention (Scott, Lawson and Curtis 2007).

Involving agency creatives in developing communications

With regard to developing concept executions for social marketing campaigns, it is highly desirable that behavioural scientists and experts in the content area be involved in the development of materials with the agency creatives and other professionals. It is insufficient to simply provide the advertising or PR agency with just a written or verbal brief. In the commercial world, ad agency personnel often take a 'tour of the factory', talk to the frontline sales people, or at least observe focus group discussions with the company's customers. For social marketing areas, it is even more crucial for agency personnel to take a 'tour of the factory', as many issues will initially be completely alien to them. It is also of great assistance to creatives in that the best ideas are based on a sound understanding of the issue.

Visits to burnt home stimulated the smoke alarms creatives

For inspiration for the Fire Authority of Northern Ireland's fire safety campaign ('Check your smoke alarm batteries every Monday'), the agency team visited and studied real fire scenes. The image then used in campaign materials was that of human handprints in the soot of burned walls (Storey 2008).

Agency creatives met the medicos for tobacco ads

When developing advertising for the Australian National Tobacco Campaign, group meetings were arranged for the agency creatives to meet with the medical specialists who dealt with smoking-related diseases, as well as behavioural science professionals working in the tobacco control area. These meetings also resulted in ad creatives visiting the specialists' laboratories. The results were the dramatic 'artery', 'stroke' and 'lung' ads that have since been adopted and adapted in several overseas jurisdictions such as Canada, New Zealand, the United States (Massachusetts) and Singapore (Hassard 1999).

Concept testing

Concept testing is an iterative process that attempts to assess which of the ideas generated in phase one are viable. It focuses on getting the right message, product or tactic. While qualitative research is the primary tool for idea generation, quantitative survey research is often carried out to confirm that acceptance of the final concept is generalisable to the total target population and acceptable to all stakeholders. Laboratory-style experiments also can be used to test different concepts by exposing different, but matched groups to different concepts and then comparing the groups' reactions.

The Freedom from Fear campaign explored three communication strategies for motivating violent men to call the Men's Domestic Violence Helpline: the potential loss of their partner and children; the negative impact on their children of the violence; and a demonstration of the remorse that often follows a violent episode. Concept testing assessed whether or not these themes would have an impact and which of these themes would have most impact on most of the target audience. This level of testing did not necessarily require any stimulus materials – it was based on the exploration of men's beliefs and attitudes in qualitative research (Francas and Donovan 2001).

Development of communication objectives

Given the outcome of the above two processes, the next step is the development of a set of communication and behavioural objectives: that is, a statement of the knowledge, beliefs and attitudes desired to be brought about in the target audience so as to lead to the desired behaviour change. This then becomes the starting point for the development of communication materials and strategies for promotion of the campaign. In the case of advertising and publicity, this would form the basis of the brief given to the advertising or public relations agency.

Pre-testing

Getting the right strategy is essential for success, whereas executing the strategy right determines the degree of success. This stage generally applies to testing specific products (Quit kits, water controllers, STD packs) or specific communication materials (press kits, advertisements, brochures, slogans). Products can be tested in groups or individually (depending on the product), or placed in people's homes for a specified time.

Copy testing is the name commonly given to testing advertising and other communication materials. Given that there are a number of ways in which a message can be executed (e.g., graphically with high emotion, different styles of music, quick cuts or extended scenes in a TV ad, etc.), pre-testing is designed to maximise the possibility that the approach taken is likely to be the most effective under the circumstances. Copy testing involves exposing a test audience to a 'draft' of the message (such as an advertisement, press release, pamphlet or video presentation) and evaluating the potential success of that message in achieving the communication objectives.

For example, with regard to the Freedom from Fear concepts noted above, each could be executed in a variety of ways. One way to demonstrate the potential loss of family could be to show a child enacting various scenarios with dolls in a doll's house: the child mimics with her dolls a man and a women arguing, followed by the female doll packing a suitcase and leaving the doll's house with two 'child dolls'. Another way could be to show a man coming home to an empty house, showing the emotions on his face as he pulls out empty dressing table drawers and looks at family photos left behind.

Testing concept executions clearly requires stimulus material, and executions are often developed in a series of group discussions. However, where a 'go no–go' decision is required with regard to, say, launching a TV ad, printing a brochure or producing a radio ad, or, as is often the case, in choosing between several different concept executions, the final testing of alternative executions is best carried out using quantitative methods (Rossiter and Donovan 1983). Quantitative copy testing involves exposing the material(s) to carefully screened members of the target audience and, where appropriate, comparing their responses to those of a similarly selected control group who are not exposed to the material(s).

Copy testing: what to measure

The following kinds of measures are usually taken after exposing people to campaign materials, although specific measures will vary by the type and objectives of the material(s):

- the thoughts and feelings generated spontaneously by the material;
- the extent to which the message is correctly understood;
- the extent to which the message is credible;
- the extent to which the message is seen to be personally relevant, important, and useful;
- the extent to which the message motivates the recommended action;
- the extent to which the audience see the recommended action as effective and themselves capable of performing the action;
- likes, dislikes and specific confusions in the material(s);
- where appropriate, the extent to which the presenter or models in the materials are credible and relevant as role models to the target audience;
- where appropriate, the extent to which any metaphors or analogies in the ads are credible and relevant.

Using copy testing: are big production budgets necessary for creating effective road safety advertising?

Based on standard advertising copy testing measures, we developed a set of measures to assess the relative effectiveness of twelve Australian and New Zealand road safety ads varying in production costs (at that time) from $15,000 to $250,000+. The twelve ads covered four road safety behaviours (speeding, drink-driving, fatigue and inattention), and included a variety of execution types within and across behaviours. One ad in each of the four behaviours was an expensive ad ($200,000 or more).

Just under 1,000 appropriately screened motor vehicle driving licence holders were recruited via street intercept methods, and randomly allocated to one of the twelve ad exposure conditions. The results showed that while the two best performing ads were highly dramatic showing graphic crash scenes, these were also the most expensive to produce, and, being 60 seconds and 90 seconds, the most expensive to air. In several cases, 30-second, low cost 'talking heads' testimonials performed equally as well as their far more expensive counterparts. We concluded that big production budgets may not be necessary to create effective road safety advertising (Figure 7.1; Donovan, Jalleh and Henley 1999).

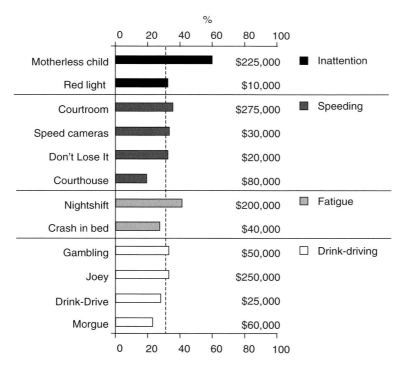

Figure 7.1 Ad impact on behavioural intentions as a driver

Donovan, Jalleh and Henley (1999)

Efficacy testing: 'can it work and can it be improved?'

Efficacy testing is what is called 'test marketing' by commercial marketers. Test marketing of new products, sales promotions, retailer agreements, distribution channels or advertising campaigns is often carried out in a limited geographical area that does not involve excessive risk or cost, and in a sample of a population with similar characteristics to the larger target audience. During the test period, surveys are carried out and sales figures recorded in the area. Efficacy testing usually involves comparing a test with a control area and may include assessments of measures such as calls to a hotline, sales of products, enquiries, etc. Diagnostic surveys measure awareness of, beliefs about and attitudes towards the intervention. If results are positive, the intervention is then introduced in all the company's markets.

Efficacy testing is designed to measure whether an intervention could work if it was implemented optimally, but under 'real world' rather than laboratory-type conditions. However, efficacy testing in social marketing areas is generally confined to school or worksite interventions, where interventions are piloted and refined before being rolled out on a broader scale. Efficacy testing of population-wide campaigns appears to be carried out infrequently in health and social marketing, usually because of time and budget restraints. One example that the first author was involved in while at the Centers for Disease Control and Prevention (CDC) involved testing two AIDS television public service announcements. People were pre-recruited to watch a particular news programme on one or other TV station for a number of nights in two locations, Springfield, Illinois and Memphis, Tennessee. People were randomly assigned to a programme that was to air an AIDS ad or to a control programme that was to contain no AIDS ads. The viewers were not told the purpose of the research. Pre-post surveys showed a significant increase in the proportion of people in the exposed group spontaneously mentioning AIDS as an 'important national issue', but no such increase in the control group (Siska *et al.* 1992).

Process research: 'is the campaign being delivered as proposed?'

Process measures are collected either during or at the end of an intervention. The questions these measures are designed to answer is whether the intervention was implemented as proposed, whether the intervention reached those it was intended to reach and if not, why not; what immediate impact the intervention had on beliefs, attitudes and behaviours related to the implementation and the intended outcomes. Aspects of concern for media-based or supported campaigns are recognition, recall and impact of the message strategies. Process research methods can range from personal interviews to recording target audience demand for information materials, etc.

The Freedom from Fear domestic violence campaign relied on paid advertising to reach violent men and encourage them to call a Men's Domestic Violence Helpline.

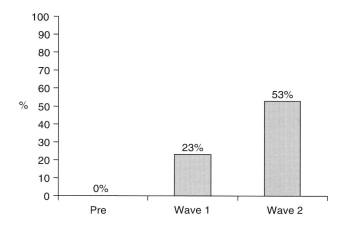

Figure 7.2 Where violent men can go for help: % spontaneously nominating a telephone helpline

Freedom from Fear campaign, Donovan, Paterson and Francas (1999)

Random telephone surveys were carried out at various intervals during the campaign to assess whether men were aware of the campaign, whether they understood the advertising messages and whether they were aware of a helpline for men to call about domestic violence. Calls to the Men's Domestic Violence Helpline were also monitored as a function of media weight. The proportion of violent men calling the Men's Domestic Violence Helpline who accepted an offer of counselling is also a process measure, as it indicates the skill of the telephone counsellors in encouraging violent callers to undergo long-term counselling.

Figure 7.2 shows that prior to the campaign, no one mentioned a telephone helpline when asked where men who used violence against their female partner could go for help. This increased to 23 per cent in the first six weeks of the campaign (wave 1). The ad was then altered to extend the time the helpline appeared at the end of the ad, along with introducing 15-second modelling ads (i.e., showing a man calling the number). After four months (wave 2), spontaneous mentions increased to 53 per cent.

This example also raises the issue of asking the appropriate question in an evaluation. In this case, the campaign aim was to have men in a situation where they realised they needed help, being able to recall from memory without prompting that a telephone helpline existed. Hence, a question presenting men with a number of options (that included a helpline) was not the appropriate question and would have exaggerated the impact of the campaign.

Outcome research: 'did it work?'

Outcome measures are designed to assess whether, and the degree to which, an intervention or media campaign has achieved what it set out to do. Short-term effects are usually called impact measures, and include intermediate objectives such as changes in beliefs, attitudes and some behaviours (such as seeking more information, calling a helpline, attending an educational seminar, wearing sun protection clothing). Longer-term effects are called outcome measures (such as reductions in heart disease and skin cancers, number of road deaths or sexual assaults or certain types of crime). These can be determined by a number of means, each with advantages and disadvantages. For example, medical registry data provide indications of skin cancer incidence and deaths.

Crime campaign outcomes

One measure of the success of crime prevention campaigns is whether or not the targeted crimes are reduced. Following a number of assaults on women by illegal mini-cab drivers, the CABWISE campaign in London was designed to discourage young women's use of illegal mini-cabs late at night by texting for the number of a legitimate local taxi service. From 2003 to 2006 the number of serious sexual assaults by illegal taxi drivers in London dropped from seventeen in 2003 to four in 2006 (Okin *et al.* 2009).

The UK 'Crime. Let's Keep It Down' campaign increased people's awareness of situational factors influencing theft likelihood and steps they could take to prevent theft. The campaign was associated with a decrease in acquisition crime of 19 per cent from 2003/4 to 2007/7 – which exceeded the campaign goal of a 15 per cent reduction (Huntley 2009).

The outcome effectiveness of many health promotion campaigns in terms of morbidity or mortality may not be known for many years. For example, the outcome of the 'slip, slop, slap' campaigns on skin cancer may take ten to twenty years to be apparent in morbidity and mortality rates for skin cancers. In the meantime, regular population surveys would be used to measure changes in knowledge and attitudes, along with self-reports of sunburn and tanning, and observational studies of people at beaches and other outdoor sporting and recreational areas to observe changes in sun protection behaviours, as well as structural changes such as the provision of shade.

Similar statements apply to campaigns such as smoking cessation campaigns and lung cancer, dietary fat campaigns and heart disease, physical activity and diabetes prevalence, energy conservation campaigns and energy use, and some road safety campaigns. Hence, these campaigns need to be evaluated in terms of intermediate measures such as beliefs and attitudes, and behavioural measures such as presenting for screening, maintenance of non-smoking, dietary habits, observation of seat belt wearing and bicycle helmet use, and sales data such as per capita sales of sunscreen, cigarettes, foods containing a high percentage of saturated fat, water and energy saving devices, 'green' labelled products (regardless of veracity), condoms, screening kits, etc.

Unfortunately, indicators such as child abuse notifications, presentations for mental illness, reports of intimate partner violence and criminal assaults are subject to different interpretations, changes in reporting and recording procedures over time, can result from a multiple of factors, and can even be unintended. For example, increased reports of assault by a male partner might be taken as indicating campaign success if following a 'break the silence' campaign, but a failure if following a 'stop the violence' campaign. On the other hand, a 'stop the violence' campaign, simply by raising the salience of the issue, could result in many women reporting violence they would not previously have reported, and perhaps others deciding to leave a violent relationship and, hence, increasing demand on women's refuges. Other outcomes such as population mental health, for example, have multiple contributors, many not under the control of the programme and many with multiple impacts. For example, an economic downturn that resulted in a sudden and substantial increase in unemployment in a community, with a resultant increase in family violence, drug and alcohol abuse, exacerbation of existing financial worries and increased job insecurity in those still employed, would have a considerable negative impact on mental health and wellbeing. In these conditions, statistical data on the number of people presenting to a physician for a mental health problem would be of little help in assessing the impact of a mental health promotion campaign (except perhaps where valid comparison data were available from other communities where the campaign was not running).

Where objective outcome measures are not available, or even where they are, most campaigns use pre–post evaluations, and, if possible, comparisons against populations where the campaign has not been implemented. For example, Hornik *et al.* (2002) describe ten projects in Jordan, Indonesia, South America, Africa and the Philippines dealing mainly with immunisation and diarrhoea issues. The campaigns involved one or more of training of volunteers and health workers, distribution of some products (e.g., vitamin A capsules), television, radio, newspapers, posters and T-shirts. Seven projects were evaluated via before–after surveys of mothers or carers of children, two used annul surveys over two or three years and two used clinical records. Only one campaign mentioned comparison with a control area.

> ### Objective outcome measures
> The 'Don't mess with Texas' campaign is evaluated by measuring littering. The Team Nutrition project (Lefebvre, Olander and Levine 1999) promoting healthier food items in school cafeterias did a plate waste evaluation to check whether students actually consumed the healthier items that they chose.

Upstream outcome indicators

Many social marketing campaigns are limited in duration and scope, and are focused downstream. Hence, the evaluations focus on individual risk beliefs, attitudes and behaviours, even when stakeholders and intermediaries have been involved in the campaign. However, as interventions move to bring about change upstream, then other performance indicators need to be taken into account. For example, interventions aimed at increasing the value a society places on its children could be evaluated in terms of changes on the ten UNICEF criteria listed in Chapter 3, and the Act–Belong–Commit mental health promotion programme described in detail in Chapter 15 includes systemic change in the state health department as in indicator of the impact of the programme. The South African Soul City Institute project outcomes include influencing legislation in areas it deals with, such as violence against women.

A comprehensive discussion of upstream indicators is beyond this book. However, the Agita São Paulo physical activity programme in Brazil provides a good example of itemising the programme's objectives, delineating the intervention components that address each of the objectives and then listing the performance indicators relevant to an evaluation of each of the intervention components. They include such indicators as changes in physical spaces and transport that result during the campaign; the support from politicians at federal, state and local level; local government integration of the campaign; and the number of policies, statutes and laws introduced or modified that support increased physical activity (Matsudo *et al.* 2006).

Don't drink the water! Literal upstream indicators

Chemical compounds in products that humans ingest make their way into our waterways. One analysis of water in the Thames in London indicated that cocaine use was fifteen times higher in London than official estimates (Goswami and Orr 2005); an estimate from the River Po near Milan found the equivalent of 4 kg of cocaine a day flowing down that river (Hawkes 2005); and it has been implied that water samples in the United States can be used as indicators of relative medication use in different counties (Petersen 2008).

Do intentions predict behaviour?

Much formative, efficacy and even impact research involves measures of behavioural intentions rather than actual behaviours. A common query then is, 'how valid are intentions as predictors of actual behaviour?' Most of the research in this area comes from consumer behaviour studies. These have generally shown a good correlation between what people say they will do and what they actually do in terms of consumer purchases. More encouraging for social marketers are the results of a meta-analysis of forty-seven interventions relating mainly to health and injury prevention where intentions and the resultant behaviour were both measured. Although this analysis showed a lesser relationship than indicated by previous correlation studies, it confirmed that attitudes and intentions are still good predictors of subsequent behaviour (Webb and Sheeran 2006).

Reviewing a number of market research studies, Urban, Hauser and Dholakia (1987) suggest a reasonable weighting for responses on a five-point intention scale would be:

Response	Weight
Definitely will	0.7
Probably will	0.35
Might or might not	0.1
Probably won't	–
Definitely won't	–

Hence, if we presented men who used violence with information about a behaviour change counselling programme and asked how likely they would be to enter the programme within the next month (the more specific the timeframe, the more accurate the prediction), the predicted uptake – all other marketing factors in place – would be as follows:

Response	Unweighted (%)	Weight	Weighted (%)
Definitely will	15	0.7	10.5
Probably will	28	0.35	9.8
Might or might not	33	0.1	3.3
Probably won't	13	0.0	0.0
Definitely won't	11	0.0	0.0
Total definitely or probably will	43%		20%

That is, our raw data suggest that 43 per cent of these men are likely to enrol in the counselling programme in the next month. However, our weighted data suggest that around 20 per cent are probably or definitely likely to, a far more realistic assessment. Note also the key statement – *all other marketing factors in place*. That is, all these estimates assume 100 per cent awareness of the service, ease of access, availability, affordability and so on. Realistic estimates must also take these factors into account for assessing actual demand. It is likely that programme timing, location and unpredicted situational factors would all reduce the estimated impact.

Just what behaviour are we trying to predict? One of the major reasons why attitudes and intentions sometimes turn out to be poor predictors of behaviour is that we have measured the wrong behaviour. This occurs in two ways:

- first, for many behaviour changes, it is trial that we want to predict not successful adoption (i.e., trying to quit smoking versus quitting smoking: 'do you intend to try to quit in the next month?' versus 'do you intend to quit in the next month?');
- second, for many targeted messages there are intermediate steps that an individual will go through before trying or adopting the behaviour (e.g., 'do you intend to seek more information about quit smoking courses?' versus 'do you intend to quit?').

Research concepts in public health

Research methods in public health are based on the disciplines of epidemiology and biostatistics.

Epidemiology can be defined as the study of the distribution and determinants of the frequency of disease. Frequency refers to quantifying the occurrence or existence of disease. Distribution refers to how the disease is distributed in populations, for example, geographically, by age or gender, and over time. Determinants refer to identifying why the disease occurs more or less frequently in one group than another. A determinant is not necessarily a cause, but might be an enabling factor.

Epidemiology does not generally deal with identifying the cause *per se*, but with what the lawyers might call 'probable cause' (tobacco company lawyers excepted, of course). That is, if lung cancer rates are considerably higher among smokers than non-smokers, and this relationship (relative risk) holds across age, gender, national and occupational groupings, then the more confident we can be in assuming that smoking is a 'probable cause' of lung cancer.

Of course, there are many variables that we need to control for, especially where 'lifestyle' and environmental factors could interact. For example, smokers are more likely than non-smokers to use alcohol and other drugs; smokers are more likely than non-smokers to work in blue collar occupations (at least these days), and, hence, are more likely to be exposed to industrial pollutants in the workplace and even in their places of residence. It is crucial that these 'covariates' are also controlled for before coming to any conclusion about the influence of smoking on lung cancer rates.

Biostatistics covers the statistical tools used in biomedical sciences. These methods allow the determination of the significance of differences between frequency measures in different sub-populations, measures of absolute and relative risk, and measures of association between variables and outcomes.

Measures of disease frequency

Prevalence and incidence are two basic ways of describing the frequency of occurrence of disease in a population.

Prevalence: Prevalence is the proportion of the population with the disease at a certain point in time (existing cases). It is expressed as per cent, per 1,000, per 100,000, etc. Prevalence is related to the onset of a disease and recovery. For example, outbreaks of curable infectious diseases are characterised by an initial rapid rise in prevalence, followed by a decline as the disease runs its natural course through the population and diseased people recover. Because prevalence indicates neither when the persons initially got the disease nor which previously diseased persons subsequently recovered or died, it is not a good measure of the overall rate or the risk of getting the disease.

Incidence: Incidence refers to how many new cases of a disease occurred in a population during a specified interval of time. It is usually expressed as number of new cases per unit of time per fixed number of people (e.g., number of new cases of cancer per 10,000 persons in one year). Because of the restriction to 'new' cases, the population in which the incidence is measured is restricted to those who are susceptible to getting the disease during the observation period (e.g., for some infectious diseases, lifetime immunity can be established and so those who had been immunised should be excluded from the population under study). This restricted population is typically called the 'at-risk population' because they are at risk of getting the disease. For this reason, incidence is often also called 'risk', because it reflects the likelihood of a person in the population of interest getting the disease within a certain period (including one's lifetime; i.e., 'lifetime risk'). Incidence is important in allowing researchers to study the impact of harmful exposures or preventive interventions on the occurrence of disease, because it doesn't depend on the length of disease course or its fatality.

Types of study designs

Studies in epidemiological and medical/public health research are usually classified into two main categories: experimental and observational designs (Lilienfeld and Lilienfeld 1980) (see Figure 7.3). In observational studies, the investigator merely observes the existing situation. In experimental studies, the investigator intervenes by manipulating exposure and other factors, and then observes the outcome. Experimental studies are usually referred to as intervention studies.

Experimental research enables researchers to determine the causal relationship between variables. Descriptive research simply describes the population of interest

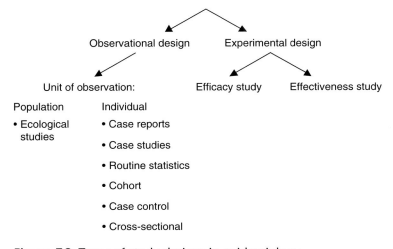

Figure 7.3 Types of study designs in epidemiology

on a number of variables, for example, attitudes and behaviours, and perhaps the correlations between these and factors such as sex and age. Descriptive research can infer, but cannot confirm, causality.

Correlation and causality: does smoking cause lung cancer?

It might be noted that smokers constitute only 28 per cent of all people, but 85 per cent of lung cancer patients. That is, if there were no causal link between smoking and lung cancer, smokers should constitute only 28 per cent of all lung cancer patients. However, there might be a third factor that causes lung cancer. For example, far more smokers than non-smokers might work in mines and other worksites where the air contains toxic irritants. Smoking may be associated with higher alcohol and junk food consumption. Hence, statistical methods such as logistic regression are used to explore all associated factors to determine whether, when all other factors are kept constant, the relationship between lung cancer and smoking still remains. However, while correlational evidence can be used to infer causality, final proof of causality depends on experimental data from the laboratory showing how the constituents of tobacco actually cause cancer.

Experimental (intervention) studies

There are two main types of experimental studies: efficacy and effectiveness. Studies of efficacy determine results under ideal conditions, whereas studies of effectiveness determine results under typical conditions. An example of an experimental study is the randomised clinical trial in which a representative sample of subjects is randomly allocated to one of several groups, each group receiving a different treatment or intervention. Measurements are made immediately following treatment or later, or they are followed in time until some event occurs. For example, a representative sample of early stage breast cancer patients are given surgical treatment and then randomised to receive chemotherapy or no chemotherapy. The patients are followed in time until death. Relative survival rates are used to assess the efficacy of the chemotherapy.

Observational studies

Observational studies can be categorised according to the unit of observation: population or individual. The most common observational studies in which the unit of observation is the population are called 'ecological' studies. In an ecological study, average rates of disease are compared with average levels of exposure to a particular agent (e.g., national heart disease rates versus national average consumption of dietary fat).

The main types of observational studies where the unit of observation is the individual are:

• *Cohort*: a representative sample of subjects is selected (the cohort) and followed in time to see if and when a certain event occurs. For example, a representative sample of coal miners may be followed for the development of respiratory disease. Cohort studies are used to obtain information on incidence rates.

- *Case control*: a representative sample of subjects with a particular characteristic (the cases), and a representative sample of subjects without the characteristic (the controls), are obtained and then information is compared concerning antecedent factors in the two groups. For example, a sample of spine injured motor vehicle casualties and a sample of non-spine injured motor vehicle casualties are obtained. Details of the accident (e.g., wearing seat belt) are then compared.
- *Cross-sectional*: measurements or observations are made on a random sample of subjects selected from a defined population at a given point in time. Cross-sectional surveys are used to obtain information on the prevalence of specified characteristics in the population and sub-populations.

Odds ratios and logistic regression

A common way to compare disease rates in different populations and sub-populations is to calculate 'risk rates' or 'risk ratios', for example, the risk rates among smokers and non-smokers of contracting lung cancer, or the risk rates among men versus women of contracting colorectal cancer.

Regardless of the type of epidemiological study, the data can be presented in 2 × 2 contingency tables of disease status versus exposure status:

		Disease status	
		Diseased	Not diseased
Exposure	Exposed	a	b
Status	Not exposed	c	d

The proportion a/(a+b) estimates the risk of disease among the exposed, while c/(c+d) estimates the risk of disease among the unexposed. The ratio of these is the *relative risk* (RR) of one group relative to the other:

RR = a(c+d)/b(a+b).

Consider the results of a cohort study on lung cancer outcomes and smoking status:

		Disease status		
		Lung cancer	No lung cancer	Total
Exposure	Smokers	28	209	237
Status	Non-smokers	7	458	465
		35	667	702

The risk of lung cancer among smokers would be 28/237 = 0.118

The risk among non-smokers would be 7/465 = 0.015.

The RR for smokers versus non-smokers is the ratio of these two risks:

$$RR = 0.118/0.015 = 7.9$$

That is, smokers are approximately eight times more likely than non-smokers to contract lung cancer.

If the above table represented the results of a case control study, it would be inappropriate to calculate relative risk because the number of cases would be determined by the investigator, and not necessarily represent prevalence in the total population. In this case, odds ratios are another way of comparing prevalence or incidence scores, where the point of reference is exposure status rather than disease status. In the example above, the odds of being a smoker (i.e., exposed) in those with lung cancer is a/c(28/7 = 4.0), and the odds of being a smoker in those without lung cancer is b/d(209/458 = 0.46). The *odds ratio* (OR) for being a smoker in those with lung cancer (the diseased group) compared with those without, is the ratio of these two odds, and therefore estimated by:

$$OR = ad/bc = 28 \times 458/7 \times 209 = 8.7$$

That is, lung cancer sufferers are 8.7 times more likely to be smokers than non-smokers.

Where the frequency of events is rare, that is, the number of diseased relative to the total number of cases is very small (as in the above example), then ORs are similar to – and often used as – estimates of relative risk.

The OR describes the relative likelihood of different groups having a disease (in a cohort study), being a substance user or excess user (in a cross-sectional survey), or being exposed to some risk factor (in a case control study), or achieving some impact threshold in an intervention trial. The reason why OR is popular in epidemiology is that it may be estimated from many different study designs. Odds ratios can be calculated for any studies, whereas RR ratios are not appropriate for case control studies and other studies where the sample sizes of the exposed/non-exposed or diseased/non-diseased are chosen by the investigator rather than occurring by chance in the population. Hence, most studies report ORs, especially case control and cross-sectional studies. Cohort and randomised control trials more commonly report relative risk and risk differences, respectively.

The above examples illustrate 'crude' ORs, where possible confounders are not taken into account (i.e., age, gender, etc.). Regression is the use of one variable (the independent or explanatory variable) to predict the value of an associated variable (the dependent or response variable). Logistic regression allows the prediction of the dependent variable holding a number of other variables constant, with the strength of the association expressed as an OR for binary comparisons (e.g., smoker versus non-smoker, sufficiently physically active to obtain health benefits versus insufficiently active, agrees with a questionnaire item versus disagrees with the statement, drinks six or more standard drinks a day versus drinks five or less standard drinks a day, and so on). Hence, this is another reason why ORs are so popular and why one of the most common data analyses in the public health literature is the reporting of ORs via logistic regression.

With regard to significance, ORs (and RRs) are usually presented with their 95 per cent confidence intervals (CIs). (A CI is a range of values within which one is confident that the true value of the measure of association is contained). Confidence intervals that do not include 1.0 represent a significance level of 0.05; that is, less than 1 in 20 that the result is due to chance.

Using logistic regression and odds ratios to identify predictors of marijuana use

Amonini (2001) administered a comprehensive questionnaire to approximately 600 14–17-year-olds. The questionnaire measured marijuana, alcohol and tobacco use, and included a large number of items measuring factors such as personality dispositions, parental relationships and parental supervision, and, for each substance, perceived morality of use, perceived social benefits, harmful health effects and perception of the laws governing use.

Table 7.2 shows the results for the personality measures for marijuana use versus non-use. The 'single factor model' shows the crude or unadjusted ORs for each variable regardless of its correlation or relationship with any other variable. These show that young people with a high tolerance of deviance are almost five times (4.99) more likely to be marijuana users than non-users, and those with a medium tolerance of deviance are over twice as likely (2.21) compared with those with a low tolerance of deviance (1.00). Similarly, greater risk seeking disposition and greater psychological reactance are related to increased marijuana use. On the other hand, a greater risk aversive disposition and greater religiosity are associated with *decreased* marijuana use: for example, those with high religiosity are one-tenth as likely (0.11), and those with medium religiosity are approximately half as likely (0.49) to be marijuana users as those with low religiosity.

As there may be sex and age differences with regard to these personality variables and marijuana use, the next column calculates ORs with sex and age held constant. The ORs remain essentially unchanged in this 'sex and age held constant' model. The third column calculates ORs controlling for all factors. That is, the results represent the extent to which each variable is independently related to marijuana use. This model shows that all the personality variables except risk aversive disposition remain significant predictors of marijuana use, at least at the 'high' level: young people with

Table 7.2 Personality measures for marijuana use versus non-use

Individual factors	Logistic regression ORs for current marijuana use (base: non-use)				
	Single factor model (SFM)	SFM with sex and age	All construct variables	P value	Confidence interval
Demographic					
Sex					
Male	1.00	1.00	1.00		
Female	0.62	0.61	0.61	0.06	0.36–1.02
Age					
14 years	1.00	1.00	1.00		
15 years	1.59	1.66	1.66	0.17	0.80–3.47
16 years	2.33	2.38	2.38	0.02	1.14–4.97
17 years	1.75	1.72	1.72	0.15	0.81–3.63
Personality					
Tolerance of deviance					
Low	1.00	1.00	1.00	0.04	
Medium	2.21	2.21	1.78	0.14	0.83–3.83
High	4.99	4.59	3.01	0.01	1.28–7.09
Risk seeking Disposition					
Low	1.00	1.00	1.00	0.00	
Medium	3.83	3.66	2.98	0.03	1.08–8.23
High	10.87	11.23	8.16	0.00	2.67–24.93
Risk aversive Disposition					
Low	1.00	1.00	1.00	0.20	
Medium	0.76	0.80	0.67	0.28	0.32–1.40
High	0.21	0.22	0.49	0.08	0.22–1.08
Psychological reactance					
Low	1.00	1.00	1.00	0.01	
Medium	3.85	3.63	2.33	0.05	0.99–5.53
High	7.14	6.71	6.59	0.00	2.02–21.53
Religiosity					
Low	1.00	1.00	1.00	0.00	
Medium	0.49	0.55	0.49	0.04	0.25–0.96
High	0.11	0.11	0.09	0.00	0.03–0.26

Amonini (2001).

a high tolerance of deviance are three times (3.01; CI 1.28–7.09) more likely to be marijuana users than non-users; those with a high risk seeking disposition are eight times more likely (8.16; CI 2.67–24.93), and those with medium risk seeking disposition nearly three times more likely; those with high reactance are 6.59 times more likely (CI 2.02–21.53); and those with high religiosity are one-tenth as likely (0.09; CI 0.03–0.26) to be marijuana users as those with low religiosity.

Research in ethnic and Indigenous communities

A number of developed countries have substantial Indigenous (or 'First Nation') populations, often considerably disadvantaged relative to the dominant ethnic group. Other countries have substantial proportions of non-Indigenous ethnic groups that may or may not have particular needs (for example, African-Americans and Hispanics in the United States, North African populations in France, the Netherlands and Italy, African, Indian and Caribbean populations in the United Kingdom, and Roma and Travellers throughout Europe and Ireland). New Zealand has a substantial Indigenous Maori population as well as a substantial Pacific Islander population. Research in minority cultural groups is therefore an issue in many countries.

From our point of view, when considering an intervention, research is necessary to first determine whether sufficient differences exist between cultural groups with regard to the basic issue (e.g., understandings of diabetes and its implications), and, if so, to inform the tailoring of the intervention for different groups. In Chapter 10 we discuss this issue with regard to segmenting by cultural group and the necessity for cultural tailoring of programmes. Following the marketing philosophy of a consumer orientation, it makes sense to do basic descriptive or phenomenological research on all cultural groups of interest anyway. Such basic understandings would provide an initial indication of the need for differentiation in intervention development, delivery and evaluation. For example, before initiating the Heartline Bali FM community radio project in Indonesia, substantial participatory research was undertaken with villagers. This included interviews with key informants, informal discussions with teenagers and group discussion with poorer families, field observations of physical features and social interaction patterns, as well as obtaining statistical information such as health services used and other population data (Pepall, Earnest and James 2006). We consider that valid cultural research can take place only in close collaboration with researchers or key individuals from the culture under study.

Researching Indigenous communities in any country presents special challenges to non-Indigenous people, especially those with an emphasis on hypothetico-deductive methodological approaches (as distinct from those with more of a phenomenological approach). Concepts of manners, interpersonal styles, use of language and the importance attached to clock time are vastly different to our dominant Western perspective, leading not only to unreliable and invalid research data, but to misunderstandings on a grand scale between communities and politicians and bureaucrats. Donovan and Spark (1997) provide a discussion of many of these issues as they pertain to survey research in Australian Indigenous communities (see box).

Guidelines for survey research in traditional Indigenous communities

Donovan and Spark (1997) suggest a number of issues to be aware of when conducting survey research in traditional Indigenous communities. These include:

- direct questioning is inconsistent with traditional culture;
- information gathering is an exchange process in Indigenous culture;
- the importance of the concept of privacy;
- English is the second, third or even fourth language for many people in remote communities;
- concepts of numeracy, intensity and specificity need special consideration;
- the concept of time is viewed very differently;
- interpersonal interaction styles are very different from European ways;
- there is a need for interaction with the community both before and after the research phase;
- community composition and situation often precludes standard evaluation techniques.

One of the implications from Donovan and Spark (1997) is that where questionnaires can be used, they not only need to take into account the above guidelines from the point of view of the respondent, but should also be mindful that the interviewer is likely to be an Indigenous person for whom English is a second or third language. Hence, questionnaires need to be clearly set out, easy to follow and be jargon free. They recommend visual illustrations wherever possible to facilitate communication. Figures 7.4(a) and 7.4(b) show visuals used by Spark (1999) in assessing health needs in remote communities.

Most significant change technique: an alternative or additional methodology for community research

A common intervention research methodology in whole community settings (including schools, worksites, towns, hospitals, etc.) is the random assignment of communities to conditions and the use of structured questionnaires to evaluate effects. This requires stable populations, relatively objective and reliable ways to sample units in the population and an acceptance of, and familiarity with, interviewing via questionnaires. However, given the nature and fluctuating composition of some communities, the conditions and lack of facilities in communities in developing countries and remote and Indigenous communities in developed countries, this is often not feasible.

In these cases the most significant change (MSC) technique (Davies and Dart 2005) is appropriate and receiving much attention in developing countries. According to Davies and Dart (2005):

40. How much does eating TOO MUCH FATTY FOOD like take-away pies, chips and deep fried chicken, cause HEART TROUBLES? (Tick one circle or dot)

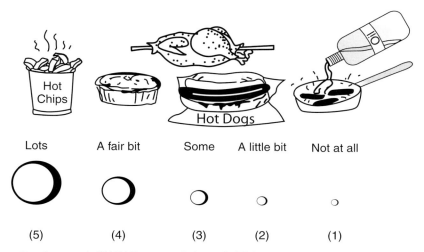

Lots	A fair bit	Some	A little bit	Not at all
(5)	(4)	(3)	(2)	(1)

41. Does eating too much SUGAR cause diabetes? (Tick one circle or dot)

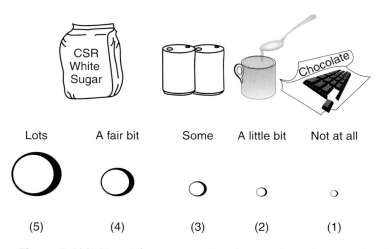

Lots	A fair bit	Some	A little bit	Not at all
(5)	(4)	(3)	(2)	(1)

Figure 7.4(a) Pictorial representations in questionnaires to aid understanding – food types

the MSC technique is a form of participatory monitoring and evaluation. It is participatory because many project stakeholders are involved both in deciding the sorts of change to be recorded and in analysing the data. It is a form of monitoring because it occurs throughout the programme cycle and provides information to help people manage the programme. It contributes to evaluation because it provides data on impact and outcomes that can be used to help assess the performance of the programme as a whole.

Essentially, the process involves the collection of stories from community members, stakeholders and field workers that relate to what they consider to have been 'significant

Read this story before Questions 8,9,10 and 11.

There is a hill and on one side there are people who are *healthy and strong* in their
bodies and on the other side are people who are *sick and weak* in their bodies.
In the middle are people who are *just okay* – not very sick, but not with good
health either. Half way down one side are people who are a fair bit strong and healthy.
Half way down the other side are people who are a bit sick.

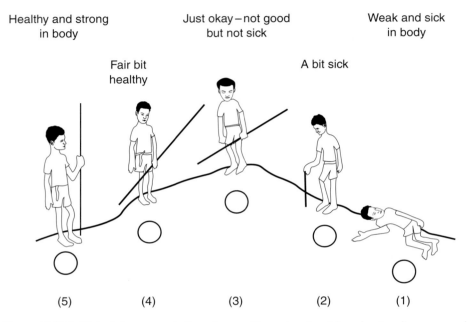

Healthy and strong in body   Just okay – not good but not sick   Weak and sick in body

Fair bit healthy   A bit sick

(5)   (4)   (3)   (2)   (1)

Figure 7.4(b) Pictorial representations in questionnaires to aid understanding – overall health

changes' in the community since the programme began. Various stories are systematically selected, read aloud in groups and the impacts discussed by the stakeholders
and programme staff. These discussions provide monitoring as well as evaluation, and
reportedly lead to greater focus on programme impact.

For example, the MSC technique was used to evaluate the impact of a three-year
(2004–7) project in Bali, Indonesia that centred on a community-oriented radio station: Heartline Bali FM (Figure 7.5). The station broadened its staff composition, and its
programming became more focused on community issues. The station aired community
service announcements and promoted community activities such as 'fun days', a village
library for children, a nutrition campaign, free medical clinics and many village religious
and cultural ceremonies (Health Communication Resources 2008). Villagers were asked
for stories about significant changes that the radio station had made in the village (see
box below). Before the campaign, very few villagers were aware of the radio station, and

Figure 7.5 Heartline Bali FM logo

those who were aware considered that it contributed little to their economy or culture. However, by the end of 2007, there was substantial awareness of the station and a general belief that the station contributed positively to the community in a number of ways.

> **'The pig project': the power of community radio in Bali**
>
> One striking story in the MSC evaluation of the Heartline Bali FM project referred to the station's 'pig project'. This project lent piglets and pig pens to disadvantaged families. When the pigs matured, the litters provided an income to the families who were also required to give two piglets back to the station, which, in turn, were lent to a further family. One family earned over 400,000 rupiah a month from their pigs in a community where most families earned less than 500,000 a month anyway. In addition to basic needs, pig recipients used the income to provide medicine for their families and to send their children to school (Health Communication Resources 2008).

Concluding comments

This chapter has covered a broad variety of topics – but that's the nature of research in social marketing. The main points to remember are these:

- qualitative research is essential for strategy development;
- good qualitative researchers are not easy to find;
- pre-testing ideas, materials, methods and measures is necessary to ensure the programme has a good chance of success;
- process and impact evaluation are crucial for answering whether and why the programme did or did not work, and for justifying further programme activities; and
- innovation in research ideas and methods is as important as innovation in programme design and implementation.

All in all, social marketers should think of research as an investment, and evaluation as a tool for improvement rather than a tool for judging.

QUESTIONS

● Discuss the differences between process and impact evaluation.

● How could you use garbage analyses to assess interventions at entertainment events?

● If you wanted to assess the differential impact of two different ads promoting alcohol moderation among college students, how would you go about it? If you exposed one ad to one group and the other ad to another group, what would you do to ensure the two groups were comparable?

FURTHER READING

Coffman, J. 2002. *Public Communication Campaign Evaluation: An Environmental Scan of Challenges, Criticisms, Practice, and Opportunities.* Cambridge, MA: Harvard Family Research Project.

Davies, R. and Dart, J. 2005. *The 'Most Significant Change' (MSC) Technique: A Guide to Its Use.* Care International, Version 1.

Hornik, R. (ed.) 2002. *Public Health Communication: Evidence for Behaviour Change.* Hillsdale, NJ: Lawrence Erlbaum.

Matsudo, S. M., Matsudo, V. K., Andrade, D. R., Araújo, T. L. and Pratt, M. 2006. Evaluation of a Physical Activity Promotion Program: The Example of São Paulo, *Evaluation and Program Planning* 29: 301–11.

Ying. L. 2009. Health Advocacy through Photovoice: A Reconsideration, *Paper presented at the annual meeting of the International Communication Association*, Sheraton New York, available at:. www.allacademic.com/meta/p15169_index.html.

8 Ethical issues in social marketing

Ethics is important in any area, but perhaps even more so in social marketing given the sensitivity of some issues in particular that social marketers are asked to address.

Commercial marketers have long been criticised for using allegedly unethical methods to target vulnerable populations, or simply using deceptive tactics against consumers in general. Marketing as an activity has been accused of being unethical in a number of ways (Murphy and Bloom 1990): creating greed and dissatisfaction; misleading because it doesn't give the full picture of a product; manipulative because it persuades people to buy things they don't need; and a waste of valuable resources that could be spent in better causes (e.g., it is said that the global Coca-Cola marketing budget could make a real difference to worldwide child poverty). Marketing is accused of focusing on selected target markets, often those that are wealthy or privileged, and neglecting others. Conversely, other marketers, such as the tobacco companies and alcohol marketers, are accused of targeting vulnerable audiences such as children, teenagers and socio-economically disadvantaged groups. Marketing is accused of being intrusive, in that television advertisements enter our homes, disrupting our leisure time, while billboards distract our attention on the road.

It has been argued that social marketers should be held to even higher ethical standards than commercial marketers because there is a greater potential for harm if social marketing practices are unethical than when commercial marketing practices are unethical (Murphy and Bloom 1990). Also, as social marketing is usually funded by governments (i.e., taxpayers), or non-profit organisations (i.e., charitable donations), the way the funding is used is a matter of public trust and should be subject to scrutiny at the highest ethical standards (Andreasen 2001).

Brenkert (2002) identified and comprehensively analysed three ethical challenges specific to social marketing:

- first, he asked who decides what social problems should be addressed and who decides whether it is a problem;
- second, he questioned the rationale that social marketers use theories and models of behaviour change more suitable to the consumer behaviour process than to solving social problems that extend beyond an individual's range; and

- third, he asked whether social marketers are acting ethically if they fail to recognise the autonomy of their target markets: their right to full participation in solving a social problem issue, rather than just having a solution marketed to them.

Brenkert called for social marketers to develop a theory of 'welfare exchange' as an alternative to the commercial market exchange; to adopt a policy of clearly explaining who has been involved in the social marketing efforts and who has paid for it; to give the target market 'some say in this process' and to use theories of behaviour change that incorporate environmental and normative perspectives as well as individual behaviour models.

People who view a social marketing campaign as unethical are likely to reject both the campaign itself and the campaign message. The result would be worse than doing nothing. Even expert members of the public, including professors of ethics, may have difficulty in separating the ethics of a social idea from the ethics of marketing the social idea (Lusch, Laczniak and Murphy 1980). This can have an adverse effect in two ways. If the social idea is seen by some as unethical, for example, gay rights, then it can reflect on the social marketer even if the marketing techniques used are ethical. Similarly, if the marketing techniques are seen as unethical, such as offering misleading or incomplete information, this can have an adverse effect on the public's response to a social idea which itself is ethical (Lusch, Laczniak and Murphy 1980). Early anti-smoking ads in Australia, for example, had to be modified because of exaggerated claims, thus providing the tobacco industry with some support for their claim that the link between smoking and health was exaggerated and 'not proven'.

Can social marketing be used to achieve unethical aims?

This question occasionally appears on the social marketing list server, usually as a warning that we have to be careful that political parties, issue organisations or even 'hate groups' might 'use' social marketing to influence people's beliefs, attitudes and behaviours with regard to achieving their own ends. However, the question suggests a view of social marketing as just a bag of techniques. From our perspective, social marketing is the application of marketing principles and tools for the common good. In simple terms, the answer to the above question is 'no' – but 'marketing' *per se*, as a set of tools and techniques, can be applied to any advocacy or persuasive task – ethical or otherwise. As we consider that social marketing is, by definition, concerned with 'ethical' goals, the primary concerns for social marketers are whether their methods are ethical and whether the relative allocation of resources is ethical.

What do we mean by 'ethics'?

The word 'ethics' is used in the broad sense to denote a moral philosophy or to refer to a system of moral or value judgements. It is the study of what people ought to do or *feel* they ought to do. When there is a legal issue our way is clearer. It's against the law to manufacture and sell illegal drugs and most would agree it's unethical to do so. But while it's legal to manufacture and sell cigarettes, not everyone would agree that it's ethical to do so. On the other hand, some would feel that while it is illegal to use cannabis, it is not a moral issue but rather one of personal choice (Amonini and Donovan 2006).

Through ethics, we attempt to come up with a system of rules based on commonly agreed values. Unfortunately, the complexity of human experience means that we can never come to an absolute agreement about what is ethical. Instead, we hold some general rules and then apply reason to each new situation. The debates over abortion and euthanasia are good examples of divergent thinking on ethical issues.

How can we tell if something's not ethical?

We know that something feels unethical when we feel a sense of shame when thinking about it. It's useful to ask yourself two questions when contemplating a potentially unethical act: (1) how would I feel if my boss, friends, peers, a journalist, or even my mother found out about it? and (2) how will I feel about it tomorrow or next year? These two questions represent the external and internal referents for what is ethical.

Deciding ethical decisions on the basis of external sources is called moral heteronomy (Benn 1988). There are two external sources of information about what is ethical: the law and cultural mores. Laws are created by society, specifically by those chosen to do so such as politicians. Laws contain sanctions if breached. Mores are also agreed upon by society, often supported by religious teachings and cultural traditions. Some mores are also laws (e.g., 'Thou shalt not kill'), but not all (e.g., 'Honour thy father and thy mother'). When you ask yourself how the people around you would regard your action, you are referring to external referents.

Deciding ethical decisions on the basis of internal moral judgements is called moral autonomy (Benn 1988). The concept of autonomy is central to ethical thought. When you ask yourself how you would feel about your action, you are making an internal reference to the self. This form of ethical reasoning is more highly prized by ethical philosophers than the external reference of moral heteronomy. For example, Kant believed that it was only by making rational and autonomous moral decisions that individuals could fulfil their greatest potential.

Ethical theories

To Aristotle (384–322 BC), a Greek philosopher, ethics was the study of virtue. Virtue was seen to be the quality that falls between two extremes or 'the golden mean'. For example, between the two extremes of cowardice and foolhardiness lies the virtue of courage (Patterson and Wilkins 1991). Ethical behaviour was seen to depend on the character of the person who performed the act. A virtuous person could perform ethical acts. To be virtuous, a person had to be of good character and had to think about their behaviour, applying reason to their choices. This is a 'non-consequential' view of ethics; that is, the act is ethical because of the nature of the person who performs it, not because of any good consequences that may follow from it. MacIntyre (1999) stated that there are two fundamental virtues: integrity and constancy. Both of these virtues set limits to how much we adapt to different situations. Integrity means that we maintain some values across all social contexts. Constancy means that we maintain values through time with 'an unwavering directedness'. Without these virtues we become compartmentalised, a 'divided self', holding many, sometimes conflicting, values that change according to the roles we are required to play.

In the eighteenth century, another non-consequentialist, Immanuel Kant (1724–1804), contributed the philosophy of the categorical imperative; that is, an act itself is ethical if through reason (logical thought) we would will that it be made a universal law, and if it emerges from a respect for humanity and from a determination to do no harm to others or to give help to others. Kant's philosophy can be summed up as the 'golden rule': 'Do unto others as you would have them do unto you'.

A British philosopher, John Stuart Mill ([1859] 1991) contributed the 'consequential' theory of utilitarianism; that is, an act is ethical if the consequences of the act are good, regardless of whether the person who performs the act is a good person (as Aristotle would have it) or whether the act was chosen for the right reasons (as Kant would require). Good consequences are those that produce the greatest happiness for the greatest number of people. Central to this theory is the egalitarian concept that everyone's happiness is equally important (Patterson and Wilkins 1991). However, this theory has been criticised for promoting a simplistic view where 'the end justifies the means' or where the welfare of some members of society is sacrificed for the benefit of the majority.

W. D. Ross ([1930] 1963), advocated an 'ethic of *prima facie* duties': fidelity, gratitude, beneficence, non-malfeasance and self-improvement. Later, John Rawls' *Theory of Justice* (1971) asserted two principles of justice: maximum freedom for all; and the distribution of wealth so that the poorest members of society would be as well-off as possible or at least not further disadvantaged. They offer alternatives to classical utilitarianism that have been absorbed to some extent into our current accepted way of thinking about ethical behaviour.

Libertarianism derives from the philosophy of John Locke ([1690] 1961), who recognised that all people have negative rights (e.g., the freedom to be free from outside interference), as well as positive rights (e.g., the right to certain benefits supplied by others). A proponent of libertarianism, Robert Nozick (1974; Lacey 2001), argued that we have a right to a say in the important decisions that affect our lives. Individuals are entitled to make informed decisions about their lives without unnecessary interference. This entitlement to negative rights such as life, liberty and property (in the broadest sense) requires that we exercise our rights only as far as they do not infringe the rights of others. This concept is particularly relevant to social marketers, who may be asked from the libertarian point of view to justify their wish to interfere in the decisions that people make, such as whether to smoke, to ride a motorcycle without a helmet or to practise unsafe sex.

Ethical organisations

It can be argued that organisations as well as individuals have moral responsibilities, and that problems arise when the organisational values are inconsistent with external morality or with the individual's own values (Tsahuridu and McKenna 2000). The individual might abdicate personal ethical responsibility, seeing it as the duty of the organisation to make the appropriate ethical decisions. The extreme example of this is the action of soldiers during wartime: 'I was only obeying orders.' In such a case, the individual is acting out of moral *anomie*, the absence of moral reasoning.

Nike and non-consequentialist thinking

Two main schools of ethical thought are labelled consequentialist and non-consequentialist. For the consequentialist school, the ethical choice produces favourable consequences. This includes the theory of utilitarianism that ethical choices produce the greatest good for the greatest number of people. This would be the argument that social marketers would use to defend their use of market segmentation, focusing limited resources where they are most likely to have the greatest good effect, even though this might mean that some needy segments, such as hard-core addicts, are neglected. The non-consequentialist school of thought holds that ethical behaviour is not determined by results, that some behaviours are intrinsically good. The social marketer who argues that hard-core addicts should be included in the target market may be arguing that this is the ethical course of action, even if it is not cost-effective. Social marketers with a strong commercial marketing background, for the most part appear to subscribe to the consequentialist school, whereas those with a public health or community action background may be more likely to subscribe to the non-consequentialist school.

An interesting example of non-consequentialist thought occurred in the late 1990s when students were shown a Nike ad advocating the message that girls who play sports suffer fewer negative and more positive events in their lives. The words included 'If you let me play ... I will like myself more. I will have more self-confidence. I will suffer less depression ... I will learn what it means to be strong. If you let me play sports.' The only evidence that Nike sponsored the ad was a single Nike 'swoosh' symbol. Many students at that time discounted any value in this message. Their antagonism arose from believing that Nike still used cheap labour in Third World countries. Their ethical thinking was non-consequentialist and harks back to ancient Greece: if the source is not seen as good, then anything that comes from it is tainted; only virtuous people can make virtuous decisions. As the years have passed and Nike's image has improved, students are less likely to make this judgement when shown the same ad.

Another difficult ethical question for the social marketer occurs when government organisations elect to run a social advertising campaign essentially for political capital. For example, a 'Just Say No' to drugs campaign that is not supported by a helpline is clearly not a well thought out campaign. We also know that some messages can backfire and increase feelings of rebellion in the target market. Is it ethical for the social marketer to contribute to a campaign that clearly will not be effective? Is it sufficient to voice objections? Only individuals can decide how far they are prepared to compromise their principles in the face of practical considerations such as keeping a job, and more strategic considerations like keeping a job in which they might later be able to make a valuable contribution to a social cause.

In May 2001, Professor Richard Smith resigned as professor of medical journalism at the University of Nottingham following the university's decision to accept £3.8 million from British American Tobacco (BAT). The money was designated to establish an international centre for the study of corporate responsibility. As editor of the *British Medical Journal*, Professor Smith conducted a poll of readers. He asked two questions: should the money be returned? and if not, should he resign as a professor at the university? There were 1,075 respondents and their viewpoint on the first question was fairly unequivocal: 84 per cent thought the university should return the money. There was less clear agreement on the issue of resigning: 54 per cent voted for resignation if the money wasn't returned. In his letter of resignation Professor Smith acknowledged that the readers were divided over whether it was better to dissociate himself entirely or stay in the organisation to continue arguing the case. He said he had decided to resign 'because I said I would do what the *BMJ*'s readers said I should do and because I've argued so strongly that the university shouldn't have taken this money' (Ferriman 2001).

Ethical principles

In Western society today, ethics has come to mean making rational choices between good and bad, deciding what actions can be morally justified, and, when faced with several morally justifiable choices, determining which is the most desirable (Patterson and Wilkins 1991). Downie and Calman (1994), considering ethical decisions in health care, concluded that the following four ethical principles should be used as a rule of thumb to guide decision-making:

- *the principle of non-malfeasance*: do not harm others physically or psychologically;
- *the principle of beneficence*: give help to others when they need it;
- *the principle of justice*: treat everyone fairly and equally;
- *the principle of utility*: make choices that produce the greatest good (or happiness) for the greatest number of people.

In line with libertarian ethical theory we would add a fifth consensus principle:

- *the principle of non-interference with the liberty of others*: allow everyone the freedom to exercise their fundamental rights as long as they do not infringe upon the rights of others.

The basis of all these ethical principles is the assumption that we ought to respect people as autonomous beings; that is, people with dignity, rights and equality, who can make rational decisions for themselves about what is right for them (Downie and Calman 1994; Dworkin 1988; Rawls 1971. Ethical dilemmas invariably arise when this assumption of autonomy is questioned. Social marketing ethical decisions are likely to arise in situations involving a person who is not fully autonomous, for example, when the person is unborn (when the issue is abortion), an addict (when the issue is smoking or drug abuse), or a prisoner (when the issue is voting rights).

Smith (2001) lists a number of moral principles that are particularly relevant in the context of social marketing:

- *Truth*: are we being entirely truthful? Is there some exaggeration or inaccuracy or omission?
- *Privacy*: are we invading the privacy of any group of people? Are we revealing information about people that is not appropriate?
- *Modelling*: are we inadvertently modelling anti-social or undesirable behaviours?
- *Morally offensive*: are we demonstrating or encouraging behaviour that society finds offensive?
- *Fair and balanced*: are we being fair to all groups?
- *Stereotyping*: are we inadvertently perpetuating inappropriate or harmful stereotypes?
- *Protecting children*: if our programmes are going to be seen by children, are they appropriate for their age?

Smith, however, cautions that such questions cannot be used as a simple ethical score card, assigning equal weight to each and achieving a minimum score before proceeding with a campaign. Ethical dilemmas occur when principles collide, such as the need to be truthful and the requirement to respect privacy. It is often difficult to decide whether one principle should take precedence over another.

The Road Crew Program to reduce drink-driving

The Road Crew Program is an innovative community-based strategy to reduce the number of alcohol-related car crashes in the United States (Rothschild, Mastin and Miller 2006). Adults are encouraged to ride in a luxury vehicle to a tavern (old limousines were purchased for the purpose) for an evening out and home again. Research had shown that people did not like to leave their cars and take a taxi home. By enlisting tavern contributions, it was possible to keep the cost nominal ($10 to $15) and the round trip was paid for at the beginning of the trip so that patrons didn't run out of money for the return journey. Marketing best practice is seen in the development of a product that appealed to the target market – a night out that would be more fun. The programme involved the target market throughout the design, including the formative research stage where it became apparent that patrons would take a ride home from the bar only if they had taken a ride there as well.

Another key element was the community involvement, including partnerships with private and public sectors.

The ethical issue that is raised around this programme is the failure to address the consumption of alcohol itself. In fact, it was expected by some that they would drink more if they knew they would be able to get a ride home. However, there was no indication that alcohol consumption increased and there was a projected decrease of 17 per cent in alcohol-related crashes in the first year.

Since the research was completed, two of the three communities involved have continued to support this programme, four new communities have adopted the programme and there is an intention to add three each year. This makes Road Crew a self-sustaining, relatively inexpensive intervention – although the ethical issue remains.

Smith (1999, 2001) makes the important point that any ethical decision is *contextual*. Several factors, and the ways in which they interrelate, need to be considered:

- *the actor* or provider, usually a government agency or non-profit organisation. How similar is the actor to the audience? What are the actor's motives? If there are several motives, are any in conflict? This can be true of joint ventures where one partner may be profit driven;
- *the offering* or product, the idea that is being sold, such as immunisation, blood donation, quit smoking. Ethical products are safe, accessible, and not too costly in terms of psychological as well as financial costs;
- *the act* or programme itself, how truthful it is, how fairly does it represent people;
- *the context* in which the act will occur, when and where the communication will take place. There are different ethical problems if the context is within a school or in mass media, for example;
- *the audience*, what are the demographics of the intended and any unintended audiences. Does the intended audience have the resources to understand and act on the communication? Who else may see the communication and think it has relevance to them particularly when using mass media?;
- *the consequences*, intended and unintended, for both audiences. If the consequences are beneficial, does that make the campaign ethical, even if it was less than truthful? Does the end justify the means, as the utilitarians believe?

Contextual ethicists argue that ethical decisions have to take into account the full cultural and historical background of all those involved, and that this is especially important in today's multicultural societies (Thompson 1995). This leads us to the difficult question of 'moral cultural relativism': can any act be defined as ethical if a society deems it to be? Examples would be the attempted extermination of the Jews in Nazi Germany, the use of child labour in garment factories, child soldiers in Africa and the invasion of Iraq. In the past, many behaviours, such as slavery, have been regarded as justified that are now no longer acceptable. Who is to say that some of our present day behaviours will later be judged as unethical? In the relativist mire, it is difficult to see how anyone can be sure that an act is ethical. Thompson (1995) answers this problem by appealing to the concept of 'moral autonomy', that the added difficulty presented by relativism should make each individual reflect carefully on their own beliefs and behaviours. This process of individual moral reasoning needs to include an informed understanding of the historical and cultural reasons why past societies may have adopted different ethical standards.

Laczniak and Murphy (1993) recommend that a checklist of eight questions be used to assess whether an action is ethical. The eight questions are paraphrased below:

- Is there a law against it?
- Is it contrary to accepted moral duties, including fidelity, gratitude, justice, non-malfeasance and beneficence?
- Is it contrary to any special obligations of the organisation?
- Is there any intention to cause harm?
- Is it likely that major harm will result?
- Is there a better alternative that would result in greater benefits?
- Are any rights likely to be infringed, including property rights, privacy rights and inalienable consumer rights, including the rights to information, to be heard, to have a choice and to have a remedy?
- Is anyone left worse off than before and, if so, is this person already disadvantaged?

If the answer to any of the eight questions is yes, the action should be reconsidered.

Codes of behaviour

The word ethics is also used in a specific way to describe a code of behaviour. Many professional organisations have a code of ethics (or code of conduct), such as the American Marketing Association's Statement of Ethics (see box below). Members of such organisations agree to abide by their professional code of ethics. For example, a fundamental aspect of marketing codes is the concept of a voluntary and fair exchange of mutual benefit to both parties. If the exchange is unfair, that is, if it benefits one party at the expense of the other, or if the consumer is coerced by false or misleading information, the practice is seen to be unethical. However, codes of ethical conduct can only give broad guidelines and social marketers face many choices that may not be specifically covered by any specific code.

AMA's Statement of Ethics

'PREAMBLE The American Marketing Association commits itself to promoting the highest standard of professional ethical norms and values for its members (practitioners, academics and students). Norms are established standards of conduct that are expected and maintained by society and/or professional organizations. Values represent the collective conception of what communities find desirable, important and morally proper. Values also serve as the criteria for evaluating our own personal actions and the actions of others. As marketers, we recognize that we not only serve our organizations but also act as stewards of society in creating, facilitating and executing the transactions that are part of the greater economy. In this role, marketers are expected to embrace the highest professional ethical norms and the ethical values implied by our responsibility toward multiple stakeholders (e.g., customers, employees, investors, peers, channel members, regulators and the host community).

ETHICAL NORMS As Marketers, we must:

1. Do no harm. This means consciously avoiding harmful actions or omissions by embodying high ethical standards and adhering to all applicable laws and regulations in the choices we make.
2. Foster trust in the marketing system. This means striving for good faith and fair dealing so as to contribute toward the efficacy of the exchange process as well as avoiding deception in product design, pricing, communication, and delivery of distribution.
3. Embrace ethical values. This means building relationships and enhancing consumer confidence in the integrity of marketing by affirming these core values: honesty, responsibility, fairness, respect, transparency and citizenship.'

The statement goes on to identify the key ethical values of honesty, responsibility, fairness, respect, transparency and citizenship (www.marketingpower.com/AboutAMA/Pages/Statement%20of%20Ethics.aspx).

At present there is no agreed on code of ethics for social marketing. However, Rothschild (2001) has proposed the following:

- Do more good than harm.
- Favor free choice.
- Evaluate marketing within a broad context of behaviour management [giving consideration to alternatives of education and law].
- Select tactics that are effective and efficient.
- Select marketing tactics that fit marketing philosophy [i.e., meeting the needs of consumers rather than the self-interests of the organisation].
- Evaluate the ethicality of a policy before agreeing to develop strategy.

Criticisms of social marketing

The concept of autonomy is central to ethical thinking. One criticism that is often levelled at social marketing is that it does not treat people like autonomous beings, but takes a paternalistic approach, treating them like children. Paternalism is the attitude that people need to be protected from self-inflicted harm, in the way that a father or mother protects a child (Downie and Calman 1994). 'Nanny state' is another term that has come to be used with reference to government regulation and social marketing, and which people often use derogatively to refer to excessive government intervention. Knag (1997) makes a distinction between old style, authoritarian 'paternalism', which chastised the individual using laws and sanctions, and a newer 'maternalism' or 'nanny state', which smothers the individual with 'education and therapy (or propaganda and regulation)'. Knag's use of the term 'nanny state' has pejorative connotations. The implication is that social marketers tell people what they should and shouldn't do as if they were children being supervised by a nanny.

At one extreme, people may be afraid that social marketing could be used by governments as a form of brainwashing, or propaganda. But recently, the debate has been more likely to focus on why social marketing often appears to be ineffective (rather than 'frighteningly effective'; Hastings, Stead and Macintosh 2002), while delivering yet more messages from 'the Ministry of Don't Do That' (Baker 2008). Other concerns relate to the potentially high level of fear being generated by such efforts (Hastings and MacFadyen 2002; Henley 2002) and maladaptive responses to guilt and shame arousal (Brennan and Binney 2010).

The ethics of motorcycle helmet legislation

The appropriateness of government intervention has been questioned in many US state legislative debates on laws to make the wearing of motorcycle helmets compulsory. The arguments for and against are summarised below. The argument against passing the laws is primarily based on John Stuart Mills' view that individuals should be able to decide for themselves if their decision doesn't affect others:

- wearing or not wearing a motorcycle helmet only affects the motorcyclist;
- helmet laws infringe the individual's constitutional right to decide a matter of personal safety that does not concern others;
- it's up to the individual to decide – even individuals who will decide to wear one should not be told they have to.

The argument for passing the laws is based primarily on the paternalistic view that the government should act to protect its citizens:

- the government has a duty to keep its citizens in good health and able to support themselves independently;
- the evidence is overwhelming that motorcycle helmets reduce injury and death from accidents;
- the decision to wear a helmet doesn't just affect the individual – in the event of injury, a carer might be impacted; in the event of death, there will be a psychological cost to the loved ones left behind;
- there is a substantial cost to society, both direct (e.g., health costs) and indirect (e.g., lost earnings).

The outcome: many of the laws that were passed in the United States to make wearing a motorcycle helmet compulsory have since been repealed following challenges to the constitutional argument that they infringe personal liberties. However, recognising that the state does have a duty to protect the vulnerable, many of those states have kept the requirement for young people (under 21) (Jones and Bayer 2007).

One argument often quoted to justify interference by the state is that the economic costs of allowing unsafe and unhealthy behaviours are borne by the community. It has been estimated in the United States that medical costs relating to diabetes (which is associated directly with obesity) increased from $44 billion to $92 billion in five years (Yach, Stuckler and Brownell 2006). The economic argument can be useful for persuading governments to invest in prevention, but is not sufficient as a fundamental justification for interference. If we say that we want people to eat more healthily because their health costs will be burdensome to the community, we imply that we would not ask them to do so if their health costs were not burdensome, even if people were dying prematurely as a result.

The studies relating to economic costs of obesity have not been as extensive as those relating to the economic costs of tobacco (Yach, Stuckler and Brownell 2006), where some have argued that prematurely dying of smoking-related diseases is less costly to the state than the costs incurred in living to old age (Barendregt, Bonneux and van der Mass 1997). This conclusion has been disputed (Rasmussen *et al.* 2004), but even if true, would not provide sufficient justification to cease tobacco control efforts. Similarly, we believe people would expect social marketing efforts relating to nutrition and physical activity to continue even if an economic analysis showed that people dying prematurely from obesity-related illnesses were costing the state less overall in health care costs than people living an additional twenty years.

Some degree of paternalism by the state is often seen as necessary and desirable because people are not equally self-reliant in every circumstance. For example, in some countries the government requires credit card companies to print interest rates on statements so that consumers are properly informed, some require people to provide for their own retirement and many require children to be vaccinated (Mead 1998). These examples of paternalism are acceptable in part because they apply to *all* members of society. The criticism of paternalistic social marketing is that it is often paternalistic towards a selected group of people, such as smokers or those considered unable to make competent decisions. Being selected out this way can create a backlash resulting in counter-productive responses so that an intervention could end up doing more harm than good.

'The government has a duty to tackle this issue which affects us all so much ...'

The former UK Home Secretary, Jacquie Smith, was quoted as saying this when the government brought in mandatory regulations to require supermarkets and licensed premises to display posters warning of health risks associated with consuming alcohol, and specifically warning women of the danger of consuming alcohol in pregnancy. This was part of a strategy to counter the problem of binge drinking and alcohol-related crime, claimed to be costing up to £13 billion a year. Inevitably, however, the strategy has been linked to accusations of the government running a 'nanny state' (Whitehead 2009).

The social determinants of health (Marmot and Wilkinson 1999) are sufficiently well understood to justify government regulation in order to reduce inequalities in areas such as housing, education and access to health services. A survey of opinion in the United Kingdom in 2004 by the King's Fund, an independent think tank, found that the public generally supported government initiatives to encourage healthier school meals, ensure cheaper fruit and vegetables, pass laws to limit salt, fat and sugar in foods, stop advertising of junk foods to children and regulate nutrition labels on food (King's Fund 2004). The UK's National Social Marketing Centre has made recommendations for social marketing strategies to improve public health, and the government has responded by making public health, especially the obesity problem, a central issue for government initiatives in the context of offering a 'helping hand' approach (Triggle 2006).

Health promoters argue that many of the behaviours they wish to change are not entirely voluntary. For example, it is argued that an individual's choices about eating fast food, consuming sweetened soft drinks and living sedentary lives have already been partly determined by commercial efforts. Thus, they argue that social marketing efforts are intended to level the playing field – educate, inform and restore true personal autonomy to people, enabling them to make rational choices (Smith 1992). For example, Kline's (2005) media education programme in Canada, with a component of 'media risk reduction', successfully educated young consumers (elementary school children) with strategies for 'tuning out' by asking them to come up with a plan for what they would do if they 'turned off TV, video games and PCs for a whole week?' The 'tune-out challenge' resulted in a reduction of media exposure (80 per cent) displaced into active leisure pursuits. A critical aspect of this intervention was the contract drawn up in advance, with the children setting their own goals and strategies (Kline 2005). In this view, the state is justified in trying to level the playing field, by using social marketing to offer information and alternative, healthier choices that can be freely accepted or rejected (Rothschild 1999).

Wikler (1978) considered the case for more punitive government intervention in the obesity debate by weighing the pros and cons of an interesting strategy: the introduction of a 'fat tax' that would require citizens to be weighed and, if found to be overweight, require them to pay a surcharge. He concluded that this level of state interference would not be justified because there are other ways to appeal to the risk taker's autonomy, through education and therapeutic efforts. Governments can use social marketing as one of these better alternatives to punitive sanctions.

A real concern is that when people are treated like children, they become like children, retaining their desires and appetites but abdicating responsibility for their individual choices to the state (Knag 1997). An example would be smokers who declare that they will continue to smoke until the government bans smoking (Brown 2001). Rothschild (1999) described marketing's role as providing a middle point between libertarianism and paternalism, offering free choice and incentives to behave in ways that benefit the common good. Joffe and Mindell (2004) advocate an alternative to the nanny state, the notion of a 'canny state', with 'less reliance on telling people what to do and more emphasis on making healthy choices easier'.

How much should people be told?

Communicating the risks of alcohol consumption during pregnancy is complicated because it is not certain that there are any risks at very low levels of consumption, nor is there any certainty about the level of consumption where the unborn child is certainly at risk. The UK's Department of Health changed its recommendation in 2007 from allowing a possible one to two units of alcohol once or twice a week to a revised guideline recommending total abstinence (Gavaghan 2009). In Australia, similarly, the National Health and Medical Research Council issued simplified guidelines in 2009 and now recommends that for women who are pregnant, planning a pregnancy or breastfeeding 'not drinking is the safest option' (NH&MRC 2009). Yet, as Gavaghan (2009) argues, this 'medical paternalism' assumes that women are unable to process the complicated scientific evidence themselves and need to have it simplified for them, even though this simplification (to an abstinence recommendation) requires a lifestyle change for many that may not be necessary or easy.

Moral imperialism

Another criticism of social marketing on a more global scale is that of 'moral imperialism' (Brenkert 2001). The criticism is that social marketing promotes the paternalistic attitude of Western society towards other cultures, particularly those in developing countries. We (in the West) see issues such as birth control and safe sex to prevent the spread of AIDS as being in the interest of the developing country. However, many health and social issues are culturally sensitive (e.g., female circumcision and women's rights in Muslim countries) and many issues are resisted on the basis of culture and religion (e.g., advocating the use of condoms in a South American country with a strong Catholic tradition) (Brenkert 2002). Social marketers have to be mindful that everything they do involves imposing values on people who may not share those values and who may have good reason for not wanting to share them.

Brenkert (2001) analysed the special ethical problems faced by international social marketers. Some of the problems identified by Brenkert are that they may not be citizens of the country in which the project takes place, and may not hold the same cultural values. They may also have more power and resources than the people to whom the social marketing effort is directed. Brenkert concluded that social marketers should recognise that not all apparently harmful values should be challenged or can feasibly be changed. Further, inherent in the use of persuasion as a means to the social marketing end is the responsibility to ensure that non-compliance must be a real option for those who are being persuaded. People must be informed what behaviour change is being attempted and why, and should have reason to trust the people who are attempting to effect the change (Brenkert 2001, 2002).

Who determines what is the social good?

As discussed in Chapter 1, we propose that social marketers use the UN Universal Declaration of Human Rights as the fundamental reference when determining what issues represent the social good. As an external ethical referent, this declaration has been debated and agreed by many to reflect the most highly regarded, basic values of our society. It provides a benchmark against which finer ethical questions can be measured. It enshrines rights of freedom, equality, privacy and education, all of which are fundamental concepts in social marketing.

The thirty Articles can be read in full at the Office of the High Commissioner for Human Rights website: www.unhchr.ch/udhr. We list some of the most relevant Articles below:

Article 1: All human beings are born free and equal in dignity and rights. They are endowed with reason and conscience and should act towards one another in a spirit of brotherhood [that is, the right to autonomy].
Article 2: These rights apply to everyone. No distinction shall be made on any basis.
Article 3: Life, liberty and security of person.
Article 7: Equal before the law and entitled to protection against discrimination.
Article 11: Presumed innocent until proved guilty according to law in a public trial …
Article 12: No one shall be subjected to arbitrary interference with his privacy, family, home or correspondence, nor to attacks upon his honour and reputation …
Article 18: Everyone has the right to freedom of thought, conscience and religion …
Article 19: Everyone has the right to freedom of opinion and expression …
Article 21.2: Everyone has the right to equal access to public service in his country.
Article 21.3: The will of the people shall be the basis of authority of government …
Article 26.1: Everyone has the right to education …

Criticism of power imbalances in social marketing

Social marketing has been criticised for the power differential that often exists between the government or organisation conducting the campaign and the often vulnerable populations who are the intended audience (Brenkert 2002). The group with the most financial power or strongest political support is likely to be able to impose its values on groups with fewer resources. At the same time, stronger groups are more able to resist political or government power. For example, in 1986, the Singapore government initiated a campaign to encourage graduate mothers to have more children. The purpose was to increase the population and to produce a more intelligent populace. It created controversy and was resisted by the educated people at whom it was directed (Teo 1992).

One of the major issues facing government departments is determining the priority needs of numerous and diverse stakeholders. In the context of road users, for example, it may be difficult to assign limited resources to groups such as pedestrians and cyclists, even when there are major environmental and health benefits to be gained, when the majority of road users are private and commercial drivers.

One way in which an imbalance of power becomes potentially unethical is when alliances are formed between powerful corporations and non-profit organisations and causes. Corporations are increasingly choosing to spend money on cause-related marketing, rather than giving donations to charitable organisations. The growth is attributed to the perception that consumers prefer to spend their money on products linked to good causes (Wymer and Sargeant 2006). Organisations see the benefits of having some control over how the money is spent and how much publicity is received for the donation. However, a difficulty may arise when the commercial partner's interests appear to be inconsistent with those of the social partner. For example, a Hong Kong charity, Caritas Integrated Service for Young People, was criticised for accepting money from the Tobacco Institute of Hong Kong for the purpose of running twenty anti-smoking programmes targeted at young people (Kwok 2000). Similarly, a US campaign to combat domestic violence and offer support to abused women was funded by the Philip Morris family of companies (Forbes 2000).

Some people have said that the tobacco industry has no role to play in preventive health care. The University of Alberta turned down an offer of $500,000 from a tobacco manufacturer and the University of British Columbia, like many other universities around the world, adopted a policy of refusing all tobacco company sponsorship (Sibbald 2000). On the other hand, the universities of Toronto, McGill and Calgary have all accepted funding from Imasco Ltd, which owns Imperial Tobacco. The University of Calgary used the money to help establish a Faculty of Nursing Learning Centre (Sibbald 2000). As mentioned earlier, Nottingham University accepted £3.8 million in 2002 from BAT to fund a professorial appointment in the field of corporate social responsibility. The website for Nottingham University's International Centre for Corporate Social Responsibility contains a 'Statement on Funding' (2009) that clearly states that 'the endowment from BAT is accompanied by a memorandum of understanding that explicitly recognises and confirms our independence and academic freedom'. At the time Nottingham University accepted this grant, the view of tobacco control advocates was that 'a chair in corporate responsibility, funded by tobacco money, can only collapse under the weight of its own shame' (Chapman and Shatenstein 2001). However, the grant led to the establishment of a centre that appears to be thriving seven years later with six academic staff, a postgraduate student programme and contributions to teaching ethics and governance in the university's MBA programme. A utilitarian ethicist would say that the end justifies the means and might even ask the question: is it ethical *not* to accept this money and run these valuable programmes? Our view is that if the primary aim of the tobacco marketer's donation is to promote corporate or brand awareness, or improve the image of the tobacco company, then it is unethical to accept the funds as it would contribute to the promotion of tobacco, and the ultimate end therefore would be harmful.

Before making an ethical decision, it is always worth considering all the choices. In the above examples, there appear to be only two choices: take the money and run the prevention programme or refuse the money and don't run the programme. However, a third possibility is to obtain the money to run the programme from a different source.

Social alliances can be a very successful strategy for both partners. However, an unfortunate consequence of the trend towards partnerships is discussed by Andreasen and Drumwright (2001). Causes that are perceived as attractive, such as breast cancer, receive greater support and exposure, whereas unattractive causes, such as AIDS, receive less support and exposure. They explain that breast cancer is seen as attractive because it affects a large number of people, is unpredictable, is not associated with undesirable behaviours and is not necessarily fatal, while AIDS is unattractive because it is associated with drug use and male homosexuality. Even within the cause of breast cancer, there are more partners keen to be associated with the more attractive activities of research than with the more mundane aspects such as providing transport to screening for disadvantaged groups. Andreasen and Drumwright (2001) caution that social alliances can be driven by a 'market mentality', where causes are supported because they are appealing, or not unappealing, in preference to causes that have a greater need of support but are less appealing. This focus on popular versus unpopular causes is not confined to corporate alliances; governments too are inclined to allocate health funds to areas seen to be (or assumed to be) popular with voters and to neglect more worthy areas that are not seen to be popular with voters (an Australian health minister was alleged to have said that he couldn't persuade his cabinet colleagues to support prostate screening because 'it's not sexy' – meaning 'not popular' with the masses).

Criticism of unintended consequences

Social marketers need to consider the possible unintended consequences of their actions. One unintended consequence is the risk of increasing 'victim blaming'. Victim blaming is the tendency to attribute people's illnesses, injuries, unemployment or other disadvantaged states to deficiencies under their personal control (i.e., 'lazy', 'lacking in self-control', 'stupid', etc.) (Schwartz *et al.* 2003). Victim blaming occurs in a variety of contexts such as obesity (O'Dea 2005; Schwartz *et al.* 2003), heart disease (Raphael 2002; Wheatley 2005), injury prevention (Bensberg and Kennedy 2002) and AIDS (Green 2003). Raphael (2003) argued that the downstream approach of focusing on the individual's need to change their lifestyle (diet, activity, etc.) draws media and the public's attention away from what we know about the contribution of social determinants of health to population health outcomes. (See Raphael 2002 website for more discussion about how 'social justice is good for our hearts'.)

It is important to address the possibility that a social marketing message may increase risk by normalising behaviours that would not be advocated otherwise. For example,

Catholic clergy are concerned that AIDS prevention campaigns in Africa advocating condom use may be inadvertently conveying the message that promiscuous sex is acceptable. Similar concerns are voiced that harm reduction strategies such as needle exchange schemes and provision of injecting rooms may 'send the wrong message' that drug use is OK (MacCoun 1998).

Interesting illustrations come from the field of edutainment. As mentioned in Chapter 5, it was thought that the US sitcom *All in the Family* would promote tolerance through the satirical depiction of the bigoted character of Archie Bunker. Instead, it appeared that viewers who were already prejudiced identified with Archie Bunker and their prejudices were reinforced (Singhal and Rogers 2004). Similarly, the Indian government produced a soap opera *Hum Log* ('We People') intended to improve the status of women. One of the characters, Bhagwanti, was intended to be seen as a negative role model, demonstrating subservient behaviour that was rewarded with abuse. The producers intended people to see Bhagwanti as an argument for women's equality. In fact, 80 per cent of female viewers saw her as a positive role model, embodying traditional female values, and many men said they thought India needed more women like Bhagwanti (Singhal and Rogers 2004).

Another potential unintended consequence is that the message might have an adverse affect on people outside the target market. For example, is it ethical to use the threat of premature wrinkles caused by smoking to try to persuade young women to quit, when this same message could lessen the self-esteem of people who already have wrinkles (Kirby and Andreasen 2001)? We might reasonably decide on a utilitarian approach here, that the end justifies the means, because the harm to wrinkled people is outweighed by the greater good done to the young women. Similarly, it is essential to consider the effect of a campaign on people for whom it may trigger unwelcome associations. For example, a campaign targeting child abusers will inevitably trigger painful memories in children and adults who have suffered abuse. It is unethical to run such a campaign without ensuring beforehand that helplines and counsellors are aware of the likely increase in demand, and are able to resource the increased demand.

Unintended consequences

A ten-year-old boy cries in the night. His mother goes in to comfort him. He says he is crying because 'daddy's going to die of lung cancer'. Her son had seen a Quit smoking advertisement showing a boy his age attending his father's funeral where the father had died from a smoking-related illness. The son had no way to resolve the anxiety raised by the advertisement; he couldn't do the quitting himself and he couldn't make his father quit (Henley and Donovan 1999a, 1999b). By being aware of potential consequences, appropriate action can be taken to minimise the effects, such as scheduling TV advertisements in late evening, when children are less likely to see them.

Ethical social marketing research

The same ethical principles apply to research. Many of the issues researched in social marketing are highly sensitive. Surveys on domestic violence, child abuse, smoking, drug abuse, etc. could all arouse in the respondent a degree of anxiety and need for further information or help. It is standard practice in social marketing research to offer respondents appropriate helpful literature to take away with them at the end of the interview, such as a Quit pack or leaflet on cancer prevention. It is also necessary to provide participants with relevant telephone numbers and website addresses for helplines and other counselling services.

The following case study illustrates some of the numerous ethical issues that can confront the social marketer. The case study is Western Australia's Freedom from Fear campaign targeting male perpetrators of intimate partner violence (Donovan, Paterson and Francas 1999; Donovan *et al.* 2000; Henley, Donovan and Francas 2007). The main focus of this campaign was to offer male perpetrators and potential perpetrators free counselling services to help them voluntarily change their behaviour. Rather than threatening imprisonment and other legal sanctions, the campaign focused on amplifying feelings of guilt and remorse in perpetrators by emphasising the effects of their violence on children. This was a universally relevant message. Perpetrators who did not have children still responded to this message, many of them recalling their own experience of violence as children.

CASE STUDY

'Freedom from Fear' domestic violence prevention campaign

Ethical question: can we ensure that the campaign will not cause physical or psychological harm? Extensive formative research ensured that the ad messages would not adversely impact on victims and children, especially victims' children. Relevant stakeholders, including women's groups, police, counsellors and other government departments were consulted throughout the development stage. Child psychologists were used in testing the ad concepts with victims and their children. Although the ads were to be scheduled in adult time, it was still regarded as crucial that any child who saw the ad would not experience clinical stress. The concepts were also tested to ensure that children did not take away the

message that they should encourage their mother's partner to call the helpline, as this might have put children in greater danger. Other checks included assessing the extent to which the ads appeared to be an unwarranted attack on men in general, and whether the ads appeared to condone violence towards women under any circumstances.

Confidentiality was a major issue; many of the callers to the helpline were admitting a criminal act. Anonymity was assured and callers were asked to give only their name when they accepted an offer to attend a counselling programme. When a referral to counselling was not possible, the helpline counsellors asked the caller to nominate an address to which they could send educational self-help booklets and audio-cassettes.

Ethical question: does the campaign give help where it's needed? There was a need to address the potential criticism that the campaign helped the perpetrator at the expense of the victim, and that these resources would be better used in providing help for victims and their children. This was done by keeping the focus on Freedom from Fear. The ultimate aim was to address the women's need to be free from the fear of violence long term by providing counselling to the perpetrator as distinct from encouraging women to seek legal sanctions such as restraining orders, which do not necessarily reduce the fear. New counselling programmes for women and children were also funded by the state government.

Ethical question: does the campaign allow those who need help the freedom to exercise their entitlements? Women and children are entitled to lives free of abuse. The campaign is contributing to their ability to claim this entitlement. The ultimate goal of the campaign is that they should be free from fear. In addition, in this non-coercive approach, the male perpetrators are being given the freedom to choose whether to seek counselling and a practical means of doing so.

Ethical question: are all parties treated equally and fairly? It would be unethical to raise hopes and motivation to change unless sufficient resources were available and accessible over a sufficient time period. This is nominally a ten-year campaign, receiving substantial funding from the state government. The resources include a helpline which is staffed by specially trained counsellors, as well as government subsidised counselling programmes. These programmes are provided in twelve locations throughout the state, six of them in regional areas. Given WA's geography, it was recognised

that access to counselling programmes would necessarily be limited in remote areas, but it was hoped to extend access in later phases of the campaign. Meanwhile, self-help materials could be sent to any location. Access to programmes was provided in non-working hours, and the helpline was staffed both day and night.

It was decided that all materials and programmes would be provided free to ensure that no financial barrier existed, or could be rationalised as existing, at any income level. Again, the focus was on the victim; it was important that victims of low income perpetrators would not be disadvantaged.

Ethical question: will the choices made produce the greatest good for the greatest number of people? By January 2005 the campaign had received over 21,000 calls, almost 13,000 of which were from the target group. Of these, 8,200 men identified themselves as perpetrators and 3,800 voluntarily entered counselling. Self-report evaluation instruments indicate that men who complete the programme say they are less likely to use physical violence and more likely to accept that they, and not their partners or their children, are responsible for the violence (Cant *et al.* 2002).

Initial estimates are that it costs about A\$2,500–\$3,000 per referral to the completion of the counselling programme. The utilitarian view is that this compares favourably with the cost, approximately A\$50,000, of treating one victim of domestic violence, including the costs of police, medical, courts, welfare and potential income loss. There is also the increased freedom from fear experienced by hundreds of women and children whose partners voluntarily sought and completed the counselling programme.

Ethical question: is the autonomy of the target market recognised? This campaign holds that many male perpetrators are fully autonomous, responsible for their actions, and able to choose to change their behaviour voluntarily. The campaign acknowledges that the perpetrator who genuinely wishes to change his behaviour has a right to treatment and to be treated with dignity in this treatment.

First do no harm: ethical issues in social advertising

In a classic illustration of why advertising creatives should not be allowed to dictate strategy and advertising content in sensitive areas, the UNIFEM-led White Ribbon Day 2006 campaign in Australia followed few of the above ethical guidelines, and particularly ignored 'first do no harm'. The worldwide White Ribbon Campaign encourages men to wear a white ribbon on 25 November to show their support for ending violence against women. In this case the Saatchi & Saatchi ad agency developed a TV community service announcement that depicted a man supposedly doing various self-harm acts for his daughter, including stepping in front of a bus. Mental health and suicide groups pleaded with the organisers to withdraw the ad, and domestic violence groups criticised the use of violence in a campaign against violence. The White Ribbon Day group ignored all such requests and rejected all criticisms. They had clearly not tested the ad against any relevant target audiences for unintended effects. This was an appalling case of ignoring ethical requirements in this area (Donovan *et al.* 2008, 2009).

Concluding comments

Social marketers need to ensure the highest ethical standards in promoting social causes. There is great potential for doing harm if social marketing practices are unethical. Ethical practice can be achieved by asking a few simple questions before proceeding with a campaign, and keeping them in mind throughout the life of the campaign. The questions are designed to alert marketers to issues relating to basic, shared ideas about what is held to be right, fair and just in our society. These questions refer to the principles of non-malfeasance (doing no harm), beneficence (doing good), justice (fair and equal treatment) and utility (providing the greatest good to the greatest number). Social marketing campaigns that fail to recognise the autonomy of a target market are justly criticised for being paternalistic. Fundamental to all ethical questions is the assumption that all people deserve to be treated as autonomous beings.

QUESTIONS

● Given that smoking rates are higher among lower socio-economic and lesser educated groups, what are the ethical issues involved in (a) charging higher medical insurance rates for smokers and (b) doctors refusing to provide medical services to smokers?

● What are some ethical issues involved in doing research with children who might have been physically or sexually abused?

● Should university researchers accept money from pharmaceutical companies to test the effectiveness of drugs? What are the arguments for and against?

FURTHER READING

Andreasen, A. 2001. *Ethics in Social Marketing.* Washington, DC: Georgetown University Press.

Brenkert, G. G. 2008. *Marketing Ethics.* New York: Wiley-Blackwell.

Donovan, R. J., Jalleh, G., Fielder, L. and Ouschan, R. 2008. When Confrontational Images may be Counter-productive: Reinforcing the Case for Pre-testing Communications in Sensitive Areas, *Health Promotion Journal of Australia* 19(2): 132–6.

Donovan, R. J., Jalleh, G., Fielder, L. and Ouschan, R. 2009. Ethical Issues in Pro-social Advertising: the Australian White Ribbon Day Campaign, *Journal of Public Affairs* 9: 5–19.

Eagle, L. 2009. *Ethics.* London: National Social Marketing Centre.

9 The competition

Recalling our new additional 4Ps presented at the end of Chapter 1, this chapter illustrates a number of objectives for changes in products and places, but with the main emphasis on product changes. We analyse the competition from three main perspectives: (1) defining the competition; (2) monitoring the competition; and (3) countering the competition. Given the importance of early childhood development for later adolescent and adult behaviours, of special interest is the 'competition for kids'. The targeting of children has gone from being virtually non-existent in the early 1950s, to specific targeting of child products, and, more recently, to an all-out drive to inculcate consumption values as the dominant cultural values. The commercialisation of schools in particular has been monitored extensively in the United States (see Annual Reports on School-House Commercialism). This monitor now includes the United Kingdom and Ireland (Molnar *et al.* 2008). Indeed, there is a growing backlash in North America (Klein 2000; Quart 2003), the United Kingdom (Glayzer and Mitchell 2008) and many other countries about marketing to teenagers and children, with food marketing being of most current interest.

Competition and the principle of differential advantage

This principle refers to an analysis of the marketer's resources versus those of the competition, with the aim of determining where the company enjoys a differential advantage over the opposition. The aim is to focus the company's resources on products or markets that exploit this differential advantage. A differential advantage could be held in technology, human resources, markets or financial backing.

Commercial organisations, as part of their strategic planning process, regularly carry out **SWOTC** analyses – audits of the organisation's strengths and weaknesses, identification of opportunities and threats facing the organisation, and analysis of their competitors. The monitoring and understanding of competitive activity is sometimes to emulate or follow such activity, while in other cases the aim is to pre-empt or counter competitors' activities.

Threats – existing and emerging – should get particular attention. This requires monitoring changes and potential changes in the various environments noted in Chapter 3, particularly technological, economic and political changes. The aim is to

217

brainstorm how to turn these threats, wherever possible, into opportunities, or at least take steps to minimise the impact of the threats. For example, rather than seeing the fragmentation of media channels as a threat to mass campaigns, it may be seen as an opportunity to provide more tailored messages to various sub-groups. Global warming is a threat, but also provides an opportunity for green products and to change people's energy habits. It may also provide an opportunity to change overall attitudes to materialism and the Western ethos of continual growth being necessary for an economy.

Defining the competition in social marketing

In commercial marketing, the competition for a particular product or brand is generally defined as those alternatives that meet the same basic needs or compete for the same resources. Burger King's competitors are not just other burger suppliers, but all fast food suppliers, including chicken and pizza suppliers (such as KFC and Pizza Hut). Competing products are those that can be substituted for the organisation's product, that is, functional alternatives. For example, if ice cream is not available, frozen yoghurt can be chosen for a family dessert. If Pizza Hut is too far away, Wendy's can be substituted, as can takeaway foods from supermarkets. For convenience foods, choices between the various alternatives are not based just on the taste of the various products, but also on price, variety of offerings, convenience of location, opening hours and associated promotion incentives (such as free Coke with every pizza, toys or movie tie-ins). Competition is based on the total bundle of benefits consumers are seeking in fast food: affordable; quick and easy to obtain; liked by the whole family; robust packaging for the takeaway journey; options for different tastes and appetite sizes; merchandise on offer and so on.

For high priced items, such as a motor vehicle purchase, the competition might not be the various automobile manufacturers, but what else can be purchased for that amount of money (e.g., home extensions, an overseas holiday, a home entertainment system or a boat).

Thus, there are clearly defined competitor entities at the *brand* level (Nando's versus KFC) and the *product category* level (all fast food entities). There are also competitive forces that may affect the whole product category or some entities more than others: a trend towards growing beards would impact all men's razor suppliers; the introduction of computers led to the demise of typewriters. These broader competitive forces have been discussed in Chapter 3.

Defining the competition is not as simple for health and social marketers, although the basic definition of all those alternatives that meet the same basic needs or compete for the same resources still applies. For example, for healthy eating many non-nutritious snack foods offer convenience, low price, good taste and a fun image. To compete, healthy snack foods must satisfy these same needs – or introduce 'new' needs. In fact, introducing 'new needs' is a common tactic in social marketing, as we are often promoting 'products' that do not provide equivalent functional benefits to those we wish to replace, or provide only some, and often at a substantial psychological or dollar cost.

Nevertheless, the lesson from the notion of functional alternatives is that when we look at our competition, we must look for the benefits people are getting from their undesired behaviours, and then devise strategies to substitute other benefits or show how the same benefits can be met by the desired behaviours. Similarly, we can identify and then highlight the disbenefits people see in their current undesirable behaviours (such as increased risk of heart disease from being sedentary), and show how these can be avoided by adopting the desired behaviour (of increased physical activity).

Overall, the competition for social marketers can be defined at a specific 'product category' level for specific behaviours, such as healthy eating, physical activity, smoking, alcohol, etc., or at a broader level in terms of any behaviour, product or idea that impacts negatively on health and wellbeing. Hence, we not only compete for teens' attention with product marketers, but also with all those groups who promote ideas and practices that have a negative impact on health and wellbeing.

Categorising the competition in social marketing

While not mutually exclusive, we propose the following categories to assist in designing strategies to monitor and counter the competition:

* competitors where *any* use of their products is harmful (tobacco, some illicit drugs, leaded petrol, some forms of asbestos);
* competitors where moderate or controlled use may be acceptable, but where excess use or abuse of their products is harmful to individuals or society as a whole (foods high in salt, sugar and saturated fats, some illicit drugs, alcohol, guns, motor vehicles, gambling, movies containing sex and violence, etc.);
* competitors defined in terms of socio-cultural beliefs and values that inhibit the uptake of healthy behaviours (attitudes to birth control inhibiting contraception, machismo attitudes inhibiting condom use and facilitating the spread of AIDS, attitudes to women that condone violence against women), or affect the health of the planet in general (such as materialism, consumption as lifestyle);
* competitors defined by beliefs and values that create conflict in society (racist organisations, some fundamentalist religious organisations, 'terrorist groups');
* competitors defined by beliefs and values that have negative consequences for many, while benefiting a select few (global corporations, commercialisation of sport, medicalisation of society, armaments suppliers, global media organisations).

For product competitors, where there is no safe level of consumption, our goal may be to drive the product marketers out of business and reduce consumption to zero. Depending on whether the products are legal (tobacco is legal, heroin is not), our primary targets may be to persuade individuals to cease use of these products and company executives to cease marketing of these products or make them safe to use. Where companies are unlikely to be co-operative, our primary goals may be to lobby bureaucrats to enforce regulations that control their manufacture and/or marketing and politicians to introduce legislation that inhibits or bans their use.

For excess use or abuse competitors, the aim is to ensure responsible use or consumption by individuals and responsible marketing by corporations. Our primary targets are individuals and product manufacturers and marketers where they are likely to be co-operative. Bureaucrats are a primary target for product regulation and governments for relevant legislation in the absence of corporate co-operation. For example, some food manufacturers appear approachable with regard to product modifications and responsible marketing, whereas tobacco marketer RJ Reynolds as recently as 2005 was denying that Joe Camel, the cartoon character with a cool persona and dark glasses, targeted youth (Heavey 2005).

In the domain of beliefs and values, our goals are to neutralise (by any ethical means) those beliefs and values that cause harm to members of a society or inhibit achievement of health and wellbeing. In some cases, our primary targets include individuals, as in mental illness de-stigmatising and anti-racism campaigns, or where socio-cultural beliefs, particularly in developing countries, inhibit the adoption of healthy practices or necessary medicines.

The competition from socio-cultural beliefs

Child drownings in Bangladesh

Drowning is a major health issue in southeast Asian countries and is attracting increased attention in places such as Bangladesh, where recent data suggest drowning accounts for 19–26 per cent of deaths of children under five years of age. Beliefs that 'evil spirits' entice children into the water or bewitch mothers who forget to keep watch over the child, along with beliefs that touching a drowning child will lead to the child's death, all contribute to these deaths and inhibit efforts to act on these drownings (Blum *et al.* 2009).

Sterility rumours impede vaccinations in Africa

Rumours that various vaccinations cause sterility have been reported in various African countries from the 1920s and still persist today. While these beliefs have a number of deeper bases, countering them is not helped by the fact that many of the organisations that conduct the vaccination programmes are also involved in family planning/birth control programmes (Kaler 2009).

More often, our targets are decisionmakers in corporations (including media owners and publishers), policymakers in the bureaucracy and lawmakers in government. Whether the primary target is the corporation for voluntary co-operation or the government to introduce and enforce legislative compliance will depend on the specific issue. For 'hate' websites, government regulation and legislation are deemed essential.

On the other hand, responsible reporting could be negotiated with the media with regard to issues such as suicide, celebrations involving alcohol and sexual issues.

There are, of course, beliefs and values associated with product and excess use competitors. In fact, many socio-cultural beliefs and values support the continuation of unhealthy lifestyles and behaviours that inhibit community wellbeing. For example, tolerance of alcohol as an integral part of celebrations facilitates adolescent binge drinking; female slimness portrayed in the media facilitates bulimia and anorexia; on a broader scale, beliefs about a subservient role of women in society facilitate sexual and physical violence against women; beliefs that economic factors have priority inhibit community welfare allocations; insufficient acknowledgement of environmental influences enhances 'victim blaming' and inadequate allocation of resources to structural change. All these are competitive forces that must be taken into account.

While health and social change organisations face competition from these external competitors, they also face internal competition for available resources. For example, heart, cancer and diabetes NGOs and research institutes all compete for donations and grants, and government departments responsible for social issues such as education and family and children's welfare compete for budget allocations with defence and infrastructure departments. The emphasis in this chapter is on external competitors. However, the lessons should assist organisations in competing for available resources, or, preferably, co-operate to meet mutual and complementary goals.

The increased attention to the obesity epidemic and the realisation that not only do physical activity and diet influence weight, but also impact heart disease, cancer and diabetes, appears to have resulted in increased programme co-operation between these sectors. For example, as part of a concerted effort to deal with obesity and overweight in Hungary (37 per cent of Hungarian adults are overweight; 23 per cent are obese), eight Hungarian NGOs, including the National Foundation of Diabetics, the National Association for Consumer Protection, the National Network of Healthier Kindergartens, the Hungarian National Heart Foundation and the National Institute for Child Health, recently called for a general banning of unhealthy food ads before 9 pm (MNSZA 2009).

Monitoring the competition

Commercial organisations monitor their competitors' activities via qualitative and quantitative research that assesses consumers' perceptions of their competitors' products and corporate image vis-à-vis their own. Competitors' annual reports, press releases, advertising, building activity, public tenders and employment notices can all be monitored to gain an insight into their activities. Independent reviews in trade magazines and the business media also provide information about competitors' activities. Similarly in social marketing, all the above sources provide useful information. However, in most cases, the most valuable information comes from the competitor's public marketing and promotional activities, supported wherever possible by internal documents outlining the company's strategies and target groups. For example, internal documents released in court cases have revealed a wealth of information about the tobacco and pharmaceutical industries' marketing tactics.

Barbie gets a credit card

Monitoring the competition includes keeping a close eye on toy marketers. In keeping with the early commercialisation of children, 'Cool Shoppin' Barbie' came with a MasterCard and cash register that had an endless 'Credit approved' response when her MasterCard was put into Mattel's toy cash register. There were fears that such a 'no limit' card might encourage irresponsible spending and could lead to youngsters accepting credit cards from banks while too young to fully understand the consequences (Associated Press 1998). The later version is part of the Barbie Fashion Fever Shopping Boutique Play Set. When all credit is used, it simply resets (Walters 2007).

The tanning doll

Cancer educators in the United Kingdom were up in arms about a French doll that takes only a minute in the sun to tan. The doll comes with a beach bag, towel, deckchair and fake suntan lotion. Cancer educators believe that the kids will get the message that it is safe to sunbathe and try to get as tanned as their doll. With skin cancer cases on the rise in Britain, these educators are 'not amused' (Williams 2001).

Given the recent focus on obesity, there have been a number of good analyses of companies' food marketing tactics and their effects (Hastings *et al.* 2003; Schor and Ford 2007; Watts and Hulbert 2008), along with presenting the findings in advocacy format – most notably in the United Kingdom (Glayzer and Mitchell 2008; Watts and Hulbert 2008; Which? 2006). Ippolito and Pappalardo (2003) provide an extensive analysis of claims in food advertising in the United States in the twenty-year period from 1977 to 1997.

Analysing the messages contained in alcohol advertising (such as social and sexual success), looking at the sports that tobacco companies sponsor (motor racing – thrills and glamour), and monitoring product placement in entertainment vehicles ('cool' images, fashion), provide a wealth of information about the benefits offered by these products. A study of alcohol advertising and promotion, for example, can assist in understanding appeals to young males. Similarly, advocacy groups need to monitor industries such as the tobacco industry and attempt to anticipate industry moves.

The media are often singled out as one of the major factors influencing people's attitudes and values with respect to products, consumption and lifestyles (Brownell and Horgen 2004; Bryant and Zillman 2002; Leiss *et al.* 2005; Pollay 1986; Strasburger 1993). Media includes paid advertising, news reporting, movies, TV programmes, lifestyle magazines, radio talkback, websites, the new social media and so on.

> **Cookie Monster cuts back on cookies**
>
> In a sign of the times, Cookie Monster now eats fewer chocolate-chip cookies and more healthy foods on the long-running 'Sesame Street' programme. The programme introduced American Fruit Stand (a parody of American Bandstand), as a way of including nutrition and exercise messages in the programme (CBC Arts 2005).

Advertising makes a specific contribution to a consumption-based society. Advertising portrays what products and brands are associated with what lifestyles, what socio-economic status, what attitudes to life and, consequently, how we can adopt and maintain a particular self-image by purchasing and consuming appropriate products (Cushman 1990). Social commentators claim that advertising has particular influence on the young, especially regarding which brands or product categories are 'in' or 'cool' (Twitchell 1996). Advertising also models for young people what various product categories are used for.

A good monitoring framework is to take the 4Ps of the marketing mix, and then systematically analyse a 'competitive industry' with respect to who is being targeted (young people, gay and lesbian groups, the elderly, etc.), and how with respect to product, place, pricing and promotion. We will look at just a few examples here, with an emphasis on monitoring what appears in the media.

Body image and eating disorders

A community-based sample in South Australia estimated that eating disorders affect about 2–3 per cent of people, 90 per cent of whom are women (Hay 1998). Studies in Europe and the United States (Hoek and Hoeken 2003; Wittchen and Jacobi 2005) show similar rates, although some studies report prevalence by specific disorder rather than overall. It is likely that the images of women portrayed in fashion magazines and advertising, particularly of beauty products, have a lot to do with this. Advertising uses sexuality and physical attractiveness to sell products, and particularly to young women. Thinness is emphasised as the ideal standard for women, although fashion models weigh almost 25 per cent less than the average female, and supermodels' slimness represents just 1 per cent of women aged 18 to 34 (Mediascope 2000a). It is not surprising then that in a US survey of girls from the fifth grade to the twelfth grade, 69 per cent reported that magazine pictures influenced their idea of body shape, and 47 per cent wanted to lose weight because of magazine pictures (Field *et al.* 1999). Unfortunately, all this leads to young women reporting dissatisfaction with their body size; girls dissatisfied with their bodies diet more and are more prone to eating disorders (Mediascope 2000a). Controlling weight is also a factor often mentioned by young women as a reason for smoking (Carter, Borland and Chapman 2001).

What we need to do is monitor the sizes of women appearing in advertising and on the fashion, entertainment and celebrity pages of magazines. Coupled with research showing the influence of these images on young girls' and women's dissatisfaction with their body image, and the link between such dissatisfaction and eating disorders, this would provide the evidence needed to undertake advocacy with editors and advertising agencies. Such lobbying has proved effective in other areas, where the proportion of women with a deep tan has declined substantially in young women's magazines in Australia (Chapman, Marks and King 1992; McDermott 2001).

Men also succumbing to body image

When GI Joe hit the stores in 1964 he had a body shape most boys could aspire to and achieve. But today's GI Joe dolls have such muscular bodies they would be difficult to emulate without steroids. A US survey found that half the boys aged 11 to 17 years chose an ideal body image possible to attain only by steroid use. Another found that 45 per cent of college men were dissatisfied with their muscle tone. No wonder steroid use has increased (Mediascope 2000b).

A campaign that purports to change the way women are targeted, at least by 'beauty' product marketers, is Unilever's 'Real Beauty' campaign for its Dove brand (www.campaignforrealbeauty.com). Reportedly based on extensive research (Etcoff *et al.* 2004), the campaign uses 'real' women rather than very slim and very attractive young models in its advertising. The campaign attracted substantial attention – and support – from a variety of quarters because of its break with traditional beauty product advertising. The campaign obtained extensive news reporting when it began, featured on *The Oprah Winfrey Show*, and enlisted the support and involvement of well-known feminist advocates and academic gender researchers (such as Naomi Wolf, Harvard's Nancy Etcoff and Susie Orbach of the London School of Economics) (Johnson and Taylor, 2008). While the campaign boosted Dove sales tremendously for the first two years, following mounting (or cumulative) cynicism and criticism from a number of quarters, sales have apparently declined since (Neff 2007).

The Dove 'Real Beauty' campaign

In a seeming contradiction to our criticisms, the Dutch company Unilever's award winning 'Real Beauty' campaign for its Dove brand not only doesn't use the usual young, slim attractive models, but uses a variety of body shapes and sizes and promotes the message 'that beauty comes in many shapes, sizes and ages'. We think that is good. But let's not forget that this was done to revive Dove's declining sales – not for the social good. However, in a good example of picking up on a socio-cultural trend, at least among many women, it was Dove's extensive market research that led to the campaign positioning. Dove also funds a Self-Esteem Foundation (launched in partnership with American Girl Scouts) to educate and inspire girls on a broader image of beauty.

The 'Real Beauty' campaign, launched in late 2004, followed the successful 'Real Women' campaign launched in the United Kingdom earlier that year, which featured real women to promote Dove's firming product.

Figure 9.1 Dove 'Real Women' ad

Noting this decline, Patton and Vasquez (2008) point out that although the media and message strategies effectively reached and resonated with women of all ages, shapes and sizes, it was probably doomed to fail in the long run because its products – designed to alter or enhance natural beauty – contradicted the campaign's primary message that natural or 'real' beauty is best. There was also the issue of Unilever's male body spray (Axe) that undermined the credibility of Dove's claim to enhancing women's self-esteem: Axe ads used the same sort of attractive young women that Dove supposedly eschewed and in scenarios that hardly enhance women's sense of self. The ads showed women being temporarily distracted from their normal routine by the body spray on a man, such that they burst out with the phrase 'Bom Chic A Wah Wah', and commenced undulating or shimmying before returning to normal.

While we agree with Patton and Vasquez that the Real Beauty campaign probably served as a catalyst for changing the way many women perceive beauty, we also believe that a greater lesson is that commercial interests are always just that – no matter what cause or issue they co-opt or adopt in their marketing strategies.

Tobacco

Tobacco litigation in the United States provided anti-tobacco activists with unprecedented access to internal tobacco company documents. These documents have provided evidence with regard to the tobacco industry's knowledge, yet public denial, of the ill-health effects of tobacco; their deliberate marketing to children; covert PR campaigns to discredit passive smoking research; using low tar cigarettes to delay or deter quitting; aggressive moves into developing countries; and their role in large-scale cigarette smuggling (ASH 2000). The evidence for targeting underage youth is particularly compelling (see Perry 1999). A UK report provides further evidence of the tobacco industry's marketing tactics from an analysis of the tobacco industry's main UK advertising agencies (Hastings and MacFadyen 2000). The Tobacco Documents Online website is a great source of information about the industry (http://tobaccodocuments.org/papers.php). All of this information provides substantial evidence for lobbying government to increase controls over the marketing of tobacco and the regulation of the industry *per se*.

Light up a 'light'

'Light' cigarettes were introduced to target smokers thinking of quitting. The cigarettes were ventilated, but this tended to be covered by the smoker's lips and fingers and, hence, did not function as claimed.

Monitoring the tobacco industry's new products, advertising, sponsorship and promotional activities is essential to: (a) ensure that the industry is not contravening promotional regulations; (b) ensure that the industry is not exploiting loopholes or legitimate activities; and (c) develop counter strategies. One way tobacco companies attempted to make cigarettes more appealing to youth in the United States was to introduce new product extensions that either used colourful, urban nightlife images on the packs (for example, Kool Mixx, Kool Smooth Fusion and Camel Exotic Blends), or contained youth friendly flavours such as berry, mocha, coconut and lime (the Marlboro Menthol 72 mm brand) (Davidson 2003; Join Together 2004).

China has a 'Health' cigarette brand

This brand doesn't mess around with words like 'light' to connote a healthier alternative; it goes straight to the point. The Xunyang Cigarette Factory 'Health' brand cigarettes are supposedly 'proved' to decrease blood sugar, regulate blood pressure, prevent arteriosclerosis and strengthen immunity as well as providing other health benefits.

In the United Kingdom, in the same vein as 'Death' cigarettes, the Shag Tobacco Company hopes to attract a cult following among university students (and no doubt other youth) to its irreverent brand name 'Shag' (Murray-West 2004).

Given the ban on advertising, the tobacco industry has constantly looked for ways to circumvent the ban, as with marketing branded clothing (such as Camel boots and Marlboro jackets and coats). Hence, studies are regularly conducted to monitor the incidence of tobacco in the major media (magazines, newspapers, movies, Internet sites, popular music, TV programmes). In Australia, movies popular with young people in the period 2000–1 included 51 minutes of smoking in 11 hours, 56 minutes of film (Donovan, Weller and Clarkson 2003). Given that 90 per cent of this portrayal showed smoking in a positive or normative light, this is equivalent to 92 × 30-second tobacco promotions. Similar studies at that time in the United States (Glantz 2002; Roberts *et al.* 1999; Roberts *et al.* 2002) indicated that tobacco incidents appeared to be increasing in popular movies and elsewhere, although more recent studies suggest that this has levelled off or declined (see box below).

Tobacco in movies

Top ten weekly movies reviewed from 1 June 2003 to 31 May 2004 by Thumbs Up! Thumbs Down! found:

* 72 per cent of all films reviewed contained some tobacco;
* of the films that contained tobacco, 37 per cent were rated R and 53 per cent were rated PG-13;
* 84 per cent of the films rated R contained tobacco;
* 77 per cent of the PG-13 films contained tobacco;
* 39 per cent of the films rated PG contained tobacco;
* incidents per hour for PG-13 films were 9.8, while incidents per hour for R rated films were 16.4;
* the average incidents per hour for all films was 10.8. This is down from 11.8 in 2002–3 reviews.

(www.scenesmoking.org/docs/tobacco_facts_revised.pdf; accessed 13 July 2009)

Such studies are important as smoking in movies has been shown to be related to initiation and continuation of smoking by adolescents (Charlesworth and Glantz 2005; Dalton *et al.* 2003) (see Figure 9.2).

Tobacco companies also target women in various ways. As noted earlier, Philip Morris assists domestic violence groups, and Philip Morris and RJ Reynolds sponsor various women's organisations in the United States, including the National Women's Political Caucus and the Center for Women Policy Studies (Eaton 2001; WHO 2001). Similarly, tobacco companies have sponsored various African-American organisations, while at the same time targeting blacks with specific brands.

In 1990, after much pressure, RJ Reynolds dropped its 'Uptown' brand, which targeted inner-city blacks, and also dropped plans for its 'Dakota' brand, which was to target young, blue collar women (Cooper-Martin and Smith 1994; Davidson 2003). A number of Internet sites of unknown origin have appeared that promote tobacco to youth and women. There is some suspicion that tobacco companies might be behind some sites.

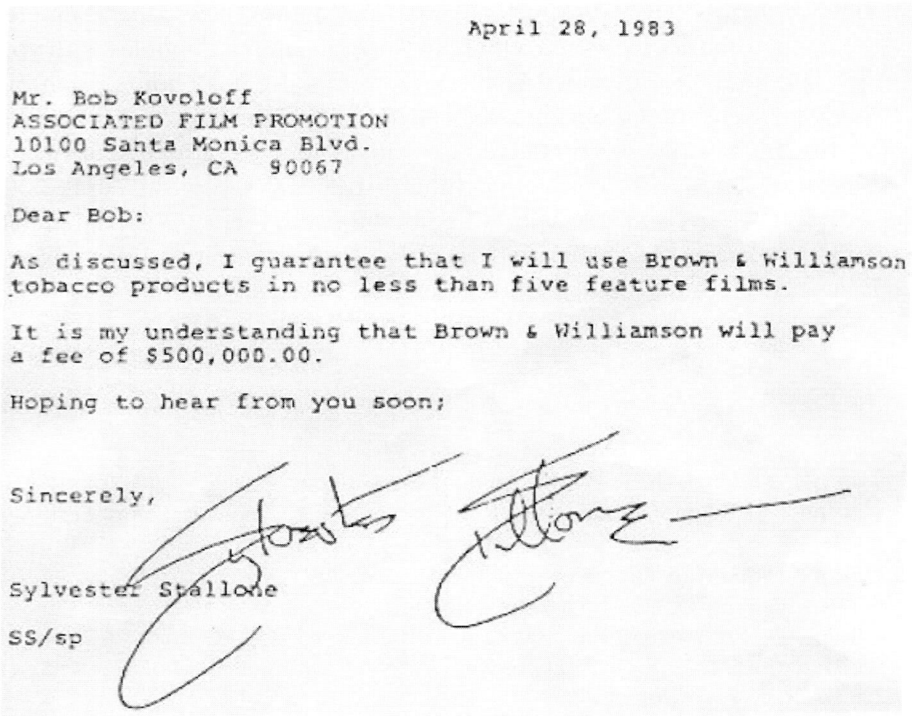

April 28, 1983

Mr. Bob Kovoloff
ASSOCIATED FILM PROMOTION
10100 Santa Monica Blvd.
Los Angeles, CA   90067

Dear Bob:

As discussed, I guarantee that I will use Brown & Williamson
tobacco products in no less than five feature films.

It is my understanding that Brown & Williamson will pay
a fee of $500,000.00.

Hoping to hear from you soon;

Sincerely,

Sylvester Stallone

SS/sp

Figure 9.2 Sylvester Stallone's product placement agreement

Smoking as art

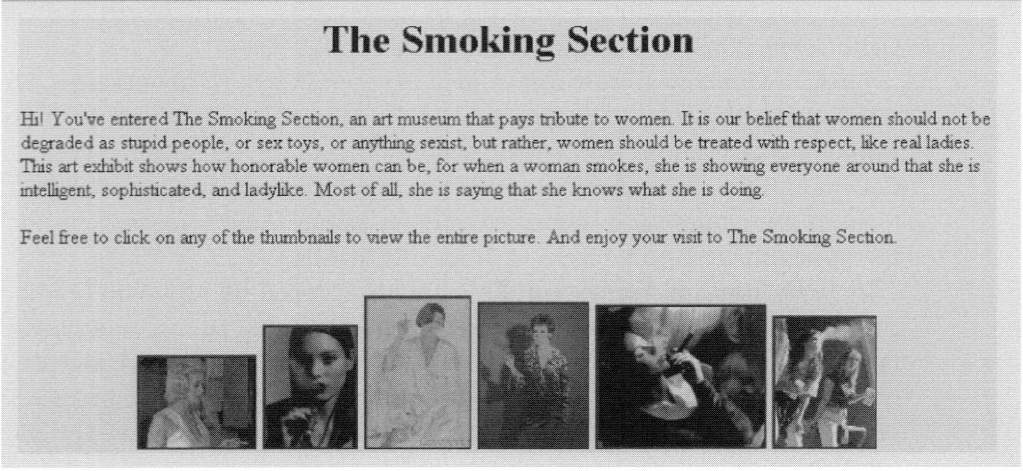

The Smoking Section

Hi! You've entered The Smoking Section, an art museum that pays tribute to women. It is our belief that women should not be degraded as stupid people, or sex toys, or anything sexist, but rather, women should be treated with respect, like real ladies. This art exhibit shows how honorable women can be, for when a woman smokes, she is showing everyone around that she is intelligent, sophisticated, and ladylike. Most of all, she is saying that she knows what she is doing.

Feel free to click on any of the thumbnails to view the entire picture. And enjoy your visit to The Smoking Section.

Alcohol

It is estimated that 23 million Europeans are dependent on alcohol in any one year, and that alcohol is responsible for 195,000 deaths in the European Union (Anderson and Baumberg 2006). Worldwide, alcohol is estimated to have cost societies from US$210 billion to US$665 billion in 2002 (Baumberg 2006). Problem drinking is most prevalent in Europe, Central America (males and females), Latin America, the Caribbean and Central Asia (males), and least in East Asia, the Pacific and Sub-Saharan Africa (Anderson 2006). Alcohol is indeed a major competitor to health and wellbeing.

From our perspective, monitoring the competition with respect to alcohol focuses mainly on targeting to young people via product characteristics and branding, trading hours, advertising and the depiction of alcohol in movies.

Drink to your health! India launches 'healthy' beer

An Indian company launched 'Ladybird Bio Beer' in 2005 promising no hangovers or other long-term health effects. On the contrary, this beer is claimed to be good for you because it won't harm the liver or cause cancers and gastric illness because it contains aloe vera, which is claimed to increase the bioavailability of vitamins B1, B6, B12, C and E in the body (Indiainfo.com 2005).

Movies and TV entertainment programmes around the globe commonly portray alcohol consumption as a normal part of life, usually depicting alcohol as a mood altering substance that serves as an aid to socialising and as a stress reducer. A content analysis of alcohol portrayal in British television soap operas revealed, on average, a visual or verbal reference to alcohol every 3.5 minutes (Furnham *et al.* 1997). None of the British programmes contained any messages about the potential harmful effects of alcohol.

In the United States, alcohol companies spend close to US$2 billion a year on advertising. Research indicates that between 2001 and 2007, in the United States there were more than two million television ads and 20,000 magazine ads for alcohol, with much of the placement directed towards youth (Austin and Hust 2005; Jernigan 2008; Siegel *et al.* 2008).

Don't like the taste of alcohol? Try an 'alcopop' or gelatin shot

US public health advocates are complaining about what they call 'starter brews' aimed at entry level consumers who don't like the taste of alcohol. Malt-based brews include personalised brands such as Mike's Hard Lemonade, Hooper's Hooch and Jed's. Teens agree that the products appear to be designed for them (i.e., underage drinkers) rather than adults and to ease them into more traditional alcoholic beverages. The sweet, lemonade taste is what primarily attracts teens to try them (BoozeNews 2001). Similarly, packaged gelatin shots ('Zippers'), in flavours such as Rum Rush, Vodka Splash and Tijuana Tequlia are causing concern because they look like the Jello snacks popular with kids (Lyderson 2002). Jones and Donovan (2001) found that a major attribute promoted by the UDL vodka-based mix that many underage young people saw as aimed at them, was that it was 'easy to drink'.

Beer advertising around the globe has over the years generally focused on the conviviality and camaraderie attainable via beer consumption, or on beer as an appropriate and normal reward for hard work (Parker 1995; Pettigrew 2000). Noble *et al.* (1990) identified 155 TV ads for alcohol in the week they studied, 47 per cent being beer ads. They reported that 35 per cent of the ads suggested that alcohol would contribute to social achievement, and 54 per cent that alcohol would contribute to sporting achievement. They noted that while beer ads were associated with sporting success, spirits ads (32 per cent of all ads) were associated with sexual or physical intimacy. These same distinctions can be seen in alcohol advertising today (see Jones and Donovan 2001; 2002).

Tobacco and alcohol feature in children's animated films

One might think that children's animated films (i.e., the very symbol of young children's entertainment) would be free of tobacco and alcohol use – except perhaps in rare circumstances. Not so. Of fifty such films reviewed, 56 per cent portrayed one or more incidences of tobacco use and 50 per cent included alcohol use. Good and bad characters were equally likely to use tobacco or alcohol. However, the most frequent tobacco portrayals were of cigars (59 per cent) rather than cigarettes (21 per cent), and wine (60 per cent) dominated the alcohol incidences, followed by beer (32 per cent). While these distributions suggest the use of alcohol and tobacco in character development, none of the films included any verbal messages about negative health effects. Given the influence of modelling on behaviours, and that character development can occur without alcohol and tobacco, there is no reason for inclusion of alcohol and tobacco use in children's animated films (Goldstein, Sobel and Newman 1999). A later report suggests that nearly half the G-rated animated films available on video-cassette in the United States show alcohol and tobacco use as normative behaviour (Thompson and Yokota 2001).

Alcohol sites on the Internet appear to have been particularly designed to appeal to youth. The US-based Center for Media Education has examined beer, wine and spirit websites found through search engines, links from other sites, or through articles in the trade press. Their reports in 1997 and 1999 showed clearly that these sites contained elements attractive to youth, such as use of cartoons, personalities, language, music or branded merchandise popular in youth culture or that would be particularly attractive to college or high school aged students; or offers of contests, interactive games, online magazines (e-zines) geared to youth, created virtual communities or chat rooms, or sponsored youth-oriented music or sports events.

As a result, the Federal Trade Commission (FTC) called on the industry to avoid content that would appeal to youth. However, a Center on Alcohol Marketing and Youth (CAMY) analysis of seventy-four websites in 2003 showed that little had changed, with games appealing to youth being a popular feature of the sites, along with downloadable screen savers and various interactive high-tech features (such as 'talking' emails using animals such as frogs and hamsters), cartoon figures and animated graphics (CAMY 2004). Similar results were found by Carroll and Donovan (2002) who examined six 'Australian' websites representing the alcohol beverage categories of beer, spirits, cider, wine, liqueurs and alcoholic sodas.

Prejudice

Examples of negative stereotyping of ethnic groups, blacks, women, the elderly, people with disabilities and other marginalised groups abound in the media (Bryant and Zillmann 2002). Some years ago negative portrayals did not appear only in the popular media: a content analysis of advertisements in medical journals found that relative to men, women were negatively portrayed, being rarely shown in technical jobs, often in provocative poses and as 'complainers', among other things (Hawkins and Aber 1988). Racism in particular appears to be alive and well throughout the world. A Ford print advertisement featuring line workers from its UK Dagenham plant featured a number of black employees. However, when the ad ran in Poland (and later by mistake back in Britain), the black and brown faces and hands had been altered to white, and one employee's beard and turban had been removed. Apparently the changes were made to suit 'local tastes'. Clearly Ford did not feel that Poland would react positively to people of colour (*Economist* 1996). In a déjà vu experience, Microsoft has just apologised for the same thing (Fried 2009). A photo on the company's US website featured a black man, an Asian man and a white woman. In the same photo on their Polish subsidiary's website, the black man's head had been replaced by the head of a white man (Edwards 2009b).

The Internet has been readily adopted by American 'hate groups', with numbers rising sharply in recent years, including an increase in Ku Klux Klan groups. Many of these sites appear to be targeting children with interactive games (the objective of one apparently is to lynch a black man) (Liu 1999).

Internet hate sites target children and youth

The Alabama-based Southern Poverty Law Center reported that the number of hate groups active in the United States was 537 in 1998, up from 474 in 1997, and that white supremacist hate sites on the Internet had increased from 163 in 1997 to 254 in 1998. These sites allow American hate groups to not only target disgruntled youth and laid-off blue collar workers in the United States, but also to reach millions around the globe.

A more recent report by the Simon Wiesenthal Center documents more than 1,400 Internet hate sites, with 120 more appearing just after the report was released. In 2000 the Simon Wiesenthal Center estimated that there were more than 3,000 websites containing hate, racism, terrorist agendas and bomb making instructions (compared with 1 in 1995). Many attract children by offering crossword puzzles and video games with racist themes. Recent research shows that the stories on some of these hate sites can influence adolescents negatively (Lee and Leets 2002).

Countering the competition

Countering the competition is, of course, what this whole book is about. Nevertheless, this section serves to introduce several strategies and tactics not covered elsewhere, as well as others covered in more detail later (especially Chapters 10, 11 and 12).

As indicated in Chapter 1, meeting the competition requires strategies aimed at: (1) the end consumer's beliefs, attitudes and behaviours; (2) those with the power to modify products, services and places; and (3) those with the power to enact legislative and environmental changes that facilitate or enforce the desired end behaviour. As we noted earlier, we can monitor competition marketers via identifying and analysing the 4Ps of their marketing mixes. We can also develop counter strategies around the these 4Ps: for example, by restricting trading hours (of bars for example) or who can purchase or use the product (age restrictions on tobacco and alcohol); by increasing the price through tax increases (cigarettes and alcohol particularly); by restricting the nature and content of advertising and promotions (guns, tobacco, alcohol, pornography); and by requiring product formulations to comply with certain regulations (added folate, iodised salt) or requiring warnings (cigarettes) or nutrient information (food products) on the packaging.

'Kapow!' to PowerMaster

Heileman's Colt 45 dominated the US malt liquor market in the 1980s (malt liquor has a higher alcohol content than regular beer and a higher market share in low income neighbourhoods). However, Heileman was losing volume overall and badly in need of a new product. Along came PowerMaster, 31 per cent stronger than Colt 45 and 65 per cent stronger than regular beer. The product was clearly aimed at inner-city blacks. The US Surgeon-General described the brewer's plans as 'socially irresponsible' and the Bureau of Alcohol, Tobacco and Firearms withdrew approval for the PowerMaster name because of its implied reference to alcohol strength. Heileman withdrew the product, although it had spent US$2 million on research and marketing for the brand (Cooper-Martin and Smith 1994; Davidson 2003). Heileman executives were clearly blind to the alcohol marketing environment in the United States at the time (academics aren't the only ones living in ivory towers).

Other examples include public health advocates in the United States arguing for taxes on sugared beverages to reduce consumption (Brownell and Frieden 2009), England's chief medical officer wanting a minimum unit price on alcohol, as Scotland also wants (Kmietowicz 2009), in Milan, parents of children under 16 caught drinking alcohol will be fined up to €500 (Willey 2009), and UK doctors wanting a complete ban on alcohol advertising (*Daily Mail Reporter* 2009).

At a broader level, we can identify unhealthy or undesirable products and behaviours and attempt to find acceptable healthy or desirable substitutes, and we can identify environmental aspects that facilitate desirable and inhibit undesirable behaviours. In fact, we commonly need to do all of these, and think laterally when we do, as the Nepalese anti-corruption authority did recently (see box below).

Pocketless trousers counter corruption in Nepal

According to the Al Arabiya news channel on 29 June 2009, as part of its anti-corruption drive, the Nepalese anti-corruption authority is issuing new pocketless trousers to all airport officials after uncovering widespread bribery and corruption at Kathmandu's Tribhuvan International Airport. 'We believe this will help curb the irregularities,' said a spokesperson for the Commission for the Investigation of Abuse of Authority (CIAA) (Al Arabiya News Channel 2009) (www.alarabiya.net/articles/2009/06/29/77322.html).

Examples of product alternatives

There are numerous examples of products that have been modified to make them more healthy or less harmful to users. Many of these changes have been brought about by consumer demand as manufacturers have seen a potentially profitable market segment for a particular product. Others have been brought about by lobbying manufacturers or by legislation following intensive advocacy.

Food and beverage products abound in such variations as low fat, high fibre, sugar free, cholesterol free, saturated fat free, vitamin boosted and low alcohol variations. Recent examples are Kellogg's folate-rich breakfast cereals, the cholesterol lowering spread Pro-activ and Brownes Dairy's Heart Plus milk. Unfortunately, the healthier alternatives are often more expensive than the regular product (Heart Plus milk is approximately 40 per cent more expensive). The National Heart Foundation's tick of approval makes it easy for consumers looking for healthy alternatives.

After much pressure by those concerned about the obesity epidemic, the major food producers are beginning to take some actions, albeit generally minor, so as to appear concerned or to avoid government intervention. For example, Kraft and PepsiCo created rating systems to designate healthier foods, and Disney is removing characters such as Mickey Mouse and Winnie the Pooh from sweets and food products it deems unhealthy to children (Warner 2005).

New to Australia, **Heart Plus** combines the great taste of reduced fat milk with omega-3. This nutrient is known to assist in the functioning of the cardiovascular system by lowering blood triglyceride (fat) levels and helping maintain a regular heartbeat. And just one 250ml glass of Brownes Heart Plus gives you 95% of a suggested daily intake of this © &™ NHF 1988 used under licence.

valuable nutrient. Heart Plus is also rich in vitamins C and E, antioxidants that help your body use omega-3 nutrients more efficiently. Folate and vitamins B6 and B12 help promote good blood flow through your arteries by lowering harmful levels of homocysteine. And of course, it's low in both fat and cholesterol. So, when you make Brownes

Heart Plus part of a life that includes a balanced diet and regular physical activity, you can drink milk to your heart's content. For more infomation please phone the customer service line on 1800 675 484 or visit the website at www.heart-plus.com.au **Heart Plus. The low fat milk with omega-3.**

Figure 9.3 Heart Plus milk

The Heart Foundation's Tick Programme helps people choose healthier foods that are lower in fat, saturated fat and sodium (salt). Many are also higher in fibre and calcium and have less sugar. All foods are independently tested and assessed against strict nutritional guidelines before getting the Tick of Approval. Random testing is carried out on the Tick products throughout the year to ensure that they always meet the strict nutrition guidelines.

There are also 'environmentally friendly' (or more so than others) cleaning products, products in recyclable packaging, motor vehicle manufacturers touting their vehicles' environmental friendliness and safety features, and, after much advocacy and against opposition from the oil, lead and chemical industries (Isaacs and Schroeder 2001), petrol is now lead free. On the other hand, many products claiming to be 'green' are not.

In a variation on this theme, in an attempt to make desirable branded products more affordable to low income youth, a National Basketball Association star (Hakeem Olajuwon) worked with Spalding to develop a shoe that sells for US$35 (versus Nikes or Reeboks around US$120) (CNAD 1997). Whether this will stop poor youth stealing the more expensive shoes from stores or other kids remains to be seen. Nevertheless, it's a 'step' in the right direction.

Gambling is an area that is only just starting to attract attention from a social marketing (Perese, Bellringer and Abbott 2005 in New Zealand) or public health (Shaffer 2003 in the United States) perspective, with most current approaches being individual-oriented: that is, identifying 'problem gamblers' and then 'counselling' them. However, the problems associated with gambling – particularly poker machines or video-lottery terminals (VLTs) – are substantial. Britons, for example, spent £50 billion on gambling in 2006, a sevenfold increase since 2001 (Womack 2006).

One way that 'socially responsible' gambling corporations (and don't be fooled by their self-described 'gaming' naming) meet some sense of social responsibility is to modify the features of their machines originally designed to increase spending and exploit addiction. For example, the Nova Scotia Gaming Corporation (NSGC; a government entity) reported around 2001 that it would replace more than 3,000 VLTs with newer models with features that after a prescribed time slow and interrupt play. Such features include a permanent clock on display, pop-up reminders of how long the player has been playing that ask if they want to continue, showing amounts wagered in dollars rather than credits and mandatory cash payouts (Blaszczynski 2003). In 2008–9, NSGC was one of the first organisations to be recognised by the World Lottery Association at their highest level of social responsibility standards. In 2009 NSGC invested more than CAD\$7.5 million in prevention, education and treatment initiatives, including the Informed Player Choice System, which provides information tools to VLT players to help them manage their play, and BetStopper, an Internet blocking software that helps parents keep their children from accessing online gambling sites (Kiley 2009). For a good example of social responsibility in action, visit www.ngsc.ca.

Examples of behavioural alternatives

For many social marketing campaigns we are concerned with behaviours other than purchasing and consumption of products and services (such as safer driving, tolerance, good parenting practices, physical activity, interacting positively with neighbours, etc.). Similarly, many food preparation (cutting off fat) and cooking behaviours (less overcooking) result in more nutrition with the same foods.

For hot chips, size does matter

Surveys in New Zealand have shown that changes in deep frying practices of hot chips could have a significant impact on fat intake from this fast food source. Similarly, changes in chip thickness would also have a significant impact. Interestingly, 89 per cent of chain outlets used thin chips (6–10 mm), while 83 per cent of independent outlets used thicker chips (12 mm or more) (Morley-John *et al.* 2002).

There is also considerable evidence that plate and serving spoon sizes have a considerable impact on how much people eat. One US study showed that when eighty-five nutrition experts attending a social event for a colleague were given either a 17-oz or a 34-oz bowl, and either a 2-oz scoop or a 3-oz scoop and allowed to serve themselves, those with a 34-oz bowl served themselves 31 per cent more than those with a 17-oz bowl, and 14.5 per cent more if they were given a 3-oz serving spoon (Wansink, van Ittersum and Painter 2006). Given that these people were all nutrition experts, this is a very significant demonstration of environmental cues that can influence our behaviour without our awareness. A similar effect occurs with regard to adjusting to serving size containers, with marketers over the years gradually increasing serving sizes of products such as popcorn at cinema complexes.

Consider positive parenting practices such as rewards for good behaviour, discussion with the child, time out and diversionary tactics. These are competing with smacking, yelling at and denigrating the child. The parent's end goal is the elimination or reduction of bad behaviours and the maintenance of good behaviours. However, for many parents, smacking and yelling are quicker and easier ways to get an immediate stop to the bad behaviour, while rewards, discussion and diversion are more time consuming methods requiring more (cognitive) effort, and are methods that many parents do not know how to go about (everybody has the skills for smacking and yelling). Campaigns can show parents how to use these methods, convince them that the end goal will be reached better by these methods, and that they are effective in the short term. While extra care is needed in messages attacking negative parenting practices, the disadvantages of such can be pointed out (e.g., a tantrum resulting from smacking, which is only exacerbated by further smacking – as many supermarket shoppers can attest to).

Alcohol consumption serves many motives, providing many benefits to young people in particular with regard to lessened social inhibitions, increased feelings of wellbeing and enhanced social and sexual interactions. However, excess alcohol consumption can sometimes preclude these benefits and result in considerable disbenefits the following day. Rothschild (1997) described a programme at the University of Wisconsin to combat binge drinking by offering appropriate alternative, non-alcohol activities and venues for students, such as keeping the recreational facilities open late on weekends and having an all-night, non-alcohol dance club. Given that intoxication reduces a drinker's ability to make sound decisions while drinking, forward planning is essential to control alcohol consumption. Hence, some campaigns urge drinkers to eat a big meal beforehand, plan to stay over if a long night's drinking is likely, appoint a designated driver before the event or plan to drink low alcohol drinks.

How the competition counters social marketing – globally

Countering the competition is a continuing battle and we are up against some of the best resourced and cleverest marketers around. No wonder that under funded advocacy groups that rely heavily on volunteers often buckle under the strain and simply fade away. One of industry's favourite tactics to deflect government action or appease vocal groups with some clout (such as medical organisations), is to adopt more stringent self-regulations with regard to marketing and product formulation (even though more honoured in the breach perhaps). The alcohol industry gets an academy award for that one. However, a more insidious current tactic that is more difficult to oppose, is where the industry purports to adopt the health issue *per se*. Hence, McDonald's promotes physical activity as its contribution to solving obesity problems in the United States, United Kingdom and China (Ives 2005). In 2005, McDonald's released its 'Commitment To Balanced, Active Lifestyles', which detailed its 'commitments' in the Asia-Pacific, Europe, Latin America, Canada and the United States (see box below).

Perhaps of lesser concern is that Disney partners with Imagination Farms to brand fruit and vegetables with Disney cartoon characters (Adelman 2006). The Imagination Farms Disney Garden website contains lots of fun things for kids to do with fruit and vegetables – but one would be forgiven for getting the impression that it's more about Disney than fruit and veg (see www.imagination-farms.com). The website has English, Spanish and French language variants.

Campaigns aimed at increasing people's levels of physical activity compete with a variety of forces. They compete first and foremost with job and family commitments, sedentary entertainments and all other leisure activities that take up an individual's free *time*. These campaigns also compete with alternative modes of transport and all other labour and time saving devices (e.g., automatic opening doors, escalators and lifts, the car, etc.). They further compete with entrenched beliefs such as only vigorous activity is likely to be of any benefit, exercise can be done only via an organised activity that requires costly equipment or clothing or both, and beliefs that other 'healthy' activities such as a good diet, not smoking and moderate drinking more than compensate for minimal exercise. It is little wonder then that physical activity levels in developed countries are either steady or decreasing, that obesity is on the rise and that physical activity campaigns have had little impact (partly because they have been under resourced and not comprehensive). Current campaigns attempt to show how people can build an increase in physical activity into their daily lives, via walking for transport, taking stairs instead of lifts and escalators, doing heavy gardening and housework and walking for leisure.

McDonald's® commitment to balanced, active lifestyles

'As a global leader, McDonald's has a long-standing commitment to be responsive to our customers' needs. And, we are committed to being part of the solution by helping our customers understand the importance of energy balance – balancing food consumption and physical activity – to achieve more balanced, active lifestyles. "it's what i eat and what i do" further extends McDonald's commitment to inspiring and motivating people to live balanced, active lives and captures the message that people should pay attention to Energy IN – the foods they eat – and Energy OUT – their level of activity or exercise – in order to find their balance. We will enlist the help of the worldwide family of Olympic athletes – including Olympians past and present, Olympic hopefuls in training and Olympic moms – to be ambassadors for the Balanced, Active Lifestyles message. Rolling out worldwide in the coming weeks and months, McDonald's team of athletes, hopefuls and moms will present a "Finding Your Balance" quiz to provide a global "pulse check" of our customers' level of knowledge about energy balance. The quiz, developed in conjunction with health professionals and physical activity experts, features basic questions about nutrition and physical activity and will also appear on our refreshed website (McDonald's 2005), www. GoActive.com.' (http://mcdepk.com/globalbalancedlifestyles/ media_downloads/global_ bal_fact_sheet.pdf, accessed 28 June 2009).

Advocacy for regulatory enforcement and change

Research has long been used by public health and other social policy-oriented organisations to support approaches to politicians to achieve legislative and policy change. For example, some twenty years ago, alarmed by Philip Morris's introduction of 15s packs of cigarettes that made them more affordable, and accompanied by a teenage-oriented advertising campaign referring to how easy they might be to hide ('Alpine 15s. They fit in anywhere'), Wilson *et al.* (1987) carried out a brief survey of children and adults who smoked. Although Phillip Morris claimed the packs were not targeted at children, the survey showed that 57 per cent of children who smoked had bought a pack of 15s in the past month compared with only 8 per cent of adult smokers. This information resulted in regulations being changed in all Australian states to prohibit small packs (Chapman and Reynolds 1987).

More recently, to support information arising from internal tobacco company documents, several research studies have provided evidence of a causal link between tobacco company marketing and youth smoking (Biener and Siegel 2000; MacFadyen, Hastings and Macintosh 2001). These sorts of data assist tobacco advocates in lobbying government to restrict tobacco marketing practices.

Advocacy for, then enforcement of, legislation as a force for social change is common around the world in areas such as violence against women, civil rights, racial and other discrimination, the rights of people with disabilities and environmental practices. This has been particularly evident in the major civil rights movements of the twentieth century in India, South Africa and the United States (Ackerman and DuVall 2000). Advocacy groups in these areas are now highly professional and well organised, although still hampered by a lack of funding.

Using the law in France to counter racism

The French cosmetics giant L'Oreal was found guilty in 2007 of racial discrimination after a French court found they had recruited women on the basis of race. The company apparently used the code BBR (bleu, blanc, rouge = French flag colours = white French = no women of African and Asian backgrounds) to inform its recruitment agency to employ only white French women to promote its range (Chrisafis 2007). The decision was upheld by France's highest court (Cour de cassation) in 2009. The case was brought by campaign advocacy group SOS Racisme (www.sos-racisme.org). L'Oreal used the theme 'Because you're worth it' in their product positioning, leading one blogger to state that 'obviously in L'Oreal's view, you're worth a lot more if you're white' (Leon 2007).

Isaacs and Schroeder (2001) describe how two women had an enormous impact on public policy and no doubt public attitudes to drink-driving in the United States. In 1978, after a drunk driver ran over and killed a teenager in her home town, a woman called Doris Aiken founded RID: Remove Intoxicated Drivers. Two years later Candy

Lightner formed MADD: Mothers Against Drunk Driving after her daughter was run over and killed by a drinking driver. The media took to their stories and they took to the media and the road, resulting in hundreds of media stories and the energising of anti-drunk driving activists throughout the United States who formed local chapters of RID, MADD and SADD (Students Against Driving Drunk). Activists provided victims' services, lobbied government officials and monitored the courts. Between 1981 and 1985 state legislatures passed 478 laws to deter drunk driving, Congress passed legislation providing extra funds to states that enacted stricter drink-driving laws, and in 1984 tied federal highway funds to a minimum drinking age of 21 years (Isaacs and Schroeder 2001).

Countering alcohol ads that reinforce sexist attitudes towards women

On the premise that sexist advertising contributes to a social context conducive to violence against women, this California campaign ('Dangerous Promises') pressured the alcohol industry to change the way in which they depicted women in their ads. After receiving a lukewarm response from brewers and spirit makers (but a positive one from wine marketers) to proposed additions to alcohol advertisers' codes of ethics, the campaign produced controversial billboard counter-ads under the banner of 'Consumers to stop sexist advertising'. One ad read: 'Bloodweiser, King of Tears – Selling Violence Against Women' (a play on 'Budweiser – King of Beers'). The aim was to attract media attention to these ads, some of which the billboard companies refused to run – hence, generating more publicity! They also established good relationships with journalists, supplying them with background data with regard to the relationship between violence, alcohol and sexist attitudes, along with numerous examples of sexist ads (such data and visuals making the journalists' jobs easier). Advertising featuring women decreased markedly in San Diego County; the brewers agreed to reconsider the code of ethics changes, while the spirits trade association agreed to an additional code dealing with sexism in advertising (Woodruff 1996).

Industry self-regulation: an oxymoron?

Industry self-regulation is often promoted as the ideal solution, rather than having government interfering in the marketplace. However, too often self-regulation appears to be adopted simply to deflect government action and is more honoured in the breach than in the observance. Nevertheless, many marketers do adhere to their own ethical and self-regulation codes of conduct. For example, with regard to body image, women's magazine editors in the United Kingdom agreed in 2000 to exclude images of very thin models from their magazines (Womersley 2000).

A number of studies have concluded that alcohol advertising and promotion encourage young people to drink and reinforces drinking habits (Collins *et al.* 2007; Ellickson *et al.* 2005; Engels *et al.* 2009; McClure *et al.* 2009; Saffer and Dave 2006). Hence, it is important to monitor alcohol marketing to ensure that responsible consumption is promoted and portrayed, especially in advertising. The strong association between alcohol and sport, particularly in beer advertising, is reflected in studies showing higher levels of consumption among physically active males versus less active males (Faulkener and Slattery 1990). Carlsberg is a long time sponsor of soccer; Carling has just signed to sponsor the Irish Football League; Famous Grouse whisky has sponsored Scottish Rugby for twenty-one years; and Bundaberg Rum is a major sponsor of the Wallabies rugby union team.

Given the link between alcohol consumption and youth ill-health and social disruption, restrictions on alcohol advertising have increasingly become an issue for debate around the world. Some countries rely on governmental regulation, whereas others use a system of industry self-regulation. However, considerable research suggests that self-regulation is of limited usefulness from a public health perspective. For example, in the United States, the Marin Institute examined complaints in the period 2004–7 to the Distilled Spirits Council of the United States (DISCUS) with regard to their Code of Responsible Marketing Practices. Of note is that complaints are judged by a code review board consisting of five representatives from major alcohol companies appointed by the DISCUS board of directors (incredible but true!). During the four-year period, seventy-eight complaints were received relating to ninety-three advertisements. Although forty-three of these ads were found to breach the code, the Marin report provides several striking examples of ads that were deemed not to breach the code – including a 'Tommy Guns' Vodka ad, featuring a Tommy gun and references to gangsters and Al Capone ('Alphonse Capone Enterprises'), which was deemed to not breach the code relating to association with violent situations, illegal activity or dangerous behaviour. Of most interest was the finding that complaints about ads of companies with a member on the DISCUS were three times less likely to be found in violation of the code (Marin Institute 2008). Jones and Donovan (2002) examined eleven alcohol advertising complaints (relating to nine separate advertisements) that were lodged with the Advertising Standards Board (ASB) by members of the Australian general public. The ASB had ruled that none of the ads breached any of the codes. Eight marketing academics ('expert judges') were given copies of the ads and the Association of National Advertisers' Code of Ethics and the Alcoholic Beverages Advertising Code. Without knowing the ASB's rulings, they were asked to judge whether the advertisements breached any of the clauses of the two codes. In contrast to the ASB's rulings, a majority of the expert judges perceived breaches of the codes for seven of the nine advertisements.

In a series of later studies, Sandra Jones and her colleagues at the University of Wollongong have consistently shown that self-regulation of alcohol advertising continues to be an oxymoron in Australia (Jones, Hall and Munro 2008; Jones, Parri and Munro 2009). For example, in a follow-up study to the above, an independent expert panel judged fourteen ads that had been complained about to the Advertising Standards

Board against the self-regulation codes. In eight of the fourteen cases, a majority of judges found the ads to breach the codes, and in none of the cases did a majority judge that there was no breach. The ASB had dismissed all the complaints (Jones, Hall and Munro 2008).

Kids are kids right? Wrong. Kids R Cu$tomer$!

The blurb on James U. McNeal's (1992) handbook on marketing to children (*Kids as Customers*) hardly repressed its delight at the opportunity provided by kids in the United States: '$9 billion of their own spending money and an influence over $130 billion of their parents' and carers' spending' – and that's much greater in 2010, with one report suggesting that American parents give grade school kids as much as $14.4 billion a year to spend on a discretionary basis. But wait, there's more! The blurb goes on to say that as future customers, children will control even more dollars and that McNeal 'shows business how to cultivate today's children into loyal customers'. 'What's more,' says the jacket, as if the billions of dollars at home aren't enough, 'McNeal urges business not to overlook the potential of … foreign children.' McNeal not only urges but leads by example, with studies in China of spending patterns and influence on parent purchasing of 4–12-year-olds, and new product information sources among 8–13-year-old children (McNeal and Ji 1999; McNeal and Yeh 1997). McNeal's book is touted as 'the indispensable marketing handbook for companies marketing to four-to-twelve-year-olds'. That's right, *four*-year-olds. 'Retailers, advertisers, product designers, and market researchers will all benefit from McNeal's extensive research …' But will the children?

McNeal's subject index lists one entry on 'Ethics in marketing to children': page 20. On page 20 we read: 'This brings up one more warning of sorts. Kids are the most unsophisticated of all consumers; they have the least and therefore want the most. Consequently, they are in a perfect position to be taken. While it is difficult to market to them successfully, as observed above, it is equally difficult to market to them ethically. Safeguards must be in place every step of the way.' We did find other references to ethical practices in the book (page 128 refers to the packaging of bubble gum to look like chewing tobacco and snuff as an unethical practice), but McNeal's book is pretty short on what these safeguards could be and there is no substantive discussion on any ethical issues.

Well, the marketers have certainly taken McNeal's and others' words to heart, pouring millions of dollars into advertising and promotions, including traditional media as well as product placement, the Internet, and tie-ins with movies and fast food chains in particular. For example, the major toy crazes of Pokemon, Cabbage Patch Kids and Tamagotchis have all been assisted by fast food promotions, and in 1996, Disney and McDonald's signed a ten-year global marketing agreement (Schlosser 2001). Not satisfied with promotion in the public domain, major marketers are turning to schools to promote their products and marketing consultants are cashing in by specialising in this area. For example, School Marketing Partners developed a school lunch menu to promote Fox's movie *Anastasia*, where the November menu featured an *Anastasia* game (actually an ad for the movie), and a come-on to buy *Anastasia* toys from Shell service stations (Orwall 1997).

The introduction of Channel One in 1990 in US schools appears to have been the foot in the door. Channel One placed television and VCR equipment in schools. In return, the schools ensured that students watched Channel One programming, where each telecast contained 2 minutes of ads for major youth marketers. But wait, there's more! Schools were then drawn into Channel One promotions with major advertisers, with teachers and principals acting as promoters, handing out coupons for JC Penney Blue Jeans and Subway, or helping kids prepare ads for Snapple or design vending machines for Pepsi Cola, or sign petitions for Reebok (Lex 1997). Lex (1997) reports that in 1991 only 2 per cent of public schools sold branded fast food, but this figure was 13 per cent by 1997 and growing, in spite of federal nutritional guidelines and sometimes higher prices.

A web-based network, the National Campaign Against Channel One (NCACO) began advocating for the removal of Channel One from schools around 2001 (and ceased around 2004). One of the major complaints was that the channel (at that time) advertised PG-13 movies (many of which we note elsewhere contain sex and violence) to younger children, and continued to promote them in other ways. Their efforts may be paying off; Molnar *et al.* (2008) report that the channel's audience is shrinking and that because it eliminated ads for sweets, soft drinks and snacks, the pool of advertisers is dwindling.

Competition for kids: school as battleground

Advertising and promotion to kids in schools in North America is big business for the corporations involved and can be a strikingly successful fund raising strategy for the schools. It has diversified from corporate sponsorships of sports, music and facilities, to include advertising posters in school hallways and on school buses, exclusive beverage deals, corporate classroom teaching materials, cafeteria franchises, exclusive vending machines, computer lab screensavers and educational TV programming interspersed with commercial ads (Aidman 1995; Molnar *et al.* 2008; Salkowski 1997; Schlosser 2001; Story and French 2004). Ads appear in the sports stadium, on the scoreboard, gymnasium, cafeteria, hallways, school buses, on textbooks, in school newspapers and yearbooks, as screensavers on school computers and even in the restrooms (Chaika 1998; Molnar *et al.* 2008; Story and French 2004).

Often it is part of the negotiated contract that advertisements will be allowed in the school buildings, on the school grounds or on the outside of the buildings (Story and French 2004). In an innovative ten-year, US$3.45 million contract, even the rooftops

Figure 9.4 Adbusters – fighting back!

of schools under the Dallas-Fort Worth airport flight path have been targeted so that passengers see Dr Pepper ads as they fly over (Kennedy 2000, cited in Killeen 2007). There have been few concerns voiced about this strategy, perhaps because the children aren't being exposed to it.

Molnar (2005) describes the various degrees of commercialism in schools as: selling *to* schools; selling *in* schools; and the selling *of* schools as marketable commodities. The latest Molnar report (Molnar *et al.* 2008) suggests that the marketing of schools is firmly established – at least in the United States. Generally, the businesses involved are soft drink manufacturers, fast food franchises, clothing and shoe companies. An exclusive beverage contract, for example, can be worth US$1.5 million to a US School District (Story and French 2004). Deals have also been made with restaurants, hotels and telecommunication organisations. Schools are not keen to accept advertising from companies involved in political, religious, alcohol, tobacco or sex products (Chaika 1998). However, violent R-rated movies have been increasingly advertised in student newspapers, a practice criticised by the Federal Trade Commission following the 1999 Columbine High School shootings (Molnar and Reaves 2001).

The FTC is now being asked to direct its attention to depictions of sex and violence in movies being promoted to children following the alleged failure of self-regulation by the Motion Picture Association of America (MPAA). In a scenario similar to that described above with regard to alcohol ads complained about, the watchdog Children's Advertising Review Unit (CARU) referred fifteen PG-13 movies to the MPAA for violence, sex, drug use and language. The MPAA decided that none contravened its self-regulation advertising rules (Edwards 2009c).

Cover Concepts (part of Marvel Entertainment) is a promotion strategy that has been highly successful in the United States, distributing free materials to more than 30 million children, including book covers, bookmarks, posters and educational comics, branded with a company's name or logo. The list of companies who advertise to children in this way includes McDonald's, Pepsi, Hershey, M&Ms and Mars (Cover Concepts website, cited in Story and French 2004).

The growth in this market has been substantial over the past decade, despite some controversy, argument and opposition. In Canada in 1999, the Ontario School Bus Association issued a policy statement arguing that external advertising on school buses could reduce the uniquely recognisable and conspicuous appearance of school buses, putting children at risk (Ontario School Bus Association 1999). A General Mills campaign for a sweetened cereal that paid elementary school teachers $250 per month to drive to school with their cars wrapped in a vinyl ad was cancelled after three weeks as a result of public protest (Tevlin 2001).

The Consumers Union in Canada issued a major report in 1998: *Captive Kids: A Report on Commercial Pressures on Kids at School*, in which they highlighted a number of disturbing trends, for example:

- *The use of biased corporate sponsored educational materials in schools.* An examination of 200 examples of corporate education materials and programmes found that 80 per cent were biased in favour of the sponsor's products or views. For example, Proctor & Gamble sponsored an educational packet that taught that disposable nappies are better for the environment than cloth nappies. They did not advise that they had commissioned the study that produced these results. Proctor & Gamble has since stopped production of the kit.
- *Requiring whole schools to participate in corporate sponsored contests.* Such a whole school contest occurred at Greenbriar High School in Georgia. A prize of $500 was offered by

Coco Cola for the best marketing idea. The students arranged themselves in T-shirts spelling 'Coke' and were photographed from a crane. One of the students in the letter 'C' suddenly revealed a T-shirt that said 'Pepsi' and was promptly suspended from the school. His suspension provided fuel for the debate on the appropriateness of such corporate activities (Schlosser 2001).

The Canadian Teachers' Federation, the Fédération des syndicats de l'enseignement and the Canadian Centre for Policy Alternatives have now released their own report on commercialism in Canadian schools to assist in advocating against this trend (Froese-Germain *et al.* 2006).

Activists ('culture jammers' such as Adbusters; see urinal ad from Campaign for Commercial-Free Schools, see Figure 9.4 above) are attempting to counter the trend in North America. For example, Arizona's State University has a Commercialisation in Education Research Unit, which gathers and publishes statistics on corporate intrusion into education. They report that the number of citations of commercialisation in the media increased from approximately 1,000 in 1990 to nearly 7,000 in 1999–2000, declining to approximately 5,500 in 2000–1 (Molnar and Reaves 2001). The authors hope that this represents a decline, but acknowledge that it may also represent people coming to accept what they see as the inevitable. As they put it, 'Cash-strapped administrators accept, sometimes solicit, and increasingly defend commercialising activities as means of making up budget shortfalls and financing everything from computers and musical instruments to art supplies and staff training' (Molnar and Reaves 2001). Given the money involved, it is not surprising that schools succumb to such overtures. The real problem comes when the school's income is tied to the quantity of product sold – which is the basis for some deals. How can such schools not encourage consumption?

McDonald's ads on school report cards. Not Ok

Local business ads on school tests. That's Ok?

First we had McDonald's rewarding Seminole County students with Happy Meal menu items for scoring As and Bs or few absences and school reports becoming promotional vehicles for Ronald (Elliott 2007) (see Figure 9.5). Then, soon after that battle was fought and won with McDonald's ceasing the promotion in 2008 (Elliott 2008), a cash strapped teacher in San Diego began to sell ads on his test papers to local businesses after the district announced it was cutting spending on school supplies (Toppo and Kornblum 2008). While some of the ads appear to be really donations, others are outright commercial. However, given the financial pressure teachers are under, the move seems to have the tacit approval of many teachers. Perhaps this is simply a sign that the United States has indeed become a 'commercial' culture when a first line solution to funding is to go commercial rather than increase pressure on politicians to restore funding.

Figure 9.5 School report card from a Seminole County public school, United States

Marketing in Schools Campaign for a Commercial-Free Childhood–Reclaiming Childhood from Corporate Marketers, an advocacy arm of the Judge Baker Children's Center at Harvard University, see www. commercialfreechildhood.org.

Until schools are adequately financed it will be very difficult to counter the trend. A group of UK companies that market to children has developed the MediaSmart[R] programme of media literacy materials for children 6–11 years. Critics view it as a cynical attempt to avoid tighter regulations, but defenders of the MediaSmart[R] programme regard it as a socially responsible effort to reduce children's vulnerability to marketing (O'Sullivan 2007). In the meantime, children are being presented with unhealthy food and beverage choices in the interest of fund raising for schools (Henry and Garcia 2004; Molnar *et al.* 2008).

Internal competition

And now a word about 'internal' competition. Threats to social marketing programmes can also come from government and political party policy. For example, public service departments charged with social change are continually forced to compromise programmes because of government policy. The highly successful Freedom from Fear campaign targeting male perpetrators, was initially shelved by the incoming Labour Government with the stated reason being that the Labour Party preferred a community action approach. However, we suspect that a further and major reason was that the Freedom from Fear campaign had been an initiative of the previous Conservative Government.

Privatisation

Privatisation is possibly today's major competitor to achieving major changes in the social determinants of crime, ill-health and social distress. Privatisation involves a move away from community responsibility via government funded programmes to an increasing tendency towards individual responsibility, with arguably significant deleterious impact on the disadvantaged in society.

What will happen to the game 'cops and robbers'?

While private detectives like Sherlock Holmes, Larry Kent and the renowned Pinkerton Agency have been around for some time, few citizens would ever have expected that their local copper might some day be an employee of a major corporation rather than a public servant. The growing reality, however, is that this may well be the case – and the cops are worried.

In Swedish writer Mankell's best-selling thriller *Sidetracked*, this exchange takes place between a couple of senior cops in Sweden:
'There's a rumour going round that staff numbers are going to be cut back on Saturday and Sunday nights.'
'That won't work. Who's going to deal with the people we've got in the cells?'
'Rumour has it that they're going to take tenders for that job from private security companies.'
'Security companies?'
'That's what I heard.'

(Mankell 2000).

Privatisation, in various forms, is a worldwide problem as governments attempt to shed responsibilities. For example, in France in May 2009, thousands of doctors and nurses marched in protest at what they considered the 'commercialisation of health care' by the French Government's attempt to impose a commercial model on the public hospital system (what we would call privatisation by degrees) (Benkimoun 2009).

Predatory corporations that lobby government to yield what many consider core areas of government to the private sector represent real competition for many government departments. In Australia in recent years this has seen areas such as public transport, prisons, energy and road transport taken over by the private sector. At the same time we have seen increasing pressure on schools, police, universities and hospitals to raise funds from the private sector, via sponsorship and other fund raising, to remain viable. While the air force has never had to call on its employees and families to have a cake sale to raise funds for a new fighter plane, school principals are having to spend more and more of their time on financial management rather than their core business of education. Similarly, we doubt that we'll see a fund raising drive by the Pentagon to make up the US$1.75 billion needed to buy an extra seven F-22 Raptor jets because the

US Senate blocked the deal. But don't worry; the Pentagon still has 187 on order (Bittle 2009).

Perhaps one of the greatest ironies in Iraq is that private contractors rather than the US armed forces provide security for visiting dignitaries, diplomats and high ranking armed forces personnel. Total spending for private security contractors in Iraq from 2003 to 2007 was between US$6 billion and US$10 billion, and, as of 2008, 25,000 to 30,000 private security employees were operating in Iraq (Congressional Budget Office 2008). Would privatised security forces – in whatever capacity – show the same regard for human rights as public servants? The Blackwater guards' killing of fourteen unarmed Iraqi citizens in 2007 (and other incidents) and the following box suggest not.

The death of Mr Ward: privatisation puts profits before prisoners' human rights

Australia's systemic racism against its Indigenous population and the privatisation of its prisoner transport system were a deadly mix for a widely respected Aboriginal elder, Mr Ward. Mr Ward was apprehended for drinking and driving in a remote area of the outback and locked up for the night in the local police station – a consequence that would not have happened to a white man in that area, let alone in a city suburb for that type of offence. Mr Ward was denied bail the next morning and transported in a private security company's van to the town of Kalgoorlie, some 400 km away, to appear in the regional court. The air conditioning in the prisoner compartment of the van did not work and was on record as faulty. The privatised prison guards did not check the prison compartment air conditioning (their cabin was ok), nor did they stop for a toilet or rest break for that whole journey. They drove non-stop in outside temperatures up to 40°C. The prison compartment had no airflow other than the non-functioning air conditioning. The inside temperature reached 50°C and Mr Ward literally cooked to death. The coroner's report was a damning indictment of Australia's human rights and humanity. The private custodial company (G4S) and the Department of Corrections both knew the prisoner transport fleet was in dire need of renewal and upgrading and had been warned several times that such a death would be the inevitable result of inaction. The coroner had this to say: 'In my view, it is a disgrace that a prisoner in the 21st century, particularly a prisoner who has not been convicted of any crime, was transported for a long distance in high temperatures in this pod.' The Human Rights Commission solicitor was less reserved and closer to the truth: 'Mr Ward's treatment during his transportation from Laverton to Kalgoorlie … was cruel, inhuman and degrading.' In our view, the profit motive – combined with a systemic disregard for Indigenous prisoners who constitute the vast bulk of prisoners requiring transport in outback areas – were directly responsible for Mr Ward's death.

Would a privatised police service put the same value on domestic violence and child abuse prevention as a government service? Would there be the same co-operation between a private police service and welfare organisations? Would a private service focus on convictions rather than prevention as a key performance indicator? What are the implications for social marketing of 'community policing' and 'neighbourhood watch'? Would householders be more inclined or less inclined to co-operate with a profit motivated police service?

In short, there are many implications of privatisation, and not just directly for government departments or units charged with social change. For example, what are the implications for Health Department campaigns within privatised prisons where there may well be a cost incurred by the prison corporation? A major task for social marketers, as we define them, is to use social marketing to ensure that governments retain what are considered the core functions of government that ensure the health and well-being of their citizens.

Concluding comments

Social marketers must continually identify and monitor their competition. This is essential to understanding why our target audiences engage in undesirable practices and for mounting advocacy campaigns against corporations marketing undesirable products and organisations promoting undesirable ideas. Monitoring means more than just looking at marketing tactics; industry manufacturing and preparation practices must also be monitored. Unfortunately, little government funded research is directed towards this aim, although there are signs that the importance of such data is now being increasingly recognised.

Our major area for competition is children and youth. In this chapter we have emphasised the targeting of youth and the schoolroom as the place where we must draw the line against commercialism. We do not want the fast food giants running school tuck shops and university canteens. We do not want principals and teachers acting as sales and commission agents for marketers. We do not want school textbooks (like McGraw-Hill's) that use brand names like Nike, Burger King and Oreo in its maths problems, or free samples of Prego spaghetti sauce for measuring viscosity, or samples of sweets that 'gush' when bitten so children can discuss the process needed to make such sweets (Peters 1999). We do not want children assuming that commercial consumption is all of, rather than just a part of, life – or, in the extreme, life itself, as in this paraphrase where professional sport's values with respect to 'winning' versus 'participating' have also declined: *'Branding isn't everything. It's the only thing.'*

But commercialism is only one of the competitors for children. Competition for kids to become healthy citizens comes also from the family, community and socio-economic conditions in which they are born and nurtured. And here we compete with government and major institutional forces. Most social marketers face competition for resources from other social marketers, and competition from political and ideological forces in government and the bureaucracy. Hence, as Andreasen (2002) discusses, perhaps social marketers need to be doing a lot more marketing of social marketing.

Overall, most commercial marketers operate on three aspects: making a product or service *attractive*, *affordable* and *available*. Hence, we need to counter on all three of these aspects – whether by education, motivation or legislation – as well as remember that before people will adopt our recommended behaviours, they must have, as the coppers would say, *motive* (see some benefit to themselves for doing it), *opportunity* (to do what we are asking them to do) and *ability* (self-efficacy). Hence, meeting the competition means ensuring that the environment actually provides opportunities for expressing the desired behaviour and might also involve skills training for the target group.

QUESTIONS

- List the major competition to programmes attempting to decrease overweight and obesity.
- What do alcohol advertisers promise young people in exchange for consuming their products?
- Should alcohol sponsorship of major sports be banned? What are the arguments for and against?
- Should schools accept deals with commercial marketers? What major marketers have a presence on your campus?

FURTHER READING

Davidson, D. K. 2003. *Selling Sin: the Marketing of Socially Unacceptable Products*. Westport, CT: Praeger.

Molnar, A., Boninger, F., Wilkinson, G. and Fogarty, J. 2008. At Sea in a Marketing-saturated World, Eleventh Annul Report on Schoolhouse Commercialism Trends: 2007–8, Boulder and Tempe, Education and the Public Interest Center & Commercialisation in Education Research Unit.

10 Segmentation and targeting

Acknowledging that different people may respond differently to different products and services and to the way information is presented to them, is a core principle in marketing. In fact, commercial marketers spend a great deal of resources identifying and determining which segments will be most profitable for them. Not surprisingly, then, market segmentation and target marketing have been emphasised from the start in the early literature defining or describing *social* marketing and its application to public health campaigns (e.g., Lancaster, McIlwain and Lancaster 1983; Manoff 1985; Novelli 1984). In today's social marketing literature, the need to target programmes at different segments of the population is taken for granted.

Market segmentation, the division of the total market into relatively homogeneous but distinct segments, and target marketing, the selection and concentration of marketing resources on one or more of these segments, together constitute the principle of selectivity and concentration. This principle follows naturally from a focus on consumer or client needs, since it acknowledges that:

- different sub-groups exist in a population;
- the differences occur on a variety of dimensions; and
- different strategies and approaches may be necessary to reach, communicate with or motivate different sub-groups.

This last point is crucial: unless the segments respond differentially to different elements of the marketing mix there is no point in segmenting.

Differences may occur in three ways:

- *locating or reaching members of the target segment*: different target audiences may be reached by different channels, inhabit different geographical areas or attend different types of entertainment;
- *communicating with members of the target audience*: different target audiences may have different values, attitudes and lifestyles, and, hence, different communication styles may be necessary to attract their attention and establish rapport; and

Table 10.1 Common bases for market segmentation	
Attitudinal	Positive, neutral, negative
Behavioural	Frequency, intensity, regularity
Demographic	Age, sex, income, education, religion, ethnicity, occupation, family life cycle
Epidemiological	Risk factor status
Geographic	State, region, city size, density (urban, suburban, rural, remote), climate, local government area, postcode, census collectors' district
Motives and benefits sought	Varies by issue (e.g., avoid disease, sensory enjoyment; peace of mind, etc.)
Psychographic	Values, lifestyle, personality
Readiness stage	Stages of change
Socio-demographic	Social class

- *motivating members of the target audience*: different target groups may be motivated for different reasons to achieve the desired behavioural response.

For example, lower socio-economic (SES) status groups may be more avid TV watchers of soap operas and reality TV shows than upper SES groups, but a message (about child immunisation) can be communicated in the same style and tone of language to both, and both may be motivated by the same factor (protection of their children). In this case, we need only select different media vehicles to reach the different groups. In other cases, we may need different ways of communicating to appeal to different groups, and their motivations to comply may be quite different.

Market segments can be described or profiled in many ways (see Table 10.1), with market researchers continually seeking better ways to delineate segments that respond differentially to different elements of the marketing mix.

Most segmentation begins with a primary initial segmentation base (e.g., users versus non-users of brand A, outgoing young males, retirees, etc.), and then these may be further sub-segmented by attitudes to the desired behaviour change, media habits, geographic location and so on. That is, regardless of the base(s) chosen for the initial segmentation (e.g., age and sex), the segments are also usually described or *profiled* on as many other variables as necessary to better understand the chosen segment(s). For example, we may segment teen smokers by age (13–16 years, 17–19 years) and sex, but then, within each segment we could further segment by employment status and occupation. We could further profile the different sub-groups on their leisure activities (e.g., type of music preferred, indoor versus outdoor orientated, passive versus active leisure pursuits, etc.) and so on.

Segmenting kids

Carolyn Heath, of the kids marketing consultancy, Logistix Kids, suggests segmenting children according to the stages of development when planning how to communicate with and motivate kids (Ligerakis 2001):

- sensory: 0–2 years;
- perceptual: 3–7 years;
- analytical: 8–12 years;
- reflective: 13–16 years.

Those interested in children's beliefs about health and morality use a similar demarcation – all based on Piaget's longstanding cognitive development stages.

For health promotion campaigns, target groups are often described in terms of *risk factor status* (e.g., smokers, the obese, the inactive, heavy drinkers, diabetics, etc.), or demographic groupings that epidemiologically appear at higher risk for the health issue in question (e.g., blue collar groups for smoking, sedentary occupations for physical activity, obese, inactive populations for diabetes, street kids for hepatitis C, etc.). Where resources are available, these are then segmented by attitude towards the desired behaviour change as this will largely determine whether or not different message strategies or interventions will be necessary for the different attitudinal groups.

According to *Marketing News* in 1987, the heaviest litterers in Texas in the late 1980s were defined as rural, pick-up truck driving, macho males, aged 18 to 34. While one motivation for all litterers was to avoid a fine of up to US$1,000, the key was to communicate with these males in a way that would engage their attention. Hence, at the beginning of the campaign the message was delivered via music by groups popular with the target audience – like the Fabulous Thunderbirds and Stevie Ray Vaughn – and through radio and TV spots by athletes such as Ed (Too Tall) Jones and Randy White.

After the first year of the campaign, littering reportedly dropped by 29 per cent overall, with deliberate littering by this target group being reduced by 41 per cent (*Marketing News* 1987). Littering was reduced 72 per cent in the first six years of the campaign (McClure and Spence 2006). 'Don't mess with Texas' continues today as one of the best-known anti-litter campaigns in the United States and has continued to work with celebrities who support the campaign, such as Lee Ann Womack, Matthew McConaughey, Jennifer Love Hewitt, Lance Armstrong and Chuck Norris. (www. dontmesswithtexas.org: 'Don't mess with Texas' is a registered trademark of the Texas Department of Transportation).

Table 10.1 indicates that there are three major ways of segmenting populations:

(1) via generally mutually exclusive classifications on one or more demographic or geographic characteristics (e.g., 18–34-year-old blue collar males living in rural Texas) (e.g., epidemiological descriptors of risk status);
(2) via generally mutually exclusive attitudinal or behavioural measures relating to the desired behaviour change (e.g., heavy regular smokers versus social smokers, readiness to change, positive versus negative attitude to change, perceived benefits of changing or not changing); and
(3) via attitudinal clusters such as in 'psychographics'.

Given an emphasis on achieving behaviour change, the focus in this book is on segmentations that are most useful for determining what strategies would most influence behaviour change. Hence, we consider that the two most useful ways for segmenting target populations for social marketing campaigns are Sheth and Frazier's (1982) attitude–behaviour segmentation and Prochaska's stage-of-change segmentation (Prochaska and DiClemente 1984). These methods should be applied even where resources are limited, since both provide the programme planner with an understanding of the beliefs and attitudes of their target groups that need to be changed, and, along with an understanding of what might motivate change, directions to achieve those changes. However, before looking at our recommended approaches, a brief word on psychographics – 'beware'.

Psychographics

One popular method in the marketing and advertising area is the psychographic or lifestyle approach. In this procedure respondents answer a number of usually general values, attitude, belief and behaviour questions (usually between fifty to a hundred). Cluster analysis or some proprietary algorithm is then used to group respondents who respond similarly to the items, and discriminant analysis is used to determine which items best differentiate the resulting clusters. Perhaps the best known psychographic approach was VALS™. The original VALS consisted of a large number of items based on Maslow's hierarchy of needs and Reisman's inner–outer directedness. VALS applied an algorithm to place people into one of nine categories reflecting their position on the above two dimensions.

The psychographic approach has particular appeal to advertising creatives, because, compared with traditional demographic segment descriptions such as *'married, 2.5 children, aged 30–45, lower-middle socio-economic level'*, psychographic segments list descriptions such as *'outgoing, active in community activities, enjoys physical activities rather than reading, prefers barbecues rather than dinner parties, etc.'*. Furthermore, psychographic segments are often given catchy segment titles such as *'swinging singles'*, *'elderly adventurers'*, or *'new age sensitive men'*. We take the view that psychographics are useful in communicating with segments, but the basic segmentation should be on dimensions that inform how to *motivate* the different segments.

Psychographic segments compared across health behaviours (e.g., the percentage of smokers in each segment) often showed little meaningful variation between segments. Furthermore, the segment descriptions gave little guidance as to which of the segments should be targeted and left the marketer in the untenable and unrealistic position of designing separate programmes for each segment. In fact, the original VALS was abandoned by many commercial marketers because of its limited power to predict differences in purchasing behaviour between segments.

The main problem with psychographic and other lifestyle/attitude–interests–opinion (AIO) segmentations is that the groups are not particularly exclusive, with considerable overlap between them. For example, 70 per cent of cluster 'A' might agree with the statement 'I prefer visiting natural wilderness areas to man-made entertainments like Disney World' versus 35 per cent of cluster 'B' agreeing with the statement. While this is certainly a substantial and statistically significant difference, 35 per cent of cluster 'B' share this characteristic with cluster 'A' and 30 per cent of cluster 'A' do not share this characteristic with their 'own' cluster.

Similarly, when applied to areas such as tobacco, we might find that 35 per cent of 'swingers', 16 per cent of 'conservatives' and 42 per cent of 'upwardly mobiles' are smokers. What do we do? Target 'upwardly mobiles' if that is also the largest segment? Such 'backward' segmentations are not useful. It is far more useful to begin with smokers and then segment smokers with respect to their attitude to – or perceived motivators for – quitting, followed by lifestyle profiling if necessary to communicate differently or to reach them through different channels.

Targeting by risk factor profile

SKIN CANCER
HAVE YOU BEEN CHECKED?

The ....LIONS CLUB has organised a FREE skin cancer screening. Specialists from the LIONS CANCER INSTITUTE will be available to examine people who feel they are at risk of having skin cancer.

If you are 16 years of age or older and have one or more of the following:

◆ A family member has had a malignant melanoma

◆ Five or more moles (not freckles) on your arms

◆ Previously had moles or skin cancers removed

◆ A mole or freckle that is changing in size or colour

◆ Fair skin that burns rather than tans

◆ Had blistering sunburn as a child

◆ Any inflamed skin sores that do not heal

then please phone .... to make an appointment.

Venue: ....

Date:...

If you are concerned but cannot attend the screening on that date please express your interest with the LIONS CANCER INSTITUTE and see your family Doctor.

Ads like this are designed to increase the appropriateness of attendees at skin cancer screening clinics (Katris, Donovan and Gray 1996).

An improvement on general attitudinal/lifestyle clustering is where the statements are specific to the product category or issue in question. One example here is Ed Maibach's segmentation with regard to Americans' beliefs about and attitudes towards 'global warming'. Maibach, Roser-Renouf and Leiserowitz (2009) surveyed more than 2,000 American adults representative of the general adult population. Six segments were identified via latent class analysis of thirty-six variables related to global warming

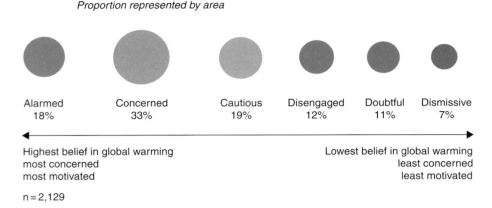

Proportion represented by area

| Alarmed 18% | Concerned 33% | Cautious 19% | Disengaged 12% | Doubtful 11% | Dismissive 7% |

Highest belief in global warming
most concerned
most motivated

Lowest belief in global warming
least concerned
least motivated

n = 2,129

Figure 10.1 Proportion of the US adult population in global warming's Six Americas

Maibach, Roser-Renouf and Leiserowitz (2009)

beliefs, issue involvement, policy preferences and climate change relevant behaviours (i.e., items such as such as perceived seriousness of effects on various populations, extent of worry, perceptions of scientists' beliefs about global warming, perceived efficacy of actions to reduce global warming, etc.).

Clustering people on these items yielded six segments (Global Warming's 'Six Americas') which were labelled: 'alarmed' (18 per cent of the population); 'concerned' (33 per cent); 'cautious' (19 per cent); 'disengaged' (12 per cent); 'doubtful' (11 per cent); and 'dismissive' (7 per cent) (see Figure 10.1).

The groups were then compared across a number of global warming behavioural intention measures, with, not surprisingly, greater support for measures to reduce global warming among the 'alarmed' and 'concerned' groups, and least among the 'dismissives'. The primary discriminators between the groups appeared to be 'how convinced people were that global warming is happening' and 'how worried' they were (see Figures 10.2 and 10.3), which suggests that an alternative procedure would be to first segment people on one or other of these measures and then compare each of these four groups on the behaviour–intention measures (as in the Sheth–Frazier framework considered next).

Behavioural clustering

An alternative is to cluster on relevant behaviours rather than beliefs and attitudes. A UK sample of more than 1,200 Devon householders was cluster analysed on a range of behaviours such as purchasing energy efficient and recycled items, reuse of glass and paper, composting, using own bags when shopping, looking for less packaging, etc. The analysis revealed four clusters that the researchers labelled 'committed

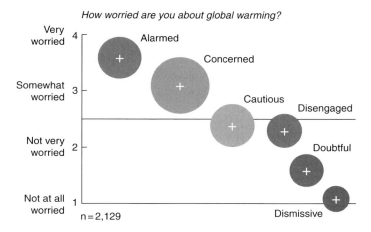

Figure 10.2 How worried about global warming are people in each of the Six Americas

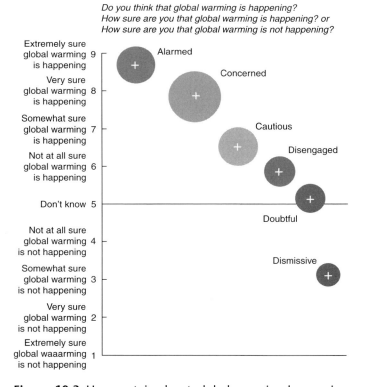

Figure 10.3 How certain about global warming happening are people in each of the Six Americas

environmentalists' (23 per cent), 'mainstream environmentalists' (33 per cent), occasional environmentalists (40 per cent) and 'non-environmentalists (3 per cent) (Gilg, Barr and Ford 2005).

Motives and benefits segmentation

Benefits segmentation is one of the most popular types of targeting in commercial marketing. This is hardly surprising, given that marketing is all about designing and delivering products and services that meet people's needs. Products and services are designed with particular attributes that provide benefits that different segments of the market are seeking. For example, toothpastes are positioned as cavity fighters or breath fresheners or teeth whiteners for flashing smiles; car models are positioned on safety or economy or power or luxury or road handling; dairy products include low fat or calcium boosted or low sugar options, etc. These market offerings recognise that although people may want multiple benefits, they can be segmented on a single primary motivating benefit. Motives–benefits segmentation, like the Sheth–Frazier and stage segmentations below, sets clear directions for action for specifically defined groups. In fact, it is often incorporated in these segmentations.

Understanding people's motives for, or benefits sought, in continuing undesired behaviours and, conversely, what might motivate cessation of undesired behaviours and adoption of desired alternatives should be at the core of all social marketing programmes anyway. This simple segmentation basis is often overlooked as people become seduced by seemingly fancy and sophisticated clustering methods that produce segments with intuitively appealing names such as 'determined smokers', 'resistant smokers' or 'status seeking social smokers'. Such segments are fine to extend our understanding of smokers, but they should not be the basis on which to develop campaigns; smokers' motivations to quit (along with perceived barriers etc.) must remain the primary focus because these determine the underlying messages and interventions.

Motives–benefits segments can then be profiled to provide insights into how to communicate with and reach the different motive–benefit segments. For example, while the negative health consequences remain relevant to varying degrees for all smokers, older smokers might be motivated to quit 'to be around for their grandchildren', whereas younger smokers might be motivated by price (tax) increases; younger adults might be motivated to exercise more for body image and fitness benefits, whereas middle-aged people might be motivated more by the benefits of weight control or cardiovascular disease risk reduction.

Sheth's and Frazier's attitude–behaviour segmentation

Sheth and Frazier (1982) present a model of strategy choice based on the concept of attitude–behaviour consistency/discrepancy (see Table 10.2). They provide a

Table 10.2 A typology of strategy mix for planned social change

	Attitude	
	Positive	Negative
Perform desired behaviour	Cell 1 Reinforcement process (a) behavioural (b) psychological	Cell 2 Rationalisation process Attitude change
Don't perform desired behaviour	Cell 3 Inducement process Behaviour change	Cell 4 Confrontation process (a) behavioural (b) psychological

Sheth and Frazier (1982).

systematic procedure not only for describing various target segments in terms of attitude and behaviour (the 'diagnosis'), but also suggest a strategy for achieving behaviour change within each of the defined segments (the 'prognosis'). Population surveys are necessary to determine the proportions falling into each of the segments. The segments can then be profiled in terms of their demographics, media habits, lifestyle variables, risk factor profiles and other relevant health beliefs and attitudes.

According to Sheth and Frazier, when attitudes and behaviour are consistent and in the desired direction (Cell 1), a *reinforcement* process is required to sustain the desired behaviour. This can be done by reinforcing the attitude, reinforcing the behaviour, or both. For example, non-smoking teenagers should be continually reminded of all the reasons why they do not smoke; adult non-smokers can be reinforced by insurance premium discounts; non-smokers should continue to congratulate reformed smokers for quitting; road safety campaigns should feed back that the campaigns have successfully reduced crashes and so on. Energy bill statements that congratulate householders for reducing their power consumption illustrate such reinforcement.

Where people hold positive attitudes towards, but do not carry out, the desired behaviour (Cell 3), an *inducement* process is required. These can be aimed at minimising or removing organisational, economic, time or place constraints. This could include actions such as providing changing rooms at the worksite to facilitate lunchtime or before/after work exercise, providing discounts to non-working mothers to attend a gym during off-peak hours and visiting worksites for blood donations; in short, making it easier for the positive attitude to be translated into action.

In some cases, the behaviour is being performed, but the attitude is negative (Cell 2). This may occur where a partner insists on the behaviour, or where the behaviour is temporarily mandatory. In these cases, **rationalisation** needs to occur to shift the individual into the positive Cell 1. Information on the benefits of the behaviour need to be communicated, along with efforts to at least neutralise negative affect and create positive affect.

Where attitudes are negative and the behaviour is not being performed (Cell 4, table 10.2), behavioural **confrontation** (e.g., restrictions on the behaviour) or psychological confrontation (e.g., 'hard-hitting' TV ads, face-to-face counselling) may be necessary.

The particular components of each of these approaches will depend on the beliefs underlying the overall attitudes towards the desired behaviour, along with an understanding of physical, social and structural facilitators and inhibitors. For example, some people positive towards increasing their levels of physical activity may simply be lazy, others may lack nearby safe facilities and others may have too many family and work demands competing for their time.

Table 10.3 Extended Sheth–Frazier segmentation model

	Behaviour		
Attitude	Always perform desired behaviour	Sometimes perform	Do not perform desired behaviour
Positive	Cell 1	Cell 4	Cell 7
Neutral	Cell 2	Cell 5	Cell 8
Negative	Cell 3	Cell 6	Cell 9

In much of our work we include a neutral category on the attitude dimension (see Table 10.3), as there are many situations where people do not have a view one way or the other. It represents the more realistic strategy of attempting to move people first from a negative to neutral, then from neutral to a positive position, rather than from a negative to a positive position in one step. Where relevant, we include two or more levels of the desired behaviour, as there are quite distinct gradations of desired and undesired behaviour for many issues (e.g., physical activity levels, alcohol frequency or amount, regular versus occasional intimate partner violence, degree of water and energy conservation, degree of recycling, etc.). Furthermore, the behavioural segmentation can be done either with regard to the desired behaviour or the undesired behaviour.

The nature of the segments also allows a determination of whether or not mass media messages are an appropriate and cost-effective method for influencing the different segments. For example, Cells 4 and 7 in Table 10.3 are far more likely than Cell 9 to respond to a media campaign, and Cell 9 probably requires a totally different approach. However, even in this case, mass media may be used to increase that target group's awareness of the issue.

A stage approach to segmentation

A segmentation model directly applicable for many areas of behaviour change derives from Prochaska's clinical work with cigarette and drug addiction (Prochaska and DiClemente 1984, 1986): transtheoretical model of behaviour change. This model now forms the fundamental basis of some social marketing frameworks (Andreasen 1995).

The stages-of-change concept divides the target population (for example, smokers, non-exercisers, coercive parents, men who use violence, drug users), into sub-segments depending on their stage in progression towards adoption of the desired behaviour (i.e., quitting, taking up exercise, using positive parenting practices, ceasing violent behaviour, stopping drug use).

Prochaska's stages are:

(1) *precontemplation* – where the individual is not considering modifying their undesired behaviour;
(2) *contemplation* – where the individual is considering changing an undesired behaviour, but not in the immediate future;
(3) *preparation* – where the individual plans to try to change the undesired behaviour in the immediate future (that is, in the next two weeks or an appropriate time frame);
(4) *action* – the immediate (six-month) period following trial and adoption of the recommended behaviour and cessation of the undesired behaviour;
(5) *maintenance* – the period following the action stage until the undesired behaviour is fully extinguished;
(6) *termination* – when the problem behaviour is completely eliminated, that is, 'zero temptation across all problem situations'.

As in the Sheth–Frazier model, Prochaska and DiClemente claim that individuals at different stages of change would have different attitudes, beliefs and motivations with respect to the (desired) new behaviour. Hence, different treatment approaches and health communication strategies may be necessary for individuals in the different stages-of-change. There is some support for these claims over a variety of areas (see Prochaska *et al.* 1994 for an analysis of twelve health problem behaviours and Nigg *et al.* 1999 for ten behaviours in an older population), but particularly smoking, nutrition and exercise (de Vet *et al.* 2008; Oman and King 1998; Spencer *et al.* 2006). The model has also been applied across a variety of countries and sub-groups, including African-American and Hispanic sub-populations in the United States, the United Kingdom (Steptoe *et al.* 2003: fruit and vegetables consumption), Holland (de Vet *et al.* 2007: fruit intake), Sweden (Kristjansson *et al.* 2003: skin cancer), Spain (Canga *et al.* 2000: smoking in diabetic patients) and fifteen European Union states (Kearney *et al.* 1999: physical activity).

Prochaska, Norcross and DiClemente (1994) describe nine activities or processes of change that individuals use to proceed through the stages of change:

- consciousness raising – increasing awareness about the problem;
- emotional arousal – dramatic expressions of the problem and consequences;
- self-re-evaluation – reappraisal of the problem and its inconsistency with self-values;
- commitment – choosing to change and making a public commitment to do so;
- social liberation – choosing social environments that foster or facilitate change;
- relationship fostering – getting help from others, professional or otherwise;
- counter conditioning – substituting alternatives;
- rewards – administering self-praise or other positive experiences for dealing with the problem; and
- environmental control – restructuring of the environment to reduce temptations and opportunities.

The processes at the top of the list are experiential, whereas those lower in the list are behavioural. The former occur more in the earlier stages of change, the latter in the later stages. The transtheoretical model also incorporates the notion of decisional balance: that an evaluation of the costs (cons) and benefits (pros) of making the change varies over the stages, with cons outweighing pros in precontemplation, pros outweighing cons in the action stage, with crossing over occurring during contemplation.

Prochaska's concept is similar to marketing's 'buyer–readiness' segmentation, which states that at any particular point in time, the market can be described in terms of those unaware of the product, those aware of the product, those informed about the product, those interested in the product, those motivated to buy the product and those who have formed an intention to buy the product (Kotler 1988) (the AIDA model: awareness, interest, desire, action). The implications of this are that marketing objectives and strategy will vary according to the relative proportions of the total market in each of these different stages.

Egger, Donovan and Spark (1993) and Donovan and Owen (1994) have suggested the potential utility of the stage model as a segmentation base in health promotion and social marketing. They delineated the various communication and behavioural objectives at the different stages as shown in Table 10.4. Mass media-based campaigns are most influential in the precontemplation and contemplation stages (by raising the salience and personal relevance of the issue), of moderate influence in the preparation stage (by reinforcing perceptions of self-efficacy and maintaining salience of the perceived benefits of adopting the recommended behaviour) and have mainly reminder influence in the action and maintenance stages where beliefs are well established and where socio-environmental influences are greatest.

As noted above, the stages of change concept has been readily adopted by health promoters and social marketers (e.g., Andreasen 1995; Booth *et al.* 1993; Maibach and

Table 10.4 Campaign objectives and relative influence of mass media by stages of change

Prochaska stages	Communication objectives	Behavioural objectives	Mass media influence
Precontemplation	Raise awareness of issue, personal relevance	Seek further information	High
Contemplation	Increase personal Relevance, build response efficacy	Form an intention to try	Moderate–high
Preparation	Build self-efficacy, reinforce reasons for trial	Trial	Moderate
Action	Reinforce reasons for adoption, maintain Motivational and efficacy support	Adoption	Low
Maintenance	Maintain reasons for adoption	Maintain new behaviour	Low

Donovan and Owen (1994).

Cotton 1995). However, for any marketing segmentation base to be meaningful, it must be shown that the different segments respond differentially to some aspects of the communication and marketing mixes directed at the segments. Hence, the utility of the stages-of-change approach in social marketing is dependent on evidence that individuals in the various stages of change do respond differentially to elements of the social marketing mix. While a number of studies have shown differences between individuals in the different stages of change, much of this has been directed towards the implications for counselling and educational interventions.

Donovan, Leivers and Hannaby (1999) tested three anti-smoking ads and analysed the results for precontemplators, contemplators and those in the ready-for-action and action stages. Figure 10.4 shows a significant relationship between the stages of change and the ads' impact on intentions to quit or cut down the amount smoked. These results support the utility of the stages of change as a segmentation variable.

The stages-of-change concept is widely used but perhaps not always properly understood, especially with regard to the various processes applicable to each of the stages (Whitelaw *et al.* 1999). Nevertheless, regardless of whether one adopts Prochaska's recommended intervention processes for the various stages, the model is very useful as a segmentation method for recruiting sub-samples for formative research and for targeting in those areas most related to addictive behaviours from whence it was derived. Further, regardless of the finer points of these models, the concept of 'buyer readiness' or 'readiness to change' is a useful one in a practical sense. The Western Australian Freedom from Fear campaign targets 'men who are aware of their problem and want to

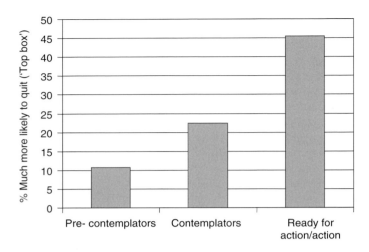

Figure 10.4 Impact of Quit ads on likelihood of quitting or cutting down by smokers' stage of change

Donovan, Leivers and Hannaby (1999)

change'. In stages terminology, that means violent men in the contemplator and ready-for-action stages (Donovan *et al.* 2000). In fact, the booklet for men explicitly states on the cover: 'For men who want to change'.

Stages of change for public opinion

At a broader level, the much respected public opinion tracker Daniel Yankelovich (1992) has delineated seven stages of public opinion change. These provide a format for segmenting whole communities, states or nations with regard to various issues such as women's rights and equality, climate controls, agricultural methods, capitalist economic models, or birth control and family planning. Yankelovich's seven stages are:

(1) **Dawning awareness**: this is when people first begin to become aware of an issue, usually through mass media news reports.
(2) **A sense of urgency**: people move from simple awareness of an issue to developing a sense of urgency about needing to form an opinion about it.
(3) **Discovering the choices**: people start to explore choices and look at the pros and cons about the issue, although there is widespread variation in the population in depth of understanding.
(4) **Resistance**: at this stage many people – through misunderstanding (or wishful thinking) – tend to opt for easy options rather than look more closely at benefits and trade-offs.

(5) **Weighing the choices**: in this stage, people more rationally and realistically weigh the pros and cons of alternatives.

(6) **Taking a stand intellectually**: at this stage, many people endorse an option in theory, but do not necessarily make any personal behavioural changes (as where people accept the need for carbon emission controls but do little about their behaviours).

(7) **Making a responsible judgement morally and emotionally**: in the final stage, people not only endorse an option, but accept the full implications of that option and modify their own behaviours to be consistent with that option.

Community readiness model

Another useful model, particularly for community-based interventions in developing countries or remote/rural indigenous communities in developed countries is the community readiness model (Kelly *et al.* 2003). This model – as its name suggests – is concerned with the stages a community must go through to get ready for an intervention, rather than the stages of progression after an intervention occurs. The model first looks at factors such as the community's current knowledge, actions and attitudes towards the issue in question, leadership in the community and community resources. It then delineates nine stages from 'no awareness' through various stages of denial, pre-planning, preparation and training, through to implementation of the intervention with a 'high level of community ownership'. This model has considerable overlap with the social mobilisation concept introduced in Chapter 1.

Personality

Segmenting by personality was popular at one stage in marketing, and particularly for beer and cigarette marketers, but appears to be rarely used today as a primary segmentation variable. However some personality scales have been found to predict some health behaviours, and particularly substance use. For example, those higher on tolerance of deviance and sensation seeking scales are more likely to use alcohol and illicit drugs, as are those with a propensity to risk taking in general.

Sensation seeking is a personality trait associated with the need for novel, complex, ambiguous and emotionally intense stimuli and the willingness to take risks to obtain such stimulation (Zuckerman 1994[2]). Given that many marijuana users were high sensation seekers, based on research with high sensation seeking teens, Palmgreen et al. (2001) developed anti-marijuana television public service announcements with high execution appeal to sensation seekers (i.e., communicating differently). Spots were placed in programmes that were watched by high sensation seeking adolescents (locating differently). Teenagers were surveyed before and after the campaign and the results analysed for high sensation versus low sensation seeking teens. The campaigns resulted in significant reductions in marijuana use in high sensation seeking adolescents whereas the (already low) usage did not change among low sensation seekers (see box below).

SENTAR: targeting by personality

Sensation seeking is characterised by a need for novel, complex, ambiguous, emotionally intense stimuli and a willingness to take risks to obtain such stimulation.

In terms of media preferences, sensation seekers prefer ads that are novel, dramatic, interesting, exciting, suspenseful, fast.

Anti-marijuana public service announcements were developed for high sensation seeking adolescents and televised in three counties in the United States.

Spots were placed in programmes with high sensation seeking audiences.

Pre-post surveys were analysed for high versus low sensation seeking teens.

Significant reductions in marijuana use in high sensation seeking adolescents; usage did not change among low sensation seekers (Palmgreen *et al.* 2002).

Selecting target audiences

Having delineated the various segments, the next step is to select one or more segments on which to concentrate. The commercial marketing literature offers only broad criteria as to how to select between segments. Similarly, with the exception of Andreasen's (1995) and Donovan, Egger and Francas' (1999) TARPARE model described below, little exists to assist public health practitioners select segments where limited resources require some prioritising.

For commercial marketers, segment size appears to be the primary determinant, although it is clear that other criteria need to be taken into account, such as the intensity of competitive activity directed at each segment, the range of products and services already available to each segment, the ease of geographically reaching each segment for tangible product delivery, access to the target segments via media channels for message delivery and the price sensitivity of different segments. These criteria provide a starting point for the TARPARE model.

TARPARE is a useful and flexible model for understanding the various segments in a population of interest, and assessing the potential viability of interventions directed at each segment, given limited resources. The model is particularly useful when, as is usually the case, there is a need to prioritise segments in terms of available budgets.

The TARPARE model

TARPARE is generally applied *after* a number of segments have been identified within a particular area of interest. That is, given a Sheth–Frazier attitude–behaviour segmentation such as that in Table 10.3, or a Prochaska segmentation (i.e., precontemplators,

contemplators and preparers for action), the TARPARE model evaluates the various segments on the following criteria:

- *T: Total number of persons in the segment.* In general, the greater the number of people, the greater the priority of the segment. This criterion is particularly important for mass interventions where small percentage shifts in large proportions of the population yield substantial benefits [e.g., reductions in driving speed and severity of injury, cholesterol shifts (Rose 1985, 1992)].

- *AR: proportion of 'At Risk' persons in the segment.* This includes a number of factors: (i) an assessment of what proportions of the segments are classified as 'low', 'medium' or 'high risk' with respect to the issue under consideration; (ii) an assessment of associated risk factors; and (iii) an assessment of *expected benefits* of risk reduction in the segment. For example, the proportion of heavy smokers might be greatest among blue collar males aged 25–35 years, but 36–50-year-old blue collar male smokers might have higher obesity levels, lower levels of physical activity and a higher incidence of diabetes. The proportion in each segment classed as 'At Risk' (high or moderate), and whose behaviour, if modified, would provide the greatest reduction in health costs, can be calculated or estimated. In general, the greater this proportion, the greater potential 'return', and hence the higher the category's priority.

- *P: Persuadability of the target audience.* This refers to how feasible it would be to change attitudes and behaviour in the segment. In general, the more persuadable, the more likely an intervention can be effective, and the higher the priority. Segments with a higher proportion of members neutral or positive to the desired behaviour would have a higher priority than segments with a high proportion vehemently opposed to the desired behaviour change.

- *A: Accessibility of the target audience.* This refers to how easy is it to reach each segment via mass communication or other channels, such as worksites, community centres, entertainment venues, schools and other institutional settings. The more accessible the target audience, the more likely an effective outcome and the higher the priority. This measure should take into account 'cost-per-thousand' data for media activities. For example, a target audience may be accessible, but the necessary media may be expensive.

- *R: Resources required to meet the needs of the target audience.* This involves assessing the financial, human and structural resources needed to service the segment. This refers to the extent to which interventions can be directed towards each segment with current services and facilities versus the need for *additional* resources. For example, various segments might be motivated to engage in increased physical activity by a particular campaign, but this may require new programmes or facilities to meet this demand (e.g., indoor running tracks, heated swimming pools).

- *E: Equity.* This refers to the need for inclusion of social justice considerations. Groups such as Indigenous people and homeless teenagers might constitute a very small proportion of the population, but for equity reasons warrant special programmes.

The TARPARE model was originally developed as a qualitative assessment, and can be usefully applied as such. The model can also be represented as a weighted multi-attribute model, where each segment's overall score is the weighted sum of its scores on each of the attributes, where the weightings reflect the relative importance of each attribute:

$$\text{Segment priority} = f\ (T.wt + AR.war + P.wp + A.wa + R.wr + E.we)$$

where w_i represents the weight attached to each factor, and

T = total number in segment
AR = % at (high) risk
P = persuadability
A = accessibility
R = additional resources required
E = equity factor

T and AR require epidemiological data; P requires an estimate based on attitudinal research; A requires a knowledge of media and entertainment habits and other lifestyle characteristics; R requires an analysis of existing resources and a survey of consumer preferences; and E requires a knowledge of policy as well as the practitioner's own ethical considerations. These factors can be measured quantitatively through surveys and questionnaires or qualitatively through such processes as focus groups. However, even with quantitative data on these attributes, the assignment of weights remains subjective, and dependent on the values of the practitioner.

TARPARE example: selecting a target segment for a physical activity campaign

Based on the Sheth–Frazier segmentation shown in Table 10.5 a quantitative analysis is shown in Table 10.6 for selection of target segments for a physical activity campaign.

In this example, all of the criteria are given equal weights, and each criterion is scored 1–5, with '5' indicating a high priority score; '3' indicating 'medium' and '1' indicating a low priority score. For example, '5' for 'At Risk' would indicate a substantial proportion of high risk people in the segment; '1' for 'Resources' would indicate that resources would be stretched to achieve campaign objectives in that segment; '3' for 'Equity' would indicate a medium strength argument for inclusion on equity grounds; and '4' for 'Persuadability' would indicate that a large proportion of the segment could be classed as contemplators or 'ready for change' (i.e., high persuadability). A number of sources are available to assist in assigning scores (Corti 1998; Egger, Donovan and Corti 1998).

Scores for each segment are summed to indicate a priority ordering. With *no weighting*, this application ranks inactive positives top priority (23), followed closely by inactive

Table 10.5 Exercise attitude – behaviour segmentation

Exercise behaviour	Attitude to exercise	
	Positive	Neutral/negative
Exercise at or near level sufficient for maximal cardiovascular benefits ('high actives')	11%	3%
Exercise at light/moderate level for some cardiovascular benefits ('medium actives')	35%	19%
Little or no exercise ('inactives')	16%	16%

neutrals/negatives (21) and medium active positives (20). Unweighted scores often yield small differences between groups.

Applying weights that reflect practitioners' values, organisational policies and available resources, generally yields clearer differences between segments. For example, to reflect a desire for maximal benefit for the greatest number with relatively little audience resistance, we would apply the following weights to segment size, at risk status and persuadability, and leave all other criteria unweighted:

- 4 to segment size (w_t)
- 3 to at risk status(w_{ar}) and
- 3 to persuadability (w_p) (total of 10)

Applying these weights, the top two segments are more clearly separated from the others:

- inactive positives: 50;
- medium active positives: 49;
- inactive neutrals/negatives: 42;
- medium active neutrals/negatives: 39;
- high active positives: 33; and
- high active neutrals/negatives: 27.

Depending on the situation, other criteria may be added. For example, in times of crisis, such as with infectious disease outbreaks, a further criterion of *Urgency* may need to be applied; that is, the extent to which action is necessary or opportunistic in the immediate short term, or whether timing is not a crucial factor. For example, a marked increase in the presentation of dengue fever cases would require an immediate public education campaign of mosquito breeding control and bite prevention to prevent an epidemic.

Table 10.6 TARPARE model for choice of target group for physical activity campaign

Target group	Size: % adult population	At risk status	Persuadability	Accessibility	Resources	Equity	Total score (unweighted)
High active positives	2 (11%)	1	5	5	1	1	15
High active neutrals/ negatives	1 (3%)	1	4	5	2	1	14
Medium active positives	5 (35%)	3	4	4	2	2	20
Medium active neutrals/ negatives	3 (19%)	3	3	4	3	2	18
Inactive positives	3 (16%)	5	4	4	4	3	23
Inactive neutrals/ negatives	3 (16%)	5	1	3	5	4	21

It is likely that different organisations will have different views on the weights they consider appropriate to each of the criteria. Some organisations may have a mass population emphasis, others might emphasise social justice considerations and others might emphasise those most at risk regardless of segment size.

Also, we have demonstrated here only an additive choice model. It may well be that some decisionmakers may use quite different decision models (Hawkins, Best and Coney 1995, 2003). For example, some organisations might first eliminate any target group below a certain size, then eliminate any group scoring low on accessibility and persuadability, then rank those remaining on social justice needs.

Andreasen (1995) suggests six factors to be taken into account when deciding resource allocation: segment size; prevalence in each segment of the problem under consideration; severity of the problem in that segment; ability of the segment to cope with the problem (termed 'defencelessness'); reachability; and responsiveness (i.e., 'probable willingness to listen'). Three of these are directly comparable with TARPARE: size; reachability (Accessibility) and responsiveness (Persuadability). Andreasen's defencelessness has some similarity with our Equity factor, and his prevalence and severity factors have some overlap with our At Risk factor. Andreasen has no factor comparable to TARPARE's Resources factor.

TARPARE was developed for application within a risk area, as in the above examples. However, it may also be applied *between* risk areas. For example, a health agency with sufficient funding for only one campaign may need to decide which of a set of pro-grammes – such as promotion of safe sex practices among teenagers, medication compli-ance among asthmatics, increasing physical activity among retired people or smoking cessation and alcohol reduction among women attempting to become pregnant or in the early stages of pregnancy – should be given priority. Models such as TARPARE may be used to determine which of these areas should be given highest priority, or, as in Andreasen's (1995) approach, the proportion of resources to be allocated to each.

Overall, the model provides a disciplined approach to target selection and resource allocation, and forces consideration of just what weights should be applied to the dif-ferent criteria – and how these might vary for different issues (e.g., HIV/AIDS interven-tions, anti-smoking campaigns, exercise promotion, parenting interventions, domestic violence campaigns, etc.), or for different objectives (e.g., increases in knowledge, changes in habitual behaviours, attitude formation or change, political lobbying, etc.). Focusing attention on the TARPARE criteria and attempting to apply these to the vari-ous segments can lead to a greater understanding of the various segments and their relative viability, regardless of which segment is selected.

Targeting opinion leaders

We may sometimes wish to select opinion leaders for formative research, or to analyse survey data by. Here is a useful ten-item agree–disagree scale (in Weimann 1991).

I usually count on being successful in everything I do.
I am rarely unsure about how I should behave.
I like to assume responsibility.
I like to take the lead when a group does things together.
I enjoy convincing others of my opinions.
I often notice that I serve as a model for others.
I am good at getting what I want.
I am often a step ahead of others.
I own many things others envy me for.
I often give others advice and suggestions.

Cross-cultural targeting

With a number of exceptions, it is common practice in most developed countries to sim-ply translate mainstream campaign materials into the languages of major migrant/eth-nic groups in the community, and/or to simply place campaign messages in the ethnic media. This is understandable, given limited resources, the number of language groups in the community and the small numbers in many of these groups. It would be far too expensive to carry out formative research with every language group and develop cul-turally specific campaign services and materials for each group. Furthermore, where there are similar motivations relevant to the desired behaviour across cultures, this may not be necessary.

However, where resources are available, it is far more effective to develop campaigns that recognise cultural differences. This is especially crucial where the underlying motivations are different, and where the ability of the message to attract attention and engage the audience depends heavily on culturally specific components. There are also some countries, or parts thereof, where there are substantial minority sub-populations based on language (e.g., French speakers in Canada, Spanish speakers in the United States) or First Nation status (e.g., Maori in New Zealand, Indians in several South American countries, Canada and the United States). More recently there have been substantial African migrations to many European countries (which is a relatively new phenomenon for some countries such as Ireland), and there are 'travellers' and 'Roma' across various parts of Europe and Ireland.

Canada's ParticipACTION campaign

This bi-lingual campaign achieved higher unaided awareness and approximately equal prompted awareness among French speakers versus English speakers in Canada. The campaign successfully reached and impacted both groups because it was led right from the start by people committed to a bi-lingual campaign that was more than just a translation of English into French. That is, campaign materials and messages were developed from a perspective that accommodated both groups, even where not all materials would be produced in both languages (Lagarde 2004).

Cultural tailoring

Based on their work in developing interventions for increasing breast and cervical cancer screening among various ethnic groups in northern California, Pasick and colleagues (1996) provide a model for developing interventions for specific target ethnic groups – which they term 'tailored' rather than 'targeted' interventions. They refer to cultural tailoring as interventions, strategies, messages or materials that conform with specific cultural characteristics that directly influence behaviour and health (Pasick, D'Onofrio and Otero-Sabogal 1996). Use of the term tailoring perhaps not only lessens objectification of the target groups, but also exemplifies a consumer orientation in that the same core service or product is to be delivered, but 'tailored' or modified so as to enhance acceptability, uptake and impact in each target group.

Pasick, D'Onofrio and Otero-Sabogal (1996) suggest research to identify the cultural dimensions relevant to the specific issue, and that these rather than broader cultural dimensions should be taken into account when developing interventions. For example, they identified *fatalismo*, a fatalistic outlook in Hispanic culture that engenders a pessimistic outlook on curing cancer and acts to inhibit screening uptake. Similarly, Vietnamese people were reported to be inhibited by the superstition that 'if you look for cancer, you will find it'. These are similar to socio-cultural beliefs such as the 'river goddess' preying on young children and other beliefs in Africa mentioned in Chapter 9.

Pasick, D'Onofrio and Otero-Sabogal (1996) suggest that there has been too much focus on the broadly defined racial or ethnic group (e.g., Vietnamese, Greek, Muslim, Chinese, etc.), and insufficient awareness of cultural dimensions specifically relevant to health. In this sense, 'culture' includes not only values, beliefs and traditions, but also the living environment, opportunities (or lack of) for healthy behaviours and opportunities (or lack of) for cultural expression. The increased involvement of churches in public health interventions in African-American communities in the United States (Yanek *et al.* 2001) and South Pacific Islander communities in New Zealand (Simmons *et al.* 2004) is an example of taking into account the important role that churches play in these communities.

Pasick and colleagues also suggest that a focus on the specific dimensions often reveals far more similarities between groups than differences. In this sense, they note that socio-economic status is a significant determinant of health that often eliminates differences between racial or ethnic groups. Similarly, the differences between sub-groups of an ethnic group are sometimes greater than between different ethnic groups.

Using a five-phase intervention model of problem identification, objective setting, theory, evaluation design and implementation, Pasick and colleagues proposed that the extent of cultural tailoring required depended on the relative importance of cultural versus other variables in each of these phases. Their model is shown in Figure 10.5, where the angle and location of the line is established by research. In the lower shaded area, cultural factors are more important; in the upper unshaded area, other factors are more important.

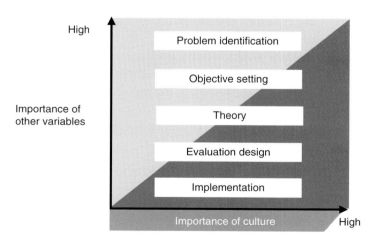

Figure 10.5 Relative importance of culture in developing interventions for ethnic groups

Adapted from Pasick, D'Onofrio and Otero-Sabogal (1996)

In their study of underage drinking, Donovan *et al.* (1997b) found a number of differences between Indigenous youth in urban settings and Indigenous youth in remote communities (e.g., interest and participation in traditional ceremonies, English literacy and use of traditional language), as well as commonalities (e.g., family and kinship ties and obligations, interest in Indigenous 'celebrities', music preferences) that had implications for under-age alcohol interventions. They also listed differences and commonalities between Indigenous youth and non-Indigenous youth in general.

Some differences between Indigenous and non-Indigenous youth were:

- greater cash resources among non-Indigenous youth;
- higher literacy and education levels among non-Indigenous youth;
- less direct exposure to alcohol abuse among non-Indigenous youth;
- greater educational and employment opportunities available to non-Indigenous youth, particularly with regard to remote youth;
- non-Indigenous society primarily marked by social drinking – Indigenous society primarily marked by 'problem' drinking;
- Indigenous youth confronted with racism;
- Indigenous youth clearly prefer Indigenous health workers, but accept non-Indigenous people who gain their trust;
- greater kinship links and responsibilities among Indigenous youth; greater face-to-face contact with relatives on an ongoing basis.

Similarities noted between Indigenous and non-Indigenous youth were:

- similar interests in music and sports – especially in salient celebrities;
- 'hanging around' focal points (e.g., shopping centres);
- sources of alcohol – parents' supplies, older siblings, friends;
- drinking behaviours – mostly quick consumption, 'binge drinking';
- types and brands of alcohol drunk;
- occasions of drinking – parties (when parents absent), parks, bushland;
- strong peer bonding and other developmental features (i.e., establishing identity, conflict with adult 'rules', wanting to assert independence, self-consciousness in dealings with the opposite sex, etc.);
- similar self-reported reasons/benefits of drinking – although 'boredom' is more important in remote Indigenous communities.

With regard to these differences, Donovan and colleagues concluded that:

- Indigenous people are essential for delivery of alcohol messages;
- the language should be clear and simple English or in the traditional language;
- alcohol messages should include, or even emphasise, negative social effects (e.g., violence, lack of money for food and other necessities, etc.), as well as health/performance effects, and, in remote areas, be linked to traditional culture; and

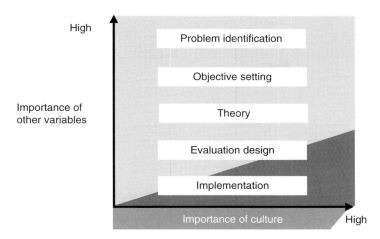

Figure 10.6 Relative importance of culture in tailoring alcohol interventions for Indigenous youth

Donovan *et al.* (1997b)

• for remote communities with licensed premises, interventions should be concurrently aimed at alcohol availability within the community.

On a broader scale, they emphasised the importance of increasing educational and employment opportunities, as well as campaigns aimed at lessening racism. Overall, in Pasick and colleague's framework, Donovan *et al.* (1997b) concluded that the problem identification, objective setting and theoretical models for under-age drinking are largely independent of cultural differences, especially for Indigenous urban youth at school. However, they concluded that cultural differences are important in expressing the *content* of the intervention materials and are crucial for *implementation*. This is depicted in Figure 10.6.

Individual tailoring

Before mass communications, personal selling was a major factor across all product and service areas, especially in non-urban areas. The 'travelling salesman' was part of the landscape and is written into folklore. Similarly, before the advent of self-service supermarkets and hypermarkets, personal selling was paramount, even for commodities and packaged goods. The best salespersons then – and now – were those who first established a good knowledge of their customer, identifying their specific and general needs. Little wonder that mass advertising was called 'salesmanship in print' by one of the first advertising legends, the copywriter John E. Kennedy (Lasker [1963] 1987).

Good salespeople, while selling the same product to every customer, *tailored* their pitch to the idiosyncrasies of each individual customer. Hence, the roominess of a Ford station wagon could be emphasised for its ability to carry golf bag and buggy, children's bassinette and toys, dog space or trade tools and equipment, depending on the potential customer's previously established needs and lifestyle. While there might be some, or even a great deal of, overlap, each individual received a customised sales pitch.

Targeted versus tailored messages

As we have seen above, targeted messages are designed for a segment of the population based on a characteristic or set of characteristics shared by members of the segment (e.g., occasional smokers, upper-SES people opposed to refugees seeking asylum, 14–24-year-old females with bulimic tendencies, etc.). Tailored messages are designed for one specific individual based on prior assessment of the individual (Kreuter *et al.* 2000, 2005). The advent of computers and interactive technology has stimulated the development of tailored messages, as individual information can be entered and analysed, and the customised message constructed and delivered in the one session.

Not quit altogether yet?

Having answered a questionnaire about recent quitting attempts, smoking behaviour, family characteristics, etc., our trying-to-quit smoker might receive the following message:

> There are a lot of rugby events being televised at the moment – and when the games are close seems to be when you find it hardest to resist the urge for a smoke. Remember this next time and make sure there are no cigarettes in the house before settling down to watch a match, and that you have a pack of those peppermint lollies you like. Your daughter Molly turns 11 in three months. That's a crucial age for kids to start experimenting with smoking, so the sooner you quit the better for her and for you.

The information required of the individual consists of a beliefs, attitudes and behaviour questionnaire, based on some model(s) of attitude–behaviour change, and, increasingly, on what stage of change the individual is in. The programmer – and here's the rub – then matches the individual's responses with a number of pre-developed messages that incorporate the individual's information. Obviously, the potential effectiveness of the tailoring will depend on (a) the nature and quality of the information entered and (b) the validity of the model used by the programmer to generate information based on the questionnaire data. If tailored messages don't work better than non-tailored messages in a particular instance (and there have been plenty of those), it doesn't mean that the concept of tailoring is not valid; we simply might have not done it properly. Overall though, Kreuter *et al.* (2000) provide evidence that, in general, tailored messages do out-perform non-tailored messages, but not always, and not always by much (e.g., Bernhardt 2001). As would be expected, studies are now moving towards the type of tailoring that seems to be most effective.

> **More jargon: 'signalling' versus 'tailoring'**
>
> Signalling refers to an executional style – graphic symbols, content and formatting – that appeals to a specific audience (e.g., the quick cuts visual style of MTV that appeals to young audiences). Tailoring refers to customising offerings based on prior knowledge of the audience's interests. SENTAR's ads above are an example of 'signalling' to engage a particular target audience.

Concluding comments

The principle of selectivity and concentration and its ramifications constitute one of the most important concepts in marketing, and hence in social marketing. It derives directly from a consumer orientation, and is plain common sense. However, the usual situation is that social marketers do not have the resources to develop campaigns and specific intervention components for all target groups no matter how they are defined. Nevertheless, given a culturally neutral message, one can ensure that different target groups can be reached and served by astute media channel and media vehicle selection, along with strategic location and delivery of services. Similarly, it is relatively simple to develop materials that contain the style of language and visual symbols of different target groups, without altering the basic information provided. However, where the target groups differ in basic motivations or require different products and services, then different campaigns or programmes must be developed for optimal effectiveness.

Various segmentation bases in Table 10.1 can be used for strategic planning at an organisational level (i.e., assigning responsibilities to different sections for different geographic areas, different age groups, occupational groups or genders, etc.). However, at the programme planning level, the segmentation must be on the basis of the targeted behaviour and the target group's attitudes and beliefs with regard to that behaviour. It is knowledge of the attitudes and beliefs about the behaviour that indicates what intervention strategy is most appropriate for each group, and what are the relevant motivational messages for behaviour change. In many cases, social marketers identify key influencers to lobby, or at whom to direct campaigns. This may range from targeting women to persuade their male partners to undergo more frequent health checks, opinion leaders to publicise screening programmes, or local political leaders and political advisers for policy and legislative changes. However, this is segmentation at an organisational planning stage. All people within these groups should then be segmented according to their attitudes and current behaviours with respect to the issue in question.

The Sheth–Frazier model is a direct application of this approach, while the stages-of-change categories assume a simultaneous application of the attitude and behaviour dimensions. Both can be applied to the same issue, although in practice, one or other appears more appropriate.

The stages-of-change approach appears most appropriate for addictive and habitual health-related behaviours, those health behaviours where there is a long period of adoption and where people see considerable barriers or disbenefits of adoption of the desired behaviour (e.g., physical activity, food habits, weight control, smoking).

The Sheth–Frazier framework seems to be more useful for health behaviours where very few are beyond the pre-contemplation stage (e.g., reducing alcohol consumption), for non-addictive health behaviours (e.g., screening behaviours) and non-health behaviours, such as anti-racism, public transport, recycling and water conservation.

The Pasick *et al.* framework appears useful in determining to what extent mainstream interventions need to be modified for different ethnic groups. This requires considerable formative research to identify not just the broad cultural dimensions that need to be taken into account (which are often already known anyway), but, more importantly, those specific to the issue in question. It is important to remember that these include not just cultural values, but all aspects of culture, including living conditions and economic and educational status.

By way of turning full circle, the advent of interactive technology combined with mass communication delivery channels has enabled the development of messages customised to individuals on a mass scale. Health professionals have been quick to pick up on this development with promising results, but there is still some way to go. There are clearly opportunities to take this approach further in a variety of social marketing areas, but we must be careful not to let the technology drive the agenda; it is the tailoring that is important, not whether the messages are delivered by computer.

QUESTIONS

● What are the basic reasons for segmentation?

● What are some obvious segmentations?

● Can the stages-of-change segmentation apply to global warming issues?

● How would you locate, communicate with and motivate (a) older smokers to quit, (b) teens who haven't started smoking?

FURTHER READING

Kreuter, M., Farrell, D., Olevitch, L., Brennan, L. and Rimer, B. K. 2000. *Tailoring Health Messages: Customising Communication with Computer Technology.* Hillsdale, NJ: Lawrence Erlbaum.

Kreuter, M. W., Sugg-Skinner, C., Holt, C. L., Clark, E. M., Haire-Joshu, D. Fu, Q., Booker, A., Steger-May, K. and Bucholtz, D. C. 2005. Cultural Tailoring for Mammography and Fruit and Vegetable Intake among Low Income African-American Women in Urban Public Health Centers, *Preventive Medicine* 41: 53–62

Maibach, E,, Roser-Conouf, C. and Leiserowitz, A. 2009. Global Warming's 'Six Americas': An Audience Segmentation, available at: http://www.climatechangecommunication.org/images/files/SixAmericas-final-v3-Web.pdf, accessed 5 April 2009.

McClure, T. and Spence, R. 2006. *Don't Mess with Texas: The Story Behind the Legend.* Austin, TX: Idea City Press.

Palmgreen, P., Donohew, L., Lorch, E. P., Hoyle, R. H. and Stephenson, M. T. 2001. Television Campaigns and Adolescent Marijuana Use: Tests of Sensation Seeking Targeting, *American Journal of Public Health* 91(2): 292.

Pasick, R. J., D'Onofrio, C. N. and Otero-Sabogal, R. 1996. Similarities and Differences Across Cultures: Questions to Inform a Third Generation for Health Promotion Research, *Health Education Quarterly* 23(Supp.): S142–S161.

Sheth, J. N. and Frazier, G. L. 1982. A Model of Strategy Mix Choice for Planned Social Change, *Journal of Marketing* 46: 15–26.

11 The marketing mix

Perhaps one of the best known concepts in marketing is the '4Ps', apparently first described by McCarthy (1960). The 4Ps have endured because they provide the four fundamentals of marketing planning and management. They refer to what the company is selling (**p**roduct), where the products and services are made available to customers (**p**lace, or distribution), how products and services are priced and paid for (**p**rice), and where and how the products and services are made known to people and they are motivated to purchase them (**p**romotion). In Chapter 2 we referred to the 'principle of customer value' as the sum total of the benefits provided by the 'mix' of these 4Ps.

This chapter will focus on these traditional 4Ps and a fifth P (**p**eople) from services marketing. Given that many health and welfare 'products' are services, lessons from services marketing can contribute to effective social marketing. We also discuss the importance of two other 'Ps' often added to the social marketing mix: **p**olicy and **p**artnerships.

Policy is highlighted because it reflects upstream activities to change the environment and particularly with regard to products and the physical environment as noted in Chapter 1. It was also noted in Chapter 9 that we can counter the competition via regulating the marketing mix of potentially harmful products (such as alcohol, gambling, guns, pornography, prostitution and tobacco), usually via advocating policy changes by decisionmakers who control the manufacture and marketing of such products. Partnerships are increasingly being recognised as an essential factor in successful social marketing as many social problems can be solved only by an integrated effort involving numerous agencies and stakeholders, such as schools, education departments, teachers, parents, health departments and health professionals, regulatory bodies and relevant industries.

Overall, policy and partnerships can be used to facilitate or enhance the effectiveness of the traditional Ps of the marketing mix: for example, bar owners having a policy requiring bar staff to be trained in safe serving practices (people); partnering with growers to deliver fresh fruit and vegetables to underserved groups (product); or negotiating with a manufacturer of fertiliser to offer discounts to Third World farmers (price).

The social marketing mix

The marketing mix covers the main areas in which decisions are made so as to maximise value to the customer. Although we discuss these elements in turn, it is important to recognise that the marketing mix refers to the blending of all the elements such that they complement each other in an integrated marketing effort. For example, products with a high price are accompanied by extensive advertising and promotion that attempt to justify the higher price, either objectively or subjectively, via appeals to sensory attributes, social status or lifestyle. Borden first used the term 'marketing mix' in 1953 to compare marketing to the process of baking, in which appropriate ingredients in the correct proportions are blended (Sargeant 2009). The total value to the customer of a product such as a particular perfume is determined not only by its fragrance, but – and arguably more so – by its packaging, brand name, brand positioning (i.e., brand image), price and the image of the outlet from where it is purchased.

- Product is anything that can satisfy a desire or need which can be offered for an exchange. Products include 'a physical good, a service, an experience, an event, a person, a place, a property, an organisation, information, or an idea' (Kotler and Keller 2005). Persons can be seen as products in political campaigns, and destinations – even countries – are products in tourism or campaigns to attract industry and commerce. Concepts of design, branding, product variation and packaging all relate to product.
- Place (otherwise called 'distribution') is the process of making the product available to the consumer, including the network or channel of organisations that may be involved, as well as the activities they perform. Concepts of logistics, retailing and wholesaling relate to place. Place also includes access factors such as opening hours, availability of public transport, availability and ease of parking, wheelchair access, ambience and store atmosphere, etc.
- Price is the total of monetary and non-monetary costs exchanged when purchasing a product or service, or adopting a practice or idea. This involves financial concepts such as availability of credit terms, discounts and automated teller machines, and psychological costs such as embarrassment (in a gym setting), withdrawal symptoms (smoking cessation), or peer derision (choosing a low alcohol beer). Time and effort costs are also included (which can be reduced by other elements of the mix, such as making the product easily obtainable and trialable).
- Promotion is the mix of activities undertaken to create awareness of the product and its benefits, and to persuade the consumer to purchase. Promotion includes advertising, direct marketing, personal selling, sponsorship, sales promotion and public relations.

The Stanford Heart Disease Prevention Program marketing mix

The Stanford Heart Disease Prevention Program was an early (1970s) attempt to apply social marketing principles in a real life field setting to 'sell' the idea of 'heart disease prevention' to a community. The success of this health promotion effort was largely due to the careful consideration given to each aspect of the campaign, including the marketing mix. The mix was identified as follows:

Product: Information about risk factors in heart disease and tangible products and services such as heart healthy recipe books and quit smoking classes comprised the product. The product line was comprehensive, including different products for different segments of the target audience, depending on their age, ethnicity and needs.

Place: The distribution strategy aimed to maximise the opportunities people had to receive and process the campaign's information and obtain the tangible products. Media channels, health professionals, community organisations and commercial organisations such as pharmacies and bookstores were enlisted to distribute the message and tangible products.

Price: The programme recognised that there would be monetary and non-monetary costs (time, social support and psychological costs) in adopting the heart healthy message. Hence, messages and products were adapted accordingly.

Promotion: Promotion strategies included mass media advertising and publicity, direct mail and community events. The programme produced a 1-hour TV special called 'Heart Health Test'. The number of viewers was significantly increased by targeting areas with a direct mail promotion that encouraged people to watch the show. They also wrote to teachers asking children to encourage their parents to watch the show (an early example of using 'pester power' in a good cause!) (Solomon 1984).

- People refers to the people involved in the delivery of services who interact with the customer. Interpersonal skills are important in any area where staff interact with customers, including supermarket checkouts. However, along with relevant knowledge and expertise, interpersonal skills are arguably far more important in the sorts of sensitive areas involved in much social marketing.
- Partnership refers to alliances with organisations that share an interest in a social marketing area. They may also have access to distribution channels, resources and audiences that can deliver the social marketing message more effectively.
- Policy refers to introducing into government, non-government organisations and businesses, small and large, policies that will help change the environment in ways that facilitate individual change. Policies may be enshrined in legislation, regulation or there may be voluntary compliance with the policies (e.g., government policy might lead to banning of tobacco advertising, a sporting club policy may lead to serving only mid-strength beer during major events, school canteens may adopt a policy of not stocking sugared carbonated beverages).

Each of these elements of the marketing mix needs to be tailored to individual market segments. The product can be modified for different segments; the place may be different for different segments; the monetary and non-monetary costs may be perceived differently by different segments; the most effective promotion strategy may vary according to the segment; different types of staff may be appropriate for different segments; and different partnerships will be appropriate in different contexts relating to different segments.

An awareness of the marketing mix concept provides public health and social change practitioners with a structured framework for considering all these aspects when planning campaigns, many of which are often overlooked by non-marketers (and even by many marketers).

France's EPODE campaign: policy

EPODE ('Ensemble, Prévenons l'Obésité Des Enfants: Together, let's prevent childhood obesity') (www.epode-european-network.com) is an innovative programme, developed in France and launched in 2004 to help prevent obesity in children. In 2008, 167 French cities were involved in EPODE (1.2 million people) and the programme is now being introduced in Belgium and Spain. The European Commission is adopting the strategies in its public health activities to address obesity (Watson 2007). The original ten cities in the pilot programme have fulfilled their initial commitment for five years and have reaffirmed their commitment for another five years, indicating sustainability of the concept (Henley and Raffin 2009).

In the context of childhood obesity, the 'upstream' advocacy role involves working to ensure individuals have access to healthy foods (such as children's school meals) and information about nutritional value of foods (as in food labels), as well as advocacy for public facilities to encourage physical activity (such as cycle paths and parks). Other possibilities include taxes on unhealthy foods or products, subsidies for healthy foods or products, regulating advertising to children (Moodie et al. 2006), making unhealthy foods less visible, more expensive, and harder to access.

Policy

Until recently, social marketing focused primarily on persuading the individual to adopt recommended behaviours (often referred to as the 'downstream' approach). However, current thinking has extended the definition of social marketing to include achieving change in the social determinants of health and wellbeing (referred to as the 'upstream' approach) (Andreasen 2006; Hastings 2006; Hastings and Saren 2003; Wilkinson and Marmot 2003). Upstream approaches attempt to bring about desired individual behaviours, often without the individual's conscious co-operation.

We consider the Ottawa Health Promotion Charter's 'Healthy Public Policy' statement (noted in Chapter 1) as a good description of policy aims for social marketers:

> Health promotion goes beyond health care. It puts health on the agenda of policymakers in all sectors and at all levels, directing them to be aware of the health consequences of their decisions and to accept their responsibilities for health. Health promotion policy combines diverse but complementary approaches including

legislation, fiscal measures, taxation and organizational change. It is coordinated action that leads to health, income and social policies that foster greater equity. Joint action contributes to ensuring safer and healthier goods and services, healthier public services and cleaner, more enjoyable environments. Health promotion policy requires the identification of obstacles to the adoption of healthy public policies in non-health sectors, and ways of removing them. The aim must be to make the healthier choice the easier choice for policymakers as well.

Alcohol is a major area for the use of policy to reduce the harm from excess consumption, particularly in terms of taxing alcohol content, regulating hours and places of availability, restricted age access, regulation of advertising and promotion and training of servers (Giesbrecht 2007). A study of alcohol policies in twenty-five countries in the Americas showed that countries with the highest impact policies (such as restrictions on access and promotion) were Colombia, Costa Rica, Venezuela and El Salvador, whereas those with the least policies were Brazil, Tobago, Trinidad, Suriname and Uruguay (Babor and Caetano 2005). Given the enormous profits involved, the alcohol industry is a formidable opponent for policy change all around the globe [for example, see Butler's (2006) analysis of alcohol policy issues in Ireland].

Product

In commercial marketing, the product generally refers to the tangible product purchased by the customer (e.g., a DVD player, wristwatch, perfume, software) or the service provided (e.g., a haircut, university degree, tree lopping, tax return lodged). In some cases, a mix of tangible products and services is purchased, as when a landscape architect supplies the trees, ornamental ponds and the overall design. In the following discussion we will use the term 'product' to include services.

However, as noted in Chapter 2, the principle of customer value emphasises that products and services are purchased not so much for themselves, but for the benefits they provide to the buyer (Lancaster 1966). You may recall Charles Revson's (of Revlon Cosmetics) statement that '... in the factory we make cosmetics; in the store we sell hope', and Levitt's more mundane example, that although people may buy a ¼-inch drill, what they want is a ¼-inch hole (Kotler *et al.* 1998).

A framework that ties these two concepts (customer benefits and product or service attributes) together is Kotler's (1988) concept of the core product, the augmented product and the actual tangible product. The core product is the underlying benefit (or benefits) that the consumer is obtaining by buying a product or service, or adopting a practice. For computers, the core product might be better management decision-making; for the practice of leaving a certain number of trees in a paddock (the actual product), the core product might be continued crop productivity through avoiding salinity; for a facial and manicure, the core product might be feeling better about

Figure 11.1 Tangible augmented product

oneself; for using condoms, the core product is peace of mind by avoiding pregnancy or a sexually transmitted infection (STI). The 'tangible' or 'observable' products' are the computer, the condom, the behavioural practices (using a condom; leaving trees), and the facial and manicure in the above examples.

The augmented product includes any additional services or tangible offerings or benefits that supplement the actual product. For computers this involves after sales service, training, warranties, associated software, a widespread consumer user network and so on. In nutrition promotion this could mean a journal for recording food consumption or a coupon for buying fresh vegetables at a discount.

In the promotion of physical activity, the core product (underlying benefit) might be a longer, healthier life through cardiovascular disease risk reduction; the actual product might be an aerobics class, and the augmented product might include a crèche, off-peak discount rates, clean, hygienic changing rooms, a discounted pedometer (Figure 11.1) or a complimentary towel. In a weight loss programme the product may be augmented with incentives, rebates, weigh-ins, social support and newsletters.

For dengue fever prevention, the tangible products might be a brochure on tips for reducing mosquito breeding and the practice of ensuring containers around the premises are emptied of water; the core product is avoidance of dengue fever and continued good health. The augmented product (if there is one) might be a free sample of insect repellent and a discount voucher for window and door screening.

As noted above, different target audiences might be seeking different core products (i.e., benefits) from the same actual product or behaviour. For example, some take up exercise to avoid specific health problems such as heart disease, while others may do so to maintain their mental health or to enjoy social interactions. Similarly, health behaviours might be promoted as delivering benefits other than health benefits if that is what is required to motivate 'purchase'. For example, men may be more motivated to 'lose their gut' so as to improve their appearance (and hence self-esteem) rather than to gain health benefits (Egger and Mowbray 1993).

For most social marketing programmes, the core product relates to the health and wellbeing of the individual, community cohesion and strength, and reduced dollar and human costs associated with preventable morbidity and premature mortality. For many social marketing campaigns, the actual product is not a tangible product and may not involve tangible augmented products either. If tangible products are available, often they are not necessary for core product 'purchase'. For example, most smokers quit smoking without calling a quitline, enrolling in a quit smoking programme or using quit tapes/instructional booklets.

Augmented product – Guaranteed Ride Home

People are much more likely to sign up for a car pooling system or agree to take some sort of public transport to work if they are assured of a guaranteed ride home in an emergency. This has led to the emergence of numerous Guaranteed Ride Home (or Emergency Ride Home) programmes now operating in the United States. When these programmes began, there were fears that people would abuse the provision, but that isn't what has happened. Interestingly, although everyone wants the guarantee, only a small proportion use it and even when they do, it is not a huge expense. The mean annual cost per registered user across fifty-five programmes surveyed was only US\$1.69 (Menczer 2007).

Product considerations in social marketing

Product considerations in social marketing differ from commercial marketing in a number of ways (Bloom and Novelli 1981; Chen 1996; Rothschild 1979), which can make formulating a product strategy in social marketing much more difficult than for goods and services.

- *Inflexibility*: commercial marketers generally have the option of redesigning their product to make it more appealing to consumers. For example, they can change its colour, shape, design or add extra features. The social product is much less flexible. For example, the social product idea 'Don't drink and drive' involves not drinking to a very specific limit, for example, a blood-alcohol level of 0.08 in the United Kingdom.
- *Intangibility*: tangible goods exist in space and time. Intangible services exist in time but not space, though they may have observable outcomes (e.g., a new hairstyle, a bank deposit). Many social marketing products are concepts or ideas that are intangible in a different way; they do not exist in space or time, but rather in our consciousness. This applies particularly to *prevention* of problem behaviours (as distinct from *cessation* of problem behaviours). For example, the 'not smoking' actual product consists of a negative attitude to smoking. Similarly, tolerance campaigns attempt to instil positive beliefs about diversity and respect for others – which may or may not have an opportunity for behavioural expression.

- *Complexity*: social products are often far more complex than consumer goods and services, requiring high levels of information processing. Whereas the commercial marketer can focus on just one benefit of a product, the social marketer may be required to convey multiple benefits, as well as being honest about any possible negative effects. For example, the decision to immunise a child could be far more complex than decisions relating to the child's clothing or haircut. Complex information may need to be conveyed to a target market with poor literacy and education. For example, an oral rehydration product was sold in Honduras as a 'tonic' for infants when research showed that Honduran mothers did not understand the concept of dehydration (Chen 1996). Pictorial aids have been found to be helpful even when the target audience is highly literate; for example, adding pictures to medication instructions assists with recall and understanding of the instructions as well as adherence to the protocols (Katz, Kripalani and Weiss 2006).

- *Controversial*: social products are often quite controversial, particularly for some segments of the target market. For example, the Western Australian Freedom from Fear campaign targeted male perpetrators of violence, arousing controversy among both men and women: some women believed that funding should go only to victims of violence, and some men believed that female perpetrators should also be targeted. For some people, some social marketing messages can be seen as an attack on their personal liberty [e.g., early opposition to the concept of random breath testing, gun owners' opposition to gun control – especially in the United States, red light cameras in Virginia seen as an 'invasion of privacy' (Jenkins 2005)].

- *Weak personal benefits*: in commercial marketing the individual consumer usually obtains the product's benefits, but for some social products the benefits are obtained by society. An individual may perceive the personal benefits of individual action to be quite weak. Examples of such social products are recycling, energy and water conservation, and not littering. Marketing social products with weak personal benefits requires that people believe in the notion of 'collective efficacy': that the recommended behaviour will achieve meaningful benefits for all if a majority of people are persuaded to adopt the behaviour (Bonniface and Henley 2008).

- *Negative frame*: social products often recommend the *cessation* of a behaviour, such as smoking, and the message may sound 'negative'. Social marketers have recognised the latter and often frame recommendations as positive statements: 'Quit' for 'stop smoking', 'Respect yourself' for 'stop drinking to excess', 'Work safe' for 'stop working dangerously', and 'Keep Australia beautiful' for 'don't litter'. However, in many cases it is more appropriate to use a negative sounding message: 'Eat less fat', 'If you drink and drive, you're a bloody idiot', 'Child abuse – no excuses, never, ever'.

Figure 11.2 Promoting incidental physical activity

The product mix in social marketing

Another important product concept in commercial marketing is the concept of a company's 'product mix': the overall assortment of products offered and how they complement each other. In a physical activity campaign, ads can emphasise the variety of ways that people can achieve the goal of '10,000 steps' per day (Figure 11.2), and people who register can purchase a discounted pedometer and receive a log book to help them plan how to gradually achieve the goal of 10,000 steps per day (Brown *et al.* 2002; Mummery and Schofield 2002).

This concept is related to the concept of market segmentation. For example, in promoting physical activity, different ways of meeting physical activity targets sufficient to provide health benefits must be available for different target groups. Hence, incidental activity is promoted to those who are time limited (or think they are), walking clubs are promoted to mothers of school age children and seniors' groups, and the concept of cumulative benefits from short periods of moderate intensity physical activity is promoted to those who would otherwise not see any benefit in these short periods. Computerised quit smoking programmes are essentially a product mix where different programme components are applied to smokers in the different stages of change.

In social marketing campaigns, we can attempt to encourage, induce or require changes in commercial products, or partner with healthy or safe product marketers, or promote our own tangible products designed to meet our goals. Here are a few examples of these:

- mosquito nets and a new medicine (artemisinin) sharply reduced malaria deaths in children in Ethiopia (dropped 50 per cent), Rwanda (60 per cent), Zambia (33 per cent) and Ghana (34 per cent) (McNeil 2008);
- motor cycle helmets were designed specifically for tropical conditions for a campaign in Vietnam (Clegg 2009) (motorcyclists called helmets 'rice cookers'; Zarocostas 2009);
- insecticide treated nets were evaluated over a two-year period in Tanzania with regard to child survival. The nets were associated with a 27 per cent increase in survival in children aged 1 month to 4 years (Schellenberg *et al.* 2001);
- increasing the insulation in poor people's homes in New Zealand resulted in warmer, drier environments and fewer school and work absences, fewer trips to the doctor and fewer hospital admissions for respiratory complaints (Howden-Chapman *et al.* 2007);
- folate in flour was introduced in the United Kingdom to prevent the development of neural tube defects in foetuses during pregnancy (Mayor 2005);
- an improved version of Golden Rice rich in pro-vitamin A was developed to help prevent dietary vitamin A deficiency, which affects over 250 million people around the world and can result in blindness and depressed immune system (Paine *et al.* 2005);
- fast food restaurant group Arby's is stopping the use of trans fat (Turner 2006), the Cargill company's new zero calorie sweetener is going ahead after trials showed that it was safe for human consumption (McKinney 2008), and St Louis-based Solae LLC, a food innovation company specialising in soy protein, has come up with a hybrid meat – part soy, part real meat – which has half the fat of regular burgers (Salter 2006);
- compact fluorescent lights (CFLs), along with various energy saving practices are commonly promoted by energy companies and green groups (Mufson 2006);
- use of an alcohol-based hand sanitiser which kills viruses associated with respiratory and gastrointestinal (GI) infections, along with hand hygiene education, significantly reduced the transmission of GI infections in families with children in child care (Sandora *et al.* 2005); and, speaking of alcohol,
- the drug baclofen, approved to treat muscle spasms, may be effective in taking away cravings for alcohol and resisting triggers to drink (Szalavitz 2009) (but again raises the issue of whether we should be seeking 'pills' or psychotherapeutic solutions for such 'ills').

> **Dolls with disabilities help children with disabilities cope**
>
> While they will never compete with Barbie and Baby Annabel, dolls with disabilities are being launched by major toy marketers. Dolls with disabilities appear to have begun in Germany when Helga Parks saw her 'Down syndrome' niece's face light up when she was given a doll with facial features similar to her own. She then began to make these 'Down' dolls, which are used in Germany in kindergartens to educate children about and destigmatise disability. Other dolls on the market include dolls with prosthetic limbs or walking frames, and blind dolls with a guide dog. Mattell recently released Becky, Barbie's friend in a wheelchair. While laypeople and the kids with disabilities appear to really appreciate dolls like themselves, the 'experts' are somewhat ambivalent as they believe such dolls might emphasise their 'differences' to other kids (Midgley 2008).

The last example above reminds us that we need to critically analyse products that claim to 'fix the problem' or be safe alternatives to risky products. For example:

- The electronic cigarette ('e-cig') claims to be the first healthy cigarette. It is free of tars and chemicals, containing only pure nicotine, and hence is claimed to function like nicotine patches. Sales are rising in Brazil, Switzerland, Sweden and the United Kingdom, but the US Food and Drug Administration refuses to allow importation of the product and the World Health Organization is calling for further safety testing (Dellorto 2009).
- Sports drinks containing carbohydrates and electrolytes are touted as a way of hydrating young athletes who might not drink enough water (sports drinks being more attractive). According to some experts, however, this is true only where kids are doing strenuous exercise in the heat for some time (Reynolds 2009).
- US scientists have developed 'exercise pills', which apparently mimic the effect of physical activity on the body. In tests with mice, sedentary mice increased their endurance running capacity by 44 per cent after a month on one of the drugs, while those allowed exercise increased their endurance running by 70 per cent (Schoofs and Winslow 2008). While these drugs may protect against obesity, diabetes and muscle wasting diseases, we have no idea of potential side effects and suspect that the major market could be athletes anyway – and we don't need more performance enhancing drugs.

Products for intermediaries

We can also distinguish between products targeted at 'end consumers' and products designed for intermediaries to do their job better. In road safety we should not only be concerned about making motor vehicles safer, but also consider products that make law enforcement more effective and, hence, serve as an increased deterrent for unsafe behaviours. For example, red light cameras, fixed and variable location speed cameras, more portable drug and alcohol detection devices, all serve to enhance road safety. Training is generally well recognised for health and social policy workers, and there are many kits that have been developed to assist these people to do their job more effectively, or at least more easily.

Kopp and Hornberger (2008) showed that providing nurses with a proper exercise and nutrition (PEN) kit along with appropriate screening tools, increased nurses' understanding of overweight and obesity and their screening and assessment practices. And in the future, overworked counsellors might have robot assistants. Perhaps not surprisingly, engineers in the United States are working on designing robots that go beyond helping with the housework, to imitating the actions of humans and even providing therapy. What have been called 'socially assistive machines' will be designed to coach and motivate people with cognitive and physical disabilities (Slomski 2009).

EPODE campaign: product

In the EPODE campaign in France, the core product is the underlying benefit to children of healthy weight management. The actual product includes tangible products (e.g., leaflets about healthy eating and physical activity), and events targeted at parents, schools, children, health professionals and other intermediaries.

One of EPODE's branding strategies is to prominently display the local city's logo in customised local materials, while minimising the national logos.

Branding in social marketing

The American Marketing Association has defined a brand as: 'a name, term, symbol, or design, or a combination of them, intended to identify the goods or services of one seller, or group of sellers and to differentiate them from those of competitors' (Sargeant 2009).

The key element of this definition in current competitive commercial marketing is the word 'differentiate'. The differentiation may be in terms of product attributes (such as this toothpaste contains 'whitening ingredient X'), or in emotive or lifestyle positionings around the brand (such as this toothpaste is for young, on-the-go professionals). It is the latter differentiation that is the hallmark of today's consumer society characterised by a surplus of parity products and services, although differentiation within product lines is often on a quality or product attribute or features basis. Twitchell (2004) refers to branding as applying a 'story' to a product or service, and such narratives being the only difference between alternative brands for parity products.

Key characteristics of a brand name are that it should be memorable, recognisable, easy to pronounce, distinctive and able to convey the product's benefits and appeal (Kotler and Keller 2005). The brand's logo is particularly important to visually draw attention to it and portray an appropriate image, as exposure to the logo is often the most frequent type of contact people will have with the brand.

However, branding is more than just 'naming' a product or campaign; it is developing brand attributes that are expressed in all areas of the marketing mix. A common phrase in the commercial literature is that of 'brand personality': the set of human characteristics associated with a brand (Aaker 1997). After much multivariate analysis, Aaker (1997) distilled a large number of traits down to five dimensions: sincerity (e.g., honest, genuine); excitement (e.g., daring, imaginative); competence (e.g., reliable, efficient); sophistication (e.g., glamorous, romantic); and ruggedness (strong, outdoorsy). (Any cigarette brands come to mind?)

How does your brand rate?*		
Modern	Neither	Old fashioned
Amateurish	Neither	Professional
Working class	Neither	Upper class
Cool	Neither	Uncool
Active	Neither	Passive
Weak, timid	Neither	Strong, powerful
Friendly	Neither	Unfriendly
Bright, bubbly	Neither	Dull, sombre

* The attributes used would be based on the brand's/campaign's desired attributes/ communication objectives.

Branding was originally restricted to manufactured products, but recent years have seen a trend towards branding primary products, particularly fruit and vegetables. While Sunkist oranges were apparently the first branded fruit (way back in 1908 by the Southern Californian Fruit Exchange growers' co-operative according to the Sunkist website), few others followed suit. However, things are changing, with Spongebob Spinach and the arrangement between Disney and fifteen growers (Imagination Farms) noted earlier. The irony is that McDonald's Happy Meals used to appear with a Disney character until Disney pulled out of sponsoring McDonald's food several years ago.

Rebranding: John the Baptist or John the Christian?

One of the best known rebranding campaigns was the repositioning of Marlboro from a cigarette for women to a cigarette for tough, masculine men who loved the great outdoors (i.e., the iconic American cowboys), an image that resonated around the globe. Now even the churches are 'rebranding': some Baptist churches in the United States fear that the name 'Baptist' has too many negative fundamentalist connotations – especially when coupled with 'Temple'. In an attempt to counter declining attendances, the Wycoff Baptist Church became 'Cornerstone Christian Church', First Baptist in New Hampshire became 'Centerpoint Church' and the Reformed Church in America near Detroit became 'Crosswinds Community Church' (Schulte 2008).

Although many social marketing campaigns have always been strongly branded (e.g., the US 'VERB, It's What You Do' physical activity campaign and the globally recognised 3Rs – Reduce, Reuse, Recycle slogan used in many countries including the United States, the United Kingdom, Australia and Japan), recent years have seen a stronger emphasis on branding in the social marketing literature and in practice. In some cases, this is simply a recognition that a 'branded', attractively packaged product is inherently more appealing than a 'generic' plain packaged product: in its efforts to combat AIDS, New York City's health department hands out 1.5 million free condoms a month in plain wrappers, but intends to repackage and brand the condoms with a distinctive 'New York City' wrapper (a subway theme) with the slogan 'We've got you covered' to attract more uptake and use of the condoms (Kugler 2007). Washington DC followed suit with its own branded condoms and the slogan 'Coming together to stop HIV in DC' (Levine 2007). Evans and Hastings (2008) provide examples of branded campaigns from a number of countries over a number of topics.

For developing social marketing brands, we suggest following the commercial brands where the brand name indicates something about the brand's use, benefits or strengths (e.g., Snugglers, Weight Watchers, Toys 'R' Us, Mr Muscle, Diet Coke, Energiser), or where the brand name has attempted to describe the product's use (e.g., Shake 'n Bake, Dial-a-Dinner, Post-It Notes). That is, we favour brands that include the overall campaign goal or end benefit, message, product or what we want people to do ('Freedom from Fear', 'Buckle Up', 'Quit', 'Break the Silence', 'Think. It's 30 for a reason', 'Don't Mess with Texas'). This is because if people only see the brand/logo displayed somewhere, at least we get our main message across, as illustrated in the specific target of '10,000 steps' physical activity brand name:

Figure 11.3 Branding a physical activity campaign

A Danish company makes products used in refugee camps and disaster areas all over the world, with the following brand names: ZeroFly – a tent tarp that kills flies; PermaNet – a mosquito net impregnated with insecticide; and LifeStraw – a filter worn around the neck that removes bacteria and some viruses and makes dirty water safe to drink (McNeil 2008).

Brands and sub-brands in the product mix

In some cases, just as in the commercial area, a campaign may have an overall brand name and various sub-brands for different products. The Freedom from Fear campaign targets men to call a helpline, which it separately brands as the Men's Domestic Violence Helpline, which also has its own logo (Donovan and Carroll 2008).

Road safety campaigns have traditionally developed quite separate brands for the different areas of road safety: that is, drinking and driving; speeding; fatigue; seat belts; inattention; etc. A striking exception is the comprehensive UK road safety campaign 'Think!' The overarching 'Think!' brand is attached to various areas of road safety, including: 'Think! Don't Drink and Drive'; 'Think! It's 30 for a Reason' (exceeding speed limit); 'Think! Always wear a seat belt'; 'Think! Don't Drive Tired'. The use of an overall campaign idea (i.e., 'Think!'), appears to integrate and strengthen all of the underlying components (Collin 2008). We recommend a look at this campaign (www. dft.gov.uk/think).

One consideration for government funded campaigns is the inclusion of government logos as well as the campaign brand. Most governments require that their logo be included. However, government branding of a campaign could reduce source credibility with a sceptical target audience. For example, some young people may not find the information contained in a government anti-marijuana campaign credible because of the government's prohibition agenda (Perman and Henley 2001). The solution is often to include the government logo but as small as possible and in a non-intrusive way.

Place

Consistent with a consumer orientation, place (or distribution) decisions in commercial marketing refer to ensuring and facilitating accessibility to the product for all target segments.

Place decisions involve matters such as physical distribution, number and type of outlets, opening hours, availability of public transport, availability and ease of parking, atmosphere in outlets and other environmental aspects such as cleanliness. For example, doctors in the United States have attracted men to cosmetic surgery by extending their opening hours and providing a more masculine setting (Cortez 2008).

Commercial marketers are well aware that, at least for fast moving consumer goods, the more widely available the product, the greater the sales. Similarly, the presence or absence of stores selling fresh fruit and vegetables in neighbourhoods significantly influences how much fruit and vegetables residents eat (Zenk *et al.* 2009). Vending machines are a clear example of making products such as cigarettes, snacks and beverages available 24 hours a day in locations other than retail outlets to make the most of impulse purchasing, and to increase the marketer's ability to reach target groups that might otherwise not be reached (e.g., shift workers in some locations, underage smokers). Vending machines in the United States have expanded their product ranges to include other items in specific locations such as sunscreen, analgesics and power cords. They may one day follow countries such as Japan, where even branded clothing can be purchased from a vending machine (Pressler 2004).

Commercial and health organisations are continually looking for outlets in high traffic locations such as major department stores, shopping malls and airports. For example, the UK Government wants to boost access in deprived areas by having doctors based in supermarkets (Day 2007), and pharmacies and walk-in clinics are beginning to appear in US airports (Yu 2008).

For social marketers, the same principles of making access easy apply. For example, the '10,000 Steps' campaign uses signposts (Figure 11.4) not only to promote the campaign, but also to facilitate walking goals by indicating distances between various points. Although some people are prepared to expend time and effort to donate blood, others are not and will do so only if the organisation comes to them. Safe sex campaigns should ensure that condoms are available not just in pharmacies, but in supermarkets and, especially for young people, the neighbourhood 7/11-type stores and petrol station mini-marts. It is even more essential that condoms are available in vending machines in nightclubs, pubs and bars where young people congregate to play the 'mating game'. This not only ensures ready access at times of need, but also avoids the problem of embarrassment inhibiting purchase in retail situations.

Place also includes available facilities (i.e., toilets and changing rooms) and the ambience of the physical environment (many social services offices are distinctly uninviting). If we want people to use public transport more, we need to ensure that the

Figure 11.4 Roadside posters facilitating uptake of the physical activity message

interiors of rail carriages/buses/ferries are clean, bright and cheery, that the seats are reasonably comfortable, and that handrails are easily accessible if one is standing. We also need to ensure people's security, both while on the vehicle and while at the pick up points.

Privacy considerations are important for many government and NGO welfare services, and safety considerations are always important. Encouraging people to walk for health benefits requires that their local area should not only have smooth paths (to avoid falls) and protected street crossings (to avoid being hit by motor vehicles), but also should be well lit at night and free of muggers.

EPODE campaign: place

EPODE builds on existing channels of distribution that already influence children's behaviour, especially parents, leisure stakeholders and teachers. Other intermediaries include school caterers, nurses, child care and kindergarten providers, dieticians, GPs, school doctors and other health professionals, social organisations, food suppliers (including supermarkets and restaurants), the leisure industry and the local media. EPODE's place strategy makes healthy choices accessible to children. Supermarkets are encouraged to present seasonal fruits, at a good price and in a place where children can pick them up themselves. They are taught the principles of nutrition and a balanced diet in school and encouraged to try healthy foods and participate in fun physical activities, including a pedestrian school bus, 'driven' by parents, to encourage walking to school (www.epode-european-network.com).

Social marketers are also interested in making it harder or less convenient for people to continue undesired behaviours in various settings. For example, a prevalence of no smoking venues makes quitting smoking easier and also makes continuing to smoke more difficult. Public health advocates attempt to reduce access to cigarettes by banning cigarette vending machines in areas where underage children have unsupervised access, and, in the case of alcohol, by restricting hours of opening and the quantity and type of alcohol that can be purchased from certain venues.

Considerations of place often overlap with partnerships in that partners are frequently chosen because they can provide access to various target groups in either physical locations (sporting and entertainment events, worksites, schools) or via memberships accessible by direct mail, email or online. That is, in some cases, intermediaries are collaborators and in other cases are simply used as delivery channels. For example, a school might simply agree to have a healthy eating component introduced into the curricula or it might be an active partner in promoting healthy eating as part of the school's own policies or mission. The UK 'Snack Right' children's nutrition project targeting parents and carers of 3–5-year-olds, used children's centres and nurseries to hold free fun and entertainment events with healthy food messages (NSMC 2009). We will consider further place issues in Chapter 13.

Intermediaries

Most commercial entities find it useful, or even necessary, to employ intermediaries to distribute their products and services through a channel or network rather than distributing directly to the end consumer themselves. In commercial marketing, intermediaries are well defined and largely exist for that purpose (i.e., retailers, wholesalers, franchises, distributors, freighters, packers, etc.). In social marketing, on the other hand, intermediaries may be teachers, employers, community groups, parents, GPs, pharmacists, other social and welfare professionals for whom delivery of our products and services is in addition to their regular task, and may be in some cases only distantly related to their primary activity.

Hence, intermediaries in social marketing in the distribution network are often much harder to control than paid intermediaries in commercial marketing. For example, not only are they usually not getting reimbursed for their co-operation, but they also may have their own ideas about how the message should be communicated, to whom and when.

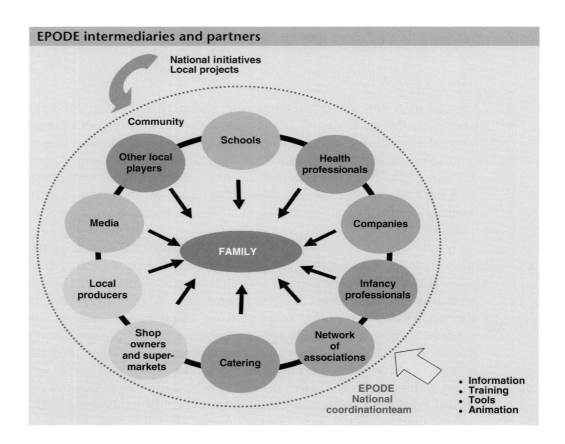

Another difficulty is that the social marketing intermediaries may need to receive some training before being able to deliver the product. This applies even to otherwise well-trained professionals. For example, GPs are often the first to admit that they lack skills in lifestyle counselling in areas such as smoking cessation, alcohol reduction, diet modification and physical activity uptake. A case in point: a survey of Canadian family doctors showed that although 43 per cent thought they should be counselling their patients to be more physically active, less than 12 per cent did so, many of them citing as a reason their lack of training in physical activity education in medical school (Kennedy and Meeuwisse 2003).

Early attempts to involve GPs in helping patients to quit smoking were not successful, partly because many smoked themselves and did not know the best ways to quit (Bloom and Novelli 1981). Many GPs may be reluctant to raise alcohol issues with their patients (McAvoy *et al.* 2001), particularly when dealing with pregnant women, despite the evidence for minimising alcohol consumption during pregnancy (France *et al.* forthcoming).

Nevertheless, general practitioners and other health professionals are an attractive channel for distributing health messages, because they are associated with strong source credibility and because they can communicate the message 'just in time' when the target audience is most likely to hear and act on it. In using intermediaries, we need to remember the marketing concept and the idea of exchange. In short, we cannot just expect GPs to help out without providing something in return, and making their involvement as easy as possible. Efforts to change the culture around alcohol consumption in pregnancy in Western Australia began with assessing the needs of health professionals for more information and materials. Having established that resources would be welcomed, several were developed and sent to every health professional in the state who would be likely to see pregnant women. These individuals were provided with a laminated fact sheet, an A4-size booklet for reference with a quick and easy questionnaire, a summary of the latest research and behavioural suggestions for overcoming time and social constraints. The pack also included a box of wallet cards to give to patients and a desk calendar to serve as a reminder of the issue. Formative research with a wide range of health professionals in metropolitan and rural areas was undertaken to develop resource materials that would be easy to use and reduce time and effort for the health professional (France *et al.* forthcoming).

Doctors prescribe physical activity

Several studies around the world have been conducted to investigate whether people will increase their physical activity levels if given a prescription to exercise by their family doctor (e.g., Bull and Jamrozik 1998; Smith *et al.* 2000). The Step Test Exercise Prescription (STEP) project was a randomised controlled trial conducted in Canada where the participants were seniors, aged over 65 years, who agreed to attend a medical clinic for the duration of the study. The findings suggested that primary care doctors could improve seniors' fitness and confidence in exercising by offering them a tailored exercise prescription. Fitness increased 11 per cent in the STEP group compared with 4 per cent in the control group and gains were sustained at six- and twelve-month follow ups in the STEP group (Petrella *et al.* 2003).

Use of non-traditional intermediaries

In recent years there has been increasing use of non-traditional intermediaries (such as taxi drivers, hair salon operators, shopkeepers) to deliver information to specific target groups in both commercial and social marketing. Here are some examples:

- in Argentina, the Buenos Aires province tourism secretariat and the La Plata municipality launched a programme to train taxi drivers and newspaper vendors to provide tourism information services (*Buenos Aires Herald* 2008);
- airport taxi drivers have been enlisted by Detroit's tourism council to give visitors a better image of the city by wearing a uniform and taking hospitality classes (Mucha 2004);
- the Power to Live Smart programme targeting African-Americans in Seattle trains barbershop and salon owners to pass on information about heart disease and stroke, and places a digital blood pressure machine (paid for by the American Heart Association) in each shop so clients can measure their blood pressure (Black 2007);
- a UK project to improve sexual health and reduce HIV transmission in ethnic minority groups works with community entities such as shopkeepers, hairdressers and taxi drivers to distribute health education materials, condoms and advice (King 2001);
- condoms for the taking appear in a self-service laundromat and other co-operating neighbourhood businesses in southeast Washington as part of the Life Guard HIV programme (Levine 2006);
- salon workers in Harlem and Washington Heights (New York) have been trained in domestic violence in an effort to reach Latino women suffering from abuse (Salazar 2008);
- in developing countries, similar community points such as brothels have been used (WHO 2000).

Although evaluations are rare at this early stage, one study reported that trained cosmetologists were effective in promoting health messages to their customers – and improved their own health behaviours at the same time (Linnan *et al.* 2005).

Churches in place strategies

Using churches is an increasingly popular place strategy, both as partnerships and as simply an access strategy. Churches are a popular strategy because in some communities the local pastor's endorsement, even for non-religious activities, is very powerful.

Furthermore, for many social marketing issues there is often a clear fit between our messages and many religious messages. Nutrition and exercise interventions in Samoan church communities in New Zealand have been very effective in achieving weight loss and increasing physical activity, showing significant differences between intervention and control communities (Bell *et al.* 2001). There are numerous examples of interventions targeting African-American (and other) communities in the United States via churches (Beasley 2006; Campbell *et al.* 2007; Peterson, Atwood and Yates 2002; Resnicow *et al.* 2001).

Others view faith groups as a means of engaging the broader community in civic activities such as social inclusion and community regeneration. The UK Economic and Social Research Council (ESRC) has produced a useful booklet offering guidance on engaging with faith groups for broader community issues ('Faith Based Voluntary Action'; available from ESRC website (www.esrcsocietytoday.ac.uk).

Computers/kiosks

Health professionals may not always be the most appropriate distributors of health advice. Prochaska and colleagues have shown that computer-based expert systems can be effective change agents with health issues such as quitting smoking, improving diet, reducing sun exposure and returning to mammography screening, as well as social issues such as bullying prevention (Grimley, Prochaska and Prochaska 1997; Pallonen *et al.* 1998; Prochaska 1997; Prochaska *et al.* 2005; Prochaska *et al.* 2007; Ruggiero *et al.* 1997). They have found that participation rates over time can remain high, and that people are more likely to continue going back to an interactive computer program than to a health professional, particularly when they have not yet managed to succeed in making the desired change. Further, computer programs will sustain high fidelity of implementation compared with systems that rely more on human performance; that is, they don't get tired of saying the same things and they don't get depressed if the patient isn't successful.

> ### Digital doctors
> Paying bills, sending lab results and scheduling appointments are increasingly being done online between doctors and patients. However, it is also possible for some diagnoses to be done online – such trials being supported by insurance companies always on the lookout for reducing medical costs (Mathews 2009).

One study effectively used an interactive computer program to encourage pregnant smokers at varying stages of change to quit smoking. The multi-media computer program was easy to use (it had touchscreen data input) and gave clear, immediate feedback with customised graphics. A surprising 67 per cent of the women said they would have used the computer program in preference to receiving one-on-one counselling from a health professional. This suggests that the use of computers would be widely accepted, as well as being highly cost-effective. One of the reasons given for the preference was that many of the women (55 per cent) felt that they would be more candid with the computer than with a person (Ruggiero *et al.* 1997).

Kiosk/computers can provide a convenient place strategy. They could be placed in doctors' waiting rooms, in health clinics, hospitals, or in other settings such as bars, shopping malls or schools. The convenience factor would need to be balanced with sensitivity to the target market, however. A study by Nicholas, Huntington and Williams (2002) looked at twenty-one kiosks in pharmacies, hospitals, information centres and doctors' surgeries. Their data suggest that information centres perform best, followed by hospitals. Surgeries performed less well, with the authors suggesting that people may be inhibited by the close proximity of others and that searching for health information may not be seen as appropriate when they are about to ask their doctor to answer their health questions.

Helplines and phone-based care

Telephone 'helplines' are a common means of making information or a service (e.g., counselling) accessible to those geographically unable to visit an outlet and those unable or unwilling to visit a service during standard working hours. Telephone helplines can either be simple pre-recorded messages or provide an interactive service. They have a number of advantages: they allow dissemination of information to large numbers of self-selected people, yet they can also provide a highly personalised service; they are convenient and private (almost everyone has easy and affordable access to a telephone and helplines are often free of charge), and they can be staffed 24 hours; they are personal, yet they also offer a degree of anonymity (Anderson, Duffy and Hallett 1992).

Most of the time helplines are reactive, that is, they simply respond to people's requests for information. However, it may be useful to consider the proactive potential of helplines. For example, the US National Cancer Institute's Cancer Information Service has adopted a policy of referring callers, where appropriate, to clinical trials or to mammography screening. They also recommend that helplines can be used as a research tool, for example, to assess the efficacy of campaigns with different minority groups (Anderson, Duffy and Hallett 1992). They may also be useful as a surveillance tool to collect data that could help predict infectious disease events (Rolland *et al.* 2006).

However, one of the major problems for helpline operators is achieving the right balance between demand and supply for crisis services. It is expensive to have a large bank of counsellors sitting idle, but it can be disastrous if suicidal people or assault victims in need of trauma counselling can't get through because 'all our operators are busy'.

Internet helplines are an alternative to telephone helplines and seem to offer even more anonymity, although concerns have been raised by some groups that the Internet is unregulated. Nevertheless, they are proving popular with boys who are generally less likely than girls to use telephone helplines (Beenstock 1999). For example, in a UK study looking at three 'mainstream' youth helplines, approximately 66 per cent of callers were female, whereas a helpline for young Muslims attracted a 50:50 split (Franks and Medworth 2005).

A variation on the above is where the 'helpline' calls the person. Automated calling systems are now being tested – similar to automated sales systems – where people respond by pressing the buttons on their phone if they want to hear all or parts of a message. Helplines may also extend to 'outreach' services, for example, where callers to a crisis line who agree, are called back for a set period until they have received appropriate formal help or are no longer in crisis. A US study involving chronically ill older people found that regular telephone contact with a social worker who kept them informed of various services halved the death rate over a 12-month period. However, the effect disappeared when the telephone calling ceased (Alkema *et al.* 2007). It may well be that the decreased mortality was not so much due to the information given but simply to the human contact.

Outreach in China: eye surgery on a train

Funded by a Hong Kong charity and staffed largely by volunteer doctors, the Lifeline Express visits towns and villages all across China to help those suffering from cataracts and who would not otherwise have access to or be able to afford treatment. Local health officials help by organising patients in advance and providing electricity and other utilities at each stop (Cody 2004).

Peer selling

Although Avon salespeople included worksites and other organisations where women congregated as sales targets, it appears that we have Tupperware to thank for the rapid adoption of peer selling (including 'pyramid selling') by marketers of such products as cosmetics, vitamins and health supplements, lingerie and sex aids, and household cleaning products.

The SafetyNet© programme that grew out of the StopAIDS project is modelled on the Tupperware method. The party is led by a trained facilitator who is gay. Such peer-led groups are effective because the informal setting allows communication of a personal nature; the relaxed atmosphere conveys positive feelings about safe sex; peer group members can share their concerns with each other; and specific information can be easily adapted to suit ethnic or different social groups. Evaluations showed significant changes in partygoers' intentions to practise safe sex (AIDS Action Committee 1989).

In Australia, an Indigenous student used 'Heartaware' parties in an attempt to teach healthy eating and food preparation habits to Indigenous people. The host was asked to invite their friends and relatives to a lunch get together. Prior to lunch, the group was given a brief talk on heart disease and risk factors. The student and a local nutrition worker then prepared lunch, explaining how the foods they chose, and how they prepared the food, lessen the risk of heart disease (Owen 2002).

A variation on this tactic is used frequently by tobacco and alcohol marketers to target young people. Individuals are paid by the tobacco and alcohol marketers to attend and mingle at parties, bars and nightclubs, and distribute cigarettes or offer to buy those around them a drink (see Chapter 9). Social marketers increasingly use 'ambassadors' for their programmes, usually enlisting high profile persons (White Ribbon Day ambassadors) or persons with local knowledge ('Snack Right' ambassadors) to take on this role.

Price

In commercial marketing, price usually refers to monetary costs incurred when purchasing goods or services. However, non-monetary costs are also involved in the purchase of commercial products. For example, there may be time costs involved in test driving a new car or travelling to a particular outlet, effort costs in switching to a new bank and psychological costs in trying a new brand of sports shoe.

Price in social marketing includes monetary costs, but most costs for most campaigns involve time, effort, physical discomfort and psychological costs. Adopting a regular exercise routine may involve monetary costs such as purchasing appropriate clothing or necessary equipment, admission fees, travel costs and babysitting costs. However, the major costs may relate to time and the lost opportunity to engage in other desired activities, perhaps effort and physical discomfort and even social embarrassment (e.g., a person with little sense of rhythm attending an aerobics class, an overweight person joining a group of slim walkers).

Cheaper low fat snacks sell

Commercial pricing strategies can be an effective way to increase compliance with a social marketing objective. One study (French *et al.* 1997) examined the effect of reducing the price of low fat snacks in nine vending machines selling low fat and regular food. At the baseline, low fat snacks made up 25.7 per cent of total sales. During the three-week intervention, when prices of low fat snacks were reduced by 50 per cent, their sales went up to 45.8 per cent of total sales. After the intervention, when prices had returned to normal, sales dropped back to 22.8 per cent. In a larger study (French *et al.* 2001), similar effects were found for adolescent and adult populations (vending machines in secondary schools and worksites). Prices were reduced by 10 per cent, 25 per cent and 50 per cent, giving increases in sales of low fat snacks of 9 per cent, 39 per cent and 93 per cent, respectively.

The most common pricing strategy is price discounting, often in partnership with a product manufacturer, for example, by electricity providers offering discounts to their customers who purchase 'ecobulbs'. A classic example was the 2009 US 'Cash for Clunkers' programme offering large cash discounts on new, lower fuel consumption cars when people traded in their old, high fuel consumption vehicles, which were then sent to the junk yard. The Car Allowance Rebate System (CARS) has proved very popular, and there are claims that the system not only stimulates the economy but will pay for itself by significantly reducing the amount of fuel the United States consumes.

Pay-as-you-drive insurance

Some insurance companies in the United States are offering discounts for low mileage drivers. This has been facilitated by various devices that can be fitted to vehicles to measure mileage. One insurance company's device (Progressive) can even measure when the vehicle is driven and to some extent how it is driven in terms of acceleration and braking behaviour. Insurance cover can then be adjusted according to mileage and driver behaviour (Levick 2009).

In general, public health promoters attempt to reduce the monetary costs of compliance by providing subsidised or free services, but overlook or minimise the inhibiting effect of these other costs. For example, the physical discomfort cost of nicotine withdrawal is one of the high costs involved in quitting smoking, along with forgoing the comfort of a cigarette in anxious situations, but this was rarely acknowledged in early anti-smoking campaigns. Similarly, targeting young males to drink low alcohol beers may involve considerable psychological costs (i.e., derisory comments from others), as well as forgoing feelings of relaxation associated with mild intoxication.

Recycling programmes, with distinctive bags or bins for different products (i.e., papers versus bottles versus cans) attempt to reduce the time and effort costs of sorting and storage of recyclable materials. Kerbside pick up eliminates the time and effort of delivering to recycling stations, and is piggybacked onto household rubbish collection to minimise forgetting and limiting effort to one occasion in the week.

Taxing cigarettes encourages quitting

There is a clear correlation between the cost and the consumption of cigarettes. In 2002, one of the recommendations of the US Interagency Committee on Smoking and Health's Sub-Committee on Cessation was to increase the tax on a cigarette pack from US$.39 to US$2.39, citing research that showed for every 10 per cent increase in price, there is a 4 per cent decrease in cigarette consumption (from smokers reducing the amount they smoke or quitting, former smokers not starting again and young people not taking it up). It was predicted that this single measure of increasing the tax by US$2 a packet would result in 4 billion fewer cigarette packs sold each year, a 10 per cent reduction in adults smoking, 4.7 million smokers quitting and 6 million young people not taking it up (Fiore et al. 2004).

Strategies to increase the monetary cost of undesirable behaviours can be used by social marketers to good effect. For example:

- Chaloupka (1995) found that college students' decisions to smoke and the number of cigarettes they smoked were highly sensitive to price, more so than adults, leading to the conclusion that substance use and abuse is reduced, especially among younger people, by policies raising the price of licit and illicit substances.
- UK researchers claim that a 50 pence minimum unit price for alcohol could save as many as 3,400 lives a year in the United Kingdom – almost the same number of people killed on the roads (O'Dowd 2009).
- London's congestion charge, introduced in 2003, served to reduce vehicular traffic in central London (a similar scheme was introduced in Stockholm in 2007).

In social marketing contexts, costs are usually short term and certain, whereas benefits are often long term and less certain (Weinstein 1988). For example, the physical withdrawal costs of giving up smoking are immediate and certain, whereas the health benefits, such as reduced risk of lung and throat cancer, are long term and a matter of probabilities. Many social marketing health campaigns stress the long-term benefits without fully addressing the short-term costs (Weinstein 1988).

EPODE campaign: price

Price is the cost of the product, both monetary and non-monetary. Price includes the concept of 'exchange' where the buyer gives up something in return for the product. In the context of childhood obesity, we are usually asking the target audience (children) to give up the instant gratification of desired foods and soft drinks or to engage in effortful activities. We may be asking parents to deny their children desired foods and also to engage in effortful activities with their children. Persuading children and parents to adopt a physical activity routine may involve some monetary costs such as purchasing shoes, clothing or equipment. However, the major costs may relate to time, effort, physical discomfort and possibly guilt.

EPODE's pricing strategy has been to stress the benefits of a healthier lifestyle, including the value of a family preparing and eating healthy food together and doing physical activities together; at the same time, the programme finds ways to make healthy products less expensive by working with supermarkets, school canteens, etc.

A key consideration when designing a pricing strategy is the concept of exchange: the target audience will weigh up the costs and benefits based on what we present to them and their previous experience. When they do this cost–benefit analysis, we need them to clearly see 'What's in it for me?' (known in marketing as 'the WIIFM'). There are three ways to help people identify the WIIFM:

- *minimise the costs of taking up recommended behaviours*: in a physical activity campaign this could mean showing how easy it is to fit 30 minutes of activity into a daily schedule;

- *maximise the costs of not taking up recommended behaviours*: this is a threat appeal strategy where the negative consequences of not adopting the recommended behaviour are shown;
- *maximise the benefits of taking up recommended behaviours*: in a physical activity campaign, this could involve focusing on the fun, fitness and social benefits as well specific health benefits.

Positive Parenting campaign: price and place working together

In the Western Australian Positive Parenting campaign, the costs of adopting the idea of positive parenting were primarily non-monetary. Time, effort and energy were required to seek out further information, read the printed materials or watch the videos and then practise the recommended positive parenting strategies. Psychological costs of embarrassment were involved in asking for help; parents might be reluctant to go to a government department and ask for help parenting their children in case they are labelled potential child abusers.

Many of these costs were reduced by the place strategy. Instead of expecting people to come in to the government office building to obtain information, product and services were brought to the target market. Information was made available in local libraries, by direct mail, on the Internet and via a helpline. The department also opened a number of parenting information centres in shopping malls. The centres are colourful, inviting and convenient (see Figure 11.5), reducing time and effort costs, as well as embarrassment costs (Henley, Donovan and Moorhead 1998).

Figure 11.5 Making place attractive

Pricing of community services: who should pay?

Governments' push towards privatisation and a 'user pays' philosophy can serve to maintain and even exacerbate inequities that already exist in society with regard to access to transport, education, recreation and health care. Crompton (1981) provides a useful discussion of pricing in the public sector. He delineates four major functions of pricing in the delivery of community services:

- equity;
- revenue production (governments can increase their revenues by charging for previously uncharged services);
- efficiency (charging for services can reduce unwarranted demand, discount pricing can be offered in low demand times to encourage shifts in demand);
- income redistribution (general taxation revenue used to supply services free to disadvantaged groups).

We are interested here primarily in equity.

The equity issue raises questions of who should pay and what share according to benefits received. If benefits are received exclusively by users, then this can be considered to have the characteristics of a private service and the total cost should be borne by the user (e.g., private parking stations). If the user benefits, but the wider community (i.e., non-users) also benefits, then the user should pay a certain amount and the community should subsidise the cost (e.g., public transport reduces air pollution). Where all members of a community benefit and there are no feasible ways of excluding some members from using the service (e.g., schools, police), then costs should be borne totally by the tax system. The question for societies is where various services will be placed. Throughout the world toll roads are becoming common, tertiary education fees have been introduced where there was previously no charge, entrance fees are charged to some national parks, energy and other essential services are being privatised, security companies are proliferating and so on. The danger is that we will reinforce existing discrepancies between the quality of life of those with high incomes and those without. Those who can afford toll costs will have less travel time than those who cannot. Although tolls may encourage the use of public transport, this depends on adequate public transport being available. It is likely that many workers will be disadvantaged by tolls.

Do local government swimming pools benefit the whole community or only users? Is there a differential benefit in low versus high socio-economic status areas? If they reduce delinquency and improve the health and wellbeing of otherwise disadvantaged groups, should they be free or heavily discounted in some areas?

Related to this discussion are those studies that attempt to assess how much people would pay for certain benefits such as reduced pollution, reduced logging in forests, electric cars and other environmental gains. The general result is that when isolated as a specific user cost, many are reluctant to pay more. However, if the cost is borne by the whole community, there tends to be more support for more costly alternatives that have environmental benefits.

Promotion

Promotion is the range of activities that create awareness of the product (or a reminder that the product exists) and its attributes, and persuades the buyer to make the purchase (Thackeray, Neiger and Hanson 2007). The promotion mix includes advertising, sales promotion, sponsorship, publicity and public relations, free merchandising (giveaways) and personal selling. It may involve mass media, localised media, outlet point-of-sale materials, in-store promotions, promotions and incentives to intermediaries, Internet sites, cross-promotions with other organisations and so on. Given that promotion is generally covered in other chapters (in particular Chapter 13 – media and Chapter 14 – sponsorship), it is discussed here only briefly.

'In NY and LA, a party's not just a party any more, it's a PR opportunity'

Similar to peer selling and the fashion event marketing of tobacco companies is the phenomenon of private parties and weddings being sponsored by marketers, even handing out 'goody bags'. So far the 'trend' appears to be confined to PR savvy people and socialites (Brown 2002).

Perhaps one area that social marketers could consider more is that of 'sales promotions'. Whereas advertising and other communication modes are intended to impact primarily on beliefs and attitudes, sales promotions are intended to act directly on behaviour (Rossiter and Percy 1997). By offering a free sample, discount or gift, sales promotions are intended to generate an intended purchase earlier than it might otherwise take place, encourage purchase of a greater quantity or, and of most interest to us, induce trial in previously resistant audience members – perhaps by making the perceived value of the 'purchase' greater than the perceived costs, or at least greater than the costs of one trial. That is, sales promotions are often targeted at 'other brand loyals' to at least trial the 'discounted' brand. However, with some exceptions (see box below), the usual sorts of sales promotions such as competitions have not worked particularly well in attracting people to cease undesirable behaviours.

'Quit and Win' contest: using sales promotion in social marketing

In 2002, ninety-eight countries participated in the 'Quit and Win' smoking cessation contest, organised by the National Public Health Institute in Finland and supported by the World Health Organization. In Taiwan alone, more than 23,000 smokers took part, agreeing to stop using all tobacco products for at least one month. Contestants' claims were verified with a test to see if they were tobacco free. A 93-year-old, Hsu Tuan, who had been a chain smoker for 75 years, gave up smoking forty cigarettes a day to win the top prize. These contests have been called a 'social marketing success story' (Lavack, Watson and Markwart 2007).

Sales promotions in our language are 'incentives' or 'facilitators'. Offers to pick people up to take them to vote or to a community meeting, or a week's free trial at a gym, or free passes to Adventure World/Movie World for all those enrolling in a parenting course would all fall into the category of 'sales promotions'.

Several 'incentive' examples have been presented throughout this chapter. These further examples indicate the variety of opportunities available, although some may be of dubious validity:

- a campaign in the Czech Republic to get people to donate blood offered them two half-litre glasses of beer in exchange (Krosnar 2004). Naturally, this attracted some criticism from health authorities (let's hope they got the blood first);
- Canadian parents who made TV and video games a reward for exercise increased their overweight children's physical activity levels by 65 per cent (Goldfield *et al.* 2006);
- offering US$100 financial incentives to low income and Hispanic participants and their obstetricians for timely and comprehensive prenatal care significantly reduced neonatal intensive care admissions, and total paediatric health care spending in the first year of life (Rosenthal *et al.* 2009);
- companies are offering employees prizes and cash rewards for losing weight and exercising (Gearon 2008).

EPODE campaign: promotion

EPODE promotes healthy behaviour to children as fun activities rather than for health benefits. For example, one theme is 'Playing is already moving!' recommending fun (non-competitive) play activities. The theme is based on research that shows that playing outside with friends can significantly increase the amount of physical activity a child gets in a day. Many of EPODE's promotion activities are focused at the local level, advertising local initiatives and events, using personal selling through doctors and teachers to promote the message. The extensive publicity the programme has received is seen as encouraging more towns to enter the programme. It could also have the effect of reinforcing a social norm around the programme's activities which would encourage families to be involved. As the promising results of the EPODE programme emerge, the campaign is being picked up as an interesting news story internationally, for example, by the *Telegraph* in the United Kingdom (Lambert 2008).

Another area that has always challenged social marketers is how to use the concept of point-of-sale advertising and promotions as in the commercial area. Road safety authorities attempt to use radio ads during drive time that ask the driver to look at their speedometer; ads on a Friday and Saturday evening remind drivers of the number of drinks to remain under 0.05 and the chances of being stopped by police. Some health promotion sponsorships require venues to strongly advertise low alcohol beers at the point-of-sale.

What we call attempting to intervene at the point of decision-making, Kotler, Roberto and Lee (2008) refer to as 'just in time' promotions: strategies that target the audience at the moment they are about to make a choice between the undesirable behaviour and alternative behaviours. For example, an individual about to order a meal may be influenced to make healthy choices by the Heart Foundation tick against certain menu items. Similarly, a good place to promote the message that infants should lie on their backs to sleep would be on the front of babies' nappies.

Another of Kotler and colleague's (2008) suggestions is that smokers who express a wish to give up could be encouraged to slip a photo of their child or children under the wrapper of their cigarette packet. However, this requires the co-operation of the smoker. Health authorities around the world are placing graphic images of ill-health effects on cigarette packs. A Canadian study of the impact of the warnings found that 44 per cent of smokers said the new warnings increased their motivation to quit, 21 per cent said that on one or more occasions they decided not to have a cigarette because of the new warnings and 18 per cent said they had asked for a different pack to avoid a particular warning. In addition, 48 per cent of non-smokers said the new warnings made them feel better about being a non-smoker (International tobacco mailing list 2002). What social marketers need to do is become more innovative in reaching our target audiences at the point of decision-making.

Perhaps the converse of that last point is to put reminders of negative consequences where they actually happened. A common occurrence around the globe is placing crosses, wreaths (and even personal effects) at the site where someone died in a road accident (known as 'roadside memorials'). In the United Kingdom, cycling groups are placing 'ghost bikes' (bikes painted white) in locations where cyclists have died in an effort to publicise the need for motorists to take care around cyclists (Gulland 2009). Until recently there had been little research on the impact that such 'memorials' have on actual behaviour, with motorists' self reports varying from 'distracting' to 'no effect' to 'a positive effect' on their behaviours. However, Canadian researcher Richard Tay conducted an on-road experiment to examine the short-term effects of roadside memorials at two intersections. The results showed that the number of red light violations was reduced by 16.7 per cent in the six weeks after the installation of the mock memorials compared with the six weeks before, whereas the number of violations at two comparison sites experienced an increase of 16.8 per cent (Tay 2009).

Praise the Lord and pass the fruit and veg: place and promotion working together

The US National Cancer Institute's '5-a-Day for Better Health Program' encourages people to eat five or more daily servings of fruit and vegetables. A randomised delayed control intervention with fifty African-American churches in North Carolina yielded a significant and substantial increase in fruit and vegetable consumption in the intervention churches. The multi component intervention was just that, involving tailored bulletins to individual participants, monthly updates, serving fruit and vegetables at church functions, distributing a cookbook, showing members how to modify their favourite recipes to be more healthy, training lay advisers, involving local grocers and promoting local produce and having the pastors promote the project during services (Campbell *et al.* 1999). A follow up study of pastors involved in the research showed that the churches had high expectations of the university researchers, but these were generally met with high levels of satisfaction with their participation (Ammerman *et al.* 2003).

People

People factors are important in all organisations, whether for profit, not for profit or government departments. Regardless of their role in the organisation, the staff members with whom the client interacts are generally the most important influence on attitudes towards the organisation. For example, a friendly, pleasant and helpful receptionist in an organisation (often lowly paid and undervalued) can make a substantial contribution to an organisation's image and repeat business. More pointedly, there would be little point in spending substantial funds on a campaign to encourage people to use public buses if the bus drivers are rude, unfriendly and reluctant or unable to give people information about the service.

The relevant factors for staffing are selecting the right people for the job and then training to ensure they do the job right. There are three main factors relevant to all people's tasks:

- interpersonal skills;
- product knowledge skills; and
- process skills.

The degree to which each is required depends on the job requirements. For example, a supermarket checkout person is required to have minimal interpersonal skills (i.e., friendly, pleasant, polite), virtually no product knowledge (with 10,000 products in the store how could they?), but the task requires competence in processing skills with regard to use of the barcode technology, cash register, EFTPOS and bagging.

Other jobs will require more extensive skills in all three areas, especially product knowledge in retail and industrial organisations (e.g., new car and computer salespeople), and interpersonal skills in service areas, including defusing client anger and dealing with problems when the process is disrupted. Process knowledge and skills appear particularly important in government welfare areas. In social marketing, especially where we are dealing with the underprivileged and disadvantaged, staff need to be patient and understanding of their clients' needs. Cultural and sensitivity training may be needed. Where people are already suffering from low self-esteem, along with a sense of helplessness and a feeling of being 'just a number', even innocent gestures may be misinterpreted and lead to a disturbance.

Many social marketing programmes involve volunteers and 'lay helpers'. However, most of their training appears to be in the content area in which they are helping rather than in dealing with the target audience as customers. Training in interpersonal skills is equally important. A crucial area is that of counselling, and particularly helpline counselling in sensitive areas such as child abuse, sexual assault, intimate partner violence, depression and suicide. In these situations, counsellors must be particularly skilled in obtaining the confidence of callers so as to keep them on the line long enough to defuse the crisis situation, then elicit their personal details so as to refer them to appropriate counselling organisations. The Freedom from Fear Men's Domestic Violence Helpline counsellors were crucial to the success of that campaign.

Partnerships

Partnerships are increasingly important for comprehensive social marketing campaigns. However, we need to distinguish between partnerships where partners share common or at least congruent goals and where they do not. In the former case, partnerships involve non-profits and governments; in the latter case partnerships involve the commercial sector.

The Prostate Net's Barbershop initiative

This programme recruited and trained local barbers within minority communities to function as lay educators. The Barbershop Initiative was launched in 2004 in conjunction with MGM Studios and their release of the movie sequel *Barbershop II* (The Prostate Net 2007: www.prostate-online.org).

In the context of obesity, 'partnerships' is an essential marketing mix element as the problem can be solved only by an integrated effort involving numerous agencies and stakeholders (Ayadi and Young 2006), including education departments, schools, teachers, parents, health departments and health professionals, regulatory bodies, the food industry, commercial marketing industry and so on. For example, funding for EPODE comes from a mix of public and private partnerships at the national and local levels. To date, national private sponsors have come primarily from the food industry, insurance and distribution sectors. To minimise concerns that these partners might exploit their involvement to promote more of their products, partners sign a charter promising that the programme will not be referred to in any product promotion, they will not intervene in any way in the programme content and they will refer to their involvement only in corporate communications.

Another key aspect of EPODE is its involvement of local authorities through the local mayors. In France, these local authorities have jurisdiction over kindergartens and primary schools, covering the primary target of children aged 3–12 years. Mayors are invited to submit an application to be an EPODE community, which involves signing a charter promising to employ a full-time project manager for the programme, organise specific activities each month in the city, participate in national meetings of project managers and commit at least €1 per capita per annum for five years, although many authorities commit much more than this (Henley and Raffin 2009).

Concern about obesity has certainly resulted in a multitude of partnerships between non-profit and for profit organisations, many featuring high visibility celebrities. The Alliance for a Healthier Generation was created in 2005 by the American Heart Association and the William J. Clinton Foundation, and is currently led by Bill Clinton and Governor Arnold Schwarzenegger of California (who replaced presidential nominee candidate Governor Mike Huckabee in 2007). The Alliance works to 'positively affect the places that can make a difference to a child's health: homes, schools, restaurants, doctors' offices and communities'.

There are also numerous partnerships addressing a variety of the problems in developing countries, particularly Africa, with regard to world hunger, HIV/AIDS, malaria, vaccination and immunisations and oral rehydration. For example, the Bill and Melinda Gates and Rockefeller Foundations launched a joint 'green revolution' effort in 2006 to develop more disease and drought resistant seeds, better distribution networks for seed and fertiliser and university level training for African crop scientists (DeYoung 2006).

Himmelman (2001) provides a useful framework for categorising partnerships along a continuum from minimal to maximal co-operation and collaboration:

- **Networking** simply involves the exchange of information for mutual benefit. Organisations may meet formally or informally to update each other on their programmes. There is little other co-operation, but the information may assist in planning to avoid competing with each other by scheduling events on the same date.
- **Co-ordinating** involves information exchange, but adds the co-ordination of plans to meet some common goal, including perhaps co-ordinating activities to have a synergistic effect.
- **Co-operating** adds the sharing of resources to information exchange and co-ordinating events and activities. At this level, organisations may pool their resources to conduct an event or promote their common goals. This is generally the level of most partnerships in social marketing.

- **Collaborating** goes even further and refers to organisations enhancing the capacity of partners for mutual gain.

For social marketing in the future, we see a need to develop and increase partnerships with:

- social entrepreneurs and social entrepreneurship foundations (such as Ashoka: www.ashoka.org), who can help deliver products and services at low cost to populations in need, particularly in developing countries;
- advocacy groups (such as the Center for Science in the Public Interest: www.cspinet.org and United for a Fair Economy: www.faireconomy.org), who can assist in bringing about changes in policies and laws;
- churches to adapting principles of liberation theology to assist in social regeneration.

Concluding comments

The marketing mix provides the social marketer with a framework for planning a comprehensive campaign. The elements of the marketing mix not only serve to remind the campaign planner of all the elements that must be considered in planning and implementing a campaign, but also provide a framework for generating ideas and an opportunity to be imaginative and innovative. The framework also serves to remind the planner that all elements need to reinforce each other. Even where one element may be given more emphasis in a particular combination, the marketing mix should still be regarded as a single entity within which each element supports and reinforces the others.

Cookin' chitlins for littluns – putting it all together

Background: A severe form of diarrhoea was affecting African-American infants in Atlanta. The bacteria causing the illness was *Yersinia enterocolitica* (YE) associated with the preparation of a traditional African-American dish: chitterlings or chitlins (made out of pork intestines). Although the problem was identified in 1989 and followed by traditional health education materials, a 1996 review showed that infants were still getting sick and some were dying, especially following Thanksgiving and Christmas holidays when this dish was traditionally served.

Formative research: Focus groups and interviews were conducted with members of the community about how they prepared the chitterlings, what chitterlings meant to them culturally and what hygiene practices they used. Some women washed the chitterlings during the cleaning process, while others pre-boiled the chitterlings before cleaning. Laboratory cultures (and the researchers' own experience) showed that the pre-boiling method eliminated the bacteria. As part of their research, the social marketers joined their participants in taste tests of chitterlings prepared each way to be sure they could honestly claim that pre-boiling made no difference to the taste!

Product: The product was the practice: 'Pre-boil your chitterlings for 5 minutes before cleaning and cooking as usual.' The primary target market was identified as older African-American women because these women were likely to prepare chitterlings and likely to have the care of babies in extended families. One difficulty was that many in the target market did not associate infants' illness with chitterlings (infants didn't often eat chitterlings but were exposed to the bacteria by being in the kitchen during preparation).

Price: Costs included the change to traditional cultural practices, the idea that pre-boiling would 'boil-in the dirt', that it involved extra work up front and that it would make a difference to the taste. These were countered by explaining that many traditional African-American grandmothers had been using the pre-boil method in their families for generations, that taste tests showed no difference in taste, that it made the whole process faster overall, as well as safer for children, and that there would be no need to exclude babies from the kitchen for extended periods (so child care problems could be avoided). (The previous health education intervention had recommended removing children from the kitchen for many hours without taking into account the inconvenience or high cost of child care in such a situation. The pre-boil method meant that children only had to be removed for a few minutes.)

Promotion: Brochures, flyers, cartoon stickers and public service announcements, as well as news releases and television news features were used. Two intermediary target markets were identified – health care providers and community leaders, and special materials were developed for each of these segments.

Place: Grocery shops were targeted to place flyers at point-of-sale next to the chitterlings. As many of the primary target market were churchgoers, and as churches were seen as a trusted source, clergy were asked to distribute leaflets at church or with newsletters. Leaflets were available in the waiting rooms of doctors, women's and infant clinics and hospitals. As well as using mass media, gospel radio talk shows popular with the target market were used, with grandmothers explaining their traditional way of preparing chitterlings, using the pre-boil method.

Outcome: A noticeable reduction in the number of hospital admissions was seen after just the first Christmas holiday (Peterson and Koehler 1997).

QUESTIONS

● Pick a well-known packaged good brand in your country. Describe what you think is that brand's marketing mix. Are different elements of the mix targeting different market segments?

● What do we mean by an *integrated* marketing mix?

● How do policy and partnerships enhance the efficacy of the marketing mix?

● How would you determine whether or not to go ahead with a partnership with a commercial organisation?

FURTHER READING

Donovan, R. J., Paterson, D. and Francas, M. 1999. Targeting Male Perpetrators of Intimate Partner Violence: Western Australia's 'Freedom from Fear' campaign, *Social Marketing Quarterly* 5(3): 127–43.

Evans, W. D. and Hastings, G. (eds.) 2008. *Public Health Branding: Applying Marketing for Social Change*. Oxford University Press.

Think! Campaign, available at: www.dft.gov.uk/think.

12 Using media in social marketing

The availability and types of media channels today have expanded substantially since the first edition of this book in 2003. However, in keeping (at least somewhat) with that old saying that the more things change, the more they stay the same, recent global award winning advertising campaigns have been characterised by an emphasis on what people are now calling 'traditional' media channels: commercial television; commercial radio; print; and ambient media (Dawson 2009; Lannon 2008). For example, the Dove campaign we noted in Chapter 9 used viral ads and the Internet, but its major impact was via television advertising and the numerous well placed billboards – that were picked up by and publicised even further in mainstream news media.

This is not to say that the 'new media' such as online advertising, viral advertising, mobile phones and 'social media' such as Facebook, Twitter, Myspace and the myriad blogs around are not important. They are, but their use and usefulness has perhaps been exaggerated. For example, during the unrest in July 2009 following the disputed election results in Iran, much was made of the fact that in the absence of journalists on the ground, information and pictures about the unrest came from people's mobile phones, the Internet and Twitter, in particular. However, these simply served as a channel to the main media, which then ensured that these images and stories received a mass audience throughout the world. Twitter and others, indeed, played a crucial role, but much the same function as incognito journalists have always done in smuggling interviews and film footage out of totalitarian states – only much faster.

The Coca-Cola Facebook–Superbowl playoff

Getting 'with it', Coca-Cola placed one of their ads on Facebook. The result: 1.6 million people viewed the ad. At far greater cost, the ad was placed in the live telecast of the Superbowl. However, compare the result: 94.5 million viewers.

From our point of view, it is not so much the media channels *per se* that are of interest, but how they are used to achieve one's objectives. In our view, innovative use of media does not equate only to technology; rather, it equates to identifying locations (or 'touchpoints') where we can reach, engage and impact our target audiences (Manning 2009), and to strategic use of creative executions that generate publicity and action (see our 'rat' example later in this chapter). Mindful of the commercial world's point-of-sale advertising, we also need to be creative in reaching target audience members at critical times; hence, the placement of anti-drug advertising in bathrooms at bars and nightclubs, 'Keep it safe. Keep it hidden. Keep it locked' signs at parking areas, 'Think!' roadside road safety billboards, drive time road safety ads on radio, sun protection warnings at beaches and swimming pools, etc. However, we probably wouldn't go as far as taking up the offer of eyelid advertising (see box).

Would you rent your eyelids as advertising space?

In a variation of paid word-of-mouth advertising, the UK-based beauty products supplier Feelunique.com was offering a pay-per-wink programme. All you had to do was have the company logo put on your eyelid and then get winking (BellaSugarUK 2008).

In this chapter we will primarily cover the main ways of using the media independent of the channel used (i.e., advertising, publicity, etc.) and the major objectives for media campaigns. We will mention, but not discuss in depth, the main channels available and how the newer channels are being used in social marketing, given that the newer technologies will no doubt change rapidly over the next few years (see Table 12.1 for a summary of the most frequently used media channels).

The importance of media in social marketing

Consistent with Ric Young's (1989) statement that information is social marketing's primary product, Richard Manoff, one of the first social marketing practitioners, called mass media 'social marketing's primary tool' (Manoff 1985). However, there continues to be some debate as to the power of the mass media, and not just among social marketers, public health professionals and other social change professions. Some argue that the mass media influence what topics we think about, but not how we think about those topics. Others claim an inordinate influence of the media – especially advertising, and particularly on children and young people with regard to promoting or exacerbating violence, sexual promiscuity, intolerance and the negative stereotyping of women, the elderly and people of colour (see Browne and Hamilton-Giachritis 2005; Bryant and Oliver 2009; Comstock 2004; Harris 2009; Leiss et al. 2005). While researchers often disagree on some issues, there is general agreement that the media can have a powerful impact as evidenced in worldwide codes for depicting suicides in news reports because of 'copycat' effects (Gregor 2004).

Table 12.1 Summary of media channels and their characteristics

Type	Characteristics
Limited reach	
Pamphlets/ brochures	Information transmission: best where cognition, rather than emotion, is desired outcome.
Fact/information sheets	Quick convenient information: use as series with storage folder, not for complex behaviour change.
Newsletters	Continuity, personalised, labour intensive, requires detailed commitment and needs assessment before commencing.
Posters	Agenda setting function: visual message, creative input required, possibility of graffiti might be considered.
T-shirts	Emotive, personal: useful for cementing attitudes and commitment to programme/ idea.
Stickers	Short messages to identify/motivate the user and cement commitment, cheap, persuasive.
Wallet cards	Much like stickers: useful for reminder information and helpline numbers.
Videos	Instructional, motivational: useful for personal viewing with adults as back-up to other programmes.
DVDs and CDs	Provides the opportunity for portable, attractive easy to use, multimedia transmitted information
Cinema	Captive audience: can target to specific audiences, emotive potential given large screen.
Mass reach	
Television	Awareness, arousal, modelling and image creation role: may be increasingly useful in information and skills training as awareness and interest in health increases.
Radio	Informative, interactive (talkback): cost-effective and useful in creating awareness, providing information.
Newspapers	Long and short copy information: material dependent on type of newspaper and day of week.
Magazines	Wide readership and influence: useful in supportive role and to inform and provide social proof.
Internet	Can serve a wide role from personal information transmission to group sessions to 'blogging'.
Mobile phones	Deliver timely, short information: supportive role, provide access to Internet sources.

Adapted from Egger, Spark and Donovan (2005).

War of the Worlds: the power of the media?

In October 1938, tens of thousands of people panicked on hearing Orson Welles' radio production of H. G. Wells' *War of the Worlds*. Thinking they were listening to a real news report of an invasion from Mars, they abandoned their homes in droves and attempted to flee to the countryside (Lowery and DeFleur 1995).

Of the different media, television has come in for most criticism, no doubt because of its capacity for dramatic, graphic images and its ability to evoke powerful emotions and to reach large segments of the population within a very short timeframe. So-called reality shows, magazine shows and daytime shows such as the Jerry Springer show, all come in for criticism for promoting values antithetical to 'desirable' social norms. Similar general criticisms are now levelled at the Internet – and video games in particular – with the Internet attracting attention because of issues such as sexual predators on the net and 'cyber bullying'.

Television and the decline of social capital

Putnam (1995a) has claimed that the advent of television has coincided with the observed decline in social capital over the past fifty years. He claims that time spent watching television has led to reduced membership and participation in community activities, and that the nature of television programming in terms of publicising and sensationalising crime and corruption has led to declines in public trust. However, this simplistic analysis has been criticised by others (e.g., Norris 1996), and we believe that it's not how much television one watches, but rather the type of shows watched that best predicts civic engagement. The current debate has now moved to whether Internet networking builds real or virtual social capital.

However, it's not just the content of television programmes; simply the act of watching television may have an impact on cognitive development. One study of 1,300 children in the US National Longitudinal Study of Youth found that, on average, a child who watched two hours of TV daily before the age of 3 was 20 per cent more likely to have attention problems at age 7 than children who watched no television (Schnabel 2009). Another study of children who viewed DVDs and videos for babies, found that viewing such videos was associated with lesser language development in babies aged 8–16 months relative to those who didn't watch such DVDs (Zimmerman, Christakis and Meltzoff 2007a, 2007b). The Walt Disney Company, producer of *Baby Einstein* (and others), was not impressed (Cressey 2007).

Although the mass media are frequently criticised for their part in the development of anti-social attitudes and behaviours among children, *Sesame Street*, the pro-social children's television programme, has been produced by the Children's Television Workshop since 1969. The programme was established with the aim of providing children (particularly disadvantaged children) with skills to equip them for school. As well as providing pre-reading skills and early numeracy skills, *Sesame Street* provides a positive social model for children, promoting sexual and racial equality. This latter objective has shown considerable benefits for white and non-white children. It has been reported that minority children watching *Sesame Street* increased cultural pride, confidence and interpersonal co-operation, and that white children showed more positive attitudes towards children of other races (Harris 2009).

The potential power of the mass media has been recognised for many years, and long before television. The Nazis may not have been the first to realise the enormous potential of the modern mass media, but they appear to have been the first to systematically exploit it on a national scale. The Nazis were also aware that 'information', and hence propaganda, could be transmitted via entertainment vehicles such as theatre and movies. Hence, the Nazis not only took control of news outlets, but also cultural and arts organisations. Goebbels ministry was known as the Ministry for Popular Enlightenment and Propaganda (Rhodes 1975). Goebbels realised that the young were particularly vulnerable and easily reachable through schools. He supplied all German schools with radios so that children could be exposed to Nazi propaganda (note the similarity to Channel One re corporate 'propaganda'; Chapter 9).

Influence of mass media on beliefs and attitudes about HIV/AIDS in China

A survey of 3,700 market workers in Fuzhou, China measured their exposure to sources of information about HIV/AIDS. Mass media such as television programmes, newspapers and magazines were nominated far more than interpersonal sources. Exposure to multiple sources – where at least one was a mass media source – was associated with increased knowledge about HIV/AIDS and less stigmatisation of people with HIV/AIDS (Li *et al.* 2009).

Effectiveness of mass media in promoting health and socially desirable causes

In the 1970s, several large-scale community health promotion trials involving the mass media were carried out. Three of the best known were the North Karelia project in Finland (Puska *et al.* 1985), the North Coast Health Lifestyle Programme in Australia (Egger *et al.* 1983), and the Stanford three and five city studies in the United States (Maccoby *et al.* 1977). These studies generally involved comparing control communities with mass media only interventions and mass media plus community-based programmes. The general conclusion from these studies was that maximum change is best achieved through the combination of mass media and community-based programmes, but that mass media alone can have some impact, albeit limited. For example, road safety advertising and publicity alone can raise awareness of an issue, and may even result in a minor short-term behaviour change. However, without concurrent visible enforcement activities, any behavioural effect may be short-lived. At the same time, the impact of enforcement activities appears to be enhanced by accompanying advertising and publicity (Elder *et al.* 2004; Tay 2005).

The effectiveness of the media, either alone or as a contributing element in social marketing campaigns has been confirmed in a number of different areas across the globe, particularly for AIDS/HIV interventions, tobacco control, road safety and sun protection, and for physical activity, general health and injury prevention, racism, domestic violence, recycling, de-stigmatisation of mental illness and crime prevention (see Cavill and Bauman 2004; Dawson 2009; Donovan and Vlais 2005, 2006; Elder *et al.* 2004; Hornik 2002; Lannon 2008; Sartorius and Schulze 2005; Singhal *et al.* 2004; Tay 2005; Wu *et al.* 2007). As with many areas, where the mass media have failed, it is not so much that mass media are ineffective, but the message has been poor, the targeting ineffective, the objectives unrealistic or the evaluation inappropriate. Where the campaigns have been based on sound social and cognitive models, where community activities are included and where all the principles of social marketing are integrated, the results have been positive.

Too often unrealistic objectives are set for the media. It is unrealistic, for example, to expect that advertising alone will have a significant impact on a man's violent behaviour, but it can have a substantial influence on encouraging the violent man to seek help for his behaviour (Donovan and Vlais 2005; Donovan, Paterson and Francas 1999).

Targeting fathers in Japan: unrealistic objectives?

Japan's Health Ministry recently sponsored a US$4 million media campaign aimed at encouraging fathers to become more involved in child rearing. The TV ads and posters featured a famous Japanese dancer holding his infant son, with the caption 'A man who does not help in child rearing cannot be called a father.' The contentious campaign created a public and media uproar as fathers took offence at the criticism of their lack of involvement (Jordan and Sullivan 1999). Japan's Prime Minister supported the campaign, saying that it increased his awareness of the importance of fathers' involvement in bringing up their children. It may be the case that focusing on the issue will encourage fathers to think about the amount of time they spend with their children. However, financial pressures on families appear to be such that men are working longer hours; hence, media only campaigns such as these would have little effect in current economic circumstances (Omori 2003).

The media can certainly stimulate help seeking (as in calls to helplines) and screening behaviours, and can contribute to significant changes in beliefs and attitudes related to more complex behaviour changes (such as racism: Donovan and Leivers 1993; Donovan and Vlais 2006). Figure 12.1 shows a clear relationship between the amount of advertising and number of calls to the Quitline for Australia's national tobacco campaign (Donovan 2000a). In short, it is crucial to determine just what are the objectives for media components of campaigns (dealt with later in this chapter).

Our experience suggests that media alone would have most behavioural effect where all or nearly all of the following apply:

- the desired behaviour change requires little or at least an acceptable time, effort, financial or psychological cost;
- social norms are important and favour the desired change;
- there are clear and substantial benefits to the individual (that outweigh any costs);

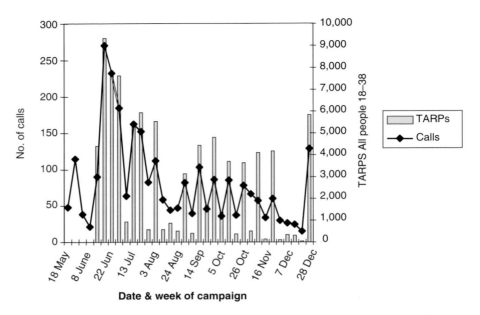

Figure 12.1 Calls to a Quitline by media weight
Donovan (2000)

- there are no major environmental inhibitors;
- the individuals' attitudes are neutral or already mildly positive towards the behaviour.

'Hard-to-reach' audiences

Some criticism of the use of mass media has centred on the claim that mass media are ineffective in reaching important target groups. In some cases this is a valid criticism in that media campaigns have been directed towards various groups that would have been more effectively targeted via some other methods.

Hard-to-reach groups are usually defined in terms of their non-responsiveness to mainstream media campaigns. However, it is important to distinguish between those who are hard-to-reach because of low access to mainstream media and those who are hard-to-reach because of apparent imperviousness to media campaigns. The latter definition is the most used (e.g., White and Maloney 1990), and accessibility is often included as a correlate of personality and lifestyle factors such as a distrust of large government organisations, a sense of fatalism and poor cognitive processing skills (Freimuth and Mettger 1990).

We suggest that Hard-to-REACH be used to refer to those simply not accessible via mainstream media and Hard-to-IMPACT be used to refer to those not responsive to media delivered messages. Groups most commonly thought of as not reachable include prostitutes, IV drug users, street kids and other homeless persons. Yet there is now considerable evidence that such groups are accessible via mainstream media, including ethnic media, although care must be taken in scheduling and vehicle selection. Furthermore, they are reachable by local 'media', including material distributed by hand (including comics) and posters in local gathering spots.

With regard to accessibility and responsiveness, as always the answer lies in carrying out adequate formative research to assess whether a potential target audience is, first, accessible and then, given accessibility, whether it is likely to be responsive to media messages. In some cases, the role of media may be limited to directing people to other campaign interventions such as telephone information services, interpreter services or needle exchange locations, rather than to belief or attitude change.

A practical model for media use in social marketing programmes

We present a three-dimensional framework for the media of methods, channels and objectives:

- five major media methods: advertising (including sponsorship); publicity (including public relations and infonews); 'edutainment'; civic journalism; and word-of-mouth;
- three major objectives for these five methods: education; motivation; and advocacy; and
- four major channels through which messages are delivered to target audiences.

The framework is shown in Figures 12.2 (methods by objectives) and 12.3 (methods by channels), where the number of asterisks indicates the relative usefulness of the methods for the various objectives and channels, respectively. We first present the five major methods then discuss the three major objectives. It can be noted that we consider the new social media as a major channel for delivery of messages via word-of-mouth (Figure 12.3).

Advertising

Advertising is generally defined as the paid placement of messages in media vehicles by an identified source, including the situation where media organisations donate time or space for the placement of social change messages that are clearly in the format of paid advertisements (community or public service announcements: CSAs or PSAs). There is a large number of advertising channels available, from direct mail to the rear of a toilet door, to shopping centre notice boards, from packaging to sporting team jumpers,

Main methods	Objectives		
	Educate (Inform)	Motivate (Persuade)	Advocate (Regulate)
Advertising and sponsorship	***	*****	**
Publicity PR and info news	***	**	***
Edutainment	***	***	***
Civic journalism	*****	***	****
Word-of-mouth	***	***	****

Figure 12.2 A framework for using media in social marketing: methods by objectives

Main methods	Main channels			
	Broadcast: TV, radio, cinema	Print: newspaper magazines outdoor	'New' technology: web, mobiles, iPods	Social media: networking, blogs, wikis
Advertising and sponsorship	* * * * *	* * * * *	* * *	* *
Publicity, PR and info news	* * * *	* * * * *	* * *	* *
Edutainment	* * * * *	*	*	
Civic journalism	*	* * * *	* *	*
Word-of-mouth		*	*	* * * *

Figure 12.3 A framework for using media in social marketing: methods by channels

from local newspapers to nationwide (and international) television networks and the worldwide web (see Table 12.1). In fact, most media vehicles, and features within media vehicles (e.g., sections in newspapers such as gardening, home improvements, etc.) exist simply to provide a channel for advertisers.

In developed countries (and even in most developing countries now), mass media advertising provides the opportunity to reach a substantial proportion of the total population in a relatively short time – and on all sorts of issues. For example, in 2005, the US Government launched a series of ads on Pakistani state television and radio promising multi-million dollar rewards for information leading to the capture of Osama bin Laden. The ads, broadcast in the Pakistani languages of Urdu, Sindhi, Baloch and Pashto, were meant to appeal to many Pakistanis' aversion to the extremist methods of al-Qaeda. The US Government had previously publicised its rewards in Pakistan on posters, matchbox covers, newspaper ads and the Internet. A contact phone number and email address (www.rewardsforjustice.net) are provided, and – not unexpectedly – promise resettlement for informants and their families (Baldauf and Tohid 2005). At the time of writing, Osama bin Laden remains at large. Advertising clearly has its limits.

In commercial marketing, advertising is the primary communication tool, although it is only one tool within the media mix (i.e., the promotion 'P'). Other elements of the communication mix include tools such as publicity, sponsorship, trade shows and in-store and shopping centre demonstrations. For example, the launch of a new product may be accompanied by extensive mass media advertising to create awareness and a tentative positive attitude towards the product; press releases may be issued about the product's technological characteristics, its social benefits or its ecological soundness; special sales representatives may be on hand in-store to describe and demonstrate the product; and entry to a sweepstake plus a substantial discount may be offered to the first 100 purchasers.

That is, in most commercial campaigns, advertising – with a defined but limited set of objectives – is only one element of an integrated campaign. This is often forgotten by inexperienced social marketers, who focus only on advertising.

Guidelines for public health advertising

- Be credible, don't exaggerate claims.
- Arouse a strong, relevant emotional response, whether positive or negative.
- For fear appeals, show relevant, disabling harmful effects in otherwise healthy individuals rather than bedridden patients, and ensure that anxiety results from a relevant self-assessment rather than just from the execution elements *per se*.
- Be sufficiently dramatic to generate word-of-mouth about the message (i.e., not just the execution).
- Use simple concrete words and visual demonstrations of effects – both positive and negative.

- Show a means of attaining the desired behaviour and a source of assistance.
- Use modelling to enhance the trial and adoption of behavioural objectives.
- Use mnemonics for informational objectives.
- Where relevant, ensure that prescriptive norms and popular norms are congruent.

(Donovan 1991)

Advertising is used to create awareness of, and at least tentative positive attitudes towards, brands and companies. This tentative positive attitude is assumed to lead to consideration of the brand at the point-of-sale (e.g., in the supermarket or department store), or requesting more information (via coupon or telephone) or visiting an outlet to inspect the product. The actual sale then is determined by the product's packaging, price, perceived value relative to competitors' offerings, the salesperson's skill (where appropriate), the product's performance (where it can be observed), acceptance of the appropriate credit card and so on; that is, all the elements of the marketing mix.

Offensive, confronting or bizarre advertising content can be used to deliberately attract attention from the news media. For example, the Dove billboards attracted considerable attention, as did the 'rat' example presented later in this chapter under advocacy.

Advertising's communication objectives

The communication objectives for the media components of social marketing campaigns can be listed as follows:

- Awareness: creating, maintaining or increasing awareness of an issue, product, service or event.
- Attitudes: creating, maintaining or increasing positive attitudes towards an issue, product, service or event.
- Behavioural intentions: creating, maintaining or increasing explicit or implicit intentions to behave in the recommended manner (including intermediate behaviours).
- Behavioural facilitation: facilitating acting on intentions by neutralising misperceptions and negatives and justifying 'costs' and other factors that inhibit adoption of the recommended behaviour.

As in the commercial area, the major roles of advertising in social change areas are, first, to create awareness of the issue, and, second, to create a tentative positive attitude towards the issue that predisposes the individual to other components of the campaign and to positive social pressures. The extent to which advertising can directly influence behaviour in health and social policy fields depends on the nature of the behaviour and the extent of prior public education. For example, non-threatening one-off behaviours, such as cholesterol testing, and even one-off behaviours with quite threatening consequences, such as HIV testing, can be influenced directly by advertising campaigns (in conjunction with easily accessible test sites).

However, addictive and more complex behaviours requiring substantial lifestyle changes can rarely be influenced directly by advertising. Advertising's role in these latter instances is to maintain salience of the issue, to sensitise the target to intervention components that might otherwise have gone unnoticed, to provide directions to sources of assistance, to generate positive attitudes towards trying to adopt the desired behaviour change, and, where the behaviour has been adopted, to reinforce that behaviour.

Sponsorship

Sponsorship is generally defined as payment for the right to associate the sponsor's company name, products or services with the 'sponsee'. The subject of the sponsorship may vary from a one-off event (e.g., a fun run), a season series (e.g., a football league), a group of individuals (e.g., a basketball team, an orchestra), or an organisation (e.g., an arts or crafts group) and its activities. Given that many high profile commercial sponsorships are accompanied by promotional activities such as advertising, product samplings, trade promotions or exclusive merchandising agreements, the more embracing term 'events marketing' is widely used, along with the term 'sports marketing' for sporting sponsorships. Sponsorship is covered in detail in Chapter 13.

Product placement

This refers to the paid placement of brands and products in movies, books and popular music. We have included this tactic under advertising, although others see it as a hybrid of advertising and publicity (Balasubramanian 1994). The tobacco companies appear to have used this tool quite extensively, along with many others: for example, Coca-Cola features extensively in *Nutty Professor II*; Tom Cruise nearly collides with an Avis truck in *M:I-2*; and in *What Women Want*, part of the story involves actually making a TV ad for Nike (Barber 2001). According to Brandchannel.com, *The Bourne Supremacy*, released in 2004, featured more than thirty trademarks.

Brandchannel.com, produced by one of the world's major branding companies (Interbrand) contains a wealth of information about product placement (among other things). They compile the 'Brandcameo Awards' in various categories. In 2008 Ford won the Overall Product Placement Award by appearing in thirty of the fifty-two number one films at the US box office from 1 January 2007 through to 30 June 2008. Ford's 58 per cent appearance rate in top films was a marked increase over its eighteen of forty-one appearances in 2005 (44 per cent) and seventeen of forty-one in 2006 (41 per cent) (Sauer 2008). The winner in 2009 was Subaru (twenty-four films), followed by Ford (twenty films) and Budweiser (twelve films) (Sauer 2009).

Patricia Cornwell's book, *Cause of Death*, includes references to numerous brands across a broad range of product categories, including cigarettes (Marlboro, Camel and

Players). Furthermore, perhaps true to its title, the book includes a sequence where the heroine smokes a Marlboro after three years without smoking. She describes the feeling as follows: 'The first hit cut my lungs like a blade, and I was instantly light-headed. I felt as I had when I smoked my first Camel at the age of sixteen. Then nicotine enveloped my brain, and the world spun more slowly and my thoughts coalesced. "God, I have missed this," I mourned as I tapped an ash' (Cornwell 1996). Hmmmm.

Ford has targeted African-Americans in some film deals, while Harley-Davidson has attempted to reach Latino youth in comic books (see box below).

Johnny Delgado is dead

This is the title of a comic about two childhood friends who are bound by the code of brotherhood, loyalty … and fate. Closer than brothers, one is destined to die and the other to secure justice as a tale of corruption and murder along the US–Mexican border unfolds. Spacedog Entertainment approached Harley-Davidson Motor Company in the developmental stages of their comic project. The lead characters in the story, Johnny Delgado and Victor Reyes, are said to personify the Harley-Davidson brand through their adventurous spirit and rebel attitudes. Growing up in a tough neighbourhood, the young boys stayed off the streets by helping out at the local motorcycle shop, where they gained their love of bikes and the freedom of the open road (Spacedog 2007).

Can advertising influence racist stereotype beliefs?

A two-week television, print and radio advertising campaign was conducted in an Australian regional city. The ads have been described in Chapter 5. The aim was to assess the feasibility of using mass media to change discriminatory beliefs.

Following formative research, an advertising campaign was developed targeting the following beliefs about Aborigines and employment:

* very few Aborigines have a job;
* very few Aborigines who have jobs hold them for a long time.

These 'objective' beliefs were identified as the basis for subjective beliefs such as Aborigines are lazy, don't want to work and can't handle responsibility. Pre–post surveys of independent samples assessed the extent to which the campaign increased people's perceptions of the proportions of Aboriginal people with a job and how many held a job for more than a year. The results are shown in Figures 12.4 and 12.5.

Prior to the campaign, substantial proportions said they just 'didn't know' what proportion of Aboriginal people in the town held a job (30 per cent) or, if employed, would last more than a year in a job (40 per cent). After the campaign, these percentages almost halved, with a substantial increase in the proportions believed to be employed (26–50 per cent increased from 25 per cent to 39 per cent) and to remain in a job more than a year (more than 50 per cent went from 8 per cent to almost 30 per cent).

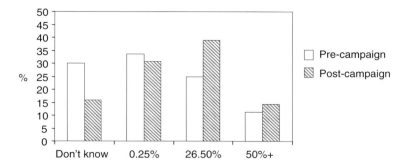

Figure 12.4 Pre–post proportions of Aborigines believed to be in paid employment

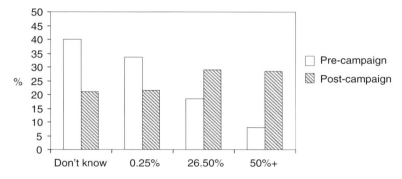

Figure 12.5 Pre–post proportions of employed Aborigines believed to remain in a job for more than a year

Donovan and Leivers (1993)

This campaign shows that even complex beliefs can be influenced by the mass media, provided the right communication strategy is used (see Donovan and Leivers 1993; Donovan and Vlais 2006).

Publicity

The high cost of advertising, and an increasing understanding of media advocacy (Chapter 4 and below) have led to social change practitioners paying more attention to unpaid placements to get their messages across. While this may involve costs to engage a public relations company to help plan and place the messages, the actual exposure is unpaid.

Publicity refers to the placement of messages in the media, usually in news or current affairs programmes, but also in feature articles or documentaries. Unlike advertising, the source of the message is seen to be a presumably unbiased journalist rather than the organisation whose product or message is the subject of the news item or feature. Publicity involves attracting the media to run a particular story or cover a particular event in a way that creates, maintains or increases the target audience's awareness of, or favourable attitudes towards, the organisation's products or message, or towards the organisation itself.

Many social marketing campaigns now involve press conferences with celebrities and staged events that attract considerable photo coverage by the media (for example the US anti-tobacco Truth campaign's placement of 'corpses' outside tobacco company offices). These events can be supported by activities such as providing the media with feature articles (for newspapers and magazines), and making experts available for interview on radio and television.

Publicity is part of the public relations mix, which refers to the activities an organisation undertakes to create and maintain positive relations with all of the organisation's 'publics', including customers, staff, suppliers, journalists and politicians. Public relations involves a number of activities other than seeking favourable publicity, such as employee magazines, loyalty magazines, educational materials, annual reports, research funding and charitable donations.

Although a publicity strategy can be a long-term, planned strategy, in practice it tends to be more short term and focused on specific newsworthy events, such as a celebrity launching a campaign. Furthermore, even if the aim is longer term, say, aiming for an article per month in a weekend newspaper, whether the article appears is up to the journalist or editor. A longer-term method that ensures continued coverage is where the news organisation itself takes responsibility for running a series of items with a socially desirable goal. This is known as civic (or public) journalism and is covered later in this chapter.

Infonews (our term) is a variation on the usual press release. It refers to the systematic placement of desired messages in news items for a specific period as part of a campaign. Journalists are provided with standard paragraphs that can accompany news about various topics. For example, in reporting any news about the tobacco industry or reports on tobacco-related illnesses, journalists can be encouraged to include closing statements such as 'tobacco kills over 40,000 people per annum in Germany'.

Similarly, reports of road crashes can include closing statements that 'crashes due to fatigue are estimated to constitute 30 per cent of crashes. Fatigue occurs not only on country roads, but in early morning traffic resulting from late nights or disturbed sleep.' For example, in co-operation with a local newspaper in the United States, the reporting of road trauma was carried out in such a way as to include information from road trauma research and how injury can be avoided. Before–after surveys following an eight-week trial of the programme revealed significant changes in people's perceptions of road trauma (Wilde and Ackersviller 1981).

Edutainment

Edutainment (or Enter–Education) refers to the deliberate inclusion of socially desirable messages in entertainment vehicles such as television and radio soap operas, films, popular music, comics, novels and short stories to achieve social change objectives (Singhal and Rogers 1999; Singhal *et al.* 2004). This may involve inserting socially desirable messages in existing or planned entertainment vehicles, or actually developing the entertainment vehicles as part of a social change programme.

With the exception of the use of theatre in health education for schoolchildren (Ball 1994), the use of edutainment in developed countries appears to consist primarily of the former, whereas in underdeveloped countries it consists primarily of the latter. In fact, edutainment is a strategy used primarily in developing rather than in developed countries (Singhal *et al.* 2004), although a recent series of three one-hour programmes on ABC TV in Australia used a well-known comedy duo to present and discuss various health problems for men (The Trouble with Men), and in the United Kingdom the BBC has produced TV programmes with the Health Education Authority. Although these programmes were entertaining, they were short-lived and each episode was self-contained, rather than embedded in an ongoing story as in a soap opera.

Guru the wise kangaroo shows Israeli kids how to behave

A thirty-episode television show targeting 7–8-year-old children featured a wise kangaroo named Guru and a sweet but naive health education elephant named Gogol. Each episode generally featured Gogol about to do the 'wrong' thing, but being interrupted by Guru, who demonstrated alternative 'right' ways. The shows were amusing and the characters likeable to enhance the likelihood of viewers modelling Guru's recommendations. The show covered topics such as safety, sun exposure, nutrition, personal hygiene and relationships. Evaluation showed substantial changes in knowledge and self-reported changes in appropriate behaviours (Tamir *et al.* 2003).

Edutainment has clear advantages for presenting potentially threatening or sensitive topics in a non-threatening way and reaching people who might otherwise not attend to the message when the source is clearly identified. That is, people might deliberately avoid a documentary or educational programme dealing with race relations, but may be quite happy to watch their favourite soap opera deal with the issue.

Edutainment appears to have been systematically adopted following a 1969 Peruvian soap opera (*Simplemente Maria*), which told the 'rags-to-riches' story of Maria, who sewed her way to social and economic success with a Singer sewing machine. Wherever the programme was televised in South America, sales of Singer sewing machines were reported to have increased substantially (Singhal and Rogers 1989). A Mexican television producer and director, Miguel Sabido, is credited with being inspired by these results to develop a series of pro-social telenovelas in Mexico and, hence, establishing the soap opera as a medium for social change. His methods have been studied and adapted by several countries, especially those where there is a strong cultural tradition of storytelling as a means of passing on knowledge. Most applications in underdeveloped countries have been directed primarily, but not exclusively, at social issues that influence economic development, particularly family planning, literacy, vocational training, agricultural methods, child rearing, female equality, family harmony and, more recently, HIV/AIDS and violence against women (Coleman and Meyer 1990; Singhal *et al.* 2004).

Edutainment: deceptive or a valid social marketing tool?

A furore broke out in the United States in December 1999/January 2000, when it was disclosed that the Office of National Drug Control Policy (ONDCP) was negotiating with TV stations to incorporate anti-drug messages into programme scripts in return for the stations not having to air a number of anti-drug PSAs. (As part of the National Youth Anti-Drug Media Campaign, US networks were required to air one free slot for every paid slot.) Some critics lambasted the stations and the ONDCP for allowing the stations to abrogate their civic responsibilities so easily. Others accused the ONDCP and the stations of deceptive conduct and social manipulation, and the ONDCP was accused of censoring television content because it allegedly wanted to approve the anti-drug programme scripts before they went to air. Only in America …

Much of the rationale for edutainment is based on Bandura's social learning theory (Bandura 1977). It is claimed that viewers will learn appropriate behaviours by observational learning (i.e., modelling). There is evidence that modelling of televised behaviours does occur (Hawton *et al.* 1999; Wharton and Mandell 1985; Winett *et al.* 1985). However, a comprehensive theory of how persuasion works via entertainment vehicles has yet to be developed. Advertising researchers have proposed that drama is 'processed' differently from lecture or argument approaches to persuasion, and that these differences might offer some advantages to persuasion by edutainment (Deighton, Romer and McQueen 1989).

Linking pro-social messages with entertainment vehicles

The Johns Hopkins School of Hygiene and Public Health developed an innovative way of using people's interest in high profile television soap operas *ER* and *Chicago Hope*: an informative 90-second health news segment dealing with the issue portrayed in that week's episode is produced to be aired immediately following the show. The segment also lists toll-free numbers and Internet links to relevant information (Cooper, Roter and Langlieb 2000).

Implementing edutainment

Achieving co-operation between social change professionals and entertainment industry professionals requires each to have a good understanding of the other's needs (Montgomery 1990). Social change professionals must accept and appreciate the commercial needs of the producers and the creative needs of the artists. They must accept that their messages must be subtle and secondary to the entertainment aspects. On the other hand, entertainment professionals must be convinced that socially desirable messages can enhance audience appeal, and hence profitability of commercial productions (Coleman and Meyer 1990). In the ONDCP situation noted above, the TV stations were required, not without good reason, to submit the scripts to the ONDCP for approval – which instigated the accusation of government censorship. The ruckus may have been avoided had the anti-drug people worked alongside the writers to jointly develop the anti-drug script components.

The potential application of edutainment in Indigenous cultures

Given the strong oral history tradition and use of storytelling to pass on cultural and religious beliefs amongst Indigenous people in countries like Australia, Canada, New Zealand and the United States, an edutainment approach could be appropriate for these groups. Ross Spark (Spark and Mills 1988; Spark, Donovan and Howat 1991; Spark *et al.* 1992), in an innovative approach to Indigenous health promotion used a community development model to elicit 'stories' from Aboriginal communities that contained health messages about issues considered important to the community. Indigenous artists co-operated with community members to express the stories in pictures. These pictures then were developed into television advertisements shown throughout the Kimberley region of Western Australia. Evaluation of the project indicated a high level of awareness of these ads among Indigenous people and substantial satisfaction with the approach (Spark 1999).

Edutainment in action: *Soul City*

Soul City is a multi-media edutainment strategy of the Institute for Health and Development Communication that has been running in South Africa since 1992

Figure 12.6 *Soul City* logo

(Figure 12.6). *Soul City* 'aims to empower people and communities through the power of mass media' (CASE 1997), using television, radio, print media, public relations and advertising, and education packages. *Soul City* (a fictitious town in South Africa) began as a television soap opera, a half-hour drama that ran weekly for thirteen weeks. It has reportedly become one of the most popular programmes on television and won the Avanti award for excellence in broadcasting two years in succession in the 1990s. The original radio drama component consisted of forty-five 15-minute episodes (in eight different languages) and was developed to reach rural audiences.

The website introduction (as at 15 August 2009) states:

> Welcome to the Soul City Institute website.
>
> Soul City Institute is a dynamic and innovative multi-media health promotion and social change project. Through drama and entertainment Soul City reaches more than 16 million South Africans. This is done through 2 main brands, Soul City targeted at adults and Soul Buddyz targeted at 8–12 year olds and adults in their lives. The second big programme that Soul City Institute is involved in is the Regional Programme which is a partnership with local organisations in eight Southern African countries. It has also been broadcast in many parts of Africa as well as Latin America, the Caribbean and South East Asia. Soul City examines many health and development issues, imparting information and impacting on social norms, attitudes and practice. Its impact is aimed at the level of the individual, the community and the socio political environment.
>
> Through its multi-media and advocacy strategies Soul City Institute aims to create an enabling environment empowering audiences to make healthy choices,

both as individuals and as communities. (www.soulcity.org.za, accessed 15 August 2009)

Soul City's original and ongoing objectives are to:

- reach as many people as possible within a broad target market, while specifically focusing on youth and women in marginalised and remote communities;
- generate discussion around health and lifestyle issues; and
- encourage changing attitudes and behaviour in relation to certain diseases and health risks.

Soul Buddyz

Soul Buddyz is designed to promote the health and wellbeing of children aged 8–12 years old. It consists of four main parts: a television series; radio series; a Lifeskills Booklet for Grade 7; and a Parenting Booklet.

The twenty-six-part television series is broadcast on SABC 1 – South Africa's most popular television channel. Each episode is approximately 26 minutes long. The drama centres on a group of children who meet after school in a park. They represent children from all walks of life and they form a firm bond. This group – the Soul Buddyz – have to deal with issues that children are facing every day of their lives. They help each other and work for their community, while having lots of fun. At the end of each episode of Soul Buddyz there is a 2-minute sequence of real children's comments about the issues that Soul Buddyz raises – this is called the 'Buddyz Buzz' and helps give some African children a voice to express their opinion on important issues affecting them (www.soulcity.org.za, accessed 15 August 2009).

There have been nine series of *Soul City*, each of which has focused on specific issues, with ongoing underlying themes of the empowerment of women, social policy/welfare issues and community action for health and development. For example, series one focused largely on mother and child health; series two on health issues including smoking and communicable diseases such as tuberculosis and STDs, as well as land and housing issues; series three included social issues such as violence, alcoholism and household energy; and series four dealt with health issues such as HIV and hypertension, as well as social issues including violence against women and teenage sexuality. The subsequent series have focused mainly on HIV/AIDS, but have covered topics such as volunteering, masculinity, violence against women and cancer. The current series is part of the OneLove Campaign being implemented in South Africa and nine other countries. A major feature of *Soul City* is that it expands its media programmes out to community activities, often using the actors to take part in community events (see box below). *Soul City* has clearly had a considerable positive impact on the knowledge, attitudes and beliefs of South African people across a range of social and health issues (Cassidy 2008; Goldstein *et al.* 2005; Usdin *et al.* 2005).

Soul City also has a strong advocacy component. In 1999, *Soul City* partnered with the National Network on Violence Against Women (NNVAW) to speed up the implementation of the Domestic Violence Act (DVA) which was passed into law the year before. Series four focused on the issue of domestic violence and the DVA was featured prominently. The campaign involved mobilising people and the news media to voice their concern about the urgent need to implement the Act (Usdin *et al.* 2005). However, on a sad note, we include the press release of 17 August 2009 reporting the murder during Women's Month of the star of series four, which was instrumental in the passing and implementation of that domestic violence legislation in South Africa in 1999. This release is also a good example of attempting to get extra information into a press release that goes beyond the story details.

Soul City media release:

Students and celebs march for OneLove at the University of Venda

Friday, 14 August 2009: This week over 350 student activists and celebrities marched from the University of Venda into Thohoyandou, waving flags and singing songs to raise awareness about the OneLove campaign. They were led by Zuluboy (Mxolisi Majozi) and Mbali Mlotshwa, who played lead roles in the *Soul City* TV series flighted earlier this year on SABC1. The OneLove campaigners were also addressed by officials from the University of Venda, Vhembe District Municipality. The OneLove march was the brainchild of Esther Tubake Mphahlele, a social sciences student at the University of Venda, who was first introduced to OneLove after she won a Metro FM competition earlier this year. She planned the march on Women's Day in an attempt to get people talking about the issues that drive multiple concurrent partnerships. 'We often hear of marches for better pay and lower tuition fees, but I wanted to get people talking about OneLove,' she said. John Molefe, *Soul City*'s Senior Executive: Marketing and Public Affairs, says that *Soul City* jumped at the opportunity to support the march. 'We were impressed that Esther took the initiative to raise awareness of OneLove on her own and are supporting her efforts to expose the invisible networks people join as a result of multiple sexual relationships.' Councillor Mashau delivered the keynote address. 'The power of this OneLove march lies in our concerted involvement to fight HIV and AIDS. We stand behind the OneLove campaign and are here today to strengthen and cement our partnership with *Soul City*,' he said. A number of prizes were given away, including the newly-released OneLove single and music DVD featuring Zuluboy. A mobile voluntary HIV testing service was offered and *Soul City* reading material was distributed. The *Soul City* TV series attracted over 6 million viewers per episode. It formed part of the OneLove campaign in South Africa, which also includes radio dramas currently on air, community dialogues across the country, OneLove seminars nationally, radio and television competitions, a website and Facebook profile.

For further information or interviews please call Onyx Marketing Communications: Despina Harito on +27 11 452 1840 or 084 453 1755/ despina@onyxmarketing.co.za.

Soul City media release:

Response to Soul City actress's murder

17 August 2009: The Soul City Institute was devastated to read of the death of Thabang Nkonyeni, an actress who played the part of Matlakala in the fourth *Soul City* television series which dealt with domestic violence. She continues to be the face of the campaigns about violence against women particularly in the training materials offered by *Soul City*. It is both tragic and ironic, that Thabang, an advocate for women's rights was murdered in her home during Women's Month. Our deepest condolences to her family and loved ones.

The reasons for her death are not confirmed, but we want to remind readers that violence against women is everyone's problem. We call on readers to take action to stop it. We do not have to tolerate it. Violence against women in South Africa has reached epidemic proportions, For example, we are known to have the highest rape statistics in the world. One in four women are said to be in abusive relationships and it is described as the country's most hidden crime.

If you are in an abusive relationship or if you know someone who is being abused, get help. Domestic violence is against the law and the police should support you. You can get an interdict to prevent an abuser harming you any further or you can lay a charge of assault. Call the national toll-free line called Stop Gender Violence for help: 0800 150 150. At the root of violence against women is a perpetrator's sense of ownership of women and the belief that women are the property of men. This gives many men a sense of entitlement over women which manifests as the 'right' to make all household decisions, control the money, have multiple sexual partners while expecting their partner to be faithful.

Common myths:
Myth: Women deserve to be beaten if they are unfaithful, disobedient or cheeky.
Fact: No one deserves to be beaten for whatever reason.
Myth: The woman must be doing something wrong.
Fact: Whatever she is doing, it is not an excuse for violence.
Myth: It can't be so bad or she would just leave.
Fact: Many women are trapped in abusive relationships because they have nowhere to go, have no money, are concerned about the children, are too scared because he's threatened to hurt her or the children. Many women want desperately to believe his promises to change. Women are often told it is their duty to stay in the marriage and make it work. They are often told they must stay for the sake of the children or that lobola has been paid and so she 'belongs' to the in-laws.
Myth: It takes two to tango.
Fact: Women are often beaten for no reason whatsoever.
Myth: Only violent men hit their partners.

> Fact: Often men who are well-respected, upstanding community members who would never dream of being violent to anyone else, are violent to their partners.
> Myth: Violence against women only happens in poor, uneducated communities.
> Fact: Violence against women cuts across racial, class, cultural and educational boundaries.
> John Molefe Senior Executive: Marketing and Public Affairs
> Soul City: Institute for Health and Development Communications Johannesburg

Use of comics

A somewhat neglected but potentially important medium that has the capacity to influence attitudes and values is that of comic books and strip comics in newspapers (Gower 1995; Kirsh 2006). Comic books have been much criticised in the past for potentially corrupting youth by endorsing, if not encouraging, the expression of various anti-social values and behaviours (State Library of Victoria 2006). On the other hand, some consider that comics in general, and strip comics in particular, might in some instances be promoting pro-social values (Videlier and Piras 1990) or could be used in classrooms to teach pro-social values (Gower 1995). In recognition of the popularity of the format of comics with young and old alike, others felt the medium could be harnessed for health education purposes in general, and this suggestion has been widely adopted, particularly for young audiences and low literacy, lesser educated populations (Beck 2006; Everett and Schaay (1994). Project Northland includes a *Slick Tracy* comic dealing with alcohol and drug issues (Komro *et al.* 2004) (Figure 12.7) and the US National Youth Anti-Drug Program also incorporates comic strip formats.

Figure 12.7 Scene from Project Nothland's *Slick Tracy* comic

* streetwize (2000)

Figure 12.8 Streetwize comics target street teens

Streetwize is a leading Australian communicator of accessible, culturally relevant and entertaining information on social issues for young people outside the school system via the medium of comic magazines (Figure 12.8).

Targeting teens with comics

New South Wales' Streetwize Communications is a non-profit organisation that develops materials appropriate for communicating social issues to young people and hard-to-reach groups. With the financial support of the NSW and Victorian Law Foundations, Streetwize produces *Krunch*, a comic aimed at conveying socially positive messages to young people in an entertaining format. Stories address such topics as school bullying, the rights of kids when their parents separate, ways of dealing with domestic violence, drug and alcohol use, Indigenous issues and the problem of coping with two cultures. All Streetwize material is produced in consultation with the community, especially young people and service providers, and involves the target audience in every stage of the development process (www.streetwize.com.au).

Civic (or public) journalism

As yet there is no specific agreed on definition of civic journalism. Jay Rosen describes public journalism in the United States as 'an unfolding philosophy about the place of the journalist in public life', which 'has emerged most clearly in recent initiatives in the newspaper world that show journalists trying to connect with their communities ... by encouraging civic participation or regrounding the coverage of politics in the imperatives of public discussion and debate' (Rosen 1994). This is not all altruistic. Media organisations hope to make themselves more valuable to their consumers by deepening their connections to the community. Nevertheless, while they may not have called it 'civic journalism' or recognised the outcome as 'increasing social capital', journalists claim to have been using mass media to improve society for as long as they have been reporting news.

Civic journalism primarily differs from standard journalism in that standard journalism thrives on conflict and disagreement, whereas civic journalism attempts to build community consensus and co-operation. For example, whereas standard journalism seeks to emphasise differences and seek interviews with those known to have extremely opposing views on a topic, civic journalism emphasises similarities and seeks to report more moderate views.

Examples of civic journalism in the United States appear to be based primarily on attempts to involve citizens more in political life. For example, in one of the first – and perhaps only – attempts to evaluate a civic journalism campaign, a field experiment supported by the Pew Center for Civic Journalism, was designed to measure directly the impact of a multimedia civic journalism project in Madison, Wisconsin. The researchers wanted to find out whether a deliberate media campaign and related activities (e.g., town hall meetings) could interest people in the elections, cause them to learn more about the candidates and the issues, and inspire them to get involved, particularly to vote. The attitudes and knowledge of the citizens were measured before, during and after the campaign. The outcomes of the project (see Denton and Thorson 1995) included:

- a high level of awareness of the programme;
- an increased interest in public affairs;

- people felt more knowledgeable;
- people aware of the programme felt more able to decide between the candidates;
- people felt encouraged to vote;
- political cynicism did not increase (despite increased awareness of how campaign publicity can be used to distort issues); and
- a substantial increase in positive feelings towards the media outlets involved in the campaign.

These results show a clear positive change in civic involvement and 'are very encouraging for those who want to improve the democratic process and to those who believe the news media can take a more active role in facilitating these processes' (Denton and Thorson 1995). The Pew Center for Civic Journalism contains a number of reports, but appears to have ceased its activities at some time in the period 2002 to 2004 (www. pewcenter.org/index.php).

Civic journalism in action: the *Akron Beacon Journal* 'Coming Together' project

While this case study began some seventeen years ago, it remains one of the best examples we are aware of in terms of civic journalism's immediate effects and as a catalyst for community activation. It is also important because of its sustainability: it spawned an organisation (Coming Together) that lasted fifteen years before running out of funds and ceasing operations in March 2008.

Following the riots that occurred in Los Angeles in 1992 after the Rodney King verdict, a journalist with the *Akron Beacon Journal* decided to do something personally about race relations in the Akron–Canton area (and surrounding counties), in Ohio. For the resulting 'A Question of Color' series of articles aimed at improving race relations in Ohio, the *Akron Beacon Journal* won the 1994 Pulitzer Prize gold medal for public service journalism, the fourth Pulitzer for the newspaper.

The overall aims of the newspaper were initially very broad: to stimulate discussion of issues; to provide reasons behind the statistics (for example, that when controlling for race, neighbourhood crime rates were similar across white and black areas of similar socio-economic status); to acquaint each group with the other's views; and to move people's beliefs and attitudes – and hence behaviours – towards some common ground. In the spirit of 'civic journalism' the idea was to present middle (rather than extreme) views, and to promote agreement rather than division and conflict (the normal fodder for journalists).

It could be argued that one of the major points of this project was that it encouraged people to express views and fears that they would not normally have expressed for fear of being labelled 'racist' or 'alarmist'. If such views are continually internalised and repressed they become more difficult to challenge and change. Expressing such views in an atmosphere of co-operation rather than confrontation is the first stage to changing negative attitudes. By the reporting of views and the reasons behind these views, the project also began to provide a greater understanding of each group's situation with respect to racial views. Apparently one of the key outcomes of the project was that whites – some of whom rarely interacted with blacks, and most of whom had never experienced discrimination of any sort and had no appreciation of blacks' experiences – became far more aware that race *was* an issue for blacks, an issue they face every day in virtually all areas of their lives. Similar ignorances exist among most non-Indigenous Australians.

Following interviews with many of those concerned with the Coming Together project, Donovan (1996) came to the following conclusions as to factors that facilitated this project:

- The personal commitment and enthusiasm of a number of individuals.
- A supportive newspaper culture – the *Journal* has a history of involvement in community issues.
- The newspaper ownership supported this community orientation with resources.
- A commitment to a long-term project (initially a year-long series of articles), not just a one-off, *ad hoc* approach.
- The extensive use of focus group research that allowed 'ordinary' people and the so-called 'silent majority' (of both races) to express their views and fears without being 'labelled', and the personalisation of stories.

The *Akron Beacon Journal's* race relations project

The *Akron Beacon Journal* instituted a year-long series of articles entitled 'A Question of Color', which dealt with five issues: racial attitudes; housing; education; economic status; and crime. Each topic was presented over three or four consecutive days, covering several pages each day, and including a number of graphics and people photos. The amount of space devoted to the series was a clear indicator to the reader of the importance placed on the issue by the newspaper.

The articles contained a mix of statistical information (proportion of home ownership by colour, proportion of occupational status by colour, etc.); traditional journalism reporting and interpretation of past and current events; the identification of major changes and non-changes over the decades; reports on the results of focus groups among blacks and whites that probed beliefs and attitudes held by the two groups towards each other (and post-group interviews with participants); and reports on survey research of the extent to which people in the community held various beliefs and attitudes. The result was articles containing strong personal components expressing attitudes and beliefs that readers could identify with. For example, the issue on schooling commenced with a quote from a 16-year-old black student whose parents bus him to a nearby, predominantly white, school: 'I think the teachers put more effort into teaching because they have more white students in their classrooms. They probably feel more comfortable with white students than with a lot of black students in a class.' Next came a map of school attendance zones, statistics on race of students, race of teachers and proportion of students in different grades passing proficiency tests. Then followed an article on the discrimination experienced by black children both inside and outside schools, with quotes from students, families and school staff. Finally, an opinion piece titled 'Who's learning in integrated schools?' looked at the impact of colour on how students are treated, what is taught, what is learnt and who benefits from the education process. The article was personalised by focusing on the prejudice experienced by two black students in a predominantly white school, and included a large photograph of the two boys with their mother.

Right from the start, the *Journal*'s readers were invited to 'Tell us what you think' about race relations and 'how blacks and whites can better understand each other', by faxing, phoning or writing to the newspaper. The newspaper periodically printed readers' contributions.

Following consultations with various community groups, the second in the series of articles was accompanied by a form inviting people and groups who wanted to become more involved in improving race relations to register with the *Journal*. This involvement of the community evolved into the 'Coming Together' community project which continued after the Question of Color series finished in December 1993. The *Journal* continued to support the project by providing office space and salaries of two part-time community co-ordinators to the end of 1995, when other funding was obtained to continue the project. The role of the community co-ordinators (one black, one white) was to assist organisations get together for various one-off or continuing events, and to produce a monthly newsletter.

- The comprehensive background research for the articles and the presentation format of the articles (i.e., use of graphics, photos).
- The timing was right – the Rodney King verdict and subsequent events resulted in a heightened awareness and urgency throughout the United States that the racial question had to be confronted.
- There was a recent release of extensive census data providing a rich source of material for the articles.
- The *Journal* acted only as facilitator, requiring the community organisations themselves to develop and implement community interactions. The journalists also remained impartial in their articles, and ensured that both sides' views were published. Extreme views on either side were not included.
- The project members and advisory council members deliberately kept the project from being 'taken over' by any particular organisation wishing to promote a specific agenda. This was done by clearly positioning the project in a race relations context, not as a movement against institutional or other expressions of racism (though these are end goals). This facilitated the participation of people and groups that might otherwise have been deterred by the perceived dominance of some particular groups.
- Other media became involved as a result of community responses (e.g., talk-back radio).

- There were no unrealistic expectations. Most of those interviewed referred to 'moving slowly', with the first goal relating to increasing 'familiarity' between the two groups, then establishing 'trust' before moving on to more concrete objectives. This principle was stated as 'learning before doing'. It was stated that 'whites are task-orientated and don't take time to develop relationships, whereas blacks required the building of trust before acting' (a similar cultural divide operates in Australia).

- In keeping with others' recommendations for civic journalism, the articles were written in a down-to-earth style and dealt primarily with concrete issues rather than abstract concepts. This made the articles comprehensible.

- Perhaps most importantly, the project told people what they could personally do to have an impact, and, furthermore, facilitated this involvement. This is crucial where people generally feel powerless or feel that their contribution would have no impact.

'No Viet Cong ever called me "nigger"'

While the term 'civic journalism' may be new, the roots of this growing ethos of news media in opposing racism stretch back many decades. Hudson cites four examples from the 1950s of the news media engendering support for civil rights and the eradication of racism in America's South. The coverage of these events – the murder of Emmett Till, the university suspension of Catherine Lucy, the first black student at the University of Alabama, the anti-apartheid bus boycott following the arrest in Alabama of a black woman for refusing to move to the back of a bus and the integration of Central High School in Little Rock, Arkansas – 'played an important part in galvanizing support for the civil rights movement in the 1950s … (awakening) America's conscience to flagrant abuses in the South' (Hudson 1999).

Hudson also points to press coverage of civil rights issues during the Second World War 'when some journalists questioned why black soldiers should have had to fight oppression overseas and then fight racism at home'. This issue was again canvassed by America's journalists after the Vietnam War, following the oft-quoted words of Muhammad Ali – who threw away his Olympic gold medal as a result of discrimination in his home town – as to why should he go to Vietnam: 'No Viet Cong ever called me "nigger".'

Word-of-mouth and viral marketing

In the commercial arena, word-of-mouth advertising generally refers to people passing on favourable (or unfavourable) reports on a product to others, and diffusion models have always considered such interpersonal exchanges an important component of how readily an innovation is adopted. While marketers sometimes tried to hurry this process along by sampling promotions and developing ad materials that generated discussion, the advent of the Internet and social network media has provided a whole new dimension to the concept. Feedback on products is now all over the net, with comments on such things as new release movies being sent instantly around in the first couple of days after release. The three major changes in this area are:

- the speed with which information spread by word of mouth can now reach millions of people all around the globe via the Internet;
- companies now make ads specifically to be spread via word-of-mouth (via YouTube or simply email, 'buzz campaigns' or 'viral marketing');
- 'stealth marketing' (not disclosing one's identity as a marketer in a communication), 'shilling' (paying someone to endorse a product without disclosing that fact) and 'infiltration' (using a fake identity in an online discussion) (Mucha 2005) appear to be increasing as marketers become far more aware of how important it is and how quickly it spreads.

Alcohol marketers are known to pay people to ask for a particular brand in a bar as well as buy for others, and tobacco companies paid college students to offer cigarettes around at parties, bars and other gatherings. Tweets have been discovered on Twitter containing paid plugs for companies including Apple, Skype, Flip, StubHub and Box. net (Weir 2009a), and the US Federal Trade Commission is now drawing up guidelines that will allow it to investigate bloggers who are paid to promote products but do not disclose that fact (Weir 2009b). Facebook supposedly allows only brand sites that are actually sponsored by the company and are clearly disclosed as such.

There is now also an Advertising Age Viral Video Chart, which in August 2009 was led by Evian's 'Rollerbabies' (infants skateboarding etc.), Nike and Microsoft (Klaassen 2009). It appears that a marked upsurge in creative executions for the Internet was sparked by T-Mobile's 'impromptu' 'flash mob' dance in Liverpool Street station, London (and various other European stations) and Cadbury's two schoolchildren wiggling their eyebrows to the old hit *Don't Stop the Rock*. These ads are marked by a fun and quirky humour, 'feel good' approach, and apparently have resulted in increased sales: Cadbury's sales reportedly increased after 'Eyebrows' and T-Mobile's sales are reportedly up 25 per cent (Hall 2009) (The ads were still on YouTube at time of publication, see www.youtube.com/watch?v=mUZrrbgCdYc.)

There have been a number of attempts to use viral marketing for socially desirable causes (see 'Take the knife' example in box below), with the 'Nicomarket' component of the European HELP tobacco control campaign being a good but apparently short-lived example. The Nicomarket viral campaign, aimed at 18–24-year-olds, featured a series of eight videos specifically developed for the Internet. These promoted ironically branded products to highlight the short-term negative impacts of smoking (such as 'Smoke' perfume, 'Nicoteeth' toothpaste, 'Nicoclean' face cleanser and 'Nicobreeze' air freshener). Each video featured a 'share with friends' email function. The website was launched Europewide in October 2007 with banner advertising on key target group websites, including MSN, Yahoo, Meetic and TillLate. The videos were also posted on key external sites with high youth visitation, such as MTV, DailyMotion, YouTube and

Metacafe. In its first year the Nicomarket website registered more than 291,000 visits, with 13 per cent of viewers forwarding the link on to others. The videos posted on external sites were also viewed 3.5 million times within the first two months (Hastings *et al.* 2008).

New media

Websites and interactive technology

The arrival of the Internet has led to enormous advances in increasing people's access to information (provided they have a PC and Internet link), and, for certain marketers, has provided a sales channel without which they could not have reached markets other than their small geographical catchment areas. However, it has not increased people's ability to interpret information, nor to judge the reliability and validity of the information provided. That is, the very accessibility of the Internet provides not only an opportunity to provide desirable social messages, but also an avenue for the dissemination of racist, violent and unhealthy messages.

This unfettered access to the web (anyone can have a website; today's search engines are very efficient) increases the need for credible social organisations not only to have a strong presence on the web, but also to continue to position themselves in the public eye as the credible, authoritative sources for information in their areas.

For social marketers, the web provides a relatively efficient and inexpensive forum for the development and dissemination of social marketing projects and materials. For example, the website of The Communication Initiative partnership (www.comminit.com) provides links to sites under seven themes: democracy/government; early childhood development; HIV/AIDS; information and communication technologies for development; media development; natural resource management; and polio. There is a wealth of information from around the globe under all of these themes, including news reports, updates and evaluations. The site also provides information on broad topics such as change theories, online research planning models and strategic thinking. There is a 'global' site, as well as a Spanish language Latin American site and an English language Africa site – each with its own themes (other useful sites for social marketers are listed in the resources section).

At the time of the first edition of this book, multimedia and interactive technology developments were offering much promise. They have delivered on this promise, and particularly the interactive aspects – which are now de rigueur on most websites, and particularly those targeting children and youth. One of the most popular interactive concepts is that of making choices at various decision points in a narrative, which then lead to very different outcomes as the story unfolds (see Figure 12.9; The Runaway

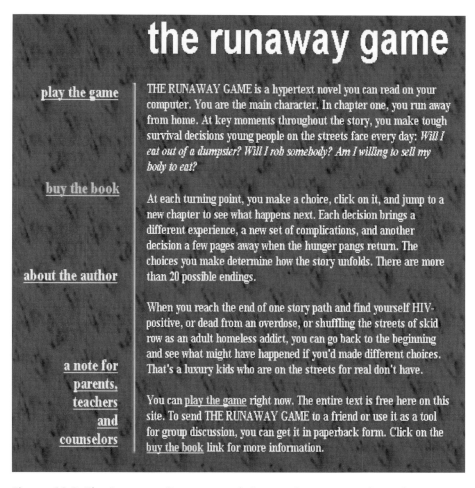

Figure 12.9 The Runaway Game: an early interactive story on the web

Game). This can be done with live actors on the stage taking directions from the audience, in books or on DVDs or websites. For example, in August 2009 the World Anti-Doping Agency (WADA) released two 'Choose your own adventure' books by Ramsey Montgomery, one targeting 8–12-year-olds that deals with cheating issues (*Always Picked Last*), and the other for older athletes dealing with the use of performance enhancing substances and supplements (*Track Star!*).

In 2009, as part of their ongoing crime reduction and prevention initiatives, the UK Metropolitan Police launched a 'choose your own adventure' YouTube campaign targeting youth carrying, or at risk of carrying, knives.

> **Take the knife?**
>
> The videos place the viewer within a group of friends. At the end of each scene, you are asked to make a decision on how the plot should unfold, which then takes you to the next video. The film begins with you at home when your friends come by and ask you to go with them. The first decision you must make is whether or not to 'take the knife'. As it turns out, 'taking the knife' leads to poor outcomes for the knife taker and his victim. At the time of publication the film could be viewed at www.youtube.com/adifferentending.

At this stage, the most opportunities for interactivity are via websites and DVDs/ CD-ROMs, although by the time this book is published, digital interactive TV (and radio) will be commonplace.

Many health organisations (often sponsored by pharmaceutical companies) have developed interactive websites where visitors can, for example, answer a questionnaire regarding their dietary habits and receive an immediate 'diagnosis' and 'prognosis' re dietary changes. Anti-tobacco campaigners are developing similar methods that classify smokers according to their stage of change, and then present messages 'tailored' to the smoker's stage of change and other characteristics (Borland, Balmford and Hunt 2004).

Mobiles

Mobile phone technology (Blackberry, iPhone, PDA, etc.) is emerging as a useful technology as its ability to access and interact with the Internet expands. For example, pan-regional broadcaster Ten Sports recently announced a deal with du Mobile and Qtel media to bring live action sport to Middle East subscribers (SportBusiness 2009).

Mobile phone ownership is growing rapidly. According to a report from the European Information Technology Observatory (EITO), it is estimated that almost two-thirds of the world's population will be using mobile phones by the end of 2009. EITO predicts that the number of mobile phone users in India is projected to increase by 32 per cent this year to 457 million, by 14 per cent to 172 million in Brazil and by 12 per cent to 684 million in China (Weir 2009c). Other data show that African ownership of mobile phones has gone from 2 per cent in 2000 to 28 per cent in 2009 (Weir 2009c), and that by 2012, almost half the population in remote areas of the globe will have mobile phones (Vital Wave Consulting 2009).

Commercial marketers are certainly aware of the potential for mobile applications, including reaching people in store during their shopping (Lin and Mooney 2009), as are charities in terms of their public relations communications and fund raising (Pearson *et al.* 2009). Similarly, mobiles are being used widely in health and injury prevention interventions. The UK Cabwise programme's use of mobiles to text the location of authorised cabbies was noted in Chapter 11, and text messaging of health-related information is becoming common as a component of health campaigns; for example, reminding British women to take their contraceptive pill, encouraging Australian AIDS patients to comply with their medication regimens and encouraging African-Americans to text STI questions to the San Francisco Health Department (Zimmerman 2007).

The UN Foundation, in conjunction with Vodafone Foundation, recently released a comprehensive report on the opportunities for mobile technology in public health (mHealth) in developing countries (Vital Wave Consulting 2009). In addition to education and awareness initiatives, they see five further areas of application: remote data collection; remote monitoring; communication and training for health care workers; disease and epidemic outbreak tracking; and diagnostic and treatment support.

Games

Like comics, DVD and video games have long been criticised for fostering anti-social attitudes and behaviours, particularly violence, with others pointing to their addictive nature and their contribution to inactivity and, hence, overweight and obesity in children (Gentile *et al.* 2004; Reichhardt 2003; Snider 2009; Vandewater, Shim and Caplovitz 2004). On the other hand, people such as Steven Johnson at New York University, in his book *Everything Bad is Good For You*, argues that games have many positive aspects, especially with regard to teaching decision-making skills (Johnson 2005). The US Army claims that its game is not only good entertainment, but also 'showcases the values the Army wants to be identified with, including teamwork, courage and honor' (Mucha 2004).

Games have been developed as part of health promotion interventions where they have generally shown that they can increase knowledge and impact on behaviour (Bandura 2004). For example, *Packy & Marlon*, an interactive video game designed to improve self-care among children and adolescents with diabetes, was evaluated in a 6-month randomised controlled trial. In the game, players take the role of animated characters who manage their diabetes by monitoring blood glucose, taking insulin injections and choosing foods, while setting out to save a diabetes summer camp from marauding rats and mice who have stolen the diabetes supplies. Each participant received a Super Nintendo video game system at an initial clinic visit and was randomly assigned to receive either *Packy & Marlon* or an entertainment video game containing no diabetes-related content. Participants were interviewed and a parent filled out a questionnaire at baseline, three months, and six months. The *Packy & Marlon* game players showed significant improvements over the control group in terms of diabetes related self-efficacy, communication with parents about diabetes and self-care behaviours and a decrease in unscheduled urgent doctor visits (Brown *et al.* 1997). This study indicates that well designed, educational video games can be effective.

The latest variation on such games are Wii 'exergames' with the Nintendo Wii selling more than 11 million consoles in the United States from late 2006 to mid 2008 (Anders

2008). The player holds the controller (like a TV remote channel changer) and an infrared camera monitors the player's movements. Players can play tennis, golf, baseball, go bowling and even boxing. And then there is Wii Fit (a wired balance board leads players through forty different exercises), Konami DanceDance Revolution (uses a mat, screen and music), the Sony Playstation Eye and Cateye Fitness GameBike (a stationary bike that links to other gaming consoles and allows the player to control the game by pedalling and steering the bike).

While research on these exergames' health and fitness benefits is limited, they do appear to provide positive behavioural and psychological effects in that people enjoy them, and they maintain higher adherence rates than traditional exercise equipment (Mark and Rhodes 2009).

Social media

Social media can be defined as electronic tools, technologies and applications that facilitate interactive communication and content exchange, with the distinct feature that the user can easily alternate between audience and author (Karjaluoto 2003). Types of social media include blogs, forums, virtual worlds, wikis and social networks (see Table 12.2). Their key characteristics are participation and connection.

As noted above, it is now commonplace for social marketers to have a presence in the social media. For example, CDC (the Centers for Disease Control and Prevention) in the United States has a presence on Twitter, Facebook, MySpace, DailyStrength, (CDC's) YouTube Channel, (CDC's) Flickr site, (CDCon) iTunes and (CDC's) Second Life Island (in addition to offering online videos, podcasts, RSS feeds and widgets on the website). CDC has used all these media in their comprehensive education and awareness campaign about swine flu (Novel H1N1 flu), the pandemic that swept the globe in 2009 (www.cdc.gov/socialmedia, accessed 16 August 2009).

Regardless of these 'new media', social marketers should not be tempted to devote excess resources simply to follow what they see as exciting new trends. As Postma (1999) reminds us, people are still people, and change at a far slower rate than technology.

While health and social marketers are enthusiastically embracing these new social media, their actual and relative impact and effectiveness have not been established to date. Their use must be carefully considered alongside other media in terms of what target audiences we wish to reach and impact, what sort of messages we want to send and what are our communication and behaviour objectives. As political campaigns both in the United States (Abroms and Lefebvre 2009) and Australia (Macnamara and Bell 2008) have shown, they have their roles. President Barack Obama's campaign in particular demonstrates the capacity of social media to mobilise one's supporters and to raise funds – which were then spent to great effect in the traditional media, particularly television.

Table 12.2 Examples of social media sites in 2009

Blogs
Image/video sharing sites: Flickr, YouTube
Internet forums
Microblogs: Twitter, Plurk
Mobile websites
Podcasts
Professional networking: LinkedIn
RSS feeds
Social bookmarking: Del.icio.us
Social networking sites: Facebook, Myspace
Social news: Digg
Virtual worlds: Second Life, Whyville
Widgets
Wikis

Choosing media and methods

The decision on whether to use advertising, publicity, civic journalism, website tech-nology edutainment, or some combination of these in any social marketing campaign is determined by the objectives of the campaign, the budget, the relative effectiveness of the different modes in reaching and impacting the target audiences, the complexity of the message, time constraints, relations with professionals in the various media, and the nature and types of media and media vehicles available.

The choice of print versus electronic media, television versus newspapers, radio ver-sus magazines and so on, also depends on budget, type of message required, target audience media habits and so on. In general, television, outdoor media and mobile phones are intrusive and therefore have the capacity to reach those who might not normally attend to a message; newspapers and websites are passive, in that only those interested in the topic will read further or deliberately access the site. Social media are more active, but again require people to access a site. An important consideration to keep in mind is that multiple channel delivery appears to have more impact than single channel delivery (Lefebvre, Olander and Levine 1999). This avoids wearout and appears to attract greater attention to, and processing of, the message when the same message appears in different media.

The US national youth anti-drug media campaign

This campaign is probably the world's most extensive interactive programme, bringing together a number of interactive websites aimed at youth, parents, teachers, media personnel and other stakeholders, placing messages on a variety of partners' websites, placing advertising on consumer websites and a major Internet service provider

[America On Line (AOL)], and developing messages and programmes for leading child–parent news content sites. A key partnership includes a deal with Marvel Comic Books which produces a special Spider Man comic book series (downloadable from the web) teaching kids anti-drug messages and media literacy skills for deconstructing what they see and hear in movies, television and popular songs (Schwartz 2000).

The primary advantages of paid advertising relate to control factors; that is, control over message content, message exposure – timing and 'location' and, hence, target audience and frequency of exposure. Advertising's major disadvantage is cost, both production costs (though creative advertising people can, and do, develop messages that don't require expensive production; see Donovan, Jalleh and Henley 1999), and media costs (by far the larger component). On the other hand, given the number of people exposed to, say, network television advertising, the cost per individual contact and impact is often quite low, especially relative to face-to-face methods.

Publicity in major media shares the ability of advertising to reach large numbers of people in a relatively short period, but has the disadvantage of less control over message content, message exposure and frequency (unless the issue is sufficiently newsworthy to attract continuing coverage for several days). A press release might be rewritten by a sub-editor in a way that omits or distorts crucial information, be relegated to the later pages of a newspaper, appear only in a very late TV or radio news spot or even be totally ignored. On the other hand, publicity is generally perceived as more credible than paid advertising (because the source is presumably unbiased, or less biased), and is less costly.

Edutainment in major media has the ability to reach large numbers of people in a relatively short period (given a popular show), but, except where the show is produced by the social marketer, has the disadvantages of less control over message content and less control over message exposure and frequency – unless the theme continues for several episodes. On the other hand, a specifically produced show may not have the reach of an already popular show. The primary advantage of edutainment (which also, but to a lesser extent, applies to publicity), is the ability to attract the attention of people who might otherwise deliberately avoid messages that appear in an obvious educational form. Where the social marketer is not directly involved in producing the show, edutainment can be quite inexpensive. However, where the social marketer is a joint or sole producer, costs can be high. On the other hand, if a show is a commercial success, the organisation might earn a profit (Coleman and Meyer 1990).

Scenarios USA

A variation on edutainment is where the target audience themselves become involved in making the production (as in Spark's approach). Scenarios USA brings together young people, film and television professionals, schools and community organisations. The young people write the script on the topic (e.g., drugs, STDs, etc.), then act in and produce the film under the guidance of professionals. The short films are then distributed as widely as possible. A major benefit of this approach is that it engages many young 'at risk' teenagers who would reject a standard approach on these issues (Joiner, Minsky and Seals 2000).

Websites are virtually de rigueur for any campaign, even if serving the same purpose as an entry in the Yellow Pages. However, websites allow target audience members to access information about the issue, and allow stakeholders to access programme information. Interactive elements can be built into the site, as well as links established to other sites. Website design becomes expensive when interactive elements are included, but the major issues are maintaining and updating the site. It is now also standard to show links to sites such as Facebook, Twitter, MySpace, Flickr and YouTube.

Civic journalism is most useful for complex issues requiring extensive information to be absorbed in a non-emotive atmosphere. The major difficulty in many countries outside the United States is that there is no established tradition of civic journalism; newspapers appear focused on advertising revenue rather than quality journalism and, hence, individual journalists appear to have little support from their editors and publishers for civic journalism initiatives.

Roles of the media in social marketing campaigns

Egger, Spark and Donovan (2005) delineate three major roles for the media components of social marketing campaigns, two of which apply primarily to the targeting of individual behaviour change and the other to the achievement of socio-political objectives or structural change. All these objectives involve the targeting of beliefs (knowledge and perceptions), attitudes (and opinions) and values. A fourth role is a 'directing' or 'public announcement' role. In this case the information is not about the issue in question, nor does it attempt to persuade; it simply directs people to further information about the issue (e.g., promoting a telephone information service), to activities associated with the issue (e.g., a cancer foundation Run For Life event), or to opportunities for community involvement in policy making (e.g., announcing a public meeting to deal with local issues).

Targeting individual behaviour change

Most uses of the mass media in health promotion and social marketing have been directed towards individual behaviour change. This is particularly so in the United States, where there is a strong cultural value on individual responsibility. The two primary communication objectives for campaigns that target individual behaviour change are:

TO EDUCATE (or INFORM);
and
TO MOTIVATE (or PERSUADE)

Education aims to create or maintain awareness, knowledge and understanding of the health issue in question. Motivation aims to bring about attitude change, behavioural intentions or explicit actions within the target group. Education is primarily a cognitive process; motivation involves cognition and emotional processes. Television advertising is most associated with, and suited to, persuasion; whereas most public health pamphlets, especially in years gone by, have focused on education.

Winning Vietnam's helmet war: education and motivation

Ogilvy & Mather's award winning campaign in Vietnam had to tackle the problem that 97 per cent of motorcyclists and their passengers were not wearing a helmet in 2007, in a situation where there were approximately 14,000 road deaths and 30,000 cases of severe brain damage and health injury per year. Wearing a helmet was mandatory only on some major highways. The advertising campaign was part of an initiative by the Asia Injury Prevention Foundation, and included lobbying the government to introduce mandatory helmet legislation, conferences and workshops on road safety, manufacturing affordable helmets designed for tropical conditions, plus education and free helmets for children. The campaign messages attacked the excuses/rationalisations that people gave for not wearing a helmet executed via a number of media: a television ad; advertising on buses (previously not available); outdoor, eye level billboards; print ads in Vietnamese and English press; postcards distributed in coffee shops and bars; and a website. The TV ad was reportedly one of the first Vietnamese ads to be posted on YouTube (www.youtube.com/watch?v=7TpWG2GD20c).

Within four months of the launch of the campaign, the proportion of motorcyclists wearing a helmet had tripled (from 3 per cent to more than 10 per cent), and the proportion wearing a helmet on highways increased from 61 per cent to 77 per cent. The campaign ads also attracted considerable publicity in Vietnamese news media. Most significantly, the advertising and subsequent publicity led to the government advancing the introduction of helmet legislation by six months, and almost universal compliance (at least initially) with the legislation. Accident and trauma data show significant declines (from 25–50 per cent) in adult head trauma and fatalities from motorcycle crashes (Clegg 2009) (Figure 12.10).

The distinction between these two roles is blurred in that the provision of information is generally not intended for its own sake, but is usually meant to lead to desired behaviour changes. It was increasing evidence that knowledge alone was insufficient to achieve attitude and behaviour change among substantial proportions of the population that led public health officials to focus more attention on how to improve the motivational power of their health messages.

Targeting socio-political change: media advocacy

As noted in Chapter 4, an ultimate goal of media advocacy is to create changes in policies that improve the health and wellbeing of communities (Wallack 1994). For

Figure 12.10 Vietnam helmet campaign

Provided by Asia Injury Prevention Foundation; photographer Dusit Pongkrapan

example, the arousal of public opinion has been used to support lobbying for legislative changes regarding restrictions on tobacco advertising and sponsorship. This sort of media use is the third major role of media:

TO ADVOCATE

It can also be described as the use of media, usually via unpaid publicity, to place a particular point of view before the public regarding some controversial issue, with the aim of involving the public in the resolution of that issue. That is, a major aim of media advocacy is to empower the public to take part in policy making (see Rogers *et al.* 1995).

Some writers view media advocacy as an alternative to and, hence, separate from, social marketing. However, we (and others such as Slater, Kelly and Edwards 2000), view media advocacy as part of a comprehensive social marketing approach. Furthermore, advocacy *per se* involves far more than just media components, and is a major tool for achieving change at the 'upstream', broader societal level.

Both individual and structural change objectives should be part of any comprehensive social change campaign. In some cases it is likely that individual targeted campaigns must have some impact first, not only on individual beliefs and attitudes towards the issue *per se*, but also on social norms towards the recommended behaviour before advocacy objectives can be achieved. For example, it is unlikely that efforts to frame smoking as a public health issue would have been as successful without prior Quit campaigns that emphasised the ill-health effects of smoking. Similarly, graphic road safety ads served to create a positive social context within which harsher penalties and surveillance methods such as speed cameras and random breath testing could be introduced with minimal public opposition.

'Cut this out and put it in bed next to your child'

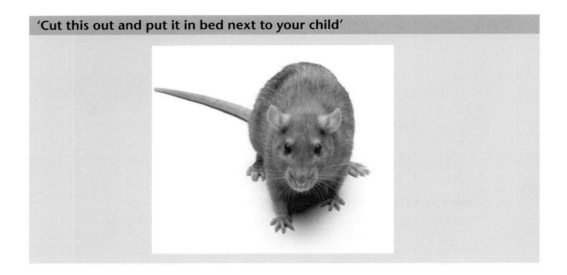

This heading and a picture of a rat constituted one of the most successful advocacy campaigns we are aware of. The year was 1967 – a very long time ago for most readers. The Rat Extermination Bill had been rejected by the US House of Representatives. Two creative 'Mad Men' – Bert Steinhauser (art director) and Chuck Kollewe (writer) at DDB – decided to do something about it. They created an *ad hoc* organisation and a print ad that appeared twice: once in the *New York Review of Books* and once in the Pelham weekly *Sun*. However, it was picked up and shown on TV, read out on radio and featured in newspaper and magazine articles. Following widespread public outcry, the bill was re-introduced and was passed. The two Mad Men even got a letter of commendation from the President – Lyndon Baines Johnson.

Why did they succeed?

An analysis of the ad copy suggests a number of reasons:

- the copy established the seriousness of the problem generally and specifically: the ad stated that rats have 'killed more humans than all the generals in history put together' … 'thousands of our children are bitten by rats each year – some killed or disfigured' (i.e., rat eradication is a legitimate public health problem);

- at the bottom of the ad was a list of all the members who had voted for the bill and all those who had voted against the bill's passage. Readers were ask to contact those who voted for the bill and 'tell them of your support', and to contact those who voted against the bill and ask them to change their mind;
- an economic argument was included: rats were claimed to cause estimated damage of US$900 million per year (versus US$40 million for pest control in the bill);
- an assurance that change was possible as they needed to persuade only sixteen members to change their vote (i.e., a realistic, achievable goal);
- a 'what's in it for me' was included: the ad stated that when the rat infested slum buildings marked for demolition were demolished, the rats, if not exterminated beforehand, would go into the restaurants and the suburbs where the readers lived.

This case is a good example of a targeted strategy being far more important than any technology. Similarly, while much is made of the Obama campaign's use of 'new' media, the fact is that all candidates in the 2008 presidential campaign used the new media – Obama's campaign simply did it better (Abroms and Levebvre 2009).

Specific objectives

There are a number of objectives that can be classified under the three overall roles of informing, persuading or advocating. However, it should be noted that the classification is not a mutually exclusive one.

Informational objectives

- informing (or educating) people about the personal and community disbenefits of various undesirable behaviours, and the benefits of alternative behaviours;
- clarifying misperceptions and/or confusions that people may have about various issues;
- reminding people of the benefits and disbenefits of which they are already aware and maintaining the salience of this knowledge.

Motivational or persuasion objectives

- reinforcing those already practising the desired behaviour;
- generating emotional arousal to increase people's motivations to cease undesired behaviours and/or to adopt various desired behaviours;
- sensitising or predisposing individuals to specific intervention components (arguably the major role as a facilitator of behaviour change);

- increasing awareness of prescriptive and, where appropriate, popular norms (Cialdini 1989) and, hence, providing social support for those who wish to adopt the recommended behaviour;
- stimulating word-of-mouth communications about the issue in question and, hence, encouraging peer (and other) group discussion and decision-making – a very important role for the diffusion of social issues.

Advocacy-related objectives (see also Chapter 4)

- increasing community awareness of the issue and placing the issue on the community's agenda (i.e., 'agenda setting');
- creating or increasing community awareness of a particular point of view with regard to the issue (i.e., 'framing' the community agenda);
- creating or maintaining a favourable attitude towards this particular view;
- creating a view that the issue is a significantly serious one for community concern (i.e., 'legitimising' the issue);
- generating a positive community mood within which regulatory and other policies can be introduced with minimal opposition and/or maximal support.

Concluding comments

The effective application of these media methods in social marketing requires close co-operation between media experts, marketing experts, content professionals and behavioural scientists with expertise in communication theory and attitude and behaviour change. A realisation of this has been a long time coming. For example, the Australian Government's first major national tobacco campaign was directed by a special advisory group (headed by a behavioural scientist), and included health promotion, social marketing and consumer behaviour experts, all with considerable experience in tobacco control.

The rat initiative demonstrates several points:

- When it comes to media, new does not always mean better – it is the end (the goal) that counts, not the means (the channel).
- Strategy should drive the creativity – not the other way around.
- We are social beings. Social networking is not new. What is new are the opportunities for non-face-to-face networking on a grand scale with 'virtual friends'.

Finally, cyber networking may decline as people miss the human contact of face-to-face interactions. This is evident in some areas where people name their cyber chat room 'fireside chats' in some vain attempt to generate some 'warmth' in the interactions. Others are going back to the 'real thing' and reviving the old concept of meeting in cafes to talk about societal issues (informing each other about place, time and topic by … social media of course).

QUESTIONS

- What methods and channels would you use to change college students' beliefs about, and attitudes towards, using marijuana?
- What methods and channels would you use to change street youths' beliefs about, and attitudes towards, marijuana?
- How has social networking changed over the last two years?
- What are the advantages and disadvantages of TV network advertising, viral advertising and mobile phone advertising to reach and impact: (a) young people; (b) retired people; (c) rural dwellers?

FURTHER READING

Abroms, L. and Lefebvre, R. 2009. Obama's Wired Campaign: Lessons for Public Health Communication, *Journal of Health Communication* 14: 415–23.

Bryant, J. and Oliver, M. B. (eds.) 2004. *Media Effects: Advances in Theory and Research.* New York: Routledge.

Dawson, N. (ed.) 2009. *Advertising Works 17: Proving the Payback on Marketing Investment.* Oxfordshire: World Advertising Research Centre.

Donovan, R. J. and Leivers, S. 1993. Using Paid Advertising to Modify Racial Stereotype Beliefs, *Public Opinion Quarterly* 57: 205–18.

Goldstein, S., Usdin, S., Scheepers, E. and Japhet, G. 2005. Communicating HIV and AIDS, What Works? A Report on the Impact Evaluation of Soul City's Fourth Series, *Journal of Health Communication* 10: 465–83.

Shrum, L. J. (ed.) 2004. *The Psychology of Entertainment Media.* Hillsdale, NJ: Lawrence Erlbaum.

Singhal, A., Cody, M. J., Rogers, E. M. and Sabido, M. 2004. *Entertainment–Education and Social Change.* Hillsdale, NJ: Lawrence Erlbaum.

Usdin, S., Scheepers, E., Goldstein, S. and Japhet, G. 2005. Achieving Social Change on Gender-based Violence: A Report on the Impact Evaluation of Soul City's Fourth Series, *Social Science & Medicine* 61: 2434–45.

13 Using sponsorship to achieve changes in people, places and policies

In social marketing, sponsorship is particularly important for gaining access to specific target audiences and for achieving policy changes that lead to healthier places, such as smoke-free areas and healthier food choices in entertainment and sporting venues. How this is done will be detailed below.

Sponsorship is generally defined as the payment for the right to associate the sponsor's company name, products or services with the sponsee. The sponsee could be an organisation (e.g., the National Heart Foundation, a national museum), a group of individuals or one individual (e.g., Michael Phelps, Tiger Woods), an event (e.g., the Olympic Games), or a season series (e.g., European Cup, Six Nations Rugby series). Sponsorship is distinguished from corporate philanthropy or simply funding an entity by the intended exploitation of the relationship by the sponsor to achieve marketing or other business objectives (Walliser 2003). Sponsorship is sometimes confused with partnerships. In our view, while some sponsorships may overlap with partnerships, a sponsor–sponsee relationship is a commercial rather than a co-operative transaction: the sponsor pays a 'fee' for certain rights via the sponsee under a contractual obligation.

In recent years, the use of sponsorship as a promotional tool has increased dramatically in both commercial marketing and in health promotion. In 1996, estimated worldwide sponsorship expenditure was US$13.4 billion (International Events Group Sponsorship Report 1996). In 2009, the International Events Group Sponsorship Report estimates it will be more than triple that amount at US$45.2 billion (SponsorMap 2009), although the rate of growth will slow to only 3.9 per cent over 2008.

The United States has the highest sponsorship expenditure (US$17.2 billion), followed by Europe (US$12.2 billion), the Asia-Pacific region (US$10.2 billion) and Latin America (US$3.6 billion). Approximately two-thirds of funds go to sport sponsorship (IEG Sponsorship Report 2006).

The growth of sponsorship

The growth in sponsorship is attributable to the inherent benefits of sponsorship (e.g., access to difficult to reach audiences), as well as to factors associated with advertising (e.g., high costs and clutter in mass media advertising), and to the phasing out of tobacco advertising in many countries around the globe. Sponsorship provides opportunities to access specific segments of an organisation's target audience (e.g., young people) and secondary audiences (e.g., employees, shareholders, politicians and clients) that are often difficult to reach through other media.

The growth in commercial sponsorship was led by the tobacco companies in an effort to continue to promote their brands following bans on television advertising, and, later, other forms of promotion (Chapman and Lupton 1994; Meenaghan 1991). The apparent success of the tobacco companies' sponsorship in maintaining brand awareness and image encouraged other companies to embrace sponsorship, particularly the major breweries and soft drink marketers. Through a 'social proof' effect (Cialdini 2001; Chapter 5), the highly visible sponsorship activities of these large companies may have been interpreted as proof that sponsorship is effective and therefore stimulated other companies to follow suit (Donovan *et al.* 1993). That also led to large companies competing for major sponsorship deals – much to the delight of the sponsees.

In fact, the rapid growth of sponsorship by alcohol, fast food and soft drink marketers of sporting teams and events and music entertainment that have the potential to reach substantial numbers of young people has caused concern in many countries as noted in Chapter 9. An Internet study of 640 sponsors (on 107 websites) of the top eight sports for 5–17-year-olds in New Zealand found that 'unhealthy' products (foods high in sugar or fat, gambling, alcohol) were over twice as common as sponsors' products classified as 'healthy'. Gambling was the most common sponsorship (19 per cent) followed by alcohol (11 per cent) (Maher *et al.* 2006).

The widespread sponsorship of sporting codes, especially those with high young male followings, has led to many countries extending alcohol advertising codes and restrictions to sponsorship. In Ireland, the 'Alcohol Marketing, Communications and Sponsorship Codes of Practice' was launched in July 2008, and a new agreement about alcohol marketing that included sponsorship was reached in February 2009 between the Scottish Government and alcohol marketers (Merrett 2009). Such controls are needed: Anheuser-Busch ranked first and Miller brewing ranked sixth in the top ten US sponsors in 2005 and 2006 (Pepsi ranked second with Coca-Cola at number four) (IEG Sponsorship Report 2006).

Vale Michael Jackson 1958–2009

When Pepsi enlisted the late Michael Jackson in 1992, the company described it as 'the biggest sponsorship deal between a musician and a corporation in history'. Apparently, when asked just how much Jackson would be paid, Pepsi's marketing chief said: 'A lot' (*The West Australian* 2009).

The entry of large companies into sponsorship programmes has been stimulated also by the growth of cause-related marketing noted in Chapter 1 and by non-profit organisations actively promoting themselves as vehicles for sponsorship. For example, Diet Coke sponsored the National Heart, Lung and Blood Institute's Heart Truth Red Dress Collection at the Mercedes-Benz (another sponsor) Fashion Show in February 2008 in New York. The Heart Truth campaign aims to increase women's awareness about heart disease. Diet Coke will also sponsor the Heart Truth Road Show, a travelling exhibit that provides free health screenings and heart disease information in US cities. The Heart Truth logo will also feature on Diet Coke cans (Zmunda 2008).

Health promotion professionals around the globe have adopted many of the concepts and tools of commercial marketing. However, it has been mainly in Australia and New Zealand that public health and health promoting organisations have enthusiastically embraced sponsorship, both as sponsors (mainly government agencies) and by actively promoting themselves to business as sponsees (non-government agencies). This has been facilitated by the fact that small-scale sponsorships at selected events are within the capacity of even small agencies to implement, and by a growing awareness among health and sporting organisations of the 'natural' fit between both types of organisations' goals. The more the perceived congruence between the sponsor and the sponsee on some overall characteristics (what is called the sponsor 'fit'), the more effective will be the sponsorship (Alay 2008; Rifon et al. 2004). Red Bull's sponsorship of UK Athletics (UKA) as the 'official drink to UKA' is an example of 'good fit'. Under the sponsorship, Red Bull has exclusive rights to provide energy drinks and drink stations across UKA offices, to coaching staff, training camps, conferences and squads. Red Bull will also provide products at all UKA competitions and have a strong field presence at all UKA televised events (SportBusiness 2009).

In Australia, the growth in health promotion sponsorship was initiated by the legislative phasing out of tobacco sponsorship and the creation of health promotion foundations in some states that replaced tobacco sponsorship funds (Furlong 1994). Funded by a tobacco tax, these foundations provide funds for health promotion research and intervention projects, and for health sponsorship. Substantial funds are distributed to sports, arts and racing organisations in return for these organisations' events being sponsored by health promoting organisations. The replacement of tobacco sponsorship with health sponsorship has occurred elsewhere; for example, in California (see Weinreich, Abbott and Olson 1999), and health sponsorship as a strategy has been adopted in New Zealand (via the Health Sponsorship Council: www.hsc.org.nz) and in Canada (via Health Canada; O'Reilly and Madill 2007). However, social marketers generally have been slow to see sponsorship as a strategy in its own right within the discipline of social marketing.

Objectives of sponsorship

Most commercial sponsorships have trading and communication objectives, while most health sponsorships have structural and communication objectives.

Trading and structural objectives

The major objective of marketing activities is to influence or reinforce consumers' attitudes and behaviour, including sales (Hoek, Gendall and Stockdale 1993). Trading objectives refer mainly to securing merchandising rights at events. For example, Heineken sponsors a number of golf tournaments, and as part of their sponsorship arrangement they seek exclusive merchandising rights so that only Heineken beer is available at these tournaments. It is hoped that (forced) trial of the product will lead to a more favourable attitude to the product and to re-purchase in other situations.

Will McDonald's have exclusive brand rights in London 2012?

According to industry website, Caterersearch, McDonald's is in talks with Olympics organisers to become the exclusive food brand at the London Olympic Games (Coca-Cola already has exclusive rights to sell non-alcoholic drinks at Olympic venues). However, local restaurant operators have criticised the potential move, arguing that food served at the London Olympics should reflect regional produce and the city's ethnic diversity. Under the proposed deal, other food operators would be able to sell their products in some Olympic sites only if they removed labels or changed packaging, and restaurants and cafés present at existing sites would have to make way for official sponsors during the event (Cutler 2009).

Trading objectives for commercial sponsorships equate to structural change for health promotion sponsorships. For example, as a condition of the health sponsorship, the sponsee may be required to establish smoke-free areas or to provide low alcohol beer at their events. Such contractual requirements can reduce the degree of exposure to cigarette smoke (Giles-Corti *et al.* 2001), induce trial of low alcohol beers and lead to the substitution of healthy foods for high fat foods (Jalleh *et al.* 1998). Healthway's sponsorship programme (described below) provides the opportunity for health agencies to work collaboratively with those in the health, recreational and cultural sectors to introduce health promoting policies in recreational settings.

Communication objectives

There are two main communication objectives for sponsorship:

- to increase awareness of an organisation, brand name or health issue among the general public or a specific target market; and

- to increase or reinforce positive attitudes towards the organisation, brand name or health issue through the association with the sponsee.

While most commercial and health sponsorships are directed primarily at consumers, they may have direct or indirect positive effects on other target groups such as potential employees, community leaders, politicians and other relevant stakeholders. Sponsorship can also be used for client entertainment, special perks for key employees and to provide incentives for the sales force and distributors.

Differences between health and commercial sponsorship objectives

Attitude and belief objectives for health and social issue sponsorships are more complex than those of commercial sponsors. Health and social marketing sponsors promote a 'message', whereas commercial sponsors are primarily concerned with brand or corporate image effects and increasing awareness of brand names, trademarks or logo symbols. Health and social issue sponsorships have additional attitude and belief objectives that can be categorised as follows:

(1) Acceptance of the message as a legitimate health or social issue.
(2) Acceptance of the personal relevance of the message.
(3) Creation or reinforcement of a perception of the social norm with regard to acceptance of the message.

How sponsorship works

Sponsorship is similar to advertising as both are used to communicate an organisation's message and image for a product, brand or service to the target market. Advertising and sponsorship both aim to increase the salience of the organisation or message. However, the process by which advertising and sponsorship achieve these communication objectives may be quite different. Advertising is a paid communication in which the medium and the message are controlled by the advertiser and can be explicitly linked to the relevant organisation or brand. Advertising is able to communicate complex messages in terms of both information and imagery (Hastings 1984). In contrast, sponsorship persuades indirectly by linking the sponsor's message to an event or organisation (Alay 2008; Meenaghan 2001; Pham 1992) (although the sponsor's contract may include advertising at the event).

Commercial sponsors are concerned primarily with brand names, trademark or logo symbols, and associating these with the 'image' attributes of the sponsee. Hence, most commercial sponsorship objectives require only limited cognitive processing, mainly via 'unconscious' associative learning. Since social marketing sponsors promote a 'message', these sponsorship objectives require conscious processing, comprehension and cognitive elaboration to achieve their objectives.

There are a number of ways in which attitude effects of sponsorship may occur:

(1) Sheer exposure may lead to feelings of familiarity and, hence, positive feelings towards the message or organisation (Donovan *et al.* 1993). In this way, sponsorship may reinforce a perception of the social norm or social acceptance of a message. Furthermore, awareness facilitates other promotional activities by sensitising the individual to such activities (Otker 1988).

(2) Sponsorship results in positive affect transfer from the event to the sponsor (Alay 2008; Keller 1993; Meenaghan 2001). Positive image or feelings (e.g., fun, enjoyment and excitement) associated with the event are transferred to the message or organisation via associative learning or cognitive inferencing.

(3) As attitudes are based on a number of beliefs, an expressed attitude towards an organisation, brand name or health message is dependent on what beliefs are most salient at the time (Klapper 1961). Hence, as sponsorship can increase the salience of a belief (Donovan *et al.* 1993), sponsorship can influence attitude.

Evaluation of sponsorship

The hierarchical communication model shown in Figure 13.1 provides a basis for understanding how sponsorship can influence behaviour. However, it is not realistic to expect sponsorship or other promotional strategies in isolation to have a direct effect on behaviour. As with mass media promotions, sponsorship is likely to be more effective in the early stages of this hierarchy, whereas other elements of the marketing strategy and environmental factors are far more influential at the later behavioural stages. Therefore, it is important to measure sponsorship effects in terms of the earlier stages in the hierarchical communication model.

Although there have been published evaluations of some high profile events (such as the Olympics; e.g., Smolianov and Aiyeku 2009), until recently the literature revealed little systematic evaluation of commercial sponsorships. Furthermore, much evaluation has focused on sponsor awareness rather than communication or purchasing effects (e.g., Alexandris *et al.* 2008; Tripodi *et al.* 2003), and on sponsor management or company managers' attitudes to sponsorships (e.g., Papadimitriou, Apostolopoulou and Dounis' (2008) and Papadimitriou and Apostolopoulou's (2009) analyses of sponsors of the 2004 Olympics in Athens). Academic papers have focused on topics such as questions of definition, the role of sponsorship in the total marketing promotions mix, the setting of goals for sponsorship, the criteria for the selection of events to sponsor, evaluation models and the development of models or theories to explain sponsorship effects (Cornwell, Weeks and Roy 2005; Madill and O'Reilly 2010; Meenaghan 2001; O'Reilly and Madill 2007; Otker 1988; Walliser 2003). Non-academic writings have focused on the benefits of sponsorship to sponsors and implementation factors (Dwyer 1997; Hobsons 1990).

Figure 13.1 Steps in a hierarchical communication model

The lack of published commercial sponsorship evaluation research may be due in part to the proprietary nature of the data (Hansen and Scotwin 1995). It may also be due to the fact that advertising forms a major part of most marketing strategies, whereas sponsorship is usually one-off or event-based. Furthermore, it is difficult to separate the effects of sponsorship from advertising, sales promotion and other promotional tools, especially for large organisations with multiple promotional activities (Rajaretnam 1994).

However, there have been a number of studies from the Department of Population Health at the University of Western Australia that represent a systematic evaluation of health sponsorship (e.g., Donovan *et al.* 1993; Giles-Corti *et al.* 2001; Holman *et al.* 1996; Jalleh *et al.* 2002). We present the results of a number of these here.

Measures of effectiveness

Sponsorship has been evaluated in three main ways: measures of media exposure; survey research on spectators' awareness and attitudes; and sales or behavioural data (Smolianov and Aikeyu 2009).

Media exposure

Sponsors often benefit from substantial publicity through media exposure associated with an event (e.g., lineage in newspapers and magazines, TV/radio mentions) (Scott and Suchard 1992). That is, sponsors reach not only the audience at events, but also

Figure 13.2 Michael Schumacher and Marlboro in the news

those who watch, listen to, or read about the event via the various forms of media (Nicholls, Roslow and Laskey 1994). Given its objectivity and ready measurement (via commercial media monitoring organisations), media exposure is the most frequently nominated measure of sponsorship effectiveness by sponsors (Pope and Voges 1994). Backing a winner has big payoffs; pictures of a winning Michael Schumacher like the one shown above appeared throughout the Formula One season in 2002 (Figure 13.2). Levels of media exposure achieved via sponsorship can then be compared with levels reached by mainstream advertising, or, more typically, can be calculated in terms of how much advertising would have been required to achieve the equivalent exposure (Nicholls, Roslow and Laskey 1994). For example, the car manufacturer Volvo spent US$5 million on sponsoring and promoting pro tennis. This was calculated to be equivalent to approximately US$35 million in media exposure, or a 7:1 ratio (Schlossberg 1996). Similarly, the value of four minutes of logo visibility during a game is estimated to be one-third to one-half the cost of buying four minutes of advertising in that game (Crimmins and Horn 1996).

Hence, sponsorship may be viewed as a cost-effective way of generating exposure. However, this comparison is valid only if sponsorship works in the same way as mainstream advertising. This is questionable as the message conveyed through sponsorship is of a much simpler nature than that which can be transmitted through advertising. Furthermore, the results of Pokrywczynski's (1994) experiments on arena displays versus advertising suggest that arena displays need eight to twenty times more exposure than a TV commercial to achieve a similar impact (Crimmins and Horn 1996). Nevertheless, despite its limitations, media exposure is a valuable process measure and a valuable comparative measure for assessing the audience reach of various sponsorships.

Sales and behavioural data

There are several methods to track sales data resulting from sponsorship. The appropriate method depends on the trading terms of the sponsorship. When sales are directly linked to a sponsored event (for example, via coupons or label redemptions), it is relatively easy to measure the impact of the sponsorship on sales. Other possible methods include comparing sales for a period around the sponsorship with the same period in prior years, or in periods before and after the sponsored event, or in the event area against national sales (Kate 1995).

Beijing sponsors claim big sales effects

According to the *People's Daily Online*, Beijing Olympics sponsors had substantial sales success. Yili Dairy became a sponsor of the Beijing Olympic Games in November 2005. Its sales significantly improved for three consecutive years from then, and in the first quarter of 2008 Yili's income reached 4.7 billion yuan, an increase of 21.5 per cent. After the Yanjing Group become the domestic beer sponsor of the Olympic Games, its brand value rose from 15.2 billion yuan in 2005 to 20.6 billion yuan in 2007, with an average annual growth rate of more than 10 per cent. However, how much was due to the sponsorship *per se* is not really known (People's Daily Online 2008).

There are few published data on the impact of sponsorship on sales that may again be due mainly to the proprietary nature of the data (Hansen and Scotwin 1995). Those that have been reported provide evidence that sponsorship can have a positive impact on sales. For example, the Los Angeles Cellular Telephone Company claimed that in 1994, every dollar spent on sponsorship of pro sports teams, ski areas, concerts and festivals produced almost $87 in incremental sales (Kate 1995). In 1992, Visa advertised that it would donate a small percentage of the value of each US transaction to the

US Olympic team. Visa's transaction volume increased by 17 per cent during the promotion. No other Visa advertising or promotion campaign had generated an increased volume of more than 3 per cent (Kate 1995).

A number of Healthway evaluation studies using self-reports indicate that health sponsorships can lead to behavioural changes among those exposed to the messages (e.g., Donovan *et al.* 1999; Holman *et al.* 1996). These will be described below.

Survey research

Besides the opportunity for a sponsor to achieve sales at the event, sponsorship aims to create a favourable image and, hence, increase the likelihood of later purchase of sponsored brands in the shopping situation (Nicholls, Roslow and Laskey 1994). In recent years a number of studies have determined the effects of sponsorship in terms of awareness and attitudinal effects (see Alay 2008; Lacey *et al.* 2007; Walliser 2003).

Awareness effects

There are two types of awareness that may result from sponsorship: awareness of the sponsors' sponsorship of an event; and awareness of the sponsors' brand name or message, regardless of any link with an event.

As noted earlier, a number of publications on the impact of sponsorships are based on major international events such as the Olympic Games and the football World Cup. The results of studies in terms of generating awareness of the sponsor's link to the event have been mixed. Since 1984, Sponsor Watch has tracked 102 official Olympic sponsors, of which only 51 per cent built a successful link between their brand and the Olympics. Of the sponsors who ran advertising during the 1992 Olympic Games, 64 per cent succeeded in creating a link between the Olympics and their brand, whereas among official sponsors who did not run advertising during the Olympics, only one sponsor (i.e., Sports Illustrated), succeeded in creating a link between the Olympics and the brand (Crimmins and Horn 1996).

It is important to assess also the awareness of a sponsor's competitors to determine the strength of the link between the sponsor and the event or organisation. For example, in the 1990s when Coca-Cola contracted to be the official soft drink of the American National Football League (NFL) for five years, prompted recognition of Coke as a sponsor among NFL football fans who regularly consumed soft drinks was 35 per cent, but 34 per cent of the sample mistakenly identified Pepsi as a sponsor of the NFL. That is, Coca-Cola's sponsorship failed to gain an advantage over its main competitor in terms of sponsor awareness. The larger the proportion of the target audience who recognise that the organisation or brand is a sponsor and its competitor is not, the stronger is the link (Crimmins and Horn 1996).

Attitudinal and intention effects

There are three attitudinal effects of interest: attitudes to sponsorship in general; attitudes to the sponsor; and attitudes to the sponsor's products or services.

Studies have found positive attitudes towards sponsorship in general. For example, the Roper Organisation for the American Coalition for Entertainment and Sports Sponsorship study found that 93 per cent of adults believed corporate sponsorships are a good thing, 76 per cent agreed that advertising and sponsorship are a fair price for the entertainment they provide, 82 per cent agreed that corporate sponsorships benefit local communities by presenting events that attract visitors and by helping to hold ticket prices down. and 76 per cent believed that corporate sponsorship is a fair price to pay to keep sports on free-to-air television (Saxton 1993). Many sponsors no doubt believe that goodwill towards sponsorship in general will, by association, flow on to their corporate reputation.

Attitudes to sponsors have been measured mainly by asking respondents to rate the sponsor on a number of statements related to corporate image. It has been argued that sponsorship is better able to influence image than traditional advertising, as advertising is too 'direct' whereas sponsorship is more 'subtle'. Hence, it has been suggested that sponsorship may be used to counter negative company images associated with unpleasant activities (insurance companies) and environmental pollution (oil companies). Some studies have found positive effects of sponsorship on company image (e.g., Alay 2008; Lacey 2007; Rajaretnam 1994; Turco 1995), while others reported little or no effect (e.g., Javalgi *et al.* 1994). No doubt Phillip Morris is hoping that its sponsorship of issues such as domestic violence will have a positive impact on its corporate image.

A number of studies have found that prompted awareness of a sponsor's link with an event can positively influence consumers' preference for the sponsor's products or services. For example, Performance Research found that 48 per cent of NASCAR fans would 'almost always' purchase a sponsor's product over that of a closely priced competitor, and 42 per cent would switch to the sponsor's brands (Crimmins and Horn 1996). Crimmins and Horn (1996) found that about 60 per cent of the adult population of the United States reported they would buy a company's product if the company supported the Olympic Games, and about 60 per cent felt they were contributing to the Olympics by purchasing the brands of Olympic sponsors. Lacey *et al.* (2007) found an increase in brand attitude and brand purchase consideration for a sponsor's motor vehicle, and this was higher for multiple attenders of the sponsored event.

A measure of attitude change less susceptible to demand effects than the above measure is simply to ask a sample of the target population to select which brand or company offers the best product or service in their category, without *any* reference to sponsorship. In Crimmins and Horn's (1996) study, Visa's advantage over Mastercard in perceived superiority doubled during the Olympic Games from 15 per cent to 30 per cent, and remained higher one month after the Olympics than it had been during the three months before the Olympics. Similarly, Seiko's average advantage over Timex in perceived superiority during the three months before the Olympics was 5 per cent which increased to 20 per cent during the Olympics. However, only about half of the Olympic sponsors who built a link to the Olympic Games had an appreciable increase in their perceived superiority.

In a study looking at a cause-related sponsorship, Irwin *et al.* (2003) surveyed nearly 450 people who attended the FedEx St Jude Classic golf tournament in Memphis, Tennessee. While the question wording no doubt inflated positive responses (all Likert scale items were phrased in the affirmative), there was substantial support for corporations supporting the tournament and meaningful causes in general. Furthermore, 74 per cent agreed that on the basis of their support for the tournament, they would be more likely to use FedEx services. Rifon *et al.* (2004), in a laboratory experiment, showed that the better the fit between the company and the cause that it sponsors, the more the sponsorship is seen as altruistic and the more positive the attitude towards the company. Back in the real world, a study in France showed that sponsorship of a professional tennis event by a government authority was viewed favourably by event attendees rather than a waste of tax money (Walliser, Kach and Mogos-Descotes 2005).

Overall then, there is substantial evidence that sponsorship can work for commercial organisations as shown above and in the various reviews and studies in Cornwell, Weeks and Roy (2005), Lacey *et al.* (2007), Meenaghan (2001) and Walliser (2003). Can it work for social marketing?

Health promotion foundations: the case of Healthway

In Australia, the first health promotion foundation was established in 1987 in Victoria (VicHealth), followed in 1991 by Healthway in Western Australia. While no two of the Australian foundations are identical, the following description of the Western Australian Health Promotion Foundation (known as Healthway) illustrates the principal concepts.

Healthway was established in 1991 under tobacco control legislation that outlawed the public promotion of tobacco products. Healthway is funded by a levy raised on the wholesale distribution of tobacco products. It uses about 60 per cent of its funds to sponsor *s*port, *a*rts and *r*acing *g*roups (SARGs) (racing includes horse, greyhound and motor car racing). SARGs may range from one-off small craft exhibitions to a series of State Theatre plays, or from coaching clinics for junior soccer players to professional league sports such as Australian Football League and National Basketball League teams.

When Healthway provides sponsorship funds (a grant) to a SARG, it simultaneously awards support funds to an independent health agency to promote a health message at the sport, arts or racing event (Figure 13.4). Health organisations (e.g., the National Heart Foundation, Cancer Foundation, Diabetes Australia, etc.) and their

Figure 13.3 Healthway's logo

messages (e.g., *Be Smoke Free, Be Active Every Day, Eat More Fruit and Veg, Be Sun Wise, Drinksafe*, etc.) for particular events are chosen primarily with regard to the nature of the event's audience or participants, and the state's health priority areas. For very small grants, and especially for rural and remote SARGs, rather than allocating funds to a health agency Healthway provides the SARG with a sponsorship support kit containing posters, decals, pamphlets and ideas for activities with regard to a specific health message.

Healthway also attempts to create healthy environments by negotiating where appropriate the introduction of smoke free areas, availability of low alcohol and non-alcohol alternatives, safe alcohol serving practices, provision of healthy food choices and sun protection measures such as shaded spectator areas and protective clothing. The latter are the equivalent of merchandising and stocking agreements in commercial sponsorship. Healthway also negotiates, where appropriate, facilitation of access by people with disabilities or low income disadvantage.

Matching sports, arts and racing events with health sponsors

In general, sponsors select organisations or events to sponsor for a combination of reasons, but the essential criteria are:

- the event's or organisation's spectators or members constitute the sponsor's target audience;
- the event's or organisation's image attributes match or, at least are not inconsistent with, the sponsor's desired corporate or brand image; and
- the cost of the sponsorship in terms of target audience numbers delivered is competitive with other means of reaching the target audience.

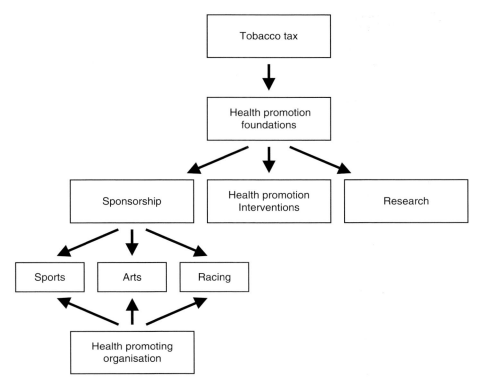

Figure 13.4 Healthway's sponsorship model

Jalleh *et al.* (2002)

In short, sponsors select events that attract their target market. In the commercial area, Schick razors sponsors the National Basketball Association's championships in the United States as basketball followers match the company's target market of 18–34-year-old males (Schlossberg 1996). The Scottish FA Cup audience consisted mostly of working-class males, one of the Scottish Health Education Group's main target groups (Hastings *et al.* 1988).

Other reasons for selecting a particular sponsee may be to pre-empt a competitor sponsoring the event (e.g., road safety authorities sponsoring a local football team to pre-empt an alcohol sponsor), the event may deliver a specific sub-group that is difficult to reach any other way (e.g., a surf carnival, a heavy metal rock concert), or the event may provide a means of reaching important opinion leaders in the community (e.g., a health authority taking a box at an international sporting event to meet local politicians, who will receive tickets to the event), or the event is popular with staff and attendance and involvement will boost morale (applies to commercial rather than social sponsorships).

> **Altruism or target marketing?**
>
> The pharmaceutical company Novo Nordisk raised a few eyebrows with its sponsorship of a one-day swimming meet in 2001. Why? Well, Novo Nordisk manufactures the performance enhancing growth hormone used by some swimming (and other) cheats. Novo Nordisk also manufactures diabetic medications and the meet was organised by US Olympic gold medallist Gary Hall Junior, a diabetic. Nevertheless, some were likening Novo Nordisk's sponsorship to that of tobacco or alcohol sponsorship – just not on! (Jeffery 2001). Just as using celebrities has sometimes had embarrassing outcomes, sponsor partnerships also need to be approached with care.

Through community surveys and surveys at events, Healthway has a good idea of the demographic and health profiles of audiences/spectators at various types of events. For example, race goers have higher than average smoking prevalence and lower than average physical activity levels; youth concertgoers have higher than average alcohol levels; football spectators have higher than average levels of physical activity, but also higher levels of alcohol consumption; arts audiences have lower than average smoking prevalence, but lower levels of physical activity; most audiences have lower than average levels of fruit and vegetable consumption, and so on.

However, some matches of message and event have to be carefully considered. For example, the National Heart Foundation's 'Eat Less Fat' and 'Eat More Fruit n' Veg' messages can yield the following sorts of problems at the races: The Eat Less Fat Stakes; The Fruit n' Veg Handicap. Similarly, the Diabetes Perth Cup just doesn't seem to match the excitement of a big race, and certainly doesn't have the glamour of the Marlboro Perth Cup.

Engaging the sponsored organisation

An important aspect is getting the sponsored organisation's staff and participants involved in or adopting the message. This appears more difficult with arts organisations that are sensitive to any sort of commercial intrusion on their 'artistic integrity', but appears to fit well with sporting organisations' members. For example, the Western Australian Football League (WAFL) is sponsored by the Office of Road Safety, primarily promoting the 'Belt Up' seat belt message. The WAFL ensures that all the players are fully aware of the sponsorship and the implications of internalising the sponsorship message. Players are asked to sign a 'pledge' to always wear their seat belt, and each player is asked to sign up eighteen friends (the number of players in a team) to also make the pledge. On the other hand, things can go wrong, as indicated in the following box. In a recent Victorian Traffic Accident Commission sponsorship deal with the Collingwood AFL club, players and officials will be given a personal breathalyser, a Cabcharge card for taxi use and a hands free mobile phone car kit in an effort to facilitate road safe behaviours all round. In addition, a code of conduct is being developed for players and officials.

> ## 'Drink drive, lose sponsor'
>
> The Victorian Traffic Accident Commission (TAC) sponsored the Richmond Tigers Aussie Rules team. The above headline appeared in a state newspaper following one of the team members being caught drink-driving. The TAC, which runs the 'Drink Drive, Bloody Idiot' campaign, was clearly not impressed, with the Tigers running the real risk of losing their sponsorship dollars. The TAC now includes penalties in its sponsorships if players or officials transgress road laws during the life of the sponsorship (Lyon 2002).

Co-operation between the health organisation sponsor and sponsee

Most major Western Australian health organisations now employ sponsorship officers (often Healthway funded), and Healthway also employs several sponsorship officers. In many cases, these health sponsorship officers have a more sophisticated understanding of sponsorship than their commercial counterparts. Similarly, many of the larger arts, sporting and racing organisations employ sponsorship officers. Co-operation between the two is essential for effective implementation of the sponsorship. Whereas initially most sponsored arts, racing and sports organisations were simply interested in the money and minimal compliance with Healthway's and the sponsor organisation's requirements, the situation has evolved to where many sponsored organisations have assumed partial responsibility for promotion of the health message and value its intrinsic benefits for its own members. Nevertheless, one must always be alert to potential problems like the following (see box).

> ## Keeping an eye on sponsees
>
> In one incident, Healthway discovered by chance that a junior football club they sponsored was to hold a raffle where the first prize was a trailer of beer, second prize was a wheelbarrow of beer and third prize was 'all you can carry'. This was hardly a 'message' that Healthway wanted to be seen to be condoning in a junior football club.

Evaluating health sponsorship: does it work?

Sponsorship, like advertising, can be used to achieve individual changes in beliefs, attitudes and behaviour. Sponsorship can also be used to negotiate structural change as a condition of the sponsorship. The Health Promotion Evaluation Unit (HPEU) at the University of Western Australia has undertaken a number of field studies, as well as designing a systematic evaluation of all the Western Australia Health Promotion Foundation's (Healthway) sponsorship activities. HPEU's research programme includes sponsorship awareness measures, as well as attempting to assess sponsorship's (actual and potential) behavioural effects and structural changes (see Donovan *et al.* 1999; Giles-Corti *et al.* 2001; Corti *et al.* 1997; Holman, Donovan and Corti 1993; Holman *et al.* 1996, 1997a, 1997b for examples). The next sections show how Healthway has used sponsorship to achieve individual and structural change.

Using sponsorship to achieve individual change

In 1992, the research team designed a system for the evaluation of health promotion and sponsorship projects sponsored by Healthway. The system, known as graduated project evaluation (GPE), attempts to systematically evaluate an organisation's sponsorship programme. GPE aims to match an appropriate level of evaluation to each sponsorship project. The GPE structure originally consisted of four evaluation levels, with the main criterion for assignment of GPE levels being the dollar amount of sponsorship (i.e., GPE level 1 for <$10,000, level 2 for $10,001–$25,000, level 3 for $25,001–$100,000 and level 4 for $100,00+) (for details of the GPE see Holman, Donovan and Corti 1993).

The evaluation required for GPE level 3 projects includes assessing the sponsored health message in terms of impact measures: health message awareness; comprehension; acceptance; intention; and action. The first three levels primarily refer to process evaluation as they relate specifically to the health message *per se*. The last two levels refer to impact and outcome evaluation as they relate to the effect of the message on behavioural intentions and actual behaviour.

In this section, we first present results from Healthway's GPE analysis. We then present examples of field studies that more directly assess the effects of sponsorship on (a) attitudes and (b) behaviour. We present the results for Healthway's early years for several reasons: first and foremost, these show the sponsorship effects that occurred immediately after introducing the sponsorship programme; second, a perusal of even the latest sponsorship literature (Madill and O'Reilly 2009; Walliser 2003) indicates that these Healthway results appear to be the only published, systematic evaluation of a sponsorship programme; third, the same methodology continues today (Ferguson, Mills and Rosenberg 2009) and is a useful extension of research methods introduced in Chapter 7.

Early GPE results: 1996/7 versus 1992/3

Data were gathered by professional interviewers at sponsored events. A combination of self-administered and interviewer administered questionnaires was used, and there were some variations by the life stage of the respondents (i.e., adult, teenager or child). Children aged 10 years or above were eligible to participate in the surveys. The questionnaires contained a core set of items so as to allow the data to be combined across projects, questionnaire type and respondent type. Interviews were conducted at the sponsored venues either during an interval or post-event. Interviewers were assigned to specific locations at the venues and were given instructions on the selection of respondents so as to ensure as far as possible, a random sample of patrons. Further details of the methodology can be found in Holman, Donovan and Corti (1993).

Table 13.1 Cognitive impact measures as a proportion of each preceding level

Measure	1992/3 (n = 5,684) Total sample (%)	1996/7 (n = 2,579) Total sample (%)
Total awareness	67	76
Comprehension	82	90
Acceptance	88	88
Intention	9	12
Action	21	23

There were thirty-three projects included in the 1996/7 sample (n = 2,579 respondents) and fifty-five in the 1992/3 sample (n = 5,710 respondents). Approximately equal proportions of males and females were interviewed at each time. In 1992/3, 49 per cent of respondents were under 20 years of age, compared with 37 per cent of respondents in 1996/7. No attempt was made to attain similar sample demographics at each time point as the samples reflect the populations attending these Healthway sponsored events at that time.

There were sixteen different messages – across seven health areas – allocated to sponsorships in 1996/7 and twenty-one (nine areas) in 1992/3. In general, the distribution of message topics was similar for the most frequently allocated messages. The most frequent health areas (messages) in both periods were smoking (Quit, SmokeFree), followed by nutrition (Eat More Fruit n' Veg), physical activity (Be Active) and sun protection (Sunsmart). Full details can be found in Donovan, Corti and Jalleh (1997) and Donovan *et al.* (1997a).

All respondents were first asked whether they could recall seeing or hearing any health messages at the event. Interviewer administered questionnaires then measured prompted awareness by presenting respondents with a list of messages and asking which they recalled seeing or hearing at the event. Respondents who were aware of the message at the event were then asked what they understood the message to mean (comprehension), and, if correct, were asked their attitude towards the message (acceptance). All respondents accepting the message (other than the child self-administered questionnaire respondents) were asked what thoughts, if any, they had about the message. Further, if they had seen the message at a previous event, they were asked whether they had taken any action as a result. Respondents' stated thoughts were analysed and those who expressed an intention to take action as a result of exposure to the message were identified. Action (and intention) includes any actions (or intentions) related to the message, not just adoption and continuation of the recommended behaviour. It also includes not only personal actions, but those related to encouraging others to adopt or continue a recommended behaviour. Table 13.1 shows the cognitive impact measures as a proportion of each preceding level in the hierarchy.

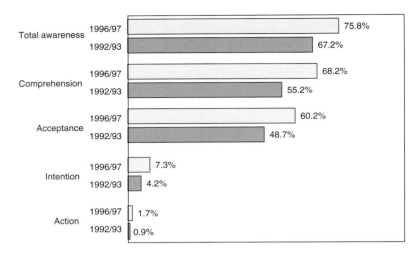

Figure 13.5 Cognitive impact measures as a proportion of the total sample 1992/3 and 1996/7

Total awareness of the sponsored health messages at events increased significantly in the four years following introduction of the programme, from 67 per cent in 1992/3 to 76 per cent in 1996/7 ($p < 0.05$). Message comprehension among respondents who were aware of the sponsored message increased slightly in 1996/7 from an already high level: 90 per cent (compared with 82 per cent in 1992/3). Acceptance of the message among those who were aware of and correctly understood the message remained high in 1996/7: 88 per cent (the same as in 1992/3).

Intention to act on the message increased, but not significantly: of respondents who agreed with the message, 12 per cent (compared with 9 per cent in 1992/3) mentioned that they would or wanted to do the recommended behaviour. Respondents who were aware of the sponsored message at a previous event were asked what they did, if anything, as a result of being aware of the health message. In both 1992/3 and 1996/7, approximately one in five of these respondents took some relevant action (21 per cent and 23 per cent, respectively).

Multiplying the preceding proportions down the hierarchy of effects provides an estimate of the percentage of the total sample sufficiently stimulated to take some relevant action as a result of exposure to a health message. These results for both 1996/7 and 1992/3 are shown in Figure 13.5. That is, of all people attending Healthway sponsored events 76 per cent were aware of a Healthway sponsored message at the event, 68 per cent correctly understood the message, 60 per cent accepted or agreed with the message, 7 per cent formed some intention to act on the message and 1.7 per cent claimed to have taken some action as a result of prior exposure. These data show a substantial increase in action over previous years (1.7 per cent compared with 0.9 per cent), and, consistent with Lacey *et al.* (2007), probably reflect the cumulative effect of many of these or related messages now being seen for a number of years at the same types of events.

This hierarchical multiplicative exercise shows the importance of achieving high levels of effects early in the hierarchy. Thus, the higher the level of awareness that can be achieved, the greater the likelihood of achieving behaviour change in the target group.

With regard to process evaluation, these data show that the sponsorship messages were receiving good exposure at events, and that the health messages used are well understood and accepted by event patrons. These are clearly necessary prerequisites for persuasion and subsequent behaviour change. Intentions to act on the health messages and behavioural outcomes are also acceptable and show an increase from 1992/3 to 1996/7. The increases achieved for all stages in the hierarchy of cognitive effects are not only likely to be related to increased exposure of audiences to health messages over time, but also to more effective sponsorship strategies being adopted by sponsorship officers. While the absolute numbers were small, commercial organisations would be quite happy to achieve behavioural effects in 1–2 per cent of the target audience

Current GPE results: 2004/5 to 2008/9

Figure 13.6 (from Ferguson, Mills and Rosenberg 2009) shows the current GPE results. The sample sizes for the years 2004/5, 2006/7 and 2008/9 were 1,851 respondents (twenty-eight events), 2,389 respondents (thirty-four events) and 2,407 respondents (thirty-four events), respectively. While some health messages had remained the same, the majority had changed since 1992/3, when they were dominated by tobacco control messages.

Figure 13.6 shows that awareness at the events in 2004/5 had declined since 1996/7, but had returned to the 1996/7 level by 2008/9. However, in spite of awareness levels remaining much the same, the implementation of the sponsorships was having far more impact on intentions and behaviour in 2008/9 than in the early years. This appears to be largely due to the sponsorship implementations being more interactive.

Field studies measuring awareness and attitudinal effects

Awareness (salience) effects

Donovan *et al.* (1993) showed that the relative salience of factors preventing heart disease varied as to whether respondents had been exposed to a 'be active' versus a 'fruit n' veg' sponsorship. The study was a quasi-experimental field design. The National Heart Foundation (NHF) was the support sponsor to the State Theatre for a series of season plays. The NHF chose two health messages to be featured during the season: 'Be active every day' and 'Eat more fruit n' veg'. The nutrition slogan was

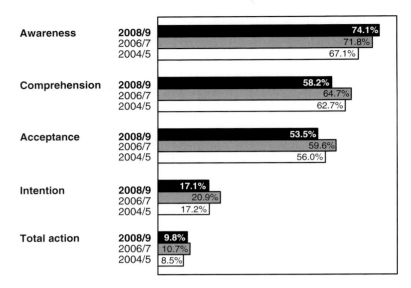

Figure 13.6 Cognitive impact measures as a proportion of the total sample 2004/5 to 2008/9

allocated to one play and the exercise slogan to another (both slogans were promoted at a third play). Face-to-face interviews were carried out as people left the theatre at the conclusion of the plays. Prior to any questions about health or sponsorship, respondents were asked: 'When you think of ways to prevent heart disease, what comes to mind?' When 'Be active' was the health message, 'exercise' responses were first to mind for 49 per cent of the sample (15 per cent responded with 'nutrition' responses); when 'fruit n' veg' was the health message, 'nutrition' responses were first to mind for 50 per cent of the sample (26 per cent responded with 'exercise' responses).

Attitudinal effects

Donovan *et al.* (1993) used a pre–post independent samples design to assess attitude effects of a health sponsor (Quit) and two commercial sponsors (a bank and a motor vehicle), at a major sporting event. Respondents in pre- and post-interviews were presented, in turn, with a set of banks and a set of motor vehicles and asked: 'If you were going to [buy a new car, open a new bank account], which of these would you be most interested in receiving more information about? And next most? And next?' Respondents were also presented with a set of health behaviours and asked: 'If you were interested in becoming more healthy, which of these would you most like more information on? And next most? And next?' The behaviours included quitting smoking or assisting someone else to do so, diet, exercise and relaxation.

The Quit sponsorship showed a near significant pre–post increase in the proportion nominating smoking behaviour (first preference: 10.4 per cent to 17.6 per cent); the car sponsor obtained a non-significant increase in pre–post preferences (first preference: 13.5 per cent to 20.0 per cent); but there was no change in preferences for the bank sponsor. There was a positive relationship between sponsor recall and sponsorship impact: Quit was recalled as a sponsor by 40 per cent versus 33 per cent for the car sponsor and 26 per cent for the bank sponsor. Donovan *et al.* (1993) concluded that sheer exposure to the Quit sponsorship appeared to result in a situational, temporary increase in positive attitudes towards attempting to quit or encouraging someone else to do so.

Further field studies were conducted to extend the Donovan *et al.* (1993) study by measuring sponsorship effects on both awareness and attitudes, and by investigating the cognitive processing that occurs as a result (Jalleh 1999). A pre–post independent samples design was used to assess sponsorship effectiveness in terms of awareness and attitude objectives at an Australian Rules football event. To allow assessment of both awareness and attitude effects without prior questions contaminating later measures, two pre- and two post-samples were taken at the event. One health and two commercial sponsors were assessed at the event: Respect Yourself (an alcohol moderation message), and two commercial sponsors, GM Holden and ANZ Bank. Only male drinkers aged 18–30 years were interviewed at the football as they are the major target group for the Respect Yourself message. Each of the evaluated sponsors had approximately the same area of perimeter and other signage at the event.

Face-to-face intercept interviewing of patrons was carried out by professional market research interviewers. Interviewers were assigned to specific locations at the venues and were given instructions on the selection of respondents so as to ensure, as far as possible, a random sample of patrons. Pre-interviews were carried out prior to entry to the event. Post-interviews were carried out in the venues from half time to the end of the event. Two sets of pre- and post-questionnaires were developed. One set of pre- and post-questionnaires focused on awareness and the other on attitude measures.

A recall (salience) measure was used to assess brand awareness: 'When you think of …[cars, banks, alcohol], what [brands, banks, health messages or slogans] … come to mind? Any others? Any others?' In both the pre- and post-awareness questionnaires, these questions were asked immediately after the preliminary screening questions. Order of presentation of brand/health issue was rotated across respondents.

The brand attitude measure followed that of Donovan *et al.* (1993). Respondents, in both pre- and post-conditions, were presented, in turn, with a set of seven banks (including ANZ) and a set of six motor vehicle manufacturers (including Holden) and asked: 'If you were going to [open a new bank account, buy a new car], which of these would you be most interested in receiving more information about? And next most? And next?' Respondents were also presented with a set of six health behaviours and asked: 'If you were interested in becoming more healthy, which of these would you

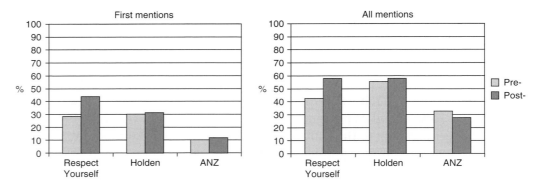

Figure 13.7 Pre–post awareness for sponsored brands and health message

most like more information on? And next most? And next?' The behaviours included quitting smoking, assisting someone to quit smoking, reducing alcohol consumption, nutrition, exercising and relaxation methods. Order of presentation of brand/health issue was rotated across respondents. In both the pre- and post-attitude questionnaires, these questions were asked immediately after the preliminary screening questions. A total of 400 football patrons was interviewed for the attitude study: pre-: n = 204 and post-: n = 196.

Awareness change

There was no impact on levels of awareness for the Holden and ANZ Bank football sponsorships, but a significant impact for the Respect Yourself sponsorship for first mentions (pre-: 28.4 per cent, post-: 43.7 per cent; p = .002) and all mentions (pre-: 42.7 per cent, post-: 58.2 per cent; p = 0.003) (see Figure 13.7).

Attitude change

There was no impact on attitude for the Holden sponsorship, a significant impact for the ANZ Bank sponsorship in terms of first mentions (pre-: 9.8 per cent, post-: 17.3 per cent; p = 0.027), and a significant impact for the Respect Yourself sponsorship for both first mentions (pre-: 1.5 per cent, post-: 8.2 per cent; p = 0.002) and all mentions (pre-: 17.6 per cent, post-: 25.5 per cent; p = 0.056) (see Figure 13.8).

The apparently greater impact of the health message may be due, at least in part, to the scarcity of health messages at these events. Respect Yourself was the only health message promoted at the football. At both venues, while the commercial brand names were the only ones in their respective product categories, there were numerous other commercial sponsors. Furthermore, since health sponsorships began in the early 1990s, they may still be a 'novelty', and as such, attract more attention relative to commercial sponsorships.

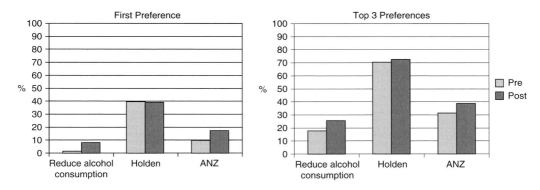

Figure 13.8 Pre–post preferences for sponsored brands and health message

The superiority of the health sponsorships over the commercial sponsorships also may be due to the implementation of the sponsorships. The health sponsor was more enthusiastic and leveraged their sponsorship more through promotional strategies such as distributing merchandise. Furthermore, Healthway had negotiated the supply and prominent display of low alcohol beer in bars at the football venue. In addition, Respect Yourself sponsored the Fremantle Dockers football team in the Australian Football League. In contrast, the commercial sponsors did not engage in any activities other than signage.

Hence, sponsorship can have a significant impact on awareness and attitude objectives; however, this impact appears to be dependent on how the sponsorship is implemented.

Field studies measuring behavioural effects

Quasi-experimental field studies are also used to assess behavioural effects. For example, as reported in Chapter 7, observational data were collected at three junior sporting codes (rugby union, basketball, Australian Rules football) before and after a mouthguard sponsorship. The sponsorship was implemented in the rugby and basketball competitions with the Australian Rules football serving as control. The sponsorship involved partnerships with dental organisations who offered high quality mouthguards at reduced prices. At competition events and training sessions, all players present on particular dates were inspected as to whether they were wearing a mouthguard. Face-to-face surveys were also undertaken with a sample of players and coaches to assess awareness of the sponsorship. Results showed a significant increase in mouthguard usage in competition events among both intervention codes (rugby: 77 per cent to 84 per cent; basketball: 23 per cent to 43 per cent) relative to the football controls (72 per cent to 73 per cent) (Jalleh *et al.* 2001).

Using sponsorship to achieve structural change

An important benefit for health sponsors is the implementation of policies that create healthier recreational and cultural environments (Giles-Corti *et al.* 2001). This is equivalent to a commercial sponsor's merchandising agreements. It involves, for example, depending on the nature of the venue and type of event, the introduction of smoke-free areas, sun protection, healthy food choices and, where alcohol is served, policies favouring the sale of low to mid strength products, as well as the implementation of responsible serving practices.

Theoretical underpinnings

Working with other sectors to create health enhancing environments in settings commonly used by people in the course of their daily lives is consistent with a social ecological approach to public health (Stokols, Allen and Bellingham 1996). It acknowledges that individual behaviour change is more likely to be sustained if it takes place in supportive social and physical environments. This is because of a dynamic interplay between observable behaviour, an individual's cognitive response and physical and social environments.

Why promote health in recreational settings?

Promoting health in recreational settings provides opportunities to reach hard-to-reach groups in the community (Olsen 1999). There is substantial evidence that large numbers of Australians regularly access these settings and many have elevated risk factors compared with the general population. This was particularly evident with those attending sports events, but also in those attending arts events for selected risk factor areas (e.g., alcohol consumption) (for more details see Holman *et al.* 1997a). A review of national health policy reports found that many referred to the potential role that recreational or cultural settings could play in achieving national health goals including injury, alcohol consumption, nutrition, sun protection and passive smoking (NHMRC 1997).

Healthway's main objective is related to tobacco control. To date, Healthway has successfully negotiated for the main areas of the football, speedway, baseball and soccer venues to be smoke-free – including outdoor seating areas.

Achieving healthy public policy reform involves a process of diffusion (Rogers 1995), which in recreational settings in Western Australia moved sport, arts and racing groups along a continuum of change. At each stage of the diffusion process, different strategies were required. Initially as part of the sponsor benefit negotiations, Healthway requested the creation of demarcated smoke-free areas. However, these policies were expanded as sponsorship agreements were re-negotiated to require organisations to

Figure 13.9 Billboard announcing baseball field being smoke-free

become completely smoke-free. In 1996, Healthway's board voted in favour of making it a condition of sponsorship that all indoor areas under the control of the sponsored organisation must be smoke free (Figure 13.9). This decision enabled Healthway to negotiate additional sponsor benefits such as policies to serve low or mid strength beers in favour of full strength beers.

A number of studies have shown that these policies have been effective. For example, following the introduction of a policy banning smoking in all indoor and outdoor seated areas at the home ground for two Western Australian-based national football teams sponsored by Healthway, spectator surveys were conducted to determine awareness of, agreement with and support for the smoke-free venue policies (Jones, Corti and Donovan 1996). Approximately three-quarters of spectators were aware of the policy (74 per cent), and the vast majority of those aware of the policy were supportive (82 per cent). There were high levels of awareness and support of the policy in smokers and non-smokers. In 1998, a similar survey was carried out. Awareness of the smoke-free policy increased to 81 per cent of respondents, and the vast majority of those aware of the policy were supportive (almost 80 per cent).

To assess the extent to which smoke-free policies at sporting events were implemented and adhered to, two observational studies were conducted (Pikora *et al.* 1999). One was conducted at Perth's premier football oval in 1997 (Subiaco Oval) and the other at the WACA, Perth's premier cricket ground in 1998. These two major venues had introduced smoke-free policies in indoor and outdoor seated areas as a result of

Table 13.2 Results of observational studies

	Subiaco Oval	WACA
Estimated number of people in the study area[a]	4,616	3,596
Estimated number of smokers in the study area	969	539
Number observed smoking in study area	8	0
Number of butts found in the study area before the game	0	0
Number of butts found in the study area after the game	6	2

[a] Based on spectator surveys of those entering the venue.

Table 13.3 Smoke-free policies in place in the majority of venues used by sports, arts and racing organisations sponsored by Healthway, 1992–7

Year	n	%
1992[a]	118	77.1
1994	292	85.9
1997	434	95.6[b]

[a] Percentages for 1992 may over-represent Healthway's influence because it includes policies within organisations and/or in the majority of venues they use.
[b] Compared with 1994: ***$p < 0.001$.

Healthway sponsorship. Some 4,616 people were observed at Subiaco Oval and 3,596 at the WACA. Using binoculars, observers systematically scanned spectators seated in randomly selected smoke-free areas throughout the grounds to determine adherence to the policy. Table 13.2 shows the results of the observations. As can be seen, there was a high level of compliance with the smoke-free policies at both events, suggesting that the policies were implemented and adhered to.

Mail surveys were conducted in mid-1992 (n = 269), 1994 (n = 511) and 1997 (n = 536) (Clarkson *et al.* 1998) of all sports, arts and racing organisations that had commenced Healthway funded projects during the previous twelve months. Response rates of 91 per cent, 78 per cent and 80 per cent, respectively were achieved. Among other things, organisations were asked whether they had introduced policies restricting smoking. As shown in Table 13.3, the percentage of organisations reporting a smoke-free policy increased significantly between 1994 and 1997 ($p < 0.001$).

Community surveys were conducted in mid-1992 (n = 2,629), 1994 (n = 2,009) and 1998 (n = 1,337) and involved randomly selected members of the general population aged 16–69 years (Clarkson *et al.* 2000). Personal interviews were used in the metro-politan area and telephone interviews were used in country areas, with the sample

Table 13.4 Smoke-free area policies present in the main sports or racing club or arts organisation in which community members involved in 1992, 1994 and 1998

	All respondents					
	n			%		
	1992	1994	1998	1992	1994	1998
Smoke-free area policies	1,059	755	506			
No smoking allowed anywhere	302	265	205	29	36	41
No smoking except for special smoking areas	119	122	126	11	16	25
Smoking allowed except for special non-smoking areas	98	60	41	9	8	8
Smoking allowed anywhere	528	295	126	50	40	25
Don't know	–	–	3	–	–	–
Not applicable/missing	–	–	5	–	–	–

applied to ensure equal numbers of male and female respondents. One of the topics included access to smoke-free policies in the principal sports, racing or arts clubs to which respondents belonged.

In 1992, 29 per cent of respondents reported that their club was entirely smoke-free, and a further 11 per cent reported that the club was mostly smoke-free with special smoking areas (see Table 13.4). In 1994, these proportions increased to 36 per cent and 16 per cent, respectively, and in 1998, they increased to 41 per cent and 25 per cent, respectively. The trend towards entirely smoke-free sports, arts and racing clubs was statistically significant (χ^2 test for trend = 10.03, $p = 0.001$)

Comment on structural impact studies

These studies indicate that with financial resources initially generated by a levy on tobacco products and an understanding of the process of bringing about change in organisations, health organisations can 'purchase' healthy structural reform in sectors outside of health.

Consistent with international research (Jeffery *et al.* 1990) and national research (Jones, Wakefield and Turnbull 1999), the results indicate that the introduction of smoke-free policies may change community norms about smoking in public. Earlier surveys of smoking and non-smoking spectators at football events indicated that there was little support for the introduction of smoke-free policies in outdoor areas. However, following the introduction of these policies in Western Australia's premier football stadium, support among spectators for the smoke-free policies increased markedly, particularly among non-smokers who have most to gain from a reduction in exposure to passive smoking. The successful introduction of smoke-free policies may indeed normalise non-smoking within recreational and cultural settings.

The extent to which smoking restrictions in recreational settings contribute to a reduction in smoking is not clear. Studies conducted in the United States and Australia indicate that policies restricting smoking in the workplace (Farkas *et al.* 1999; Farrelly *et al.* 1999; Owen and Borland 1997) and in households (Farkas *et al.* 1999) are associated with a reduction in smoking by smokers and lower rates of smoking by adolescents (Farkas *et al.* 2000). They also significantly reduce non-smokers' exposure to tobacco smoke and consequent respiratory and other diseases (Wilson and Thomson 2002). Although there is some evidence that the impact of smoking restrictions may diminish over time, it appears that in the long term the net result is a reduction in cigarette consumption. While the direct influence on smokers of smoke-free policies in recreational settings remains unknown, it is likely these policies create supportive environments and positive social norms for non-smoking behaviours (Thomson and Wilson 2006).

Concluding comments

Giles-Corti *et al.* (2001) suggest that lessons from Healthway's experience have wider application, particularly in developing countries where the tobacco industry actively uses tobacco advertising and sponsorship to market tobacco products.

Healthway's approach to achieving reform in recreational and cultural settings is instructive and may be applied elsewhere.

- First, it involved working collaboratively with other agencies including those in health, recreational and cultural sectors.
- Second, it involved a 'small wins' incremental approach (Weick 1984) that increased the prevalence of smoke-free policies, while gaining the support of various stakeholders, including the general public.
- Third, it involved comprehensive evaluation of its sponsorship activities, including community attitudes towards reform.
- Finally, it involved communicating evaluation results to all stakeholders.

Since the use of health and commercial sponsorships will continue to grow in the future, more research is required to build the knowledge base of how sponsorship works and its impact on those exposed to the sponsorship. Overall, a number of studies provide evidence that health sponsorships have an impact on awareness of health issues, attitudes towards various healthy behaviours and on intentions and behaviour; however, this impact appears to be dependent on how the sponsorship is implemented.

QUESTIONS

● How does sponsorship differ from advertising and other promotional strategies?

● How would you determine what organisation or event you would sponsor if you wanted to (a) reduce violence against women or (b) reduce alcohol consumption?

● How many alcohol sponsors are there of sporting teams and events in your locality? How would you argue for their removal?

FURTHER READING

Holman, C. D. J., Donovan, R. J., Corti, B., Jalleh, G., Frizzell, S. K. and Carroll, A. M. 1996. Evaluating Projects Funded by the Western Australian Health Promotion Foundation: First Results, *Health Promotion International* 11: 75–88.

Jalleh, G. J., Donovan, R. J., Giles-Corti, B. and Holman, C. D. J. 2002. Sponsorship: Impact on Brand Awareness and Brand Attitudes, *Social Marketing Quarterly* 8(1): 35–45.

Ireland Alcohol Marketing, Communications and Sponsorship Codes of Practice 2008. Available at: www.iapi.ie/download.php?s=taskforces&f=1235666539_Alcohol_sponsorship-Legal_alcohol.pdf, accessed 7 October 2009.

Meenaghan, T. 2001. Understanding Sponsorship Effects, *Psychology and Marketing* 18(2): 95–122.

Walliser, B. 2003. An International Review of Sponsorship Research: Extension and Upgrade, *International Journal of Advertising* 22(1).

Planning and developing social marketing campaigns and programmes

This chapter presents a number of models that assist in developing and implementing social marketing interventions. Although we have used the terms 'campaign' and 'programme' interchangeably in much of this book, or have simply referred to 'interventions', we first note the differences between planning for what might be called a 'campaign' and what might be called a 'programme'. We then re-present our communication campaign planning model from Chapter 5 and extend it to campaign components before presenting more comprehensive models applicable to developing larger scale programmes.

Campaign versus programme

The public health area generally avoids the distinction between these two terms by referring to 'interventions'; that is, actions taken to alter or influence a state of affairs, where actions may be paid or unpaid media activities, changes in policies and regulations, development of school curricula modules, health worker training and so on. However, even public health professionals generally distinguish between a 'campaign' and a 'programme', although the distinction is often based on interventions that make substantial use of mass media ('campaigns') versus those that do not ('programmes').

For our purposes the term campaign is more applicable to limited scope, limited duration interventions, whereas the word programme is more applicable to broad scope, longer duration interventions. The Freedom from Fear initiative that targets men who use violence against their female intimate partners to call a helpline and enrol in a counselling course is usually referred to as the 'Freedom from Fear campaign'. Although there are secondary target groups, there is a single primary target group being encouraged to take clearly defined actions, and primarily during the period when the helpline number is publicised. A broader initiative addressing the issue of violence against women would include other target groups and other strategies, such as interventions targeting how police and the justice system respond to violence against women; interventions targeting young men in their teenage years, and especially as they begin to form relationships with women; interventions targeting young women in those same years as to how they might identify and avoid disrespectful and abusive relationships; adequate refuges and counselling for women and children victims of male violence;

interventions targeting media and entertainment images, including pornography, that demean or condone violence against, women and so on. Where these various components are integrated and co-ordinated to achieve an overarching goal over the long term, we would describe this as a programme to reduce violence against women.

In practice, a comprehensive programme can be viewed as including a number of campaigns with limited scope and limited duration. For example, within the overall programme against violence against women, there may be a short-term advocacy campaign targeting lawmakers and police to introduce temporary exclusion orders where rather than women (and children) having to seek the safety of a refuge, men who use violence are removed from the home after a violent incident and not allowed to return for 24, 48 or 72 hours depending on the incident. Hence, we need both broad and limited scope planning models.

The multi-level, multi-strategy Agita São Paulo physical activity intervention in Brazil is a good example of a comprehensive programme consisting of a number of specific campaigns (Matsudo *et al.* 2003). This programme covers the 40 million people within the state of São Paulo and involves over 300 state and local partners. The programme targets individuals to increase their levels of physical activity and targets municipalities and state departments to introduce policies that encourage physical activity, including in architectural, transport and natural geographic domains. The programme uses a variety of methods, including mass and targeted media, mass events, community meetings, training, etc. to achieve its goals in each of its targeted areas (see Matsudo *et al.* 2003, 2004). This is also a very good example of evaluation methods over a broad variety of domains (Matsudo *et al.* 2006).

Communication planning model as campaign planning model

In Chapter 5 we introduced the six-step communication model and showed how this could be used as a communication planning model by reversing the steps from exposure to effects. That model focused on developing communication components of a campaign. However, the framework can be applied to any intervention component:

Step 1:   What is the overall programme goal that the campaign must help to achieve?

Step 2:   What specific objectives do we want this particular campaign to achieve?

Step 3:   Who do we need to impact to achieve our goal and what do we want them to do? (target segments).

Step 4:   What overall strategies or types of intervention will be necessary to reach each of these target groups? (education, regulation, changes in risky products and places, etc.).

Step 5:   For each target group, what place, price, product, promotion and people mix will bring about the desired behaviour change?

Step 6:   For each target group, how will we monitor progress towards the specific behavioural objectives and evaluate the intervention components?

For example, given the importance of early childhood as outlined in Chapter 3, a nation may adopt an overall policy goal of 'creating a more positive socio-cultural environment so that the nation's children are protected from harm and have the opportunity to maximise their development potential', based on the following:

- the importance of early childhood as crucial not just for the health and wellbeing of children *per se*, but also in their future years as teens and adults;
- levels of child abuse and neglect are unacceptably high;
- many children currently fail to optimise their full potential;
- children represent a nation's human capital; and
- the greater the wellbeing of children, the greater economic and other contributions they will make as adults to the nation's wealth.

We might then develop a five-year programme to first change the way a society views and values its children, so that legislative, policy and resource allocations can be shifted to provide more facilities and services that will afford greater protection for children and greater optimisation of their potential. Following the above six-step model, at step 3 we might identify the following primary target groups: parents and carers; professionals working directly with children and youth (such as teachers, junior coaches, paediatricians, community nurses, etc.) and the tertiary institutions providing their training; urban planners and designers; local, state and federal politicians; journalists and media professionals; and children and youth themselves.

We would then identify an appropriate strategy and tools (intervention types) to reach and impact each of these. For example we might consider:

- mass media advertising, publicity and edutainment targeting parents, carers and the general population (and indirectly, all other target groups);
- use of political lobbyists and evidence-based reports for politicians on how early interventions such as prenatal courses, parenting courses, pre-school programmes, access to child care, etc. improve the health and wellbeing of children and enhance their development potential;
- evidence-based reports for urban planners on how the built environment can be made safer for children and enhance their involvement in healthy social and recreational activities;
- media packs showing the impact that negative reporting on children and youth has on children and youth, as well as the general population; and
- relevant curriculum materials for educators.

Given an overall strategy and specific goals for each target group, we would then begin to develop the specific product, place, price and promotion strategies for each along with relevant evaluation methods. Opinion polling on children's issues would monitor changes in beliefs and attitudes in the general population, and measures such as the introduction of child friendly policies in local governments and federal budget allocations to children's services would indicate progress at those levels.

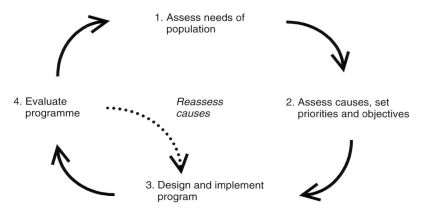

Figure 14.1 Green's basic steps in programme planning and implementation

Green (1999)

Overall programme planning models

A number of planning models have been described or proposed in the social marketing and health promotion literature. Perhaps the simplest distillation is that above originating in health promotion (Figure 14.1; Green 1999).

In this model, phase 1 implies an epidemiological approach to identifying populations at risk and determining needs overall. In the health area this is reflected in a nation's defined health priorities.

In phase 2, risk factors are identified, both behavioural (e.g., alcohol, tobacco, physical inactivity, diet, unsafe driving behaviours, criminal offences) and structural (e.g., poor housing, unemployment, unsafe work environments, racial and other discrimination, abuse), along with Green's predisposing, enabling and reinforcing factors (Green and Kreuter 2005).

Phase 3 attempts to bring about changes in the determinants of the behaviours and conditions being targeted, hence, delivering the desired social outcomes. Evaluation of programmes leads eventually to re-assessments in phase 1, and, in the short term, to re-assessment of programme components and assessments in phase 2.

Based apparently on a model from the Center for Communications Programs at the Johns Hopkins University, the Academy for Educational Development (AED), Washington DC, used a similar framework to that above (Day and Monroe 2000) (Figure 14.2).

In a further variation, Egger, Spark and Donovan (2005) delineate their five-stage SOPIE model for health promotion interventions: situational analysis; objective setting; planning; implementation; evaluation. The SOPIE approach has been used in Pacific Island countries to help structure interventions aimed at reducing chronic non-communicable diseases, such as diabetes and obesity, as well as in smaller-scale

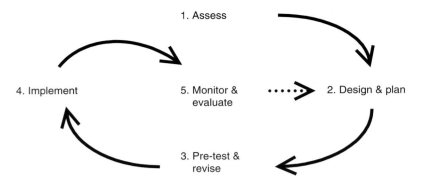

Figure 14.2 AED's basic steps in programme planning and implementation

Day and Monroe (2000)

Table 14.1 The SOPIE model for health promotion interventions
• **Situational analysis**: identifying the issue, specifying the problem, identifying potential target audiences and strategies, assessing resources, formative research.
• **Objective setting**: defining overall goals and campaign goals, specific behavioural and communication objectives for the target audiences.
• **Planning**: devising message strategies, developing and pre-testing materials, selecting media, identifying supporting components.
• **Implementation**: developing detailed programme procedures, involving other sectors and stakeholders, programme management.
• **Evaluation**: campaign monitoring, process and outcome evaluation.
Egger, Spark and Donovan (2005)

social experiments, such as in encouraging older people to eat more fibre. The stages of the process are shown in Table 14.1 (from Egger, Spark and Donovan 2005).

An important point is that all of the above models stress that planning is an iterative process whereby objectives, strategies and methods are continually revised in the light of what is viable given such things as the nature and extent of the problem, the nature and accessibility of the target audience(s) and the limitations of financial and other resources.

One point we would add is the need to maintain political support for interventions with long-term outcomes. This should be built in to the implementation phase. It is vital to brief and support incoming ministers and heads of department when changes occur in cabinet or in governing parties.

Lawrence Green's PRECEDE–PROCEED model

The PRECEDE–PROCEED model is probably the most widely used planning model in the health promotion literature and in practice, and is being increasingly applied also in social marketing. A recent survey of members of the Australian Health Promotion Association found that the PRECEDE–PROCEED was the model most frequently used for programme planning and implementation (Jones and Donovan 2004), and Green's website lists about 1,000 publications referring to the model, with most of them involving an application of it. Applications range from the usual areas of tobacco, nutrition, physical activity, sun protection, road safety and alcohol, to occupational health, domestic violence, periodontal treatment and juvenile rheumatoid arthritis [and even how to get university professors to be more productive: 'Using the PRECEDE–PROCEED Model to Increase Productivity in Health Education Faculty' (Ransdell 2001)].

The PRECEDE–PROCEED model has been applied in a variety of countries, including India, Nepal, Taiwan, France, the Netherlands, Australia, Canada, France and Spain, and among various ethnic sub-groupings in the United States and Canada (see www.lgreen.net/precede.htm; includes a version of the model in Japanese). The model is shown in Figure 14.3 and the use of the model to develop a mental health intervention is shown in Figure 14.4 (from Wright *et al.* 2006).

The value of Green's model (which has undergone a number of modifications since first presented as just PRECEDE), is that it makes explicit that the factors analysed in the planning and development phases (the PRECEDE phases) are the same factors to be considered in the implementation and evaluation phases (PROCEED).

PRECEDE is an acronym for *P*redisposing, *R*einforcing and *E*nabling *C*onstructs in *E*ducational (and *E*nvironmental) *D*iagnosis and *E*valuation. According to Spark (1999), who applied the model to his Ph.D. thesis on health promotion in Indigenous communities, the PRECEDE framework was novel in that it focused on outcomes rather than inputs, forcing the health practitioner to begin the planning process from the outcome end (which we do with the basic communication planning model). It was also comprehensive in that each of the original five phases in PRECEDE allows a different 'layer' of assessment: social; epidemiological; behavioural; educational; and administrative.

During the decade following the publication of PRECEDE, there was an acknowledgement in the international public health community that health education, with its emphasis on behavioural or lifestyle-related choices and individually-oriented programmes, was neglecting the importance of social factors in the aetiology of many diseases. This was crystallised in the declaration of the Ottawa Charter for Health Promotion, at a World Health Organization sponsored conference in 1986 in Ottawa, Canada (noted in Chapter 1). The Ottawa Charter described five principles for health promotion action as the basis for a 'new public health': strengthening community action; developing personal skills; building healthy public policy; reorienting health services; and creating supportive environments (World Health Organization 1986).

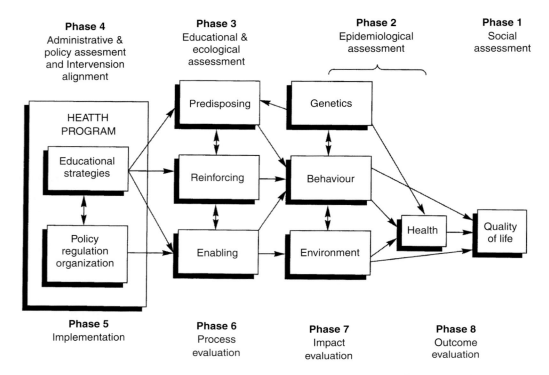

Figure 14.3 The PRECEDE–PROCEED model for health promotion planning and evaluation

Green and Kreuter (2005)

Reflecting this broadened scope, Green amended the PRECEDE model to give greater emphasis to environmental factors and expanded it to include PROCEED: an acronym for *Policy, Regulatory* and *Organisational Constructs* in *Educational* and *Environmental Development*. PROCEED includes resource mobilisation and evaluation, and is essentially an elaboration and extension of the original administrative diagnosis phase of PRECEDE. Overall, the addition of PROCEED to the original model gave greater emphasis to the contribution of structural factors and community organisation processes to programme implementation.

The social assessment involves assessing people's perceptions of their own needs and how the issue at hand impacts on their quality of life. For example, asthmatics and diabetics face certain restrictions on their lifestyle, have to comply with a medication schedule and have to visit a medical practitioner more often than average. Epidemiological analyses identify the relative importance of various health problems in various sub-groups of the population and the behavioural and environmental factors related to those health problems. For example, young males account for a higher proportion of road crashes than other groups; alcohol, speed and not wearing a seat

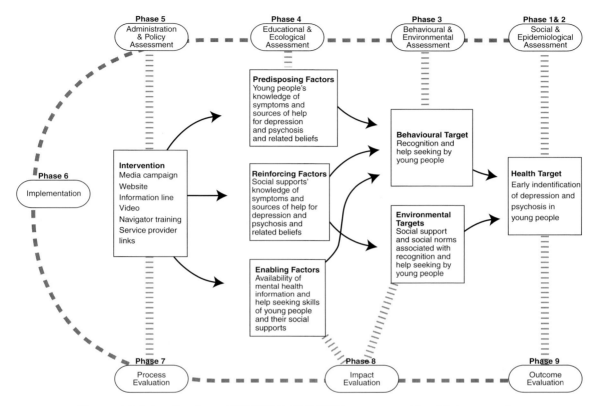

Figure 14.4 Application of PRECEDE–PROCEED to a mental health intervention

belt are related to crashes, severity of injury and mortality. Phases 1 and 2 correspond to the needs assessment phases in Figures 14.1 and 14.2.

Behavioural and environmental analyses look at the factors arising from epidemiological analyses in more depth, as well as behaviours and environmental aspects that may arise from clinical or other evidence. In road safety, the use of seat belts, driver education, driver skills, exceeding the speed limit, driving while tired, vehicular modifications, roadworthiness of vehicles, road conditions and placement of warning signs all require analysis in terms of such things as how important are they, how changeable are they and what resources are required to change them.

The educational and ecological assessment is the 'heart' of the model: it identifies the factors that must be changed to initiate or facilitate the desired behaviour and environmental changes. These factors then become the targets for the programme. The model proposes three types of factors:

• **predisposing factors** – individuals' beliefs, attitudes and perceptions that influence their decision to act (e.g., a belief that alcohol increases feelings of wellbeing and reduces one's shyness predisposes one to consume alcohol, a belief that alcohol is a poison or may lead to loss of control predisposes one to not consume alcohol);

• **reinforcing factors** – environmental factors that serve to reward or punish expression of the behaviour (e.g., friends' approval of one's speeding or drinking alcohol serves to reinforce the behaviour, a parent's clear disapproval of drug use serves to inhibit that behaviour);

• **enabling factors** – individual and environmental factors that make a behaviour possible (or not possible) to occur (e.g., having time and money facilitates joining a health club, smoke-free policies facilitate smoking cessation; i.e., skills, resources, support policies and services).

For example, following research with regard to drink-driving among male drivers in rural areas, Batini and Donovan (2001) proposed the following classification of factors as influencing drink-driving in these areas.

Predisposing factors

• *Convenience*: most believe that it's simply easier to drive rather than seek out alternatives. They believe it's easier to drive home than collect their car the next day (includes fear of damage to or theft of car if left overnight).

• *Cultural acceptance*: rather than being morally unacceptable behaviour, drinking and driving is very much seen as being culturally acceptable – the actual social norm in their towns. However, they do distinguish between the terms 'drinking and driving' versus 'drunk driving', the latter being generally considered far less acceptable.

• *Personal safety*: in some towns many were fearful of being assaulted while walking home after having consumed alcohol.

Enabling factors

• *Lack of enforcement*: most participants knew that the police can't be everywhere all the time. Many knew when the police 'knock off' for the evening. High profile 'blitzes' (e.g., booze bus, random breath test stop) are highly visible and easily avoided (via the 'bush telegraph'). There was a known lack of funding for regular patrols and a perception that if they have got away with it before, they can get away with it again.

• *Lack of public transport*: for many, there are simply no (or very limited) public transport options, particularly within the smaller towns. In addition, those living out of town cite the distance as being too far to walk (e.g., 30 km, 50 km, etc.) (Figure 14.5).

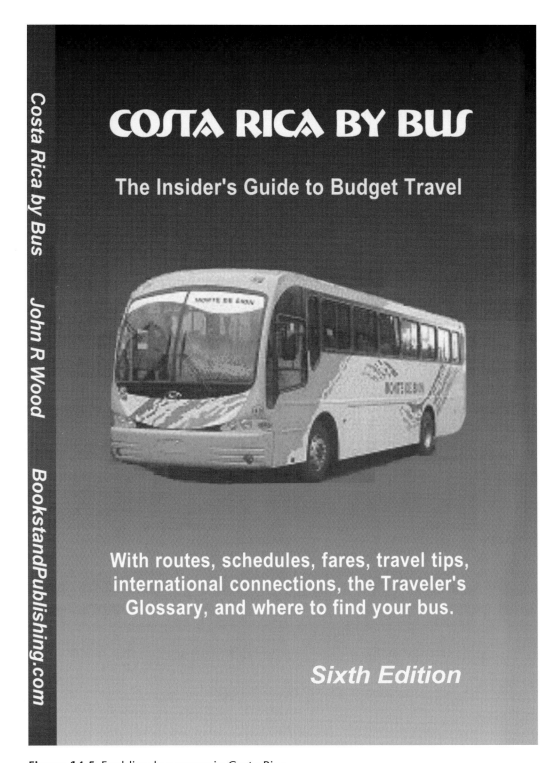

Figure 14.5 Enabling bus usage in Costa Rica

Reinforcing factors

- *Expense of alternatives*: many are reluctant to pay the fare for a 30–50 km taxi ride, often viewed as a 'waste of good drinking money'.
- *Confidence*: while aware of the 0.05 blood-alcohol limit, many feel perfectly capable of driving above this limit, citing that they've 'driven from an early age on the farm' and have the 'ability to handle country roads'. Others try to drive more 'carefully' after drinking (e.g., slower, concentrate more, etc.). There is a perception that if they have been able to successfully drive home after consuming alcohol before, they can do it again.

Predisposing, enabling or reinforcing?

People sometimes have difficulty determining whether a factor should be classified as 'enabling' or 'reinforcing' or 'predisposing'. However, 'correct' classification is not crucial. What is crucial is being able to identify the factors in the first place and then being able to elaborate the implications of the factors – which should not be affected by their classification.

The educational and organisational analysis identifies what needs to be done. The next phase looks at how it can be done. Administrative and policy assessment involves assessing resources and looking at educational, motivational and regulatory alternatives for influencing the factors identified in phase 4. It involves establishing intersectoral collaboration where necessary and developing relationships with intermediaries.

Planning and designing the intervention are an outcome of phases 1–5, along with setting of process, impact and outcome objectives. Implementation (phase 6) can include pre-testing of methods and materials, perhaps even carrying out efficacy (or pilot) trials of the intervention. Process, impact and outcome evaluation were covered in Chapter 6. Process evaluation should be ongoing to ensure that timelines are met and to enable valid assessments of impact and outcomes (i.e., failure to meet attitudinal and behavioural objectives might be due to non-delivery of communication materials, call analyses might reveal that only 20 per cent of calls to a helpline are being answered before the caller hangs up).

Applying PRECEDE–PROCEED to increasing fruit and vegetable consumption

In Chapter 11 we referred to the Black Churches United for Better Health Project ('Praise the Lord and pass the fruit n' vegs'). Campbell *et al.* (1999) used the PRECEDE–PROCEED model to develop a set of activities (their marketing mix) based on the predisposing, enabling and reinforcing factors identified as determinants of fruit and vegetable consumption.

They report the following activities to address predisposing factors:

- Tailored bulletins – each individual received personalised, tailored messages and feedback based on questionnaire data with regard to their beliefs, attitudes and current behaviours, barriers, social support and stage of change.

- Printed materials – monthly packages of brochures, posters, banners, idea sheets, church bulletin inserts were provided to each church's Nutrition Action Team (church members recruited by the pastor to organise and implement activities).

The following activities addressed enabling factors:

- Gardening – churches were encouraged to plant fruit and vegetable gardens, and training was available for 'master gardeners'. (Note: a programme in Queensland encouraged schools to plant gardens as a way of creating and sustaining positive attitudes towards fruit and vegetable consumption; Viola 2002).
- Educational sessions – Nutrition Action Team members attended educational sessions and were trained to conduct cooking sessions showing how to achieve 'five-a-day' guidelines.
- Cookbook and recipe tasting – a trained 'cookbook person' in each church showed members how to modify their favourite recipes to meet the 'five-a-day' guidelines and conducted taste tests on the modified products. Recipes were included in a cookbook distributed to all participants.
- Serving more fruit and vegetables at church functions – a 'practise what you preach' orientation to enable more trial of fruit and vegetable dishes.

The following activities addressed reinforcing factors:

- Lay health advisers – 'natural helpers' were identified and trained on social support to assist others advance through the stages of change.
- Community coalitions – each county formed a coalition of relevant stakeholders such as local grocers, farmers and church members who received training in community action and organised community events.
- Pastor support – pastors were encouraged to promote the campaign in their sermons and church announcements, received a newsletter keeping them informed of all activities, reviewed educational materials and were involved in generating tailored messages.
- Grocer–vendor involvement – promotional materials such as recipe cards, coupons and farmer's market posters were distributed to church members and local stores.

Concluding comments

Planning and designing social marketing interventions follows a logical common-sense sequence. Regardless of terminology in the different models, and regardless of whether it is a campaign or a programme being planned, most approaches begin with some sort of problem identification, then move to a selection of goals, followed in turn by identification and consideration of alternative strategies to achieve those goals, testing and refinement of the strategies before full implementation, monitoring the implementation and using that information to further refine or revise the programme components, and evaluation of outcomes on an ongoing basis.

A key point to remember is that subsequent stages can be only as good as the preceding stages, and the needs assessment/problem identification stage is the most important of all. Another key point is that the process is iterative and recursive with later stages informing earlier stages, especially when pre-testing of methods and materials begins.

Finally, no social marketing programme, no matter how successful in achieving its objectives, is immune from political interference. Programme planning could therefore include a political contingency component where possible.

QUESTIONS

- How would you use the PRECEDE–PROCEED model to plan an alcohol moderation campaign on your campus?
- What does it mean to say that these planning models are 'recursive' and 'iterative'?
- What are some of the predisposing, enabling and reinforcing factors underlying:
  (a) marijuana use; (b) sexual-orientation discrimination; (c) mental illness stigmatisation;
  (d) dating violence against women?

FURTHER READING

Centers for Disease Control (CDC). The website contains an interactive logic model which is useful when planning a social marketing campaign such as the one developed for the VERB physical activity campaign in the United States (Huhman, Heitzler and Wong 2004), available at: www.cdc.gov/pcd/issues/2004/jul/04_0033a.htm.

Egger, G., Spark, R. and Donovan, R. J. 2005. *Health Promotion Strategies and Methods,* 2nd edn. Sydney: McGraw-Hill.

Green, L. W. and Kreuter, M. W. 2005. *Health Promotion Planning: An Educational and Ecological Approach,* 4th edn. New York: McGraw-Hill.

Matsudo, S. M., Matsudo, V. R., Andrade, D. R., Araújo, T. L., Andrade, E. L., de Oliveira, L. C. and Braggion, G. F. 2004. Physical Activity Promotion: Experience and Evaluation of the Agita São Paulo Programme using the Ecological Móbile Model, *Journal of Physical Activity and Health* 2: 81–97.

15 Case study: the Act–Belong–Commit campaign promoting positive mental health

The *Act–Belong–Commit* community-based social marketing campaign targets individuals to engage in activities that enhance mental health. It simultaneously encourages community organisations offering such activities to promote their activities under the *Act–Belong–Commit* banner. The campaign provides a simple framework for mental health promotion professionals to communicate with, and gain the co-operation of, potential partners and stakeholders within and outside the health system.

The campaign was developed as an upstream or primary prevention intervention. However, the campaign messages are also appropriate for at-risk individuals and groups (secondary prevention), and for people recovering from a mental illness (tertiary prevention). Hence, as it evolves the campaign is developing a number of programme components and partners for secondary and tertiary prevention.

The campaign is conducted by Mentally Healthy WA, a group based within the Faculty of Health Sciences at Curtin University in Western Australia (WA). This chapter draws on a number of publications available from the website (e.g., Donovan, James and Jalleh 2007; Donovan *et al.* 2003a, 2006a; Jalleh *et al.* 2007).

Background: mental illness and the need for mental health promotion

Mental health disorders are a highly significant component of global disease burden when disability as well as death is taken into account. Using measures of disability-adjusted life years, projections by Murray and Lopez (1996) show that mental health conditions could increase their share of the total global burden by almost half by 2020: from 10.5 per cent to 15 per cent

The growth of mental health problems and consequent demand for treatment services have led to growing international interest in promotion, prevention and early intervention for mental health. However, interventions to date have been largely directed towards those suffering mental health problems, early identification of at risk individuals or de-stigmatisation of the mentally ill (for examples, see Davis and Tsiantis 2005; European Commission 2004; Jane-Llopis *et al.* 2005; Saxena *et al.* 2005; Wright *et al.* 2006). The United Kingdom recently commenced a major de-stigmatising campaign called 'Time to change' (www.time-to-change.org.uk), with similar goals to the 'Say it out loud' campaign launched in May 2008 by the Illinois Children's Mental Health Partnership and the Illinois Department of Human Services, Division of Mental Health (www.mentalhealthillinois.org).

While there are a number of school and worksite interventions aimed at building positive mental health (Durlak and Wells 1997; Morrow, Verins and Willis 2002; Stewart *et al.* 2004), and various 'mental health' organisations provide tips on maintaining or building mental health (see Iceland's ten commandments of mental health), there is little published literature on populationwide mental health promotion campaigns that target people to be proactive about maintaining and building their own (and others') mental health other than the Victorian Health Promotion Foundation's (VicHealth) 'Together we do better' campaign (Walker, Moodie and Herrman 2004) and California's 1982 'Friends can be good medicine' campaign (Hersey *et al.* 1984; Taylor *et al.* 1984). The WHO and World Federation for Mental Health joint publication, *Mental Health Promotion: Case Studies from Countries*, describes thirty-five programmes from around the world, none of which is a comprehensive communitywide positive mental health promotion campaign (Saxena and Garrison 2004).

10 COMMANDMENTS OF MENTAL HEALTH

1. Think positively; it's easier
2. Cherish the ones you love
3. Continue learning as long as you live
4. Learn from your mistakes
5. Exercise daily; it enhances your well-being
6. Do not complicate your life unnecessarily
7. Try to understand those around you and encourage them
8. Do not give up; success in life is a marathon
9. Discover and nurture your talents
10. Set goals for yourself and pursue your dreams

PUBLIC HEALTH INSTITUTE OF ICELAND

www.publichealth.is

Background: origins of the campaign

Given the increasing awareness of the need for positive mental health promotion, the Western Australian Health Promotion Foundation (Healthway; see Chapter 13) commissioned qualitative research with people in general as well as mental health professionals to inform a mental health promotion campaign in Western Australia (Donovan *et al.* 2003a).

The research suggested two possible starting points for a mental health promotion campaign:

- targeting individuals in general to be more proactive about their own mental health; and
- targeting individuals in authority over others to be more aware of their impact on their charges' mental health.

The former would encourage individuals to engage in activities that enhance mental health (such as social, arts and sporting organisation membership, community involvement, physical and mental activities, hobbies, engaging in meaningful activities, volunteering, etc.), while simultaneously encouraging community organisations that offered such activities to promote their activities under a mental health and well-being message. The latter would focus on interactions between those in authority and those under their charge or care (such as supervisors and their workers, parents and their children, teachers and their students, coaches and their trainees, service personnel and customers, etc.), with the aim of replacing coercive, negative styles with encouraging, positive styles.

ABC guide to promoting mental health via targeting individuals in authority

A tentative ABC guide for targeting individuals in authority over others has been developed by the Mentally Healthy WA group: actively involve (those in your care) – build (their) skills – celebrate (their) achievements. This guide suggests three major ways that individuals in charge can enhance the mental health of those in their care. The fundamental notions are that each and every individual in their care should be given the opportunity to actively participate in the group or organisation's activities and relevant decisions, be provided with challenges that increase their skills and sense of self-efficacy and have their achievements recognised. These three concepts are based on individuals' beliefs about factors influencing one's mental health or vulnerability to illness, and are consistent with the literature, particularly Hawkins and Catalano's concept of bonding (Hawkins *et al.* 1992), and concepts of control and reward imbalance (Oxenstierna *et al.* 2005; Vezina *et al.* 2004).

Healthway decided to begin with the individual/community organisation focus and invited the Curtin group to develop and implement a campaign. After a six-month feasibility study to recruit intervention sites and personnel, and to develop and pre-test communication materials, the *Act–Belong–Commit* campaign was piloted in six towns in regional Western Australia from October 2005 for a two-year period. Mentally Healthy WA then obtained funding to launch the campaign statewide for the period 2008–10.

In this chapter we focus mainly on the development, implementation and evaluation of the pilot study, and then provide a summary of the campaign's progress at 2009.

The *'Act–Belong–Commit'* ('A–B–C') message provides a simple mnemonic that represents three major domains of factors that the research literature and people in general consider contribute to good mental health (Donovan *et al.* 2003a; Ross and Blackwell 2004; Rychetnik and Todd 2004; Shah and Marks 2004). These are presented briefly below and elaborated later in the chapter.

- '**Act**' means that individuals should strive to keep themselves physically, socially and cognitively active. Being active is a fundamental requirement for mental health.
- '**Belong**' refers to being a member of a group or organisation (whether face-to-face or not), such that an individual's connectedness with the community and sense of identity are strengthened. A sense of belonging is considered fundamental to good mental health.
- '**Commit**' refers to the extent to which an individual becomes involved with (or commits to) some activity, cause or organisation. Commitment provides a sense of purpose and meaning in people's lives.

The research literature confirms that each of these domains is considered fundamental to human psychological wellbeing.

Overall goals of the pilot campaign

The pilot campaign was designed with two overall goals:

(1) the development of a sustainable campaign model that could be incorporated into the state Health Department's portfolio of health promotion activities, in the same way that various physical health promotion campaigns are (such as tobacco control, physical activity, nutrition, sun protection, sexual health, etc.). At the time we commenced this campaign, there was no such populationwide mental health promotion initiative in the state (or elsewhere in Australia); and

(2) the development of a mental health promotion model that positioned mental health as a whole of community issue, not just an issue for the health system.

Campaign goals

Our formative research showed that other than taking some actions when they were 'stressed' or in some 'crisis' situation, people rarely considered what they could or should be doing for their mental health on an ongoing, proactive basis. This was in marked contrast to the salience and proactive intentions about their physical health.

Hence, an overall campaign goal is to reframe people's perceptions of mental health away from simply the absence of mental illness, to the belief that people can (and should) act proactively to protect and strengthen their mental health.

Related goals are to increase individuals' awareness of things they can (and should) do to enhance or improve their own mental health and to increase individuals' participation in individual and community activities that strengthen mental health and reduce vulnerability to mental health problems.

At the community level, the overall goal is to build cohesion in communities via fostering links between community organisations around a unifying theme of positive mental health. A related goal is to build links between those in the community dealing with mental health problems and those in the community with the capacity to strengthen positive mental health.

Overall strategy and planning

The overall strategy can be described as a community-based social marketing approach. *Act–Belong–Commit* project officers (one full-time or two half-time FTEs) were appointed in each pilot town. Western Australia Country Health Service (WACHS), the division of the Western Australian Health Department responsible for health services outside the metropolitan area, agreed to assign one of their health promotion staff in each town to implement the campaign for half their working time. The campaign funded an additional half-time FTE person. At that time WACHS' commitment was only for the pilot intervention.

The project officers all received a two-day training module in the state's capital city at the commencement of the campaign. The primary goals of the project officers were to establish working partnerships with appropriate organisations and to try to achieve at least one co-branded event per month in each town. With the help of the Mentally Healthy WA manager who visited and delivered public presentations to community meetings in the towns, project officers used their own networks in the towns to form a local steering group to organise and plan activities for the duration of the pilot. Project officers were encouraged to form partnerships outside the health and welfare systems. The campaign's main focus in the first twelve months was on establishing partnerships and relationships in the six towns.

The project officers developed a twelve-month plan at the beginning of each year. This involved first holding a community meeting of those individuals and organisations interested in the campaign. Attendees were separated into small groups and asked to identify a number of activities or issues they would like to see undertaken as part of the campaign in their town. The whole meeting then discussed all suggestions and agreed on a list of priorities. These meetings also allowed the project officer to identify those keenly interested in being full partners in the campaign, those interested in limited co-operation on some events and others who simply wished to be kept informed of activities as they occurred. All of these received a monthly 'newsletter' on activities in that town. The project officer, in conjunction with a small group called the management or steering committee, then set out their objectives for the next twelve months.

Project officers were encouraged to target individuals and groups that might be isolated or could particularly benefit from inclusive activities. This resulted in some towns targeting Indigenous groups or older adults or women's networks or youth or people with a disability. However, each town was free to set its own specific objectives.

A 'customer' orientation ensured that potential partner organisations were offered resources and services of benefit to them in *exchange* for their promoting the *Act–Belong–Commit* message. Organisations were offered the project officer's organisational assistance for event planning, assistance in applying for funding from relevant funding bodies (e.g., governments, charities and arts and sporting funding bodies), merchandise and promotional opportunities for their organisation via their association with the *Act–Belong–Commit* campaign. Potential partners were aware that the campaign would be placing advertisements in the local newspaper and generating press releases on mental health promotion issues and co-branded events.

In essence the campaign aims to increase individual and community wellbeing by increasing and strengthening connections between community members via their participation in family and community events and organisations, as well as increasing collaborations between community organisations that offer activities conducive to good mental health and wellbeing. This is depicted in Figures 15.1 ('before' *Act–Belong–Commit*) and 15.2 ('after' *Act–Belong–Commit*) where people are shown on the right-hand side and organisations on the left-hand side. Lines show people's participation in organisations and connections between organisations. Towns with high social capital will already have many strong connections between people and organisations. In Figure 15.2 the Mentally Healthy WA project officer builds these connections: getting people to participate in community organisations' activities and getting the organisations to collaborate more – hence, increasing and strengthening connections between and among people and organisations in the town.

For the first twelve months of the *Act–Belong–Commit* campaign, the main promotional strategy consisted of paid advertising and unpaid publicity in local newspapers. A set of four launch press advertisements was developed and placed in local newspapers. Later, three more lengthy ads dealing with specific issues were developed.

In the second twelve months of the campaign, a television advertisement was launched to increase populationwide awareness of the campaign messages. The advertisements were supplemented by publicity and press releases for events in the towns (examples available on the website).

The advertising and publicity were designed to sensitise people to local organisations' promotion of their activities, and, in conjunction with these promotions, to get people to participate in specific events or become more active in organisations of which they were already members.

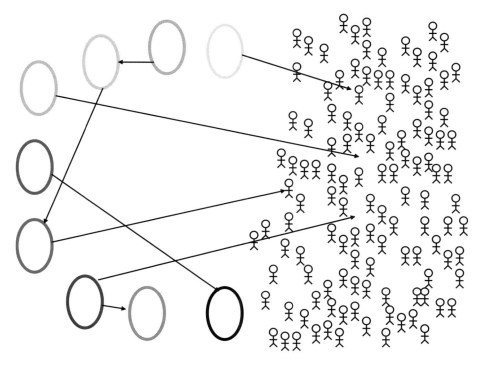

Figure 15.1 Community organisations and community members prior to *Act–Belong–Commit*: unconnected or weakly connected

Campaign target groups

Our two primary target groups were:

- individual community members; and
- office holders or owners of community organisations or businesses that offered activities conducive to good mental health (e.g., libraries, sporting and recreational clubs, tourism operators, volunteer associations, walking groups, educational institutions, eco-environmental groups, arts and craft groups, etc.).

In a sense these constituted, respectively, 'end consumers' and 'retailers' (partners). These organisations provided both a channel through which to deliver messages (i.e., posters and banners at events) as well as the 'products' (behaviours) for end consumers to 'purchase' (i.e., adopt or participate in).

Journalists for the local media also constituted a target group, and in a couple of towns a local journalist was an active member of the steering committee. In return for our paid advertising, we expected – and generally received – good use of our press releases and coverage of local events held under the *Act–Belong–Commit* banner. In all

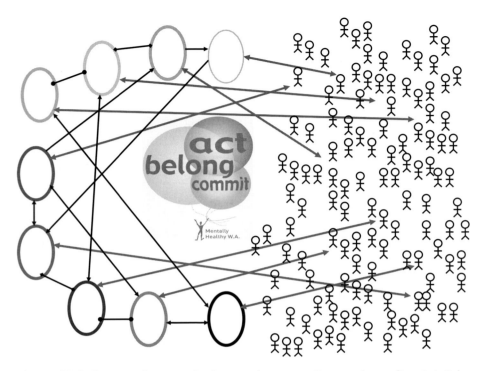

Figure 15.2 Community organisations and community members after *Act–Belong–Commit*: more connections, more strongly connected

such cases we provide good quality photos and attempt to make the releases interesting to the paper's readers. Other mutually beneficial newspaper features have been negotiated in some towns (e.g., one town's newspaper featured a 'club-of-the-month', describing the club's activities and contact details, along with the *Act–Belong–Commit* logo and message).

Communication and behavioural objectives

For individuals in general, the primary objectives were to increase the salience of mental health, to encourage them to think proactively about their mental health, to increase their awareness of what they could and should do to increase or maintain good mental health, and to encourage them to engage in activities that would enhance their mental health.

For community organisation office holders, the primary objectives were to increase their awareness that the activities they provided were good for participants' mental health, to encourage them to form partnerships with the *Act-Belong–Commit* campaign (and other community organisations) and, hence, promote their activities on the additional benefit that participation in their activities is beneficial to mental health. It was expected that partnering with *Act–Belong–Commit* would help organisations undertake activities to increase attendance, participation, membership and volunteerism in their organisations, and to form partnerships with other organisations to achieve these aims.

For journalists, the primary objectives were to establish working relationships to facilitate the use of press releases and coverage of local events held under the *Act–Belong–Commit* banner.

The campaign brand name encapsulates both the communication and behavioural objectives of the campaign (i.e., what people can and should do for good mental health):

- ACT: maintain or increase levels of physical activity (e.g., walk, garden, dance, etc.), cognitive activity (e.g., read, do crossword puzzles, play cards, etc.) and social activity (e.g., say hello to neighbours, have a chat to a shopkeeper, maintain contacts with friends, etc.);
- BELONG: maintain or increase levels of participation in groups if already a member or join a group, maintain or increase participation in community events and with family and friends; and
- COMMIT: take up a cause or challenge (e.g., volunteer for a good cause, learn a new, challenging skill, etc.).

A person can ACT by reading a book, BELONG by joining a book club, COMMIT by becoming the secretary/organiser for the book club or by occasionally reading challenging books rather than just 'pulp fiction'.

Campaign development and branding

The formative research identified a number of factors that people perceived to impact on positive mental health, ranging from economic and socio-cultural factors to individual personality and lifestyle factors. There was near universal support for the concepts that remaining active (physically, socially and mentally), having good friends, being a member of various groups in the community and feeling in control of one's circumstances were necessary for good mental health. There was also widespread agreement that having opportunities for achievable challenges – at home, school or work, or in hobbies, sports or the arts – are important for a good sense of self. Helping others (including volunteering, coaching, mentoring) was frequently mentioned as a great source of satisfaction, as well as providing a source of activity and involvement with others.

These findings were used to develop the overall campaign message strategies as well as the umbrella brand Mentally Healthy WA and the *Act–Belong–Commit* campaign brand.

The 'Mentally Healthy WA' brand

Formative research with a broad variety of individuals about their understanding of mental health indicated that people not only rarely thought proactively about their mental health, but that the term 'mental health' primarily had connotations of 'mental *illness*' (e.g., 'schizophrenia', 'psychiatry', 'manic depression', 'depression', etc.).

On the other hand, the term 'mental*ly* health*y*' had primarily positive connotations (such as 'alert', 'happy', 'able to cope', 'socially adept', 'emotionally stable', etc.). Hence, it was decided to brand the overall campaign as the 'Mentally Healthy WA' campaign and use the term 'mentally healthy' as often as possible in conjunction with the term 'mental health' to neutralise these negative connotations and build positive connotations to the term 'mental health'.

Other features of this umbrella brand name were:

- inclusion of the state ('WA') as part of the brand to stimulate a sense of community and ownership); and
- the brand format can be easily adapted by other states or countries (or individual towns) (e.g., 'Mentally Healthy Hawaii', 'Mentally Healthy UK'). The Mental Health Council of Australia (the peak body for organisations dealing with mental illness) now uses 'Mentally Healthy Oz' (and the *Act–Belong–Commit* logo) in its national campaign around World Mental Health Week.

The *Act–Belong–Commit* campaign brand

We wanted the campaign brand to go beyond slogans or belief statements such as 'together we do better' and 'friends are good medicine' and to connect directly to the actions we wanted people to take (in the same way that other health promotion/injury prevention campaigns include their basic desired behaviour in their branding or logo, such as Quit, Belt Up, DrinkSafe, 2 Fruit n' 5 Veg, Eat less fat, etc.).

Given the potential complexity of the mental health/illness area, we also imposed the requirement that the campaign's primary messages be 'as simple as ABC' to act on. This resulted in searching for behaviours beginning with the letters 'A', 'B' and 'C' that reflected the formative research and literature.

We chose the verbs 'act', 'belong' and 'commit' as they not only provide the opportunity to tell people that maintaining good mental health 'is as easy as A–B–C', but they also represent the three major domains of factors that the literature and people in general consider contribute to good mental health (Baumeister and Leary 1995; Donovan 2004; Donovan *et al.* 2003a, 2005, 2006b; Ross and Blackwell 2004; Rychetnik and Todd 2004; Shah and Marks 2004).

These three domains may be viewed as a hierarchy of increasing contribution to an individual's sense of self and mental health.

Act: There is substantial evidence from a variety of sources that individuals with higher levels of physical, cognitive and/or social activity have higher levels of wellbeing and mental health, and that such activities can alleviate mental problems such as anxiety and depression.

Belong: Many activities can be done alone or as a member of a group (e.g., read a book versus join a book club, go for a walk alone or join a walking group, play solitaire or bridge games). In some cases there are synergistic effects: belonging to a book club not only adds a connectedness dimension but is also likely to expand the cognitive activity involved; joining a walking group is likely to expand the physical activity while adding a social connection. Regular involvement in social activities, whether via hobby groups, professional interest groups, family and friends is likely to result in a strong personal support group, one of the most important factors for maintaining mental (and physical) health. Involvement in local community activities and organisations also builds social cohesion (or social capital) which is important for individuals' mental health. The California based 'Friends are good medicine' and VicHealth's 'Together we do better' campaigns are examples of campaigns that focus on the 'belong' domain.

Commit: Meeting challenges provides a sense of accomplishment, feelings of efficacy and a stronger sense of self (Csikszentmihalyi 1990; Csikszentmihalyi and Csikszentmihalyi 2006). There is widespread agreement in the general population that volunteering and activities undertaken to benefit the community at large, especially where these involve the disadvantaged, add to self-esteem and self-worth, particularly in the retired elderly. Volunteering and greater participation in community activities and organisations have substantial implications for community cohesion and social capital, and hence quality of life (ESRC 2004).

In short, positive mental health relies on people keeping physically, socially and mentally active, participating in group activities, keeping up social interactions, getting involved in community activities and taking up causes or setting goals and achieving them.

The visual brand

The *'Act–Belong–Commit'* logo was required to reframe good mental health as more than the absence of illness and to reflect people's positive connotations to the term 'mentally healthy'. Balloons were chosen to signify 'lightness', sociability and generally positive affect and energy (Figure 15.3). Another reason for choosing balloons was that the three balloons could be displayed easily at sponsored/branded events. Project officers were provided with a good supply of 'act', 'belong' and 'commit' balloons in the appropriate colours and anchors and a gas cylinder. Trios of balloons at events reinforced brand recognition as well as adding to the sociability/fun atmosphere of the

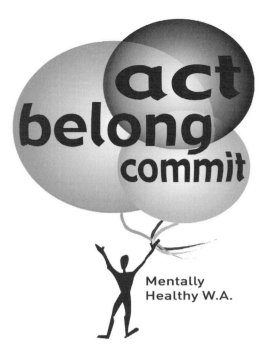

Figure 15.3 *Act–Belong–Commit* brand/logo

event. The balloons proved popular with children who asked for them – thus serving to bring their parent or carer into contact with the brand.

A single non-gender character holding the balloons was chosen to have non-specific appeal. This also has the advantage of potential adaptation in other promotional areas (such as an animated TV ad), and by other partners (the Mental Health Council of Australia sought permission to add a 'child' figure, which was consistent with their own logo of a similar adult character shown in a protective pose with a child figure).

Several variations were tested to ensure that the brand was seen as 'friendly' and was generally 'liked'. We also ensured that the logo achieved high ratings on 'easy to read' and 'easy to remember'.

The marketing mix

Product

The core product offered to individuals was good mental health and feelings of well-being in exchange for their taking up activities suggested in the *Act–Belong–Commit* messages. The core product offered to organisations was facilitation in reaching their own organisational goals in exchange for promoting their activities under, or in conjunction with, the *Act-Belong–Commit* brand.

Actual products offered to *individuals* were all the activities offered by organisations that promoted their activities under or alongside the *Act–Belong–Commit* banner. Actual products offered to *organisations* were the skills of the project officers who helped organise events, obtain sponsorship funding and publicity for organisations and their activities, along with merchandising items (e.g., posters, frisbees, T-shirts, drink bottles, stickers, hats, bookmarks, fridge magnets and stress balls). All of these served to establish and maintain a good relationship with these partners. Some of these promotional products were also distributed to attendees at various events.

People

The manager appointed to implement the campaign (Dr Ray James), had considerable expertise and experience in health promotion and community health. He also had extensive contacts in the State Health Department in country areas. His personal contacts facilitated the recruiting of individuals in the country towns willing to take on the campaign.

The project officers in each town were required to have health promotion expertise and good interpersonal skills. The project officers offered their expertise to community organisations in return for their partnership co-operation.

A small management group or steering committee (six to ten people) was set up in each town consisting of representatives of the main partner organisations in each town. This group served to support the project officer as well as provide links to other organisations in each town.

Promotion

An umbrella media advertising and publicity campaign was developed to support project officers' interactions with community organisations and to meet the communication objectives for individuals. In the latter case, the advertising and publicity were designed to sensitise people to local organisations' promotion of their activities, and, in conjunction with these promotions, to get people to participate in specific events or become more active in organisations of which they were already a member.

An initial set of four press ads was developed (see Figure 15.4) for the launch and first six months of the campaign. The ads were designed to appear on consecutive right-hand pages for maximal impact (note that the ads feature the original website address). Donovan *et al.*'s (2003a) summary of people's understanding of mental health suggested that people in Western Australia would be responsive to mental health promotion messages if delivered in everyday language. Hence, the ad content deliberately avoided technical jargon and the notion that mental health concepts were complex. The copy refers to people already knowing what's good for their mental health, with 'health experts now confirming that knowledge'. All the ads were pre-tested for understanding,

Figure 15.4 Launch ads to appear on right-hand side of four consecutive pages

credibility and potential impact, and included the website and a local telephone number. The media spend for the advertisements was AU$105,000 per annum. Production costs were approximately AU$5,000. Radio interviews provided further opportunities to reach the community.

Television was not used in year one as the first year was primarily to establish partnerships and because of the substantially greater cost of television advertising. After sufficient partnerships were established, a 30-second television advertisement was developed and began airing in February 2007. The production cost was AU$55,000 and the media spend was AU$67,000. The television ad featured animated characters engaging in various activities (playing tennis, playing chess, attending a musical event, planting trees, officiating a wheelchair athletes' basketball game) while an announcer said: 'Keeping mentally healthy is as important as keeping physically healthy. And it's as easy as a, b, c: act, belong, commit', and then proceeded to 'define' these three terms. The ad ended with 'Keeping mentally healthy helps you cope better with problems and stress. And you'll simply feel happier too.' The ad was pre-tested for understanding,

Figure 15.5 Scenes from television ad

message credibility and potential impact (see Figure 15.5) (All ads appear on the web-site: www.actbelongcommit.org.au).

Newsletters were circulated by most towns – either monthly or quarterly – among collaborating organisations and others who had registered an interest, with the aim of keeping people informed and maintaining individuals' interest by recounting person-alised, local stories about the campaign's implementation.

A website was developed, but primarily to allow the project officers in each of the towns to exchange information about their various activities and events, rather than as a resource for the general population.

Price

While individual participation in some events and activities required a monetary out-lay, most of the co-branded events to date have not; what they have required are psy-chological costs such as time (primarily), effort, or shyness being overcome or dealing with potential social embarrassment (e.g., in attending an intergenerational concert and meeting, greeting and conversing with strangers). There were no monetary costs for organisations collaborating with the campaign. This was clearly an attraction for small, local community organisations.

Place

There were two levels of place: first, our campaign project officers were physically located in each town. In a commercial sense these were our 'sales offices' in each town.

The organisations that collaborated with the campaign (e.g., local government organisations, businesses, libraries, tertiary and technical education services, sporting and arts clubs/groups, professional associations, schools, worksites, recreational groups, including Indigenous and other ethnic groups and so on) become a second level of place, in that their premises (or use of public spaces) are where the 'behaviours' are engaged in.

Pilot campaign evaluation

As a pilot project, one of the major aims was simply to observe and learn from the implementation process so that learnings could be transferred to future and larger scale campaigns. Another aim of the pilot was to assess community reaction in general, and particularly how community organisations responded to, and collaborated with, the campaign. In terms of sustainability, we were particularly interested in to what extent the campaign would be absorbed or internalised by collaborating organisations. Much of these learnings are presented in case studies for each town. Five of the six original pilot towns provided a narrative of the development and implementation of the campaign in those towns. The case studies reflect the unique set of circumstances in each of the towns, and can be found in full at www.actbelongcommit.org.au ('Implementing the *Act–Belong–Commit* Pilot Campaign: Lessons from the Participating Towns').

Partnerships and collaborations: process evaluation

For the first twelve months of the campaign, the emphasis was on establishing partnerships in the towns and building brand awareness and knowledge among potential partners. During this period, nearly sixty key partnerships were established, more than a hundred co-branded community events and activities were held, and the campaign generated a total of 124 campaign-related press articles in the local newspapers (27,538 cm^2).

Mail surveys of officeholders in organisations that actively collaborated with the campaign were conducted in September 2006 and January 2008. The aim was to assess the impact of such collaborations on their organisation and their attitudes towards the collaboration. The organisation was asked to indicate the impact – if any – of the collaboration on the capacity of the organisation in terms of producing media releases and articles, promoting events or activities, increasing staff level of expertise, increasing public awareness of their organisation and applying for funding and grants. Participating organisations indicated that the collaboration had a positive impact in all of these areas, and primarily in increasing staff expertise and promotion of events and activities.

Respondents were also asked to provide an overall rating on a ten-point scale, of how beneficial they considered their collaboration with the campaign to have been and whether they would be willing to collaborate with the *Act–Belong–Commit* campaign in running events or activities in future. The overall mean beneficial rating was almost eight out of ten and 100 per cent stated they would be willing to collaborate with the campaign in the future.

During the pilot intervention, project officers assisted community organisations to obtain over AU$400,000 in sponsorship funding (primarily from Healthway).

Population effects: impact evaluation

Benchmark and two twelve-month follow-up telephone surveys (random selection) of the intervention town residents (n = 200 per town) were conducted, along with telephone surveys of metropolitan residents and non-intervention rural town residents (n = 1,000). The final survey was undertaken in October 2007.

Campaign awareness after the first twelve months of limited local newspaper advertising varied from 20 per cent to 30 per cent in the various towns. After television advertising was introduced, campaign reach increased to 64 per cent combined across intervention sites. Women were more likely to be aware of the campaign than men (72 per cent versus 58 per cent), and people aged under forty slightly more likely than over forties (70 per cent versus 60 per cent). There was almost universal correct understanding of the *Act–Belong–Commit* brand message among those aware of the campaign in the intervention towns (only 8 per cent said 'don't know').

Among those aware of the campaign in the intervention towns, 24 per cent indicated that they had changed the way they thought about mental health, and 14 per cent that they had changed their behaviour in some way as a result of the campaign. Most changes in thinking related to simply being more aware of mental health issues, knowledge about *Act–Belong–Commit* ways to keep mentally healthy and more positive/less stigmatised views of mental illness. Most changes in behaviour were consistent with the three *Act–Belong–Commit* domains. Other responses referred to being more accepting of people in general and those with a mental illness.

Systemic impact

Prior to this pilot campaign, the Health Department had no communitywide mental health promotion programme. Towards the end of the pilot programme, WACHS proactively approached Mentally Healthy WA (MHWA) with an offer to continue funding six half-time project officers for a period of six months while MHWA sought funding to expand the campaign statewide. After funding for a limited statewide expansion was confirmed, WACHS agreed to implement the *Act–Belong–Commit* programme in its total jurisdiction, with health promotion officers incorporating *Act–Belong–Commit* in their job requirements, albeit to differing degrees depending on local priorities.

In addition to incorporation into the State Health Department's non-metropolitan jurisdiction, several metropolitan local government areas and two non-health state government departments approached MHWA at or prior to the end of the pilot requesting involvement in any statewide expansion.

Another goal was to position mental health in a community context and not just a 'health' issue. This was achieved by attracting partnerships with a wide variety of community organisations, government departments and NGOs, including arts, crafts, theatre, sporting groups, libraries, educational groups, animal care, multicultural dancing and cooking events, land-care groups, etc. One measure of success here was that a number of non-health organisations that became aware of the pilot in the rural areas were ready and waiting for the campaign to go statewide.

Conclusion from the pilot

The pilot programme indicated that changes in the way people view mental health are achievable and that a community-based approach utilising existing community organisations is feasible and, indeed, attractive to a variety of non-health-related government, non-government and commercial organisations. However, achieving change is facilitated where system change occurs at the same time. From our perspective, although the organisation and general population survey data are encouraging, our achievement of system change within WACHS is considered a major step forward.

However, the lessons from tobacco control are quite clear: efforts must be adequately resourced, multi-faceted and sustained. In that context, our results suggest that with the right resources and support, a community-based social marketing programme to improve mental health has the potential to enhance individual and community well-being on a populationwide basis.

The statewide campaign 2008–10

The campaign was launched statewide in mid-2008 with an enhanced website for general use. Currently the campaign has memoranda of understanding with about thirty WACHS and community partners, including several metropolitan local government entities.

Government departments that partner with the campaign include the Department for Sport and Recreation and the Department of the Environment. The former has a common goal of increasing participation in community sporting and recreational clubs and the latter has a common goal of people caring for and enjoying time in natural environments. Both are very much aware of the mental health and community cohesion benefits of participation in their activities.

Department for Sport and Recreation partnership

In early 2009, *Act–Belong–Commit* partnered with the Department of Sport and Recreation (DSR) to encourage people to *Act–Belong–Commit* by joining a club. The *Act–Belong–Commit* television ad was altered by inserting a well-known television presenter after the first few scenes who says: 'Joining a club is a great way to Act, Belong, Commit', while the camera focuses on the DSR's website where people can find clubs in their area. The presenter then says: 'Go on. Join up, join in and enjoy life more' and the ad returns to the original final scenes. The joint exercise provided double the time that each would have obtained separately for the advertising budgets. The television advertising was accompanied by the poster in Figure 15.6 being distributed to DSR sites, clubs and doctors' surgeries throughout the state, along with a brochure about the association between joining a club and good mental health.

Figure 15.6 Partnership with the Department of Sport and Recreation

New products and new target groups recently or in development include:

- a seniors version of print ads and radio ads;
- training module for peer–educator workshops for retirees/seniors;

- materials for schools (adolescents);
- whole-of-school adoption of the campaign;
- module for incorporation in pain clinics (courses for people to manage chronic pain);
- module for use by primary physicians;
- seminars/workshops for health sector and non-health sector professionals;
- seminars/workshops for general public;
- self-help booklet for general public;
- Indigenous and other cultural adaptations;
- worksite project: *Actively involve–Build skill –Celebrate achievements.*

Why has the campaign been successful?

There are a number of characteristics of the campaign that have contributed to its success so far. However, we believe that the main ingredient was that we took a truly genuine consumer orientation into all of our planning and implementations:

- the campaign messages and their execution were based on what people told us in the formative research and were pre-tested for understanding, credibility and potential impact;
- the basic messages were simple and easy to follow;
- the views of mental health professionals were assessed before campaign planning began;
- the campaign was not imposed on other groups; rather we offered them something of value in return for their co-operation; and
- each town was given the autonomy to set its own objectives, target groups and types of events.

Other features were:

- the project officers had very good people connections and very good professional and interpersonal skills;
- a multi-disciplinary development group and a strong articulate consumer representative on the Curtin management group;
- partnerships were built on shared goals and vision; and
- the project was new, positive in outlook and could incorporate a wide variety of activities (i.e., non-restrictive, non-prescriptive).

Concluding comments

As far as we are aware, there are no similar, comprehensive, populationwide mental health promotion campaigns in any other jurisdiction. Existing initiatives that include

Connect...

Be active...

Take notice...

Keep learning...

Give...

Aked et al (2008); Developed by nef (the economics foundation; http://www.neweconomics.org) for the Foresight Mental Capital and Wellbeing Project (http://foresight.gov.uk).

Figure 15.7 Five Ways to Wellbeing

'mental health promotion' in their titles or objectives (such as those mentioned earlier in the United Kingdom and Illinois), are primarily concerned with de-stigmatisation or target people with a mental illness. However, we expect that as more reports appear that focus on building positive mental health [see the Aked *et al.* (2008) UK new economics foundation report; Figure 15.7], then mental health promotion will be more widespread. It is suggested that the community-based social marketing approach described above will serve as a model for such campaigns.

QUESTIONS

● What do you think the Curtin group should do if they were approached by the following to hold a co-branded event – and why?

  ● a day long family music festival held in a vineyard in a rural area;

  ● a rock concert that was sponsored by a spirits marketer; or

  ● a pool competition in a local bar.

● What sort of partners would be most suitable for an *Act–Belong–Commit* campaign in your region?

● How would you go about implementing the *Act–Belong–Commit* campaign in your university?

FURTHER READING

Bryant, C. A., McCormack Brown, K. R., McDermott, R. J., Forthofer, M. S., Bumpus, E. C., Calkins, S. A. and Zapata, L. B. 2007. Community-Based Prevention Marketing: Organizing a Community for Health Behavior Intervention, *Health Promotion Practice* 8: 154 (DOI: 10.1177/1524839906290089, originally published online 21 August 2006.

Donovan, R. J., James, R., Jalleh, G. and Sidebottom, C. 2006. Implementing Mental Health Promotion: The Act–Belong–Commit Mentally Healthy WA Campaign in Western Australia, *International Journal of Mental Health Promotion* 8(1): 29–38.

ACKNOWLEDGEMENTS

The Mentally Healthy WA pilot intervention was funded largely by Healthway, supported by WA Country Health Services, Lotterywest, the Office of Mental Health and Pilbara Iron Ltd. The 2008–10 intervention is funded by Healthway, WA Country Health Services, Lotterywest and the Office of Mental Health.

REFERENCES

Aaker, J. L. 1997. Dimensions of Brand Personality, *Journal of Marketing Research* 34(Aug.): 347–56.

ABC News 2008. China Milk Scare Escalates, 28 September, available at: www.abc.net.au/ news/stories/2008/09/22/2370263.htm, accessed 21 June 2009.

Abraham, C. and Sheeran, P. 2005. Health Belief Model, in M. Conner and P. Norman (eds.), *Predicting Health Behaviour: Research and Practice with Social Cognition Models*, 2nd edn. Buckingham: Open University Press, pp. 28–80.

Abroms, L. and Lefebvre, R. 2009. Obama's Wired Campaign: Lessons for Public Health Communication, *Journal of Health Communication* 14: 415–23.

Ackerman, P. and Duvall, J. 2000. *A Force More Powerful: A Century of Nonviolent Conflict.* New York: St. Martin's Press.

Action on Smoking and Health (ASH) 2000. PR in the Playground: Tobacco Industry Initiatives on Youth Smoking, available at: www.ash.org.uk.

Adelman, J. 2006. Kids Bite on Cartoon Fruit, Post-Tribune, 6 September, available at: www.highbeam.com/doc/1N1–1148A31B5B760F50.html.

Aidman, A. 1995. *Advertising in Schools*, ERIC Digest, ERIC Identifier ED389473, available at: www.ed.gov/databases/ERIC_Digests/ed 389473.html, retrieved 27 October 2001.

AIDS Action Committee 1989. SafetyNet© Programme: Small Group Parties for Safer Sex Education, *Australian Journal of Public Health* 79(9): 1305–6.

Ajzen, I. 1988. *Attitudes, Personality, and Behavior.* Chicago, IL: Dorsey Press.

Aked, J., Marks, N., Cordon, C. and Thompson, S. 2008. *Five Ways to Well-being: The Evidence.* London: Nef and the Foresight Commission.

Al Arabiya News Channel 2009. Airport Workers in Kathmandu get Bribe-proof Garment: Nepal Fights Bribery with Pocketless Pants, available at: www.alarabiya. net/articles/2009/06/29/77322.html#000, retrieved 29 June 2009.

Alay, S. 2008. Female Consumers' Evaluations of Sponsorship and their Response to Sponsorship, *South African Journal for Research in Sport, Physical Education and Recreation* 30(2): 15–29.

Alderson, W. 1957. *Marketing Behavior and Executive Action.* Homewood, IL: Irwin.

Alexandris, K., Douka, S., Bakaloumi, S. and Tsasousi, E. 2008. The Influence of Spectators' Attitudes on Sponsorship Awareness: A Study in Three Different Leisure Events, *Managing Leisure* 13(1): 1–12.

Alkema, G., Wilber, K., Shannon, G. and Allen, D. 2007. Reduced Mortality: the Unexpected Impact of a Telephone-based Care Management Intervention for Older Adults in Managed Care, *Health Serv Res* 42(4): 1632–50.

Allen, J., Fuller, D.A. and Glaser, M. 1994. Understanding Recycling Behaviour: A Public Policy Perspective, in D.J. Ringold (ed.), *Marketing and Public Policy Conference Proceedings*. Chicago, IL: American Marketing Association, vol. 4.

Ammerman, A., Corbie-Smith, G., St George, D., Washington, C., Weathers, B. and Jackson-Christian, B. 2003. Research Expectations among African-American Church Leaders in the PRAISE! Project: A Randomized Trial Guided by Community-based Participatory Research, *American Journal of Public Health*, 93(10): 1720–7.

Amonini, C. 2001. 'The Relative Influence of Morality, Legitimacy, and Other Determinants on your Alcohol, Tobacco and Marijuana Use', unpublished doctoral dissertation, Graduate School of Management, University of Western Australia, Perth.

Amonini, C. and Donovan, R. J. 2006. The Relationship between Youth's Moral and Legal Perceptions of Alcohol, Tobacco and Marijuana and Use of these Substances, *Health Education Research: Theory and Practice*, 21(2): 276–86.

Amr, H. and Singer, P. 2008. To Win the 'War on Terror', We Must First Win the 'War of Ideas': Here's How, *The Annals of the American Academy of Political and Social Science*, 618: 212–22.

Anders, M. 2008. As Good as the Real Thing?, *ACE FitnessMatters*, July/August, 7–9.

Anderson, D. M., Duffy, K. and Hallett, C. 1992. Cancer Prevention Counseling on Telephone Helplines, *Public Health Reports* 107: 278–83.

Anderson, P. 2006. Global Use of Alcohol, Drugs and Tobacco, *Drug and Alcohol Review* 25(6): 489–502.

Anderson, P. and Baumberg, B. 2006. *Alcohol in Europe: A Public Health Perspective*. London: Institute of Alcohol Studies.

Andreasen, A. 1995. *Marketing Social Change: Changing Behavior to Promote Health, Social Development, and the Environment*. San Francisco, CA: Jossey-Bass.

　2001. *Ethics in Social Marketing*. Washington, DC: Georgetown University Press.

　2006. *Social Marketing in the 21st Century*. Newbury Park: CA: Sage.

Andreasen, A. and Drumwright, M. 2001. Alliances and Ethics in Social Marketing, in A. Andreasen (ed.), *Ethics in Social Marketing*, pp. 95–124. .

Andreasen, A. R. 2002. Marketing Social Marketing in the Social Change Marketplace, *Journal of Public Policy and Marketing* 21(1): 3–14.

APA Public Affairs Office 2007. Peer Pressure Best Motivator when it comes to Energy Saving, Psychologists tell House Panel, 25 September.

Asbury, H. 2002. *The Gangs of Chicago*. New York: Basic Books.

Associated Press, The 1998. Barbie needs limit … *Marketing News*, 27 April, 32(9).

Austin, E. W. and Hust, S. J. 2005. Targeting Adolescents? The Content and Frequency of Alcoholic and Nonalcoholic Beverage Ads in Magazine and Video Formats November 1999–April 2000, *Journal of Health Communication* 10(8): 769–85.

Ayadi, K. and Young, B. 2006. Community Partnerships: Preventing Childhood Obesity, *Young Consumers: Insights and Ideas for Responsible Marketers* 7(4): 35–40.

Babor, T. and Caetano, R. 2005. Evidence-based Alcohol Policy in the Americas: Strengths, Weaknesses, and Future Challenges, *Rev Panam Salud Publica (Pan American Journal of Public Health)*, 18(4–5): 327–37.

Backer, T. E., Rogers, E. M. and Sopory, P. 1992. *Designing Health Communication Campaigns: What Works?* Newbury Park, CA: Sage.

Bagozzi, R. P. and Moore, D. J. 1994. Public Service Advertisements: Emotions and
    Empathy Guide Prosocial Behaviour, *Journal of Marketing* 58: 56–70.
Bagozzi, R. P. and Warshaw, P. R. 1990. Trying to Consume, *Journal of Consumer Research*
    17: 127–40.
Baker, M. 2008. How Do you Sell Respect to Roadhogs?, Business Respect 140, available at:
    www.businessrespect.net/page.php?Story_ID=2296.
Baker, M. J. 1996. *Marketing: An introductory Text,* 6th edn. London: Macmillan.
Baker, T. A. and Wang, C. C. 2006. Photovoice: Use of a Participatory Action Research
    Method to Explore the Chronic Pain Experience in Older Adults, *Qualitative Health
    Research* 16(10): 1405–13.
Balasubramanian, S. K. 1994. Beyond Advertising and Publicity: Hybrid Messages and
    Public Policy Issues, *Journal of Advertising* 23: 29–46.
Baldauf, S. and Tohid, O. 2005. Chasing bin Laden with TV ads in Pakistan Offering Cash,
    21 February, retrieved 17 August 2009 from www.usatoday.com/news/world/2005–
    02–21-al-qaeda-ads_x.htm.
Ball, S. 1994. Theatre and Health Education: Meeting of Minds or Marriage of
    Convenience? *Health Education Journal* 53(2): 222–5.
Bandura, A. 1977. *Social Learning Theory.* Englewood Cliffs, NJ: Prentice-Hall.
    1986. *Social Foundations of Thought and Action: A Social Cognitive Theory.* Englewood
    Cliffs, NJ: Prentice-Hall.
    2004. Health Promotion by Social Cognitive Means, *Health Education & Behavior*
    31(2): 143–64.
Banks, S. M., Salovey, P., Greener, S., Rothman, A. J., Moyer, A., Beauvais, J. and Epel, E. 1995.
    The Effects of Message Framing on Mammography Utilization, *Health Psychology*
    14: 178–84.
Barber, L. 2001. Product Misplacement, *The Weekend Australian Review*, 20–21 January, p. 23.
Barendregt, J. J., Bonneux, L. and van der Maas, P. J. 1997. The Health Care Costs of
    Smoking, *New England Journal of Medicine* 337(15): 1052–7.
Barr, S. and Gilg, A. 2006. Sustainable Lifestyles: Framing Environmental Action in and
    around the Home, *Geoforum* 37: 906–20.
Batini, C. and Donovan, R. J. 2001. Drinking and Driving in the Great Southern: Perceptions
    of Practices, Priorities and Preventives, Stage One Qualitative Research Report to
    Great Southern Public Health Services, Perth, Western Australia: NFO Donovan
    Research.
Baumberg, B. 2006. The Global Economic Burden of Alcohol: A Review and some
    Suggestions, *Drug & Alcohol Review* 25(6): 537–51.
Baumeister, R. and Leary, M. R. 1995. The Need to Belong: Desire for Interpersonal
    Attachments as a Fundamental Human Motivation, *Psychological Bulletin*
    117(3): 497–529.
BBC News 2007. Brown Defends New Citizen Juries, retrieved 20 June 2009 from http://
    news.bbc.co.uk/2/hi/uk_news/politics/6980747.stm.
Beasley, S. 2006. Faith Healing, retrieved 9 July 2006 from www.balitmoresun.com/news/
    health/bal-hs.churches07jul07,0,617581.story?col.
Beck, R. 2006. Popular Media for HIV/AIDS Prevention? Comparing Two Comics: Kingo
    and the Sara Communication Initiative, *Journal of Modern African Studies*
    44(r4): 513–41.

Becker, M. H. 1974. The Health Belief Model and Personal Health Behaviour, *Health Education Monographs* 2: 324–473.

Beenstock, S. 1999. Meg@hurts, *Times Educational Supplement*, 26 March, pp. B8–9.

Bell, A., Swinburn, B., Amosa, H. and Scragg, R. 2001. A Nutrition and Exercise Intervention Programme for Controlling Weight in Samoan Communities in New Zealand, *International Journal of Obesity Related Metabolic Disorders* 25(6): 920–7.

BellaSugarUK 2008. Would you Rent your Eyelids as Advertising Space?, retrieved 2 April 2009 from http://uk.fashion.popsugar.com/2620233.

Belz, F. and Peattie, K. 2009. *Sustainability Marketing: A Global Perspective.* Chichester: Wiley.

Benkimoun, P. 2009. French Doctors Protest over Commercialisation of Care, *BMJ* 338: 1233.

Benn, S. I. 1988. *The Theory of Freedom.* New York: Cambridge University Press.

Bennett, R. 1998. Shame, Guilt and Responses to Nonprofit and Public Sector Ads, *International Journal of Advertising*, 17(4), 483–99.

Bensberg, M. and Kennedy, M. 2002. A Framework for Health Promoting Emergency Departments, *Health Promotion International* 17(2): 179–88.

Bernhardt, J. M. 2001. Tailoring Messages and Design in a Web-based Skin Cancer Prevention Intervention, *The International Electronic Journal of Health Education* 4: 290–7, retrieved from www.iejhe.org.

Berwick, D. M. 2003. Disseminating Innovations in Health Care, *The Journal of the American Medical Association* 289(15): 1969–75.

Bevins, J. 1988. Reducing Communication Abuse, *Workshop Proceedings Vol. I.,* Third National Drug Educators Workshop. Fremantle, WA, 22 September.

Biener, L. and Siegel, M. 2000. Tobacco Marketing and Adolescent Smoking: More Support for a Causal Influence, *American Journal of Public Health* 90(3): 407–11.

Binder, D. 1996. *Fair Play for Kids: A Handbook of Activities for Teaching Fair Play,* 2nd edn. New York: McGraw-Hill.

Bittle, S. 2009. Clipping the Raptor, Trimming the Budget, retrieved 23 July 2009 from www.publicagenda.org/blogs/clipping-raptor-trimming-budget.

Black, C. 2007. How to Get a Healthy Heart with that Brand-new Do, 29 April, retrieved 15 May 2007 from http://seattlepi.nwsource.com/printer2/index.asp?ploc=t&refer=http://seattlepi.nwsour

Blasi, A. 1980. Bridging Moral Cognition and Moral Action: A Critical Review of the Literature, *Psychological Bulletin* 88: 593–637.

Blaszczynski, A. 2003. *Harm Minimization Strategies in Gambling: An Overview of International Initiatives and Interventions.* Sydney: University of Sydney.

Bloom, P. N. and Novelli, W. D. 1981. Problems and Challenges in Social Marketing, *Journal of Marketing* 45(Spring): 79–88.

Blue, C. L. 1995. The Predictive Capacity of the Theory of Reasoned Action and the Theory of Planned Behavior in Exercise Research: An Integrated Literature Review, *Research in Nursing & Health* 18: 105–21.

Blum, L., Khan, R., Hyder, A., Shahanaj, S., El Arifeen, S. and Baqui, A. 2009. Childhood Drowning in Matlab, Bangladesh: An In-depth Exploration of Community Perceptions and Practices, *Social Science & Medicine* 68(9): 1720–7.

Boer, H. and Seydel, E. R. 1996. Protection Motivation Theory, in M. Conner, and P. Norman (eds.), *Predicting Health Behaviour.* Buckingham: Open University Press, pp. 95–120.

Bombardier, C., Laine, L., Reicin, A., Shapiro, D., Burgos-Vargas, R., Davis, B., Day, R., Ferraz, M., Hawkey, C., Hochberg, M., Kvien, T. and Schnitzer, T. 2000. Comparison of Upper Gastrointestinal Toxicity of Rofecoxib and Naproxen in Patients with Rheumatoid Arthritis. VIGOR Study Group, *New England Journal of Medicine* 343(21): 1520–8.

Bonniface, L. and Henley, N. 2008. A Drop in the Bucket: Collective Efficacy Perceptions and Environmental Behaviour, *Australian Journal of Social Issues* 43(3): 345–58.

Boocock, S. S. 1995. Early Childhood Programs in other Nations: Goals and Outcomes, *The Future of Children* 5(3): 94–114.

Booth, M. L., Macaskill, P., Owen, N., Oldenburg, B., Marcus, B. H. and Bauman, A. 1993. Population Prevalence and Correlates of Stages of Change in Physical Activity, *Health Education Quarterly* 20: 431–40.

Booth-Butterfield, S. and Reger, B. 2004. The Message Changes Belief and the Rest is Theory: the '1% or less' Milk Campaign and Reasoned Action, *Preventive Medicine* 39(3): 581–8.

BoozeNews 2001. Statement of George A. Hacker on the Marketing of 'Alcopops' to Teens, 9 May, retrieved 20 April 2003 from www.cspinet.org/booze/alcopops_statement.htm.

Borland, R., Balmford, J. and Hunt, D. 2004. The Effectiveness of Personally Tailored Computer-generated Advice Letters for Smoking Cessation, *Addiction* 99(3): 369–77.

Boster, F. J. and Mongeau, P. 1984. Fear-arousing Persuasive Messages, *Communication Yearbook* 8: 330–75.

Boston University School of Public Health 2004. Flavored Cigarettes Appeal to Minority Youth. Join Together, 25 August, retrieved 21 October 2004 from www.jointogether. org/sa/news/summaries/reader/0,1854,574308,00.html.

Boutelle, K., Jeffery, R., Murray, D. and Schmitz, M. 2001. Using Signs, Artwork, and Music to Promote Stair use in a Public Building, *American Journal of Public Health* 91(12): 2004–6.

Bowman, D., Heilman, C. M. and Seetharaman, P. B. 2004. Determinants of Product-use Compliance Behavior, *Journal of Marketing Research* 41(3): 324–38.

Braun, S. 2003. The History of Breast Cancer Advocacy, *The Breast Journal* 9(Supp.2): S101–S103.

Brenkert, G. G. 2001. The Ethics of International Social Marketing, in A. Andreasen (ed.), *Ethics in Social Marketing.* Washington, DC: Georgetown University Press, pp. 39–69.

2002. Ethical Challenges of Social Marketing, *Journal of Public Policy & Marketing* 21(1): 14–36.

Brennan, L. and Binney, W. 2010. Fear, Guilt, and Shame Appeals in Social Marketing, *Journal of Business Research* 63(2): 140–6.

Brook, S. 2004. Anti-smoking Ads Help 1 Million Quit, 3 November, retrieved 4 November 2004 from www.guardian.co.uk/media/2004/nov/03/advertising.society.

Brown, D. 2001. Depressed Men: Angry Women: Non-stereotypical Gender Responses to Anti-smoking Messages in Older Smokers, Unpublished masters dissertation, Edith Cowan University, Perth, Western Australia.

Brown, G. 1985. Tracking Studies and Sales Effects: A UK Perspective, *Journal of Advertising Research* 25(1): 52–64.

Brown, L. 2002. In for the Showbag, *The Australian*, 31 May, p. 17.

Brown, S., Lieberman, D., Gemeny, B., Fan, Y., Wilson, D. and Pasta, D. 1997. Educational Video Game for Juvenile Diabetes: Results of a Controlled Trial, *Informatics for Health and Social Care* 22(1): 77–89.

Brown, W. J., Mummery, K., Eakin, E., Trost, S., Schofield, G. and Abernethy, P. 2002. 10,000 Steps Rockhampton: Top Down and Bottom Up Approaches to Increasing Levels of Physical Activity, in S. Miilunpalo and R. Tulimaki (eds.), *Health Enhancing Physical Activity (HEPA): Evidence-based Promotion of Physical Activity,* Book of Abstracts. Tampere, Finland: UKK Institute.

Browne, K. and Hamilton-Giachritsis, C. 2005. The Influence of Violent Media on Children and Adolescents: A Public Health Approach, *The Lancet* 365(9460): 702–10.

Brownell, K. and Frieden, T. 2009. Ounces of Prevention – The Public Policy Case for Taxes on Sugared Beverages, *New England Journal of Medicine* 360(18): 1805–8.

Brownell, K. and Horgen, K. 2004. *Food Fight: The Inside Story of the Food Industry, America's Obesity Crisis, and What We Can do About It.* Chicago, IL: Contemporary Books.

Brownlee, S. 2001. The Big Fat Question. *Self,* December, pp. 124–7, 162–3.

Bryant, J. and Oliver, M. (eds.) 2009. *Media Effects: Advances in Theory and Research*, 3rd edn. New York: Routledge.

Bryant, J., and Zillmann, D. (eds.) 2002. *Media Effects: Advances in Theory and Research*, 2nd edn. Hillsdale, NJ: Lawrence Erlbaum.

Buchanan, D. R., Reddy, S. and Hossain, Z. 1994. Social Marketing: A Critical Appraisal … Social Marketing and Communication in Health Promotion, *Health Promotion International* 9(1): 49–57.

Buenos Aires Herald 2008. Taxi Drivers, Salesman Trained for Tourism, *Buenos Aires Herald,* 12 October.

   2008. La Rioja to Ban Raffle of Plastic Surgeries, *Buenos Aires Herald*, 12 October.

Bull, F. C. and Jamrozik, K. 1998. Advice on Exercise from a Family Physician can help Sedentary Patients to become Active, *American Journal of Preventative Medicine* 15(2): 85–94.

Burdette, A. M. and Hill, T. D. 2008. An Examination of Processes Linking Perceived Neighborhood Disorder and Obesity, *Social Science and Medicine* 67(1): 38–46.

Butler, S. 2006. Tipping the Balance? An Irish Perspective on Anderson and Baumberg, *Drugs: Education, Prevention and Policy* 13(6): 493–7.

Campaign for a Commercial-Free Childhood 2009. Access Marketing in Schools, CCFC, available at: www.commercialfreechildhood.org.

Campbell, M., Hudson, M., Resnicow, K., Blakeney, N., Paxton, A. and Baskin, M. 2007. Church-based Health Promotion Interventions: Evidence and Lessons Learned, *Annual Review of Public Health* 28: 213–34.

Campbell, M. K., Demark-Wahnefried, W., Symons, M., Kalzbeek, W. D., Dodds, J., Cowan, A., Jackson, B., Motsinger, B., Hoben, K., Lashley, J., Demissie, S. and McClelland, J. W. 1999. Fruit and Vegetable Consumption and Prevention of Cancer: The Black Churches United for Better Health Project, *American Journal of Public Health* 89(9): 1390–6.

Canadian Broadcasting Corporation 2005. Cookie Monster Cuts Back on his Favourite Food, CBC – Arts, 8 April, retrieved 9 April 2005 from www.cbc.ca/arts/story/2005/04/08/cookie050408.html?print.

Canadian Centre for Policy Alternatives 2006. Commercialism in Canadian Schools: Who's Calling the Shots?, cited 30 June 2009, available at: www.policyalternatives.ca/documents/National_Office_Pubs/2006/Commercialism_in_Canadian_Schools.pdf.

Canga, N., De Irala, J., Vara, E., Duaso, M., Ferber, A. and Martinez-Gonzalez, M. 2000. Intervention Study for Smoking Cessation in Diabetic Patients: A Randomized Controlled Trial in Both Clinical and Primary Care Settings, *Diabetes Care* 23(10): 1455–60.

Cant, R., Downie, R., Fisher, C., Henry, P. and Froyland, I. 2002. Evaluation of Perpetrator Programs for Mandated and Voluntary Participants in Western Australia, Centre for Research for Women, Perth, Western Australia.

Caragay, A. B. 1992. Cancer-preventive Foods and Ingredients, *Food Technology* 46(4): 65–8.

Cardwell, D. 2007. City to Reward the Poor for Doing the Right Thing, *New York Times*.

Carroll, T. and Donovan, R. J. 2002. Alcohol Marketing on the Internet: New Challenges for Harm Reduction, *Drug and Alcohol Review* 21: 83–91.

Carter, S., Borland, R. and Chapman, S. 2001. *Finding the Strength to Kill your Best Friend: Smokers Talk about Smoking and Quitting.* Sydney: Australian Smoking Cessation Consortium and GlaxoSmithKline Consumer Healthcare.

Carter, S. P, Carter, S. L. and Dannenberg, A. L. 2003. Zoning out Crime and Improving Community Health in Sarasota, Florida: 'Crime Prevention Through Environmental Design', *American Journal of Public Health* 93(9): 1442–5.

Cassidy, J. 2008. Medicine and the Media – The Soap Opera that Saves Lives, *British Medical Journal* 336(7653): 1102–3.

Casteel, C. and Peek-Asa, C. 2000. Effectiveness of Crime Prevention through Environmental Design (CPTED) in Reducing Robberies, *American Journal of Preventative Medicine* 18(4S): 99–115.

Cavill, N. and Bauman, A. 2004. Changing the Way People think about Health-Enhancing Physical Activity: Do Mass Media Campaigns have a Role?, *Journal of Sports Science* 22(8): 771–90.

Center on Alcohol Marketing and Youth (CAMY) 2004. *Clicking with Kids: Alcohol Marketing on the Internet.* Washington, DC: Georgetown University.

Center for a New American Dream (CNAD) 1997. Poverty, Race and Consumerism, available at:www.newdream.org.

Chaika, G. 1998. The Selling of our Schools: Advertising in the Classroom, *Education World*, retrieved 29 October 2001 from www.education-world.com/ a_admin/ admin083.shtml.

Chaiken, S. 1987. Heuristic versus Systematic Information Processing and the Use of Source versus Message Cues in Persuasion, *Journal of Personality and Social Psychology* 45: 805–18.

Chaloupka, F. J. 1995. Public Policies and Private Anti-health Behavior, *The Economics of Health and Health Care* 85(2): 45–9.

Chapman, S. 2004. Advocacy for Public Health: A Primer, *Journal of Epidemiology and Community Health* 58: 361–5.

2007. *Public Health Advocacy and Tobacco Control: Making Smoking History.* Oxford: Blackwell Publishing.

Chapman, S. and Lupton, D. 1994. *The Fight for Public Health: Principles & Practice of Media Advocacy.* London: BMJ Publishing Group.

Chapman, S. and Reynolds, C. 1987. Regulating Tobacco – The South Australian Tobacco Products Control Act 1986, *Community Health Studies* 11(1): 9–15.

Chapman, S. and Shatenstein, S. 2001. The Ethics of the Cash Register: Taking Tobacco Research Dollars, *Tobacco Control* 10(1): 1–2.

Chapman, S., Marks, R. and King, M. 1992. Trends in Tans and Skin Protection in Australian Fashion Magazines, 1982 through 1991, *American Journal of Public Health* 82: 1677–80.

Charlesworth, A. and Glantz, S. A. 2005. Smoking in the Movies Increases Adolescent Smoking: A Review, *Pediatrics*, 116(6): 1516–28.

Chaudary, N. K., Solomon, M. G. and Cosgrove, L. A. 2004. The Relationship between Perceived Risk of Being Ticketed and Self-reported Seat Belt Use, *Journal of Safety Research* 35(4): 383–90.

Chen, P. 1996. Social Marketing: Principles and Practices for Planned Social Change, *Media Asia* 23(2): 79–85.

Chou, S., Rashad, I. and Grossman, M. 2005. *Fast-food Restaurant Advertising on Television and its Influence on Childhood Obesity.* Cambridge, MA: National Bureau of Economic Research.

Chrisafis, A. 2007. You're Worth It – If White: L'Oréal Guilty of Racism, *The Guardian*, 7 July, retrieved 26 June 2009 from www.guardian.co.uk/world/2007/jul/07/france. angeliquechrisafis.

Chu, G. C. 1966. Fear Arousal, Efficacy, and Imminency, *Journal of Personality and Social Psychology* 4: 517–24.

Cialdini, R. 2001. *Influence: Science and Practice.* Neeham Heights, MA: Allyn & Bacon.

Cialdini, R. B. 1984. *Influence: The New Psychology of Modern Persuasion.* New York: Quill.
  1989. Littering: When every Litter Bit Hurts, in R. E. Rice and C. K. Atkin (eds.), *Public Communication Campaigns.* Newbury Park, CA: Sage.

Cialdini, R. B., Reno, R. R. and Kallgren, C. A. 1990. A Focus Theory of Normative Conduct: Recycling the Concept of Norms to Reduce Littering in Public Places, *Journal of Personality and Social Psychology* 58(6): 1015–26.

Cina, A., Bodenmann, G., Hahlweg, K., Dirscherl, T. and Sanders, M. R. 2006. Triple P (Positive Parenting Program): Theoretical and Empirical Background and First Experiences in German Speaking Areas, *Journal of Family Research* 18: 66–88.

Clarkson, J., Corti, B., Pikora, T., Jalleh, G. and Donovan, R. J. 1998. *Organisational Survey 1992–1997. Healthy Environment Policies in Sponsored Organisations.* Perth: Health Promotion Evaluation Unit, The University of Western Australia.

Clarkson, J., Donovan, R. J., Giles-Corti, B., Bulsara, M. and Jalleh, G. 2000. *Survey on Recreation and Health 1992–1998: Vol. 5: Health Environments in Recreation Venues.* Perth: Health Promotion Evaluation Unit, The University of Western Australia.

Clegg, A. 2009. Public Awareness Campaign for Helmet Wearing: Winning Vietnam's Helmet War, in N. Dawson (ed.), *Advertising Works: Proving the Payback on Marketing Investment.* Henley on Thames: World Advertising Research Center.

Close, H. and Donovan, R. J. 1998. *Who's My Market? Researching Audience for the Arts.* Sydney: Australian Council.

Cody, E. 2004. In China, Eyesight Fixed by Rail, 8 August, retrieved 9 August 2004 from www.washingtonpost.com/ac2/wp-dyn/A48723–2004Aug7?language=printer.

Cohen, D., Scribner, R. and Farley, T. 2000. A Structural Model of Health Behavior: A Pragmatic Approach to Explain and Influence Health Behaviors at the Population Level, *Preventative Medicine* 30(2): 146–54.

Coleman, P. L. and Meyer, R. C. (eds.) 1990. *Proceedings from the Enter–Educate Conference: Entertainment for Social Change*. Baltimore, MD: Johns Hopkins University Centre for Communication Programs.

Collin, W. 2008. Innovative Uses of Media, in J. Lannon (ed.), *How Public Service Advertising Works*. Henley-on-Thames: World Advertising Research Centre.

Collins, M. 1993. Global Corporate Philanthropy – Marketing Beyond the Call of Duty?, *European Journal of Marketing* 27(2): 46–59.

Collins, R. L., Ellickson, P. L., McCaffrey, D. and Hambarsoomians, K. 2007. Early Adolescent Exposure to Alcohol Advertising and its Relationship to Underage Drinking, *Journal of Adolescent Health* 40(6): 527–34.

Committee on Environmental Health 2009. The Built Environment: Designing Communities to Promote Physical Activity in Children, *Pediatrics* 123(6): 1591–8 (doi:10.1542/peds.2009–0750).

Community Agency for Social Enquiry (CASE) 1997. *Let the Sky be the Limit: Soul City Evaluation Report*. Braamfontein, South Africa.

Comstock, G. 2004. Paths from Television Violence to Aggression: Reinterpreting the Evidence, in L. Shrum (ed.), *The Psychology of Entertainment Media*. Hillsdale, NJ: Lawrence Erlbaum.

Cone 2008. Past. Present. Future. The 25th Anniversary of Cause Marketing, retrieved 16 October 2008 from www.coneinc.com.

Congress of the United States 2008. Contractors' Support of US Operations in Iraq: A CBO Paper: Congressional Budget Office.

Conner, M. and Norman, P. (eds.) 2005. *Predicting Health Behaviour: Research and Practice with Social Cognition Models*, 2nd edn. Buckingham: Open University Press.

Conner, M. and Sparks, P. 1996. The Theory of Planned Behaviour and Health Behaviours, in Conner and Norman (eds.), *Predicting Health Behaviour,* pp. 121–63.

Consumers Union 1998. Captive Kids: A Report on Commercial Pressures on Kids at Schools, retrieved 27 October 2001 from www.igc.org/consunion/other/captivekids/summary.htm.

Cooper, C., Roter, D. and Langlieb, A. 2000. Using Entertainment Television to Build a Context for Prevention News Stories, *Preventative Medicine* 31(3): 225–31.

Cooper, P., Tomlinson, M., Swartz, L., Landman, M., Molteno, C., Stein, A., McPherson, K. and Murray, L. 2009. Improving Quality of Mother–Infant Relationship and Infant Attachment in a Socio-economically Deprived Community in South Africa: Randomised Controlled Trial, *British Medical Journal* 338: b974.

Cooper-Martin, E. and Smith, N. C. 1994. *Target Marketing: Good Marketing or Bad Ethics,* Georgetown University, School of Business Administration, Working Paper Series, MKTG-1777–15–1294.

Cornwell, P. 1996. *Cause of Death.* Boston, MA: Little Brown.

Cornwell, T., Weeks, C. and Roy, D. 2005. Sponsorship-linked Marketing: Opening the Black Box, *Journal of Advertising* 34(2): 21–42.

Cortez, M. 2008. Cosmetic Surgery Losing Stigma for US Men, rises 17% in 2007, 26 February, retrieved 26 February 2008 from www.bloomberg.com/apps/news?pid=sid=aFwrVHhd3N.A&refer=healthcare#.

Corti, B. 1998. 'The Relative Influence of, and Interaction Between, Environmental and Individual Determinants of Recreational Physical Activity in Sedentary Workers and Home Makers', unpublished doctoral dissertation, Department of Public Health, The University of Western Australia, Perth, Western Australia.

Corti, B., Holman, C. D. J., Donovan, R. J., Frizzell, S. K. and Carroll, A. M. 1997. Warning: Attending a Sport, Racing or Arts Venue may be Beneficial to your Health, *Australian and New Zealand Journal of Public Health* 21(4): 371–6.

Coyle, S. L., Boruch, R. F. and Turner, C. F. (eds.) 1989. *Evaluating AIDS Prevention Programs.* Washington, DC: National Academy Press.

Craig-Lees, M., Joy, S. and Browne, B. 1995. *Consumer Behaviour.* Brisbane: John Wiley.

Cressey, D. 2007. Is baby DVD research Mickey Mouse Science? *Nature*, 448: 848–9, published online 22 August, available at: www.nature.com/nature/journal/v448/n7156/full/448848b.html, accessed 22 May 2010.

Crimmins, J. and Horn, M. 1996. Sponsorship: From Management Ego Trip to Marketing Success, *Journal of Advertising Research* 35(4): 11–21.

Crompton, J. L. 1981. The Role of Pricing in the Delivery of Community Services, *Community Development Journal* 16(1): 44–54.

Crowe, D. 2000. Crime Prevention through Environmental Design, National Crime Prevention Institute, University of Louisville.

Csikszentmihalyi, M. 1990. *Flow: The Psychology of Optimal Experience.* New York: Harper Perennial.

Csikszentmihalyi, M. and Csikszentmihalyi, I. 2006. *A Life Worth Living: Contributions to Positive Psychology.* New York: Oxford University Press.

Curry, A., Latkin, C. and Davey-Rothwell, M. 2008. Pathways to Depression: The Impact of Neighborhood Violent Crime on Inner-city Residents in Baltimore, Maryland, USA, *Social Science and Medicine* 67(1): 23–30.

Curtis, K., McCluskey, J. and Wahl, T. 2007. Consumer Preferences for Western-style Convenience Foods in China, *China Economic Review* 18: 1–14.

Curtis, V. 2003. Talking Dirty: How to Save a Million Lives, *International Journal of Environmental Health Research* 13(1): S73–S79.

Cushman, P. 1990. Why the Self is Empty: Toward a Historically Situated Psychology, *The American Psychologist* 45(5): 599–611.

Cutler, M. 2009. Worldwide Olympic Partner McDonald's is in Talks with London, available at: www.sportbusiness.com/news/170181/catering-industry-warns-over-mcdonald-s-2012-exclusivity.

Daily Mirror Reporter 2009. Ban Alcohol Advertising and Introduce Minimum Price for Drinks, Demand Doctors, *Mail Online*, 20 July 2009.

Dalton, M., Sargent, J., Beach, M., Titus-Ernstoff, L., Gibson, J., Ahrens, M., Tickle, J. and Heatherton, T. 2003. Effect of Viewing Smoking in Movies on Adolescent Smoking Initiation: A Cohort Study, *The Lancet* 362(9380): 281–5.

Daniels, L. 1977. *Fear: A History of Horror in the Mass Media.* London: Granada Publishing.

Darnton, A. 2008. Reference Report: An Overview of Behaviour Change Models and Their Uses, GSR: Government Social Research.

Davidson, D. 2003. *Selling Sin: The Marketing of Socially Unacceptable Products*, 2nd edn. Westport, CT: Praeger.

Davies, R., and Dart, J. 2005. The 'Most Significant Change' (MSC) Technique: A Guide to its Use, Care International, Version 1.

Davis, H. and Tsiantis, J. 2005. Promoting Children's Mental Health: The European Early Promotion Project (EEPP), *International Journal of Mental Health Promotion* 7(1).

Dawson, N. (ed.) 2009. *Advertising Works 17: Proving the Payback on Marketing Investment.* Henley on Thames: World Advertising Research Centre.

Day, B. A. and Monroe, M. C. (eds.) 2000. *Environmental Education & Communication for a Sustainable World: Handbook for International Practitioners.* Washington, DC: Academy for Educational Development and GreenCom.

Day, M. 2007. UK Government Invites Bids for General Practices in Supermarkets, *British Medical Journal* 334(7594): 605.

De Musis, E. A. and Miaoulis, G. 1988. Channels of Distribution and Exchange Concepts in Health Promotion, *Journal of Health Care Marketing* 8: 60–8.

de Vet, E., de Nooijer, J., de Vries, N. and Brug, J. 2007. Comparing Stage of Change and Behavioral Intention to Understand Fruit Intake, *Health Education Research* 22(4): 599–608.

2008. Testing the Transtheoretical Model for Fruit Intake: Comparing Web-based Tailored Stage-matched and Stage-mismatched Feedback, *Health Education Research* 23(2): 218–27.

Deighton, J., Romer, D. and McQueen, J. 1989. Using Drama to Persuade, *Journal of Consumer Research* 16: 335–43.

Dellorto, D. 2009. FDA Hazy on e-cigarettes' Safety, CNN.com 2009 (cited 18 March 2009), available at: http://edition.cnn.com/2009/HEALTH/03/13/ecigarettes.smoking.

Denton, F. and Thorson, E. 1995. *Civic Journalism: Does it Work?* Washington, DC: Pew Center for Civic Journalism.

Department of the Environment for Northern Ireland 2005. Northern Ireland Seat Belt Survey, retrieved 24 June 2009 from www.doeni.gov.uk/ni_seatbelt_survey_apr_2005.pdf.

DeYoung, K. 2001. Organisations Find Big Changes in Bush's A-list, *The Washington Post*, 17 May, p. 21, retrieved 28 May 2001 from www.washingtonpost.com/wp-dyn/articles/A36643–2001May16.html.

2006. Gates, Rockefeller Charities Join to Fight African Hunger, 13 September, retrieved 14 September 2006 from www.washingtonpost.com/wp-dyn/content/article/2006/09/12/AR20060912013.

Dichter, E. 1964. *Handbook of Consumer Motivations.* New York: McGraw-Hill.

Dillard, J. P., Plotnick, C. A., Godbold, L. C., Friemuth, V. S. and Edgar, T. 1996. The Multiple Affective Outcome of AIDS PSAs: Fear Appeals do More than Scare People, *Communication Research* 23: 44–72.

Dixon J. M., Hinde S. J. and Banwell C. L. 2006. Obesity, Convenience and 'Phood', *British Food Journal* 108(8): 634–45.

Doane, D. 2005. The Myth of CSR: The Problem with Assuming that Companies can do Well While also Doing Good is that Markets don't really Work that Way, *Stanford Social Innovation Review* Fall.

Donovan, R. J. 1991. Public Health Advertising: Execution Guidelines for Health Promotion Professionals, *Health Promotion Journal of Australia* 1: 40–5.

1995. *Guidelines for creating effective road safety advertising.* Report to Federal Office of Road safety. Perth, WA: Donovan Research.

1996. *Using Newspapers and Community Action to Further the Aboriginal Reconciliation Process: A Submission to the Council for Aboriginal Reconciliation.* University of Western Australia, Perth, WA.

1997. *A Model of Alcohol Consumption to Assist in Developing Communication Strategies for Reducing Excessive Alcohol Consumption by Young People.* Report to Health Department of Western Australia. Perth, WA: Donovan Research.

2000a. Tracking phase two of the national tobacco campaign. In K. Hassard (ed.), *Australia's National Tobacco Campaign: Evaluation Report: Vol. 2.* Canberra: Commonwealth Department of Health and Aged Care, pp. 115–54.

2000b. Understanding the social determinants of health. *Social Marketing Quarterly*: 6(3) 55–7.

2001. The effect of tobacco warnings: Expert statement. Submitted by Canadian Cancer Society, in the case of *JTI-MacDonald Corp., Imperial Tobacco Canada Ltd and Rothman, Benson & Hedges Inc.* v. *Attorney General of Canada*, Montreal.

2004. North Queenslanders' Beliefs about Mental Health and Mental Health Promotion. Townsville: Report to Queensland Health, Tropical Public Health Unit.

2009. Towards an Understanding of Factors Influencing Athletes' Attitudes Towards Performance Enhancing Technologies: Implications for Ethics Education, in T. Murray, A. Wasunna , E. Parens and K. Maschke (eds.), *Enhancing Technologies in Sport: Ethical Conceptual and Scientific Issues.* Baltimore, MD: The Johns Hopkins University Press.

Donovan, R. J. and Batini, C. 1997. *Strategy Development and Concept Testing Research for Road Safety Campaign,* Summary Report to Marketforce, Donovan Research, Perth, Western Australia.

Donovan, R. J. and Carroll, T. 2008. Public Health Branding Down Under, in W. D. Evans and G. Hastings (eds.), *Public Health Branding: Applying Marketing for Social Change.* Oxford University Press.

Donovan, R. J. and Egger, G. 1997. *A Conceptual Framework for Achieving Drug Compliance in Sport,* Report to Australian Sports Drug Agency, Donovan Research, Perth, Western Australia.

2000. *Men's Health Beliefs: A Qualitative Research Report to the 'Healthy Blokes' Project,* Centre for Behavioural Research in Cancer Control, Donovan Research, Perth, Western Australia.

Donovan, R. J. and Francas, M. 1987. *Child Value,* Report to Department for Community Services, Donovan Research, Perth, Western Australia.

1990. Understanding Motivation and Communication Strategies, *Australian Health Review* 13: 103–14.

Donovan, R. J. and Henley, N. 1997. Negative Outcomes, Threats and Threat Appeals: Towards a Conceptual Framework for the Study of Fear and Other Emotions in Social Marketing Communications, *Social Marketing Quarterly* 4(1): 56–67.

Donovan, R. J. and Holden, S. J. S. 1985. Projective Techniques in Attitude Research, *Australian Marketing Researcher* 9: 55–62.

Donovan, R. J. and Jalleh, G. 1999. Positive versus Negatively Framed Product Attributes: The Influence of Involvement, *Psychology & Marketing* 28(4): 215–34.

2000. Positive versus Negative Framing of a Hypothetical Infant Immunisation: The Influence of Involvement, *Health Education and Behaviour* 27(1): 82–95.

Donovan, R. J. and Leivers, S. 1993. Using Paid Advertising to Modify Racial Stereotype Beliefs, *Public Opinion Quarterly* 57: 205–18.

Donovan, R. J. and Owen, N. 1994. Social Marketing and Population Interventions, in R. K. Dishman (ed.), *Advances in Exercise Adherence,* 2nd edn. Chicago, IL: Human Kinetics, pp. 249–90.

Donovan, R. J. and Spark, R. 1997. Towards Guidelines for Researching Remote Aboriginal Communities, *Australian and New Zealand Journal of Public Health* 21(1): 89–95.

Donovan, R. J. and Vlais, R. 2005. *Review of Communication Components of Social Marketing/ public Education Campaigns Focusing on Violence against Women,* Report to VicHealth, Melbourne, Australia.

2006. *A Review of Communication Components of Anti-racism and Pro-diversity Social Marketing/Public Education Campaigns,* Report to VicHealth, Melbourne, Australia.

Donovan, R. J., Corti, B. and Jalleh, G. 1997. Evaluating Sponsorship Effectiveness: An Epidemiological Approach to Analysing Survey Data, *Australian Journal of Market Research* 5(2): 9–23.

Donovan, R. J., Egger, G. J. and Francas, M. 1999. TARPARE: A Method for Selecting Target Audiences for Public Health Interventions, *Australian and New Zealand Journal of Public Health* 23(3): 280–4.

Donovan, R. J., Jalleh, G. and Henley, N. 1999. Effective Road Safety Advertising: Are Big Production Budgets Necessary?, *Accident Analysis and Prevention* 31: 243–52.

Donovan, R. J., Jalleh, G. and Jones, S. 2003. The Word 'Cancer': Reframing the Context to Reduce Anxiety Arousal, *Australian and New Zealand Journal of Public Health* 27(3): 291–3.

Donovan, R. J., James, R. and Jalleh, G. 2007. Community-based Social Marketing to Promote Positive Mental Health: The Act–Belong–Commit Campaign in Rural Western Australia, in G. Hastings (ed.), *Social Marketing: Why Should the Devil Have all the Best Tunes?* London: Butterworth Heinemann.

Donovan, R. J., Leivers, S. and Hannaby, L. 1999. Smokers' Responses to Anti-smoking Advertisements by Stage of Change, *Social Marketing Quarterly* 5(2): 56–63.

Donovan, R. J., Paterson, D., and Francas, M. 1999. Targeting Male Perpetrators of Intimate Partner Violence: Western Australia's 'Freedom from Fear' Campaign, *Social Marketing Quarterly* 5(3): 127–43.

Donovan, R. J., Weller, N. and Clarkson, J. 2003. *Incidental Smoking in the Media Study,* Report to the Commonwealth Department of Health and Aged Care, Centre for Behavioural Research in Cancer Control, Curtin University, Perth, Western Australia.

Donovan, R. J., Close, H. K., Woodhouse, M. and Hogben, J. 1979. *The Resident and Urban Renewal.* Melbourne: Australian Housing Research Council.

Donovan, R. J., Corti, B., Holman, C. D. J., West, D. and Pitter, D. 1993. Evaluating Sponsorship Effectiveness, *Health Promotion Journal of Australia* 3(1): 63–7.

Donovan, R. J., Egger, G., Kapernick, V. and Mendoza, J. A. 2002. A Conceptual Framework for Achieving Drug Compliance in Sport, *Sports Medicine* 32(4): 269–84.

Donovan, R. J., Francas, M., Paterson, D. and Zappelli, R. 2000. Formative Research for Mass Media-based Campaigns: Western Australia's 'Freedom from Fear' Campaign

Targeting Male Perpetrators of Intimate Partner Violence, *Health Promotion Journal of Australia* 10(2): 78–83.

Donovan, R. J., Henley, N., Jalleh, G. and Slater, C. 1995. *Road Safety Advertising: An Empirical Study and Literature Review,* Report to Federal Office of Road Safety, Donovan Research, Perth, Western Australia.

Donovan, R. J., Henley, N., Watson, N., Zubrick, S., Silburn, S. and Williams, A. 2005. People's Beliefs about Factors Contributing to Mental Health: Implications for Mental Health Promotion, *Health Promotion Journal of Australia* 18(1): 50–6.

2006a. The Impact on Mental Health in Others of Those in a Position of Authority: A Perspective of Parents, Teachers, Trainers and Supervisors, *Australian e-Journal for the Advancement of Mental Health*, 5(1).

Donovan, R. J., Jalleh, G., Clarkson, J., Corti, B. and Pikora, T. 1997a. *Sponsorship Monitor Evaluation Results 1996/97,* Health Promotion Evaluation Unit, Department of Public Health and Graduate School of Management, University of Western Australia, Perth, Western Australia.

Donovan, R. J., Jalleh, G., Clarkson, J. and Corti, B. 1999. Evidence for the Effectiveness of Sponsorship as a Health Promotion Tool, *Australian Journal of Primary Health – Interchange* 5(4): 81–91.

Donovan, R. J., Jalleh, G., Fielder, L. and Ouschan, R. 2008. When Confrontational Images may be Counterproductive: Reinforcing the Case for Pre-testing Communications in Sensitive Areas, *Health Promotion Journal of Australia* 19(2): 132–6.

2009. Ethical Issues in Pro-social Advertising: The Australian White Ribbon Day Campaign, *Journal of Public Affairs* 9: 5–19.

Donovan, R. J., James, R., Jalleh, G. and Sidebottom, C. 2006b. Implementing Mental Health Promotion: The Act–Belong–Commit Mentally Healthy WA Campaign in Western Australia, *International Journal of Mental Health Promotion* 8(1): 29–38.

Donovan, R. J., Mick, L., Holden, S. J. S. and Noel, J. 1997b. *Underage Drinking Amongst Aboriginal and Islander Youth in the Northern Territory,* Report to Northern Territory Department of Health, Donovan Research, Perth, Western Australia.

Donovan, R. J., Watson, N., Henley, N., Williams, A., Silburn, S., Zubrick, S., James, R., Cross, D., Hamilton, G. and Roberts, C. 2003a. Mental Health Promotion Scoping Project, Curtin University of Technology: Centre for Behavioural Research in Cancer Control, Perth, Western Australia.

Downie, R. S. and Calman, K. C. 1994. *Healthy Respect. Ethics in Health Care,* 2nd edn. Oxford University Press.

Doyle, S., Kelly-Schwartz, A., Schlossberg, M. and Stockard, J. 2006. Active Community Environments and Health: The Relationship of Walkable and Safe Communities to Individual Health, *Journal of the American Planning Association* 72(1): 19–31.

Drumwright, M. E. 1996. Company Advertising with a Social Dimension: The Role of Noneconomic Criteria, *Journal of Marketing* 60: 71–88.

Durlak, J. and Wells, A. 1997. Primary Prevention Mental Health Programs for Children and Adolescents: A Meta-analytic Review, *American Journal of Community Psychology* 25(2): 115–52.

Dworkin, G. 1988. *The Theory and Practice of Autonomy.* Cambridge University Press.

Dwyer, C. 1997. Sponsorship, *The Australian Financial Review Magazine*, November, pp. 20–2.

Eaton, L. 2001. Tobacco Companies Exploit Women, says WHO, *British Medical Journal* 322: 1384.

Economic & Social Research Council (ESRC) 2004. The art of happiness … is volunteering the blueprint for bliss?, Press Release, September, available at: www. esrcsocietytoday.ac.uk/ESRCInfoCentre/PO/releases/2004/september/art.aspx, accessed 23 May 2010.

Economist, The 1996. Think Global, Act Prejudiced?, 24 February, p. 77.

Edwards, J. 2009a. Church of Scientology runs Commercials on CNN, 16 June, retrieved 18 June 2009 from http://industry.bnet.com/advertising.

   2009b. Microsoft Edits Black Person out of Ad; Everyone Offended, retrieved 27 August 2009 from http://industry.bnet.com/advertising/10003668/microsoft-edits-black-person-out-of-ad.

   2009c. MPAA under Fire as FTC asked to Examine Violent Movie Ads Targeting Kids, 24 June, BNET Advertising, Industry News and Insights by Jim Edwards, retrieved 26 June 2009 from http://industry.bnet.com/advertising/10002751/mpaa-under-fire-as-ftc-asked-to-examine-violent-movie-ads-targeting-kids.

Egger, G. and Mowbray, G. 1993. A Qualitative Assessment of Obesity and Overweight in Working Men, *Australian Journal of Nutrition and Diet* 50(1): 10–14.

Egger, G., Donovan, R. J. and Corti, B. 1998. *Development of National Physical Activity Guidelines,* Report to Commonwealth Department of Health and Aged Care, Health Promotion Evaluation Unit, University of Western Australia, Perth, Western Australia.

Egger, G., Donovan, R. J. and Spark, R. A. 1993. *Health and the Media: Principles and Practices for Health Promotion.* Sydney: McGraw-Hill.

Egger, G., Spark, R. and Donovan, R. J. 2005. *Health Promotion Strategies and Methods*, 2nd edn. Sydney: McGraw-Hill.

Egger, G., Bolton, A., O'Neill, M. and Freeman, D. 1996. Effectiveness of an Abdominal Obesity Reduction Programme in Men: The Gut Buster 'Weight Loss' Programme, *International Journal of Obesity* 20: 227–31.

Egger, G., Donovan, R. J., Giles-Corti, B., Bull, F. and Swinburn, B. 2001. Developing National Physical Activity Guidelines for Australians, *Australian and New Zealand Journal of Public Health* 25(6): 561–3.

Egger, G., Fitzgerald, W., Frape, G., Monaem, A., Rubinstein, P., Tyler, C. and Mackay, B. 1983. Results of a Large-scale Media Anti-smoking Campaign in Australia: The North Coast Healthy Lifestyle Programme, *British Medical Journal* 287(6399): 1125–288.

Elder, J. P., Geller, E. S., Hovell, M. F. and Mayer, J. A. 1994. *Motivating Heath Behaviour.* New York: Delmar.

Elder, R., Shults, R., Sleet, D., Nichols, J., Thompson, R. and Rajab, W. 2004. Effectiveness of Mass Media Campaigns for Reducing Drinking and Driving and Alcohol-involved Crashes: A Systematic Review, *American Journal of Preventative Medicine* 27(1): 57–65.

Ellickson, P., Collins, R., Hambarsoomians, K. and McCaffrey, D. 2005. Does Alcohol Advertising Promote Adolescent Drinking? Results from a Longitudinal Assessment, *Addiction* 100: 235–46.

Elliott, B. 1995. The Inapplicability of the Exchange Concept to Social Marketing, Marketing and Public Policy Conference, Atlanta Georgia.

Elliott, S. 2007. Straight As, with a Burger as a Prize, *The New York Times*, 6 December, retrieved 27 June 2009, from www.nytimes.com/2007/12/06/business/media/06adco.html.

2008. McDonald's Ending Promotion on Jackets of Children's Report Cards, *The New York Times*, 18 January, retrieved 27 June 2009 from www.nytimes.com/2008/01/18/business/media/18card.html.

Engels, R., Hermans, R., van Baaren, R., Hollenstein, T. and Bot, S. 2009. Alcohol Portrayal on Television Affects Actual Drinking Behaviour, *Alcohol and Alcoholism* 44(3): 244–9.

Etcoff, N., Orbach, S., Scott, J. and D'Agostino, H. 2004. The Real Truth about Beauty: A Global Report. Findings of the Global Study on Women, Beauty and Well-being, Dove, a Unilever Beauty Brand.

European Commission 2004. Actions against Depression: Improving Mental Health and Wellbeing by Combating the Adverse Health, Social and Economic Consequences of Depression, Health and Consumer Protection Directorate-General, Luxembourg.

Evans, W. and Hastings, G. (eds.) 2009. *Public Health Branding: Applying Marketing for Social Change*. Oxford University Press.

Everett, K. and Schaay, N. 1994. Country Watch: South Africa, *AIDS Health Promotion Exchange* 1: 7–8.

Farkas, A. J., Gilpin, E. A., Distenfan, J. M. and Pierce, J. P. 1999. The Effects of Household and Workplace Smoking Restrictions on Quitting Behaviours, *Tobacco Control* 8: 261–5.

Farkas, A. J., Gilpin, E. A., White, M. M. and Pierce, R. P. 2000. Association Between Household and Workplace Smoking Restrictions and Adolescent Smoking, *Journal of the American Medical Association* 284(6): 717–22.

Farrelly, M. C., Evans, W. N. and Sfekas, A. E. S. 1999. The Impact of Workplace Smoking Bans: Results from a National Survey, *Tobacco Control* 8: 272–7.

Farrer, F. 2000. *A Quiet Revolution: Encouraging Positive Values in our Children*. London: Rider.

Faulkener, R. A. and Slattery, C. M. 1990. The Relationship of Physical Activity to Alcohol Consumption in Youth, 15–16 Years of Age, *Canadian Journal of Public Health* 81: 168–9.

Fawcett, S., Lewis, R., Paine-Andrews, A., Francisco, V., Richter, K., Williams, E. and Copple, B. 1997. Evaluating Community Coalitions for Prevention of Substance Abuse: The Case of Project Freedom, *Health Education Behavior* 24(6): 812–28.

Fennell, G. 1978. Consumers' Perceptions of the Product-use Situation, *Journal of Marketing* 42(2): 38–47.

Ferguson, R., Mills, C. and Rosenberg, M. 2009. Sponsorship Monitor Evaluation Results 2008/2009, Perth, Health Promotion Evaluation Unit, School of Sport Science, Exercise and Health, The University of Western Australia.

Fernald, L., Gertler, P. and Neufeld, L. 2008. Role of Cash in Conditional Cash Transfer Programmes for Child Health, Growth, and Development: An Analysis of Mexico's Oportunidades, *Lancet* 371(9615): 828–37.

Fernald, L. C. and Gunnar, M. R. 2009. Poverty-alleviation Program Participation and Salivary Cortisol in Very Low-income Children, *Social Science Medicine* 68(12): 2180–9.

Ferriman, A. 2001. Editor Resigns from Post after Tobacco Gift, *British Medical Journal* 322: 1200, available at: http://bmj.com.cgi/content/full/322/7296/1200/e.

Festinger, L. 1957. *A Theory of Cognitive Dissonance.* Stanford University Press.

Field, A., Cheung, L., Wolf, A. M., Herzog, D. B., Gortmaker, S. L. and Colditz, G. A. 1999. Exposure to the Mass Media and Weight Concerns Among Girls, *Pediatrics* 103(3), retrieved 20 April 2003 from www.pediatrics.org/cgi/content/full/103/3/e36.

Finch, J. 2006. The Impact of Personal Consumption Values and Beliefs on Organic Food Purchase Behavior, *Journal of Food Products Marketing* 11(4): 63–76.

Fine, S. H. 1990. *The Marketing of Ideas and Social Issues,* 2nd edn. New York: Praeger.

Fiore M. C., Croyle R. T., Curry S. J., Cutler C. M., Davis R. M., Gordon, C., Healton, C., Howard K. K., Orleans T. C., Richling, D., Satcher, D., Seffrin, J., Williams, C., Williams L. N., Keller P. A. and Baker T. B. 2004. Preventing 3 million Premature Deaths and Helping 5 million Smokers Quit: A National Action Plan for Tobacco Cessation, *American Journal of Public Health* 94(2): 205–10.

Fishbein, M. 1967. *Readings in Attitude Theory and Measurement.* New York: Wiley.

Fishbein, M. and Ajzen, I. 1975. *Belief, Attitude, Intention and Behaviour: An Introduction to Theory and Research.* Reading, MA: Addison-Wesley.

Fishbein, M., Bandura, A., Triandis, H. C., Kanfer, F. M. and Becker, M. H. 1991. Factors Influencing Behavior and Behavior Change: Final Report to NIMH, Paper presented at NIMH Theorist's Workshop. Rockville, Maryland.

Flatt, K. 2005. Ten Campaigning Tips for Lobbying MPs: Charity Parliamentary Monitor. London: nfpSynergy.

Forbes, A. 2000. Differences Social Marketing–Commercial Marketing, Message posted to social marketing list server, 3 April, archived at: soc-mktg@listproc.georgetown.edu.

Foster, P. 2009. Nine held over Shanghai Building Collapse, 29 June, retrieved 5 July 2009 from www.telegraph.co.uk/news/worldnews/asia/china/5685963/Nine-held-over-Shanghai-building-collapse.html.

Fox, K. F. A. and Kotler, P. 1980. The Marketing of Social Causes: The First 10 years, *Journal of Marketing* 44(Fall): 24–33.

Francas, M. and Donovan, R. J. 2001. *Perpetrator Research,* Report to Domestic Violence Prevention Unit, NFO Donovan Research, Perth, Western Australia.

France, A., Donovan, R. J., Watson, C. and Leivers, S. 1991. A Chlamydia Awareness Campaign Aimed at Reducing HIV Risks in Young Adults, *Australian Health Promotion Journal* 1(1): 19–28.

France, K., Henley, N., Payne, J., D'Antoine, H., Bartu, A., O'Leary, C., Elliott, E. and Bower, C. forthcoming. Health Professionals Addressing Alcohol Use with Pregnant Women in Western Australia: Barriers and Strategies for Communication, *Substance Use and Misuse.*

Franco, M., Diez Roux, A. V., Glass, T. A., Caballero, B. and Brancati, F. L. 2008. Neighborhood Characteristics and Availability of Healthy Foods in Baltimore, *American Journal of Preventative Medicine* 35(6): 561–7.

Franks, M. and Medforth, R. 2005. Young Helpline Callers and Difference: Exploring Gender, Ethnicity and Sexuality in Helpline Access and Provision, *Child & Family Social Work* 10(1): 77–85.

Freedman, J. L. and Fraser, S. C. 1966. Compliance without Pressure: The Foot-in-the-door Technique, *Journal of Personality and Social Psychology* 4: 195–202.

Freimuth, V. S. and Mettger, W. 1990. Is there a Hard-to-reach Audience? *Public Health Reports* 105: 232–8.

French, S. A., Jeffrey, R. W., Story, M., Breitlow, K. K., Baxter, J. S., Hannan, P. and Snyder, M. P. 2001. Pricing and Promotion Effects on Low-fat Vending Snack Purchases: The CHIPS Study, *American Journal of Public Health* 91(1): 112–17.

French, S. A., Jeffrey, R. W., Story, M., Hannan, P. and Snyder, M. P. 1997. A Pricing Strategy to Promote Low-fat Snack Choices through Vending Machines, *American Journal of Public Health* 87(5): 849–51.

Frewer, L., Scholderer, J. and Lambert, N. 2003. Consumer Acceptance of Functional Foods: Issues for the Future, *British Food Journal* 105(10): 714–31.

Fried, I. 2009. Microsoft Apologizes for Race-swap Photo Incident, 25 August, retrieved 27 August 2009 from http://news.cnet.com/8301–13860_3–10317763–56. html?part=rss&subj=news&tag=25.

Froese-Germain, B., Hawkey, C., Larose, A., McAdie, P. and Shaker, E. 2006. *Commercialism in Canadian Schools: Who's Calling the Shots?*. British Columbia: Canadian Teachers Federation.

Frost & Sullivan. 2008. U.S. Functional Beverages Market: A Young Market with Growing Popularity, 29 May (cited 21 June 2009), available at: www.flex-news-food.com/ console/PageViewer.aspx?page=16777&str=U.S.%20Functional%20Beverages%20 Market:%20A%20Young%20Market%20with%20Growing%20Popularity.

Fulton, M., and Giannakas, K. 2004. Inserting GM Products into the Food Chain: The Market and Welfare Effects of Different Labeling and Regulatory Regimes, *American Journal of Agricultural Economics* 86(1): 42–60.

Furlong, R. 1994. Tobacco Advertising Legislation and the Sponsorship of Sport, *Australian Business Law Review* 22(3): 159–89.

Furnham, A., Ingle, H., Gunter, B. and McClelland, A. 1997. A Content Analysis of Alcohol Portrayal and Drinking in British Television Soap Operas, *Health Education Research* 12(4): 519–29.

Gavaghan, C. 2009. 'You can't handle the truth'; Medical Paternalism and Prenatal Alcohol Use, *Journal of Medical Ethics* 35(5): 300–3.

Gearon, C. 2008. Firms Offer Payouts to Those Who Work Out, 14 October, retrieved 15 October 2008 from www.washingtonpost.com/wp-dyn/content/article/2008/10/10/ AR2008101002658_pf.html.

Geller, E. S. 1989. Applied Behavior Analysis and Social Marketing: An Integration for Environmental Preservation, *Journal of Social Issues* 45: 17–36.

Gentile, D., Lynch, P., Linder, J. and Walsh, D. 2004. The Effects of Violent Video Game Habits on Adolescent Hostility, Aggressive Behaviors, and School Performance, *Journal of Adolescence* 27: 5–22.

Gibbons, S., Ebbeck, V. and Weiss, M. 1995. Fair Play for Kids: Effects on the Moral Development of Children in Physical Education, *Research Quarterly for Exercise & Sport*, 66(3):47–55.

Gibbons, S., Ebbeck, V., Gibbons, S. and Ebbeck, V. 1997. The Effect of Different Teaching Strategies on the Moral Development of Physical Education Students, *Journal of Teaching and Physical Education* 17: 5–98.

Giesbrecht, N. 2007. Reducing Alcohol-related Damage in Populations: Rethinking the Roles of Education and Persuasion Interventions, *Addiction* 102(9): 345–9.

Giles-Corti, B., Clarkson, J., Donovan, R. J., Frizzell, S. K., Carroll, A. M., Pikora, T. and Jalleh, G. 2001. Creating Smoke-free Environments in Recreational Settings, *Health Education & Behavior* 28(3): 341–51.

Gilg, A., Barr, S. and Ford, N. 2005. Green Consumption or Sustainable Lifestyles? Identifying the Sustainable Consumer, *Futures* 37: 81–504.

Gintner, G. G., Rectanus, E. F., Achord, K. and Parker, B. 1987. *Parental History of Hypertension and Screening Attendance: Effects of Wellness Appeal versus Threat Appeal.* Hillsdale, NJ: Lawrence Erlbaum.

Gladwell, M. 2000. *The Tipping Point: How Little Things Can Make a Big Difference* London: Little Brown.

Glantz, S. 2002. Rate Movies with Smoking 'R'. *Effective Clinical Practice* 5: 31–4.

Glayzer, A. and Mitchell, J. 2008. How Parents are being Misled: A Campaign Report on Children's Food Marketing, British Heart Foundation, London.

Godin, G. 1994. Social Cognitive Models, in R. K. Dishman (ed.), *Advances in Exercise Adherence,* 2nd edn. Chicago, IL: Human Kinetics, pp. 113–36.

Godin, G. and Kok, G. 1996. The Theory of Planned Behavior: A Review of its Applications to Health-related Behaviors, *American Journal of Health Promotion* 11(2): 87–98.

Goldberg, M. E. 1995. Social Marketing: Are we Fiddling while Rome Burns? *Journal of Consumer Psychology* 4(4): 347–70.

Goldfield, G., Mallory, R., Parker, T., Cunningham, T., Legg, C., Lumb, A., Parker, K., Prud'homme, D., Gaboury, I. and Adamo, K. 2006. Effects of Open-loop Feedback on Physical Activity and Television Viewing in Overweight and Obese Children: A Randomized, Controlled Trial, *Pediatrics* 118(1): 157–66.

Goldstein, A. O., Sobel R. A. and Newman, G. R. 1999. Tobacco and Alcohol use in G-rated Children's Animated Films, *Journal of the American Medical Association* 281: 131–6.

Goldstein, S., Usdin, S., Scheepers, E. and Japhet, G. 2005. Communicating HIV and AIDS, What Works? A Report on the Impact Evaluation of Soul City's Fourth Series, *Journal of Health Communication* 10: 65–483.

Gordon, S. 2009. Promise of Cash Prompts Smokers to Quit: Financial Incentives Tripled Rates of Cessation, Study Found, US News and World Report, 11 February, retrieved from http://health.usnews.com/articles/health/healthday/2009/02/11/promise-of-cash-prompts-smokers-to-quit.html.

Goswami, N. and Orr, J. 2005. The Thames: Awash with Cocaine, retrieved 19 August 2009 from www.telegraph.co.uk/news/uknews/3325948/The-Thames-awash-with-cocaine.html.

Gower, D. 1995. Health-related Content in Daily Newspaper Comic Strips: A Content Analysis with Implications for Health Education, *Education* 116(1): 37–42.

Grant, D. and Iserson, K. 2005. Who's Buying Lunch: Are Gifts to Surgeons from Industry Bad for Patients?, *Thoracic Surgery Clinics* 15: 33–542.

Green, E. 2003. New Challenges to the AIDS Prevention Paradigm, *Anthropology News* 506, available at: www.aaanet.org/press/an/infocus/hivaids/0309_green.htm.

Green, L. W. 1999. Health Education's Contributions to Public Health in the Twentieth Century: A Glimpse through Health Promotion's Rear-view Mirror, *Annual Review of Public Health* 20: 7–88.

Green, L. W. and Kreuter, M. W. 2005. *Health Promotion Planning: An Educational and Ecological Approach,* 4th edn. New York: McGraw-Hill.

Gregor, S. 2004. Copycat Suicide: The Influence of the Media, *Inpsych* August 2004: 5–28.

Grimley, D. M., Prochaska, G. E. and Prochaska, J. O. 1997. Condom Use Adoption and Continuation: A Transtheoretical Approach, *Health Education Research* 12(1): 61–75.

Grunwald, M. 2009. How Obama is Using the Science of Change, retrieved 14 April 2009 from www.time.com/time/printout/0,8816,1889153,00.html.

Gruskin, S., Plafker, K. and Smith-Estelle, A. 2001. Understanding and Responding to Youth Substance Use: The Contribution of a Health and Human Rights Framework, *American Journal of Public Health* 91(12): 1954–63.

Gulland, A. 2009. Watchdog Warns Government over Inaccurate Data on Road Casualties, *British Medical Journal* 338: 1906.

Hahn, A. and Craythorn, E. 1994. Inactivity and Physical Environment in Two Regional Centres, *Health Promotion Journal of Australia* 4(2): 43–5.

Haire, M. 1950. Projective Techniques in Marketing Research, *Journal of Marketing* 14: 49–656.

Halfon, N., Russ, S., Obeklaid, F., Bertrand, J. and Eisenstadt, N. 2009. *An International Comparison of Early Childhood Initiatives: From Services to Systems.* New York: The Commonwealth Fund.

Hall, E. 2009. Why do U.K. Videos Always Seem to go Viral?, retrieved 18 August 2009 from http://adage.com/print?article_id=138478.

Handler, H., Knabe, A., Koebel, B., Schratzenstaller, M. and Wehke, S. 2005. The Impact of Public Budgets on Overall Productivity Growth, WIFO Working Papers 255, WIFO, Vienna.

Hansen, F. and Scotwin, L. 1995. An Experimental Inquiry into Sponsoring: What Effects can be Measured? *Marketing and Research Today* 23(3): 173–81.

Harachi, T. W., Ayres, C. D., Hawkins, D., Catalano, R. and Cushing, J. 1996. Empowering Communities to Prevent Substance Abuse: Process Evaluation Results from a Risk- and Protection-focused Community Mobilization Effort, *Journal of Primary Prevention* 16: 233–54.

Hardy, F. [1950] 1972. *Power Without Glory.* Hawthorn, Victoria: Lloyd O'Neill.

Harris, R. J. 2009. *A Cognitive Psychology of Mass Communication,* 5th edn. New York: Routledge.

Harrison, J. A., Mullen, P. D. and Green, L. W. 1992. A Meta-analysis of Studies of the Health Belief Model with Adults, *Health Education Research: Theory & Practice* 7(1): 107–16.

Harvey, B. 2001. Firms Fight for Police Job, *The West Australian*, 18 January, p. 4.

Hassard, K. (ed.) 1999. *Australia's National Tobacco Campaign: Evaluation Report, Vol. 1.* Canberra: Commonwealth of Australia.

Hastings, G. 1984. Sponsorship Works Differently from Advertising, *International Journal of Advertising* 3: 171–6.

  2006. Ten Promises to Terry: Towards a Social Marketing Manifesto, *Social Marketing Quarterly* 12(2): 59–62.

  2007. *Social Marketing: Why should the Devil have all the Best Tunes?* Oxford: Butterworth-Heinemann.

Hastings, G. and Donovan, R. J. 2002. International Initiatives: Introduction and Overview, *Social Marketing Quarterly* 8(1): 3–5.

Hastings, G., Freeman, J., Spackova, R. and Siquier, P. 2008. HELP: A European Public Health Brand in the Making, in D. W. Evans and G. Hastings (eds.), *Public Health Branding: Applying Marketing for Social Change.* Oxford University Press.

Hastings, G. and Haywood, A. 1994. Social Marketing: A Critical Response, *Health Promotion International* 9(1): 59–63.

Hastings, G., MacAskill, S., McNeill, R. and Leathar, D. 1988. Sports Sponsorship in Health Education, *Health Promotion* 3: 161–9.

Hastings, G. and MacFadyen, L. 2000. *Keep Smiling: No One's Going to Die*. London: British Medical Association.

         2002. Controversies in Tobacco Control: The Limitations of Fear Messages, *Tobacco Control* 11(1): 73–5.

Hastings, G., MacFadyen, L. and Anderson, S. 2000. Whose Behavior is it Anyway? The Broader Potential of Social Marketing, *Social Marketing Quarterly* 6(2): 46–58.

Hastings, G. and Saren, M. 2003. The Critical Contribution of Social Marketing: Theory and Application, *Marketing Theory* 3(3): 305–22.

Hastings, G., Stead, M. and MacFadyen, L. 2002. Reducing Prison Numbers: Does Marketing Hold the Key? *Criminal Justice Matters* 49(1): 20–5.

Hastings, G., Stead, M. and Macintosh, A. 2002. Rethinking Drugs prevention: Radical Thoughts from Social Marketing, *Health Education Journal* 61(4): 347–64.

Hastings, G., Stead, M. and Webb, J. 2004. Fear Appeals in Social Marketing: Strategic and Ethical Reasons for Concern, *Psychology & Marketing*, 21(11): 961–86.

Hastings, G., Stead, M., McDermott, L., Forsyth, A., MacKintosh, A. M., Rayner, M., Godfrey, C., Caraher, M. and Angus, K. 2003. Review of Research on the Effects of Food Promotion to Children: Final Report, Centre for Social Marketing, the University of Strathclyde, Glasgow.

Hawkes, N. 2005. Where Rivers Run High on Cocaine: Analysis of Waste Water in Italy shows a Startlingly High Level of Drug Abuse, 5 August, retrieved 19 August 2009 from www.timesonline.co.uk/tol/news/world/article551797.ece.

Hawkins, D., Best, J. and Coney, A. 2003. *Consumer Behavior: Building Marketing Strategy*. Tata: McGraw Hill.

Hawkins, D. I., Best, R. J. and Coney, K. A. 1995. *Consumer Behavior: Implications for Marketing Strategy*. Chicago, IL: Irwin.

Hawkins, J. D., Catalano, R. F. and Miller, J. Y. 1992. Risk and Protective Factors for Alcohol and other Drug Problems in Adolescence and Early Adulthood: Implications for Substance Abuse Prevention, *Psychological Bulletin* 112: 64–105.

Hawkins, J. D., Catalano, R. F. and associates 1992. *Communities that Care: Action for Drug Abuse Prevention*. San Francisco, CA: Jossey-Bass.

Hawkins, J. D., Catalano, R. F., Kosterman, R., Abbott, R. and Hill, K. G. 1999. Preventing Adolescent Health-risk Behaviors by Strengthening Protection during Childhood, *Archives of Pediatrics & Adolescent Medicine* 153(3): 226–47.

Hawkins, J. W. and Aber, C. S. 1988. The Content of Advertisements in Medical Journals: Distorting the Image of Women, *Women & Health*, 14(2): 43–59.

Hawton, K., Simkin, S., Deeks, J. J., O'Connor, S., Keen, A., Altman, D. G., Philo, G. and Bulstrode, C. 1999. Effects of a Drug Overdose in a Television Drama on Presentations to Hospital for Self-poisoning: Time Series and Questionnaire Study, *British Medical Journal* 318: 972–7.

Hawton, K., Simkin, S., Deeks, J., Cooper J., Johnston, A., Waters, K., Arundel, M., Bernal, W., Gunson, B., Hudson, M., Suri, D. and Simpson, K. 2004. UK Legislation in

Analgesic Packs: Before and After Study of Long-term Effect on Poisonings, *British Medical Journal* 329: 1076–9.

Hawton, K., Townsend, E., Deeks, J., *et al.* 2001. Effects of Legislation Restricting Pack Sizes of Paracetamol and Salicylate on Self-poisoning in the United Kingdom: Before and After Study, *British Medical Journal* 322, 1–7.

Hay, P. J. 1998. Eating Disorders: Anorexia Nervosa, Bulimia Nervosa and Related Syndromes – An Overview of Assessment and Management, *Australian Prescriber* 21: 100–3, retrieved 20 April 2003 from www.australianprescriber.com/magazines/vol21no4/eating_disorders.htm

Health Communication Resources 2008. Community Radio and Social Change: An Impact Evaluation in Bali, Indonesia, retrieved 24 June 2009 from www.comminit.com/en/node/274976/307.

Heavey, S. 2005. R.J. Reynolds COO Defends Cigarette Ads in Trial, Reuters, 1 April, retrieved 9 April 2005 from www.health-news.org/breaking/1014/rj-reynolds-coo-defends-cigarette-ads-in-trial.html.

Heckman, J. J. 2006. Skill Formation and the Economics of Investing in Disadvantaged Children, *Science*, 312(5782): 1900–2.

Henley, N. 1995. Fear Literature Review, in R. J. Donovan, N. Henley, G. Jalleh and C. Slater (eds.), *Road Safety Advertising. Report to Federal Office of Road Safety*, Perth: Donovan Research, pp. 92–120.

1999. Using Threat Appeals in Social Marketing, in M. Harker, D. Harker, P. Graham and M. J. Baker (eds.), *Marketing Trends in Australasia: Essays and Case Studies*. Basingstoke: Macmillan, pp. 230–42.

2002. 'You Will Die!' Mass Media Invocations of Existential Dread, M/C 5(1), available at: http://journal.media-culture.org.au/0203/youwilldie.php.

Henley, N. and Donovan, R. J. 2002. Identifying Appropriate Motivations to Encourage People to Adopt Healthy Nutrition and Physical Activity Behaviours, *Journal of Research for Consumers* 4 (December), available at: www.jrconsumers.com.

2003. Young People's Response to Death Threat Appeals: Do they Really Feel Immortal? *Health Education Research* 18(1): 1–14.

1999a. Threat Appeals in Social Marketing: Death as a Special Case, *International Journal of Nonprofit and Voluntary Sector Marketing* 4(4), 300–319.

1999b. Unintended Consequences of Arousing Fear in Social Marketing, Australia and New Zealand Marketing Academy Conference, November, Sydney, New South Wales.

Henley, N. and Raffin, S. 2010. Social Marketing to Prevent Childhood Obesity: The EPODE Program, in E. Waters, B. Swinburn, R. Uauy and J. Seidall (eds.), *Preventing Childhood Obesity: Evidence, Policy and Practice*. Oxford: Wiley-Blackwell – BMJI Books.

Henley, N., Donovan, R. and Francas, M. 2007. Developing and Implementing Communication Messages, in L. Doll, S. Bonzo, J. Mercy and D. Sleet (eds.), *Handbook of Injury and Violence Prevention*. New York: Springer.

Henley, N., Donovan, R. J. and Moorhead, H. 1998. Appealing to Positive Motivations and Emotions in Social Marketing: Example of a Positive Parenting Campaign, *Social Marketing Quarterly* 4(4): 48–53.

Henry C. J. and Garcia A. C. 2004. Exclusive Beverage Arrangements in U.S. and Canadian Schools: A Review of Practices and Policy Perspectives, *Foodservice Research International* 15: 107–17.

Henry, P. 2001. An Examination of the Pathways Through which Social Class Impacts Health Outcomes, *Academy of Marketing Science Review*, retrieved 26 April 2001 from www.amsreview.org/amsrev/theory/henry03–01.html.

Herrick, T. 2004. For these Educators, the Diet of Worms isn't just History, *Wall Street Journal*, 1, A10.

Hersey, J. C., Klibanoff, L. S., Lam, D. J. and Taylor, R. L. 1984. Promoting Social Support: The Impact of California's 'Friends Can Be Good Medicine' Campaign, *Health Education Quarterly* 11(3): 293–311.

Higbee, K. L. 1969. Fifteen Years of Fear Arousal. Research on Threat Appeals: 1953–1968, *Psychological Bulletin* 72: 426–39.

Himmelman, A. 2001. On Coalitions and the Transformation of Power Relations: Collaborative Betterment and Collaborative Empowerment, *American Journal of Community Psychology* 29(2): 277–84.

Hoad, A. 2008. Reducing Negative Behaviour, in J. Lannon (ed.), *How Public Service Advertising Works*. Henley on Thames: World Advertising Research Centre.

Hobsons 1990. *Hobsons Sponsorship Yearbook 1991*. Cambridge: Hobsons Publishing.

Hoek, H. W. and van Hoeken, D. 2003. Review of the Prevalence and Incidence of Eating Disorders, *International Journal of Eating Disorders* 34(4): 383–96.

Hoek, J. A., Gendall, P. and Stockdale, M. 1993. Some Effects of Tobacco Sponsorship Advertisements on Young Males, *International Journal of Advertising* 12: 25–35.

Hofstetter, C. R., Hovell, M. F. and Sallis, J. F. 1990. Social Learning Correlates of Exercise Self-efficacy: Early Experiences with Physical Activity, *Social Science Medicine* 31(10): 1169–76.

Hollingsworth, P. 2001. Convenience is Key to Adding Value, *Food Technology* 55(5): 20.

Hollingworth, W., Ebel, B., McCarty, C., Garrison, M. M., Christakis, D. and Rivara, F. 2006. Prevention of Deaths from Harmful Drinking in the United States: The Potential Effects of Tax Increases and Advertising Bans on Young Drinkers, *Journal of Studies on Alcohol* 67(2): 300–8.

Holman, C. D. J., Donovan, R. J. and Corti, B. 1993. Evaluating Projects Funded by the Western Australian Health Promotion Foundation: A Systematic Approach, *Health Promotion International* 8(3): 199–208.

Holman, C. D. J., Donovan, R. J., Corti, B., Jalleh, G., Frizzell, S. K. and Carroll, A. M. 1996. Evaluating Projects Funded by the Western Australian Health Promotion Foundation: First Results, *Health Promotion International* 11, 75–88.

Holman, C. D. J., Donovan, R. J., Corti, B. and Jalleh, G. 1997a. The Myth of 'Healthism' in Organised Sport: Implications for Health Promotion Sponsorship of Sport and the Arts, *American Journal of Health Promotion* 11(3): 169–75.

Holman, C. D. J., Donovan, R. J., Corti, B., Jalleh, G., Frizzell, S. K. and Carroll, A. M. 1997b. Banning Tobacco Sponsorship: Replacing Tobacco with Health Messages and Creating Health-promoting Environments, *Tobacco Control* 6(2): 115–21.

Homel, R., Carseldine, D. and Kearns, I. 1988. Drink-driving Countermeasures in Australia, *Alcohol, Drugs and Driving* 4(2): 113–44.

Hornik, R. (ed.) 2002. *Public Health Communication: Evidence for Behaviour Change*. Hillsdale, NJ: Lawrence Erlbaum.

Hornik, R., McDivitt, J., Zimicki, J., Yoder, P., Contreras-Budge, E., McDowell, J. and Rasmuson, M. 2002. Communication in Support of Child Survival: Evidence and Explanations from Eight Countries, in Hornik (ed.), *Public Health Communication.*

Howden-Chapman, P., Matheson, A., Crane, J., Viggers, H., Cunningham, M., Blakely, T., Cunningham, C., Woodward, A., Saville-Smith, K., O'Dea, D., Kennedy, M., Baker, M., Waipara, N., Chapman, R. and Davie, G. 2007. Effect of Insulating Existing Houses on Health Inequality: Cluster Randomised Study in the Community, *British Medical Journal* 334(7591): 460.

Hubert, D. 2000. *The Landmine Ban: A Case Study in Humanitarian Advocacy, Occasional paper No. 42,* Thomas J. Watson Jr. Institute for International Studies, Brown University, Providence, Rhode Island.

Hudson, D. 1999. *Panel Discusses Crucial Role of Media in Civil Rights Movement.* First Amendment Center.

Huhman, M., Heitzler, C. and Wong, F. 2004. The VERBTM Campaign Logic Model: A Tool for Planning and Evaluation, *Preventing Chronic Disease* 1(3): 1–6.

Humpel, N., Owen, N. and Leslie, E. 2002. Environmental Factors Associated with Adults' Participation in Physical Activity: A Review, *American Journal of Preventative Medicine* 22(3): 188–99.

Huntley, A. 2009. Acquisition Crime, Cutting the Cost of Crime: How Advertising turned a Nation of Victims into a Nation of Crime Prevention Officers, in N. Dawson (ed.), *Advertising Works 17.* Henley on Thames: World Advertising Research Centre.

IEG Sponsorship Report 2006. Projection: Sponsorship Growth to Increase for fifth Straight Year, available at: www.sponsorship.com/iegsr/2006/12/25/9279.asp.

indianinfo.com. 2005. First Beer Launched in Kerala Market Today, 17 August, retrieved 27 June 2009 from http://news.indiainfo.com/2005/08/17/1707bio-beer.html.

International Events Group Sponsorship Report 1996. 1996 Annual Sponsorship Survey, cited in T. B. Cornwell, and I. Maignan 1998. An International Review of Sponsorship Research, *Journal of Advertising* 27(1): 1.

International tobacco mailing list 2002. Archived at: http://lists.essential.org/mailman/listinfo/intl-tobacco.

Ippolito, P. and Pappalardo, J. 2003. *Nutrition and Health Advertising.* New York: Novinka Books.

Irwin, R., Lachowetz, T., Cornwell, T. and Clark, J. 2003. Cause-related Sport Sponsorship: An Assessment of Spectator Beliefs, Attitudes, and Behavioral Intentions, *Sports Marketing Quarterly* 12(3): 131–9.

Isaacs, S. L. and Schroeder, S. A. 2001. Where the Public Good Prevailed, *The American Prospect* 12(10), available at: www.prospect.org.

Ives, N. 2005. McDonald's says it's time to exercise, *The New York Times*, 9 March, retrieved 14 March 2005 from www.nytimes.com/2005/03/09/business/media/09adco.html.

Jalleh, G. 1999. Evaluating Sponsorship Effectiveness: Health vs Commercial Sponsorship, unpublished Master of Public Health thesis, University of Western Australia, Perth, Western Australia.

Jalleh, G. and Donovan, R. J. 2000. *Evaluation of Westar Rules and the West Australian Country Football League 'Belt up' Sponsorship,* Centre for Behavioural Research in Cancer Control, Curtin University, Perth, Western Australia.

2001. Beware of Product Labels! *Journal of Research for Consumers*, 2, retrieved 20 January 2003 from www.jrconsumers.com.

Jalleh, G., Donovan, R. J., Clarkson, J., March, K., Foster, M. and Giles-Corti, B. 2001. Increasing Mouthguards Usage among Junior Rugby and Basketball Players, *Australian and New Zealand Journal of Public Health* 25(3): 250–2.

Jalleh, G., Donovan, R. J., Giles-Corti, B. and Holman, C. D. J. 2002. Sponsorship: Impact on Brand Awareness and Brand Attitudes, *Social Marketing Quarterly* 8(1): 35–45.

Jalleh, G., Donovan, R., James, R. and Ambridge, J. 2007. Process Evaluation of the Act-Belong-Commit Mentally Healthy WA Campaign: First 12 Months Data, *Health Promotion Journal of Australia* 18(3): 217–20.

Jalleh, G., Hamilton, A., Clarkson, J., Donovan, R. J. and Corti, B. 1998. *Healthy Food Choices at Healthway Sponsored Events,* Health Promotion Evaluation Unit, Department of Public Health and Graduate School of Management, University of Western Australia, Perth, Western Australia.

Jamie's School Dinners 2009. Channel 4, 2009, cited 21 June 2009, available at: www.channel4.com/life/microsites/J/jamies_school_dinners.

Jane-Llopis, E., Barry, M., Hosman, C. and Patel, V. 2005. Mental Health Promotion Works: A Review, *Promotion & Education* 2(Supp.): 9–25, 61, 67.

Janz, N. and Becker, M. 1984. The Health Belief Model: A Decade Later, *Health Education Quarterly* 11: 1–47.

Javalgi, R., Traylor, M., Gross, A. and Lampman, E. 1994. Awareness of Sponsorship and Corporate Image: An Empirical Investigation, *Journal of Advertising* 23(4): 47–58.

Jeffery, C. R. 1971. Crime Prevention through Environmental Design, *American Behavioral Scientist* 14(4): 598.

Jeffery, N. 2001. Sponsor Quizzed over Unsporting Conduct, *The Australian*, 11 October, p. 20.

Jeffery, R. W., Forster, J. L., Schmid, T. L., McBride, C. M., Rooney, B. L. and Pirie, P. L. 1990. Community Attitudes toward Public Policies to Control Alcohol, Tobacco, and High-fat Food Consumption, *American Journal of Preventive Medicine* 6(1): 12–19.

Jenkins, C. 2005. Va. may end trial use of red-light cameras, retrieved 15 August 2009 from http://pqasb.pqarchiver.com/washingtonpost/access/789187271.html?dids=78 9187271:789187271&FMT=ABS&FMTS=ABS:FT&fmac=&date=Feb+5%2C+2005&aut hor=Chris+L.+Jenkins&desc=Va.+May+End+Trial+Use+of+Red-Light+Cameras%3B+L egislators+Table+Bills+To+Extend+Programs.

Jernigan, D. 2008. Intoxicating Brands: Alcohol Advertising and Youth, *Multinational Monitor* 29(1): 23–7.

Job, R. F. S. 1988. Effective and Ineffective Use of Fear in Health Promotion Campaigns, *American Journal of Public Health* 78(2): 163–7.

Joffe, M. and Mindell, J. 2004. A Tentative Step Towards Healthy Public Policy, *Journal of Epidemiology and Community Health* 58(12): 966–8.

Johnson, K. L., Raybould, A. F., Hudson, M. D. and Poppy, G. M. 2007. How Does Scientific Risk Assessment of GM Crops Fit Within the Wider Risk Analysis? *Trends in Plant Science* 12(1): 1–5.

Johnson, S. 2005. *Everything Bad is Good for You.* London: Penguin.

Johnston, J. and Taylor, J. 2008. Feminist Consumerism and Fat Activists: A Comparative Study of Grassroots Activism and the Dove Real Beauty Campaign, *Journal of Women in Culture and Society* 33(4): 942–66.

Joiner, K., Minsky, M. and Seals, B. F. 2000. By and for Youth: Lessons from the Sahel and Paris come to the USA, *Social Marketing Quarterly* 6(3): 138–51.

Jones, K., Wakefield, M. and Turnbull, D. 1999. Attitudes and Experiences of Restaurateurs Regarding Smoking Bans in Adelaide, South Australia, *Tobacco Control* 8: 62–6.

Jones, M. M. and Bayer, R. 2007. Paternalism & its Discontents Motorcycle Helmets Laws, Libertarian Values, and Public Health, *American Journal of Public Heath* 97(2): 208–17.

Jones, S. and Donovan, R. J. 2001. Messages in Alcohol Advertising Targeted to Youth, *Australian and New Zealand Journal of Public Health* 25(2): 126–31.

2002. Self-regulation of Alcohol Advertising: Is it Working for Australia, *Journal of Public Affairs*, 2(3): 153–65.

2004. Does Theory Inform Practice in Health Promotion in Australia?, *Health Education Research* 19(1): 1–14.

Jones, S., Corti, B. and Donovan, R. J. 1996. Public Response to a Smoke-free Policy at a Major Sporting Venue (letter), *Medical Journal of Australia* 164: 759.

Jones, S. C., Hall, D. and Munro, G. 2008. How Effective is the Revised Regulatory Code for Alcohol Advertising in Australia?, *Drug and Alcohol Review* 27(1): 29–38.

Jones, S., Parri, G. and Munro, G. 2009. Adolescent and Young Adult Perceptions of Australian Alcohol Advertisements, *Journal of Substance Use* 1–18.

Jordan, M., and Sullivan, K. 1999. Japan Urges Dads To Spend More Time With Kids – Ad Campaign Sparks Renewed Debate, 13 May, available at: http://community. seattletimes.nwsource.com/archive/?date=19990513&slug=2960369.

Kahneman, D. and Tversky, A. 1979. Prospect Theory: An Analysis of Decision-making under Risk, *Econometrica* 6: 621–30.

1982. The Psychology of Preferences, *Scientific American* 46: 160–73.

Kaler, A. 2009. Health Interventions and the Persistence of Rumour: The Circulation of Sterility Stories in African Public Health Campaigns, *Social Science Medicine* 68(9): 1711–19.

Kane, R. L., Johnson, P. E., Town, R. J. and Butler, M. 2004. A Structured Review of the Effect of Economic Incentives on Consumers' Preventive Behavior, *American Journal of Preventive Medicine* 27(4): 327–52.

Kaptchuk, T. J. 2003. Effect of Interpretive Bias on Research Evidence, *British Medical Journal* 326(7404): 1453–5.

Karjaluoto, E. 2008. A smashLAB White Paper: A Primer in Social Media, retrieved 15 August 2009 from www.smashlab.com/files/primer_in_social_media.pdf.

Karlsen, S. and Nazroo, J. Y. 2002. Relation between Racial Discrimination, Social Class, and Health among Ethnic Minority Groups, *American Journal of Public Health* 92(4): 624–31.

Kate, N. T. 1995. And Now, a Word from our Sponsor, *American Demographics*, June, 46–52.

Katris, P., Donovan, R. J. and Gray, B. N. 1996. The Use of Targeted and Non-targeted Advertising to Enrich Skin Cancer Screening Samples, *British Journal of Dermatology* 135: 268–74.

Katz M. G., Kripalani, S. and Weiss B. D. 2006. Use of Pictorial Aids in Medication Instructions: A Review of the Literature, *American Journal of Health-System Pharmacy* 63: 2391–7.

Katz, D., Mansfield, P., Goodman, R., Tiefer, L. and Merz, J. 2003. Psychological Aspects of Gifts from Drug Companies, *The Journal of the American Medical Association* 290(18): 2404–5; author reply 2406–7.

Kawachi, I., Kennedy, B. P., Lochner, K. and Prothrow-Smith, D. 1997. Social Capital, Income Inequality, and Mortality, *American Journal of Public Health* 87(9): 1491–8.

Kearney, J., de Graaf, C., Damkjaer, S. and Engstrom, L. 1999. Stages of Change towards Physical Activity in a Nationally Representative Sample in the European Union, *Public Health Nutrition* 2(1A): 115–24.

Keller, K. L. 1993. Conceptualizing, Measuring and Managing Customer-based Equity, *Journal of Marketing* 57: 1–22.

Kelly, K. J., Edwards, W., Comello, M., Plested, B., Thurman, P. and Slater, M. 2003. The Community Readiness Model: A Complementary Approach to Social Marketing, *Marketing Theory* 3(4): 411–26.

Kennedy, M. F. and Meeuwisse, W. H. 2003. Exercise Counselling by Family Physicians in Canada, *Preventive Medicine* 37: 226–32.

Kerr, N., Yore, M., Ham, S. and Dietz, W. 2004. Increasing Stair Use in a Worksite through Environmental Changes, *American Journal of Health Promotion* 18(4): 312–15.

Kiley, L. 2009. Email to Donovan, 24 July 2009.

Killeen, K. 2007. How the Media Misleads the Story of School Consumerism: A Perspective from School Finance, *Peabody Journal of Education* 82(1): 32–62.

King, A. C., Jeffery, R. W., Fridinger, F., Dusenbury, L., Provence, S., Hedlund, S. A. and Spangler, K. 1995. Environmental and Policy Approaches to Cardiovascular Disease Prevention through Physical Activity: Issues and Opportunities, *Health Education Quarterly* 22(4): 499–511.

King, D. 2001. Promoting Sexual Health through High Street Shops, HEDIR listserv, 1 November.

King's Fund 2004. Improving Health in London: Case Study: Health in a Lunch-box (cited 6 September 2009, available at: http://librarycatalogue.kingsfund.org.uk/uhtbin/cgisirsi/x/0/0/5?searchdata1=105735{CKEY}&library=ALL.

Kirby, S. and Andreasen, A. 2001. Marketing Ethics to Social Marketers. A Segmented Approach, in A. Andreasen (ed.), *Ethics in Social Marketing*. Washington, DC: Georgetown University Press, pp. 160–83.

Kirsh, S. 2006. Cartoon Violence and Aggression in Youth, *Aggression and Violent Behavior* 11: 547–57.

Klaassen, A. 2009. Miley Cyrus nudges Walmart onto viral video chart, retrieved 18 August 2009 from http://adage.com/print?article_id=138423.

Klapper, J. T. 1961. *The Effects of Mass Communication*. Glencoe, IL: The Free Press.

Klein, N. 2000. *No Logo*. Toronto: Knopf.

Kline, S. 2005. Countering Children's Sedentary Lifestyles: An Evaluative Study of a Media-risk Education Approach, *Childhood* 12(2): 239–58.

Kmietowicz, Z. 2009. Target Cheap Drinking as we did Passive Smoking, says Chief Medical Officer, *British Medical Journal* 338: b1124.

Knag, S. 1997. The Almighty, Impotent State: or, the Crisis of Authority, *Independent Review* 1(3): 397–413.

Kohlberg, L. 1976. *Moral Stages and Moralisation: The Cognitive Developmental Approach*, ed. T. Lickona. New York: Holt, Rinehart and Winston.

Kollmuss, A. and Agyeman, J. 2002. Mind the Gap: Why do People Act Environmentally and What are the Barriers to Pro-environmental Behavior? *Environmental Education Research* 8(3): 239–60.

Komro, K., Perry, C., Veblen-Mortenson, S., Bosma, L., Dudovitz, B., Williams, C., Jones-Webb, R. and Toomey, T. 2004. Brief Report: the Adaptation of Project Northland for Urban Youth, *Journal of Pediatric Psychology* 29(6): 457–66.

Kopp, M. and Hornberger, C. 2008. Proper Exercise and Nutrition Kit: Use of Obesity Screening and Assessment Tools with Underserved Populations, *Journal of Pediatric Nursing* 23(1): 58–64.

Kotler, P. 1988. *Marketing Management: Analysis, Planning, Implementation and Control.* Englewood Cliffs, NJ: Prentice-Hall.

2001. *A Framework for Marketing Management.* Upper Saddle River, NJ: Prentice Hall.

Kotler, P. and Andreasen, A. R. 1987. *Strategic Marketing for Nonprofit Organisations.* Englewood Cliffs, NJ: Prentice-Hall.

Kotler, P., and Keller, K. 2005. *Marketing Management.* Englewood Cliffs, NJ: Prentice Hall.

Kotler, P. and Lee, N. 2009. *Up and out of Poverty.* Philadelphia, PA: Wharton School Publishing.

Kotler, P. and Roberto, E. L. 1989. *Social Marketing: Strategies for Changing Public Behaviour.* New York: The Free Press.

Kotler, P. and Zaltman, G. 1971. Social Marketing: An Approach to Planned Social Change, *Journal of Marketing* 35: 3–12.

Kotler, P., Roberto, N. and Lee, N. 2008. *Social Marketing: Improving the Quality of Life.* Thousand Oaks, CA: Sage.

Kotler, P., Armstrong, G., Brown, L. and Adam, S. 1998. *Marketing,* 4th edn. Sydney: Prentice-Hall.

Kotler, P., Chandler, P. G., Brown, L. and Adam, S. 1994. *Marketing Australia and New Zealand,* 3rd edn. Sydney: Prentice-Hall.

Kreuter, M., Farrell, D., Olevitch, L., Brennan, L. and Rimer, B. K. 2000. *Tailoring Health Messages: Customising Communication with Computer Technology.* Hillsdale, NJ: Lawrence Erlbaum.

Kreuter, M. W., Sugg-Skinner, C., Holt, C. L., Clark, E. M., Haire-Joshu, D., Fu, Q., Booker, A., Steger-May, K. and Bucholtz, D. C. 2005. Cultural Tailoring for Mammography and fruit and Vegetable intake among Low Income African-American Women in Urban Public Health Centers, *Preventive Medicine* 41: 53–62.

Kristjansson, S., Helgason, A., Marsson-Brahme, E., Widlund-Ivarson, B. and Ullen, H. 2003. 'You and your skin': A short-duration Presentation of Skin Cancer Prevention for Teenagers, *Health Education Research* 18(1): 88–97.

Krosnar, K. 2004. Czech Republic offers Free Beer to Blood Donors, *British Medical Journal* 329(7470): 819.

Kugler, S. 2007. Branded Condoms NY: New York Plans Official City Condom, 26 January 2007, retrieved 27 January 2007 from www.nyc.gov/htm/doh/html/ah/ah/shtml.

Kulik, J.A. and Carlino, P. 1987. The Effect of Verbal Commitment and Treatment Choice on Medication Compliance in a Pediatric Setting, *Journal of Behavioural Medicine* 10(4): 367–76.

Kwok, Y. 2000. Charity Defends using Tobacco Industry Cash, *South China Morning Post,* 12 April, message posted on international tobacco admin list server, archived at intl-tobacco@lists.essential.org.

Lacey, A. R. 2001. *Robert Nozick.* Princeton University Press.

Lacey, R., Sneath, J., Finney, Z. and Close, A. 2007. The Impact of Repeat Attendance on Event Sponsorship Events, *Journal of Marketing Communications* 13(4): 243–55.

Laczniak, G. R. and Murphy, P. 1993. *Ethical Marketing Decisions: The Higher Road.* Needham Heights, MA: Allyn & Bacon.

Lagarde, F. 2004. The Challenge of Bilingualism: ParticiPACTION Campaigns Succeeded in Two Languages, *Canadian Journal of Public Health* 95(Supp.2): S30–S32.

Lambert, V. 2008. The French Children Learning to Fight Obesity, *The Telegraph*, 8 March, pp. 1–6.

Lancaster, K. J. 1966. A New Approach to Consumer Theory, *Journal of Political Economy* 14: 132–57.

Lancaster, W., McIlwain, T. and Lancaster, J. 1983. Health Marketing: Implications for Health Promotion, *Family and Community Health* 5: 41–51.

Landers, J., Mitchell, P., Smith, B., Lehman, T. and Conner, C. 2006. 'Save the Crabs, Then Eat 'Em': A Culinary Approach to Saving the Chesapeake Bay, *Social Marketing Quarterly* 12(1): 15–28.

Lannon, J. (ed.) 2008. *How Public Service Advertising Works.* Henley on Thames: World Advertising Research Centre.

Lasker, A. D. [1963] 1987. *The Lasker Story: As He Told It.* Lincolnwood, IL: NTC Business Books.

LaTour, M. S., Snipes, R. L. and Bliss, S. J. 1996. Don't be Afraid to Use Fear Appeals: An Experimental Study, *Journal of Advertising Research* 36(2): 59–67.

Lavack, A., Watson, L. and Markwart, J. 2007. Quit and Win Contests: A Social Marketing Success Story, *Social Marketing Quarterly* 13(1): 31–52.

Lee, E. and Leets, L. 2002. Persuasive Storytelling by Hate Groups Online, *American Behavioral Scientist* 45(6): 927–57.

Lefebvre, R. C. and Flora, J. A. 1988. Social Marketing and Public Health Intervention, *Health Education Quarterly* 15: 299–315.

Lefebvre, R. C., Olander, C. and Levine, E. 1999. The Impact of Multiple Channel Delivery of Nutrition Messages on Student Knowledge, Motivation and Behavior: Results from the Team Nutrition Pilot Study, *Social Marketing Quarterly* 5: 90–8.

Lehman, D., Hawkins, J. D. and Catalano, R. F. 1994. Reducing Risks and Protecting our Youths: A Community Mission, *Corrections Today* 56(5): 92–100.

Lehrer, J. 2008. Grape Expectations: What Wine can Tell us About the Nature of Reality, retrieved 25 February 2008 from www.boston.com/bostonglobe/ideas/articles/2008/02/24/grape_expectations.

Lehrman, S. 1999. GM Backlash leaves US Farmers Wondering how to Sell their Crops, *Nature,* 9 September p. 107.

Leidig, M. 2006. Becker Promotes Condom use in Germany, *British Medical Journal* 332(7545): 812.

Leiss, W., Kline, S., Jhally, S. and Botterill, J. 2005. *Social Communication in Advertising: Consumption in the Mediated Marketplace,* 3rd edn. New York: Routledge Taylor & Francis.

Leon 2007. L'Oreal found Guilty of Racism. Sox First, available at: www.soxfirst.com/50226711/loreal_found_guilty_of_racism.php, accessed 21 May 2010.

Leventhal, H. and Cameron, L. 1994. Persuasion and Health Attitudes, in S. Shavitt and T. C. Brock (eds.), *Persuasion: Psychological Insights and Perspectives.* Boston: Allyn & Bacon, pp. 219–49.

Leventhal, H. and Trembly, G. 1968. Negative Emotions and Persuasion, *Journal of Personality* 36: 154–68.

Levick, D. 2009. Progressive's MyRate Plan Pegs Customers' Driving Style to Rates, 17 June, retrieved 20 June2009 from www.courant.com/business/hc-progressive-insurance.artjun17,0,2006781.story.

Levin, I. P. and Gaeth, G. J. 1988. How Consumers are Affected by the Framing of Attribute Information Before and After Consuming the Product, *Journal of Consumer Research* 15(December): 374–8.

Levine, S. 2006. The Condoms? Please, Take One, 1 December 2006, retrieved 4 December 2006 from www.washingtonpost.com/wp-dyn/content/article/2006/11/30/AR2006113001462.html.

2007. 250,000 Condoms Deployed for HIIV Awareness, Prevention, 16 February, retrieved 19 June 2008 from www.wahsingtonpost.com/wp-dyn/content/article/2007/02/15/AR20070215016.

Lewis, G., Morkel, A. and Hubbard, G. 1993. *Australian Strategic Management: Concepts, Context and Cases.* Sydney: Prentice Hall. (Case 21; Smoking and health: An industry under siege.)

Lex, L. 1997. School's Back, and so are the Marketers, *The Wall Street Journal*, 15 September, p. B1.

Li, L., Rotheram-Borus, M., Lu, Y., Wu, Z., Lin, C. and Guan, J. 2009. Mass Media and HIV/AIDS in China, *Journal of Health Communication* 14(5): 424–38.

Ligerakis, M. 2001. Never Underestimate the Power of Kids, *B&T Weekly*, 23 February, p. 8.

Lilienfeld, A. M. and Lilienfeld, D. E. 1980. *Foundations of Epidemiology.* New York: Oxford University Press.

Lin, C. and Mooney, A. 2009. How Mobile makes Bricks-and-mortar Retail Accountable, retrieved 19 August 2009 from http://adage.com/digitalnext/post.php?article_id=137371.

Link, B. G. and Phelan, J. C. 1995. Social Conditions as Fundamental Causes of Disease, *Journal of Health and Social Behavior* (Extra issue): 80–95.

1996. Why are Some People Healthy and Others Not? The Determinants of Health of Populations, *American Journal of Public Health* 86(4): 598–9.

Linnan, L., Ferguson, Y., Wasilewski, Y., Lee, A., Yang, J., Solomon, F. and Katz, M. 2005. Using Community-based Participatory Research Methods to Reach Women with Health Messages: Results from the North Carolina BEAUTY and Health Pilot Project, *Health Promotion Practice* 6(2): 164–73.

Liu, C. 1999. Online Hate Sites Target Children, Report Warns, *The West Australian*, 30 March, p. 30.

Locke, J. [1690] 1961. *An Essay Concerning Human Understanding*, ed. J. W. Yolton. London: J. M. Dent.

Lomas, J. 1998. Social Capital and Health: Implications for Public Health and Epidemiology, *Social Science and Medicine* 47(9): 1181–8.

Lonczak, H., Abbott, R., Hawkins, J., Kosterman, R. and Catalano, R. 2002. Effects of the Seattle Social Development Project on Sexual Behavior, Pregnancy, Birth, and Sexually Transmitted Disease Outcomes by age 21 years, *Archives of Pediatric Adolescent Medicine* 156(5): 438–47.

Lord, C. G., Ross, L. and Lepper, M. R. 1979. Biased Assimilation and Attitude Polarisation: The Effects of Prior Theories on Subsequently Altered Evidence, *Journal of Personality and Social Psychology* 37: 2098–109.

Lowery, S. A. and DeFleur, M. L. 1995. *Milestones in Mass Communication Research,* 3rd edn White Plains, NY: Longman.

Lucidi, F., Grano, C., Leone, L., Lombardo, C. and Pesce, C. 2004. Determinants of the Intention to use Doping Substances: An Empirical Contribution in a Sample of Italian Adolescents, *International Journal of Sport Psychology* 35: 133, 148.

Lucidi, F., Zelli, A., Mallia, L., Grano, C., Russo, P. and Violani, C. 2008. The Social-cognitive Mechanism Regulating Adolescents' Use of Doping Substances, *Journal of Sports Sciences* 26: 447–56.

Lusch, R. F., Laczniak, G. R. and Murphy, P. 1980. The 'Ethics of Social Ideas' vs the 'Ethics of Marketing Social Ideas', *The Journal of Consumer Affairs* 14(1): 156–64.

Lyderson, K. 2002. In Iowa, there's not always room for Jello, *Washington Post*, 3 July, p. A2.

Lyon, K. 2002. Drink Drive, Lose Sponsor, *The West Australian*, 5 February, p. 105 (reproduced from *The Age*).

Mabry, M. 1999. Give us this Day our Daily Meds, retrieved 19 August 2009 from www.newsweek.com/id/88802.

Maccoby, N., Farquhar, J., Wood, P. D. and Alexander, J. 1977. Reducing the Risk of Cardiovascular Disease: Effects of a Community-based Campaign on Knowledge and Behavior, *Journal of Community Health* 3(2): 100–14.

MacCoun, R. J. 1998. Toward a Psychology of Harm Reduction, *American Psychologist* 53(11): 1199–208.

MacFadyen, L., Hastings, G. and MacKintosh, A. M. 2001. Cross-sectional Study of Young People's Awareness of and Involvement with Tobacco Marketing, *British Medical Journal* 322: 513–17.

MacIntyre, A. 1999. Social Structures and their Threat to Moral Agency, *Philosophy* 74: 311–29, retrieved 4 October 2001 from www.royalinstitutephilosophy.org/articles /macintyre_lecture.htm.

Mackenbach, J. 2009. Politics is Nothing but Medicine at a Larger Scale: Reflections on Public Health's Biggest Idea, *Journal of Epidemiology and Community Health* 63: 181–4.

Macnamara, J. and Bell, P. 2008. E-Electioneering: Use of New Media in the 2007 Australian Federal Election, University of Technology, Sydney and Media Monitors, Broadway, NSW.

Madill, J. and O'Reilly, N. 2010. Investigating Social Marketing Sponsorships: Terminology, Stakeholders, and Objectives, *Journal of Business Research* 6(2): 133–9.

Maher, A., Wilson, N., Signal, L. and Thomson, G. 2006. Patterns of Sports Sponsorship by Gambling, Alcohol and Food Companies: An Internet Survey, *BMC Public Health* 6: 95.

Maheswaran, D. and Meyers-Levy, J. 1990. The Influence of Message Framing and Issue Involvement, *Journal of Marketing Research* 27: 361–7.

Maibach, E. 1993. Social Marketing for the Environment. Using Information Campaigns to Promote Environmental Awareness and Behavior Change, *Health Promotion International* 8(3): 209–24.

Maibach, E. W. and Cotton, D. 1995. Moving People to Behavior Change: A Staged Social Cognitive Approach to Message Design, in E. Maibach, and R. L. Parrott (eds.), *Designing Health Messages*. London: Sage.

Maibach, E., Abroms, L. and Marosits, M. 2007. Communication and Marketing as Tools to Cultivate the Public's Health: A Proposed 'People and Places' Framework, *BMC Public Health* 7: 88.

Maibach, E., Roser-Renouf, C. and Leiserowitz, A. 2009. Global Warming's Six Americas 2009: An Audience Segmentation Analysis, A Yale Project on Climate Change and George Mason University Center for Climate Change Communication Report.

Maiman, L. A. and Becker, M. H. 1974. The Health Belief Model: Origins and Correlates in Psychological Theory, *Health Education Monographs* 2(4): 336–53.

Mair, J. S. and Mair, M. 2003. Violence Prevention and Control through Environmental Modifications, *Annual Review of Public Health* 24: 209–25.

Manger, H., Hawkins, D., Haggerty, K. and Catalano, R. 1992. Mobilizing Communities to Reduce Risks for Drug Abuse: Lessons on Using Research to Guide Prevention Practice, *The Journal of Primary Prevention* 13(1): 3–22.

Mankell, H. 2000. *Sidetracked*. London: Harvill Press.

Manning, N. (ed.) 2009. *The New Media Communications Model: A Progress Report*, ed. N. Dawson, *Advertising Works 17: Proving the Payback on Marketing Investment*. London: IPA/WARC.

Manoff, R. K. 1985. *Social Marketing*. New York: Praeger.

Marin Institute 2008. Why Big Alcohol can't Police Itself: A Review of Advertising Self-regulation in the Distilled Spirits Industry, Marin Institute.

Mark, R. and Rhodes, R. 2009. Active Video Games: A Good Way to Exercise, *WellSpring* 20(4).

Marketing News. 1987. Campaign gets 'Bubbas' to quit messin', *Marketing News*, 19 June, p. 16.

Marks, A. 1997. *Private Sector Collaboration in Social Marketing Health Research: Examples from South Africa,* Paper presented to the Innovations in Social Marketing Conference, Boston.

Marmot, M. G. 2000. Social Determinants of Health: From Observation to Policy, *Medical Journal of Australia* 172: 279–83.

Marmot, M. G., Rose, H., Shipley, M. and Hamilton, P. J. S. 1978. Employment Grade and Coronary Heart Disease in British Civil Servants, *Journal of Epidemiology and Community Health* 32(4): 244–9.

Marmot, M. G., Smith, G. D., Stansfield, S., Patel, C., North, F., Head, J., White, I., Brunner, E. and Feeney, A. 1991. Health Inequalities among British Civil Servants: The Whitehall II Study, *Lancet* 338(8758): 58–9.

Marmot, M. G. and Wilkinson, R. 1999. *Social Determinants of Health*. Oxford University Press.

2006. *Social Determinants of Health,* 2nd edn. Oxford University Press.

Marteau, T., Ashcroft, R. and Oliver, A. 2009. Using Financial Incentives to Achieve Healthy Behaviour, *British Medical Journal* 338: b1415.

Mathews, A. 2009. The Doctor will Text You Now: Patients Visit with their Physicians Online as more Insurers begin Paying for Digital Diagnoses, 1 July, retrieved 1 July 2009 from http://online.wsj.com/article/SB10001424052970203872404574257900513900382.html.

Matsudo, S. M., Matsudo, R, Araujo, T. L., Andrade, E. L., de Oliveira, L. C. and Braggion
     G. F. 2003. The Agita São Paulo Program as a Model for Using Physical Activity,
     American Journal of Public Health 14(4): 265–72.

Matsudo, S. M., Matsudo, R. M., Andrade, D. R., Araújo, T. L., Andrade, E., de Oliveira, L.
     and Braggion, G. 2004. Physical Activity Promotion: Experience and Evaluation of
     the Agita São Paulo Program using the Ecological Mobile Model, *Journal of Physical
     Activity and Health* 2: 81–97.

Matsudo, S. M., Matsudo, V. R., Andrade, D. R., Araújo, T. L., and Pratt, M. 2006.
     Evaluation of a Physical Activity Promotion Program: The Example of Agita São
     Paulo, *Evaluation and Program Planning* 29: 301–11.

Matsumoto, Y., Sofronoff, K. and Sanders, M. R. 2007. The Efficacy and Acceptability of
     the Triple P – Positive Parenting Program with Japanese Parents, *Behaviour Change*
     24(4): 205–18.

Mayer, S. E. 1997. *What Money Can't Buy. Family Income and Children's Life Chances.*
     Cambridge, MA: Harvard University Press.

Mayor, S. 2005. UK Report Recommends Fortification of Flour with Folate, *British Medical
     Journal* 331(7528): 1292-a, retrieved 3 December 2005 from www.bmj.com.

McAuley, E. and Jacobson, L. 1991. Self-efficacy and Exercise Participation in Sedentary
     Adult Females, *American Journal of Health Promotion* 5(3): 185–92.

McAvoy, B. R., Donovan, R. J., Jalleh, G., Saunders, J. B., Wutzke, S. E., et al. 2001. General
     Practitioners, Prevention and Alcohol – A Powerful Cocktail? Facilitators and
     Inhibitors of Practising Preventive Medicine in General and Early Intervention for
     Alcohol in Particular: A 12-nation Key Informant and General Practitioner Study,
     Drugs: Education, Prevention and Policy 8(2) : 103–17.

McCarthy, E. J. 1960. *Basic Marketing: A Managerial Approach.* Chicago, IL: Richard Irwin.

McClure, A. C., Stoolmiller, M., Tanski, S. E., Worth, K. A. and Sargent, J. D. 2009.
     Alcohol-branded Merchandise and its Association with Drinking Attitudes and
     Outcomes in US Adolescents, *Archives of Pediatric Adolescent Medicine* 163(3): 211–17.

McClure, T. and Spence, R. 2006. *Don't Mess with Texas: The Story Behind the Legend.*
     Austin, TX: Idea City Press.

McCoy, M. 2000. Good Business for Good Citizens, *The Qantas Club*, Winter, pp. 6–11.

McDermott, L. 2001. An Investigation of Socio-cultural Factors which Promote the
     Desirability of a Suntan among Adolescents, unpublished Masters thesis, University
     of Queensland.

McDonald's Corporation and Affiliates 2005. McDonald's Commitment to Balanced,
     Active Lifestyles. Global Program Fact Sheet, retrieved 21 August 2009 from http://
     mcdepk.com/globalbalancedlifestyles/media_downloads/global_bal_fact_sheet.pdf.

McGuire, W. J. 1985. Attitudes and Attitude Change, in G. Lindsey and E. Aronsen (eds.),
     The Handbook of Social Psychology, Vol. II, 3rd edn. New York: Random House, pp.
     233–346.

McKee, N. 1992. *Social Mobilisation and Social Marketing.* Pennang, Malaysia: Southbound.

McKenzie-Mohr, D. and Smith, W. 1999. *Fostering Sustainable Behavior: An Introduction to
     Community-based Social Marketing, 2nd edn.* Gabriola Island, British Columbia: New
     Society.

McKinney, M. 2008. Cargill's new No-calorie Sweetener gets a Nod, 15 May, retrieved 19
     May 2008 from www.startribune.com.

McNeil Jr., D. 2008. Nets and new drug make inroads against malaria. *New York Times*, retrieved 5 February 2008 from www.nytimes.com/2008/02/01/health/01malaria. html.

McNeal, J. U. 1992. *Kids as Customers: A Handbook of Marketing to Children*. New York: Lexington.

McNeal, J. and Ji, M. 1999. Chinese Children as Consumers: An Analysis of their New Product Information Sources, *The Journal of Consumer Marketing* 16(4): 345–64.

McNeal, J. and Yeh, C. 1997. Development of Consumer Behavior Patterns among Chinese Children, *Journal of Consumer Marketing* 14(1): 45–59.

Mead, L. (1998. Telling the Poor What to Do, *Public Interest*, 6 January, available at: www. britannica.com/bcom.

Mechanic, D. 1999. Issues in promoting health, *Social Science and Medicine* 48: 711–18.

Mediascope 2000a. Body Image and Advertising, Issue Briefs, Mediascope Press, Studio City, California, retrieved 20 April 2003 from www.mediascope.org/pubs/ibriefs/ bia.htm.

2000b. *Muscle Madness: The Ugly Connection between Body Image and Anabolic Steroid Use*, Issue Briefs, Mediascope Press, Studio City, California.

Meenaghan, T. 1991. The Role of Sponsorship in the Marketing Communications Mix, *International Journal of Advertising* 10(1): 35–47.

2001. Understanding Sponsorship Effects, *Psychology and Marketing* 18(2): 95–122.

Menczer, W. B. 2007. Guaranteed Ride Home Programs: A Study of Program Characteristics, Utilization. and Cost, *Journal of Public Transportation* 10(4): 131–50.

Merrett, N. 2009. Alcohol Sport Sponsors Agree to Scottish Restrictions, 5 February (cited 26 June 2009), available at: www.beveragedaily.com/content/view/print/235230.

Meyerowitz, B. E. and Chaiken, S. 1987. The Effect of Message Framing on Breast Self-examination Attitudes, Intentions, and Behavior, *Journal of Personality and Social Psychology* 52: 500–10.

Midgley, C. 2008. Dolls with Disabilities Divide Opinion, *The Weekend Australian*, 12–13 July, p. 17.

Milberger, S. M., Davis, R .M. and Holm, A. L. 2009. Pet Owners' Attitudes and Behaviours Related to Smoking and Second-hand Smoke: A Pilot Study, *Tobacco Control* 18(2): 156–8.

Mill, J. S. [1859] 1991. *On Liberty and other Essays, ed.* J. Gray. Oxford University Press.

Molnar, A. 2005. *School Commercialism: From Democratic Ideal to Market Commodity*. New York: Taylor & Francis.

Molnar, A. and Reaves, J. A. 2001. *Buy me! Buy me! The Fourth Annual report on Trends in Schoolhouse Commercialism. Year 2000–2001,* Commercialism in Education Research Unit, EPSL-0109–101-CERU. Arizona State University, Tempe, Arizona.

Molnar, A., Boninger, F., Wilkinson, G. and Fogarty, J. 2008. At Sea in a Marketing-saturated World: The Eleventh Annual Report on Schoolhouse Commercialism Trends: 2007–2008, Boulder and Tempe, Education and the Public Interest Center & Commercialism in Education Research Unit 2008 (cited 14 August 2009), available at: http://epicpolicy.org/publication/Schoolhouse-commercialism-2008.

Montgomery, K. C. 1990. Promoting Health through Entertainment Television, in C. Atkin and L. Wallack (eds.), *Mass Communication and Public Health: Complexities and Conflicts*. Newbury Park, CA: Sage.

Moodie, R., Swinburn, B., Richardson, J. and Somaini, B. 2006. Childhood Obesity – A Sign of Commercial Success, but a Market Failure, *International Journal of Pediatric Obesity* 1(3): 133–8.

Morales, T. 2002. Functional Beverages: Are they Worth your Money?, retrieved 21 June 2009 from www.cbsnews.com/stories/2002/07/29/earlyshow/health/health_news/main5166.

Morgan, K. and Sonnino, R. 2007. Empowering Consumers: The Creative Procurement of School Meals in Italy and the UK, *International Journal of Consumer Studies* 31: 19–25.

Morley-John, J., Swinburn, B.A., Metcalf, P.A. and Raza, F. 2002. Fat Content of Chips, Quality of Frying Fat and Deep-frying Practices in New Zealand Fast Food Outlets, *Australian and New Zealand Journal of Public Health* 26: 101–7.

Morrow, L., Verins, I., and Willis, E. (eds.) 2002. *Mental Health and Work: Issues and Perspectives.* Adelaide: Aussinet: the Australian Network for Promotion, Prevention and Early Intervention for Mental Health.

Moxey, A. O'Connell, D., McGettigan, P. and Henry, D. 2003. Describing Treatment Effects to Patients, *Journal of General Internal Medicine* 18: 948–59.

Mucha, T. 2004. The Brand called Detroit City: Seeking to Repair its Battered Image, Detroit Turns to its Taxi Drivers. Good Idea. No, Seriously, *Marketing Focus*, 5 August.
2004. War Gaming. Retrieved May 30, 2004.
2005. Psst. Have you Heard about the Word-of-mouth Industry? As it grows up, marketers want to give it the sheen of respectability.

Mufson, S. 2006. Change the Light Bulbs and Plug those Leaks, *Washington Post*, 25 June, retrieved 26 June 2006 from www.washingtonpost.com/wp-dyn/content/article/2006/06/24/AR2006062400087.html.

Mugford, S., Mugford, J. and Donnelly, D. 1999. *Social Research Project: Athletes' Motivations for Using or not Using Performance Enhancing Drugs.* Canberra: Australian Sports Drug Agency.

Mulilis, J-P. and Lippa, R. 1990. Behavioral Changes in Earthquake Preparedness due to Negative Threat Appeals: A Test of Protection Motivation Theory, *Journal of Applied Social Psychology* 20(8): 619–38

Mummery, K. and Schofield, G. 2002. 10,000 Steps Rockhampton, Health Promotion Queensland, Inaugural Seminar, 20 September, Brisbane.

Murphy, P.E. and Bloom, P. N. 1990. Ethical Issues in Social Marketing, in S. Fine (ed.), *Social Marketing. Promoting the Causes of Public and Nonprofit Agencies.* Boston, MA: Allyn & Bacon.

Murphy, T. 1994. Patients Encouraged to Reveal Abuse, *Australian Doctor*, 15 July, p. 50.

Murray, C. and Lopez, A. (eds.) 1996. *The Global Burden of Disease: A Comprehensive Assessment of Mortality and Disability from Diseases, Injuries and Risk Factors in 1990 and projected to 2020.* Cambridge, MA: Harvard University Press.

Murray-West, R. 2004. First Death, then Shag – Welcome to the World of Cult Student Cigarettes, *The Telegraph*, 1 February, retrieved 21 October 2004 from www.telegraph.co.uk/education/3325420/First-Death-then-Shag – welcome-to-the-world-of-cult-student-cigarettes.html.

National Academy of Sciences, Institute of Health 2000. Promoting Health: Intervention Strategies from Social and Behavioral Research, National Academies Press,

retrieved 18 April 2003 from: books.nap.edu/books/0309071755/html/6.html#
pagetop.

National Health and Medical Research Council (NHMRC) 1997. *Health-promoting Sport, Racing and Arts Settings. New Challenges for the Health Sector.* Canberra: AGPS.
2009. Australian Guidelines to Reduce Health Risks from Drinking Alcohol.

National Social Marketing Centre (NSMC) 2007. Snack Right, retrieved 3 June 2009 from
www.nsms.org.uk/public/CSView.aspx?casestudy=37.

Neff, J. 2007. Unilever: Don't let Beauty Get too Real, *Advertising Age* 78(16): 1–42.

New Tang Dynasty Television 2009. Survey: Most Consumer Goods Sold in Southern
China Below Standard, retrieved 5 July 5 from http://english.ntdtv.com/ntdtv_en/
ns_china/2009–07–02/117428800071.html.

NFO Donovan Research 2000. *Qualitative Research for the 'Smarter Than Smoking' Project,*
Report to Smarter Than Smoking Management Group, Perth, Western Australia.

Nicholas, D., Huntington, P. and Williams, P. 2002. The Impact of Location on the Use
of Digital Information Systems: Case Study Health Information Kiosks, *Journal of
Documentation* 58(3): 284–301.

Nicholls, J. A., Roslow, S. and Laskey, H. A. 1994. Sports Event Sponsorship for Brand
Promotion, *Journal of Applied Business Research* 10(4): 35–41.

Nicol, P. W., Watkins, R. E., Donovan, R. J., Wynaden, D. and Cadwallader, H. 2009. The
Power of Vivid Experience in Hand Hygiene Compliance, *Journal of Infection Control*
72: 36–42.

Nigg, C., Burbank, P., Padula, C., Dufresne, R., Rossi, J., Velicer, W., Laforge, R. and
Prochaska, J. 1999. Stages of Change across Ten Health Risk Behaviors for Older
Adults, *Gerontologist* 39(4): 473–82.

Noble, G., Martin, D., Ford, J., Harbilas, R., Hornsey, A., Noble, E. and Nolan, J. 1990.
Portrayals of Driving and Alcohol in Popular Television Programmes Screened in Australia.
CR 90, Canberra: Federal Office of Road Safety.

Norman, P. and Connor, M. 1996. The Role of Social Cognition Models in Predicting
Health Behaviours: Future Directions, in M. Conner and P. Norman (eds.), *Predicting
Health Behaviour.* Buckingham: Open University Press, pp. 197–225.

Norman, P., Bennett, P. and Lewis, H. 1998. Understanding Binge Drinking among Young
People: An Application of the Theory of Planned Behaviour, *Health Education
Research: Theory and Practice* 13(2): 163–9.

Norris, P. 1996. Does Television Erode Social Capital? A Reply to Putnam, *PS: Political
Science and Politics* (September): 474–80.

Nottingham University Business School 2009. ICCSR Statement on Funding, retrieved
31 May 2009 from www.nottingham.ac.uk/business/ICCSR/assets/Statement%20
on%20Funding.pdf.

Noussaire, C., Robin, S. and Ruffieux, B. 2004. Do Consumers Really Refuse to Buy
Genetically Modified Food, *Economic Journal* 114: 102–20.

Novelli, W. D. 1984. Developing Marketing Programs, in L. W. Frederickson , L. J.
Solomon and K. A. Brehony (eds.), *Marketing Health Behavior: Principles, Techniques
and Applications.* New York: Plenum.

Nozick, R. 1974. *Anarchy, State and Utopia.* New York: Basic Books.

Nussbaum, M. 1986. *The Fragility of Goodness: Luck and Ethics in Greek Tragedy and
Philosophy.* New York: Cambridge University Press.

Nutbeam, D. 1998. Evaluating Health Promotion – Progress, Problems and Solutions, *Health Promotion International* 13(1): 27–44.

O'Dea, J. A. 2005. Prevention of Child Obesity: 'First, do no Harm', *Health Education Research* 20(2): 259–65.

O'Dowd, A. 2009. UK Government may Consider Minimum Price for Alcohol, *British Medical Journal* 339: b2929.

Office of National Drug Control Policy (ONDCP) 1997. National Youth Anti-Drug Media Campaign, Washington, DC.

O'Keefe, D. J. 1990. *Persuasion: Theory and Research*. San Francisco, CA: Sage.

Okin, G., Sangster, V., Thurner, R. and Adam, F. 2009. CABWISE: Creating a Brand to Help Prevent Rapes, in N. Dawson (ed.), *Advertising Works 17: Proving the Payback on Marketing Investment*. Henley on Thames: World Advertising Research Centre.

Olsen, C. K. 1999. Countering Pro-tobacco Influences at the racetrack, *American Journal of Public Health* 89(9): 1431–2.

Oman, R. F. and King, A. C. 1998. Predicting the Adoption and Maintenance of Exercise Participation using Self-efficacy and Previous Exercise Participation Rates, *American Journal of Health Promotion* 12(3): 154–61.

Omori, M. 2003. The Participation of Japanese Fathers in Child Rearing, archive of CRN homepage topics for discussion, retrieved 15 August 2009 from www.childresearch. net/index.html.

Ontario School Bus Association 1999. Policy Statement No. 1000. External Advertising on School Buses, retrieved 29 October 2001 from www.shantz-coach.com/ external.html.

O'Reilly, N. and Madill, J. 2007. Evaluating Social Marketing Elements in Sponsorship, *Social Marketing Quarterly* XIII(4): 1–25.

Orleans, C. T., Gruman, J., Ulmer, C., Emont, S. L. and Hollendonner, J. K. 1999. Rating our Progress in Population Health Promotion: Report Card on Six Behaviors, *American Journal of Health Promotion* 14(2): 75–82.

Ornstein, R. E. 1986. *Multi Mind.* London: Macmillan.

Orwall, B. 1997. Why are School Kids Eating Dimitri's Fudge? *The Wall Street Journal*, 24 November, p. B1.

Osterhus, L. T. 1997. Pro-social Consumer Influence Strategies: When and How do They Work? *Journal of Marketing* 61(Oct.): 16–29.

O'Sullivan, T. 2007. Get MediaSmart®: A Critical Discourse Analysis of Controversy around Advertising to Children in the UK, *Consumption Markets & Culture* 10(3): 293–314.

Otker, T. 1988. Exploitation: The Key to Sponsorship Success, *European Research* 16(2): 77–86.

Owen, J. 2002. Unpublished Ph.D. Progress Report, University of Western Australia, Perth, Western Australia.

Owen, N. and Borland, R. 1997. Delayed Compensatory Cigarette Consumption after a Workplace Smoking Ban, *Tobacco Control* 6: 131–5.

Owen, N., Humpel, N., Leslie, E., Bauman, A. and Sallis, J. 2004. Understanding Environmental Influences on Walking; Review and Research Agenda, *American Journal of Preventative Medicine* 27(1): 67–76.

Oxenstierna, G., Ferrie, J., Hyde, M., Westerlund, H. and Theorell, T. 2005. Dual Source Support and Control at Work in Relation to Poor Health, *Scandinavian Journal of Public Health* 33(6): 455–63.

Packard, V. 1967. *The Hidden Persuaders*. New York: David Mackay.

Paine, J., Shipton, C., Chaggar, S., Howells, R., Kennedy, M., Vernon, G., Wright, S., Hinchliffe, E., Adams, J., Silverstone, A. and Drake, R. 2005. Improving the Nutritional Value of Golden Rice through Increased Pro-vitamin A Content, *Nature Biotechnology* 23(4): 482–7.

Pallonen, U. E., Velicer, W. F., Prochaska, J. O. *et al.* 1998. Computer-based Smoking Cessation Interventions in Adolescents: Description, Feasibility, and Six-month Follow-up Findings, *Substance Use and Misuse* 33(4): 935–65.

Palmgreen, P., Donohew, L., Lorch, E. P., Hoyle, R. H. and Stephenson, M. T. 2001. Television Campaigns and Adolescent Marijuana Use: Tests of Sensation Seeking Targeting, *American Journal of Public Health* 91(2): 292–6.

Palmgreen, P., Donohew, L., Pugzles Lorch, E., Hoyle, R. and Stephenson, M. 2002. Television Campaigns and Sensation Seeking Targeting of Adolescent Marijuana Use: Controlled Time Series Approach, in R. Hornick (ed.), *Public Health Communication*. Hillsdale, NJ: Lawrence Erlbaum.

Papadimitriou, D. and Apostolopoulou, A. 2009. Olympic Sponsorship Activation and the Creation of Competitive Advantage, *Journal of Promotion Management* 15: 90–117.

Papadimitriou, D., Apostolopoulou, A. and Dounis, T. 2008. Event Sponsorship as a Value Creating Strategy for Brands, *Journal of Product & Brand Management* 17(4): 212–22.

Paradies, Y. 2006. A Systematic Review of Empirical Research on Self-reported Racism and Health, *International Journal of Epidemiology* 35(4): 888–901.

Parker, B. 1995. *Snakebites, Hammers and Hand Grenades*. Working paper, Bradley University, Peoria, Illinois.

Parker, D., Manstead, A. S. R. and Stradling, S. G. 1995. Extending the Theory of Planned Behaviour: The Role of Personal Norm, *British Journal of Social Psychology* 34: 127–37.

Pasick, R. J., D'Onofrio, C. N. and Otero-Sabogal, R. 1996. Similarities and Differences Across Cultures: Questions to Inform a Third Generation for Health Promotion Research, *Health Education Quarterly* 23(Supp.): S142–S161.

Patterson, P. and Wilkins, L. 1991. *Media Ethics, Issues and Cases*. Dubuque, IN: Wm. C. Brown.

Patton, C. R. and Vasquez, R. 2008. Dove's Campaign for Real Beauty: A Case Analysis, in R. A. Oglesby and M. G. Adams (eds.), *Business Research Yearbook: Global Business Perspectives, vol. XV*, a publication of the International Academy of Business Disciplines, pp. 850–61.

Pearson, L., Allocco, O., Terrey, H. and Saxton, J. 2009. Sending an SMS: The Potential of Mobile Phones and Text Messaging for Charities and Non-profit Organisations, nfpSynergy, Charities Aid Foundation & Institute of Fundraising.

Peek-Asa, C. and Zwerling, C. 2003. Role of Environmental Interventions in Injury Control and Prevention, *Epidemiologic Review* 25: 77–89.

People's Daily Online 2008. Sponsors clearly Benefit from Olympics, retrieved 11 August 2009 from http://english.peopledaily.com.cn/90001/90776/90882/6482371.html.

Pepall, E., Earnest, J. and James, R. 2006. Understanding Community Perceptions of Health and Social Needs in a Rural Balinese Village: Results of a Rapid Participatory Appraisal, *Health Promotion International* 1–9.

Pereira, M., Kartashov, A., Ebbeling, C., Van Horn, L., Slattery, M., Jacobs, D. and Ludwig, D. 2005. Fast-food Habits, Weight Gain, and Insulin Resistance (the CARDIA study): 15-year Prospective Analysis, *The Lancet* 365(9453): 36–42.

Perese, L., Bellringer, M. and Abbott, M. 2005. Literature Review to Inform Social Marketing Objectives and Approaches, and Behaviour Change Indicators, to Prevent and Minimise Gambling Harm, Auckland University of Technology, Wellington.

Perman, F. and Henley, N. 2001. Marketing the Anti-drug Message: Source Credibility Varies by Use/non-use of Marijuana, *Australia and New Zealand Marketing Academy Conference 2001,* Massey University, New Zealand.

Perry, C. L. 1999. The Tobacco Industry and Underage Youth Smoking: Tobacco Industry Documents from the Minnesota Litigation, *Archives of Pediatric and Adolescent Medicine* 153: 935–41.

Persaud, R. 2000. Suicide Rate Rises after Funeral of Princess of Wales, *British Medical Journal* 321: 1246.

Peters, C. 1999. Teacher, there's a Brand Name in my Math Problem!!, ZNET Daily Commentaries, 23 August, available at: www.zmag.org.

Petersen, M. 2008. *Our Daily Meds: How the Pharmaceutical Companies Transformed Themselves into Slick Marketing Machines and Hooked the Nation on Prescription Drugs,* 1st edn. New York: Farrar, Straus and Giroux.

Peterson, E. A. and Koehler, J. E. 1997. Changing Traditions: Preventing Illness Associated with Chitterlings, Paper presented to the *Innovations in Social Marketing Conference,* Boston, Massachusetts.

Peterson, J., Atwood, J. and Yates, B. 2002. Key Elements for Church-based Health Promotion Programs: Outcome-based Literature Review, *Public Health Nursing* 19(6): 401–11.

Petrella, R. J., Koval, J. J., Cunningham, D. A. and Paterson D. H. 2003. Can Primary Care Doctors Prescribe Exercise to Improve Fitness? The Step Test Exercise Prescription (STEP) Project, *American Journal of Preventative Medicine* 24(4): 316–22.

Pettigrew, S. F. 2000. Culture and Consumption: A Study of Beer Consumption in Australia, Ph.D. thesis, University of Western Australia, Perth, Western Australia.

Petty, R. E. and Cacioppo, J. T. 1983. Central and Peripheral Routes to Persuasion: Application to Advertising, in L. Percy and A. Woodside (eds.), *Advertising and Consumer Psychology.* Lexington, MA: Lexington Books.

1986. Elaboration Likelihood Model of Persuasion, *Advances in Experimental Social Psychology* 19: 123–93.

Pham, M. T. 1992. Effects of Involvement, Arousal, and Pleasure on the Recognition of Sponsorship Stimuli, in J. F. Sherry Jr. and B. Sternthal (eds.), *Advances in Consumer Research*, Provo, UT: Association for Consumer Research, pp. 85–96.

Piercy, N. F. 2008. *Market-led Strategic Change: Transforming the Process of Going to Market*, 4th edn. Oxford: Butterworth-Heinemann.

Pikora, T., Phang, J. W., Karro, J., Corti, B., Clarkson, J., Donovan, R. J., Frizzell, S. and Wilkinson, A. 1999. Are Smoke-free Policies Implemented and Adhered to at Sporting Venues? *Australia and New Zealand Journal of Public Health* 23(4): 407–9.

Pokrywczynski, J. 1994. An Examination of the Exposure Potential of In-stadium Advertising in Displays during Televised Sports Coverage, in L. N. Reid (ed.),

Proceedings of the 1992 Conference of the American Academy of Advertising, American Academy of Advertising, pp. 150–5.

Pollay, R. 1986. The Distorted Mirror: Reflections on the Unintended Consequences of Advertising, *Journal of Marketing* 50: 18–36.

Pomazal, R. J. and Jaccard, J. J. 1976. An Informational Approach to Altruistic Behavior, *Journal of Personality and Social Psychology* 33: 317–26.

Pope, N. K. and Voges, K. E. 1994. Sponsorship Evaluation: Does it Match the Motive and the Mechanism? *Sport Marketing Quarterly* 3(4): 37–45.

Postma, P. 1999. *The New Marketing Era*. New York: McGraw-Hill.

Prentice-Dunn, S. and Rogers, R. W. 1986. Protection Motivation Theory and Preventive Health: Beyond the Health Belief Model, *Health Education Research: Theory & Practice* 1(3): 153–61.

Pressler, M. 2004. Convenience, No Store: Vending Machines are being Stocked with More than Snacks, 10 April, retrieved 14 April 2004 from www.washingtonpost.com/ac2/wp-dyn/A359–2004Apr9?language=printer.

Privat, M., Aubel, C., Arnould, S., Communal, Y., Ferrara, M. and Bignont, Y-J. 2009. Breast Cancer Cell Response to Genistein is Conditioned by BRCA1 Mutations, *Biochemical and Biophysical Research Communications* 379, 785–9.

Prochaska, J. O. 1997. Interactive Communication Technologies and Risk Reduction. Keynote Address at *Innovations in Social Marketing Conference*, Boston, Massachusetts.

Prochaska, J. O. and DiClemente, C. C. 1984. *The Transtheoretical Approach: Crossing the Traditional Boundaries of Therapy*. Illinois: Dow-Jones/Irwin.

   1986. Toward a Comprehensive Model of Change, in W. R. Miller, and N. Heather (eds.), *Treating Addictive Behaviours: Processes of Change*. New York: Plenum Press.

Prochaska, J. O., Norcross, J. C. and DiClemente, C. C. 1994. *Changing for Good*. New York: Avon Books.

Prochaska, J. O., Evers, K. E., Prochaska, J. M., Van Marter, D. and Johnson, J. L. 2007. Efficacy and Effectiveness Trials: Examples from Smoking Cessation and Bullying Prevention, *Journal of Health Psychology* 12(1): 170–8.

Prochaska, J. O., Velicer, W. F., Rossi, J. S., Goldstein, M. G., Marcus, B. H., Rakowski, W., Fiore, C., Harlow, L. L., Redding, C. A., Rosenbloom, D. and Rossi, S. R. 1994. Stages of Change and Decisional Balance for 12 Problem Behaviours, *Health Psychology*, 13: 39–46.

Prochaska, J. O., Velicer, W. F., Redding, C., Rossi, J. S., Goldstein, M., DePue, J., Greene, G. W., Rossi, S. R., Sun, X., Fava, J. L., Laforge, R., Rakowski, W. and Plummer, B. A. 2005. Stage-based Expert systems to Guide a Population of Primary Care Patients to Quit Smoking, Eat Healthier, Prevent Skin Cancer, and Receive Regular Mammograms, *Preventive Medicine* 41: 406–16.

Public Agenda 2008. *Public Engagement: A Primer from Public Agenda*. Center for Advances in Public Engagement, available at: www.publicagenda.org/cape.

Purdue, W., Gostin, O. and Stone, L. 2003. Public Health and the Built Environment: Historical, Empirical and Theoretical Foundations for an Expanded Role, *Journal of Law, Medicine and Ethics* 31: 557–66.

Puska, P., Toumilehto, J., Salonen, J., Neittaanmaki, L., Maki, J. and Virtamo, J. 1985. The Community-based Strategy to Prevent Heart Disease: Conclusions of the Ten years of the North Karelia Project, *Annual Review of Public Health* 6: 147–93.

Putnam, R. D. 1995a. Tuning in, Tuning out: The Strange Disappearance of Social Capital in America, *PS: Political Science and Politics* (December): 664–83.

1995b. Bowling Alone. America's Declining Social Capital, *Journal of Democracy* 6: 65–78.

2000. *Bowling Alone. The Collapse and Revival of American Community.* New York: Simon & Schuster.

Quart, A. 2003. *Branded: The Buying and Selling of Teenagers.* London: Arrow.

Raats, M. M. 1992. The Role of Beliefs and Sensory Responses to Milk in Determining the Selection of Milks of Different Fat Content, unpublished doctoral thesis, University of Reading, UK.

Rajaretnam, J. 1994 The Long-term Effects of Sponsorship on Corporate and Product Image: Findings of a Unique Experiment, *Marketing & Research Today* 21(1): 62–73.

Rangan, V. K., Karim, S. and Sandberg, S. K. 1996. Do Better at Doing Good, *Harvard Business Review* 7(3): 42–54.

Ransdell, L. 2001. Using the PRECEDE–PROCEED Model to Increase Productivity in Health Education Faculty, *International Journal of Health Education* 4(1): 276–82.

Raphael, D. 2002. Social Justice is Good for our Hearts: Why Societal Factors – Not Lifestyles – Are Major Causes of Heart Disease in Canada and Elsewhere, available at: www.cwhn.ca/resources/heart_health/justice2.pdf.

2003. Barriers to Addressing the Societal Determinants of Health: Public Health Units and Poverty in Ontario, Canada, *Health Promotion International* 18(4): 397–405.

Rasmussen, S., Prescott, E., Sorensen, T. and Sogaard, J. 2004. The total Lifetime Costs of Smoking, *European Journal of Public Health* 14(1): 95–100.

Rawls, J. 1971. *A Theory of Justice.* Cambridge, MA: Harvard University Press.

Reichhardt, T. 2003. Playing with Fire? *Nature*, 424(July): 367–8.

Resnicow, K., Jackson, A., Wang, T., De, A., McCarty, F., Dudley, W. and Baranowski, T. 2001. A Motivational Interviewing Intervention to Increase Fruit and Vegetable Intake through Black Churches: Results of the Eat for Life Trial, *American Journal of Public Health* 91(10): 1686–93.

Retallack, S. 2006. Ankelohe and Beyond: Communicating Climate Change, 16 May, retrieved 26 July 2009 from www.opendemocracy.net.

Reynolds, G. 2009. Phys Ed: Are Sports Drinks Actually Good for Kids? *The New York Times*, 4 August, available at: http://well.blogs.nytimes.com/2009/08/04/phys-ed-are-sports-drinks-actually-good-for-kids.

Rhodes, A. 1975. *Propaganda: The Art of Persuasion: World War II.* London: Angus & Robertson.

Rice, G. 2006. Pro-environmental Behavior in Egypt: Is there a Role for Islamic Environmental Ethics? *Journal of Business Ethics* 65(4): 373–90.

Rice, R. E. and Atkin, K. J. 1989. *Public Communication Campaigns.* Newbury Park, CA: Sage.

Rifon, N., Choi, S., Trimble, C. and Li, H. 2004. Congruence Effects in Sponsorship: The Mediating Role of Sponsor Credibility and Consumer Attributions of Sponsor Motive, *Journal of Advertising* 33(1): 29–42.

Rippetoe, P. A. and Rogers, R. W. 1987. Effects of Components of Protection–motivation Theory on Adaptive and Maladaptive Coping with a Health Threat, *Journal of Personality and Social Psychology* 52(3): 596–604.

Robberson, M. R. and Rogers, R. W. 1988. Beyond Fear Appeals: Negative and Positive Appeals to Health and Self-esteem, *Journal of Applied Social Psychology* 18: 277–87.

Roberfroid, M. B. 2002. Functional Foods: Concepts and Application to Insulin and Oligofructose, *British Journal of Nutrition* 87(2): 139–43.

Roberts, D., Christenson, P. G., Henriksen, L. and Bandy, E. 2002. *Substance Use in Popular Movies and Videos*. Office of National Drug Control Policy. Washington, DC.

Roberts, D., Henriksen, L., Christenson, P. G. and Kelly, M. 1999. *Substance Use in Popular Movies and Music*. Office of National Drug Control Policy. Washington, DC.

Rogers, E. M. 1995. *Diffusion of Innovations,* 4th edn. New York: The Free Press.

Rogers, R. W. 1975. A Protection Motivation Theory of Fear Appeals and Attitude Change, *Journal of Psychology* 91: 93–114.

　1983. Cognitive and Physiological Process in Fear Appeals and Attitude Change: A Revised Theory of Protection Motivation, in J. Cacioppo, and R. Petty (eds.), *Social Psychophysiology*. New York: Guilford Press.

Rogers, T., Feighery, E. C., Tencati, E. M., Butler, J. L. and Weiner, L. 1995. Community Mobilization to Reduce Point-of-purchase Advertising of Tobacco Products, *Health Education Quarterly* 22(4): 427–42.

Rolland, E., Moore, K. M., Robinson, V. A. and McGuinness, D. 2006. Using Ontario's 'Telehealth' Health Telephone Helpline as an Early-warning System: A Study Protocol, *BMC Health Services Research* 6(10): 1–7.

Rose, G. 1985. Sick Individuals and Sick Populations, *International Journal of Epidemiology* 14(1): 32–8.

　1992. *The Strategy of Preventive Medicine*. Oxford University Press.

Rosen, J. 1994. Public Journalism: First Principles, in J. Rosen, and D. Merritt Jr., (eds.), *Public Journalism: Theory and Practice*. Dayton, OH: Kettering Foundation.

Rosenstock, I., Strecher, V. and Becker, M. 1988. Social Learning Theory and the Health Belief Model, *Health Education Quarterly* 15: 175–83.

Rosenstock, I. M. 1974. Historical Models of the Health Belief Model, in M. H. Becker (ed.), *The Health Belief Model and Personal Health Behavior*. Thorofare, New Jersey: Charles B. Slack.

Rosenthal, M., Li, Z., Robertson, A. and Milstein, A. 2009. Impact of Financial Incentives for Prenatal Care on Birth Outcomes and Spending, *Health Services Research* 44: 1465–79.

Ross, H. S. and Mico, P. R. 1980. *Theory and Practice in Health Education*. Palo Alto, CA: Mayfield.

Ross, R. and Blackwell, A. 2004. *The Influence of Community Factors on Health: Annotated Bibliography*. New York: PolickLink and the California Endowment.

Ross, W. D. [1930] 1963. *The Right and the Good*. Oxford: Clarendon Press.

Rossiter, J. R. and Donovan, R. J. 1983. Why you Shouldn't Test Ads in Focus Groups, *Australian Marketing Researcher* 7: 43–8.

Rossiter, J. R. and Percy, L. 1987. *Advertising and Promotion Management*. New York: McGraw-Hill.

　1997. *Advertising Communications and Promotion Management,* 2nd edn. New York: McGraw-Hill.

Rossiter, J. R., Percy, L. and Donovan, R. J. 1991. A Better Advertising Grid, *Journal of Advertising Research* 31, 11–22.

Rothman, A. J. and Salovey, P. 1997. Shaping Perceptions to Motivate Healthy Behavior: The Role of Message Framing, *Psychological Bulletin* 121(1): 3–19.

Rothman, A. J., Bartels, R., Wlaschin, J. and Salovey, P. 2006. The Strategic Use of Gain- and Loss-Framed Messages to Promote Healthy Behavior: How Theory Can Inform Practice, *Journal of Communication* 56: S202–S220.

Rothman, A. J., Salovey, P., Antone, C., Keough, K. and Martin, C. D. 1993. The Influence of Message Framing on Intentions to Perform Health Behaviors, *Journal of Experimental Social Psychology* 29: 408–33.

Rothschild, M. 1999. Carrots, Sticks, and Promises: A Conceptual Framework for the Management of Public Health and Social Issue Behaviors, *Journal of Marketing* 63(4): 24–37.

Rothschild, M. L. 1979. Marketing Communications in Nonbusiness Situations or Why it's so Hard to Sell Brotherhood like Soap, *Journal of Marketing* 43: 11–20.

1997. A Marketing View of Behavior Management in the Social and Public Domains, *Innovations in Social Marketing Conference*, Boston, Massachusetts.

2001. Ethical Considerations in the Use of Marketing for the Management of Public Health and Social Issues, in A. Andreasen (ed.), *Ethics in Social Marketing*. Washington, DC: Georgetown University Press, pp. 17–38.

Rothschild, M. L., Mastin, B. and Miller, T. W. 2006. Reducing Alcohol-impaired Driving Crashes through the Use of Social Marketing, *Accident Analysis & Prevention* 38(6): 1218–30.

Rudd, C. 2003. Merging General Practice-driven Reforms and Public Sector Strategies in the 1990s: A Framework for Health Policy, unpublished doctoral dissertation, University of Western Australia, Perth.

Rudd, R. E., Kaphingst, K., Colton, T., Gregoire, J. and Hyde, J. 2004. Rewriting Public Health Information in Plain Language, *Journal of Health Communication* 9(3): 195–206.

Rudd, R. E., Moeykens, B. A. and Colton, T. C. 1999. Health and Literacy. A Review of Medical and Public Health Literature, in *The Annual Review of Adult Learning and Literacy*. National Center for the Study of Adult Learning and Literacy, vol. 1, ch. 5, retrieved 28 April 2003 from http://ncsall.gse.harvard.edu/ann_rev/vol1_5.html

Ruggiero, L., Redding, C. A., Rossi, J. S. and Prochaska, J. O. 1997. A Stage-matched Smoking Cessation Program for Pregnant Smokers, *American Journal of Health Promotion* 12(1): 31–3.

Rychetnik, L. and Todd, A. 2004. VicHealth Mental health Promotion Evidence Review: A Literature Review Focusing on the VicHealth 1999–2002 Mental Health Promotion Scoping Project. Sydney: University of Sydney.

Sabbag, R. 2003. *Smokescreen: A True Adventure*. Edinburgh: Canongate.

Saffer, H. and Dave, D. 2006. Alcohol Advertising and Alcohol Consumption by Adolescents, *Health Economics* 15(6): 617–37.

Salazar, C. 2008. Salon Workers get Lesson in Violence, 6 January, retrieved 19 June 2008 from www.nydailynews.com/ny_local/bronz/2008/01/06/2008–01–06_salon_workers.

Salkowski, J. 1997. We'll Return to History Class after these Messages. Schools Learn how to Ad; Multiply their Revenues, 8 April, StarNet Dispatches, retrieved 29 October 2001 from http://dispatches.azstarnet.com/features/ad.htm.

Sallis, R., Hovell, M. F., Hofstetter, C. R., et al. 1990. Distance between Homes and Exercise Facilities Related to Frequency of Exercise among San Diego Residents, *Public Health Reports* 105(2): 179–85.

Salmon, C. T. (ed.) 1989. *Information Campaigns: Balancing Social Values and Social Change.* Newbury Park, CA: Sage.

Salovey, P. and Williams-Piehota, P. 2004. Field Experiments in Social Psychology: Message Framing and the Promotion of Health Protective Behaviors, *American Behavioral Scientist* 47: 488–505.

Salter, J. 2006. Company Comes up with 'hybrid' Hamburger, 27 June, retrieved 29 June 2006 from www.obesitydiscussion.com/forums/diet-forum/company-comes-up-hybrid-hamburger-1359.html.

Sanders, M. R. 2001. Helping Families Change: From Clinical Interventions to Population-based Strategies, in A. Booth, A. C. Crouter, *et al.* (eds.), *Couples in Conflict.* Hillsdale, NJ: Lawrence Erlbaum, pp. 185–219.

Sanders, M. R., Markie-Dadds, C., Tully, L. A. and Bor, W. 2000. The Triple P-Positive Parenting Program: A comparison of enhanced, standard, and self-directed behavioral family intervention for parents of children with early onset conduct problems. *Journal of Consulting and Clinical Psychology* 68(4): 624–40.

Sanders, M. R., Markie-Dadds, C. and Tully, L. A. 2001. Behavioural Family Therapy Reduced Disruptive Behaviour in Children at Risk for Developing Conduct Problems, *Evidence-Based Mental Health* 4(1): 20–4.

Sandler, D. M. and Shani, D. 1993. Sponsorship and the Olympic Games: The consumer perspective, *Sport Marketing Quarterly* 2(3): 38–43.

Sandora, T. J., Taveras, E. M., Shih, M. C., Resnick, E. A., Lee, G. M., Ross-Degnan, D. and Goldmann, D. A. 2005. A Randomized, Controlled Trial of a Multifaceted Intervention including Alcohol-based Hand Sanitizer and Hand-hygiene Education to Reduce Illness Transmission in the Home, *Pediatrics* 116(3): 587–94.

Santora, M. 2004. Burgers for the Health Professional, 26 October (cited 21 June 2009), available at: www.nytimes.com/2004/10/26/nyregion/26fast.html.

Sargeant, A. 2009. *Marketing Management for Nonprofit Organizations.* Oxford University Press.

Sartorius, N. and Schulze, H. 2005. *Reducing the Stigma of Mental Illness.* Cambridge University Press.

Sauer, A. 2008. Brandcameo produce placement awards, retrieved 17 August 2009 from www.brandchannel.com.

Sauer, A . 2009. Brandcameo product placement awards, retrieved 17 August 2009 from www.brandchannel.com.

Saxena, S. and Garrison, P. 2004. Mental Health Promotion: Case Studies from Countries. Geneva: World Health Organization and World Federation for Mental Health.

Saxena, S., Ommeren, M., Tang, K. and Armstrong, T. 2005. Mental Health Benefits of Physical Activity, *Journal of Mental Health* 14(5): 445–51.

Saxton, E. 1993. Motorsports, *Marketing News*, December, p. 5.

Schellenberg, J., Abdulla, S., Nathan, R., Mukasa, O., Marchant, T., Kikumbih, N., Mushi, A., Mponda, H., Minja, H., Mshinda, H., Tanner, M. and Lengeler, C. 2001. Effect of Large-scale Social Marketing of Insecticide-treated Nets on Child Survival in Rural Tanzania, *The Lancet* 357(9264): 1241–7.

Schlossberg, H. 1996. *Sports Marketing.* Oxford: Blackwell Business.

Schlosser, E. 2001. *Fast Food Nation: What the All-American Meal is doing to the World.* London: Allen Lane, Penguin Press.

Schnabel, J. 2009. Media Research: The black box, *Nature* 459(7248): 765–8.

Schoofs, M. and Winslow, R. 2008. Just Sitting Back to get in Shape: Two Pills do the Work of Exercise, 1 August, retrieved 5 August 2008 from http://online.wsj.com/article/SB121751115798400781.

Schor, J. B. and Ford, M. 2007. From Tastes Great to Cool: Children's Food Marketing and the Rise of the Symbolic, *Journal of Law, Medicine & Ethics* 35(1): 10–21.

Schulte, B. 2008. Shrinking Flock Examines its Identity, 8 June 2008, retrieved 9 June 2008 from www.wahsingtonpost.com/wp-dyn/content/article/2008/06/07/AR200806070092.

Schwartz, B. 2000. *Fact Sheet: Interactive Program.* Washington, DC: Fleishman Hillard. Posted on Social Marketing Listserve, 9 January.

Schwartz, M. B., Chambliss, H. O., Brownell, K. D., Blair, S. N. and Billington, C. 2003. Weight Bias among Health Professionals Specializing in Obesity, *Obesity Research* 11(9): 1033–9.

Schwartz, S. H. and Tessler, R. C. 1972. A Test of a Model for Reducing Measured Attitude-behavior Discrepancies, *Journal of Personality and Social Psychology* 24(2): 225–32.

Schwarzer, R. and Fuchs, R. 1996. Self-efficacy and Health Behaviours, in M. Conner and P. Norman (eds.), *Predicting Health Behaviour.* Buckingham: Open University Press, pp.163–96.

Scott, B. E., Lawson, D. W. and Curtis, V. 2007. Hard to Handle: Understanding Mothers' Hand washing Behaviour in Ghana, *Health Policy and Planning* 22: 216–24.

Scott, B. E., Schmidt, W. P., Aunger, R., Garbrah-Aidoo, N. and Animashaun, R. 2008. Marketing Hygiene Behaviours: The Impact of Different Communication Channels on Reported Hand washing Behaviour of Women in Ghana, *Health Education Research* 23(3): 392–401.

Scott, D. and Suchard, H. 1992. Motivations for Australian Expenditure on Sponsorship: An Analysis, *International Journal of Advertising* 11: 325–32.

Services Marketing Today 1994. American Marketing Association Customer Satisfaction Congress Report, July/August.

Shaffer, H. 2003. A Public Health Perspective on Gambling: The Four Principles, *AGA Responsible Gaming Lecture Series* 2: 1–27.

Shah, H. and Marks, N. 2004. *A Well-being Manifesto for a Flourishing Society.* London: New Economics Foundation.

Sheppard, B. H., Hartwick, J. and Warshaw, P. R. 1988. The Theory of reasoned Action: A Meta-analysis of Past Research with Recommendations for Modification and Future Research, *Journal of Consumer Research* 15: 325–43.

Sherif, C. W., Sherif, M. and Nebergall, R. E. 1965. *Attitude and Attitude Change: The Social Judgment–Involvement Approach.* Philadelphia, PA: W. B. Saunders.

Sherman, D., Mann, T. and Updegraff, J. 2006. Approach/Avoidance Motivation, Message Framing, and Health Behavior: Understanding the Congruency Effect, *Motivation and Emotion* 30(2): 165–9.

Sheth, J. N. and Frazier, G. L. 1982. A Model of Strategy Mix Choice for Planned Social Change, *Journal of Marketing* 46: 15–26.

Shilton, T. 2006. Advocacy for Physical Activity – from Evidence to Influence, *Promotion and Education* 13(2): 118–26.

Shonkoff, J. and Phillips, D. A. 2000. *From Neurons to Neighborhoods: The Science of Early Childhood Development*. Washington DC: National Academy Press.

Shu, L. L., Gino, F. and Bazerman, M. H. 2009. *Dishonest Deed, Clear Conscience: Self-Preservation through Moral Disengagement and Motivated Forgetting (Working Paper)*, Boston, Massachusetts: Harvard Business School.

Sibbald, B. 2000. U of A refuses Tobacco-sponsored Scholarship Donation, *Canadian Medical Association Journal* 164(1): 81.

Siegel, M., King, C., Ostroff, J., Ross, C., Dixon, K. and Jernigan, D. 2008. Comment – Alcohol Advertising in Magazines and Youth Readership: Are Youths Disproportionately Exposed? *Contemporary Economic Policy* 26: 482–92.

Simmons, D., Voyle, J., Fou, F., Feo, S. and Leakehe, L. 2004. Tale of Two Churches: Differential Impact of a Church-based Diabetes Control Programme among Pacific Islands people in New Zealand, *Diabetic Medicine* 21(2): 122–8.

Simpkin, A., Robertson, L., Barber, V. and Young, J. 2009. Modifiable Factors Influencing Relatives' Decision to offer Organ Donation: Systematic Review, *British Medical Journal* 338: b991.

Singhal, A. and Rogers, E. M. 1989. Prosocial Television for Development in India, in R. E. Rice, and C. K. Atkin (eds.), *Public Communication Campaigns*. Newbury Park, CA: Sage.

  1999. *Entertainment-Education: A Communication Strategy for Social Change*. Hillsdale, NJ: Lawrence Erlbaum.

  2004. The Status of Entertainment-education Worldwide, in A. Singhal , M. Cody , E. Rogers and M. Sabido (eds.), *Entertainment-education and Social Change: History, Research and Practice*. Hillsdale, NJ: Lawrence Erlbaum.

Singhal, A., Cody, M., Rogers, E. and Sabido, M. 2004. *Entertainment-education and Social Change*. Hillsdale, NJ: Lawrence Erlbaum.

Siska, M., Jason, J., Murdoch, P., Yang, W. S. and Donovan, R. J. 1992. Recall of AIDS Public Service Announcements and their Impact on the Ranking of AIDS as a National Problem, *American Journal of Public Health* 82: 1029–32.

Slater, M. D., Kelly, K. and Edwards, R. 2000. Integrating Social Marketing, Community Readiness and Media Advocacy in Community-based Prevention Efforts, *Social Marketing Quarterly* 6(3): 125–37.

Sloan, A. E. 2000a. The Top Ten Functional Foods, *Food Technology* 54(4) (April): 33–51.
  2000b. Adding value in 2000+, *Food Technology* 54(1) (January): 22.
  2001. Clean foods, *Food Technology* 55(2) (February): 18.

Slomski, A. 2009. 'I'm Here to Make You Feel Better', 10 March, available at: www.washingtonpost.com/wp-dyn/content/article/2009/03/09/AR2009030902247.html.

Smith, A. 1992. Setting a Strategy for Health, *British Medical Journal* 304(6823): 376–9.

Smith, B. 1998. Forget Messages … Think about Structural Change First, *Social Marketing Quarterly* 4(3): 13–19.

  1999. Ethics and the Social Marketer: Is the Glass Half-full, Half-empty, or Hemorrhaging? *Social Marketing Quarterly* 5(3): 74–5.

Smith, B. J., Bauman, A. E., Bull, F. C., Booth, M. L. and Harris, M. F. 2000. Promoting Physical Activity in General Practice: a Controlled Trial of Written Advice and Information Materials, *British Journal of Sports Medicine* 34: 262–7.

Smith, M. 2000. Germany Opposes Cigarette Curbs, *Financial Times*, 30 June, message posted to anti-tobacco mailing list, archived at anti-tobacco@lists.essential.org; http://lists.essential.org/mailman/listinfo/anti-tobacco.

Smith, W. A. 2001. Ethics and the Social Marketer: A Framework for Practitioners, in A. Andreasen (ed.), *Ethics in Social Marketing*. Washington, DC: Georgetown University Press, pp. 1–16.

Smolianov, P. and Aiyeku, J. 2009. Corporate Marketing Objectives and Evaluation Measures for Integrated Television Advertising and Sports Event Sponsorships, *Journal of Promotion Management* 15: 74–89.

Snider, M. 2009. Study: Video-game-playing Kids Showing Addiction Symptoms, retrieved 21 April 2009 from www.usatoday.com/life/lifestye/2009–04–20-gaming-addiction_N.htm.

Snipes, R. L., LaTour, M. S. and Bliss, S. J. 1999. A Model of the Effects of Self-efficacy on the Perceived Ethicality and Performance of Fear Appeals in Advertising, *Journal of Business Ethics* 19(3): 273–85.

Solomon, D. 1984. Social Marketing and Community Health Promotion, in L. W. Frederiksen , L. J. Solomon and K. A. Brehony (eds.), *Marketing Health Behavior. Principles, Techniques, and Applications*. New York: Plenum Press, pp.115–36.

Song, Y., Gee, G., Yingling, F. and Takeuchi, D. 2006. Do Physical Neighborhood Characteristics Matter in Predicting Traffic Stress and Health Outcomes? *Transportation Research* Part F (10): 164–76.

Spacedog Entertainment 2007. Harley-Davidson Rides onto the Comic Book Scene in New Releases, retrieved 17 August 2009 from www.spacedogentertainment.com/news/news-details/10.

Spark, R. 1999. *Developing Health Promotion Methods in Remote Aboriginal Communities*, unpublished doctoral dissertation, Curtin University, Perth, Western Australia.

Spark, R. and Mills, P. 1988. Promoting Aboriginal Health on Television in the Northern Territory: A Bicultural Approach, *Drug Education Journal of Australia* 2(3): 191–8.

Spark, R., Donovan, R. J. and Howat, P. 1991. Promoting Health and Preventing Injury in Remote Aboriginal Communities: A Case Study, *Health Promotion Journal of Australia* 1(2): 10–16.

Spark, R., Binns, C., Laughlin, D., Spooner, C. and Donovan, R. J. 1992. Aboriginal People's Perceptions of their Own and their Community's Health: Results of a Pilot Study, *Health Promotion Journal of Australia* 2(2): 60–4.

Sparks, P., Shepherd, R. and Frewer, L. J. 1995. Assessing and Structuring Attitudes toward the Use of Gene Technology in Food Production: the Role of Perceived Ethical Obligation, *Basic and Applied Social Psychology* 16: 267–85.

Spencer, L., Adams, T. B., Malone, S., Roy, L. and Yost, E. 2006. Applying the Transtheoretical Model to Exercise: A Systematic and Comprehensive Review of the Literature, *Health Promotion Practice* 7(4): 428–43.

SponsorMap 2009. Global Sponsorship Spend remains Positive for 2009, SponsorMap, retrieved 10 August 2009 from www.sponsormap.com/global-sponsorship-spend-remains-positive-for-2009.

Sports Business International 2009. Red Bull extends UK athletics partnership, *SportBusiness*.

Squires, S. 2005. To lose well, think positive, *The Washington Post*, 22 March, p. HE01, retrieved 23 March 2005 from www.washingtonpost.com/wp-dyn/articles/A55828–2005Mar22.html.

State Library of Victoria 2006. Heroes & Villains: Australian comics and their creators. Curator's Essay, retrieved 4 March 2008 from www.slv.vic.gov.au/programs/exhibitions/catalogues/heroesvillains/essay.html.

Staunton, C. E., Hubsmith, D. and Kallins, W. 2003. Promoting Safe Walking and Biking to School: the Marin County Success Story, *American Journal of Public Health* 93(9): 1431–4.

Stead, M., Hastings, G. and Eadie, D. 2002. The Challenge of Evaluating Complex Interventions: A Framework for Evaluating Media Advocacy, *Health Education Research* 17(3): 361–4.

Steptoe, A., Perkins-Porras, L., McKay, C., Rink, E., Hilton, S. and Cappuccio, F. 2003. Behavioural Counselling to Increase Consumption of Fruit and Vegetables in Low Income Adults: Randomised Trial, *British Medical Journal* 326(7394): 855.

Stewart, D., Sun, J., Patterson, C., Lamerle, K. and Hardie, M. 2004. Promoting and Building Resilience in Primary School Communities: Evidence from a Comprehensive 'health promoting school' Approach, *International Journal of Mental Health Promotion* 6(3): 26–33.

Stokols, D. 1992. Establishing and Maintaining Healthy Environments: Towards a Social Ecology of Health Promotion, *American Psychologist* 6–22.

—— 1996. Translating Social Ecological Theory into Guidelines for Community Health Promotion, *American Journal of Health Promotion* 10(4): 282–98.

Stokols, D., Allen, J. and Bellingham, R. L. 1996. The Social Ecology of Health Promotion: Implications for Research and Practice, *American Journal of Health Promotion* 10(4): 247–51.

Stoll, S. and Beller, J. 1998. Character Development: Can Character be Measured? *Journal of Physical Education* 69: 19–24.

St-Onge, M. 2005. Dietary Fats, Teas, Dairy, and Nuts: Potential Functional Foods for Weight Control? *American Journal of Clinical Nutrition* 81: 7–15.

Storey, R. 2008. Initiating Positive Behaviour, in J. Lannon (ed.), *How Public Service Advertising Works*. Henley on Thames: World Advertising Research Centre.

Story, M. and French, S. 2004. Food Advertising and Marketing directed at Children and Adolescents in the US, *International Journal Behavioral Nutrition and Physical Activity* 1(1): 3.

Story, M., Kaphingst, K., Robinson-O'Brien, R. and Glanz, K. 2008. Creating Healthy Food and Eating Environments: Policy and Environmental Approaches, *Annual Review of Public Health* 29: 253–72.

Stout, P.A. 1989. *Fear Arousal and Emotional Response to AIDS Messages*, paper presented at the Annual Convention of the Association for Consumer Research, New Orleans.

Stout, P. A. and Sego, T. 1994. *Emotions Elicited by Threat Appeals,* unpublished paper, University of Texas.

Strasburger, V. C. 1993. Children, Adolescents, and the Media: Five Crucial Issues, *Adolescent Medicine: State of the Art Reviews* 4(3), retrieved from Children Youth and Family Consortium Electronic Clearinghouse at www.cyfc.umn.edu.

Streetwize Communications 2008. Streetwize, retrieved 12 February 2008 from www.streetwize.com.au/publications_aboriginal.html.

Strong, J. T., Anderson, R. E. and Dubas, K. M. 1993. Marketing Threat Appeals: A Conceptual Framework and Implications for Practitioners, *Journal of Managerial Issues* 5: 532–46.

Sutton, S. R. 1982. Fear-arousing Communications: A Critical Examination of Theory and Research, in J. R. Eiser (ed.), *Social Psychology and Behavioural Medicine*. New York: Wiley.

1992. Shock Tactics and the myth of the Inverted U, *British Journal of Addiction* 87: 517–19.

Swinburn, B., Egger, G. and Raza, F. 1999. Dissecting Obesogenic Environments, *Preventive Medicine* 29(6): 563–70.

Szalavitz, M. 2009. Treating Alcohol Addiction: A Pill instead of Abstinence?, 29 July, retrieved 30 July 2009 from www.time.com/time/health/article/0,8599,1913016,00.html.

Tabachnick, J. 2003. Stop it Now! An Innovative Social Marketing Campaign Targeting Sexual Abusers and the People who know Abusers, *Social Marketing Quarterly* 9(1): 42–4.

Tamir, D., Shabtai, A., Weinstein, R., Dayan, I., Avraham, M. and Tamir, M. 2003. Television Entertainment and Health Education for Children in Israel, *Health Education* 103(4): 245–53.

Tanner, J. F., Day, E. and Crask, M. R. 1989. Protection Motivation Theory: An Extension of Fear Appeals Theory, *Journal of Business Research* 19: 267–76.

Task Force of the National Advisory Council on Alcohol Abuse and Alcoholism 2002. How to Reduce High-risk College Drinking: Use Proven Strategies, Fill Research Gaps, April, Final report of the Panel on Prevention and Treatment, US Department of Health and Human Services, retrieved 19 April 2003 from www.collegedrinkingprevention.gov/images/Panel02/FINALPanel2.pdf.

Tay, R. 2005. Drink-driving Enforcement and Publicity Campaigns: Are the Policy Recommendations Sensitive to Model Specification? *Accident Analysis Prevention* 37(2): 259–66.

2009. Drivers' Perceptions and Reactions to Roadside Memorials, *Accident Analysis and Prevention* 41(4): 663–9.

Taylor, R. L., Lam, D. J., Roppel, C. E. and Barter, J. T. 1984. Friends can be Good Medicine: an Excursion into Mental Health Promotion, *Community Mental Health Journal* 20(4): 294–303.

Teo, J. 1992. Evaluation of a social Marketing Program to Encourage Graduate Mothers in Singapore to have more Children, unpublished paper, Edith Cowan University, Perth, Western Australia.

Tevlin, J. 2001. General Mills ad Campaign turns Sour after Protest; Teachers' Cars had Ads for Reese's Puffs Cereal, *Star Tribune*, 31 August.

Thackeray, R., Neiger, B. L. and Hanson, C. L. 2007. Developing a Promotional Strategy: Important Questions for Social Marketing, *Health Promotion Practice* 8: 332–6.

Thaler, R. and Sunstein, C. 2008. *Nudge: Improving Decisions About Health, Wealth, and Happiness*. New York: Yale University Press.

The Hungarian National Heart Foundation (MNSZA) 2009. Limit Commercials of Unhealthy Foods to Children: Ban Junk Food Ads!, retrieved 16 June 2009 from www.mnsza.hu/english/program_tvwf.php.

The Jefferson Center 2009. The Jefferson Center: For New Democratic Processes (cited 20 June 2009), available at: www.jefferson-center.org/index.asp?Type=NONE& SEC={C6DC82A7-A6F4–4FF9-B232-ED7B8D7E2B2D}.

The Prostate Net 2007. Barbershcp Initiatives, retrieved 19 June 2008 from www.prostate-online.or/barber.html.

The West Australian 2009. Michael Jackson 1958–2009, Liftout, 1 July, available at: Wanews.com.au.

Thomas, K. 1997. Health and Morality in early modern England, in A. M. Brandt and P. Rozin (eds.), *Morality and Health*. New York: Routledge, pp.15–34.

Thompson, C. J. 1995. A Contextualist Proposal for the Conceptualization and Study of Marketing Ethics, *Journal of Public Policy and Marketing* 14(20): 177–202.

Thompson, K. and Yokota, F. 2001. Depiction of Alcohol, Tobacco, and other Substances in G-rated Animated Featٮre Films, *Pediatrics* 107(6): 1369–74.

Thompson, S. 2006. Breast Cancer Awareness Strategy Doubles Sales of Campbell's Soup, retrieved 3 October 2006 from www.gwu.edu/~nsarchiv/NSAEBB/NSAEBB8/nsaebb8i.htm re Salvador Allende.

Thomson, G. and Wilson, N. 2006. One Year of Smokefree Bars and Restaurants in New Zealand: Impacts and Resۂonses, *BMC Public Health* 6: 64.

Todt, O., Muñoz, E., González, M., Ponce, G. and Estévez, B. 2009. Consumer Attitudes and the Governance of Food Safety, *Public Understanding of Science* 18: 103–14.

Toppo, G. and Kornblum, J. 2008. Ads on tests add up for teacher, *USA Today*, 1 December, retrieved 2 April 2009 from www.usatoday.com/news/education/2008–12–01-test-ads_N.htm.

Triandis, H. C. 1977. *Interpersonal Behavior*. Monterey, CA: Brooks/Cole Publishing Co.

Triggle, N. 2006. From nanny state to a helping hand, 25 July, available at: http://news.bbc.co.uk/1/hi/health/5214276.stm.

Tripodi, J., Hirons, M., Bednall, D. and Sutherland, M. 2003. Cognitive Evaluation: Prompts used to Measure Sponsorship Awareness, *International Journal of Market Research* 45(4): 435–55.

Tsahuridu, E. and McKenna, R. J. 2000. Moral Autonomy in Organisational Decisions, *Current Topics in Manageme٠t* 5, 167–85.

Turco, D. M. 1995. The Influence of Sponsorship on Product Recall and Image among Sport Spectators, in K. Grant and I. Walker (eds.), *World Marketing Congress Proceedings*. Melbourne: Academy of Marketing Science, vol. 7(3), pp.11.6–10.

Turner, D. 2006. Arby's to Cut Trans Fat from Fries, 29 November, retrieved 30 November 2006 from www.usatoday.com/money/industries/food/2006–11–29-arbys-transfat_x.htm.

Twitchell, J. B. 1996. *ADCULTUSA: Triumph of Advertising in American Culture*. New York: Columbia University Press.

2004. *Branded Nation: the Marke¯ing of Megachurch, Colleg Inc., and Museumworld*. New York: Simon & Schuster.

Tyler, T. R. 1990. *Why People Obey the Law*. New Haven: Yale University Press.

1997. Misconceptions about Wΐy People Obey Laws and Accept Judicial Decisions, *American Psychological Socieٮy Observer, September*, pp. 12–46.

UNICEF. 2008. The Child Care Transition, in *Innocenti Report Card 8*. Florence, Italy: UNICEF Innocenti Research Centre.

Urban, G. L., Hauser, J. R. and Dholakia, N. 1987. *Essentials of New Product Management.* Englewood Cliffs, NJ: Prentice Hall.

Usdin, S., Scheepers, E., Goldstein, S. and Japhet, G. 2005. Achieving Social Change on Gender-based Violence: A Report on the Impact Evaluation of Soul City's fourth series, *Social Science & Medicine* 61: 2434–45.

Vandewater, E., Shim, M. and Caplovitz, A. 2004. Linking Obesity and Activity Level with Children's Television and Video Game Use, *Journal of Adolescence* 27: 71–85.

Vasquez, V., Minkler, M. and Shepard, P. 2006. Promoting Environmental Health Policy through Community-based Participatory Research: a Case Study from Harlem, New York, *Journal of Urban Health* 83(1): 101–10.

Vaughn, R. 1980. How Advertising works: A planning model, *Journal of Advertising Research*, 20(5): 27–33.

    1986. How advertising works: A planning model revisited. *Journal of Advertising Research*, 26(1): 57–66.

Vezina, M., Bourbonnais, R., Brisson, C. and Trudel, L. 2004. Workplace Prevention and Promotion Strategies, *Healthcare Papers* 5(2): 32–44.

VicHealth Centre for Tobacco Control 2001. *Tobacco Control: A Blue Chip Investment in Public Health.* The Cancer Council of Victoria, Melbourne.

Videlier, P. and Piras, P. 1990. Health in Strip Cartoons, *World Health Forum* 11: 14–31.

Vidmar, N. and Rokeach, M. 1974. Archie Bunker's Bigotry: A Study in Selective Perception and Exposure, *Journal of Communication* 24: 36–47.

Vila, B. 1994. A General Paradigm for Understanding Criminal Behavior: Extending Evolutionary Ecological Theory, *Criminology* 32: 311–60.

Vining, J. and Ebreo, A. 1992 Predicting Recycling Behavior from Global and Specific Environmental Attitudes and Changes in Recycling Opportunities, *Journal of Applied Social Psychology* 22(20): 1580–607.

Viola, A. 2002. Building Healthy Queensland Communities Inaugural Seminar, Brisbane. Health Promotion Queensland.

Vital Wave Consulting 2009. The opportunity of mobile technology for healthcare in the developing world, Washington, DC and Berkshire, UK: UN Foundation-Vodafone Foundation Partnership.

Waitzkin, H., Iriart, C., Estrada, A. and Lamadrad, S. 2001. Social Medicine then and now: Lessons from Latin America, *American Journal of Public Health* 91(10): 1592–601.

Walker, L., Moodie, R. and Herrman, H. 2004. Promoting Mental Health and Wellbeing, in R. Moodie and A. Hulme (eds.), *Hands on Health Promotion.* Melbourne: IP Communications.

Wall Street Journal 2008. States ask Baby-products Makers to avoid BPA, 13 October, retrieved 14 October 2008 from http://online.wsj.com/article/ SB122392061604129235.html.

Wallack, L. 1990. Improving Health Promotion: Media Advocacy and Social Marketing Approaches, in C. Atkin and L. Wallach (eds.), *Mass Communication and Public Health: Complexities and Conflicts.* Newbury Park, CA: Sage.

    1994. Media Advocacy: A Strategy for Empowering People and Communities. *Journal of Public Health Policy,* 155(4): 420–36.

Wallack, L. and Dorfman, L. 1996. Media Advocacy: A Strategy for Advancing Policy and Promoting Health. *Health Education & Behavior,* 23(3): 293.

Wallack, L., Dorfman, L., Jernigan, D. and Themba, M. 1993. *Media Advocacy and Public Health: Power for Prevention.* Newbury Park, CA: Sage.

Walliser, B. 2003. An International Review of Sponsorship Research: Extension and Upgrade, *International Journal of Advertising* 22(1).

Walliser, B., Kach, M. and Mogos-Descotes, R. 2005. Legitimizing Public Authorities as Sponsors: An Inquiry into the Factors that Related to the Perception and Memorization of their Sponsorship, *International Review on Public and Non Profit Marketing* 2: 51–8.

Walsh, D. C., Rudd, R. E., Moeykens, B. A. and Moloney, T. W. 1993. Social Marketing for Public Health, *Health Affairs* 12(2): 104–19.

Walters, C. 2007. Barbie teaches Credit Cards 101: 'you never run out of money!', *Consumerist*, 8 October, retrieved 26 June 2009 from http://consumerist.com/consumer/indoctrination/barbie-teaches-credit-cards-101-you-never-run-out-of-money-308326.php.

Wansink, B., van Ittersum, K. and Painter, J. E. 2006. Ice cream Illusions Bowls, Spoons, and Self-served Portion Sizes, *American Journal of Preventative Medicine* 31(3): 240–3.

Warner, M. 2005. Under Pressure, Food Producers Shift to Healthier Products, retrieved 17 December 2005 from www.nytimes.com/2005/12/16/business/16food.html.

Warzana, A. 2000. Physicians and the Pharmaceutical Industry: Is a Gift ever just a Gift? *Journal of the American Medical Association* 283(3): 373–80.

Watson, R. 2007. Steps to a Leaner Europe, *British Medical Journal* 335(7632): 1238.

Watts, R. and Hulbert, L. 2008. *Through the Back Door: An Exposé of Educational Material Produced by the Food Industry.* London: British Heart Foundation.

Webb, D. J. and Mohr, L. A. 1998. A Typology of Consumer Responses to Cause-related Marketing: From Skeptics to Socially Concerned, *Journal of Public Policy & Marketing* 17(2): 226–38.

Webb, T. and Sheeran, P. 2006. Does Changing Behavioral Intentions Engender Behavior Change? A Meta-analysis of the Experimental Evidence, *Psychological Bulletin* 132(2): 249–68.

Weick, K. 1984. Small Wins: Revising the Scale of Social Problems, *American Psychologist* 39: 40–9.

Weimann, G. 1991. The Influentials: Back to the Concept of Opinion Leaders? *Public Opinion Quarterly* 55: 267–79.

Weinreich, N. K., Abbott, J. and Olson, C. K. 1999. Social Marketers in the Driver's Seat: Motorsport Sponsorship as a Vehicle for Tobacco Prevention, *Social Marketing Quarterly* 5(3): 108–12.

Weinstein, N. D. 1988. The Precaution Adoption Process, *Health Psychology* 7: 355–86.

Weir, D. 2009a. FTC to probe bloggers who take money to hawk stuff, BNet Industries, retrieved 7 July 2009 from http://industry.bnet.com/media/10002941/ftc-to-probe-bloggers-who-take-money-to-ha.

2009b. Pay per tweet scandal in U.S. = Secret sponsor deal in U.K, BNet Industries, retrieved 7 July 2009 from http://industry.bnet.com/media/10001712/pay-per-tweet-scandal-in-us-secret-sponsor.

2009c. Two out of three globally using mobile phones, BNet Industries, retrieved 15 August 2009 from http://industry.bnet.com/media/10003652/two-out-of.

Weitzman, E. and Kawachi, I. 2000. Giving Means Receiving: The Protective Effect of Social Capital on Binge Drinking on College Campuses, *The American Journal of Public Health* 90(12): 1936–9.

Weststrate, J. A., van Poppel, G. and Verschuren, P. M. 2002. Functional Foods, Trends and Future, *British Journal of Nutrition* 88(2): 233–5.

Wharton, R. and Mandell, F. 1985. Violence on Television and Imitative Behavior: Impact on Parenting Practices, *Pediatrics* 75(6): 1120–2.

Wheatley, E. 2005. Disciplining Bodies at Risk: Cardiac Rehabilitation and the Medicalization of Fitness, *Journal of Sport & Social Issues* 29(2): 198–221.

Which? 2006. *Food Fables: Exploding Industry Myths On Responsible Food Marketing To Kids – Campaign Report.* London: Which?

White, S. L. and Maloney, S. K. 1990. Promoting Healthy Diets and Active Lives to Hard-to-reach Groups: Market Research Study, *Public Health Reports* 105: 224–31.

Whitehead, T. 2009. Supermarkets must Display Pregnant Women Alcohol Warning Posters, available at: www.telegraph.co.uk/.../Supermarkets-must-display-pregnant-women-alcohol-warning-posters.html.

Whitelaw, S., MacHardy, L., Reid, W. and Duffy, M. 1999. The Stages of Change Model and its Use in Health Promotion: A Critical Review, Health Education Board of Scotland Research Centre.

Wiebe, G. 1952. Merchandising Commodities and Citizenship on Television, *Public Opinion Quarterly* 15: 679–91.

Wiegman, O., Taal, E., Van Den Bogaard, J. and Gutteling, J. M. 1992. Protection Motivation Theory Variables as Predictors of Behavioural Intentions in Three Domains of Risk Management, in J. A. M. Winnubst and S. Maes (eds.), *Lifestyles, Stress and Health: New Developments in Health Psychology.* Leiden: DSWO Press, pp. 55–70.

Wikler, D. I. 1978. Persuasion and Coercion for Health: Ethical Issues in Government Efforts to Change Life-styles, *Health and Society* 56(3): 303–38.

Wilde, G. J. S. and Ackersviller, M. J. 1981. Accident Journalism and Traffic Safety Education, Report No. TP 3659 E/CR 8202, Transport Canada, Traffic Safety, Ottawa.

Wilkinson, R. and Marmot, M. 1998. Social Determinants of Health. The Solid Facts, World Health Organisation Europe, Copenhagen, available at: www.who.dk/document/E59555.pdf.

Wilkinson, R., and Marmot, M. (eds.) 2003. *Social Determinants of Health: The Solid Facts,* 2nd edn. World Health Organization.

Willey, D. 2009. Milan to Enforce Teen Drink Ban, BBC News, retrieved 20 July 2009 from www.newvote.bbc.co.uk/mpapps/pagetools/print/news.bbc.co.uk/2/hi/europe/815772.

Williams, A., Zubrick, S. and Silburn, S. 2001. *Foundations of Social and Emotional Development: A Continuum,* Report for Students at Educational Risk Project, Education Department of Western Australia.

Williams, C. 2001. Doll that gets a tan, *Daily Mail*, 15 June, p. 27.

Wilson, D. H., Wakefield, M. A., Esterman, A. and Baker, C. C. 1987. 15's: They Fit in Everywhere, Especially the Schoolbag, *Community Health Studies* 11(1): 16–20.

Wilson, D. K., Kaplan, R. M. and Schneiderman, L. J. 1987. Framing of Decisions and Selections of Alternatives in Health Care, *Social Behavior* 2: 51–9.

Wilson, N. and Thomson, G. 2002. Still Dying from Second-hand Smoke at Work: A Brief Review of the Evidence for Smoke-free Workplaces in New Zealand, *The New Zealand Medical Journal* 115(1165): U240.

Winett, R. A., Leckliter, I. N., Chinn, D. E., Stahl, B. and Love, S. Q. 1985. Effects of Television Modeling on Residential Energy Conservation, *Journal of Applied Behaviour Analysis* 18(1): 33–44.

Wittchen, H. and Jacobi, F. 2005. Size and Burden of Mental Disorders in Europe – a Critical Review and Appraisal of 27 Studies. *European Neuropsychopharmacology* 15(4): 357–76.

Witte, K. 1993. Message and Conceptual Confounds in Fear Appeals: The Role of Threat, Fear and Efficacy, *The Southern Communication Journal* 58(2): 147–55.

   1998. Fear as Motivator, Fear as Inhibitor. Using the Extended Parallel Process Model to Explain Fear Appeal Successes and Failures, in P. A. Andersen, and L. K. Guerrero (eds.), *The Handbook of Communication and Emotion: Research, Theory, Applications, and Contexts*. San Diego, CA: Academic Press, pp. 423–50.

Witte, K. and Allen, M. 2000. A Meta-analysis of Fear Appeals: Implications for Effective Public Health Campaigns, *Health Education and Behavior* 27(5): 591–615.

Wolf, S., Gregory, W. L. and Stephan, W. G. 1986. Protection Motivation Theory: Prediction of Intentions to Engage in Anti-nuclear War Behaviors, *Journal of Applied Social Psychology* 16(4): 310–21.

Wolff, C. G., Schroeder, D. G. and Young, M. W. 2001. Effect of Improved Housing on Illness in Children under 5 years old in northern Malawi: Cross-sectional Study, *British Medical Journal* 322: 1212–13.

Womack, S. 2006. Britons Spend more on Gambling than Fresh Fruit or Vegetables, retrieved 19 January 2006 from www.telegraph.co.uk/news/1539923/Britons-spend-more-on-gambling-than-fresh-fruit-or-vegetables.html.

Womersley, T. 2000. Magazines ban Anorexic Models, *Electronic Telegraph*, 20 April, retrieved 20 April 2003 from www.telegraph.co.uk/news/main.jhtml?xml=%2Fnews%2F2000%2F06%2F22%2Fnbody22.xml.

Woodruff, K. 1996. Alcohol Advertising and Violence against Women: A Media Advocacy Case Study, *Health Education Quarterly* 23(3): 330–45.

World Health Organization (WHO) 1986. The Ottawa Charter for Health Promotion, *Health Promotion International* 1: 3–5.

World Health Organization 1995. Development Communication in Action, Report of the inter-agency meeting on advocacy strategies for health and development, WHO, Geneva.

World Health Organization 2000. 100% condom use programme in entertainment establishments, Regional Office for the Western Pacific, Manila, Philippines, retrieved 21 April 2003 from www.google.com.au/search?q=cache:8VJehkmprWMC:www.wpro.who.int/pdf/condom.pdf+%22teahouses%22+%22health+education%22&hl=en&ie=UTF-8.

   2001. Women and the tobacco epidemic: Challenges for the 21st century, retrieved from http://tobacco.who.

World Health Organization. 2002. World Report on Violence and Health: Summary, WHO, Geneva.

Wright, A., McGorry, P. D, Harris, M. G, Jorm, A.F. and Pennell, K. 2006. Development and Evaluation of a Youth Mental Health Community Awareness Campaign – The Compass Strategy, *BMC Public Health* 6(215): 1–9.

Wu, Z., Luo, W., Sullivan, S. G., Rou, K., Lin, P., Liu, W. and Ming, Z. 2007. Evaluation of a Needle Social Marketing Strategy to Control HIV among Injecting Drug Users in China, *AIDS* 21: 115–22.

Wurtele, S. K. and Maddux, J. E. 1987. Relative Contributions of Protection Motivation Theory Components in Predicting Exercise Intentions and Behavior, *Health Psychology* 6(5): 453–66.

Wymer, W. and Sargeant, A. 2006. Insights from a Review of the Literature on Cause Marketing, *International Review on Public and Non Profit Marketing* 3(1): 9–15.

Wynne-Jones, J. 2009. Church Blesses Fathers with Beer: Bottles of Beer will be Given to Fathers who attend Church, in an Alternative 'Blessing' for Father's Day, 20 June, retrieved 22 June 2009 from www.telegraph.co.uk/news/newstopics/religion/5587035/Church-blesses-fathers-with-beer.html.

Yach, D., Stuckler, D. and Brownell, K. D. 2006. Epidemiologic and Economic Consequences of the Global Epidemics of Obesity and Diabetes, *Nature Medicine* 12(1): 62–6.

Yanek, L., Becker, D., Moy, T., Gittelsohn, J. and Koffman, D. 2001. Project Joy: Faith-based Cardiovascular Health Promotion for African-American Women, *Public Health Reports* 116(Supp.1): 68–81.

Yankelovich, D. 1992. How Public Opinion Really Works, *Fortune* 126(7): 102–5.

Yen, I. H. and Syme, S. L. 1999. The Social Environment and Health: A Discussion of the Epidemiologic Literature, *Annual Review of Public Health* 20: 287–308.

Ying, L. 2009. Health Advocacy through Photovoice: A Reconsideration, *Annual Meeting of the International Communication Association,* Sheraton New York, New York.

Young, E. 1989. *Social Marketing in the Information Era,* American Marketing Association Conference, Social Marketing for the 1990s, Ottawa, Canada.

Yu, R. 2008. Health Care Businesses take off at Airports, *USA Today,* 8 April, retrieved 11 April 2008 from www.usatoday.com/travel/flights/2008–04–07-airport-clinics-pharmacies_N.htm.

Yunus, M. and Jolis, A. 1999. *Banker to the Poor: Micro-lending and the Battle against World Poverty.* London: Aurum Press.

Zaltman, G. and Coulter, R. H. 1995. Seeing the Voice of the Customer: Metaphor-based Advertising Research, *Journal of Advertising Research* 35: 35–51.

Zaridze, D., Brennan, P., Boreham, J., Boroda, A., Karpov, R., Lazarev, A., Konobeevskaya, I., Igitov, V., Terechova, T., Boffetta, P. and Peto, R. 2009a. Alcohol and Cause-specific Mortality in Russia: a Retrospective Case-control Study of 48,557 Adult Deaths, *The Lancet* 373(9682): 2201–14.

Zaridze, D., Maximovitch, D., Lazarev, A., Igitov, V., Boroda, A., Boreham, J., Boyle, P., Peto, R. and Boffetta, P. 2009b. Alcohol Poisoning is a Main Determinant of Recent Mortality trends in Russia: Evidence from a Detailed Analysis of Mortality Statistics and Autopsies, *International Journal of Epidemiology* 38(1): 143–53.

Zarocostas, J. 2009. Deaths from Road Traffic Injuries will nearly Double to 2.4 million a year unless Safety Measures are Strengthened, *British Medical Journal* 338: b2464.

Zenk, S., Lachance, L., Schulz, A., Mentz, G., Kannan, S. and Ridella, W. 2009. Neighborhood Retail Food Environment and Fruit and Vegetable Intake in a Multiethnic Urban Population, *American Journal of Health Promotion* 23(4): 255–64.

Zimmerman, F., Christakis, D. and Meltzoff, A. 2007a. Associations between Media Viewing and Language Development in Children under age 2 years, *Journal of Pediatrics* 151: 364–8.

2007b. Television and DVD/Video Viewing in Children younger than 2 years, *Archives of Pediatric Adolescent Medicine* 161: 473–9.

Zimmerman, R. 2007. Don't 4get ur pills: Text messaging for health, retrieved 19 August 2007 from http://online.wsj.com/article/SB119551720462598532.html.

Zmunda, N. 2008. Diet Coke dresses Heidi Klum in Red to Promote Heart Health Brand Sponsors Fashion Week Runway Show as part of Year long Partnership, *Madison+Vine: News.*

Zubrick, S. R., Ward, K. A., Silburn, S. R., Lawrence, D., Williams, A. A., Blair, E., Robertson, D. and Sanders, M. R. 2005. Prevention of Child Behavior Problems through Universal Implementation of a Group Behavioral Family Intervention, *Prevention Science* 6(4): 287–304.

Zuckerman, M. 1994. *Behavioral Expressions and Biosocial Bases of Sensation-seeking.* Cambridge University Press.

Zuckerman, M. and Reis, H. T. 1978. Comparison of Three Models for Predicting Altruistic Behavior, *Journal of Personality and Social Psychology* 36(5): 498–510.

INDEX

[Names of campaigns are listed as sub-headings under 'campaigns (named)' or 'case studies'. Where there is extended discussion 'see' references point to the main entry.]

intimate partner violence *see* violence, domestic
involvement, in motivational model, 139

journalism, civic, 344–8
    evaluation, 344–5
    as publicity strategy, 334
    race relations and, 345–8
    versus journalism, standard, 344
journalists as target group, 413–14, 415
juries *see* citizen juries

Kelly *see* community readiness model
knowledge attitude behaviour change model,
    125–6

laddering examples, 162–3
latitude of acceptance, 100, 101–2, 380–7
legal advocates *see* advocacy
legal environment monitoring, 47
legislative change, 13–14, 205, 375
    advocacy and, 13–14, 239–40, 358–61
    and social marketing, 47, 66, 366
    see also policy change
legitimacy, in motivational model, 142–6
libertarianism, 198, 200
liking principle, *see under* persuasion
lobbying, 12, 50, 85
logistic regression *see* regression, logistic
logos, 296, 368, 417–18

Maibach *see* Global Warming's 'Six Americas'
marijuana use
    campaign against, 267–8
    cannabis marketing [box], 24
    moral perceptions, 145–6
    personality and, 267–8
    research concepts, 187–9
market research, 28, 37–8
    question examples, 37
    see also research
market segmentation, 35, 89, 252–5, 279–80,
    284–5
    audience analyses, 274–5, 276–9
    behavioural clustering, 258–60
    of children, 254
    common bases, 253, 255, 260
    consumer orientation and, 35

Global Warming's 'Six Americas', 79–80, 257–8
    models, 255, 260–2, 263–4, 267, 271
    personality and, 267–8
    physical activity example, 270–3
    process, 35
    profiling, 256–7, 260
    psychographics, 255–60
    stages of change concept, 263–7, 290
    see also target marketing
marketing, 1, 4, 21
    advertising *see main entry* advertising
    business and, 2–3, 4
    cause-related, 10, 211, 366
    children as targets, 222, 242–7, 292
    concepts, 4, 12, 28–35, 41, 43, 301
    defined, 3–4, 23–7, 28
    downstream and upstream approaches, 44–6,
      211
    environment and, 39–40
    ethical considerations, 195, 242
    not-for-profit, 9
    orientations, 412
    principles, 23–5, 27–8, 35–6, 43
    process, 23, 26, 28, 38–40
    religion and, 4–5
    research, 28, 37–8
    social change and, 3
    societal, 11
    strategic planning of *see* campaign planning
    see also commercial marketing; social
      marketing; target marketing
marketing mix, 12, 33–5, 282–318, 418–21
    4 Ps, 12, 17–19, 33–5, 223–5, 282–5
    in *Act–Belong–Commit* campaign, 418–21
    definition, 282–5
    partnerships, 282–5, 315–17
    people, 34, 284, 314–15, 419
    place, 17, 18, 33, 223–5, 282–5, 297–306, 318,
      421
    policy, 282–6
    political change, 18–19
    price, 33, 223–5, 282–5, 306–11, 318, 421
    product, 17, 18, 19, 33, 34–5, 40–1, 223–5,
      233–6, 282–5, 286–96, 318, 418–19
    promotion, 12, 33, 223–5, 282–5, 311–14, 318,
      419–21